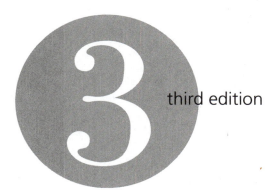

third edition

TERRORISM

An Investigator's Handbook

[william e. dyson]

 LexisNexis®

 anderson publishing
A member of the LexisNexis Group

Terrorism: An Investigator's Handbook, Third Edition

Copyright © 2008 Matthew Bender & Company, Inc., a member of the LexisNexis Group
Newark, NJ

ISBN: 978-1-59345-5309

Phone   877-374-2919
Web Site www.lexisnexis.com/anderson/criminaljustice

Terrorism: An Investigator's Handbook/William E. Dyson
p. cm.
Includes index.
ISBN: 978-1-59345-5309 (softbound)

Cover design by Tin Box Studio, Inc./Cincinnati, OH

EDITOR Elisabeth Roszmann Ebben
ACQUISITIONS EDITOR Michael C. Braswell

Dedication

Robert R. Glendon—The senior FBI Special Agent who mentored my early career and encouraged me to concentrate in the area of terrorism, and a dear friend who taught me the value of professionalism and dedication.

Dr. Richard H. Ward—Dean of the Henry C. Lee College of Criminal Justice and Forensic Sciences, University of New Haven, New Haven, Connecticut, a close friend who encouraged me to prepare this volume, and who assisted, advised, and counseled me along the way.

William Reed—President of the Institute For Intergovernmental Research (IIR) in Tallahassee, Florida, who encouraged me to stay in the field of terrorism after my retirement from the FBI, and who gave me advice and counsel. Sadly, my friend Bill died July 16, 2000.

Preface

The attacks of September 11, 2001, changed the United States forever. Terrorism, once on the minds of a relative few in the population, immediately became the concern of the entire nation. Although the attacks occurred in New York City, the Washington, D.C., area, and to a certain extent in Pennsylvania where one of the hijacked airplanes crashed, every American felt its impact. The attacks dominated all forms of the media, and even seven years later, few Americans can go more than several days without finding something in the media relating to terrorism that probably would not have been found prior to that horrible day in 2001. Average Americans constantly see expressions of increased security that are in part a result of those attacks. They hear of deficit spending, and know that much of it emanated from those fatal attacks and the wars in Afghanistan and Iraq that followed. They hear the president talking about a "war on terrorism," and they observe more American flags flying today than they have seen in years.

Terrorism presents a greater threat to world security today than it has presented at any time in history. Modern technology has made it possible for a small group of dedicated individuals to perpetrate actions that could result in tens of millions of dollars in damage and the deaths of thousands of people. Prior to the 1940s, it would have required a military unit to create such carnage. The law enforcement community must at least be aware of the potential threat. Agencies operating in the most vulnerable areas must be prepared to respond rapidly to a terrorist attack. Considering the seriousness of the situation, prevention of the attack is far more desirable than having to respond to an attack. However, if the attack cannot be prevented, the response must be rapid, professional, and appropriate. Law enforcement agencies owe that to the community they serve, and the community will expect it from them.

Unlike common criminals with whom law enforcement deals on a regular basis, terrorists represent a true threat to the very nature and structure of the country. They do not intend to use the democratic process to achieve their ends. They want a change, and they will use extreme violence to get what they want. They may claim that they do not wish to harm innocent people; however, to many terrorists, the ends justify the means. Consequently, if innocent parties are harmed, that is acceptable. Terrorists are selfish and self-righteous. They know what they want, they are certain that they are correct, and they intend to get what they want regardless of who is harmed.

Although to many people, terrorism means violence perpetrated by foreigners, and more specifically by Islamic extremists, the fact is that terrorism in the modern world encompasses much more than this. Most of the "attacks" that have occurred in the twenty-first century inside the United States have been perpetrated by single-issue, special-interest extremists seeking to protect animals and the environment in accordance with their beliefs. Some of their attacks have been relatively minor in nature, involving vandalism and related threats. However, others have been quite serious. The August 1, 2003, Earth Liberation Front (ELF)-claimed arson of a condominium complex under construction in San Diego, California, resulted in a loss of some $50 million, and would rank in financial terms as one of the worse terrorist attacks in United States history.

Advances in modern communication and transportation have made it possible for terrorists to attack anywhere. What this means is that no law enforcement agency can feel that it is immune from the terrorist threat. Attacks can happen in even the smallest hamlet or the most rural area. Political extremists can live and travel anywhere. Terrorism presents a challenge to all law enforcement officers.

This handbook introduces law enforcement professionals to the field of terrorism investigation. It describes how terrorists operate and how they differ from other criminals. It outlines how investigations should be conducted against terrorists. It warns law enforcement officers about the pitfalls that await them in conducting probes of terrorism. It offers suggestions that the officer can use to improve his or her investigation of a terrorist group. It helps the law enforcement profession to better prepare prosecutable cases against terrorists.

Law enforcement officers are likely to discover that a terrorism investigation will be among the most difficult they will ever experience. If they can master such a case—prevent a terrorist attack, solve a terrorist incident, apprehend a fugitive terrorist, help to convict a terrorist in court—they will have developed skills and knowledge that will enable them to be much better investigators than before. Any criminal investigator will benefit from the information contained in this handbook.

Foreword

The primary focus of this volume is in the area of domestic terrorism occurring in the United States. International terrorism will not be specifically addressed except for that happening inside the country. Much of what is covered in this volume would also be applicable to international terrorism investigations conducted in industrialized nations. This manuscript is intended to explore the best techniques that law enforcement can employ to conduct terrorism investigations in America. It takes the position that virtually all investigative techniques that law enforcement officers normally use in criminal investigations can also be applied to terrorism cases. However, it is argued that often these techniques must be used in a different manner with respect to terrorism. The author believes that terrorists are unique within the criminal world. Terrorists do not behave like the average criminals routinely encountered by authorities. The vast majority of the terrorist attacks that have occurred in the United States during the past 40 years, and especially those perpetrated during the twenty-first century, have been committed by home-grown domestic extremists. These attacks have occurred in just about every state, and have been committed by right-wing, left-wing, and single-issue/special-interest militants. The attacks have involved vandalisms, arsons, and bombings—among other crimes intended to engender fear. Most have caused property damage with only a few intended to result in bodily harm. Some have been relatively minor, employing vandalism, including broken windows and acid damage to vehicles. Others, like the April 19, 1995 bombing of the Murrah Federal Building in Oklahoma City, were designed to cause fatalities. The August 1, 2003, arson attack perpetrated by the Earth Liberation Front (ELF) in San Diego, California, was one of the most costly attacks in United States history, causing some $50 million in damage. Multiple attacks also seemingly carried out by the ELF on August 22, 2003, resulted in millions of dollars in damage to vehicles at several California car dealerships and arson destruction of a Chevrolet dealer's warehouse. Just three days before the September 11, 2001, attacks the Animal Liberation Front (ALF) set a fire that completely destroyed a McDonald's restaurant in Tucson, Arizona. On April 1, 2001, likely anarchists caused approximately $1 million in damage to sports utility vehicles at a Chevrolet dealership in Eugene, Oregon.

Despite the fact that most terrorist attacks in the United States are carried out by domestic terrorists, the September 11, 2001, attacks and the February 26, 1993, bombing of the World Trade Center in New York clearly demonstrate that international terrorists represent a threat to the security of the United States. In June 2007, authorities announced the arrests of several members of an alleged Islamic extremist cell who were conspiring to bomb a jet fuel line into New York's John F. Kennedy International Airport. One of the conspirators was a foreign-born naturalized United States citizen, while the other plotters lived in foreign countries. In addition, there have been several arrests of individuals living in the United States who were allegedly conspiring to perpetrate terrorist attacks in the country on behalf of foreign ideologies. In May 2007, five men were arrested for allegedly conspiring to attack soldiers at the Fort Dix Army Base in New Jersey in connection with Islamic extremism. The techniques covered by this volume can be applied to investigations conducted against such foreign conspiracies in the United States.

It is not the purpose of this manuscript to present a history of terrorism or to describe past and current terrorist groups. An effort has been made to explore the development of terrorism as a concept, and to explain why this problem is so much greater today than at any other time in history. Efforts have been made to describe the various types of terrorism. However, the bulk of the book focuses on the area of investigation. It is intended to offer suggestions and advice with respect to the investigation of terrorist individuals and groups. It is hoped that law enforcement officers will be able to use the information contained in this volume to solve terrorist attacks and to place the offenders into custody. When applying suggestions in this volume, investigators must consider and follow the policies and procedures of their department and the laws and statutes of their city and state and of the federal government.

Contents

SECTION I

The Nature of Terrorism and the Threat It Presents

① An Overview of Terrorism

Terrorism presents a greater threat to national and transnational security today than it has presented at any time in history. This has been demonstrated repeatedly since the twenty-first century began. The September 11, 2001, attacks at the World Trade Center and the Pentagon were probably the worse terrorist incidents in history—certainly in the history of the United States. The October 12, 2002, attacks on the Island of Bali caused ripples around the world. The May 2003 suicide attacks in Casablanca, Morocco, that killed 45 people; the August 2003 attack on the JW Marriott Hotel in Jakarta, Indonesia; the November 2003 suicide bomber attacks on the British Consulate and British HSBC Bank in Istanbul, Turkey, that killed more than 25 people (including the British Consul-General) and wounded 450 others, and the March 2004 train bombings in Madrid, Spain, which killed 191 people and wounded 2,000 others, all illustrate how serious the threat has become. As the century progressed the terrorist threat has continued as was manifested through attacks like the September 1-3, 2004, Chechen separatist takeover of a secondary school in Beslan, Russia, that resulted in 322 people being killed, including 155 children, and 500 people being wounded; the bombings of three underground trains and one public bus in London, England, on July 5, 2005 that killed 54 people and injured some 700 others; the simultaneous bombings on July 23, 2005 at the Red Sea resort of Sharm el-Sheikh in Egypt that killed almost 90 people and wounded 120 others; the triple suicide bombings of tourist hotels in Amman, Jordan on November 9, 2005 that killed some 60 people, and wounded more than 300 others; the multiple bombs that exploded on July 11, 2006 on the Indian railway system around Bombay that killed around 185 people and wounded more than 700 others; the October 16, 2006, attack on Sri Lankan sailors near the towns of Dambulla and Sigiriya that killed more than 100 sailors and wounded more than 150 others; the attempted car bombings in a crowded entertainment area of London, England, on June 29, 2007 and the related suicide car bombing of the Glasgow International Airport in Scotland on the following day; the October 19, 2007, bombing of a procession in Karachi, Pakistan, that was carrying former Prime Minister Benazir Bhutto from the airport as she returned to the country from years of exile, that killed almost 140 people and wounded more than 300 others; the subsequent December 27, 2007 suicide attack in Rawalpindi, Pakistan that killed Mrs. Bhutto and some 20 others; and the May 13, 2008, seven-bomb attack by militants in the Indian city of Jaipur, which killed at least 80 people and wounded between 150 and 200 others. Even the domestic single-issue militant group, the Earth Liberation Front, proved that it could cause a catastrophic attack when it perpetrated an arson in San Diego, California, on August 1, 2003, that caused $50 million in damage. These examples are only a few of the horrific attacks that have occurred around the world during the first eight years of the twenty-first century.

As the term is used today, terrorism is *the illegal use of extreme force and violence for the purpose of coercing a governmental entity or population to modify its philosophy and direction.* Traditionally, terrorism has been employed by a small minority of a population who are unwilling or unable to wait for the majority to concur with, or implement their program. Or it has been employed by oppressed people who have not had any option other than to use force to make change. Terrorism can also be deployed by a minority who realize that the majority plans to make changes that they do not desire. Certainly the Ku Klux Klan of the 1960s who attacked local blacks and visiting white civil rights workers in the southern United States, did so in an effort to maintain long-established segregationist policies that they feared that society no longer accepted and that the government was going to change. In the later twentieth century, single-issue extremists came on the scene; and by the twenty-first century had become the most prolific terrorists functioning in the United States. These people often do not seek to overthrow the government. Instead they seek to make changes in a particular area of concern such as abolishing abortion. Many single-issue extremists do not come from the oppressed or the extreme minority, and they are not reactionaries seeking to return to the past. Although most people reject their use of violence, the ultimate goal that single-issue militants are seeking may be shared by a large part of the population.

There are numerous definitions of terrorism. Indeed, many government and private entities that are involved in the field have their own definition of the term. Some of these definitions consist of a single sentence, while others can be several pages long. Regardless of their authorship, all definitions of terrorism stress extreme violence and fear generated in furtherance of political and social objectives.

Historical Terrorism

A review of recorded history reveals that violent attacks that would fall under the current definition of terrorism have occurred periodically throughout the ages. It can be assumed that terrorism probably dates to when humans first began to live in a communal environment. Perhaps the first terrorist incident occurred in a cave when several members of the community attempted to force a change in leadership by setting a fire or causing a rockslide.

Attempting to determine the exact role that terrorists have played in shaping the history of the world is not particularly easy. It appears that throughout most of history, terrorism has been more of a bothersome irritant to the governments in power than an actual threat to them. There are some instances in which terrorists have played a significant role in a movement that has caused a drastic government change. However, in most situations in which a major alteration of government has occurred, terrorists at best appear to have occupied only peripheral roles in a movement. The significance of the terrorist role in these revolutions is open to question. The movement would probably have succeeded without terrorist attacks. The seeds of discontent were well-sown. At best, the terrorists hastened the inevitable revolution.

Many cite the American Revolution against the British as an example of a terrorist success. Incidents like the Boston Tea Party and the burning of Chief Justice Thomas Hutchinson's Boston residence did occur. Today, these actions would be labeled as terrorist incidents. However, it appears that the movement toward freedom was well under way in the American colonies for a variety of reasons. The violent colonist-perpetrated terrorist attacks at most quickened the process, but did not cause the revolution.

Probably the single most successful form of terrorist attack that has been used throughout history is the assassination of a nation's leader. Unlike today, when self-rule democratic governments are quite common in advanced countries, during much of the world's history single leadership was more the rule. In such situations, assassinating the monarch or dictator would result in some kind of change in managerial direction and style. However, assassinations of top leaders have not been very common throughout history. And many of the attacks that have occurred have not been terrorist incidents. Some were coups by military leaders, relatives, and advisors to the leader. These were more selfish than terroristic in nature. Others were committed during mass rebellions. Mentally ill people have also been responsible for assassinations.

Throughout history, terrorists have faced serious problems trying to make an impact and in accomplishing their ultimate objectives. Although they have advocated rapid changes in government policies, they have often lacked the tools necessary to foster these changes. Frequently they have had some success in generating extreme fear within limited perimeters, but they have usually been unable to cause mass hysteria. Further, terrorists have experienced great difficulty in communicating their philosophy to the masses. Even in instances in which they have perpetrated a violent attack such as an assassination or bombing, terrorists have experienced difficulty in claiming credit for that act, or in providing their explanation for committing it.

Modern Terrorism

A number of the factors that tended to impede terrorists during most of history vanished during the twentieth century. Many of the innovations that occurred during that period, particularly during the second half of the millennium, were beyond the imagination of people living during the nineteenth century or earlier. By the 1960s, the era of modern terrorism began. It was at about that time that, perhaps for the first time in history, it had become possible for a small group of individuals to cause catastrophic damage and to almost instantly communicate their reasons for doing so. Rapid technological advances are likely to continue into the future, although probably not as profoundly as during the twentieth century.

There are four main areas in which twentieth and twenty-first century advances have had a profound impact on terrorists: communications, technology, weapons, and transportation.

Communications

Advances realized during the twentieth century in the area of communications surpassed those made in any other period of history. These advances have enabled terrorists to promulgate their message faster and more thoroughly than ever before. These advances have enabled terrorists to communicate with their comrades and with sympathizers and members of other groups. These advances have also enabled terrorists to learn how to perpetrate more frightening attacks than previously envisioned.

Prior to the beginning of the twentieth century, communication was largely comprised of personal verbal exchanges and letters. Written communication, in the form of books, periodicals, and newspapers, had existed for several hundred years, but their availability was limited. Information was not readily available, and by modern standards the accuracy of what was available was often questionable. Compounding the problem was the large illiteracy rate in even the most advanced nations. Consequently, many people could not benefit from the written forms of communication that were available. The situation improved a great deal during the nineteenth century with the development of the telephone and telegraph, but these forms of communication were not readily available to the masses and were not always reliable.

The twentieth century saw the telephone become so commonplace that most residents of advanced nations had access to one before the century ended. Even people residing in the least developed nations of the world presently have some access to telephones. Today, many people living in industrialized nations regularly carry cellular telephones. Many American teenagers and even younger children have their own cell phones. These devices have become so compact that they can be carried in a shirt pocket and resemble a credit card. The newest cell phones even allow the caller to transmit images, send text messages, and access the Internet. This means that people can be verbally contacted at any time regardless of their location.

Developments in radio and television have made possible rapid and direct, verbal and visual contacts between people all over the world. The Internet has done the same. E-mail has become so commonplace that even children have their own e-mail addresses. Internet chat rooms are used regularly by millions of people. These developments could not have even been imagined by our forefathers who lived two centuries ago.

The terrorist has benefited from these advances in communications technology. For the first time in history, any terrorist can present his or her message to a large audience with relatively little effort. Any attack that a terrorist perpetrates will receive rapid worldwide attention. If the terrorist wants to cause fear, he or she has mass communication to help spread the word. People around the world saw the aftermath of the violent attacks on New York's World Trade Center in 1993 and on Oklahoma City's Murrah Federal Building in 1995 before many of the rescue workers arrived on the scene. Had the perpetrators of these attacks chosen to do so, they could have given advance warnings to local television stations, thereby giving the entire world an opportunity to actually view a terrorist attack as it was happening. To an extent, that is exactly what occurred on September 11, 2001, in the United States. Millions of people turned on their television sets after hearing of an airplane striking one of the World Trade Center towers and saw the second plane crash into the other tower. Terrorists thrive on publicity for their cause. Modern communications technology clearly enables the terrorists to receive maximum exposure.

Modern communication has also made it possible for people having strong views on a subject to find others who hold similar beliefs regardless of where they may live. Prior to the twentieth century, people seeking a change in government and society may not have realized that there were others who held similar views; and even if they did, may not have had any way to converse with them.

Technology

Many of the basic aspects of life that we take for granted did not exist or existed only in a rudimentary manner prior to the twentieth century. Possibly the most important of these developments is the controlled use of electricity. Related to this is the development of items capable of storing electricity—batteries.

The development of the personal computer has altered the world as it has never before been changed. Today, computers are involved in almost every aspect of our lives. Everything from food production to home heating has been affected. Almost every profession has been altered in some respect by computers. In-home use of the personal computer has steadily increased, and soon almost every adult and teenager in America and other industrial nations will be online. An ever-increasing number of schools and employers will only accept applications sent to them via the Internet. E-mail has become a very common means of communication.

For the terrorist, the personal computer has been helpful in a variety of ways. It enables rapid, inexpensive, worldwide communication. Never before have terrorists been able to promulgate their message with such speed. Terrorists have also benefited from the knowledge that is available via the Internet. They can learn how to construct bombs or find sources from whom they can obtain such devices. They can learn about modern weapons and find sources for them. They can locate targets to attack. They can contact one another with relative security.

Because the computer has become so integral to the functioning of the government and the civilian sector, terrorists can generate great fear by attacking them. Bombing a bank may send a message that a group wants a change in a country's monetary system. However, tampering in some way with a bank's computer system so that large sums are "misfiled" among thousands of accounts could actually create fear that would make the bomb appear insignificant by comparison.

Of course, for the terrorist, the computer itself can be used as a weapon. Computers are widely deployed to manage and control systems so that certain activities occur at certain times. For example, aspects of a city water system are likely to be controlled by a computer that regulates the amount of chemicals that are added to ensure purity. Certainly, any computer that directs or manages such a function can be instructed or programmed to misdirect or mismanage that function. One can visualize a terrorist programming the computer that manages a city's electrical power to suddenly send a surge of current through the power lines—blowing out transformers, damaging anything run by electric power, and causing fires.

Weapons

Terrorists attempt to publicize and engender support for their beliefs. What sets the terrorist apart and makes him unique is his willingness to use violence to persuade and coerce others to follow his agenda. If true fear is to be generated, the terrorist must use weapons that are capable of causing mass hysteria. Consequently, many terrorist attacks that occurred before the mid-twentieth century were suicidal in nature. The primitive level of weapons available often forced the terrorist to have direct contact with his victim—a factor that usually led to his being apprehended or killed. It is difficult to imagine John Wilkes Booth being able to kill President Lincoln without having been in his immediate presence. Even as late as 1963, when President Kennedy was killed, it was difficult for an assassin to ensure success without being physically close to his target. The weapons that have been available to violent agitators throughout most of history, including knives, bows and arrows, swords, and spears all have required close proximity to the target. Early firearms did not improve the situation very much. Even the explosives that became available during the Middle Ages required that the perpetrator be close to his target.

The lack of sophisticated weapons had a chilling effect on would-be terrorists throughout most of history. No one will be able to determine how many would-be terrorists remained inactive because they lacked the weapons that would have enabled them to commit violent attacks. Although many terrorists are truly willing to sacrifice their lives to further their cause, almost all would like to live long enough to see progress. Most have not been interested in committing suicide attacks.

Great advances took place in weapons technology during the twentieth century. Many believe that the advances that will take place in the twenty-first century will far surpass what occurred during all of the twentieth century. The terrorist no longer believes that he must give up his life in order to perpetrate certain violent attacks. Modern sniper rifles are such that an assassin no longer needs to be anywhere near his victim. The shooter could be so far away that the victim and his or her bodyguards would have no idea where the shot originated. This makes escape possible.

The size and scope of the terrorist arsenal has been greatly expanded due to improvements in weapons technology. Whereas in previous centuries assassination was likely to be the tactic that would yield the best results and make the greatest impact, this was certainly not the case during the latter part of the twentieth century. In fact, in the United States and Europe, assassination has not been a common terrorist tactic for the past several decades. The modern terrorist has a wide array of weapons available to enable him to generate extreme fear. His arsenal might include missiles, rockets, and other projectiles that can be fired accurately many miles from a target.

Explosives are now so sophisticated that they can easily be concealed and detonated remotely. Indeed, one terrorist sent a chilling message to the law enforcement community in the early 1970s when he placed time-delayed explosive devices in safe deposit boxes in banks across the country. Although one device accidentally exploded prematurely, the rest were found when the perpetrator warned that they were concealed in the banks. There is every reason to believe that most of the devices would have exploded as designed about six months after placement. This extremist's message was clear—technology had developed to such a level in the 1970s that even a person with little knowledge of explosives or electricity could create and hide an explosive device that would detonate months later. The advances that have occurred since that time make it theoretically possible that a device could be placed years prior to the intended time of detonation. A bomb could literally be placed into a structure as it was being constructed, and detonated many months later after the building was completed.

Weapons of Mass Destruction. Over the years, various advances have been heralded as the ultimate weapon that could destroy humankind. At one time the crossbow was even given that distinction. However, today there are weapons that can literally threaten whole populations with a single blow. The crossbow may have made armor obsolete, but it did not really threaten civilization. The atomic bomb does pose an actual threat to the population of the world. So do biological agents and certain chemicals.

The bubonic plague killed hundreds of thousands of people in Europe during the Middle Ages. The difference today is that, while previous epidemics were "natural" occurrences, epidemics can now be deliberately created by people. It is not beyond the realm of possibility that a terrorist group could unleash a disease that might literally kill much of a nation's population.

Dangerous substances have always existed; however, the ability to control and use them has never been greater than it is today. During the early part of the twentieth century, some countries created chemical weapons, including cyanide, chlorine, and mustard gas. Eventually, most nations became so convinced that these chemical agents represented such a grave threat to the world's population that they agreed to never use them, even in war. The Sarin gas attacks in Japan in the 1990s demonstrated that an organized group outside a government agency could create and use a chemical agent in an attack that could conceivably destroy entire segments of a population.

Conventional Weapons. So-called weapons of mass destruction might enable a terrorist group to wipe out a population. However, this may not be desirable or necessary. Weapons of mass destruction are difficult to procure and use. Detonating a nuclear weapon would probably require assistance from a hostile foreign power. Procuring, storing, and using enriched nuclear fuel may be well beyond what most terrorist groups would want to do. Chemical and biological weapons are very dangerous to create, store, and use. They are also difficult to use with precision. Consequently, there may be unintended victims, including members of the terrorist group.

There are other weapons that are either presently on the market or that will soon be available. These include devices that employ lasers, sound waves, oxygen deprivation, pressure, and electrical current. Many can be engineered to specifically target certain individuals. Most are military weapons that the terrorist groups would have to procure from a government through theft. The military will continually update the quality and accuracy of their non-nuclear missiles. Part of this includes an ever-increasing number of small, handheld rocket devices of the light anti-tank weapon (L.A.W.) variety that Puerto Rican terrorists have used in attacks on government buildings.

Transportation

Being able to travel and move quickly is important to terrorists. Until the twentieth century, truly fast transportation did not exist. For the most part, travel was limited to walking or riding animals. Travel on water certainly dates to before recorded history; however, this form of transportation has always been limited to natural or man-made waterways. For much of history, water travel was also limited by natural currents, wind, and human power—all of which were restrictive and not always reliable. Rail transportation developed several hundred years ago. However, like water travel, trains have always been restricted in where they can operate. The limitations presented by various modes of travel have affected terrorists adversely.

Most of what terrorists did prior to the late twentieth century was local in scope. If they decided to travel a distance to commit a violent attack, they had to cope with the difficulties of transporting their weapons. Once they had committed the attack, they faced the problem of escape. One can imagine a terrorist assassin patiently waiting at the local rail depot to catch a train for his "getaway." Similarly, one can visualize a terrorist riding his horse gingerly along a dirt trail with a suitcase full of nitroglycerin-based dynamite dangling from the saddle.

The advances in transportation during the twentieth century eclipsed the advances that had been made during any previous century. The development of the internal combustion engine and other power plants enabled vehicles to be created that could transport anyone just about anywhere. These power systems have also given us more control over water travel. We can now travel on, over, and under water. Possibly the greatest advancement in the area of transportation has been the development of aircraft that are capable of flying almost anywhere.

Many people who lived just 200 years ago never ventured more than few hundred miles from their homes. Today, high school and college students routinely take spring or summer break trips that involve more miles than their nineteenth-century ancestors traveled in their entire lives. Modern businesspeople can have breakfast in New York and dinner in California. Two millennia ago months would have been required to travel between the coasts, and very few people would even considered such a trip.

The New Breed of Terrorists

The advances in transportation, communication, weapons, and technology have enabled a much more sophisticated terrorist to develop during the twentieth century. This modern terrorist has the ability to wreak havoc of massive proportions against his victims, and then of being able to flee apprehension. Never before in history has it been possible for small groups of individuals to cause such mayhem and still have a real chance of not being identified or apprehended.

Modern weapons technology makes it possible for very few people to cause a great deal of damage. Modern communications technology enables people to learn how to conduct terrorist attacks and how to obtain information about weapons. It also enables virtually anyone to gain an almost instant worldwide audience to express his or her views. Modern transportation enables the rapid movement of weapons and allows terrorists to escape easily. These factors have helped the traditional terrorist, who wants to overthrow or otherwise force his government to modify its actions and philosophy, to thrive.

These advances have also encouraged a largely heretofore unknown type of terrorist to develop. This has been the single-issue or special interest extremist. This terrorist does not seek to overthrow his government, or to even greatly change it. This person's concern, for which he is willing to employ violence, involves a specific issue. In some cases it is a relatively general matter such as "the environment" while in other situations it is a small portion of a general concern such as the protection of a particular species of animal. More likely than not, prior to the latter part of the twentieth century, these people did little more than voice their dissatisfaction, if they even did that. When they did resort to violence, it was usually so limited that it garnered little or no publicity, caused little damage, and resulted in no major change.

Today, one can find single-issue terrorism involving such topics as animal rights, the environment, and abortion. While many people have sympathies regarding these concerns, violent extremists who are willing to conduct terrorist actions comprise only a small number of these people. The near future will likely see other single-issue terrorists emerge in light of the success that some current single-issue terrorists have achieved. For example, in England, animal rights extremists have virtually brought the fur industry to an end by liberating animals from farms, setting fires in stores that sell furs, and attacking people wearing furs.

Religious violence has existed throughout history. It can be quite fanatical in that participants may be willing to give up their lives in order to enter a desirable afterlife. Religion is very much a part of some of the current terrorist activity in the world. Many fanatic Islamic extremists are driven by religion and politics. Some have become suicide bombers in the belief that they will end up in paradise because they have died for their religion. Some right-wing extremists in the United States base their violent philosophy on their religion. They claim that their efforts to force the exclusion of Jews, blacks, and others are inspired by the Bible.

The Twenty-First Century Challenge to Law Enforcement

The many advances of the twentieth century have helped make terrorism a major problem for governments and the law enforcement community. Unlike most criminal activities, terrorism represents a direct threat to some aspect of the government or population. Terrorists thrive on publicity, and with the help of modern technology, are able to garner it despite efforts that a government may take to suppress information about violent attacks. Terrorists want to cause fear. People expect their government to protect them so that they can live in peace. Governments must address terrorism if for no other reason than to make it appear that they are providing security to their citizens.

While it is true that contemporary technology has created a new kind of terrorist who represents a significant threat to organized governments, it must be realized that twenty-first century technology has also positively affected law enforcement. Indeed, the police community has never had better tools to counter crime at any other time in its history. As recently as the 1930s and 1940s, police agencies relied on call boxes, sirens, and light beacons to contact their patrol officers. Now all police vehicles have radios, and many have computers. It is now commonplace for officers to carry cellular telephones, lightweight portable radios, and pagers. In fact, the cell phone is rapidly becoming a basic item of police equipment. Similarly, video cameras have become commonplace in police work. Some surveillance teams use cell phones instead of police radios for communication when following suspects, and regularly employ video cameras. It is likely that camera cell phones and hand-held Internet devices will soon find their way into everyday police work. The six-shot revolver and shotgun common in police work 50 years ago have been replaced by highly sophisticated automatic weapons. Police have access to all modes of modern transportation, which is a far cry from the horse on which the sheriff of the nineteenth century relied.

The primary challenge presently facing law enforcement with respect to terrorism is that, unlike terrorists of the past, modern terrorists have the capability to perpetrate horrendous attacks resulting in numerous casualties and vast amounts of property damage. Terrorists today can cause mass hysteria. Terrorists operating as late as the early twentieth century had difficulty causing such fear.

Another factor that the law enforcement community must consider involves the terrorist approach to arrest and prosecution. The modern terrorist realizes that he may be apprehended in connection with either his violent political actions or criminal activities undertaken to support his political endeavors. In the past, terrorists probably believed that discovery by law enforcement meant death or a prison sentence. Many modern terrorists do not view arrest as the end of their activities. Instead, they try to view it from a positive standpoint. To these people the arrest itself, as well as the subsequent court proceedings, can be used as a forum through which their philosophy can be promoted. Court proceedings can serve as a vehicle through which to criticize the government and law enforcement. Further, the court can be used to gather information about law enforcement investigative techniques and to identify informants. Once convicted and sent to prison, the terrorist can actively spread his philosophy to a captive inmate audience in an effort to recruit them or to encourage them to formulate their own anti-government political agenda.

In conjunction with this philosophy, many terrorist groups have legal supporters who follow the political cause and who are prepared to give legal counsel and advice when required. To a certain extent, terrorists and their legal support network, including actual attorneys, paralegals, self-taught legal advisors, and even "jailhouse lawyers," develop an expertise in challenging the work of law enforcement agencies in court. They admit to little if anything, and they will accuse investigators, witnesses, prosecutors, and magistrates of wrongdoing.

What this means for law enforcement is that great care must be given to case development and prosecution. Carelessness and poor investigative techniques will not go unnoticed by the terrorists. Modern technology has greatly enhanced the ability of terrorists and other criminal defendants to challenge law enforcement in court. A defense attorney can quickly locate expert witnesses by using a computer. Similarly, he or she can locate manuals outlining correct procedures and policies that govern the behavior of investigators. Defense attorneys can carefully organize and correlate the discovery material given to them by the court, and combine this information with the results of their own investigative efforts. In short, defense attorneys are now better able to uncover poor police work than in the past.

If in the past terrorists did not know how to challenge law enforcement investigative techniques, they have had the opportunity to learn through several highly publicized criminal trials held during the latter part of the twentieth century. One was the O.J. Simpson murder trial, in which millions watched what had originally appeared to be an open-and-shut case collapse before their eyes. Defense attorneys repeatedly dwelled on what they suggested were questionable police investigative activities—most of which would have been accepted without protest during trials held only a few years earlier.

Exacerbating the situation is the fact that terrorist groups gather intelligence and, to some extent, exchange information with other radical groups. Anything that an established terrorist group learns from a court case will be maintained, studied, and shared so that errors will not be repeated in the future. This was illustrated in a situation in which a federal agent was sent to New York to assist in the investigation of a terrorist-perpetrated armored truck robbery that resulted in the deaths of two law enforcement officers and one guard. When the agent served a search warrant on the apartment of a suspect, he was shocked to find a copy of an official government report on another terrorist group that he had authored several years earlier. It was apparent that a defense attorney involved in a court case in a distant city had copied the report from materials turned over to him in discovery, and had subsequently passed it to the New York group.

How Law Enforcement Addresses the Current Terrorist Threat

Modern terrorism manifested itself in the United States during the 1960s. It primarily arose from opposition to the Vietnam War. With time, other social issues also became involved. Many of the more vocal anti-war activists were also "leftist" oriented. They believed that the war was actually an example of imperialism, which in turn was a natural outgrowth of capitalism. They further argued that capitalism was responsible for all of the social ills that plagued the country, including denial of civil rights, sexual discrimination against women, oppression of homosexuals, and abuse of prison inmates. Many of its earliest adherents were college-age whites, both male and female. As peaceful anti-war protests grew larger and more militant, covert bands of people began committing acts that would be described as terroristic by today's standards.

Also during the 1960s there were concerted efforts to integrate the schools in the southern United States. These endeavors were met with opposition, some of which was violent and deadly. Murders, bombings, and arsons often occurred during this era. The violent extremists who sought to maintain segregation were regarded as "rightist" oriented. Their attacks would clearly constitute terrorism under the current definition of the term.

During the 1960s, the term *terrorism* was only one of a number of words used to refer to the violent acts committed to protest the philosophy of the government and/or to force a change in society. Such words as militant, revolutionary, radical, extremist, communist, or Klansman were just as likely to be used for the perpetrators of such attacks. Because the bombings and other attacks were not being grouped together under any single term like terrorism, it may never be possible to determine exactly how many violent actions occurred during the 1960s and early 1970s. No one was keeping track of such statistics. Things changed during the early 1970s when the term terrorism came to be accepted as an encompassing descriptor for both leftist and rightist political violence.

Bombings, arsons, and other attacks of the era were all investigated. However, there was no coordinated law enforcement effort. Although the FBI, as the largest federal law enforcement agency, responded to many of the violent incidents, it did not have an official mandate to be the lead federal agency with respect to what would later be designated as terrorist attacks. Local agencies almost always responded to violent attacks, but there was often confusion between and within agencies as to who should perform what function at the crime scene. Compounding this problem was the fact that there were few bomb technicians employed by law enforcement agencies, and there was no centralized training facility for these specialists. The Redstone Arsenal school for police bomb technicians was not established until the early 1970s. When viewed from modern standards, crime scene investigations were often poorly conducted. Bombings and arsons frequently were so destructive that it was assumed that nothing worthwhile could be recovered. Some law enforcement agencies made little effort to develop intelligence on would-be and actual terrorists. Other agencies went to the opposite extreme and investigated so many political activists that they did not have time to concentrate on the really dangerous extremists.

During the 1970s, several terrorist groups—including the Weather Underground Organization and the New World Liberation Front—bombed many buildings. The law enforcement community was largely unsuccessful in solving these attacks. The Weathermen actually exploded bombs inside the United States Capitol and the Pentagon. Several terrorists ended up on the FBI's Ten Most Wanted Fugitives list, which until that time usually meant that the subject would be quickly apprehended. Unfortunately, that did not occur, and these people remained on the list for years. By the late 1970s various law enforcement agencies, including the FBI, came under pressure concerning its intelligence-gathering practices. As a result, the federal government adopted much stricter guidelines that for the most part precluded federal agencies from conducting investigations without there being a clear criminal violation. Picketing, demonstrating, and otherwise exercising one's First Amendment rights under the United States Constitution did not constitute such criminality. Many other law enforcement agencies also adopted guidelines that similarly limited intelligence gathering against dissidents.

Bombings and other terrorist attacks continued during the late 1970s and into the early 1980s. The violent Puerto Rican Armed Forces for National Liberation (FALN) organization perpetrated more than 100 attacks during this period. Most of them remained unsolved as the 1970s ended. Other groups, such as the United Freedom Front and the Armed Resistance Unit (also called the Red Guerrilla Resistance) also successfully attacked targets with relative ease. The latter group even succeeded in detonating a bomb inside the United States Capitol. A group of Black Liberation Army and former Weather Underground Organization members staged a series of blatant armored truck robberies on the east coast of the United States during the late 1970s and early 1980s. They met their demise on October 20, 1981, in an armored truck robbery and subsequent chase that saw two law enforcement officers and one armored truck driver murdered. The combined force of federal, state, and local law enforcement officers who successfully investigated this incident and ultimately identified and charged all of the conspirators subsequently became the New York Terrorism Task Force.

By the early 1980s, the tide began to turn in favor of the law enforcement community. By this time, law enforcement had come to realize that terrorists were unique. They were not profit-motivated, but were politically driven. They did not act like normal criminals. Many did not even consider themselves criminals, and most believed that their actions, no matter how violent, were justified. They trusted one another and worked well together. They developed a support network unlike that of any other criminal underground. They could be defeated, but law enforcement would have to try to understand them in order to accomplish this objective. While it was common during the 1960s and 1970s for investigators to overlook terrorist communiqués in which the group claimed credit for an attack, investigators of the 1980s religiously studied these terrorist releases. The value of detailed and careful investigations was becoming apparent. If the terrorist was to be countered, it had to be done legally and professionally. Physical evidence had to be collected because it was necessary in order to ensure a conviction. Bomb scenes could not be ignored. Quality evidence that could help solve the case could be recovered.

Possibly the most important development was the concept of cooperation between agencies. The New York Joint Terrorism Task Force demonstrated this concept in an outstanding fashion. At the same time, a group of investigators from the Chicago Police Department, the Illinois State Police, and the FBI were joining together into an entity known as the Chicago Joint Terrorism Task Force. This task force targeted the FALN in a manner that was totally different from the way law enforcement agencies had ever investigated a terrorist organization. Within a year, the task force had discovered clandestine bomb factories and identified various covert terrorist group members.

This case came to a conclusion with arrests in June 1983, which prevented a series of bombings scheduled for July 4, 1983. The success of these task forces led to the development of additional units, so that by the late 1990s there were more than 20 operational terrorism task forces functioning across the United States. As direct result of the September 11, 2001, attacks, the federal government placed great emphasis on the task force concept, and soon every FBI office was involved in such an entity. By 2008 there were more than 100 terrorism task forces functioning across the United States.

These factors—the task force concept, the recognition of terrorism as a specialty, focusing on people committing crimes rather than those exercising their constitutionally protected rights, and taking great care with respect to conducting investigative techniques, especially in the area of gathering evidence—made the difference. Members of terrorist groups functioning during the 1980s soon found themselves incarcerated for lengthy prison terms. Since that time, virtually every left and right-wing terrorist group that has attempted to establish itself as a serious threat to the United States government has been quickly thwarted by the law enforcement community.

Today, law enforcement must continue to address the threat of terrorism before violent attacks occur. With modern weapons, no law enforcement agency can take the risk that a clandestine cell will not perpetrate a crime of mass destruction. Before the advent of modern terrorism in the 1960s, a law enforcement agency could take a "wait and see" attitude, especially if it had never before experienced a terrorist attack. Even if a group did perpetrate an incident, its magnitude might not be great enough to justify spending a large amount of time and effort to investigate the incident or to counter the group. In view of such tragic events as the Sarin gas attacks in Japan, and bombings at the World Trade Center and the Murrah Federal Building, the attacks of September 11, 2001, and the many devastating attacks around the world during the twenty-first century, law enforcement agencies cannot ignore the threat posed by terrorists.

Terrorism investigations must be well-organized and coordinated with other law enforcement agencies. Investigations must be done correctly, and must be properly documented. Careless investigations can return to haunt the agency that conducts them. Even though both may engage in similar illegal actions, the terrorist is different from the common criminal. Often his political motivation causes the terrorist to act differently from other individuals who commit crimes. The philosophy of the terrorist group must be studied and understood by investigators. Just as coaches study game films and the team philosophy of their opponents, law enforcement officers must attempt to understand the mindset of the terrorist they investigate.

Law enforcement officers must use a variety of investigative techniques in their quest to solve terrorism cases. Terrorists are smart and cunning. They study their craft well. Attempting to resolve a terrorism investigation by using a limited number of techniques is likely to fail. Even if a small number of techniques yield positive results, it is wise to develop the case through a variety of investigative avenues, because terrorists will challenge every article of evidence presented in court.

Law enforcement should make efforts to prevent terrorist attacks rather than waiting for them to happen. Government buildings and key asset facilities must be properly protected. Government leaders must be guarded. Efforts must be made to monitor, if not restrict, dangerous weapons and hazardous products from falling into the hands of terrorists. In many instances, adequate laws and policies exist, but are not properly enforced.

While no one wants a terrorist attack to occur, it is inevitable that some will. It is important that law enforcement agencies respond to such attacks in an organized and professional manner. Many terrorism cases will be proven in court through forensic evidence. Thus it is important that extensive crime scene investigations be conducted. Modern technology has greatly enhanced the ability of law enforcement professionals to gather evidence at crime scenes and other locations.

2 Defining, Delineating, and Dissecting Terrorism

The *Random House Webster's Dictionary* (1998) defines *terrorism* as "the use of violence and threats to intimidate or coerce, esp. for political purposes." It is very different from the one that appeared in the 1967 *Random House Dictionary of the English Language*, which states: "1. the use of terrorizing methods. 2. the state of fear and submission so produced. 3. terroristic method of governing or of resisting a government." The same dictionary's primary definition of the word *terror* was: "intense, sharp, overmastering fear: to be frantic with fear." The 1982 *American Heritage Dictionary* defined *terrorism* as "the systematic use of terror, violence, and intimidation to achieve an end." Its primary definition of *terror* was: "intense, overpowering fear." The definitions cited from the 1967 and 1982 dictionaries were typical of what was contained in similar publications of their era.

It can be seen that the definition of terrorism has changed over time. It has always implied the use of extreme violence intended to generate fear. This could be caused by a variety of factors. A local street gang could induce fright on the part of neighborhood residents. A motorcycle gang riding down the main street of a small community could generate extreme fear to the townspeople. A labor union overturning company trucks during a strike could greatly alarm the business owner. Similarly, strikers could be frightened by "union busters" brought in by the company to clear away picketers. A robber could cause extreme panic in his victim if he suddenly shot out the windows of the person's store. Although all of these examples could be described as terrorism and may well have been considered terrorism 50 years ago, such would not be the case today.

During the past two decades, the term *terrorism* has been used so often with respect to violent political actions that most people assume that any extreme violence labeled as terrorism has been conducted for political purposes. If a newspaper's headline proclaims that a terrorist attack has occurred at a downtown building, few readers would think that an entity such as a street gang, labor union, or a marauding band of motorcycle club members was involved. They would, instead, believe that the attack was politically motivated.

The use of the term *terrorism* to describe politically motivated violence in the United States is relatively new. As recently as the 1960s and the early 1970s, the perpetrators of destructive attacks conducted in conjunction with the anti-Vietnam War movement were only called "terrorists" by a few. It was just as common for people to label the extremists of the era as "revolutionaries," "insurrectionists," "militants," "new left radicals," "Bolsheviks," "Communists," anarchists, "mad bombers," or by their own group name, if it was known. Ku Klux Klan members and others who viciously attacked black and white civil rights activists during the 1950s and 1960s were similarly not called terrorists. Terms like "segregationists" or "Klansmen" were used, if any term at all was employed to describe them. Of course, there were occasions when the media might describe the victim of a politically oriented violent attack as having been "terrorized," but that term was probably used no more during the era than were descriptive words like "frightened," "scared," or "shocked."

The fact that there was no single term to refer to extreme political violence during that period was to have a negative effect on the efforts of the law enforcement community to combat this form of criminal activity. It was difficult to develop a common strategy to deal with the problem, or to even estimate the magnitude of the threat, when the investigators involved could not even agree on a name for it, much less what constituted it. Police agencies often experienced difficulty determining which operational unit within their department should be assigned to handle a case involving political violence. Developing unique procedures for handling these crimes was an almost impossible situation under these circumstances.

By the early 1970s, the term *terrorism* began to be applied to acts of extreme political violence. The perpetrators came to be called terrorists. It may never be known whether it was the news media, academics, or the law enforcement community who first employed the term with regularity. However, today all of these entities use it almost exclusively to refer to extreme, violent, politically motivated activities.

Despite the fact that modern dictionaries have similar definitions for terrorism, there is still no universally accepted definition in the law enforcement community or in the population in general. Various federal agencies that deal with terrorism each seem to have their own definition of the term. Sometimes state, county, and local agencies will use one of the federal agencies' definitions; however, they often will construct their own. (Non-federal agencies that are members of joint terrorism task forces usually accept the FBI's definition of terrorism because the FBI is the lead agency in these bodies.) In addition to that, there almost seems to be an unwritten rule that anyone who authors a publication concerning terrorism must create a unique definition of the term. Think tanks and private organizations involved in the area of terrorism also have their own definitions.

Most investigative agencies and private entities that have interest in and concern about the danger presented by political extremists create definitions of terrorism that are inclusive enough to support their interests. The FBI defines terrorism as:

> … the unlawful use of force or violence against persons or property to intimidate or coerce a government, the civilian population, or any segment thereof, in furtherance of political or social objectives.

The second word of the FBI's definition is "unlawful." Although many other entities fail to address the issue of legality when defining terrorism, the FBI, as a law enforcement agency, believes that it is important to stress that terrorism is criminal in nature. An entity more involved in intelligence gathering would likely not emphasize the criminality of terrorism.

The definition of terrorism used by the U.S. State Department mentions subnational groups and clandestine state agents. Given the international responsibilities of this agency, it is natural that the State Department would include such words in its definition. Federal and state agencies that have only tenuous connections to terrorism, but that want to be included in such investigations, would probably define terrorism broadly.

Special interest and civil rights groups that choose to have their own definition of the word terrorism will likely tailor one that will reflect their entity's interest. An organization representing a specific ethnic or religious group will want to ensure that their definition of terrorism is broad enough to cover individuals who use force and violence in an effort to exclude their members from the general population. Similarly, a freedom-of-choice group might want anti-abortion violence to be considered terrorism. An association of fur breeders would likely want animal rights activists who wreak havoc on fur farms to be classified as terrorists. A timber company might expect that extremists who vandalize their equipment in an effort to stop timbering would be classified as terrorists.

Despite all of the different definitions, almost everyone in the field believes that terrorism involves the use of extreme violence intended to force a change in the government and society. Most accept that terrorist acts are illegal. However, there are some special-interest organizations that would like an expanded definition that would place some legal activities, including marches, demonstrations, leafleting, and similar forms of protests, within the scope of their understanding of terrorism. They become particularly adamant about this if the activity involves implied threats of violence or the violation of any relatively minor laws, including marching without a permit, blocking public access, and impeding traffic. Most law enforcement and government agencies do not consider such forms of protest activity to be within the realm of terrorism even if they escalate into riots. (An exception might occur if it can be determined that the riot was staged, and that certain people committed pre-planned violent acts during the seemingly spontaneous riot.)

As if defining terrorism were not difficult enough, describing and characterizing the specific types of terrorism also present a myriad of difficulties.

A variety of factors, including advances in transportation and communication, have caused the lines separating the different types of terrorism to become blurred. Also, the political causes involved are often difficult to categorize or place into a universally acknowledged type of terrorism. Just as some large corporations are becoming multinational and difficult to identify with a specific country, some terrorist organizations are also becoming international in scope.

Issues Related to Terrorism

There are certain questions with respect to terrorism that must be addressed in order to understand the concept.

Does a terrorist have to seek the overthrow of the government? Through most of history, terrorists did indeed seek major changes in, or the toppling of, governments. Certainly those who attempted to kill the leader of a country wanted significant change. In the modern era of terrorism, however, there are many single-issue extremists who do not want the overthrow of the government. Indeed, a good number are supportive of the government and use violence in an effort to force the government to take action with respect their cause, such as banning abortion or outlawing genetic engineering.

Does a terrorist have to attempt to kill people? Obviously, a political extremist will generate great fear by killing his opponents or members of the population in general. However, not all terrorists want to kill people. An international terrorist group like al Qaeda clearly believes that deaths will promulgate their cause. By contrast, domestic groups like the New World Liberation Front of the 1970s and the United Freedom Front of the 1980s usually went out of their way to avoid killing anyone. The Puerto Rican independence group FALN had it both ways. While they usually placed bombs and incendiaries that were seemingly meant to cause only property damage, in at least three of their attacks they clearly intended to kill people.

Does a terrorist have to frighten the entire population? If one would view al Qaeda's September 11, 2001, attacks as a standard, the answer would be a resounding "Yes." That attack affected the entire country. However, that tragic event was not typical. The fact is that many terrorist attacks are directed against the government, law enforcement, certain people, businesses, or other specific entities. These attacks are intended to cause alarm, fear, and concern on the part of the targeted victims, not necessarily in the whole population.

Does a terrorist have to employ physical violence? Traditionally, terrorists have used brute force to generate fear. Beating, shooting, bombing, burning, assaulting, and killing would accomplish their objective. In the modern world, the aim remains as it always has been, generating fear. Today that can be accomplished in a variety of ways. Letting animals out of cages will scare people involved in the fur business. Sending a virus to the computers of a bank will likely scare a bank president just as much as if someone punched him or her in the nose. Animal rights activists in 2002 and 2003 stole credit cards belonging to businessmen whom they opposed, and charged large amounts of merchandise to their accounts. In mid-2007 the Animal Liberation Front (ALF) tampered with a company's Web site, forcing that firm to sell its shares in an animal testing company that the ALF was protesting against. These actions got the message to the victims just as effectively as would have firebombing the firms' company vehicles.

Is there a minimal amount of damage that must be done before an attack can be classified as being terrorism? Obviously, large attacks involving visible damage as well as deaths and injuries will likely garner more attention than would a broken window or a car damaged with acid. However, all of these forms of attack qualify as terrorism if the motive is to generate fear in order to force social change.

Types of Terrorism

All terrorist attacks fall within the following two broad categories regardless of the political cause involved or the composition of the group perpetrating the act.

Domestic Terrorism

Domestic terrorism is politically oriented extreme violence that is perpetrated by residents of a country within that country in order to force a change in government or in how society functions.

International Terrorism

International terrorism is politically oriented extreme violence that is perpetrated by residents or representatives of one or more countries against the interests of another country, or by members of a violent foreign politically directed organization not affiliated with the country being attacked for the purpose of forcing a change in government or in how society functions.

On the surface, these definitions appear straightforward, but they are sometimes difficult to distinguish. A number of violent political attacks could fall into either of these categories. If a United States-based group, such as the FALN, bombs a building in the United States in an effort to gain freedom for Puerto Rico, this is clearly a domestic terrorism incident. However, this was not so clear when in 1986 the Libyan government allegedly conspired with a Chicago street gang known as the El Rukns to perpetrate violent attacks in the United States. Some considered this domestic terrorism because the perpetrators and targets were located within the United States. Others contended that the situation was international in nature because it was being done on behalf of a foreign government. Another situation occurred one year earlier, when a group of Indian Sikhs were arrested while conspiring in the United States to assassinate India's then-Prime Minister Rajiv Gandhi during a visit to the United States. Although the conspirators lived in the United States and the attack was to occur in the United States, the political cause was in India. During the mid-2000s there have been several conspiracies perpetrated by residents of the United States intended to attack targets inside of the United States in support of foreign extremist philosophies. One involved a group of men in New Jersey who in 2007 allegedly conspired to attack soldiers at the Fort Dix Army base on behalf of Islamic extremism. Some would describe such plots as domestic terrorism, while others would say that the foreign philosophical influence was sufficient to classify these conspiracies as international terrorism.

The United States is home to people of every national origin. Some are recent immigrants, students, visitors, or even illegal aliens, while others were born in the United States. The problems existing in the homelands of these people often accompany them, and can erupt in violence in this country. The question of whether an incident is domestic or international arises when the political cause is foreign (international), but the perpetrators or targets are Americans (or located in the United States). If a domestic terrorist group attacks a foreign entity or person inside the United States, some people would classify that incident as domestic, while others would call it international because of the foreign nature of the target.

During the latter part of the 1970s, a group of ethnic Serbians who resided in the United States engaged in a terrorist bombing conspiracy against the Yugoslavian government and its diplomatic presence in the United States. Similarly, during the early 1980s, two prominent Turkish officials were assassinated in the United States by residents of Armenian descent living in the United States, based upon a Turkish-Armenian dispute dating back to 1915. Although the latter conspirators were probably influenced, and possibly directed by, foreign extremists, the former activists apparently were self-directed. Because these incidents occurred in the United States and involved people legally living in the United States, they could easily be classified as domestic terrorism. However, an equally good argument could be made that they were international in nature because the victims were foreign and the issues behind the attacks had nothing to do with the United States.

Although most of the questionable situations involve recent immigrants, questions can also arise with respect to situations perpetrated by American citizens concerning domestic issues. If an American terrorist group attacks a United States company operation located in another country, or attacks a United States consulate or military facility located abroad, is that domestic terrorism because the targets, perpetrators, and cause are all United States-related? If so, is it still domestic if a foreign-based terrorist group provides assistance in the operation?

In the United States, there is a tendency to think of international terrorists as being from abroad or under foreign direction, committing violent attacks against the United States. The idea of American citizens perpetrating attacks in other countries is sometimes difficult to envision. However, in March 1998, a group of Michigan residents were arrested for allegedly raiding a fur farm in Ontario, Canada—a short distance across the border. Hundreds of thousands of dollars' worth of damage was done. This action would seem to fit most definitions of international terrorism, yet many people would probably be reluctant to label these animal rights extremists as "international terrorists" because their actions seemed to be more of an extension of the numerous similar attacks that were occurring in the United States at the time. Furthermore, many people do not think of Canada as being a foreign country in the same sense that they regard European and Asian countries as foreign. Had these animal extremists attacked a Canadian government building, it would have made it much easier for people to have accepted a characterization of them as international terrorists.

The FBI's definitions of domestic and international terrorism address some, but not all, of these issues:

> Domestic terrorism is the unlawful use, or threatened use, of force or violence by a group or individual based and operating entirely within the United States or Puerto Rico without foreign direction and whose acts are directed at elements of the U.S. Government or its population, in furtherance of political or social goals.

> International terrorism is the unlawful use of force or violence committed by a group or individual, who has some connection to a foreign power or whose activities transcend national boundaries, against persons or property to intimidate or coerce a government, the civilian population or any segment thereof, in furtherance of political or social objectives.

The State Department does not specifically define domestic terrorism; however, it does offer the following definition of international terrorism:

> The term "international terrorism" means terrorism involving citizens or the territory of more than one country.

Specific types of terrorism can constitute either domestic or international terrorism. Some types of terrorism can be both. A particular movement may usually attack targets within their own country for specific purposes, yet have an agenda that involves the use of violence in other countries as well. The Revolutionary Armed Forces of Colombia (FARC) is recognized as a terrorist force in Colombia, and has staged numerous attacks in their homeland, yet the group has also staged operations in other South American countries, including Ecuador and Venezuela. It would be incorrect to characterize FARC as an international terrorist group, because their activities are so much a part of Colombia, yet their activities in neighboring countries cannot be properly described as domestic in nature.

Specific Types of Terrorism

Left-Wing Extremism

In its purest form, left-wing extremists would like to see the creation of a nation in which the means of production will be commonly owned. Every person will receive what he or she needs, and every person will contribute what he or she can best provide. Education will be available to all in accordance to natural skills and abilities. Medical needs will be met as required. Everyone will be equal in the eyes of the state. In essence, there will be a classless, peaceful society. Most supporters of this socialist concept believe that some form of transition period must occur between the present form of government and the society that will ultimately be created. This is usually referred to as the "Dictatorship of the Proletariat." In theory, this transition is occurring in Cuba and was occurring in the former Soviet Union prior to its breakup and in China during the Mao Tse-Tung era.

Not all left-wing extremists envision the same ideal state. Some would retain some private ownership or other aspects of the present government. Others would oppose any private enterprise. Many differ on the methods for achieving the ends, and on the time required to bring them about. Not all socialists agree with what common ownership of the means of production involves. Most seem to accept that any strong, dictatorial government that is necessary to bridge the transition from capitalism to socialism will eventually be replaced by something that will be weak and not oppressive. However, the exact kind of government that will ultimately develop is unclear to many left-wing adherents.

Probably the most vocal left-wing extremists of the early twenty-first century are anarchists. In theory, they would advocate no government at all because the term originates from the Greek words an, meaning "without," and arkos, meaning "ruler." However, many of the modern adherents of this philosophy are practical enough to realize that in a technologically developed and crowded country, the idea of everyone being on his or her own will not work. So they talk about direct democracy and very localized government—tribal or town councils—but no large, distant, amorphous ruling body. They all seem to agree that capitalism is wrong and causes many social evils, and must be replaced. While a number of the modern anarchists in the United States will accept being described as socialists, they tend to shun the term *communism*. To them the idea of having a "dictatorship of the proletariat" is unnecessary and a change from capitalism to socialism can be made rapidly without the need for a strong government to "educate" the masses. In fact, some believe that the doctrine of communism is hypocritical in the sense that the communist party dictators have no intention of ever stepping down from power, and are therefore no different or better than the oppressive government that was overthrown.

Right-Wing Extremism

On the surface, it would seem that if left-wing extremists seek a classless society with everyone being equal, which in the end will almost run itself, right-wing proponents must want the exact opposite—a strong central government that owns the means of production and rigidly controls the lives of its residents, or a government that offers citizenship to a chosen class with others being denied full membership or excluded completely. A fascist state with all of its nationalist and supremacist philosophies comes to mind. As a matter of fact, almost everyone agrees that a fascist Nazi dictatorship is a right-wing form of government. A monarchy would also qualify as a right-wing government.

However, the continuum is not a straight line with the left wing on one side and the right wing on the other side. It is better viewed as being multidimensional, with right-wing philosophies extending away from the left wing in varying directions. Fascism or Nazism would be located at one extreme away from the left wing. Along that line would fall groups like the National Alliance and the Aryan Nations. However, followers of a concept like the Posse Comitatus and related theories, including the Freemen and sovereign citizens, would be equally far from the left wing in another direction. Generally, Posse Comitatus followers fear the idea of a central government and prefer a localized authority that only loosely governs in accordance with the desires of the people. In reality, the Posse Comitatus and related philosophies would prefer virtually no government and are, therefore, anarchist in nature.

Fascism and the Posse Comitatus have little in common other than the fact that they express similar hatreds, prejudices, and fears and oppose the current United States government. Nonetheless, both are usually classified as being right-wing in philosophy. The Ku Klux Klan, militias, tax protest groups, survivalists, and certain religious groups, including Christian Identity and the World Church of the Creator, more recently renamed the Creativity Movement and largely defunct by 2008 (which some do not accept as being an actual religion), are also characterized as right-wing in nature. Some of these groups would fall close to fascism/Nazism, while others would seem to be more related to the Posse. However, a few of these entities have their own paths away from the left-wing apart from fascist and posse adherents.

Both left-wing and right-wing groups can be domestic or international in nature. A person like Benjamin Smith, who went on a murderous rampage in Illinois and Indiana in July 1999, could be described as having been a right-wing domestic terrorist because he had been a very prominent member of the World Church of the Creator. The now-defunct Weather Underground Organization could correctly have been characterized as having been a left-wing domestic terrorist group. The leftist-oriented Kurdish Worker's Party (PKK) is an international Turkish-based terrorist group that has perpetrated violent attacks in various parts of the world. The revolutionary organization 17 November is usually described as being a leftist-oriented Greek domestic terrorist group, although some might also consider it international in nature because it has attacked American and Turkish targets inside Greece.

Single-Issue or Special Interest Terrorism

Single-issue extremism is likely to be the most bothersome terrorism problem that will face governments in the future. Although they may not commit the most violent and deadly attacks, they will likely be responsible for the greatest number of incidents. The single-issue terrorist does not have an overall political agenda. Often, he is not trying to bring down the government in favor of another form of authority, nor is he attempting to abolish the government altogether. He usually does not favor a drastic change in the economic system, and he does not want to greatly alter the way in which people live. His concern may be such that his issue could be characterized as being "leftist" or "rightist," but these terms are usually not best applied to such causes. Many single-issue terrorists are fairly satisfied with the way that their country is being run in general. However, the single-interest terrorist has a specific concern that he wants addressed immediately. He is willing to use extreme violence—even murder—to achieve his objective. For many single-issue terrorists, their cause has become their entire focus in life. While they may be able to express opinions on other political issues, they do not address them in their violent agenda.

It must be noted that many broad-based domestic and international terrorist groups also hold positions with respect to issues that single-issue groups might champion. For example, a white right-wing or black separatist group might oppose abortion because they want members of their own race to multiply. However, it would be wrong to classify people from either of these groups as being single-issue, anti-abortion terrorists. Similarly, some domestic and international terrorist groups hold views on animal and environmental issues that generally concur with those held by single-issue extremists in these areas, yet they should not be categorized as single-issue terrorists. This is particularly true of anarchists whose members often promote activism in connection with both animal and environmental issues, and who have perpetrated terrorist attacks in both areas.

Broad-based domestic and international terrorist groups often view single-issue extremists as dedicated people and ideal recruits for their movements. While such groups may be able to convince some members of single-issue causes to join them, many have no desire to expand their field of interest.

The primary single-issue/special-interest terrorist causes currently include:

- animal rights
- environmental or "eco" issues
- anti-abortion
- anti-genetic engineering

(It should be noted that the FBI generally lumps anti-genetic engineering attacks together with environmental issues. A separate category is listed because there have been upwards of 50 attacks in this area in the United States during the twenty-first century.)

Violent extremist attacks based on these issues have occurred in the United States during the past two decades. There is every reason to believe that such actions will continue in the future, especially in the animal rights and environmental issues areas, in which there have been hundreds of attacks within the past five years.

Anarchists have become deeply involved in animal, environmental, and anti-genetic engineering issues during the past 10 years. These people seek the overthrow of the government and blame the U.S. government for many of the problems relating to these issues. Specifically, they believe that the capitalist system causes problems, and that an effective way of resolving the issues is to eliminate captialism. Investigators may find it difficult to differentiate between true single-issue extremists and anarchists who hold single-issue views. It is possible that a group perpetrating animal or environmental attacks may be comprised of both single-issue and anarchist militants.

It is likely that additional single-issue terrorist causes will arise in the future. One of these areas involves opposition to the expansion of technology. Already there are people who fear the loss of human dignity to computers and other machines. Theodore Kaczynski (known as the "Unabomber"), who detonated bombs across the country between May 1978 and April 1995, was driven by this concern. It remains to be seen whether organized groups of people will employ violence for this cause.

Another area that is already a concern of some right-wing groups is immigration. There are people who are so concerned about this situation that they may turn to violence in an effort to force an end to what they feel is the all-too-open immigration of foreigners into the United States. Still another area of potential single-issue concern is land use. Environmental terrorists are already involved in aspects of this issue. However, this is far from being a totally environmentalist concern. There are others who believe that they should be permitted to do as they please with their own land, or that they should have free access to government property. In many respects, their view of land use is counter to what many environmentalists desire.

When the overall history of terrorism is reviewed, it can be seen that the phenomenon of single-issue terrorism is a relatively recent development. There was some such activity in response to the Industrial Revolution in Europe, when a few workers rebelled against machinery by sabotaging it, but this was something of an aberration. The rapid technological progress that has occurred probably best accounts for the rise in single-issue terrorism. The advances that have taken place during the past century have overshadowed the developments that occurred in any other similar period in history. The rapid advances continually raise new issues of concern. Improvements in communication during the past 50 years have resulted in almost instantaneous information transmission. People have come to realize that their concerns about a specific issue are shared by others. What was previously a personal concern can quickly become a movement or cause.

In the past, many people often had no way to vent their anger about different issues. Now, anyone can learn how to build a bomb, procure a weapon, or sabotage something. People can now communicate with one another over great distances and, if necessary, plan violent attacks. Today, anyone who is angry about a particular issue can either become a terrorist himself, or can join others who are terrorists.

Religious Terrorism

Religious terrorism refers to the use of extreme violence by religious fanatics for the purpose of forcing changes in the government or on the part of the population. Some people believe that violent struggles within a particular religion or church constitute religious terrorism. Most people, however, include only situations in which the target is a government or a specific geographical area, or all or part of the general population. An example might be an effort by a terrorist group to violently force the government to transform itself into a theocracy based on their religion.

Religious terrorism is often entwined with other forms of terrorism. For example, a right-wing extremist may derive some of his views with those of the Christian Identity Church. Middle Eastern extremists seeking a homeland for Palestinians may allow Islamic extremists to influence their views and actions. These people may become convinced that their political views and actions are blessed by God. An extremist may believe that he is a Phineas Priest following God's mandates as he sees them outlined in the Bible.

National or Ethnic Terrorism

There are people who will use force and violence to forge a homeland for their ethnic or national group. Often they are considered domestic terrorists because their battle is with the government that controls the area where their group resides. The Puerto Rican independence movement is an excellent example of this situation. Violent terrorist groups have attacked American interests on various parts of Puerto Rico and on the island of Vieques for many years in an effort to force the U.S. government to allow Puerto Rico to become a sovereign nation.

Sometimes these conflicts are international, because the ethnic group is spread across several countries, or they view another country as being responsible for the plight of their people. In Europe, the battle for freedom for Northern Ireland from English control has gone on for may years. It has involved both England and Northern Ireland, with some attacks against the English occurring in other European countries. The Irish terrorists have also used other countries to procure funding and weapons. The English-Irish conflict could also be characterized as religious terrorism in that the violent groups seeking Irish freedom are Catholic and the English are Protestant.

Race-Based or Hate Terrorism

The fact that an individual or group hates someone because they belong to another race, nationality, creed, sexual orientation, or age, or for any other reason, does not automatically make them terrorists. To be considered a terrorist, the bigot or hate group must commit violent attacks against those they despise in an effort to cause them extreme fear. Conceivably, the person or group could also attack the government in an effort to force it to create restrictions against the hated group. Furthermore, they could attack businesses, organizations, and citizens whom they believe are sympathetic to the targeted group in an effort to convince them to disassociate from the hated group.

Most people who hate enough to commit violent attacks also harbor views that would better classify them in other forms of terrorism. For example, many right-wing terrorist groups have agendas of hate against some non-whites and Jewish people. Some religious terrorists have hatred for particular groups of people. Ethnic terrorists also commonly hold such hatreds.

Narco-Terrorism

Narco-terrorism became a buzzword that was frequently used by the media in the United States during the late 1980s and early 1990s. Like the term terrorism, narco-terrorism does not have a universally accepted meaning. Most definitions include the following:

> Narco-terrorism is the use of extreme force and violence by producers and distributors of narcotics against a government or population, intended to coerce that body to modify its behavior in their favor.

There is little question that narco-terrorism has existed in foreign countries, particularly in South America, for decades. Drug cartels have attacked government buildings, law enforcement facilities, police officers, and courts with regularity in nations such as Colombia and Peru. Furthermore, some politically oriented extremist groups have become involved in the drug trade to support themselves. These groups have employed violent attacks to promote both their political agendas and to protect their drug income from government intervention.

In the early 1990s there was a fear that, as the U.S. government initiated efforts to curtail foreign drug trafficking into the United States, the foreign drug cartels and political organizations would respond by attacking facilities and government/law enforcement personnel within the continental United States. Similarly, there was concern that indigenous drug distributors would follow suit and also violently attack the government in an effort to force the government to ease enforcement of narcotics statutes.

As a matter of fact, the United States government did increase its war against drugs during the 1990s, and did take overt actions directed at the foreign drug organizations. They indicted cartel leaders for violations of U.S. laws, initiated extradition proceedings against foreign drug dealers, prosecuted foreign drug lords, and funded foreign government initiatives against the drug cartels. The much-feared reprisals did not occur in the United States, although there have been some attacks on American facilities and citizens abroad by drug distributors. United States-based drug groups did not emulate the violent actions of their foreign counterparts.

Today, the threat of narco-terrorism within the United States has not materialized. Illegal drug distributors in the United States have not violently attacked the government or law enforcement. Foreign-based drug cartels have not initiated violent attacks within the United States as had been feared. The concern about violent attacks has not forced the United States government to alter its war on drugs. The threat of terrorism has not caused the general population to demand that the government reduce its efforts to counter drug trafficking.

The term *narco-terrorism* has been used by some to refer to virtually any violent action taken by those engaged in the narcotics business. Such people would even use the term to describe a violent turf battle between rival drug distributors. Some have gone so far as to use the term to describe illegal acts done by drug users in their efforts to get money to buy drugs. A few have suggested that terrorist groups that sell narcotics to support themselves are committing narco-terrorism. However, the term is used most often to describe situations in which drug producers or distributors attempt to force the government to permit them to operate as they choose.

Computer or Cyber-Terrorism

The personal computer has become a significant part of the lives of most of the populations of developed nations. Anyone who attacks a computer can have an impact on many people. If the attack is designed to destroy or alter data, or to cause something to malfunction or fail, it can certainly cause fear. Merely attacking the computer for the sheer joy of being able to do so, as is the case for many hackers, does not constitute political terrorism even though it may do damage and cause fear. Similarly, stealing information from the computer of another person, a business, or the government may be of concern to the victim, but it is not political terrorism unless the perpetrator is attempting to force the victim to change his or her thinking or policies. Political terrorism requires that there be an effort on the part of the perpetrator to use fear to exert pressure on the government or the population to modify its behavior.

There is little question that terrorists can use computers to accomplish violent ends. Indeed, it is remarkable that it has not already been widely done. It is a virtual certainty that some terrorist groups will attack the cyberworld at some point in the near future. The first attacks will likely be in the arena of finance, and will involve banking facilities as well as government facilities.

Other targets could involve virtually anything that is controlled by computers. In theory, if something is controlled by a computer, it could be misdirected by a computer. Even if something is not controlled by a computer, it could conceivably be put under the control of a hostile computer. In theory, a computer that controls the water supply for a city could be programmed to pollute that water by changing the purification procedure. An airplane flown via a computer could be programmed to fly into a building. A computer-directed missile could be aimed at one of the country's own cities.

The computer is a tool that can be used by virtually any political terrorist to perpetrate an act that could result in extreme violence and fear. Computers also can be targets or victims of terrorist attacks.

The Concepts of Revolution and Civil War

Revolution and civil war involve the use of extreme violence for political purposes. It is incorrect to refer to such events as terrorism. The concept of terrorism implies a small minority of people involved in perpetrating acts of violence. Indeed, terrorism has been described as the "weapon of the weak." This is not to suggest that a large percentage of a particular population may not generally favor the cause championed by a group of terrorists. However, it is only a small group of people who believe that they must actually employ violence to ensure that the cause is achieved.

In some instances, revolutions and civil wars can develop from terrorism. As the terrorists attract publicity for their attacks against symbols of the government, their cause may gain popularity with the citizens. It is also possible that members of the population may turn to the terrorists for support because they become convinced that the government can no longer protect them. At some point the terrorist cause may evolve into an insurrection, with people battling each other, as in a civil war, or battling the government. Most terrorist causes will not ultimately evolve into a revolution. There is no clear line of demarcation between terrorism and a revolution or civil war. Certainly if 50 percent of a given population is involved in violent attacks, a revolution has occurred. However, if only one or two percent of the population is engaging the government in violent attacks, it may be appropriate to describe the situation as terrorism. It is also probably appropriate to describe a situation as revolutionary if one-quarter of the population is engaged in the violence. At what point below that percentage terrorism becomes insurrection, revolution, or civil war is unclear.

In some situations, all of the terms may be proper. In South America, some violent groups have taken control of huge amounts of rural land. This seems to be a situation that is best described as civil war or revolution. Yet these groups have no control over other parts of the country—often large cities—where they may occasionally engage in violent attacks such as bombings or assassinations in order to intimidate the government. In this case, the group is functioning in a terroristic manner.

The Concept of Guerrilla Warfare

Guerrilla warfare involves a clandestine hit-and-run method of attack. Almost all of the violent actions undertaken by terrorists could be characterized as being "guerrilla" in nature. Guerrilla-style tactics are also employed during civil wars, revolutions, and in full-fledged war involving two or more countries. In the latter situations, however, it is likely that many of the engagements will be direct battles between the warring factions.

Some authorities believe that there is a guerrilla warfare phase between terrorism and civil war/revolution. They see the terrorist cause developing into a paramilitary force that is more involved in engaging the government in limited battle than attacking it without response as in a bombing or an assassination. They believe that if the government is unable to combat the guerrilla stage, it will ultimately develop into an insurrection and revolution.

Recent Terrorist Tactics

Leaderless Resistance

Leaderless resistance is a term that describes a tactic that has been quite popular in recent years and has been employed with great success by such groups as the Animal Liberation Front and the Environmental Liberation Front. Abortion activists and right-wing extremists have also used leaderless resistance. Although it is a tactic that could be used in a civil war/revolution situation, it is more likely to be used by terrorists. In employing leaderless resistance, a small group of terrorists undertakes violent action entirely on its own, without the direction or knowledge of anyone else in the movement. The attack on the Murrah Federal Building seems to fall within the concept of leaderless resistance. This action supposedly was taken against the government to avenge what had happened in Waco, Texas, two years earlier. The Branch Davidian complex fire in April 1993, during which more than 80 Branch Davidian members died following a 51-day standoff, was a popular right-wing extremist issue. However, no one associated with established right-wing terrorist groups appears to have had advance information concerning Timothy McVeigh's plans in Oklahoma City, and no group seemed to have planned it.

In September 2000, a civil suit resulted in a judgment against Richard Butler, which gave every indication that his Aryan Nation compound in Hayden Lake, Idaho, would be seized. The reaction of many of his supporters was that white supremacists should move toward leaderless resistance as opposed to operating openly—with compounds, Web sites, and public demonstrations—as Butler had done for years.

In leaderless resistance, the action taken by the perpetrators directly relates to the cause and seemingly benefits the movement. The fact that no one outside the actual perpetrators knows who carried out the attack makes solving it very difficult for law enforcement.

Lone Wolf Terrorism

The lone wolf is a variation of the leaderless resistance concept. In this situation, one person elects on his or her own to perpetrate a violent attack based on the philosophy of the group to which he or she belongs. No one involved with the cause knows that the action is to take place, and after it happens no one knows who did it unless the person admits to it. Buford Furrow's alleged attack on a Jewish community center in California in August 1999 seems to fit into the lone wolf philosophy. The targets, Jewish children and a Filipino-American postal worker, are those that many right-wing terrorist groups would favor. However, there is no evidence that anyone involved in any right-wing organization was aware of Furrow's plans. Benjamin Nathaniel Smith's two-state shooting spree in July 1999, which targeted blacks, Jews, and Asian-Americans, resulting in two deaths and numerous injuries, also appears to have been a lone wolf action. Smith had been heavily involved with the World Church of the Creator (WCOTC) prior to the incident; however, he had abruptly resigned from the church just before he began his rampage. Law enforcement agencies were unable to develop any evidence to show that the WCOTC as a group, or any of its members, was aware that Smith intended to stage the violent attacks that ultimately resulted in his suicide.

Summary

There are many definitions for the term *terrorism*. However, all address the use of extreme force and violence intended to make a government or population modify its direction or politics. Terrorism has existed throughout history. It can take a variety of forms, including left-wing, right-wing, special interest-single issue, religious, ethnic, and hate. It can be domestic in nature, involving a single country, or it can be international in scope. The concepts of guerrilla warfare, civil war, and revolution also involve extreme violence for political purposes. However, these differ from terrorism in the sheer numbers of people usually involved. Terrorists may operate as individuals but operate more commonly in relatively small groups. A terrorist cause can develop into a civil war or revolution, and insurgents involved in either of these forms of conflict could call upon terrorists to assist them. A recent trend that has developed in the United States among right-wing and special-interest groups is the concept of leaderless resistance, in which groups encourage independent bands of people to commit whatever cause-related act they choose, without any direction. Associated with this is the concept of lone wolf terrorism, in which one person commits violent acts for a cause without the direction or knowledge of the group's leadership.

3 **Religious-Based Terrorism**

Terrorists are a different breed of criminal. Religious-based extremists are in many respects unique within the overall terrorist community. All terrorists are driven by their political beliefs. In the case of religious terrorists, many of their basic political beliefs are derived from, related to, and bolstered by their faith convictions. Most religious terrorists believe that their God supports and directs them. For some, it means that dying for the cause will result in a desirable afterlife. Therefore, religious terrorists are often among the most dedicated extremists. Some are willing to kill enemies of their political cause if they are convinced that their God will approve of it. Others will actually kill themselves if they believe that it will further their cause and that their God will be pleased by their actions. Many, but not all, suicide bombers are driven in part by their religious beliefs.

Foreign Religious-Based Terrorism

The United States is possibly the most diverse civilization in the world. Virtually every culture on earth is represented. Almost every language in the world is spoken by someone living in the United States. Many of the early settlers came in search of religious freedom, or because they were driven from their homeland due to their religious beliefs. The tradition of religious dissenters coming to the United States continues to the present day. Some of the animosities that exist in other countries have been brought to the United States by citizens of these lands who have immigrated to America. Religious beliefs are often a part of foreign hostilities and conflicts.

Foreign-based religious extremists have attacked American interests in various parts of the world on a number of occasions. However, until recently there have been few attacks within the United States. Some of these extremists have targeted foreign consulates, people, and businesses inside of the country, but not the United States itself. Examples include Armenians, Serbs, Croats, and Sikhs. In some instances, the target has been something identified with the United States, but not actually part of the government. The bombing of the World Trade Center in New York in 1993 was done by Middle Eastern religious terrorists. Members of this same group were arrested in New York

City later in 1993 as they conspired to bomb major landmarks in that city and to assassinate prominent politicians and foreign leaders. The tragic attacks of September 11, 2001, reinforced the message to Americans that the United States could indeed be attacked by foreign religious political zealots. In that instance the Pentagon, a symbol of America's military might, was struck along with the World Trade Center.

Although Irish terrorists are not known to have committed violent attacks in the United States, during the past 20 years there have been several arrests of people affiliated with the terrorist Provisional Irish Republican Army (PIRA) who have attempted to purchase weapons in the United States for use against their English targets. Irish terrorists have also used the United States as a source of revenue for their cause. The struggle in Northern Ireland has largely been religious in nature, with the Catholic Irish battling the Protestant British. The first part of the twenty-first century has seen relative peace in Northern Ireland

Foreign-based religious terrorists have made a number of attacks against American interests and citizens abroad. Because of statutes passed in the United States during the latter part of the twentieth century, American law enforcement officers—primarily from the FBI—have been conducting investigations in the countries where these attacks have been staged. In such cases the involved country must grant permission for United States law enforcement officers to function in their territory. Since September 11, 2001, the trend with respect to American investigators conducting investigations in foreign countries has greatly increased.

Domestic Religious-Based Terrorism

When asked about religious terrorism, most Americans probably think of foreign fanatics. This is because of the attacks that such groups have made on American targets abroad, and because some foreign religious zealots such as the "Blind Sheikh" Omar Abdel Rahman have engaged, or are engaged, in radical political activity in the United States.

These people fail to realize, however, that there are native-born religious-based political extremists residing in the United States who pose an internal terrorist threat. Their religious beliefs form the foundation of their political extremism. Some have committed terrorist attacks. Others may do so in the future because they believe that their religions condone such actions. Many of these extreme religions are not themselves political terrorist movements. However, some of their adherents also belong to extreme political groups that have staged attacks in the past or may stage attacks in the future.

Christian Identity

The Christian Identity religion is based in the United States but traces its roots to eighteenth-century England. Originally called British- or Anglo-Israelism, Christian Identity developed a philosophy of its own in the United States, particularly following World War II. The primary theme of the religion is that the white people of England and most of western Europe descended from the missing tribes of Israel who were carried away from the promised land by invading Assyrians in 721 B.C. Because many of the early settlers to the Americas came from Europe, it is presumed that they, too, are directly descended from those taken from the promised land. Men like Wesley Swift, William Potter Gale, and Richard Girnt Butler did much to formalize Christian Identity beliefs in the United States from the 1950s to the present. Through studying the Bible they concluded that the "chosen people" are descended from Adam, who was created by God in his image. To them, Adam was of the white race. They believed that although God may have also created non-white people, he did not give them souls and therefore they are less than human. These non-white people have been called "mud people."

Christian Identity adherents believe that Satan physically seduced Eve, resulting in "half-devil" Cain being born. Being the product of evil, Cain had little choice but to kill his half-brother, Abel, who was the offspring of Adam and Eve. After Cain was banished from the Garden of Eden, he fathered many children through liaisons with the "mud people." Swift, Gale, Butler, and their supporters became convinced that, through the years, the descendants of Cain spread throughout the earth and continue to live today as what the world knows as Jews. To "true believers," Jews must be feared and hated. Non-whites are not considered equals.

Christian Identity is not organized in the same way as many of the Christian denominations in the United States. There is no pope or recognized leader or council of elders who direct the church. Therefore, Christian Identity doctrine will vary from place to place with respect to the interpretation of certain biblical passages. However, the basic tenets concerning the chosen people and the status of non-whites and Jews is fairly consistent. Christian Identity followers are often quite religious and regularly study the King James version of the Bible. Because they believe that they are the true "chosen people," some follow the rules of Kosher as outlined in the Book of Leviticus.

Most of the people who joined Christian Identity after World War II were converts. For the most part they had been raised in Protestant churches. With the passage of time, however, there has been an increasing number of individuals raised from birth in the Christian Identity religion. Because many of these people have also been home-schooled, at least during their early years, they are ingrained with the Christian Identity teachings of scorn and hate for, and separation from, non-whites and Jews.

A religion that advocates hatred for certain groups of people, for whatever reason, is likely to promote violence by its followers. The right-wing terrorist group known as The Order, founded in the early 1980s by Robert Mathews, was heavily influenced by Christian Identity members, although Mathews himself was probably not a member of this religion. The armed compound at the Arkansas-Missouri border in the late 1970s and early 1980s known as the Covenant, the Sword, and the Arm of the Lord (CSA) was heavily influenced by the Christian Identity religion. Buford Furrow, who in 1999 fired a gun into a Jewish day care center, wounding children, and who subsequently shot to death a Filipino postal worker, was a Christian Identity follower. Members of the Christian Identity religion belong to a variety of right-wing extremist organizations in the United States, including the Ku Klux Klan and Posse Comitatus.

Creativity Movement
(formerly known as the World Church of the Creator)

The Creativity Movement previously calling itself the the World Church of the Creator (WCOTC), was founded by Ben Klassen, a Ukrainian who was raised in Canada and Mexico before settling in California, where he worked as an engineer. He later moved to Florida, where he enjoyed success in the real estate business and served as a state legislator in the mid-1960s. Klassen originally called his religion the Church of the Creator, but Matt Hale expanded the scope of the movement by adding "World" to its name. Many of the basic tenets of the religion are contained in Klassen's books, *Nature's Eternal Religion* (1973) and *The White Man's Bible* (1981). The religion marks several holidays, the two most significant of which revolve around Klassen. February 20 is recognized as "Klassen Day" because it marks Klassen's birthday, and February 21 is designated as "Founding Day," because it is the date on which *Nature's Eternal Religion* was originally published. Klassen committed suicide on August 6, 1993.

Many critics refuse to recognize the Creativity Movement as a true religion because it does not worship a deity. Church members generally accept the fact that there may have been a deity that created the earth. However, they believe that if such an entity existed, it is no longer present. Klassen gave himself the title of "Pontifex Maximus" (Supreme Leader) of the church. His successor, Matt Hale, also assumed that title. Hale, who is a law school graduate and a concert violinist, also refers to himself by the title of "Reverend." The Creativity Movement describes itself as being a racial religion for the white race.

The Creativity Movement urges its members to memorize five fundamental beliefs:

1. We believe that our race is our religion.

2. We believe that the white race is nature's finest.

3. We believe that racial loyalty is the highest of all honors, and racial treason is the worse of all crimes.

4. We believe that what is good for the white race is the highest virtue, and what is bad for the white race is the ultimate sin.

5. We believe that the one and only, true and revolutionary white racial religion—creativity—is the only salvation for the white race.

The Creativity Movement encourages its members to love, aid, and abet white people, while hating their enemies—namely non-whites and Jews. Although the Creativity Movement informs its followers that their church membership could be revoked if they commit illegal acts or encourage others to do so, its hatred for non-whites and Jews could serve to cause followers to commit violent acts. In 1993, George Loeb, a church minister, murdered Harold Mansfield, a black Gulf War veteran, in Florida. More recently, in 1999, Benjamin Smith allegedly went on a shooting rampage in Illinois and Indiana over the July Fourth holiday. Smith killed Ricky Byrdsong, a former basketball coach at Northwestern University, who was black, and Won-Joon Yoon, a Korean graduate student in Bloomington, Indiana. He also shot several Jewish people exiting a Chicago synagogue and a black minister in Southern Illinois. Smith had been an extremely active member when the group was known as the WCOTC, and had been recognized as the "Creator of Year" by the church. Smith committed suicide as authorities in southern Indiana were attempting to arrest him.

At one time the WCOTC was a rapidly expanding religion that used the Internet to spread its message. It was actively recruiting among Skinheads and other young white people. Its battle cry of "RAHOWA" had become well-known across the United States and in Europe. This term is derived from the first two letters of the three-word phrase, "Racial Holy War." Law enforcement officers had come to realize that if they observed graffiti containing RAHOWA, they should be aware that the group had at least some supporters functioning in their area.

Things began to come apart for the WCOTC in late 2002, when it became apparent that a civil suit filed by the TE-TA-MA Truth Foundation of Oregon demanding that the WCOTC cease using that name because they held a copyright on it, was going to force the WCOTC to give up the name that they had spent years promoting. On January 8, 2003, Hale was arrested when he arrived at the federal building in Chicago for a hearing in the matter. On the previous day a federal grand jury had indicted Hale on charges of conspiring to kill United States District Court Judge Joan Humphrey Lefkow, who was presiding magistrate in the copyright case. Hale's incarceration, combined with Judge Lefkow's ruling that the WCOTC could no longer use their name, dealt the WCOTC a crippling blow. The group renamed itself the Creativity Movement, and temporarily relocated to Riverton, Wyoming, where they were not warmly welcomed by local residents. On April 26, 2004, Hale was convicted in federal court in Chicago of soliciting to murder Judge Lefkow, as well as three counts of obstruction of justice. A year later on April 6, 2005, Hale was sentenced to 40 years in prison. This sentence ensured that the Creativity Movement leader will spend most of the rest of his life in federal custody.

Following Hale's sentencing, the Creativity Movement almost disintergrated. Lacking a leader and unable to use its well-known WCOTC name or its Web site, the group could no longer spread its message of hate and white supremacy. Pockets of followers continus to exist several years after Hale's sentencing; however, the group no longer holds much prominence in the extremist movement.

Odinism

Odinism, or Wodenism, is an ancient Norse religion that gained popularity in the United States during the 1980s and 1990s. Certainly not all people who practice this religion are extremists. Many people are drawn to it because of its emphasis on nature. Right-wing extremists have turned to Odinism as a kind of rejection of Christianity. They believe that Christianity's "love thy neighbor" and "turn the other cheek" doctrines have weakened the white race. They have come to believe that Odinism is a white-Aryan religion that stresses the survival of the white race. They believe that the spirit of Wotan (also known as Odin and Woden) permeates their souls, and causes them to want to fight to preserve their race. These extremists have also adopted the warlike stance of some of its gods, especially Thor, the god of thunder. Many Skinheads have laid claim to this religion, and have adorned their bodies with tattoos of Odinist symbols.

It would be unreasonable to believe that many right-wing adherents have a true understanding of the tenets of the long-dead Odinist religion. They seem to have taken from it the warlike virtues and symbolism that fits their needs. Some right-wing followers of Odinism also continue to hold some of the Christian beliefs of their childhood.

Literal Interpreters of the Bible

There are few religions that advocate murder and terroristic violence as a matter of course. In fact, most of the major religions emphasize love and compassion. However, it is possible for a fanatical member of almost any religion to find something in the sacred scriptures of his or her faith that would justify terrorist action. Judeo-Christian holy texts contain many passages that, if taken literally or out of context, could be used by extremists to validate terrorist attacks.

An excellent example involves the story of Phineas that is told in the Old Testament (Num. 25). Phineas appeased the wrath of God when he slew Zimri, who was an Israeli, and Cozbi, who was a Midian, because they engaged in an unacceptable sexual relationship (Cozbi was not of the chosen people). Some extremists have taken this biblical account to be a message from God that true believers should take action when they see a transgression against God's laws. Some Christian extremists also cite Chapters 8 and 9 of Ezekiel to not only legitimize their violence, but to describe how it should be accomplished.

In 1996 a small group of white male religious zealots calling themselves the "Phineas Priesthood" staged bank robberies and bombings in and around Spokane, Washington. Three men were subsequently arrested and convicted in this case. The men all espoused a right-wing extremist philosophy, but apparently acted without direction from any organization. Like Phineas, they believed that they had the right to enforce God's laws. As far as they were concerned, the banks they robbed engaged in usury—a practice that they believed was contrary to God's teachings.

Of course, Christians are not the only literal translators of religious scripture. Muslim extremists also find justification in the Koran for their violent actions.

Religious-Based Anti-Abortion Activism

Many, but not all, extreme anti-abortion activists base their views upon the Bible. Some cite the Sixth Commandment, "Thou shalt not kill" (Exod. 20:13), as justification for their actions. They believe that abortion is murder and violates God's law. Others have gone deeper into scripture and have found passages that they believe specifically outline God's abhorrence of abortion and authorize them to act on God's behalf against abortion providers. Although deeply religious, people who believe that they are carrying out God's will by committing violent attacks against abortion providers, including doctors, are dangerous terrorists. It would be difficult to find any other political extremist who would be more dedicated to his cause than one who believes that God sanctions what he or she is doing.

Dealing with Religious-Based Terrorists

The investigation of a religious-based terrorist group is similar to the investigation of any other terrorist group. However, there are certain factors relating to religious-based extremists that are worthy of note. Such people are likely to be more willing to die for their cause than are other terrorists. Most terrorists realize that their number is small; consequently, the death of even a single group member can have a major negative impact on their cause. Therefore, many members will be reluctant to die even though they have totally dedicated their lives to their political agenda.

Religious fanatics, especially those who believe that dying while struggling for their cause will result in eternal life, are much more likely to go out in a blaze of glory. Posse Comitatus member, tax protester, and

Christian Identity follower Gordon Kahl was a good example of this. Kahl allegedly shot and killed two U.S. Marshals in North Dakota in 1983 when they attempted to arrest him for a probation violation that arose out of a tax evasion conviction. He fled and remained a fugitive for four months until being cornered in a farmhouse in Arkansas. During the shootout, a law enforcement officer was killed and Kahl died when the farmhouse caught fire and was destroyed. Robert Mathews, the leader of The Order, chose to burn to death rather than surrender. Mathews is generally believed to have been an Odinist, although some say he was a Christian Identity adherent. In this respect, religious-based terrorists are likely to present an even greater threat to law enforcement officers than other terrorists.

Religious-based terrorists truly know their group's theology. Many law enforcement officers are not in a position to debate such people on the subject of religion. If the person in question insists upon talking about religion, it may make it almost impossible to conduct a standard interview of him. Nonetheless, it may be valuable for an investigator to converse at length with such an extremist, because he may make incriminating statements and possibly even confess to crimes insofar as he believes that his actions were sanctioned by his God. Undercover and informant operations will require knowledge of the targets' religious views. For example, an undercover officer or informant who does not have at least some knowledge of the King James version of the Bible will experience difficulty getting close to devout Christian Identity or Phineas Priesthood members. Penetrating a religious-based terrorist group with an informant or undercover agent is almost certainly going to be more difficult than penetrating other terrorist groups.

Religious terrorists also present unique legal issues for investigators. Law enforcement officers usually do not investigate church activities. The United States Constitution prohibits the establishment of a state religion, and also prohibits the placement of restrictions on the free exercise of religion. This can present a myriad of problems for investigators, because some terrorists are religious fanatics, and others can try to shield their activities behind a church. Law enforcement officers can find themselves facing issues like: Can an agency send an undercover officer or informant into a church service or meeting? Can a church service be observed? Can a church telephone be tapped, or can a church building be wired in order to listen to conversations? Can a pastor be interviewed about church members? What constitutes a privileged conversation? For that matter, what qualifications must a person have to even be considered a minister, and what constitutes a church or a religion? Under what circumstances can a search warrant be issued for a church? Of course, all of these questions can also be applied to mosques, synagogues, temples, and other religious structures, and to rabbis, imams, priests, and other clerics. All of the aforementioned issues can present serious difficulties in court, and could result in an otherwise excellent case being dismissed due to investigative violations. Civil liability on the part of the department and the investigators is also a possibility, if a court deems that the church's freedom to function has been infringed. Investigators should work very closely with their department's legal counsel or prosecutor when investigating religious terrorists.

The religious terrorist is motivated by his or her beliefs, and is usually governed by the rules and restrictions of his or her religion. Obviously, a successful investigator must make an effort to become knowledgeable about the religious terrorist group that he or she is investigating. Such information can help the investigator to combat the group. It may identify the kind of target that the group will attack and suggest the best times for such an attack to occur. It could help to identify who in the group will most likely carry out attacks. It could also open avenues through which the investigator can interview group members in a meaningful manner. Additionally, a study of the group's religious beliefs and practices will likely identify who in the group has the most power and influence, and therefore is the most culpable with respect to prosecution.

④ What Investigators Need to Know About Terrorists

In the United States it is not illegal to be terrorist per se. It does not violate the law to belong to a terrorist organization, including those listed by the U.S. State Department. Further, it is not against the law to criticize or otherwise speak against the government. In some countries, any and all of these "crimes" can result in a person being jailed. However, it must be understood that in America a person claiming to be a terrorist or saying that he is a member of a militant group like al Qaeda is not likely to be given a free pass by the law enforcement community. Such utterances would at the very least give investigators the right to give a cursory look into the background and activities of the person. Claiming membership in a clandestine extremist group that has perpetrated terrorist attacks in the United States or against American citizens or American-owned property abroad could logically cause detectives to consider that person to be a suspect in such illegal actions. Indeed, such a person could possibly find him- or herself in court explaining why he should not be held culpable for the violent actions perpetrated by "his" group. Of course, a person claiming membership in a specific terrorist organization could also find himself being sued by victims of that group's attacks.

Law enforcement officers have a responsibility to investigate terrorist attacks. While merely speaking out against the government may be perfectly legal, taking violent action in an effort to force the government or population to modify its behavior does violate the law. Terrorists are criminals. Their violent political actions could include just about anything that will frighten people. Within this area fall such crimes as bombings, arsons, kidnappings, physical threats, assassinations, airline hijackings and, sadly, using an airliner as a missile. Although some terrorists have outside funding, including wealthy benefactors, surface supporters, their own employment, and even foreign governments, many find it necessary to raise funds through illegal means. Some of these activities could involve robberies, including banks and armored trucks, burglaries, extortion, kidnapping for ransom, and white-collar crimes. Furthermore, most terrorists find it necessary to commit crimes in order to acquire the tools and implements required for them to commit both terrorist attacks and to raise funds. Some instrumentalities of the crime, like vehicles and explosives, are often stolen. Others, including firearms, might be purchased and later illegally altered to make them untraceable. Some may be purchased or rented "legally," but through the illegal use of false identification. A safe house or storage locker are likely to be procured through fictitious documentation. Some items gathered for use in a terrorist attack, including explosives and dangerous chemicals or biological agents, are almost certainly not going to be stored in accordance with federal or state statutes.

Terrorists can commit just about any crime in furtherance of their cause. Often they follow the philosophy of the "ends justifying the means." Although it might seem to be "macho" to hold up a supermarket or crowded movie theatre, a clandestine group is just as likely to turn to something less glamorous. One terrorist group in the United States created and sold counterfeit music tapes to raise funds. A few have even violated their own "ethics and morals" by selling drugs to support themselves. Of course, when their revolution ultimately succeeds, their "new" government would ban narcotics. Selling stolen goods and transporting cigarettes from low-tax states to high-tax states have also been used by terrorists in the United States to raise revenue. Creating false and misleading "charities" is still another illegal vehicle employed by terrorists—particularly with respect to support of foreign groups.

Terrorist groups sometimes use a fund-raising criminal action to make a political statement. In this respect, a group might rob a bank for the money, but then issue a claim of credit stating that the robbery was intended to be an attack on the capitalist system. A right-wing group could take proceeds from a Jewish or minority firm, and claim that the whole action was motivated by white supremacy.

Training is another reason for terrorist groups to commit criminal actions that on the surface do not appear to be have political extremist overtones. Obviously, any terrorist group wants to avoid apprehension in connection with a violent political attack. Indeed, they desire that the operation come off so smoothly that authorities will find themselves left without a clue. For some terrorists, only a "trial by fire" can prove that the group can function with precision during a clandestine political attack. To them, a criminal action that involves weapons or real danger fills the training bill. If group members can remain calm and work as a team during such an endeavor, it can be reasoned that they would do the same during a political attack. The fact that such an action will yield funds for the group's treasury is an extra benefit to be derived from this form of training.

The fact that terrorists violate many of the laws that common criminals break does not mean that they are similar to other law violators, or that they should be investigated in the same manner. Investigators soon learn that terrorists are different from most other lawbreakers. They are not driven by a selfish profit motivation. Their political cause is what moves them. Most criminals are well aware that their actions violate the law. And most do not try to justify their crimes, although in court they may offer excuses for them. For the terrorist, the crime, whether it be a political attack or an action to raise funds, is justified because it promotes the cause. He is not violating the law for his own benefit. Instead, he is doing it as part of a progression that will ultimately result in a better world. Some anti-government terrorists do not even recognize the country's laws as being valid. These factors are noteworthy, because they mean that terrorists will often act differently from other criminals. For example, investigators are sometimes able to develop good robbery suspects from a group of possible candidates, by determining which ones are living beyond their means. This technique is not going to work with respect to terrorists, because the fruits of their criminal activity go to the "cause" with no benefit to them. The terrorist will be driving the same old car a week after the bank robbery, whereas the more common criminal might suddenly have a new SUV in his driveway.

"Know thy enemy" is a philosophy that law enforcement officers should embrace with respect to terrorism investigations. Understanding the terrorist will go a long way toward having success in investigating him. Knowing the extremist will also make it much easier to try to co-opt him. The wise investigator will make every effort to learn as much as he can about the political movement. He should know how the members perceive it, and how they fit into it. It helps greatly to know what kind of support each member can expect to receive from his group should he be questioned or arrested by the police or be called before a grand jury. Similarly, it would behoove the investigator to know the kind of assistance group members would receive if they were forced to flee.

The following are questions that an investigator studying a terrorist should attempt to resolve during the course of an investigation:

Philosophy of the Group to Which the Terrorist Belongs

What is the political philosophy of the terrorist group to which the subject belongs?

What aspects of this philosophy does the subject strongly support, and what aspects does the subject least support?

Does the subject fully understand the group's philosophy, and can he verbally defend it?

Is the group's philosophy rational?

Is the philosophy based on religion, and if so, which religion?

Is there a "Bible" or "manifesto" that outlines the group's philosophy?

Does the philosophy include deadlines and ends—is there an exact doomsday?

Does the philosophy revolve around one person? If so, what will occur if something happens to that person?

Do other terrorist groups follow similar political philosophies? If so, what keeps them from merging or keeps the subject from joining one of these other groups?

Does the terrorist group exclude anyone because of their race, creed, religion, national origin, age, sex, sexual orientation, or for any other reason?

Is the political cause popular, such that many non-terrorists might lend sympathy to members of the group?

Did the group split from another organization, and does that other group continue to exist? If so, was the subject a part of the other group?

Group Rules and Policies with Respect to Its Members

Under what rules does the terrorist group permit the subject to operate?

Are all group members treated equally and if not, how is the subject treated in comparision with other members?

Is there a written document that outlines the group's rules and regulations or operating procedures?

Does the subject need group permission to do certain things?

Does the subject live in a commune or safe house?

Is the subject a member of a covert cell?

Does the subject live totally under a false identity?

Is the subject forbidden to talk with law enforcement personnel?

Is the subject expected or permitted to carry a firearm or other weapon?

Does the subject receive direct financial assistance from the group, or is he (and possibly his family) entirely on his own?

What are the subject's options if he is arrested, or if he is merely confronted by a law enforcement officer?

Is the subject regarded as an obedient member or a maverick and rule violator?

Can the subject leave the group, and if so, what does he lose?

Group Structure and How the Individual Fits Into It

What is the group's hierarchy and structure?

Is there a written document outlining the structure?

Is the structure cellular in nature?

Where does the subject fit within the group's structure?

Does the subject have power and authority in the group?

Does the subject have expertise needed by the group, and does it give him some form of special status?

Does the subject know the identities of all group members above, below, and at the same level as himself?

Does the subject have any close associates in the group?

Is the subject in a sexual relationship with another group member, and if so, do other members know about it and approve of it?

Personal Aspects of the Terrorist's Commitment to the Cause and Group

Is the subject a "thinker" or a "doer" with respect to the political movement?

Is the subject involved in recruitment for the cause?

Has the subject actually committed a violent act?

Will the subject kill someone if it is deemed politically justified?

Would the subject perpetrate a suicide attack?

How did the subject get involved in the cause? Who recruited him?

Does the subject have any outside interests that are separate from the political cause?

Does the subject have friends who are not involved in the cause? If so, who are they, and what kind of contact does the subject maintain with them? Does the group know about them?

Does the subject have any forms of personal problems, including physical or mental illness, sexual deviation, or narcotics/alcohol addiction; and does the group know about them?

How Does the Subject Fit into the Group?

Is he a "perfect fit" or is there something about him that makes him different from other group members?

Are other group members likely to directly assist the subject should he be injured or arrested?

Does the subject have a particular skill or expertise that the group needs?

Does the subject have any "secrets" relating to himself or his family of which the terrorist group is not aware?

Are there things going on in the group that affect the subject of which the subject is unaware?

Has the subject belonged to terrorist groups in the past? If so, why did he leave them?

How Does the Subject Regard Himself with Respect to the Group?

Is the subject a confident, self-assured member, or is he constantly concerned about his status and membership?

Is the subject popular with other group members?

Does the subject need the group more than the group needs the subject?

Is the subject jealous of any other group members, and if so, why?

How will the subject hold up in custody away from the group? Has he ever been incarcerated?

Skills of Value Possessed by the Subject

Is the subject proficient in using weapons?

Is the subject knowledgable about explosives, and has he used them in the past?

Does the subject possess skills in flying an airplane, piloting a boat, speaking a foreign language, programming a computer, or in any other area that may be of value to the group?

Has the subject been in the military or had experience in law enforcement?

Has the subject attended a terrorist training camp, and if so, where, when, and what did he study?

Does the subject train others in the group?

Does the subject author philosophical papers for the group?

Outside Support for the Terrorist

Does the subject have legal support through his political movement, and if so, are the subject's legal advisors members of the terrorist group?

Is there an "underground" to support the subject should he become a fugitive or just decide to conceal himself from government scrutiny?

Is there a surface political network to support the subject and his cause?

Will the group's members and supporters raise funds for the subject, procure legal support, protest his situation, write letters, gather names on petitions, and otherwise provide him with assistance?

If the subject was forced to flee, where would he logically go?

Does the subject have a foreign haven where he could go when in trouble, and if so, is the subject able to speak the language of that country, and has he ever been there before?

The Terrorist's Relationship with His or Her Family

What happens to the subject's family if he is arrested, injured, or killed doing a political action or is forced to go underground?

What family members, if any, are aware of his involvement in the terrorist group, and which members support the group's cause?

Is anyone in the family an actual member of the group?

Which family members are likely to cooperate with law enforcement agencies?

Will his political cause provide direct support to the subject's family?

Will the subject's family be pressured by the group to provide assistance to the subject?

Will the subject divorce himself from his family, if the group so demands it?

Was the subject raised in a radical political setting?

Summary

Being a terrorist per se is not illegal in the United States. Neither is being a member of a terrorist group. However, terrorist groups conspire to and actually violate laws and therefore commit criminal offenses. Some of the statutes they violate are directly connected with violent political attacks, including the illegal use of explosives and weapons. However, many of the laws that are broken by terrorists relate to raising funds for the group and gathering the means and materials required by the group in order for it to function. "Know thy enemy" is a motto that investigators should follow with respect to investigating terrorist groups and their members. It is important for the investigator to know the philosophy of the terrorist organization, how the group is structured, how it functions, how its members are governed and controlled by the group, and how they relate to other members of the organization.

SECTION II
Investigative Techniques

5 An Overview of Investigative Techniques as They Apply to Terrorism

There are no investigative techniques that can only be employed in terrorism investigations. Conversely, there are no investigative techniques employed in ordinary criminal cases that cannot also be applied in at least some terrorism investigations. Nonetheless, terrorism investigations are different in many respects from the average criminal matters that investigators normally address. While the investigative techniques employed may be essentially the same, their application is often different. If nothing else, the use of certain techniques is more constrained in terrorism cases. The terrorist is motivated by his political objectives, which are all-consuming. His whole life is controlled by his political goals. His values and mores are governed in many respects by his political agenda. If his activities result in a profit, it is for the benefit of his political organization and not for himself.

Most terrorists live in a state of fear. Because they seek to overthrow or at least force a change in the operation and philosophy of the government, they come to regard the government and its law enforcement agencies as the enemy. They both hate and fear them. They fear opposing organizations. They fear entities that they themselves have targeted, such as certain minorities and businesses. They often fear the media, although they seek its publicity to promote their cause. They also fear their fellow group members, knowing that any one of them could turn on them or be a police operative.

Clearly, people who live in a state of fear avidly promote security measures. For many terrorists, security is a prominent aspect of their lives. They are on constant alert for people who might be monitoring their activities. They are always apprehensive about strangers. They are even suspicious of people they have known for a while. They fear that the government will turn their friends and associates against them. They fear that their telephones are being monitored, and that their homes and vehicles are "bugged." There is little question that their extreme emphasis on security restricts their ability

57

to function. Just trying to communicate with one another can present a major difficulty for terrorists. When they meet with one another, security issues consume much of their time.

Their extraordinary emphasis on security is what makes the terrorist difficult to investigate. Few criminals practice security to the extent that the average terrorist does. Neither the terrorist nor the common criminal wants to be arrested. Perhaps the main difference between the two is that the criminal assumes that somewhere along the way he or she will probably be caught. For him or her, it is an unpleasant cost of doing business. By contrast, the terrorist does not assume that apprehension is inevitable. He will abort a mission if he believes that law enforcement is aware of his activities. While the ordinary criminal is not likely to actually commit an illegal act in the presence of authorities, he is probably not going to completely abandon his project either. He may delay his activities for a short period or alter his target somewhat. Some terrorists would literally drop out of their movement rather than risk compromising their fellow conspirators. If a terrorist group comes to suspect that law enforcement has identified its safe house, it will not only abandon that location, but will probably also discontinue the operation that involved the safe house. The group might actually relocate to another city. Few criminal conspirators would go to such extremes to avoid apprehension.

Another factor that differentiates the terrorist from the ordinary criminal involves the extent of knowledge that many terrorists have about law enforcement operations. A number of the leftists of the 1960s, 1970s, and 1980s, and the rightists and special interest groups of the last 25 years have trained their members with respect to police investigative techniques. Not only has verbal training been given to members, but pamphlets and books that outline how law enforcement agencies operate have also been published. Security information has also been made readily available online. Many of these security materials are extremely accurate. Obviously, people who know how police operate can take actions intended to interdict and foil the investigators.

Many common criminals have a "macho" attitude with respect to police operations. They believe that they will be able to detect someone who is following them, or that they will be able to identify an informer or undercover officer. Some also believe that they can successfully undergo a police interview without revealing valuable information. The fact is, most average criminals overestimate their ability to outsmart law enforcement. Police often are able to observe such people without them ever being aware of the surveillance. By using skillful interview practices, investigators usually glean information of value and even confessions when they converse with criminals. The average criminal often fails to identify informants in their midst. Many criminals are not even aware of some investigative techniques such as trash covers, pen registers, and mail covers.

In the case of terrorists, however, the situation is different. Investigators soon find that it is much more difficult to follow someone who knows exactly how police surveillance is done. It is a challenge to interview a person who is familiar with interviewing techniques or who absolutely refuses to say a word to them. Penetrating a conspiracy with an informant or an undercover officer becomes a problem when the conspirators assume that they will be targeted, and have a good idea of how the law enforcement agency will attempt to accomplish their mission.

In addition to the documents that various groups create and distribute themselves, terrorists also seek out materials designed specifically for law enforcement training. Right-wing extremists often review military manuals and police training guides. Some terrorists actually read the same police textbooks that law enforcement agencies use in their academies. Such publications are available at gun shows, in some gun shops, at extremist book stores, army surplus retailers, and through Internet sites.

The fact that many terrorists are aware of law enforcement investigative techniques does not mean that these methods of developing information cannot be employed. It simply means that greater care must be used during the investigation.

When the terrorist is apprehended, it is unlikely that he will cooperate with authorities. He has probably been schooled about what to expect while in custody, and he has been taught how to respond. He usually knows how to avoid being successfully interviewed. In many instances, the terrorist knows that he can expect adequate legal assistance; consequently, he can stall interrogations of any sort by demanding that his attorney be present. He also knows that he will receive political support, which might include everything from public demonstrations, courtrooms packed with supporters, letter-writing campaigns, and help in escaping from custody. If nothing else, he knows that he will become something of a hero or martyr to his cause. Because he was arrested for political activities, the terrorist often does not experience guilt for what he has done. The terrorist is not likely to confess to his crime even if he was literally caught in the act of committing it. In fact, many political extremists do not believe that their actions violate any valid law. Furthermore, the terrorist is often not going to agree to a plea bargain unless it is very much in his favor or can benefit his political agenda. In virtually all of these respects, the terrorist is quite different from the average criminal with whom law enforcement officers are accustomed to dealing.

When the terrorist case goes into court, the investigator will find a unique situation. The terrorist's political cause will permeate the proceedings. Accusations of prejudice, bias, and illegal activities will be lodged against the investigators, the prosecutor, and the judge. Everything will be challenged. In many respects, the investigator, his department, the prosecutor, the court, and the government will find themselves "on trial" during the course of the proceedings.

What this means for the law enforcement investigator is that terrorism cases are usually complex and difficult to resolve. A variety of investigative techniques must be employed. Throughout the investigation, great attention to detail must be given. Carelessness and mistakes must be avoided. Proper and prompt documentation of the results of every investigative technique is imperative. Rules and procedures with respect to the use of these techniques must be followed. Investigative techniques must be used with care. Investigators must constantly ask themselves whether the application of a particular technique will alert the subject to the law enforcement agency's interest in him. If the response is yes, or even maybe, the technique probably should not be used as it normally would. The terrorist will practice extreme security when carrying out his clandestine activities. Similarly, the investigator must use extreme care when investigating the terrorist.

Summary

Every investigative technique normally used to solve criminal cases can be used in a terrorism investigation. Conversely, there are no techniques that can be applied only to terrorism violations. Terrorists fear law enforcement agencies and usually practice security procedures that can make it difficult for police investigators to monitor their activities and arrest and prosecute them. Many terrorist groups study law enforcement operations and alert their members about how officers use investigative techniques. This factor differentiates terrorists from many ordinary criminals who often assume that they know how police function, but who in actuality are quite naïve in this respect. Terrorists are unlikely to cooperate with authorities when arrested and will often use court proceedings as a forum through which to promulgate their political views. What this means for the law enforcement officer is that he or she must use great care in conducting terrorism investigations.

6 **What the Terrorist Knows About Law Enforcement**

In order to understand the need to modify basic investigative techniques to fit the terrorist, it is important to have an understanding of what political extremists know about law enforcement.

Many terrorist group members and their surface supporters have either no arrest records at all, or have only been detained for minor violations revolving around protest-type activities. A number of political terrorists in the United States, particularly animal and environmental extremists and anarchists, are relatively young and could hardly be characterized as "worldly." Others, particularly sovereign citizen and militia types, may be older, may come from rural areas, and are not well educated or particularly sophisticated. Very few can be classified as hardened criminals. In fact, many extremist groups are hesitant to accept people with extensive criminal records for fear that the "baggage" that these people carry could cause police to take notice of them, and give authorities reason to monitor the group's activities. Clandestine terrorists can only succeed if they are able to blend into the community beyond the attention of law enforcement. Because many terrorists are relative novices with respect to criminality, it is easy for investigators to assume that they will have something of an advantage over them. They may believe that because they have had success in solving crimes perpetrated by experienced criminals, they should not have any difficulties dealing with amateurs who may never have even received so much as a traffic citation. As many law enforcement officers have discovered, the terrorist can prove to be a very challenging adversary.

Despite their seeming naïveté, terrorists are quite familiar with law enforcement investigative techniques. In fact, many political extremists know more about police operations than do people who have lengthy arrest records. Hardened criminals are likely to have knowledge of the arrest and court process, because they have been through it many times. However, they really do not know all that much about how law enforcement officers actually conduct their investigations. The very fact that they keep getting arrested would seem to suggest that they have yet to learn how to avoid the police.

Professional criminals are likely to have been interrogated many times and have lied repeatedly—yet they still seem to believe that they can fool and mislead the investigator conducting the interview. They have fallen victim to informants despite their belief that they can spot a "squealer" a mile away. They have been repeatedly tailed during investigations, yet did not realize it until the surveillance logs were presented in court.

Security is at the heart of every clandestine terrorist organization. Without it the group would soon perish. The terrorist is motivated to create the fear necessary to promulgate the political cause and escape to continue the endeavor. It is the cause that gives their lives meaning; consequently, everything must be done to keep their group functioning. Whereas the common criminal thinks first of himself, and will very likely sell out his partners in exchange for a deal with authorities, terrorists think as a group, and will go out of their way to protect each other so that the political struggle can continue even if they are forced out of it.

Terrorist Training Materials

Following the coalition invasion of Afghanistan that resulted from the September 11, 2001, attacks, authorities located copies of a document commonly referred to as the al Qaeda Training Manual. It is a rather large and detailed guide for clandestine al Qaeda members to follow in order to maintain security, support themselves, and to carry out political attacks. There is no indication that the manual was ever intended for release outside of the terrorist organization. The document is a "must-read" for all law enforcement officers working any form of terrorism case. Even though it is intended for a specific group, and has many aspects that apply only to al Qaeda or similarly oriented entities, the guide nonetheless is of value to even local street investigations, because it illustrates the kind of materials that extremist groups provide to their members. The U.S. Department of Justice has made available selected portions of a copy of the al Qaeda Training Manual that was located by the Manchester, England, Metropolitan Police Department during a search of computer files located in the home of an al Qaeda member. This can be accessed at www.usdoj.gov/ag/manualpart1_1.pdf. In December 2002, Indonesian authorities recovered a 40-page operation guidebook used by the Indonesian Islamic terrorist group Jemaah Islamiyah.

Investigators should be aware that many groups, particularly domestic entities in the United States, have documents that instruct their members with respect to operations. Investigators should make every effort to obtain these documents. In addition to written materials, some terrorist groups provide verbal lessons to their new recruits and conduct training exercises. It is important that investigators become aware of what information is being passed on to members of the group they are targeting. Furthermore, there has been a trend during recent years for groups to encourage people to perpetrate acts under their banner, or at least against targets that they think should be hit. Under this "leaderless resistance" concept, the heart of the group leadership is not even interested in who is doing the action—they just want it done, and they want it accomplished securely and properly. In order to ensure that this occurs, they must publish materials relating to security, targets, and clandestine operations in general. The Internet is certainly the best way to transmit this information. This has opened a whole new avenue for law enforcement officers who in the past had to turn an informant or rely on searches in order to obtain such documents.

In some cases the documents used by clandestine terrorists are put out by the group itself and are meant only for group members to see. In other instances, the materials may be released by supporters of the group for use by clandestine operatives, overt operatives, and by those engaged in leaderless resistance. Obviously, the released manuals are much more accessible to law enforcement. The materials generally deal with the following topics: security from the police and government, target selection, attack preparation, and clandestine operations. The al Qaeda Training Manual deals with all of these issues.

Security

Security-related documents are probably the most common materials that extremist groups—whether clandestine or overt—make available to their own members, people they want to follow leaderless resistance, and supporters. It is expected that clandestine extremists become familiar with these materials and follow them. Surface support people who are not actually covert and are not likely to engage in actual criminal activities are also encouraged to follow at least some of the suggestions in these documents. Certainly overt activists should adhere to security rules in cases in which they are working with clandestine operatives—such as when asked to provide them with shelter or financial support. In the modern world it is likely that security materials will be conveyed via the Internet—some intended for surface people, others intended only for clandestine group members.

"What to do if contacted by law an enforcement agency" is a common subject covered in security documents. Most guides discourage group members from having anything to do with police. Some groups instruct their members to merely close the door or walk away without saying a word when approached by investigators. Other manuals instruct the person to state, "I have nothing to say," and then not say anything more. The white supremacist Aryan Nations group (South Carolina faction) advocates this along with other security suggestions in a document titled "Activist Tips" (www.aryan-nations.org/ activist_tips.htm). Still other security documents encourage the member to get the investigator's name and tell him to "see my lawyer." A few of the documents explain the reason for noncooperation. They point out that police are skilled interviewers who generally follow the philosophy that something of value can be gained from every interview even if the person lies or swears at the officer. A few guides point out that if a person is innocent and provides investigators with an alibi, it allows the officer to eliminate him or her as a suspect, thereby permitting the investigator to home in on the actual guilty person. These manuals suggest that if everyone refuses to talk, the officer is stuck with an unmanageable number of suspects.

Spotting informants and identifying tactics employed by law enforcement officers to penetrate terrorist groups are topics often covered in security manuals. Extremist groups will also provide instruction with respect to spotting electronic coverage and some will even show their members pictures of "bugging" devices. The Animal Liberation Front puts out a very short, yet high-quality document titled, "Warning Signs of Covert Eavesdropping or Bugging" (www.animalliberationfront.com/ALFront/Activist%20Tips/ Security/Warning_Signs_of_Covert_Eavesdropping_or_Bugging.htm) which, if followed, could well result in a member becoming aware that he is the subject of electronic law enforcement coverage. Other topics covered by various security manuals address detecting and thwarting police physical surveillance, safe use of telephones, fax machines and the mail, and computer privacy. In the latter area, the following Web site, http://security.resist/ca/ compintro.shtml, which describes itself as "Helping activists stay safe in our oppressive world," publishes information explaining methods that political activists should follow to ensure computer security.

Target Selection

The fact that a person is a member of a clandestine group or is working in a leaderless resistance capacity on behalf of a particular cause does not necessarily mean that he knows what is politically correct to attack. Furthermore, there is no guarantee that the person will be aware of the location of logical targets. For years the Animal Liberation Front published a list of fur farms because such entities do not often appear in city directories or telephone books, and would-be attackers might not know where they would be located. More recently, the animal rights movement has targeted the animal testing firm Huntingdon Life Sciences (HLS). Various animal rights activist Web sites regularly release the names and addresses of people employed by HLS and by companies that do business with HLS.

Many groups release, in one fashion or another, communiqués or verbal statements in which they claim credit for attacks that they have perpetrated. Usually the communiqué or statement names the victim and outlines why a certain target was chosen. Other group members can use these communiqués as guides to the types of targets that are acceptable to strike. Leftist-oriented groups of the 1960s to 1980s, including the Weather Underground Organization, the United Freedom Front, the Armed Resistance Unit, and the FALN, issued such documents often via mail or verbally outlined their grievances by telephone. Groups today tend to use the Internet, although the telephone is still used on occasion. Animal rights activists and environmental terrorists will often leave behind spray-painted messages at the scene of the crime.

Attack Preparation

Many groups teach their members how to construct explosive and incendiary devices or how to perpetrate attacks involving vandalism. The idea is that over time the group has developed a method that works (or has borrowed a proven method from someone else). Consequently, the organization wants to ensure that all of their devices and vehicles of attack will function, and they do not want experimentation. The Animal Liberation Front previously published via the Internet, a document titled "Wake Up Time" that explained in detail, and with diagrams, how to construct a simple electrical timer that could be used as a delay in an incendiary device. That guide, which is almost certainly still in the hands of some activists, even went into detail with respect to security in connection with building the device in order to make it more difficult for police to trace. For a while in the early 2000s another how-to-do guide titled, "Arson-Around with Auntie ALF" was made available to extremists on the Internet by an entity calling itself "Auntie ALF, Uncle ELF and the Anti-Copyright gang."

There are various guides distributed by, or on behalf of, domestic extremist groups that cover security, targeting, and "how to" issues. The now-defunct Bioengineering Action Network at one time maintained a Web site that contained a document titled "The Nighttime Gardener," which provided a variety of instructions concerning security and methodology with respect to staging anti-genetic engineering attacks. The Army of God Manual is a fairly large document intended to be used by anti-abortion extremists in their campaigns to stop abortions. The publication offers numerous illegal suggestions on disabling abortion clinics (www.armyofgod.com/AOGhistory.html).

Clandestine Operations

A number of groups offer manuals that deal with how a group should function. They cover everything from the establishment of a safe house, to obtaining disguise materials, to procuring quality false identification. The al Qaeda Training Manual devotes a good deal of material to this—which is obviously of extra importance to this group, because their members could be entering countries that are markedly different from their nation of origin. The Animal Liberation Front's "The A.L.F. Primer," which was once readily available on the Internet, also covers a good deal of this kind of information.

Some of the manuals go into detail with respect to the hierarchy of their specific organization. In essence, the guides will explain how the organization is supposed to function. Indonesian authorities report that the Jemaah Islamiyah guide found in December 2002 includes flowcharts depicting the organization's leadership.

Why Political Extremists Study Security-Related Manuals

Terrorists are extremely disciplined. Their political cause is the most important thing in their lives. They quickly realize that security is key to the success of the cause. A person who has such dedication will go out of his way to follow security procedures even if it limits his ability to function. He would prefer to take three hours traveling to a safe house and getting there without being detected rather than take one hour to arrive at the location only to have a police surveillance team successfully follow him. He would gladly travel 10 miles to mail a letter rather than do it at his local post office. He would rather use a pay telephone even though he has a telephone in his residence or a cell phone in his pocket. He will meet people at a chilly park bench before he will have them come to his home.

The extremist knows that his group's security manuals and verbal training are intended to foster security. He will follow what the group instructs him to do because he is a true believer. If the group leader instructs him to read a security document, he will do so not because the leader is going to give him an examination to prove that he did as ordered, but because he knows that it is for the good of the political movement.

Many of the documents concerning security and clandestine operations are available on the Internet and could be read by common criminals. Yet few do it—a factor that is to the advantage of the law enforcement community. Most common criminals believe that they have a certain street sense that enables them to be a step ahead of the law. They certainly do not commit crimes because they want to get arrested—if they wanted that, they could throw a rock through the window of the police station. The common criminal believes that he knows what is necessary to outsmart the police. He does not think that he needs security manuals. Furthermore, if he were going to use such guides, he would not use those produced by political extremist organizations. Criminals generally tend to look at such people as kooks or weirdos, off in some distant world of unreality. This being the case, they are certainly not going to give much credence to their ideas concerning security. Another reason revolves around the issue of discipline. While political extremists are quite disciplined, common criminals tend to be the exact opposite. Even if the leader of a street gang, narcotics cartel, or the Mafia ordered his underlings to study a security manual, many would not do so unless they were convinced that they would be tested and punished if they failed the examination.

Why Law Enforcement Officers
Should Study Extremist Materials

The value of law enforcement officers reading and carefully studying clandestine "how-to-function" documents is akin to a football coach having the opposing team's playbook. Documents addressing a group's security measures can give an officer a good idea of which investigative techniques will likely be the most useful and effective, and which may not be of value. If a group's security documents tell members not to talk to a law enforcement officer under any circumstances, the investigator will know that straightforward contacts will probably not develop much information. If, on the other hand, a group's security information permits members to talk to police, but tells them to have a witness present, the officer knows what to expect and can prepare accordingly. If an investigator notices that a group's security directions are flawed in some manner, he may be able to capitalize on such a failing. For example, if the group's security manual addresses everything from police interviews to electronic coverage, but makes no mention about trash covers, the investigator may want to consider using this technique, especially on a newer member who may not have even considered the fact that police might look in his garbage.

Knowing how group members are supposed to operate can help the investigators separate overt supporters from the clandestine functionaries who really should be targeted. As an illustration, seeing a person pick up a document in a particular manner to avoid leaving fingerprints could strongly suggest that individual is clandestine, if the terrorist group's operational manual instructs members to handle documents in that manner.

The very security procedures that a terrorist group employs to protect its operations can actually lead to its downfall. Investigators should make a concerted effort to learn whatever they can about a group's security and general operational policies. "Know thy enemy" is the philosophy that must be followed. Efforts should be made to determine which policies are rigidly enforced and which are optional. They should know whether leaders and senior members make an effort to carefully explain the reasons behind certain rules and directions. If new recruits are taught to follow operational rules in a rote manner, law enforcement investigators can capitalize on this failing. People who blindly do things without knowing the reasoning behind it are apt to make mistakes or become careless when under tension or pressed for time. If nothing else, they will not know how to function if something impedes them from following the "rules."

The fact that a group member is using security procedures outlined by the terrorist group can be used against him or her in court. It is for this reason that terrorist investigations must be carefully conducted, and often require more attention to detail than other criminal investigations. Frequently the investigator will be well under way on his case before he encounters instructional manuals used by the group. If he has been careful in the early stages of investigation, he might be able to review previous interview, surveillance, and informant documentation and determine that information is contained therein that shows that the person is practicing group-mandated security procedures.

How to Locate Terrorist Manuals and Guides and Determine Security Procedures

Some manuals and operational guides are readily available on the Internet. The investigator need only look at Web sites operated by supporters of the clandestine terrorist group.

The more covert directives are for members only and are not likely to be readily accessible on the Internet although some of the documents may be located on secure sites. If the group is clandestine and is perpetrating terrorist attacks, it is very likely that there are certain written or unwritten guides concerning security and operations. The very fact that the investigator realizes this much is important because it puts him or her on alert for this information, which can be located in several ways:

Informants. If the investigator has a source inside the group, he or she should ask about such manuals and about any specific verbal training of which the source is aware, concerning everything from dealing with police to bomb making. Periphery informants may not have ready access to such materials, but could encounter some of it, if they know to be alert for it. Frequently an informant will be exposed to group security procedures either by being told about them, seeing manuals and guides regarding them, or simply by observing the members of the group employing them. However, because informants are not trained investigators, and sometimes do not realize exactly what their handling officers are seeking, they may not volunteer the information. Informants must be specifically asked about security procedures to ensure that the information is obtained.

Former group members. Someone who was once in the group and left for any reason, including arrest or banishment, is likely to know about security training. He may no longer have any written materials, but he should be able to provide information about what is contained in such documents. He certainly should know what verbal and hands-on instruction he received.

Members of related groups. Sometimes members of brother groups have access to, or are aware of, verbal and written training and security materials.

Surface support group members. Even though the covert materials may only be intended for members who are clandestine, groups sometimes make some of their training available to certain support people, because if these people need them to perform a task, it is important that they also practice correct security measures.

Searches. Anytime a terrorist-related search is done, efforts should be made to locate training/security materials. If at all possible, the search warrant should be written so that such items can be taken. For example, if an affidavit is being prepared for a search for bombs in a suspected safehouse/bomb factory, it is logical that there may be diagrams about bomb construction. Therefore, a request to look for such documentation should be included in the affidavit.

Surveillance. Surveillance personnel monitoring political extremists should always be alert for anything that seems unusual or that appears during multiple coverages. For example, different suspects within a group who during each surveillance are seen stopping to look into store windows might have been taught to use the reflection in the glass to detect surveillance. An investigator could conceivably assemble his own "manual" of security for the group based upon what he sees members doing. If at some later date the investigator encounters a person willing to talk about the group, he could determine the type of training that person received, and ascertain if his own observations were correct.

Terrorist Training

Not all of the instruction that extremist groups provide to their members is in the form of written materials or verbal lessons. Some involves practical exercises in which group members not only learn how to conduct attacks, but also practice new techniques. Not all groups do this. Militias of the 1990s and those operating today periodically stage firearms training sessions in open areas. While many of these groups are not terrorists per se, a number of them are anti-government, and some members of such groups have been arrested for terrorism-related violations. Other right-wing and left-wing extremists have also conducted field exercises. Even international terrorist groups have staged training exercises in the United States.

What is taught in such sessions can be of value to law enforcement officers. It may help to solve cases, especially if it can be ascertained that a device used in an attack is similar to one that a particular extremist cell used in a practice session. Some of the training sessions may not even be legal—possibly staged on public property in violation of a statute, or on private property without the permission or knowledge of the owner. The session may involve explosives, which in most cases will violate the law—if for no other reason than illegal possession or transportation of the explosives. Illegal firearms, including automatic weapons, may also be used.

Investigators who learn that an extremist field training session was held at a particular location would do well to conduct a search of that area for evidence that may be of value at some future date. For example, shell casings could be compared with those found at the scene of a previous terrorist attack. Remains of an incendiary or explosive device from a training location could be held for comparison with evidence recovered from a future arson or bombing. Remains of bullets, explosives, or incendiaries could be mentioned in applications for electronic coverage or arrest warrants. The fact that bullets from an illegal firearm were found at a location where training took place could be of value in an affidavit for a search warrant of an individual's residence seeking that firearm.

Summary

Security is a key element in the successful operation of a clandestine terrorist group. Rather than leaving each member to his own resources to determine how to best protect themselves and the organization, many groups offer their members manuals, guides, or at the very least, verbal training related to various elements of security. They also provide them with "how-to" directives with respect to covert operations, target selection, and staging attacks. It is important that law enforcement officers be alert for information that a group provides with respect to security so they can better tailor the techniques that they use against the group.

⑦ Interviewing

The interview could easily be described as the "mother of all investigative techniques." It was probably the first investigative technique ever employed by law enforcement, and is likely to be the most commonly used. It is difficult to imagine any investigation being conducted without at least one attempted interview.

For criminal justice purposes, an interview is a directed verbal discourse with a suspect, witness, victim, or other involved party. Ideally, an interview involves one or two law enforcement interviewers and a single interviewee. It is not wise for an investigator to interview two or more people at the same time, because the strongest person present is likely to influence the weaker interviewees. On occasion, someone representing the interests of the interviewee, such as an attorney, probation officer, youth counselor, interpreter, or parent may be present during an interview. In such situations, care must be taken to ensure that statements attributed to the person being interviewed are in fact made by him or her, and not by others present during the interview.

Special care must be taken in conducting interviews with terrorist group members and their close sympathizers. Although many terrorists will refuse to submit to an interview, a number of those who agree to the interview will insist that their attorneys be present. In such situations, it is likely that the attorney will also be a group member or at least a sympathizer. Consequently, it will not be unusual for such an attorney to interject political rhetoric into the interview and to attempt to interrogate the investigators on philosophical issues. The attorney may also attempt to determine how much information the investigator has and from what sources he gathered his evidence. Left-wing group members are often more likely to want to have an attorney present than are right-wing extremists. Investigators should be aware that not all people functioning as legal counsel for extremists are in fact licensed attorneys. This is particularly true with respect to right-wing situations, in which the so-called legal representative may have only attended a week-long course on common law matters or tax avoidance. Investigators will find it to their advantage to have an exchange of credentials with attorneys during which they display their police badge and ID card while at the same time asking to study the lawyer's identification.

A recent trend with respect to interviews involving certain right-wing terrorists is for them to invite "witnesses" to be present during the proceedings. As with sympathizer attorneys, these "witnesses" are not impartial participants. They hold similar political beliefs, and are sometimes mentors of the person being interviewed. Regardless, if the attorney or a "witness" is permitted to be present during an interview, it is important that only statements made by the person being interviewed be documented as emanating from him or her. There is no prohibition against creating separate documentation in which statements made by people observing the interview are recorded. In particular, if such observers make incriminating statements, their comments should be documented.

During an interview concerning a right-wing activist's involvement in the distribution of fraudulent financial documents, a "witness" might attempt to assist the interviewee by stating that everyone, including himself, is distributing the documents in question. Because this would be an admission of a crime, a separate interview report should be prepared documenting this person's statement.

There is no attorney-client privilege that would somehow protect an attorney from statements that he might make during the course of a law enforcement interview of his client. It is true that investigators should advise subjects and certain other suspects of their constitutional rights concerning self-incrimination prior to an interview. However, investigators are not obligated to advise others, such as attorneys and "witnesses" who voluntarily accompany an interviewee, about their constitutional rights. If, during the interview of a subject, his attorney or "witness" blurts out an admission to a criminal act, the investigator would be wise at that point to advise that person of his or her privilege against self-incrimination before questioning him or her any further about the admission.

Many investigations begin with an interview. A citizen files a complaint with a police agency. An officer talks to the victim of a crime. An investigator interrogates people in an effort to develop a case from information that he has received from an informant or other source. Many investigations conclude with at least an attempted interview of the subject of the case. In between the initial complaint and the attempt to obtain a confession, numerous other interviews are likely to take place.

An interview is a technique that may be used at any time during the course of an investigation. Often interviews just happen and the investigator has little or no time to prepare for them. There are, however, interviews that are scheduled by the investigator and therefore can be carefully organized and planned. It is during these interviews that investigators can best employ a specific method of interrogation in order to learn the complete truth from the interviewee.

In many respects, interviews conducted in terrorism investigations are not much different from those conducted in any other important case. However, terrorist interviews will probably be complex and lengthy because politics are bound to creep into them, and lawyers and "witnesses" may be present. Furthermore, it is possible that the terrorist subject has had specific training with respect to the various interviewing techniques that investigators use. Some terrorist groups make pamphlets outlining law enforcement interview methodology available to their members. The ordinary criminal rarely has any insight with respect to the interview techniques that an investigator will use against him or her.

In terrorism cases, investigators should be mindful that they may be conducting the only interview they will ever get with the subject. It is possible that, upon reflection and contacts with fellow terrorists, the subject will not submit to any further meetings with law enforcement personnel. As a result, terrorist interviews must be conducted carefully and in detail. Information developed must be diligently explored. Efforts must be made to identify evidence, witnesses, and other elements that can be used to confirm the subject's statements, if he should later recant or refuse to testify. Interviews with terrorists must be properly documented in a timely manner. If important information is developed, the investigators should assume that subsequent use of the information will be challenged in court.

Investigators should realize that many terrorists, particularly on the leftist side, will refuse to allow themselves to be interviewed about anything. In fact, some terrorist groups actually school their members against talking with any law enforcement agency. Groups give their members brochures that warn against even exchanging greetings with law enforcement officers, much less talking with them. These documents suggest that law enforcement personnel are highly skilled at eliciting information from people. They warn that even the most innocuous question can cause the person being interviewed to provide damaging information that the investigative agency did not previously have.

Samples of leaflets that have been distributed to people associated with terrorist groups for the purpose of discouraging them from submitting to law enforcement interviews can be seen on pages 74 and 75.

While it is true that many terrorist groups caution their members against talking with law enforcement personnel, there are some organizations that welcome law enforcement contacts. These people are usually affiliated with certain right-wing, special-interest, or ethnic groups. A few of these groups actually seek to recruit law enforcement officers into their organizations. They believe that if they can present the officer with the "facts" about the situation, they can at least gain his or her sympathy, if not support. During the 1970s, various Yugoslav terrorists operating in the United States believed that law enforcement would be sympathetic to them because they were anti-Communist and anti-Russian. During the 1990s, some militia-type extremists believed that local law enforcement officers would buy into their fears of transnational government. Some anti-abortion advocates believe that they

DON'T TALK TO THE F.B.I.

Hot on the heels of Reagan's "anti-terrorist" crusade, the FBI is back in town. Many people have questions about what to do when confronted by the FBI. Here are some guidelines.

DON'T TALK TO THE FBI!

You don't have to. There is no law requiring any of us to talk to an FBI agent, a cop or any other investigator. Every bit of information given to the FBI, no matter how unimportant it might seem, becomes part of their intelligence gathering on the movement; a piece of the puzzle they are fitting together to be used to destroy people and organizations. Often the FBI comes and says something like, "Your name has come up in the course of an investigation into a bombing conspiracy. If you can just answer a few questions, we're sure we can clear this up." The purpose of statements like these is to catch us off guard, to scare us and get us to talk.

Some people think we can outsmart the FBI, turn their questions around and get information from them. Experience has shown that this is dangerous: our questions and answers often provide insights for the FBI to go on. Likewise, the FBI will try to catch us up if we make statements that they can prove are false. When this happens they can threaten us with perjury charges. The best thing to do is REFUSE TO TALK.

DON'T LET THE FBI INSIDE YOUR HOUSE!

If they come to your door, don't let them inside. If they get a foot in the door, demand that they leave at once.

Legally they can only enter your home if they have search or arrest warrant. If they say they have a warrant demand to see it and demand to see their I.D. If they wai to ask a few questions, show you pictures of people, as about who uses your phone, etc. say "No, I have nothin to talk to you about." If you have a lawyer, tell them tha she/he will contact them. The FBI will try to intimidat you if sweet talking fails, or vice-versa. This is why w must be clear and firm in our refusal to cooperate. Some times they will try to intimidate us by threatening to hav us subpoenaed to a grand jury. However, cooperatin with the FBI by answering a few questions will not sto; anyone from being subpoenaed. It only encourages then to see you as potentially talkative before a grand jury.

Not only are activists being visited by the FBI, but fam ily members, neighbors and co-workers are being ap proached as well. Often the FBI will threaten to harass ou parents or friends. These kinds of slimy threats are no thing new, but still they can present problems. In mos cases, it makes sense to try to educate relatives and friend *before* the FBI shows up. The FBI's history of dirty trick: is widely known and we can draw on this as we talk tc people.

The government and FBI want to use their fear tactics lies and spies to put us on the defensive. Now is the time to build a real wall of resistance, to refuse to be isolated o turned back. The FBI, which was vilified during the 1960s, and rejuvenated in the 1970s, must again be the target of our contempt and our outrage in 1984.

the FBI is in town...

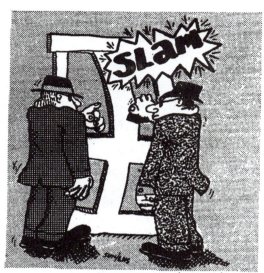

and snooping for bits and snatches of information. They ask questions of our friends and acquaintances about us and our activities. Through the use of Grand Juries, they attempt to delve into our personal lives in ways which otherwise would be unavailable to them. They seek information from those who may know nothing of the activities being investigated, sometimes breaking into people's houses or just generally harassing them.

It is public knowledge that one of the primary goals of the FBI in the last decade has been to crush the Left through harassment, prosecutions, and undercover disruption. The budgets of police agencies at every level continue to soar.

That is no big surprise. This is a time of economic and political crises in the United States. The government has suffered recent setbacks with the people's victories in Vietnam and Cambodia, Watergate, the CIA and FBI exposes, and ever-increasing inflation and unemployment.

In such a period, the FBI and other police agencies have their tasks cut out for them: divide, disrupt, intimidate, slander and jail people. They are especially eager to capture those who have been forced or have chosen to go underground; to cut off the support of their friends; and to paint the entire radical movement as a criminal enterprise.

With the recent nationwide upsurge of FBI and Grand Jury activity, the government is attempting to intimidate several specific communities. First, the attacks center on the women's and gay communities. The FBI alleges that these groups have aided and abetted underground fugitives. They continue to single out the Native American movement and their struggle for sovereignty. They are seeking information about us, and as recently seen in Kansas, South Dakota, San Francisco, and New York, about our people's lawyers.

Our collective response will be crucial in determining the extent to which they succeed in isolating us from each other.

 don't talk!

can engender support from officers who are Catholic, or who are members of other churches that also oppose abortion. Similarly, animal rights supporters believe that they can convert investigators who love pets to their cause.

Interviews with terrorists who want to recruit the officer are difficult to conduct. A skilled and talented interviewer who is willing to devote the time can probably acquire some information, but it will be a challenge. Such interviews frequently end up as political tirades that may result in the subject becoming even more entrenched in his views. Law enforcement officers would be wise to avoid engaging in political debates with interviewees. This is not to suggest that officers should refrain from discussing (not debating) certain aspects of a subject's political beliefs. Indeed, some statements made by a subject concerning his beliefs can be used as evidence against him in court.

Officers should make an effort to understand the political philosophy of the subject they plan to interview. Often such subjects live in a world of their own that is quite apart from the mainstream of society. This can certainly be true of people who reside in communes or compounds, or who have been raised in a closed political society, including homeschooling. It is valuable for the officer to be knowledgeable about concepts that are unique to that person's beliefs. An investigator interviewing a right-wing subject should be cognizant of such terms as "Aryan," "common law court," "de jure" and "de facto" government, "Uniform Commercial Code," and "sovereign citizen." In fact, it would be valuable for the investigator to discuss such terms as they arise during the interview. The investigator probably should not give the appearance of being an "expert" in the subject's political philosophy. The investigator would probably elicit more cooperation if he or she indicated that he or she was aware of a given concept, but was uncertain of its exact meaning. An interviewer might say, "I've heard the terms de facto and de jure government used, but I am really confused about what they mean—could you explain them to me?" An officer who responds with complete ignorance to the subject's political rhetoric is likely to fail in his efforts to interview that person.

Some terrorists' political beliefs are heavily based in religion. It is important that the investigator understand the subject's spiritual beliefs. It not only helps in understanding the subject's mindset and statements, but it also helps to avoid interview-ending blunders. Some extremist religions have restrictions and prohibitions that could easily be violated by a naïve interviewer. For example, an investigator who offered coffee or a cigarette or a certain food item to a person whose religion banned that item might offend the subject to the extent that he would be uncooperative.

The interviewing officers should never agree with, or show support for, any illegal actions that a terrorist mentions during an interview. It is a mistake for an officer to assume that he can win a subject's confidence by claiming to support terrorist activities conducted by the subject and his group. Such statements can later be used against that officer if he is a witness in court. Also, if at some later date the subject decides to leave his group and turns to law enforcement for help, he is not likely to talk to an officer who has told him that he supports such acts as bombings or assassinations. If an investigator thinks that he must show some empathy for the person's beliefs in order to keep the interview going, he could say something like, "From what you have told me about the situation, I can see how you could be angry and want to do something."

What Is Sought during an Interview

Regardless of whether an interview is spontaneous or well-planned and scheduled, the investigator conducting it should ask the following questions:

Who?

What?

When?

Where?

Why?

How?

Just about any interview that addresses these six questions will be complete. Unfortunately, due to time constraints and distractions, and the fact that the people being interviewed are reluctant to respond to all questions, many interviews fail to include responses to all of these questions. Before allowing an interviewee to leave, a wise investigator will review his or her notes to determine whether he has resolved these six questions. Most investigators realize a failing in one of these areas when they attempt to document the results of their interview and realize that it does not flow properly because something logical is missing from their narrative.

Interview Methods

With experience, investigators tend to adopt, develop, and refine their own methods for conducting interviews. Some investigators use a variety of methods, depending on the situation. Others tend to use a single method that they find most comfortable. Some investigators do what comes naturally to them. Others adopt an established interview method, or copy one used by a respected peer. There are a variety of interview methods that can be used. Several of them are described below.

Routine or Conventional. This form of interview is the most common and is more conversational than it is interrogative. The investigator using this method is attempting to get responses to the basic "who, what, when, where, why, and how" questions. He or she is not trying to intimidate, trick, or even convince the person being interviewed. This method is often used with complainants, victims, or suspects in an investigation. There are no threats involved. The questions are straightforward. What happened? When, why, and how did it happen? Who did it? Where were you when it happened?

Confrontational. This form of interview is used almost exclusively when interviewing subjects, suspects, and people believed to be less than candid, because it essentially mandates that the interviewer challenge the person being questioned. A sense of fear and threat is generated. The interviewer makes clear that he or she is demanding nothing less than a complete response, and expects to receive it immediately. The interviewer attempts to convey that he has the ability to determine when someone is lying to him, so the person being interviewed had better be truthful.

There is no friendliness or empathy expressed in this kind of interview. There are glares, grunts, growls, table pounding, yelling, impatient gestures, and some sarcasm on the part of the interviewer. Crying, begging, complaining, or vomiting will get the person being interviewed nowhere. The interviewer makes it seem as though he already knows the truth, but nonetheless wants the satisfaction of hearing the subject say it out loud.

If this method is properly executed, the subject will think to himself, "get me out of this room and away from this person." Many terrorists will not allow themselves to be bullied, and therefore will not respond to this method of interrogation. Virtually no sympathizer attorney will permit a client to submit to this kind of interview.

The confrontational method is not without its faults. Some people are completely turned off by dominating people, and may refuse to cooperate primarily because of the way they are treated by the interviewer. A more serious problem involves the risk of a coerced confession. The person being interviewed may become so controlled by the investigator's demanding personality that he or she will admit to guilt or whatever the investigator proposes.

In one terrorism investigation, a demanding interviewer forcefully suggested that several people had been present during a particular clandestine meeting. When the subject claimed to be unsure about that fact, the interviewer let it be known that he already knew the facts, and expected the subject to confirm them if any kind of deal was to be made to reduce charges against the subject. The subject agreed to the "facts" as outlined by the interviewer, and the results of the interview were documented. When the subject subsequently testified against fellow group members in court, he confirmed that the meeting had occurred as outlined in the written report of his earlier interview. Following his testimony and the resultant cross-examination by the defense attorney, the subject realized that one of the people that the prosecutor had claimed was present at the clandestine meeting was not in fact at that meeting. On the following day the subject recanted this part of his statement. The change in the witness's testimony destroyed his credibility with respect to his entire statement, and weakened the prosecutor's case.

In this example, it is likely that the interviewer's confrontational method caused the subject to cooperate more quickly and completely than he might have if another interview method had been used. However, this method almost certainly caused the subject to agree to "facts" about which he was uncertain.

"Just the Facts." Sergeant Joe Friday of the long-running *Dragnet* radio and television programs used a machine-gun approach to interviewing that has often been mirrored by law enforcement officers. It is possible that the actors in those programs copied the technique from actual detectives, because in the early *Dragnet* radio programs, Joe Friday did not use the method as intensively as he did in later episodes. When using this technique, Sergeant Friday puts up with no nonsense from anyone, including witnesses, victims, and subjects. He frequently tells people that he wants "just the facts." His questions are intended to eliminate all irrelevant information and conversation. He comes across as neither friendly nor cold. Instead, he is all business and impatient to get things done. He can be threatening and loud, but only when it appears that someone is lying to him, or being disrespectful to his position as a police officer. The objective of this method is to get the interviewee into a pattern of quickly and concisely responding to every question asked, without giving him or her enough time to concoct a lie or story.

As investigators mature, many tend to use the "just the facts" method to a certain extent. Witnesses, victims, and average citizens often ramble and veer off on tangents as the investigator is attempting to develop facts. Some guilty people trying to hide the truth attempt to change the direction of the interview in an effort to avoid having to address the issue by lying. To deal with this, an investigator must take action, such as employing the "just the facts" interview method, to quickly learn the details of what has occurred. Some investigators even find this method permeating their communication skills to the extent that they constantly try to limit all of their conversations, including when off-duty, to getting "just the facts."

The "just the facts" method of interviewing has the potential failing of alienating certain people, especially innocent victims and bystanders. Some people enjoy making everything they have to say into a "story" that includes irrelevant information. Interviewers who refuse to listen to such stories come across as callous and uncaring. More problematic for the interviewer is that, when forced to stick to the facts, some people forget to mention important things that they would probably have included if permitted to give a rambling account.

Following a bank robbery, investigators using the "just the facts" method of interviewing quickly interrogated tellers and customers in order to obtain a description of the offender. However, one investigator chose to allow a witness to ramble though her account of the robbery, which included her reason for being in the bank, and an outline of her health problems. After some time, the woman told about how the robber had bumped into her as he limped out of the bank. As it turned out, the offender had an artificial leg. Although the other witnesses had all noticed the limp, none had mentioned it, because they had been rushed by interviewers.

Best Buddy. As the title suggests, the officer using this method attempts to elicit cooperation and information by demonstrating that he is friendly and easygoing. The interviewer wants to be perceived as a kind, understanding person who will try to help the person being interviewed. The officer using this method is not usually time-driven. He will ramble on about sports, the economy, and just about anything else that he believes will make the interviewee feel more comfortable. He wants to convince the interviewee that they both "put their pants on in the same way," and that they both make "human" mistakes. The interviewer wants to convey the impression that "I'm your friend, we're very much alike, you can tell me."

Another way to use this method is to employ a "smile campaign." Whenever the investigator encounters people that he hopes to ultimately interview, he will give them a warm smile and a wave of his hand. If possible, he will greet these people with a friendly "Good morning" or "Have a great day." If all goes well, the person will eventually warm up and respond with a smile and a comment. As time passes, the interviewer will attempt to expand his comments until such time as he is actually engaging the subject in a conversation. Hopefully a formal interview will eventually be possible.

Terrorists like to talk about their cause. The interviewer using the "best buddy" method with political extremists may find himself engrossed in endless philosophical discussions with the subject. In the long run, this may be a good thing, because it may convince the person being interviewed that the investigator is truly concerned about what is the most important aspect of his life, namely his political existence. Unfortunately, some terrorists will ramble indefinitely about their political philosophy, and they will never really respond to the investigator's law enforcement questions.

The "best buddy" method can work well if the investigator detects that the subject harbors some guilt for what he has done. The fact that a subject is a dedicated terrorist does not mean that he wanted to kill an innocent person with a bomb. In such a situation, an investigator may want to discuss what can be done for the victim's family, or what can be done to ensure that innocent people will not be harmed in future bombing attacks.

The "best buddy" interviewer can often have some success in convincing people to cooperate by offering them more palatable-sounding alternatives to the criminal activity under investigation. Statements like the following can be used: "You're not like all of those other killers—you didn't really mean for the person to die." "You had no way of knowing that a little bomb like that would do so much damage." "It looked like that fur store was flaunting how badly it treated animals by the display that it had in its front window." "Seeing pictures of those discarded fetuses could make anyone angry."

Good Guy-Bad Guy. In this interview method, two investigators work in tandem in order to elicit cooperation. One investigator assumes the role of the "bad guy," who is unbending and nasty. He makes it seem that he is convinced that the interviewee is "no good" and not worthy of any favors. As far as the "bad guy" is concerned, there is already enough evidence to "hang him," so why should he waste his time listening to lies? In contrast, the "good guy" investigator presents an understanding façade, making it seem that he either believes the interviewee, or that he at least has some empathy for him. During the interview, the two investigators act as though they do not like each other, and that they do not want to work together. The concept behind this method is to encourage the interviewee to cooperate with the "good guy" because he and the "good guy" have a common opponent, namely the "bad guy." It is designed to show that the "bad guy" is more forceful than the "good guy." Consequently, if something does not happen to end the interview quickly, the "bad guy" will push the "good guy" out of the picture, and the interviewee will be left at the mercy of the "bad guy." In some situations, a third interviewer will enter the scene and take the side of the "bad guy" in an attempt to encourage the subject to try to even the odds by joining the "good guy," thereby cooperating with the "good guy."

The "good guy-bad guy" interview method is very commonly used. In fact, many salespeople, particularly in the automobile industry, have perfected it with great success. One wonders how many people have purchased cars from the "good guy" salesperson because they became convinced that a "bad guy" salesperson or manager was preparing to terminate the "good guy" for being too honest or decent.

The "good guy-bad guy" method will only work if the two investigators are on the same page and meet the demands required of their roles. This may be difficult, especially if the officers do not work with one another on a regular basis. Both officers often end up in playing the "bad guy," which essentially turns the method into a kind of "double-whammy" confrontational interview. Unfortunately for law enforcement, this method has received a great deal of exposure in films and television. Most terrorists, particularly leftist-oriented terrorists, will be able to identify it almost immediately and counter it. Some extremist publications specifically describe this method of interview, and warn their followers not to be deceived by it. The method might work in certain political extremist interviews if one officer can feign a curiosity or interest in an aspect of the subject's cause while the other investigator appears to care less.

The Wanderer. Like the fabled television detective, Columbo, the investigator using this interview method has a tendency to wander from point to point, often asking easily answered questions that have nothing to do with the topic. The objective of this method is to keep the interviewee off-balance so that he or she cannot remember each answer that he or she has given, because the investigator has veered off on tangents. If the subject is telling the truth, it is likely that he or she will respond similarly to a question no matter how many times it is asked. If the subject is lying, he or she may experience difficulty recalling his or her story if intervening discussion on other topics has occurred. The trick is for the interviewer to keep track of the various inconsistencies and then spring them on the interviewee. It is hoped that a confession will result as the subject comes to realize that the investigator is not as weird or confused as he or she believed. Even if a confession does not occur, it is still likely that the officer will learn some information that he would not have learned otherwise.

The "wanderer" method is difficult to use effectively. The outgoing "in charge" personalities of many law enforcement investigators make it difficult for them to pretend to be confused bunglers. The method can also be time-consuming, and can prove problematic if it is tape-recorded or videotaped, because a jury asked to watch a tape of such an interview could become confused and believe the investigator to be less than competent.

The Perfect Dummy. In this method, the investigator paints himself as a less-than-bright person. Moreover, he is very slow and methodical, seemingly wanting to make sure that his notes are absolutely correct. In fact, the investigator tries to convince the person being interviewed that his notes are at least as important to him as is the resolution of the case. This interviewer constantly makes statements like, "Let me make sure that I have this right." "So in summary ..." "I'm a little confused about ..." "Now, let me get this straight." The objective of this method is to make the subject wait before he can give his whole story. People who have concocted a lie have a tendency to want to state it, and then, if need be, explain and defend their lie. With this method of interview, the person is constantly being interrupted while trying to tell his lie. He finds himself repeatedly restating parts of his tale before he can get the whole story out. This can be a very effective method, because it has the tendency to confuse the person being interviewed and can cause him or her to forget parts of a rehearsed story. Even worse for the interviewee, it can cause him or her to mix true statements with false statements. Unfortunately, this interview method is difficult to conduct. This method should not be done in the presence of another investigator, unless that investigator is fully aware of what is happening. This method is likely to be difficult to employ with political extremists. Leftists and some right-wing subjects will not tolerate it. Less-educated extremists (particularly some right-wing Ku Klux Klan-types) and foreign terrorists may become lost, especially if there is a language barrier.

In one particularly difficult interview, an investigator repeatedly interrupted a subject's story and kept regressing, supposedly to get his notes correct. Not only did the subject become increasingly upset with the investigator's apparent over-concern for keeping detailed notes, so did the other officer involved in the interview. At one point, this officer butted into the interview, stating "he already answered that question, don't you remember? He said ..." Several minutes later, the interviewing officer sprang the trap. He suddenly rattled off inconsistency after inconsistency to the subject. Taken totally off-guard, the subject confessed.

Following the interview, the other officer advised that up until the confession, he had believed that the subject might be innocent. He also admitted that, during the course of the interview, he had come to suspect that the interviewing investigator was one of the dumbest people that he had ever encountered. Clearly, the two officers had not collaborated concerning interview methods prior to the interview.

The Open End. In this interview method, the investigator refrains from asking specific questions. All inquiries are general and vague. In many respects, the open-end interview is the exact opposite of the "just the facts" interview method. Time is not a factor in the open-end method. The idea is to get the subject talking. If he chooses to ramble or go off on tangents, only minimal effort will be expended to bring him back on course. The investigator avoids giving the subject any information that may assist him in constructing a story. Instead of asking whether the subject attended a particular function, the investigator might ask the subject what he did on Saturday evening. Instead of asking about his business relationship with a particular person, the investigator might ask what he knows about that person. If the investigator receives a positive response, he might follow up by asking additional vague questions. One purpose of the "open end" interview is to keep the subject guessing about the depth of the interviewer's knowledge. Another purpose is to keep the subject believing that he, the subject, has control over the direction of the interview. In order to keep that control, however, the subject comes to believe that he must provide some information. Unfortunately for the subject, he does not know how much information will be needed to appease the interviewer; consequently, he may end up giving more information than he otherwise would have.

Terrorists are taught to not cooperate with law enforcement. For this reason, many will not respond to open-ended questions. Those who do respond will often go into long philosophical diatribes, and may never provide any pertinent information. However, some may make damaging admissions while talking about their politics. Most lawyers will not tolerate an open-ended interview. They will demand that their client be asked specific questions.

Obnoxious. The obnoxious interviewer attempts to solicit cooperation by making himself so unpleasant that the person being interviewed does not even want to be in the same room with him. If this method is to succeed, it must be done in such a manner that the subject believes that the investigator conducting the interview is not just acting, but is in fact an obnoxious person. If a second investigator is involved in the interview, he facilitates the scenario by doing things to suggest that he, too, does not want to be in the room with the "obnoxious" interviewer. The "obnoxious" interviewer does not use threats or intimidation to gain cooperation. In fact, he does the exact opposite by feigning friendship, empathy, and understanding. Tricks that are used to facilitate the "obnoxious" interview method include:

> Poor physical hygiene—disheveled, body odor, bad breath, smelly cigar, generally unkempt appearance
>
> Bad manners—complete with belching, passing gas, sloppy eating, noisy gum chewing, snorting, nose-picking, and scratching in inappropriate places
>
> Invading the subject's personal space—by standing too close and going nose-to-nose with him, but not in a threatening manner

Offering food and drink in an unappealing manner—"Want a bite of my sandwich?" "Want a swig of my soda?" "I have a candy bar in my pants pocket, want to split it?"

Speaking too softly or too loudly (but not shouting at the person), speaking in a mumbled voice, blocking one's mouth with a hand when speaking. Generally making it difficult to be understood. Repeatedly using annoying phrases like, "You know what I mean?" "You know?"

Making repeated ethnic, religious, cultural, age, race, and sexual jokes, comments, and remarks that are not funny. It is best not to make any of these comments about the subject or his culture, but instead direct the remarks toward other people, including the interviewer's boss, partner, and other police officers. (Care must be used here because the subject could tell his attorney about such comments, and the attorney could ask the officer about them in court to the embarrassment of the police agency.)

Being a know-it-all, but giving the subject enough bad information to "prove" to the subject that the interviewer is a jerk. Offering simple authoritative solutions to all of the complex issues currently in the news.

The idea behind the "obnoxious" interview method is to make the interrogation so unpleasant that the subject wants to leave as soon as possible, and make the subject not want to undergo any additional interviews with this person.

Eclectic. Most investigators use an eclectic interviewing system in which they employ aspects of several interview methods during an interrogation. They tend to take a pragmatic approach in which they shift methods depending upon the subject's mood and response. Initially, such an interviewer might be very confrontational in an effort to intimidate the subject into telling the truth. When the investigator sees that he is succeeding, he may change to become a "best buddy" to the subject in an effort to encourage the subject to tell everything, because the interviewer has enough empathy to understand why he did what he did. If the subject begins to ramble, the interviewer may begin to ask rapid-fire questions in an effort to get "just the facts." At certain points during an interview, the investigator may ask very specific questions, while at other times he may ask only open-ended questions. If, during the interview, the investigator notices that some of his habits seem to irritate the subject, he may capitalize on these habits. During some parts of the interview, the investigator may make it clear that he is very knowledgeable about the topic of discussion, while at other times he may feign ignorance about what is being discussed.

The lines separating the various interview methods are not crystal clear. Aspects of an investigator's personality will enter into any interview. In fact, recent events in the investigator's personal life will often manifest themselves during an interview. An investigator who is suffering from a headache, or who had an argument with his spouse prior to coming to work, or who is going through financial difficulties, may not perform the role of "good guy" during an interview as well as he normally does. Conversely, this same investigator might be capable of doing the best "confrontational" interview of his career under these same circumstances.

There are other tactics that can be employed in connection with most of the methods discussed above. If the interview is conducted in a police station, two-way glass can be used so that observers can watch what is happening. It is possible that an observer will see things that the interviewers may miss. It also gives the interviewers a chance to leave the room and observe the subject, to see how he behaves when alone.

Some investigators have been trained in body language; consequently, they observe what the subject does with respect to everything from his hands to his feet. They watch his expressions and listen to his voice. These people may not be able to learn exactly what happened through these observations; however, many can readily detect a lie or a misleading or deceptive statement just from the subject's body movements. People talented in this field can even make correct assessments by viewing a subject through two-way glass without even hearing his or her voice. Some recent research suggests that people have a tendency to use certain words more often when they are being untruthful than when they are being honest.

Legal Aspects of Interviews

Regardless of the interview method used, the purpose of the interview is to develop all the facts that the interviewee knows. From a law enforcement perspective, the interview must be done legally and in accordance with departmental policies and procedures. Although law enforcement agencies in some countries may use torture, beatings, and other forms of physical and mental abuse as a part of their interview techniques, it is illegal for American law enforcement agencies to engage in such practices. The end does not justify the means. Just because the subject ultimately confesses to something that he did in fact do, it does not justify beating the person in order to force him to make that confession.

The law in the United States requires the police agency to make it clear to suspects that they do not have to submit to an interview, and that they have the right to consult with legal counsel before being interviewed. An advice of rights is not required to be given during all law enforcement interviews. Usually crime victims, complainants, or non-involved witnesses are not informed of their constitutional rights regarding self-incrimination. If, however, during the course of an interview with such a person, he or she makes admissions of guilt, that person should be advised of his or her rights before additional questions are asked.

For example, under normal circumstances, an investigator would not give an advice of rights to a victim teller in a bank robbery. If, however, during the questioning of that teller, she made admissions that she was involved as a co-conspirator in the crime, the investigator should suspend the interview, and advise her about self-incrimination before resuming his questions. This would be based on the assumption that the officer could not allow the teller to simply walk away from the interview after having confessed to a criminal violation.

While the exact wording of advice of rights statements may vary somewhat between agencies, they all contain essentially the same warnings. These are the *Miranda* rights, which arose from the 1966 *Miranda v. Arizona* Supreme Court decision. Essentially this court decision held that people who are subjected to custodial interrogation must be informed of certain rights. Custodial interrogation occurs when a person has been taken into custody or otherwise deprived of his or her freedom of action in any significant way. Most law enforcement agencies have printed "Advice of Rights" forms and cards that their investigators can read to people they intend to interview. This is a wise policy. Even if an investigator has memorized the form, it is best for him to read it to the subject. If he does not do so, a subject may be able to successfully argue in court that the officer failed to inform him of a particular right, such as the right to consult an attorney. Many agencies require their investigators to have the subject read and sign a form that outlines his or her rights prior to a formal interrogation being conducted.

There are gray areas concerning the advice of rights. The main ones involve exactly when a subject is considered a suspect, and when a law enforcement officer deprived the subject of his or her freedom. It is to the law enforcement agency's benefit to conclude that the person did not become a suspect until he made admissions during the interrogation. The defense will counter that the law enforcement's agency interviewed the subject because they had evidence of his guilt. In the long run, it is probably to everyone's advantage to give the subject the benefit of the doubt and to advise him of his rights whenever any question arises. It is reasonable to assume that if an investigator has even the slightest concern regarding this issue, a defense attorney will also have questions and will raise them in court. If in doubt, advise the subject of his or her rights.

The *Miranda* warning involves the following points:

> The person has the right to remain silent and, if he or she waives this right, he or she has the right to stop talking at any time during the interview;
>
> Anything said by the person can be used against him or her;

> The person has a right to receive advice from legal counsel and has the right to have legal counsel present during questioning;
>
> If the person is indigent, legal counsel will be appointed to represent him or her.

Some have claimed that, in their enthusiasm to solve a case, investigators have attempted to skirt the advice of rights requirement by claiming that the person being interviewed was not a "suspect" at the time of the interrogation. Suspects have also claimed that investigators have attempted to trick them into forgoing their rights by having a second investigator attempt to interview the subject after he or she has been read his or her rights by the first investigator, and he or she refused to submit to an interview with him. Still other subjects have claimed that investigators have tried to convince them to reconsider their decision not to talk to them. Some subjects have accused investigators of giving them confusing advice concerning the method through which they could consult an attorney. None of these practices is wise.

A subject should be advised of his or her rights when an interview is anticipated. If the subject refuses to submit to an interview based upon the advice of rights, the law enforcement agency should not attempt an interview. Similarly, if a subject asks for an attorney, the law enforcement agency should not attempt to interview him until he has conferred with an attorney. The law enforcement agency certainly should not try to convince the subject to forgo his right to consult with an attorney.

Obviously, there are situations in which a person will change his or her mind and voluntarily decide to submit to an interview after having declined initially. This is a sensitive situation. The investigator must make it clear that the subject's action is voluntary and not coerced. It is probably best that there be a second investigator, and perhaps another witness, present to confirm the willingness of the person to talk with the investigator. It would be wise to have the person sign a document outlining the voluntary nature of the interview. If the process can be videotaped, this may be a way of ensuring that there are no doubts about whether it is voluntary. It can become a sticky problem if the initial refusal to submit to the interview was made in the presence of, or under the counsel of, an attorney. If that attorney is not consulted prior to a subsequent interview, both the client and the attorney could later accuse the government of denying the subject his or her right to counsel by virtue of ignoring the counsel's advice.

Departmental policies must be followed with respect to interviews. If they are not followed, a defense attorney may be able to have a confession declared inadmissible because the investigator violated his own department's procedures. Even if the judge does not exclude such an interview, the investigator's violation of departmental policy can have a negative effect on the jury with respect to the investigator's credibility. Departmental policies could involve such things as requiring management authority to conduct interviews, rules about retaining notes, requirements that more than one

The *Miranda* Rights Interrogation Form used by the FBI.

INTERROGATION; ADVICE OF RIGHTS
<u>YOUR RIGHTS</u>

Place _____

Date _____

Time _____

Before we ask you any questions, you must understand your rights.

You have the right to remain silent.

Anything you say can be used against you in court.

You have the right to talk to a lawyer for advice before we ask you any questions and to have a lawyer with you during questioning.

If you cannot afford a lawyer, one will be appointed for you before any questioning if you wish.

If you decide to answer questions now without a lawyer present, you will still have the right to stop answering at any time. You also have the right to stop answering at any time until you talk to a lawyer.

<u>WAIVER OF RIGHTS</u>

I have read this statement of my rights and I understand what my rights are. I am willing to make a statement and answer questions. I do not want a lawyer at this time. I understand and know what I am doing. No promises or threats have been made to me and no pressure or coercion of any kind has been used against me.

Signed _____

Witness: _____

Witness: _____

Time: _____

investigator be present during an interview, and procedures for documenting the results of interviews.

Some agencies have translated their advice of rights forms into various languages to accommodate non-English-speaking subjects. Investigators should use care with respect to using such forms. If the interview is conducted in English, but the subject signs a foreign language rights form, the subject may later claim that his admissions were invalid because he did not understand the questions. He could use the rights form as proof that the investigators were aware of his language limitations. There is certainly nothing wrong with using a foreign language rights form if the interview is conducted in that same language. In fact, it is a very good idea to do this, because if that person signed an English language form, and was subsequently interviewed in another language, he could later claim that he did not understand his *Miranda* rights.

Some right-wing extremists have used a unique tactic with respect to the rights and waiver form that can cause problems for investigators if not handled when it occurs. The subject will read and sign the *Miranda* rights form, but will also include with his signature a phrase like, "under threat, duress, and coercion" or a part thereof, or just letters, like "TDC." Obviously, a court will take a very dim view of an interview that has been conducted under threat or duress. It is important that the investigator immediately address this issue with the subject. If he insists upon leaving those words on the *Miranda* form, the interview should probably not take place. The investigator should also be alert for the subject using such a phrase or letters on any other forms that he might be asked to sign to include a permission to search document or a signed statement. Some anti-government subjects may try to include the term "Uniform Commercial Code" or "UCC," in conjunction with their signature. These people refuse to recognize the authority of the federal government or even of state governments. However, they still see the value of being able to move freely within the country, so they have embraced the UCC as an authority to do this. The UCC is a code of law governing the sale of goods and other transactions. In itself this term or letters will probably not negate the voluntary nature of an interview. However, because the subject chose to bring the UCC into the process, the interviewer should ask the person to discuss the nature of this term, and he should include that explanation in the documentation of the interview.

Right-wing extremists have also attempted to intimidate investigators by reading them "their rights." In some instances, they have even presented the officer with a card similar to the *Miranda* rights form used by police agencies. Usually, their "rights" card outlines some aspects of the U.S. Constitution, and reminds the officer that he or she can be sued. Investigators should not allow such warnings to negatively affect their planned interview. However, the officer should avoid signing any kind of warning form in exchange for the subject signing a *Miranda* rights form.

If there was a legal or procedural flaw in how an interview was conducted, the law enforcement agency involved should inform the prosecutor's

An Arabic version of the *Miranda* Rights Interrogation Form used by the FBI.

استجواب : الاعلام بالحقوق

حقوقـك

المكان ــــــــــ

التاريخ ــــــــــ

الوقت ــــــــــ

قبل ان نسالك اية اسئلة يجب ان تفهم حقوقك

لك الحق ان تبقى صامتا

اى شىء تقوله يمكن استعماله ضدك فى المحكمة

قبل ان نوجه اليك اية اسئلة لك الحق ان تستشير محاميا لكى تحصل منه على اية نصيحة
ولك الحق ايضا فى ابقائه معك اثناء الاستجواب

ان لم يكن فى استطاعتك ماليا توكيل محام سوف يعين لك واحد قبل بدء الاستجواب
اذا كانت تلك رغبتك

اذا قررت ان تجيب الان على الاسئلة بدون حضور محام يمثلك فمن حقك ان تتوقف
عن الاجابة فى اى وقت حتى تستشير محاميا .

التنازل عن الحقوق

قرأت هذا البيان المتعلق بحقوقى وفهمت ما هى تلك الحقوق . اننى راغب فى ان
ادلى ببيان وان اجيب على الاسئلة ولست اريد محاميا فى الوقت الحاضر . اننى اعلم وافهم
ما اقم بعمله الان . لا وعود او تهديدات وجهت الى ولا ضغط او اكراه من اى نوع استعمل
ضدى

التوقيع

شاهد ــــــــــ

شاهد ــــــــــ

الوقت ــــــــــ

office as soon as possible. Attorneys representing terrorists will carefully scan an investigation for any such errors. The best way to deal with such a problem is not to commit the violation in the first place.

Location of Interviews

Ideally, all interviews should be conducted at a location and time most conducive to convincing the interviewee to cooperate. Often this is not possible. Interviews with witnesses frequently occur at the crime scene or shortly after the incident. In the latter case, immediacy is often important; consequently, the witness must be contacted at his or her home or place of employment, rather than at the police station. For many suspects and subjects, law enforcement agencies often face a major problem just trying to convince them to submit to an interview. Forcing them to come to the office may give them extra time during which they may to decide to refuse to cooperate, or during which they can formulate a story.

Suspects and others should be interviewed at locations controlled by law enforcement officials. The room in which the interview is conducted should lend itself to the interview method that will be used by the investigators. The room used for a "just the facts" interview should be stark and businesslike, with few distractions. In contrast, a "homey" room containing some comfortable chairs and maybe some plants and pictures on the wall might go well with a "best buddy" interview. A messy, dim, poorly furnished room would likely complement an investigator using the "obnoxious" interview method.

Items that can facilitate an interview should be located close to the room that will be used. Paper, pencils or pens, a tape recorder or a videocassette recorder, drinking water, and a bathroom all fall within this category. Support personnel should also be available. This might include a stenographer, another officer to witness all or part of the session, a photographer, a supervisory investigator to render management decisions as required, and a translator (if needed).

Likewise, investigative tools should be available for use during the interview. These might include a photo album or photo spread that could be employed if the subject cooperates, or if he claims only to know people by sight and not by name. Other tools could include advice of rights forms, fingerprint cards, forms for taking handwriting samples, a telephone, and handcuffs and leg restraints, which might be needed should the subject become belligerent or despondent.

Some agencies expend considerable time planning a major interview, especially in a terrorism investigation. They employ behavioral scientists to work with investigators in creating a profile of the subject's personality. The objective is to determine how an interview can be conducted in order to elicit the most cooperation. After determining what they believe will have the greatest impact on the subject, these agencies literally construct an area where the interview will take place. For example, if the investigators conclude that the subject is nervous, and might cooperate if convinced that arrest is imminent, they will create an interview room that fulfills the subject's fears. They might lead the subject into the interview room through what appears to be an investigation work area. In this workspace might be a file cabinet bearing the subject's name on several drawers. On the floor might be a box with the subject's name thereon and a notation, such as "bank records" or "telephone records." There may be surveillance photographs of the subject tacked on a poster board propped against a wall. Another feature might be a small sign identifying a portion of the work area as being associated with the subject—"The Smith Task Force."

When the subject enters the interview room, he clearly sees several large volumes near where the interviewer is seated. During the interrogation, the interviewer will "refer" to these files. A large photo album labeled "Surveillance" might also be on the desk near the interviewer. Comments made during the interview itself could include remarks that clearly suggest that the interviewer knows everything about the subject. These could include asking the subject "How do you like your Jones 2008 computer?" "Is your father still restoring that old Model T?" "Would you like a Grape Nehi?" (the subject's favorite soda), "Did you ever find your grandfather's pocket watch?" "Did you get to spend much time with your old school friend, Lester, when he was in town last week?"

All of the props are intended to lead the subject to conclude that he is the target of a large-scale investigation involving a significant number of investigators. Furthermore, they are intended to show the subject that a broad variety of investigative techniques have been employed against him. Hopefully, the subject will conclude that his only option is to cooperate, because the investigators already know everything that they need to know in order to prosecute him.

While it is probably best to conduct interviews in locations within the control of the law enforcement officer, there are some benefits to talking to subjects in their own homes, provided that the officer is not in danger. Such interviews can be particularly valuable in terrorist investigations. The primary advantage of such an interview is that it allows the officer to see the subject's surroundings. It is possible that there might be illegal items such as automatic weapons or narcotics within view of the officer. Some political extremists believe that they have a legal or religious right to have such things and therefore may not conceal them. Even items that are not illegal may be of value in a subsequent prosecution. The fact that the officer views a book on making explosives inside a subject's residence could be later used as an element of probable cause in a search warrant application.

Some subjects are so involved in their cause that they decorate their homes with banners, flags, and other outward manifestations of their movement. Any of these items can become the subject of discussion. Obviously, the person would not display items that did not have some meaning to him. Consequently, the investigator is likely to get a response if he asks about something, or compliments it. A simple comment like, "Where did you get a Nazi flag made of such fine material?" could cause a proud right-winger to give a lengthy response about his cause. Of course, all of these materials could be used as evidence against the subject. A visit to a subject's home can also reveal the variety of items that the subject owns. This would enable a prosecutor to expand search warrant parameters. For example, if an interviewer observes that the subject has a computer, a wall safe, a gun cabinet, or file cabinets in his home, he can ensure that these items are listed in a search warrant.

The Use of Deception during Interviews ●

Many investigators have questions about how honest or dishonest they should be when conducting interviews. They realize that if they truthfully inform a subject that they have no evidence against him, he will probably not confess, and may lie to them. If, however, they tell the subject that they have proof that he committed the crime, he might be willing to cooperate in the hope of making a "deal." Investigators also realize that, in order to use certain interview methods, they must feign everything from anger and confusion to empathy in order to be effective. While this is not dishonesty, it is certainly deceptive.

Subjects often ask interviewers to explain how they learned certain facts. Not wanting to appear unfriendly, interviewers are forced to give misleading responses in order to protect informants, wiretaps, and other sources of information. Conversely, to engender cooperation, some investigators find it valuable to lead subjects to believe that they employ techniques like wiretaps or surveillance when in fact that might not be the case. Investigators will frequently cite an anonymous tip as their source of information. When the subject presses the issue, the investigator will respond by asking a question like, "Now why would someone tell us this if it wasn't true?" In actuality, the source of the information might have been an established informant or an undercover officer.

There are no specific regulations that clearly define the amount and type of deception that can be used during an interview. It is difficult for an investigator to conduct an interview with a suspect or other person without using some amount of deception. For some officers, shaking hands and extending a cheerful greeting to the subject is deceptive because the investigator may have good reason to loathe the person, and would certainly not associate with him off the job.

Training programs offered by both law enforcement agencies and other entities teach the use of deception during interviews. Some of these courses are outstanding with respect to the effectiveness of the tactics that they present. They instruct investigators about how to create an ideal environment that will induce a suspect to confess to the crime. If the law enforcement officer and the subject were operating on a level playing field, there would be few problems with employing these techniques, because only a guilty subject would confess to committing the crime.

Fortunately for law enforcement agencies, it is rare that the two sides participating in any form of interview are true equals. The investigator almost always has a better sense of the playing field. The interviewee is usually somewhat apprehensive, and believes that he is in a subordinate position. With respect to law enforcement interviews, the investigator is often better educated than the interviewee. In most situations, he possesses greater knowledge of the law and court system. Of greater pertinence is the fact that he is able to lead the person being interviewed to believe that he has the power to release him from custody or to place him in custody.

Among the strategies taught in interrogation courses such as those offered by John E. Reid and other companies are the following:

> Ask questions in such a manner as to give the person two or more choices, all of which involve an admission of guilt. A person might be asked whether he checked the building to make sure that there was no one inside before he placed the bomb. By responding affirmatively, the person is admitting to the bombing. However, he may think that he is clearing himself in the death of the night security officer who died in the explosion.

> Along this same line, offer the person possible "outs" that he can use to avoid punishment. Options usually involve blaming someone or something else for the action. "That new law the government passed was enough to make even the most peaceful person take action." "No one could stand to see a river polluted like that." "Your group's leader has a personality that makes people do whatever he wants them to do."

> Avoid asking questions that can be answered with a simple "yes" or "no." Such questions will often yield one-word responses. Ask open-ended questions, particularly ones that will yield an admission of guilt. "What happened to the gas can after the fire at the abortion clinic?" "Where did Fred get the bolt cutters that he used to cut the lock on the gate at the fur farm?"

> Try to motivate the person to express some concern for the people targeted in the crime. However, during these questions, avoid directly asking him if he was the cause of the suffering. Possibly show pictures and get the person to express some sorrow. Mention an innocent person who was not the intended victim. "Isn't it sad that this little girl will have to grow up without a father?" "What do you think of the old couple's handicraft store that was destroyed when that meat market was set on fire?"

Avoid threatening the person with prison. Instead, make him or
her believe that he or she will be free to go when the interview is
over. Of course, make it clear that the interview cannot be considered over until all of the issues have been resolved. A person who
believes that he is going to go to jail following the interview may
see no reason to cooperate. Similarly, a person who thinks that he
will ultimately go to prison may not be willing to answer questions.
If the person asks what will happen to him, it is best for the interviewer to outline a variety of punishments that people convicted
of crimes can receive, even though the case in question may not
qualify for some of the lesser alternatives given.

In theory, these interrogation techniques help motivate a guilty person
to confess the truth in order to relieve himself from his guilt, or in the hope
that he can get a break or make the whole thing "go away." Unfortunately,
some innocent but very frightened people might confess to crimes that they
did not commit. Fearing the worst and believing that they will be sent home
with a "slap on the wrist," they may ultimately admit to the violation. Having
no details about the crime, they agree with the facts posed by the interviewer.
Of course, this is not what anyone wants to have happen. Certainly no investigator would want a person to confess to perpetrating a terrorist attack if he
did not actually do it. If nothing else, it may allow the person who is actually
guilty to remain free to commit additional attacks.

Investigators who are trained in interrogation methods as outlined above
must always apply ethics to what they do. They must ensure that the person
is confessing because he actually committed the crime, and not because he
wants to go home, or fears that he must confess to avoid the death penalty.
Documentation of such interviews is extremely important. Only the details
of the crime that were provided by the subject should be credited to him. If
the subject only concurred with something that the interrogator presented,
the documentation should reflect this. As an example, "Joe Smith replied,
'yes' when asked if he stole the victim's watch after killing him" as opposed
to "Joe Smith advised that after killing him, he stole the victim's watch."
The facts of the two statements are essentially the same; however, the latter
makes it appear that the subject clearly confessed and provided a detail possibly known only to the killer (the theft of the watch).

Some things that an investigator might say during the course of an interview could come back to haunt him in court. Other statements could lead to
civil suits being filed against him. The purpose of a law enforcement interview is to develop correct information. However, the ends cannot be used to
justify the means. A law enforcement officer cannot just say anything that
he wants during an interview. Deception cannot be used to deprive a person
of his or her constitutionally protected rights. For example, with respect to
advice of rights, investigators must be truthful. An investigator cannot read a

subject his rights and then proceed to trick the subject into waiving them by giving the subject an incorrect interpretation of their meaning. An investigator cannot tell a subject that his or her right to consult an attorney only applies to a courtroom situation.

An issue that disturbs some investigators involves deceptive statements that could slander or otherwise harm another person. Again, there is no clear-cut answer. In some old movies, detectives can be seen telling a subject that his partner or a specific relative had already confessed, and identified the subject as a co-conspirator. This can present a major problem, especially when dealing with terrorists. Telling a member of an extremist political group that another group member is cooperating with law enforcement could result in that person being killed. Investigators could find themselves being sued for libel if they told interviewees that specific individuals had accused them of committing crimes when it was not true. Furthermore, giving an interviewee false information about someone else can lead to a variety of problems. For example, telling a suspect that his alibi witness is unreliable because he is a pedophile, could destroy that person's reputation if the suspect subsequently spreads this incorrect information in the community.

Others Present During Interviews

It is best if interviews involve only one or two law enforcement officers and the interviewee. Unfortunately, that will not always be the case. Interviewees may demand to have an attorney present, especially after being advised of their constitutional rights. Some subjects will only agree to submit to an interview if a specific person is present during the questioning. The agency may be forced to agree to this in order to be able to talk to the person. Sometimes the agency may be able to reach some form of compromise with the subject, and an observer acceptable to both parties can be present for the interview.

Attorneys

Attorneys are the observers that investigators are most likely to encounter during interviews. They are also probably the most likely to become vocal and involved in the interview. They are the only observer that cannot be removed from an interview without the specific consent of the subject. An investigator who forces a disruptive lawyer to leave an interview and then continues to talk to the subject is asking for trouble in court.

Some law enforcement officers prefer not to interview a subject if an attorney is present. Unless the officer has some reason to believe that the attorney will attempt to encourage the subject to submit to an interview, most investigators will probably find it easier to interview a subject on a one-on-one basis without anyone else in the room. Clearly, the presence of an attorney will temper the interview. Being an outsider, the attorney is likely to pick up on what the investigator is attempting to do, and take action to negate it. It may be very difficult for investigators to use the "best buddy" or "good guy-bad guy" methods of interviewing in the presence of an attorney who should realize what is occurring. Certainly, any competent attorney is going to limit how far an investigator using the "confrontational" method can go. The investigator who uses either the "wanderer" or "perfect dummy" methods will discover that the attorney will demand that specific questions be asked.

The presence of an attorney could present a serious challenge to an investigator attempting to conduct an interview with a terrorist. Questions concerning political motivations will probably be met with resistance from an attorney. If the attorney is a supporter of the political cause, he or she may become engaged in a philosophical debate with the investigator. He or she may also use political reasons to justify his or her client not responding to certain questions.

Usually law enforcement officers will have no reason to challenge an attorney's credentials. However, in certain political extremist cases, particularly those involving sovereign citizens, investigators should ensure that the person functioning as the suspect's "legal advisor" is indeed a licensed attorney. Some "legal advisors" have only attended a short course on common law practices and should not be afforded attorney privileges. If the subject is demanding an attorney and the investigator determines that the person who arrives to represent him is not an actual attorney, the investigator should make this information clear to the subject. In one case involving a black extremist group, it was discovered that an "attorney" being given lawyer visitation rights in a prison had never passed the bar examination, and therefore could not qualify as attorney under prison regulations.

Translators

On occasion, an interviewee will claim an inability to speak English and will want to bring his own translator to the interview. This is not a good practice. If a translator is required, the law enforcement agency should provide the translator. If a member of the agency cannot perform the function, efforts should be made to use a translator from a private company, university, other government agency, or a language training school. An interview conducted with a person using his own translator is of little value and could present serious problems in court. The interviewer has no way of knowing whose answer he is documenting. It is possible that the translator is not even giving the questions to the subject properly or that the translator is not giving the correct response to the investigator. If nothing else, the investigator may have difficulty explaining to a jury that the subject "told" him anything. A good defense attorney will remind the jury that the only "telling" was done by the translator.

Parent/Guardian

Youthful offenders may ask that a parent, guardian, or counselor be present. Although in most cases it would probably be easier if the offender were interviewed alone, common sense dictates that someone be permitted to accompany the juvenile. This will help to preclude the juvenile from later claiming that he was immature and did not understand what was happening, or that the adult interviewer terrified him into confessing to something that he did not do. On the positive side, a reasonable adult can sometimes encourage a youthful subject to cooperate. Investigators should stand firm in refusing to allow friends and peers of the subject to be present during an interview. While an older (in most cases, adult) brother or sister may be an acceptable observer, younger siblings should be restricted from interviews. Minors do become involved in political extremist groups, and do perpetrate terrorist attacks. This is true in single-issue/special-interest terrorism. Some groups recruit youths via the Internet. Because parents are not usually involved in the political activity, they are not likely to be supporters of their child's political cause and, therefore, will not necessarily be adversaries of the interviewing officers.

Witnesses

A trend during the 1990s with some right-wing extremists in the United States was for them to insist upon having a "witness" present during interviews. Such people were almost always sympathizers or fellow members of the group. Sometimes the "witness" was the subject's mentor. A "witness" might even be a minister possibly associated with a Christian Identity church or some other less-than-mainstream religion. While it is undesirable to have such people present during an interview, it may be acceptable if that is the only way that the subject will consent to the interview.

Other Observers

It is not good practice to allow friends, associates, business partners, relatives, "do-gooders," clergy, civic leaders, employers, or anyone else to sit in during an interview. If these people have information that is of value to the investigation, they should be interviewed separately.

Regardless of who is present during an interview, the subject's statements must be the only ones attributed to him in the written documentation of the interview. On occasion an observer will make a statement and the subject will acknowledge it as being correct. This is unacceptable. The investigator must make sure that the subject himself makes the statement, or that he acknowledges it when the interviewer poses it in the form of a question. The investigator must also be careful to avoid using an attorney's clarifications in his documentation of the subject's remarks. Sometimes lawyers will attempt to temper a subject's admission by saying something like, "in other words, he means …"

Recording Interviews

At the Interviewer's Request

Modern technology has made it possible for law enforcement officers to tape-record and videotape virtually every interview they conduct. Whether this should always be done is open to question for several reasons. The quality of such tapes could be poor in instances in which the interviews take place outside, such as at a crime scene. Transporting equipment, especially camcorders, during the course of a normal workday could be a serious inconvenience for investigators. The major problem with respect to recording all interviews involves transcribing the recordings. The time required to do this could impair the operations of a law enforcement agency. It is easier to prepare an interview report that summarizes an interview than it is to prepare a verbatim transcript. Furthermore, it is often necessary to prepare a summary of the verbatim transcript anyway, in order to effectively use the information.

Limiting audio or video recording to interviews with important suspects as opposed to witnesses, victims, and complainants is probably a wise compromise, if a department decides to record interviews. Clearly, it is better that a special room within the department's facility be wired for sound and video, rather than taking the equipment to interviews. If nothing else, the equipment could be permanently installed to ensure quality recording. A skilled technician could also be available to handle problems.

There are some advocates of recording and videotaping who believe that it will eliminate all charges of police brutality with respect to interviews. Of course, this is not exactly true. A subject who chooses to recant could always argue that he was threatened, beaten, or offered an inducement to cooperate before entering the interview room. He might even argue that the recording equipment intimidated him.

The primary difficulty with recorded statements is that they can limit the interview methods available to the investigators. Knowing that the tape could end up in court, investigators are likely to tone down their normal approach. When using the "good guy-bad guy" interview method, the "bad guy" will not want to appear so bad that the jury will dislike him when he appears in court. Similarly, the user of the "obnoxious" method is likely to clean up his act for fear that the judge and jury will discount his testimony because they do not like him. The use of misleading and incorrect statements will be curtailed. If they are not, the defense counsel may use them to discredit the officer. Under normal circumstances, it is likely that such tactics will not be mentioned in court, and that the jury will not be fully aware of them. If a tape and transcript of the interview are entered into evidence, the jury will learn what the interviewing officers told the subject. For example, if the interviewer convinced the subject to confess by telling him that his fingerprints were found at the crime scene, the jury will become aware of this. If the fingerprint evidence is not presented in court, the jury will know that the interviewing officer lied to the subject.

Investigators must remember that once a decision to record an interview has been reached, all future interviews with that subject should also be recorded. Consequently, if it appears that a series of interviews will be required to completely debrief the subject, the investigator should plan at the outset to either record all or record none. Courts will take a very dim view of disputed information allegedly developed during a later interview that, unlike earlier interviews, was not recorded. The defense will be able to argue quite effectively that the interview in question was deliberately not recorded so that the investigator could incorrectly claim that the subject had made admissions during it. A similar problem could arise if a department institutes a general policy to record confessions and other important interviews. If, for some reason, a particular interview that yields valuable information is not recorded, the defense will argue that the interviewing investigator violated department policy, adding that the omission was deliberate because the investigator wanted to use improper tactics during that interview.

At the Subject's Request

Because audio and video recording devices have become so readily available, many people use them regularly. More and more law enforcement personnel are encountering people who will not submit to an interview unless they can record the conversation. Some departments frown upon this. Others have no policy on recording interviews. The wise investigator will discourage the subject from recording an interview. However, if the subject insists, the investigator will have to decide whether the value of the interview is worth the cost. The investigator must remember that the subject's recording belongs to him. He could release it to the media or give it to a terrorist group to maintain in a library. The subject could alter the tape to portray the investigator in a bad light and use the tape to discredit the police department.

The problem could become more complicated if the subject asks to record the interview at a location other than at a police facility. Investigators often contact subjects at their residence, place of employment, or other location that is more familiar to the subject than to the investigator. Allowing a recording in the subject's domain creates a myriad of potential problems. The investigator will have no idea of how many people may be recording the conversation, or what they will do with it.

If an investigator decides to allow the subject to record the interview, he should use similar equipment to make a recording for his department, even if the subject promises to make a copy of his tape available to the agency. It is important that there be one accurate, complete, and correct copy of the inter-view tape on file for anyone, including a court, to review. The subject's copy could easily be altered. The subject should never be permitted to have the only copy of a recording of an official interview. In view of the small size of modern recorders, a wise investigator should assume that any interview that he has with a subject in the subject's domain is being recorded and possibly filmed even though the subject has denied such action and the interviewer cannot see the equipment!

Unique Features of Interviews with Terrorists

An actual interview conducted with a terrorist may not be all that differ-ent from those conducted with other criminal subjects. There are, however, some unique features with respect to the overall interview process that are worthy of comment.

First, motivating the terrorist to agree to an interview can be a challenge. Some are "underground," therefore any law enforcement contact with them will cause the group to scatter. This will undo all of the hard work that went into identifying the existence of the covert cell. As a result, direct contact with underground subjects must be done with extreme caution. If enough evidence exists to arrest the clandestine members, nothing will be lost by attempting to interview them. If something is discovered that strongly suggests that the group member will cooperate when contacted, and not reveal the contact to other group members, it may be appropriate to attempt to interview him. For example, if a law enforcement agency learns through a wiretap that a member of a white supremacist group actually has black ancestors, the investigator may feel confident that contacting that subject and revealing the incriminat-ing information will cause him to cooperate.

Interviews with people who have valuable information but are not them-selves members of the group can also present problems for investigators in terrorism cases. Some relatives of group members will not provide informa-tion even if they do not support the subject's political philosophy. They tend to view their relative as a well-meaning, non-criminal idealist who may be using the wrong means to do the right thing. In contrast, there are many rela-tives of terrorists who do support the overall political philosophy, if not the specific cause of the subject. These people usually prove to be uncooperative. Interviews with relatives of terrorists are often more difficult than interviews with relatives of ordinary criminals.

Some people who have information about terrorists are often too afraid to cooperate with investigators. Additionally, there may be many sympathizers for the overall cause with which the terrorist is associated. Although they may disagree with the use of violence, these people find it difficult to cooperate with law enforcement with respect to the political activities of the terrorist. For example, there may be many people in a particular state who are concerned about federal interference in local affairs. Although these people are essentially peace-loving and do not agree with a local terrorist environmental group, they may not cooperate with investigations into violent attacks committed against federal properties by that group.

The terrorist is politically motivated and his entire existence is connected with his cause. It is therefore very easy for the subject who has submitted to an interview to reflect on what he has done, and to refuse to submit to a second interview. It is important for an interviewer who has encountered a terrorist willing to submit to an interview to obtain from him an overall account of what he knows. Furthermore, it is important to try to elicit incriminating statements from the subject. In connection with this, investigators should try to obtain information that will support admissions that the suspect has made. For example, if the subject admits to having made a bomb, investigators should have him carefully describe how the device was constructed and have him draw a diagram of it. In addition, efforts should be made to determine where he procured the parts, where he tested it, where his workshop is located, and any brand names or other descriptions of the bomb's components. This is important because it will enable the investigator to develop proof that the subject was truthful in his admission even if he subsequently retracts his statements.

Interviews with religious-based terrorists can be difficult, but can yield valuable information. The investigator should ask the subject to explain how the Bible or other religious documents and doctrines support his beliefs. If the person is a "true believer," he should have little difficulty responding. The person will often justify his actions by stating that God's laws supersede man's laws. It will not be unusual at this juncture for the subject to admit to violating specific man-made laws. For example, an anti-abortion extremist may use the Bible to justify killing an abortion doctor, and claim that God's laws concerning this are more binding than are the country's laws. This is essentially a confession of guilt that can be used to convict the person.

Encouraging Unwilling Subjects to Submit to an Interview

Encouraging a subject to submit to an interview is a problem that many investigators face. This is especially true in complex investigations, including terrorism investigations. Many investigators naturally have good interrogation skills, and virtually all have undergone training in this area. If they can convince a subject to engage in conversation, they can probably develop some information of value, if not a complete confession.

Obviously, if a subject refuses to submit to an interview or asks to confer with an attorney, the investigator should not continue to question him. Confusion about the length of time that an investigator must wait until approaching a subject for another interview sometimes occurs. A general rule of thumb is that if a subject is advised of his rights and refuses to be interviewed, an investigator should not contact him again about the same case. If a subject refers the investigator to an attorney, the investigator should not attempt to conduct another interview unless that attorney concurs. Along the same lines, an investigator should not attempt to skirt this rule by asking another investigator in his department to attempt to interview the subject about the case. This policy would also cover investigators assigned to task forces. A local police officer working on a joint terrorism task force cannot ask an FBI agent who is also assigned to that task force to interview someone who has already refused to be interviewed. This is not to say, however, that an FBI agent could not interview the subject concerning another investigative matter.

What this means is that an investigator or law enforcement agency cannot make repeated contacts with a subject after that subject has exercised his constitutional right not to submit to an interview in a case. Agencies that violate this policy will often face problems in court. Any admissions a subject makes after having invoked his right not to be interviewed will probably be inadmissible as evidence against him. Furthermore, the subject could seek a restraining order against an agency that continually contacts him after he has refused to be interviewed. He could also seek a civil remedy against the police department.

A problematic situation that arises in terrorism investigations is that attorneys claiming to represent a subject might contact the law enforcement agency instructing them not to interview the subject. In some instances the attorney contact will occur before the agency has even attempted to talk to the person. These attorneys are usually members of, or closely affiliated with, the extremist cause. Their purpose is to protect the group from prosecution. Knowing that law enforcement officers can usually obtain something of value from any interview they conduct, these attorneys want to ensure that people affiliated with the political cause have absolutely no contact with law enforcement investigators. This situation presents difficulties for law enforcement officers who have been trained to respect the wishes of the person to be interviewed. They find themselves unsure of what path to take when told by someone else not to interview the person.

When facing such a dilemma, the investigator should seek advice from the department's legal counsel or from the prosecutor's office. If the attorney contact arose from an actual attempt made by an investigator to conduct an interview with the subject, the investigator should probably accept the attorney's request as legitimate. If, however, the attorney contact does not come as a result of an effort to interview the subject, it is likely that the legal counsel and the prosecutor's office will inform the investigator that he is free to attempt to interview the subject if he so desires. This situation will sometimes occur when an agency begins to interview group members, or after a terrorist attack has occurred. The group's attorney will respond by trying to prevent any contact with group members, by telling the law enforcement agency that he represents the people that he anticipates will be contacted, and that he does not want them to be interviewed. In a touch of irony, such efforts by attorneys can actually backfire in that the attorneys may give out the names of group members that the law enforcement agency did not previously know.

There are several things that an investigator can do to encourage subjects to submit to interviews.

Prepare for the Interview

Probably the smartest tactic that an investigator can use in attempting an interview with a reluctant subject is to be well prepared. This does not just mean having high-quality questions for the subject to answer, although this is certainly important. It also does not just mean having good knowledge about the subject's activities and about his group, although this, too, is beneficial to a good interview. Instead, the most valuable aspect of preparation is determining the best time to contact the person, and knowing just how to break the ice with respect to beginning a conversation with him. Informants, wiretaps, undercover agents, surveillance, and various other investigative techniques can yield the intelligence needed for the investigator to make the best approach to the subject.

The idea is to contact the subject when he is vulnerable and initiate the conversation in such a way that it will cause him to respond. For example, through a wiretap, the investigator learns that a particular group member is not in favor of the bombing that the group had perpetrated a week earlier. The investigator might initiate his contact with the subject by stating that something must be done to curtail careless attacks like the one last week in which an innocent person was almost killed. In another example, an investigator learns from an undercover agent that the subject believes that a particular group member is too sadistic. The investigator might initiate the interview with the subject by stating that his department is concerned about the sadistic nature of this person because they fear that he is causing the group to move in that direction. In both of these examples, the subject might make some kind of response before refusing to be interviewed. The subject may even agree to an interview. Obviously, an investigator can capitalize on any kind of personal problem that the subject is having including poor health, financial difficulties, or marital conflicts.

Claim a Lack of Information or Knowledge

Another method that can be considered is for the investigator to begin the contact by feigning misunderstanding or confusion about something that the person's group has done. Even though the interviewee has been taught not to cooperate with the law enforcement officers, he might automatically respond to the investigator's comment in the same manner that he would if a member of the general public had raised the issue to him. The investigator might say something like, "I just don't understand why anyone would want to bomb the statue in the park" or "I'm really concerned about the hundreds of minks that died after being released from their cages."

Another thing that can be done is to confuse philosophies and heroes. An officer might state that he just does not understand the group's Marxist beliefs, when in fact the group is involved in animal rights. An investigator may remark that the Christian Identity Church, which the subject attends, has similar beliefs to those held by the African Methodist Episcopal Church down the street. Again, the idea is to say something at the outset that will create an almost knee-jerk response from the subject.

Conduct an Informational Interview

In this form of contact, the investigator makes it clear from the start that he is there to tell the subject some facts. He then proceeds to do just that. If done properly, it can catch the subject off-guard, and he might listen and even ask questions. If a conversation follows, the investigator can also make inquiries. The following are examples of how an informational interview might go:

> "I'm Detective Bell of the Nob Hill Police Department. I want you to know that we are aware of your membership in the XYZ group. This group is bad news. We know that they have bombed buildings and shot people, and we intend to get every one of them. Their program to protect the fire ants is illogical, and the people of this country aren't going to tolerate their activities any longer."

> "Good morning. I am Sergeant Jones of the Hatfield Sheriff's Office. I have been directed by the Sheriff to inform you that we are aware that your group is providing false documentation to illegal aliens. We have brought our information to the county prosecutor, and he is presently drawing up an indictment. We have also informed immigration authorities about this, and they plan to seek federal warrants for members of your group. I strongly suggest that you hire a lawyer and follow his or her advice. You can give your lawyer my business card."

Both of these examples contain enough information to cause fear and anger, yet no questions have been asked. In the first example, the detective has, in effect, ridiculed the group's political objectives. In the latter example, the sergeant has revealed that his agency and a federal agency have enough evidence about the group's illegal activities to assemble an indictment.

Use the Grand Jury

The grand jury hears evidence and returns indictments. Most terrorists have at least heard of the grand jury system and some even oppose it as a part of their political agenda. Sometimes subjects will voluntarily agree to submit to an interview if they are given a grand jury subpoena. Investigators should take advantage of this. Unless there is a rule forbidding such practice, investigators should try to serve these subpoenas in the hope that they may prompt an interview.

The grand jury can be combined with an informational interview. The investigator may contact the subject and immediately inform him that a grand jury is hearing evidence concerning him, and that he will soon be called to testify before it. This may induce some questions.

Use of Other Agencies

If a subject refuses to submit to an interview with one agency, that agency cannot ask another agency that has similar jurisdiction to attempt an identical interview. However, on occasion, two or more agencies will be investigating different cases involving the same subject. As a result, each agency may attempt its own interview. If the subject cooperates with one agency and makes admissions, there is no reason why that agency cannot ask whether the subject has committed any other crimes. If fact, they probably should ask this question if any kind of plea bargain is being discussed. If a subject cooperates with one agency, he may agree to cooperate with others.

Investigators should avoid treading in the gray area with respect to constitutional rights. If a subject refuses to submit to an interview with one agency, no one from this agency should accompany an investigator from another agency who attempts to interview the same person about one of their cases. Similarly, an agent should not falsely identify himself when trying to interview someone who has already declined to be interviewed. For example, a militia member refuses to talk to a federal investigator and accuses his agency of being part of a United Nations conspiracy to take over the United States. Another investigator from that same federal agency cannot then approach the subject for an interview identifying himself as a deputy sheriff or local detective.

Task Forces

Law enforcement agencies should not use task forces or any other kind of cooperative police effort among agencies as a vehicle for depriving people of their constitutional rights. However, this does not preclude the members of a joint task force operation from carefully planning interviews. There is no reason the agencies cannot select whom they believe would be the best person to conduct an interview with a subject. In some cases it may be reasoned that the subject would be more likely to accept an officer from a federal agency than an officer from a local agency. In another case, it may be reasoned that a local detective would be best received by the suspect. Many right-wing subjects will talk to a sheriff's deputy before they will talk to either a city officer or a federal agent.

Documentation

In law enforcement, documenting an interview can be just as important as the actual conversation between the investigator and the subject. While it is true that if the fruits of the interview itself are what is sought and what drives the investigator, it is the documentation that records the results of the discourse for future reference. Old-time cops in the United States, including territorial marshals and sheriffs of the Old West, rarely took notes during interviews, and hardly ever returned to their offices to write reports. Indeed, many of these men were unable to read or write. Similarly, movies depicting police of the early twentieth century rarely show officers taking notes.

Things are very different today. Most courts are reluctant to accept verbal evidence that has not been documented. This is especially true if the verbal evidence is coming from a sworn law enforcement officer. One problem that must be addressed involves the rules of discovery that mandate that the prosecution reveal to the defense the evidence that they plan to present during the trial. The prosecution is bound to experience significant difficulties in turning over evidence that has never been reduced to writing (or possibly a tape-recording).

During a trial, particularly a trial involving terrorists, arguments can be made by defense attorneys that the police conducted illegal investigative techniques. Defense attorneys can argue that prosecutors are concealing facts that they should know. For this reason, the prosecutor must present a logical path of investigation so that no unresolved doubts exist. The defense will try to show examples where "gaps" appear in the trail of logical investigation. They will demand to know what led the investigator from point "A" to point "C." Often the jump was made because a victim, witness, suspect, subject, or other person told the investigator something during an interview. If that interview was never documented, the defense will claim that it never actually occurred. They will argue that the investigator engaged in an illegal act such as a wiretap or an improper search to gain the information.

Terrorism cases are almost always complex investigations. As such, they require a great deal of correlation, structure, and organization. Solid documentation of the fruits of all the investigative techniques employed is required.

The investigator should convert his interview notes into a well-written report as soon as possible. The original raw notes should be retained in agency files. It is possible that if the person interviewed later recants, the officer who conducted the interview may have to produce his or her notes as "proof" of what the subject said during the interview. Computers have had a strong impact on law enforcement. Many law enforcement officers now use laptop computers. This has made documenting interviews easier than ever before.

Pretext Interviews

Pretext interviews are law enforcement discourses in which the interviewee is not aware that he is being contacted in connection with an investigation. The interview may be with an individual or individuals who are able to provide information regarding an investigation. Some investigators take a "shotgun" approach to pretext interviews. They figure that anything gained from such an interview is more than they had before, therefore they play them by ear and ask whatever they can. This is not a good way to conduct such an interview. If an investigator decides to conduct a pretext interview, he or she should have specific areas of concern that he or she wants to address. The pretext interview should be done in such a manner that those questions can be asked with a reasonable expectation of receiving a response. Pretext interviews are fraught with danger. Investigators involved in terrorism cases should probably avoid using pretext interviews except as a last resort. Pretext interviews fall into two broad categories—covert and overt.

Covert

In the covert pretext interview, the law enforcement officer conducts the interview without informing the person being contacted that he is an investigator. In covert pretext interviews, the investigator is not working in an undercover capacity per se. He simply does not inform the interviewee of his official position. Often he does not even identify himself by any name and, if he does, he often does not have identification to support the name he uses. The following are examples of the covert pretext interview:

An investigator arranges to sit next to the target at a sporting event or in a small restaurant. He then engages the target in small talk. If successful, the investigator expands his conversation to include topics he is interested in. If at a sporting event, the investigator might lament difficulties that he had in getting to the stadium. He might ask the target if he normally drives, and if so, where he parks. If in a restaurant, the investigator might tell the subject about a family situation in the hope that the target will respond with comments about his family.

> An investigator arranges to encounter the target as he stands near a protest demonstration staged by a group with whom the subject has an affiliation. He asks the target, "What's going on?" and tries to engage the target in a conversation that will include questions about the group.

Overt

In the overt pretext interview, the investigator plainly identifies himself as a law enforcement officer, but he claims to be looking for something entirely different from the actual topic of interest. By catching the person off-guard, the investigator hopes to learn information that he might not normally be able to learn from the target. He also hopes to avoid alerting the target to the officer's knowledge about him and the fact that he is being investigated. The following are examples of how an overt pretext interview might work:

> The officer visits the target's residence and informs him that he is investigating recent burglaries in the neighborhood. He warns the target to lock his doors and windows at night, and he asks the target if he has observed any suspicious people around the area. He then attempts to engage the target in general conversation, during which he will insert questions that he wants answered. He might ask the target about his work schedule and whether there are times that his home is unoccupied.

> An officer pulls over the target's car for a valid traffic violation and engages him in conversation in the hope of developing information. He uses the traffic stop to examine the target's driver's license and vehicle registration, and to look into his car.

Pretext interviews may yield valuable information, but there are two main problems associated with them:

> **Accuracy:** The information provided by the target of a pretext interview may be inaccurate, or completely incorrect. In a pretext interview, the investigator is a stranger. The target has no obligation to tell him the truth. In the case of overt interviews, the target is aware that he is talking to a law enforcement officer. There is a tendency for the interviewee to be on guard, and tell the police officer what he believes the officer wants to hear.

Legality: Great care must be used in pretext interviews to ensure that the subject's constitutional rights are not violated. If the subject has already refused an official interview or referred investigators to his attorney, he should not be subjected to a pretext interview. Pretext interviews that enable an officer to do something that he could not normally do should be avoided. Using a pretext interview to search a person's house may seem like a clever idea, but it is illegal. Stopping a vehicle can also be a problem. A law enforcement officer often has the authority to make a traffic stop, but only if there is, in fact, a violation. Stopping someone for speeding when he or she was driving within the speed limit is improper.

Regardless of how the pretext interview is conducted, the fruits of it should be documented to reflect that a pretext was used. It is improper and highly misleading to make it appear that a target voluntarily provided information to a law enforcement officer when the target was unaware that he was even talking to a police investigator. It is also unwise to make it appear that the results of a pretext interview are as accurate as are the results of most other investigative techniques.

Summary

The interview is the most common investigative technique that an officer will use. It is difficult to imagine any case not involving at least one interview. Some cases are largely built on the fruits of interviews. Terrorism case interviews are often not as easy to conduct as interviews in many ordinary criminal matters. Some terrorists, particularly left-wing terrorists, will refuse to talk with law enforcement officers. Many terrorists who are willing to submit to an interview will use the time to promote their political views. Some will even attempt to recruit the interviewing officers to their cause. The purpose of an interview is to develop answers to the basic questions that an investigator must ask: who, what, when, where, why, and how. There are a variety of different methods that can be used when interviewing a suspect. They can range from straightforward questions to the use of devious tactics intended to develop information without the person even realizing that he is cooperating. The method used will depend on the degree of reluctance that the interviewee has demonstrated, and the skill of the interviewer. If the subject is the target of an investigation, as opposed to being a witness or victim, he must be advised of his *Miranda* rights.

The location of the interview can affect the success of the technique and, therefore, should be considered when planning the discourse. The investigator is not required to provide information about the case to a subject during an interview, and the investigator may use deception when talking to the person. It is quite possible that other people may be present during an interview with a subject. Under normal circumstances the other person in an interview will be an attorney; however, in some instances a parent or translator might be in the room. Some right-wing extremists will bring "witnesses" into an interview. These people are almost never attorneys, but instead are sympathizers to their political cause. Recording an interview has some value, but an investigator should not allow the subject to be the only person making a recording.

Documentation is one of the most important aspects of the interview process. If the results of the interview are not reduced to written form, it will be extremely difficult to use them as evidence against the subject.

8 Polygraph Examinations

The polygraph, commonly called the lie detector, is not really an investigative technique in and of itself. It is actually a form of interview. The polygraph is a mechanical device that is designed to detect physiological changes that occur when a person makes an untruthful statement. While many people firmly support the accuracy of the polygraph, the fact is that it has little value as evidence in court. Indeed, only New Mexico routinely allows polygraph examination results to be admitted in evidence in criminal trials. The United States Supreme Court ruled in 1998 that a criminal defendant does not even have the right to present evidence in his own defense that he has passed a polygraph test. Justice Clarence Thomas ruled that there is "simply no consensus that polygraph evidence is reliable." He continued by stating that "to this day, the scientific community remains extremely polarized" about the question.

Polygraph examinations can be administered to anyone who is willing to submit to them. However, because of the time involved, the need for a skilled polygrapher, and the associated costs, polygraphs cannot be given to every agreeable subject. Individuals who are unwilling to undergo a polygraph examination should not be forced to do so. It is not advisable, and probably not legal, to physically force a person to be connected to a polygraph machine. The validity of such a forced examination would be questionable at best, and few polygraphers would conduct such an examination.

Although polygraph examinations are usually administered to subjects and suspects, they can also be given to witnesses and victims if there is some question about the honesty of their statements. The fact that a person is being truthful does not necessarily mean that the person's information is accurate. Instead, it means that the person believes that the information that he or she is providing is correct. Peoples' observations are not always correct even though they may be convinced in their mind that they are accurate. This is a good reason for an investigator to conduct a thorough interview in which he asks the basic "who, why, where, what, when, and how" questions. A good interview might reveal that the person simply was not in a position to "know" what he honestly believes that he "knows." A witness might be certain in his identification of a suspect, yet through an interview the investigator may realize that the witness was too far away to get a clear view of the suspect or that something was obstructing his view. If that person is adamant in his identification, it may not make sense to give him a polygraph examination. He may pass, yet be discredited by a defense attorney during trial.

The fact that a polygraph examination indicates that a person is being deceptive can be important for a law enforcement officer to know. However, the test in itself does not disclose the person's reason for being untruthful, and, of course, does not reveal what the true facts are.

Some companies use polygraph examinations to screen potential employees before they even conduct a serious interview with them. In law enforcement, however, the situation is different. The polygraph should not be used as an initial step at the beginning of the investigative process. It should be used only after the subject has been interviewed about the matter at hand. As in the case of an interview, a person cannot be compelled to submit to a polygraph examination. Many laypeople have the mistaken belief that the polygraph is used in association with a normal law enforcement interview. They believe that the subject is hooked up to a polygraph machine while being interrogated for hours by investigators. The fact is, polygraph examinations are administered by trained professionals. Even though many are sworn law enforcement officers and may have spent many hours working the streets, most polygraphers concentrate on the polygraph and do not regularly handle investigations. If they are active investigators, they usually do not administer tests in their own cases.

In the United States, polygraph examinations are usually limited to a few pertinent questions—possibly three or four key issues—that are interspersed with several "test" questions. The notion that someone is connected to a polygraph machine while undergoing a lengthy interrogation is simply not correct. Certain foreign law enforcement agencies ask more and broader questions when administering polygraph examinations than do most polygraphers in the United States.

Usually the polygraph process is begun after one or more comprehensive interviews have been conducted with a subject. During these interviews, the subject would have made statements of supposed fact, such as comments outlining specific activities. In addition, the interviewing investigators would usually have asked the subject pointed questions concerning guilt that would have yielded negative responses. The polygraph deals with facts more than theories. The polygraph will not be used to determine whether a person really believes in a political philosophy that he openly espouses. The purpose of the polygraph examination is to determine whether the subject was honest in his denials of guilt, and with respect to his statements of activity. In some instances, the subject will offer to take a polygraph examination in order to "prove" that he is being honest. More often, however, it is the investigators who suggest that the subject undergo the examination in order to demonstrate honesty. Some agencies administer polygraph examinations to informants to assure themselves that the sources are truthful. If nothing else, an informant who believes that he may be forced to take a polygraph test will likely think twice about providing false or exaggerated information to his handling officer.

For many law enforcement officers, the polygraph examination itself is not the most important aspect of the technique. In fact, some investigators who openly support the use of the polygraph actually have strong reservations about its accuracy. For many investigators, the polygraph offers its greatest value as a coercive force to convince a person to tell the truth. Many investigators do not mention the polygraph until after a subject has given a fairly detailed statement and has denied guilt. The investigators then inform the subject that they are almost completely convinced of his or her truthfulness, and will only need a successful polygraph examination to become fully convinced. It is at this point that some subjects begin to recant or alter their previous statements. Other subjects refuse to take the test. Of course, either response gives investigators reason to suspect that the subject is being untruthful. Investigators can respond by challenging the subject's honesty and conducting a re-interview. Another tactic is for investigators to lead the subject to think that they believe him, but that their supervisor insists on the polygraph before allowing the investigators to look for the "real" perpetrator of the crime.

After the subject agrees to take the polygraph examination, the polygrapher will conduct his own interview with the subject. He usually tells the subject that his intent is not to fail him on the test, but instead to create a situation in which he will pass the test. The polygrapher is being honest in his comments. He does in fact want the subject to be truthful. Of course, if the subject is guilty, he wants the subject to admit via the polygraph that he perpetrated the criminal act and thereby pass the test. In order to create such an environment, the polygrapher explains to the subject that he must carefully go through the polygraph questions with the subject prior to the administration of the actual test. The polygrapher then reviews with the subject each question that will be asked during the examination. He makes it clear that the subject must be able to respond with a "yes" or "no" answer to each question. Consequently, it is important that he ask the question in such a manner that the subject can truthfully respond to every aspect of the question. The subject is instructed to be absolutely certain that every word in the question is correct. It is here that untruthful subjects often start to make changes in their previous statements as they attempt to eliminate from questions the words that they believe are causing them the greatest anxiety. Some subjects may want to eliminate some questions entirely, which of course conveys a message to the polygrapher. It does not take much before a trained polygrapher will develop a strong indication that the subject is being untruthful. Many polygraphers can accurately predict how well a subject will perform on a polygraph examination after only a short interview with the subject.

A large number of scheduled polygraph examinations are never completed. Some subjects reconsider and decide not to take the test. Some have lawyers who will not permit them to take the test. Many other subjects end up confessing guilt during the polygrapher's pre-test interview. The questions that end up on the examination they finally do take are therefore quite different from the questions that were originally proposed.

For some subjects, the polygraph offers a glimmer of hope of beating the charge. They are guilty, and have no real way of mitigating what they have done. For them, the polygraph is a million to one gamble. They believe that if by some miracle they can pass the test, the investigators will become convinced that they are innocent. They think that because they are willing to take the polygraph the investigators might be convinced that they have the wrong person. As a matter of fact, very few truly guilty people will beat the polygraph examination.

After the initial polygraph examination, the polygrapher talks with the subject again. If the subject has shown deception, the polygrapher attempts to convince the subject to tell the truth. At this point, many subjects admit that they have given some false or misleading information and attempt to modify the wording of the questions so that they can respond to them sufficiently well to pass the test. A few subjects will even confess at this point.

Another polygraph examination is possible at this point if the questions have been modified so that the subject can now respond to them well enough to pass the test. Most examiners will not ask the exact same questions during a subsequent examination unless it is clear that the subject did not initially understand them well enough to give an honest answer. This is rare, indeed, because the pre-test interview is designed to ensure that the subject understands what he or she will be asked.

Polygraph examinations have become fairly common in law enforcement despite the fact that they usually cannot be introduced in court. Their primary value appears to be in inducing subjects to be truthful. Investigators imply that while a subject can lie to them, he or she cannot lie to the machine. Therefore, the subject should tell the truth to the interviewers rather than go through the humiliation of failing a polygraph examination.

Many police agencies employ their own polygraph examiners. Some are sworn law enforcement officers while others are skilled technical employees. Some police agencies use polygraph operators who are employed by other, larger police agencies. A small local department might use a state or county police polygraph operator. There are also private polygraph professionals who are occasionally hired to conduct law enforcement polygraph examinations.

Polygraph examinations are based upon the principle that a person's body will react in a measurable way when that person makes an untruthful statement. For most people, the examination will probably function accurately. For a few people it may not. Clearly, if a person believes that he is telling the truth even though his statement is in fact incorrect, he will probably pass a polygraph examination. However, most polygraph operators are also highly skilled interviewers. Consequently, they are often able to determine whether the basis for the person believing something to be true is unsound during the pre-test interview.

> In a terrorism investigation, a highly reliable witness placed a man at the scene of a bombing shortly before the explosion occurred. When located sometime later, the man denied being at the location on the date and time in question, although he admitted being there on another occasion. He was positive that he was not present on the significant date and time because he had attended an event at a distant location. The man passed a polygraph examination. It was later learned that the man had confused the date on which he had attended the other event. The man had passed the polygraph examination despite giving incorrect information because he was convinced at the time of the test that he was at another location at the time in question.

Some people suffer from mental problems that range from delusions to an inability to differentiate fact from fiction. Such people are likely to provide unreliable results on a polygraph. Polygraph operators will usually be able to identify such people during a pre-test interview, and will probably not administer the examination.

Some cultures have views concerning honesty that are different from those held by most Americans. If such a person feels absolutely no guilt in providing incorrect information in a given situation or circumstance, he or she will probably not have the same kinds of physiological responses that the average American has when making an untruthful statement. Many polygraph operators believe that they can still identify untruthful statements from such a person, although their examination may have an "inconclusive" result.

In such a situation the examiner will usually try to home in on the actual incident rather than on a crime per se. Rather than ask whether the subject "murdered" the victim, they might ask specifically if the subject stabbed the victim. In that way, the issue is the stabbing, not the murder. Even if the person feels no guilt about the murder and does not believe that it was wrong, he knows that he stabbed the victim. As a result, he will probably fail the polygraph if he claims that he did not stab the victim.

There are a variety of "tricks" that some people claim will allow a person to defeat the polygraph. These range from attempting some form of self-hypnosis to doing things like putting pins in their shoes to cause pain while being asked questions. None of the "tricks" has consistently proven effective in combating the accuracy of the polygraph. Experienced polygraph examiners have seen many of these "tricks" and can quickly identify what the person is attempting to do.

The skill, experience, and expertise of the polygrapher all influence the results of an examination. Highly talented polygraphers will have few failures because they obtain confessions during pre-test interviews. Less experienced polygraphers may have more inconclusive results because their questions will not be as clear and the subjects will have difficulty responding to them. Some polygraphers have problems with subjects who do not speak English.

Some polygraphers experience problems because they either do not receive or do not request sufficient background information on the subject before administering an examination. A few polygraphers have less-than-satisfactory results because they fail to note equipment failures.

In one terrorism case, a subject passed a polygraph examination even though many investigators were convinced that he was being untruthful. One year later, another polygraph operator reviewed the results of the examination, and discovered that the test revealed an impossible straight line for the galvanic skin response. Clearly, that gauge was malfunctioning or the operator had failed to connect the person to the monitor.

In another terrorism case, the polygrapher administered an examination to a subject who had not slept in more than 30 hours. The investigators never informed the examiner of the situation, and the examiner never asked the subject or the investigators about this probably because he had no reason to suspect that anything was out of the ordinary.

In still another examination, the polygrapher was unable to communicate with the subject because he spoke a foreign language. To solve the problem, he asked a bilingual officer to participate in the examination as a translator. What the polygrapher did not know was that the bilingual officer had conducted a lengthy, highly confrontational, and threatening interview with the subject earlier in the day, and the subject was very afraid of that officer.

In all three of the above examples, there are questions about the validity and accuracy of these polygraph examinations. Highly experienced polygraph operators would never have administered examinations under the circumstances outlined in these examples had they been aware of all of the facts.

Terrorists are usually reluctant to submit to interviews with law enforcement officers. They often have attorneys who are sympathetic to the cause and who will instruct them not to speak to investigators. A person who will not submit to an interview is not going to undergo a polygraph examination. Even in cases in which a subject is willing to submit to an interview, many terrorist subjects are going to be unwilling to agree to take a polygraph examination unless they believe that they will pass it.

⑨ Records Checks

Records checks are probably the easiest investigative resource available to an investigator; however, many investigators fail to use them to their full potential. The fact is, every government agency, civic group, educational institution, bank, private company, utility, and nonprofit organization maintains written records in one form or another. These records involve what they do, who they contact, with whom they have business dealings, and their employees. The records check investigative technique involves surveying all entities that can provide information on the subject of an investigation. Very often an investigator can assemble an extensive profile on a subject though agency checks without ever leaving his or her office. Indeed, technology has made the process even simpler for investigators. A modern investigator can access numerous records by simply pressing a few keys on his or her computer keyboard. If that cannot be accomplished, many departments have the ability to communicate with other agencies for records via the telephone or facsimile (fax) machine. Many larger agencies have clerical employees who can be assigned to research records at various agencies. For many good investigators, the first few hours of time that they devote to a new case involves records checks.

Records checks are extremely important in terrorism investigations because they can almost always be performed without the subject's knowledge. In fact, if the investigator has any suspicion that a particular agency cannot be trusted to maintain the confidentiality of the check, that agency should not be contacted. If the information held by that agency is deemed important, any approach for a records check should be done through a trusted person within that agency. Absent that, a court order with an instruction not to reveal the inquiry is a possible solution. Terrorists are always alert for law enforcement coverage of their activities. If they are deeply clandestine, any hint that law enforcement has learned of their activities can cause terrorists to abort their mission and possibly relocate. If this happens, much of the intelligence developed on that subject will be worthless. Furthermore, if an informant, undercover agent, or other source provided the information that led to the investigation of the subject, that person may come under suspicion, and therefore will be of little future value. It is important that a law enforcement agency develop as much information as possible on a terrorist subject from a safe distance before employing investigative techniques that can be more easily detected by the subject. Agency checks fall into several categories.

Agency Records Checks

As logical as it may seem, some law enforcement investigators fail to run the names of their subjects through the complete records of their own agency. This should be the first step in any investigation. It is imperative that an investigator assure himself that a new subject is not already being investigated by another member of his department. Clearly, problems could arise if one investigator's subject is a fugitive in another investigator's case, or if the subject is a department informant. It is important to know what history the subject has with the department. Previous arrests and closed investigations can yield valuable information and can save a great deal of time. It makes no sense for an investigator to duplicate what has already been done by other investigators. Furthermore, if the subject has had a good experience with the police agency, such as having his stolen car recovered or receiving a rapid response to a burglary of his residence, the investigator may be able to capitalize on that.

Along this same line, the names of relatives and close associates of the subject should be checked through department records. Not only can information about these people provide intelligence with respect to the subject, it can also yield information about potential informants who might be able to assist in investigating the subject. With respect to terrorists, it would be wise for investigators to also check agency files with respect to the subject's organization. Anything developed about a terrorist group will be of value with respect to investigations of subjects who are members of that group.

Records checks should be thorough. This is especially important in terrorism investigations, in which many subjects have never been arrested. Some agencies maintain centralized record systems in which a single request will yield everything that the department knows about the subject. Most departments, however, maintain separate records for various functions that the agency performs. Some departments separate sensitive files from other records. Consequently, a check of a police department's arrest records will often not necessarily reflect that a subject has been a complainant, witness, victim, applicant, involved in an automobile accident, received a traffic citation, or issued a permit to carry a concealed weapon. It is also likely that such a check will not reveal that the subject's name has appeared in an intelligence file.

Some agencies maintain records of people whose names have been checked against their files by other agencies. Teachers, city workers, taxi drivers, gambling casino workers, and employees of firms holding city contracts are examples of the kinds of individuals whose names might be checked through police records. Certainly this information could lead an investigator to a heretofore unknown employment, or at least to an employment application. Some law enforcement departments maintain separate file systems for their own employees and for informants. An investigator should know whether his subject falls within either of these categories.

Even the worst criminal or the most violent terrorist could have been the victim of a crime or could have been involved in a traffic mishap. Sometimes very valuable information can be found in non-arrest police records, because people let their guard down in such situations and may provide information that they would not normally give to a law enforcement officer. For example, a terrorist involved in animal rights violence who happens to witness a man beating a woman in a restaurant parking lot may be very cooperative when giving a witness statement to police and may even provide personal background information that, for the security of his political group, would best be kept secret. Similarly, a terrorist may be quite cooperative with a police officer who is investigating the theft of his car.

Checking one's own department records should not be limited to the outset of an investigation. As aliases are developed and the identities of additional friends and relatives surface, these names should also be checked against the agency's files. Furthermore, it is a good idea to occasionally recheck the subject's name against agency records. Sometimes a subject will be arrested or have other contact with the agency, and that information will not reach the case investigator even though that investigator has placed a "stop" with the records custodian. This is particularly important if more intrusive investigative techniques are being conducted on the subject. It would be important to know that if on the evening a trash cover was conducted, the subject had notified police of a possible burglar behind his residence. Similarly, an investigator would want to know that the subject had alerted police about an attempted car theft on the day that a surveillance team member had placed a tracking device on the subject's car.

Other Law Enforcement Agency Records Checks

A wise investigator will check the name of a newly assigned subject through the logical law enforcement agencies within his geographic area to determine what information, if any, they have on the subject. Usually the agencies within a particular area have established systems through which they can check each other's records. Such checks may be accomplished through the completion of a form, a telephone call, or via computer. Efforts should be made to conduct thorough checks with any agencies the subject might have had contact with. Clearly, such files as victim, accident, and complainant should be checked in the subject's town of residence. Investigators should realize that they are not usually going to be able to receive as much information from other agencies as they will receive through checks conducted within their own department. Privacy statutes and civil lawsuits have caused agencies to place restrictions on what can be released and exchanged with other agencies. This is particularly true with respect to intelligence files.

Under most circumstances, inquiries can be made of other law enforcement agencies without fear of jeopardizing an investigation. Caution might be required if the subject is a law enforcement officer. Even greater caution is required if there is reason to believe that the law enforcement agency being checked has members who are somehow connected with the criminal activity being studied. If a department is looking into police corruption in another law enforcement agency, it may not want to conduct a routine check of the name of one of the officers suspected of involvement in that illegal activity. In some parts of the United States, right-wing extremist groups have penetrated some law enforcement agencies, usually smaller ones. Checking the name of a right-wing terrorist subject through a penetrated agency could compromise the case. In some instances, it might be better not to conduct a check of a particular law enforcement agency's records. In other situations, it might be wise to work through a trusted person within that department, or to establish a joint operation with internal affairs investigators employed by that agency.

Task forces can do much to enhance and speed up agency checks. The various task force member agencies should be able to check their own agency records in a faster and more thorough manner than could outside agencies. As a result, a task force investigator is likely to obtain a much more complete package of other agency information about his subject than he would if he had to rely on normal interagency methods.

Credit Bureaus

Virtually every adult in the United States has some kind of record with a credit bureau. Most credit bureaus cooperate with law enforcement agencies and will provide them with information contained in their files. Many, however, will charge the agency a fee that could be fairly sizable if many names are run through their files. The information in credit files can offer excellent lead material for an investigator. It can include intelligence regarding banking, loans, credit cards, vehicles, debts, property ownership, and general financial standing. There are two main problems involved in credit bureau checks: the information may be inaccurate or out-of-date.

Most credit bureaus record the name of any firm, agency, or person that requests a review of an individual's credit. Consequently, if the subject visits a credit bureau, and demands to personally review his file, he may well discover a notation that a particular law enforcement agency received information from that file on a specific date. In some investigations, especially those involving terrorism, such a disclosure could have a very negative effect on the police agency's investigation. It is also conceivable that if a person does not have a credit file, and a police agency checks for one, the credit bureau may create a file to reflect the existence of that individual, and record in it the fact that a police agency had run a check on that name.

Credit bureaus can be very valuable in terrorism investigations with respect to determining false identification. Many terrorists employ false documentation from time to time. Most clandestine terrorists live their lives under false identities. Unlike ordinary criminals, who often fabricate false identities or buy false identification from a street outlet, terrorists frequently create high-quality identification that is backstopped. As such, they will attempt to establish a credit history so that their identification can be used to rent vehicles, apartments, and hotel rooms. Credit bureau records can help an investigator determine the origin and use of a terrorist's false identification. However, the risk of detection must be considered before a law enforcement investigator institutes a credit bureau records check. A terrorist may personally check his false identity's credit bureau file just to ensure that no questions have arisen about documentation. If such a person discovers that a police inquiry has been made about his false identity, it is likely that he will abandon it and possibly even cease his clandestine activities.

City, County, and State Agencies

Virtually every city, town, and village has a department that maintains its records. In large cities, there can be scores of specialized agencies manned by hundreds of city employees, each of whom is responsible for maintaining a particular form of record. In small municipalities, one town clerk may handle all of the records. These records can yield a variety of interesting facts that may be of value in an investigation. Often the information itself is of little value, but when combined with other facts developed about a subject, it can become significant. For example, the check of a city building department may reveal that the subject was issued a building permit for the construction of a wine cellar in his basement. On the surface this may not seem important, but if the subject is a suspected terrorist about whom nothing has been developed to suggest any actual interest in wine, an investigator might suspect that the reinforced basement room may have a more sinister use than merely storing wine.

A wise investigator will know his town. He will know what is required for people to live and work in the town. He will know what city services are available. He will know how the town affects its residents. He will know what taxes people must pay. He will know where licenses and permits are required. As he comes to know the subject, he will realize what rules and regulations apply to him, and he will seek out the agencies within the community that should have records on the subject. If the subject works, the investigator will know that he must pay taxes. If the subject has a pet, he will know if it should be registered. If the subject owns property, he will know what records exist in the city concerning property ownership, taxes, and zoning regulations. If the subject owns a car, the investigator will know who in the city will have ownership records.

Every agency that has an impact on the subject should have some form of record on that person. If an involved agency does not have a record, it may mean that the subject has failed to do something that he should have done, such as paying a local income tax or registering his dog. This kind of information could prove to be of great value as the case against the subject develops. If, for example, the subject has failed to pay his property taxes, this could provide a legitimate reason for an investigator to conduct an interview with him without having to reveal that the agency is aware of other criminal or terrorist activity on his part.

City Records

The following represents some of the many city departments that will have records that can be reviewed for information on the subject:

Property Taxes—In large cities there will be an official with a title such as city tax assessor or treasurer who maintains records outlining ownership of all properties in the city, and the name of the taxpayer on that property. Smaller towns may not have an official who is solely responsible for this function; however, there will be someone handling these records. Often there is a court associated with the assessor's office, because property owners usually have some rights with respect to tax appeals.

City Taxes—In large cities, an official will be responsible for the collection of sales taxes, city income tax, business taxes, excise taxes, and any other taxes levied by the city. Smaller towns will probably not have as many different taxes, but someone will be responsible for those that are in place.

Licenses—Almost every municipality has some form of licensing for businesses that operate within its borders. Such records can contain a wealth of information about the owners of the enterprise. Cities also issue a variety of other licenses, certificates, inspection stickers, and permits, including those for animals, vehicles, use of city facilities, professions, and special events.

Property Ownership—Large cities have an official with a title similar to recorder of deeds, who is responsible for recording all property ownership and real estate transactions in the city.

Building Records—Most cities require building permits for construction within their boundaries. Usually, an official heads a department that oversees building inspectors who must approve work that is done to ensure that it meets city building codes.

Streets—Large cities have an official with a title such as street commissioner, whose job it is to construct, repair, and clear city streets. For the most part, the records of this department will not contain information on individuals; however, it is possible that information on some citizens might appear in the street department files. It is possible that someone has complained about the streets, had his car towed on street cleaning day, or been assessed a fee or tax for street improvement. It is also possible that during a storm a person's tree fell onto a street, or a city-owned tree or pole toppled onto a person's house.

Sanitation—Someone must be responsible for waste disposal. In large cities, the municipality may actually conduct the waste disposal function, maintain a fleet of garbage trucks, and operate its own city dump. In other areas, the city may hire an independent contractor to perform these tasks. In many areas there is a fee for refuse removal, which means that there will be customer records. Some towns require residents to schedule special pickups for large items—which could result in a record of the request and perhaps a description of the item.

Health—Most large cities have a health department that maintains records of health problems, communicable diseases, and child inoculations. These records are sometimes easier to review than are the records of private physicians.

Welfare—Larger communities have welfare departments that are responsible for dealing with people having a variety of needs, including unemployment, poor health, old age, child care, and disabilities. Small towns may refer much of this responsibility to the county and state, but they may still maintain some records and probably offer some services.

Vital Statistics—Someone must maintain city birth, death, marriage, divorce, and similar records. In cities, large departments handle this function, which is now primarily maintained in computerized lists. In small towns, a city clerk may still perform the duty by hand. In some areas the county or state government maintains the bulk of these records.

City Employment—All municipalities must maintain records of their own employees. In large cities there is likely to be a fully staffed personnel department.

Voting—Some records concerning voting will be maintained by the city, although it is likely that more comprehensive records will be maintained by the county and state.

County and State Records

Vital Statistics—These records will reflect births, deaths, divorces, adoptions, and similar records.

Welfare—These records will show who is receiving specialized assistance due to financial needs, physical or mental problems, and disabilities.

Health—These records will reflect records of contagious diseases and inoculations.

Voting—State and county voting records may contain valuable information.

Disaster Services—Most states have an agency that is responsible for providing assistance during major catastrophes, including floods, tornadoes, hurricanes, earthquakes, and similar events. If a person has been a victim, or has made a claim in connection with a disaster, there will be records to that effect.

Taxes—Although there are strict regulations concerning the release of information from these records, some information can be obtained by law enforcement agencies (it may require a subpoena or some other form of court order). Sales tax records for small businesses are usually easier to obtain. These records can reflect the background of the business and its owner, as well as its payment record.

Driver's License—All states issue drivers' licenses. These records contain basic identifying data and usually have photographs. Many states maintain copies of the photographs. Some states, such as Illinois, do not keep copies of driver's licenses on file, but descriptive information is maintained. License bureaus also have detailed driving histories of people holding licenses. Sometimes these histories can be very valuable because they may reflect otherwise unknown vehicles in which a subject was driving, and may show places where he or she has traveled (based on traffic citations and accidents).

Vehicle Registration—All states register vehicles and registration documents contain owner information. Usually the recent ownership history of a particular vehicle can be traced through the agency that issues vehicle licenses. This could be quite valuable in terrorism investigations, because a terrorist might "sell" his vehicle to himself or another group member using false identification.

Professional Licensing—There are a variety of professions and industries that are regulated and licensed by the state. These include physicians, dentists, attorneys, barbers, and certain skilled trades, as well as movers, cable companies, financial institutions, and contractors.

Courts

Courts exist at local, county, state, and federal levels. Courts handle a variety of responsibilities. In addition to general criminal courts, there are courts that handle bankruptcy, labor disputes, zoning, domestic relations, and a number of other specialties. Furthermore, other courts handle civil matters that range from small claims to major class action lawsuits involving large corporations. Court records can contain a wealth of information. They should be checked if there is any indication that the subject has been involved in a proceeding in that court.

Courts maintain very accurate records and therefore are excellent sources of information. Judges have a great deal of power within their jurisdiction. They can order people to provide information about themselves and to produce records as needed in court. As a result, it may be possible to locate information in court records that the subject might refuse to provide anywhere else.

Court records can be very valuable in certain right-wing extremist cases in which the subjects have filed liens on the properties of law enforcement officers, judges, prosecutors, and city officials, or have sued these people for some reason. Such extremists may also have been engaged in zoning disputes, property rights arguments, and the refusal to pay income and property taxes—all issues that likely ended up in court.

Schools

Educational institutions maintain fairly complete records on their students. Much of what is contained in student files can be of intelligence value to law enforcement agencies. Unfortunately, obtaining school records may not be as easy as it once was. City school records are usually available to some extent to local law enforcement agencies. Federal agencies will often be required to produce some form of legal document or a release from the student before being able to view these records. Private school record procedures vary, but more likely than not a court order or parental consent will be required to access these files. Universities and colleges have become quite fearful of civil liability and consequently most are reluctant to give any law enforcement agency access to their files. Some will verify attendance and graduation, but will give little more information without the production of a court order or subpoena.

State law enforcement agencies are sometimes able to obtain student information through a college security department where retired police officers are employed, or through some other campus contact. This is quite risky. If the information ends up in court, the prosecutor may find it impossible to locate anyone willing to testify about the origin of the information. Not only could it cost the government its case in court, it could also result in civil suits being filed against the police agency. It is usually best for a law enforcement agency to follow the procedures for record procurement that the educational institution has established.

Private schools—including everything from general educational institutions to technical training centers, to fly-by-night educational operations—have varying rules with respect to opening their records. Most legitimate institutions will require the consent of the student, if not a court order.

Many legitimate educational institutions have alumni associations that may or may not be connected to the school. These entities may be willing to assist law enforcement agencies in locating former students. Some schools, particularly technical institutions, have employment offices that assist their students in finding jobs. In some instances such offices will maintain employment applications of former students.

The Internet has also entered the picture with respect to school attendance. Private companies advertise on the Internet that for a fee they will locate graduates of schools. While claiming that they offer their services to help reunite school friends, collection agencies and private detectives are also likely to use these companies to find people. Such firms may be of value to the law enforcement community as well.

Public Utilities (Gas, Water, Electricity, Sewer)

Public utilities maintain some personal information about their customers and their property. Because most customers pay by check or credit card, utility companies can at least provide information about these payment vehicles. The actual record of service usage itself may be of some interest. A clandestine bomb factory, used only to construct bombs, may be identified by an investigator because of its unusually low electricity and water usage. Conversely, a person raising marijuana plants in his basement may have an extraordinarily high electric bill. Public utility companies usually cooperate with local police agencies, although they will often demand subpoenas from federal agencies.

Employment

Employment records contain a wealth of information about people who work, have worked, or who even applied for a position. Many large firms require that potential employees to submit lengthy applications that contain everything from a listing of previous employers to arrest records, education, and family history. There is no set pattern for obtaining employment records. Some companies make them readily available, while others require court orders. Many large firms will refer requests for information to their legal counsel, who in turn will want to know about the nature of the inquiry. Most law enforcement agencies cannot reveal the reason they are seeking the information. Companies tend to be more cooperative if they believe that the employee may present a threat or embarrassment to their firm. However, investigators usually do not want to reveal much information about subjects to most employers, because the mission of the investigator is to gather intelligence, not give it away to others.

Care has to be used in contacting employers in terrorism cases. If the employer believes that the employee could be a terrorist, he may terminate or transfer him out of fear. Investigators might be wise not to use a volatile term like *terrorism* when interviewing an employer unless he truly believes that the nature of the threat posed by the employee requires such notification.

Banking and Financial Institutions

Banking records can be very revealing and in many instances can be used as evidence to prove wrongdoing. However, most financial institutions are reluctant to release information about customers without a court order. Bank officers wish to avoid civil suits, and are well aware that financial records could be subpoenaed. Law enforcement officers can usually obtain subpoenas for bank records through their prosecutor's office, if they can show that the subject's activities may involve the misuse of funds. Despite the problems of procuring banking records, they are worth the trouble. On occasion, banks will assess a fee to the law enforcement agency or the prosecutor's office for the work that they must do to gather and duplicate the records.

Telephone

In the modern world everyone uses a telephone, and just about anyone who has a residence will have access to a telephone. Today most people also now have cellular telephones in addition to their home telephones, and some people have actually discontinued their home telephone service completely in favor of their cell phone. Most people have some, if not a great deal of access, to telephones at their place of employment. Telephone usage records are often worth a great deal to an investigator. Excellent evidence can be developed from such records in light of the fact that some people tend to be careless with respect to telephone use. Even a highly sophisticated terrorist may occasionally slip and make an unwise telephone call because he is in a hurry, does not wish to venture outside on a cold night to use a pay telephone, or believes that his cell phone is secure.

Members of the Puerto Rican independence terrorist group FALN used a "safe house" telephone to contact their fugitive leader, William Guillermo Morales, in Mexico. This careless use of the telephone led to the arrest of Morales, who had been a fugitive for almost five years.

Some form of court order is almost always required to obtain telephone records. Costs may be charged by the telephone company in connection with expenses incurred to compile the records.

The cost of fax machines has dropped dramatically during the past decade. In the twenty-first century, many people have fax machines in their homes, and many of them have separate telephones dedicated to these machines. Records of fax machine transmissions can also be of value to law enforcement investigators.

Military

Law enforcement agencies, particularly federal agencies, have some access to military records with respect to veterans and their dependents that can be of value. Membership in a reserve unit will mean that there will be an active file on a person.

Medical Records

Medical records that are maintained by physicians, clinics, hospitals, and insurance companies can provide information of value. They are usually very difficult to secure without the patient's permission. A court order to produce medical records may also be difficult to obtain, depending on the reason the investigator gives for requesting the documents.

Newspapers, Magazines, and Other Publications

Publishers usually have records of what they print, often in the form of microfilm or stored on their server. The main problem with this information, particularly with respect to newspapers, is that it may not be entirely correct. Newspapers have to meet a deadline, and do the best they can to print an accurate account of an incident. Early in a story, they do not have all the facts, so the initial accounts may be incomplete or inaccurate. The investigator should review all the stories the newspaper has about his subject, rather than just the first story concerning a particular incident. Public libraries are also a source for newspapers and other publications. Some of the stories released by many major publications can be accessed via the Internet without having to make a specific request to the publisher. A subscriber to a private service like LexisNexis will have the ability to easily scan a large number of newspapers and other publications using a person's or group's name and a variety of other key words to locate information that appeared in print during the twenty-first century and earlier.

Directories

Although often forgotten, there are a number of public access directories that can yield valuable information to investigators. Many people forget about the telephone directory, which may reflect an otherwise unknown current or previous address for a subject. There are city directories available for most larger communities in the United States. These directories indicate the current address and telephone number of every person having a listed telephone number on a given street. These directories also reflect length of residency. There are other directories that identify members of a number of professions, including doctors and lawyers. School yearbooks are another valuable resource that can yield useful information. Public libraries often maintain copies of local school yearbooks, as do alumni associations.

Many directories are now available online. An investigator may do well to take the information that he does know about a new subject, and check it against what is available on the Internet. If, for example, the investigator believes that the subject has a certain skill or certification, he may be able to locate a directory on the Internet that can verify this and provide information about the subject.

There are a variety of other agencies and groups that maintain records that may yield good information about a subject. Some will provide law enforcement investigators with whatever they want, while others will provide limited information. Still others will not produce any information without a court order. Obviously, the latter situation can be very frustrating. An investigator may go to extreme lengths to procure a court order, only to discover that the entity has no record on the subject.

The following represents some of the other entities that may have records of investigative value:

- Insurance industry

- Stockbrokers

- Professional associations

- Licensing and certification agencies

- Newspapers and magazine subscription services

- Retail sales outlets, including department stores, automobile dealers, appliance stores, and catalog/mail-order companies

- Delivery services

- Communication service providers

- Rental agencies of any kind, particularly vehicles

- Student, fraternity, and alumni associations

- Labor unions

- Pharmacies

- Funeral homes

- Private post box services

- Gambling casino membership clubs

- Airline frequent flyer and hotel membership programs

- Health and fitness clubs

The Internet

The Internet has opened a whole new world of information availability to the law enforcement investigator. In some instances new forms of records that were not previously retained or assembled in a user-friendly configuration are now available simply because of the capabilities of modern computer technology. However, probably the most valuable information for the investigator can be found in records that always existed but were not generally known to the law enforcement community, or were inaccessible to investigators. Following the tragic September 11, 2001, attacks, communities became concerned about targets within their domain that could be attacked by terrorists. Many investigators were amazed to find that all kinds of sensitive and potentially compromising data was available on the Internet. Such things as the blueprints of government buildings, including courthouses and police stations, grids reflecting utility services in a town, and even personal information about city officials and law enforcement personnel was sometimes found on the Internet. These discoveries led investigators to explore what else was available. They soon learned that almost anything they could imagine was retrievable on the Internet in some fashion, if not in the exact form that they wanted.

A good investigator would be wise to run names of new subjects—individuals, groups, businesses, or enterprises—through an Internet search engine to determine whether any information is available. This should be particularly done in terrorism investigations, because political extremists often use the Internet to promulgate their causes. Of course, opposing groups respond on the Internet by criticizing and offering alternate views. Furthermore, there are many entities who oppose terrorism, support civil rights, or represent special interests, including certain nationalities, hobbies, and businesses, who regularly distribute material on the Internet that is either critical of, or supportive of, extremist viewpoints. Stories involving political extremism are much more likely to appear in some form on the Internet than will accounts of most other criminal offenses. Any information gleaned from the Internet can be used to enhance the knowledge of the investigator and give him logical leads to follow.

The keys to success with respect to the Internet revolve around the nature of the question and to whom it is asked. Various search engines can be probed, and some Web sites offer their own search capabilities. The question should be asked in a variety of ways. If a name is so common that it generates too many "hits" to make a search feasible, the range can be restricted by adding to the inquiry a term that may help home in on the subject. For example, if the subject of the inquiry is person believed to be a white supremacist who has been involved with explosives, perhaps the person's name can be queried with additional words such as "bomb," "white supremacist," or the name of an overt or covert extremist group with which the subject might have an association. Certainly, if the group that has perpetrated a terrorist attack has a Web site, or a surface-support organization for that group has a site, these sites should be studied for any information that can be used for evidence or for leads.

Every investigator must realize that the Internet is not necessarily a reliable and accurate source. It is important to know the origin of the entry, and to make direct contact with this source if possible. In terrorism investigations, a fair amount of information revolving around political extremism emanates from established civil rights or business-oriented sources that an investigator can personally contact for information. Other information will have come from magazines, newspapers, and related publications, and will often reflect a byline. If feasible, the investigator can make personal contact with the author to determine the credibility of the sources used. Great care should be used in employing Internet information as a basis for search or arrest warrants or in applications for electronic coverage. However, the Internet can provide some decent lead material. It may also offer an opening for conducting interviews without letting the subject become aware of an investigator's knowledge of him. The subject can be told that someone reported to the police agency that he had seen information on the Internet that the subject was involved in bombing buildings. The investigator can tell the subject that he was assigned by his boss to determine if this information was true, and if not, ascertain why someone would have put it out on the Internet. The investigator can even play the role of the "good guy," telling the subject that he thought it only fair that he inform the subject about the Internet entry so that the subject could make an effort to correct it.

The Internet is still a relatively recent development in the area of law enforcement. Investigators should review their agency's policies with respect to its use, and if found to be lacking, should contact their department's legal counsel or the prosecutor's office for advice before using it in their investigations. One of the main areas of concern will involve the placement of Internet information into a file. In terrorism cases, documentation of the steps of investigation is important, because in court subjects are likely to challenge whatever they can, especially if such an inquiry can result in embarrassment to the police department. Consequently, if something gleaned from the Internet results in a change in the direction of an investigation, or leads an investigator to take a specific action, it is important that this information be somehow reflected in the file. If it is not, the defense may argue that the investigator's actions were caused by information that he gained from an illegal technique, an undisclosed electronic coverage, or an informant whose existence had not been disclosed.

Chat rooms are an area where information of undetermined reliability can be developed. However, law enforcement officers should use great care in going into such locations to gather information. If the investigator must sign in with a false identity or do anything to conceal his real reason for being in the chat room, his activities are probably undercover in nature, and should be guided by his department's regulations governing undercover operations. A wise investigator will not enter a chat room in connection with an official police investigation until he has consulted his legal counsel for advice.

Summary

Records checks should be one of the very first avenues of investigation undertaken. In some instances, records of an investigator's own department will reveal information of value. Many records checks can be conducted from the police agency without coming near the subject. Care should be taken to ensure that the subject does not become aware of the records checks. This is important in terrorism investigations, because clandestine extremists will sometimes flee if they become aware that the police know of their activities. The Internet is a wealth of information concerning both people and things. It may not always be accurate, but it can provide an investigator with good lead material.

⑩ Surveillance

From a law enforcement perspective, the investigative technique known as surveillance involves the visual observation of a person or targeted location by law enforcement personnel for the purpose of developing information that can ultimately lead to a prosecution. Surveillance is a basic investigative technique that probably dates to law enforcement's earliest days. Modern technology has given law enforcement many tools to enhance surveillance; however, the technique continues to consist mainly of personal observations of people and locations by investigators. (It is noted that the term *surveillance* could also include technical coverage of a subject or location. For the purposes of this text, this form of coverage will be treated in Chapter 18, Sensitive Technical Techniques.)

Movies, old-time radio shows, and television police programs have so publicized surveillance that virtually every criminal and terrorist knows of the technique. Fortunately for law enforcement, many of the depictions are very misleading, and fail to reflect the true nature of this investigative tool. The entertainment media has often made it seem that surveillance is something that law enforcement can perform instantaneously, and with little chance of detection. Many older "cop" dramas have included scenarios in which a suspect is released from custody so that he can be "tailed" from the police station, observed meeting cohorts, and ultimately arrested while committing a crime. In actuality, surveillance involves a great deal more work and sophistication than is shown in such stories. This is particularly true with respect to observing political extremist subjects.

The Value of Surveillance

Surveillance is a valuable investigative tool because it involves actual, real-time observation as opposed to something historical or hearsay. Such observations are greatly valued in affidavits for search and arrest warrants and requests for technical coverage. Law enforcement personnel make excellent witnesses in court proceedings. The confidence of a prosecutor increases with each sworn investigator that he is able to place on the stand to offer testimony based upon personal observation. This is extremely important in terrorism investigations, in which the defense is likely to challenge every aspect of the government's case. The violent nature of a terrorist group can intimidate non-law enforcement witnesses. Such people can be further confused and their testimony negated by defense attorneys. The most successful terrorist prosecutions rely on law enforcement witnesses, forensic evidence—including fingerprints, and investigation supported by photographic and technical means. Cases based heavily on civilian eyewitnesses and informant testimony are destined to experience some problems in court. Not only can surveillance develop excellent evidence, it can also result in the subject actually being seen engaging in criminal activity, resulting in his arrest.

Drawbacks of Surveillance

As valuable a technique as it is, surveillance has drawbacks that make it difficult to use on a regular basis. Surveillance is one of the most manpower-intensive and time-consuming investigative techniques available to law enforcement agencies. Positive results can never be guaranteed, even in surveillances that employ large numbers of investigators. Some surveillances can extend for months without producing anything of value. The technique is also quite taxing on agency resources, including vehicles and radio and photographic equipment.

Surveillance can also be a risky technique to use in a terrorism investigation. Truly committed terrorists are more dedicated to their political cause than they are to themselves. They will take no action that will jeopardize their group. Many terrorists would literally quit their movement before they would allow law enforcement to use them to identify their group's clandestine activities. A terrorist who realizes that his cover has been breached by law enforcement is not likely to lead investigators to a safe house or to other covert group members. For this reason, a law enforcement agency that has identified a covert terrorist must use great care in acting upon this information. A poorly arranged surveillance that alerts the subject that his cover has been blown will likely negate the value of the information that the agency had previously developed on the subject. In short, an agency may be better served by doing nothing with the information that it has developed about a clandestine terrorist than by initiating a weak surveillance that ultimately renders the information worthless because the subject detects the coverage and responds by ceasing his activity within the terrorist group.

Smaller police agencies that lack personnel and resources may not be able to make satisfactory use of surveillance in any of their investigations. Some smaller departments might get some use of the technique if they limit their coverage to restricted durations in which they can muster all of their manpower for short periods. Another solution to the dilemma has been joint operations wherein several small agencies join together to conduct surveillances. A variation of this would have one or more smaller agencies join with a larger state or federal agency in order to successfully use the technique. Obviously, a joint operation will require the initial agency to share its information with the units assisting it. For some departments, this can present a problem, especially if the information justifying the surveillance came from a confidential informant or from grand jury testimony.

Larger departments often have sufficient manpower to support a secure surveillance; however, mere manpower and resources do not ensure productive use of this technique. The keys to success are dedication and the willingness to do everything possible to avoid detection. Some larger law enforcement agencies maintain specialized squads of investigators who are assigned to conduct surveillance on a full-time basis. One major federal agency employs squads of nonsworn, but highly trained personnel who only do surveillance. Professional surveillance teams become highly skilled and have the vehicles and the equipment needed to succeed.

Unfortunately, specialized surveillance units often serve the entire department and become accustomed to moving from target to target. They never become familiar with any particular investigation. More problematic is the fact that these teams learn that when a unit within the department finally does get their service after having waited for weeks or even months, that unit expects tangible results. The teams have come to know that units will not be satisfied with repeated surveillance logs that show that the subject was lost in traffic. Despite the fact that these teams are aware that they should not be detected by the target, and despite the fact that they have the skills and equipment to enable them to avoid discovery, they find themselves being forced to take unnecessary chances in order to avoid being criticized for losing the subject. If these specialized teams are to be used in a terrorism investigation, they must be convinced that it is better to repeatedly lose the subject than it is to be detected even once.

Another failing of specialized teams involves some of the personnel assigned to them. All too often an officer who is experiencing problems handling investigative assignments is "dumped" into a specialized unit such as a surveillance team, in the hope that he can succeed somewhere in his chosen profession. Similarly, on occasion, an officer who no longer wants to endure the hard work associated with his regular daily assignments will volunteer to work on a specialized unit in the hope of lessening his burden. However, highly specialized surveillance teams require top-level employees. Even one unprepared officer can compromise a good surveillance team and jeopardize the security of an operation.

Common Criminal Surveillance versus Terrorist Surveillance

In many criminal investigations the fact that the subject becomes aware that he is under surveillance is not a case-ending crisis. Professional criminals tend to view law enforcement as a necessary adversary that they must overcome in order to conduct their business. They are well aware that their activities violate laws. They are also aware that they will encounter law enforcement on a periodic basis. Professional criminals realize that they could on occasion become the targets of police surveillance, especially if they have arrest records or are associating with known offenders. Although they are smart enough not to commit illegal acts in the presence of surveilling law enforcement officers, criminals are usually not intimidated enough to become law-abiding citizens merely because they learn of police interest in them. A detected surveillance might cause a criminal to lay low for a few hours, days, or even weeks; but most criminals will eventually resume their former illegal activities. Some career criminals regard the very idea of losing a police surveillance to be a challenge rather than a deterrent. Criminals are profit motivated. They must commit illegal acts in order to reap the reward. There is little true loyalty among criminals. Often one will sell out another in exchange for a lesser sentence or some other deal. A member of a criminal group who determines that he is being surveilled may not inform his fellow conspirators, even though their security will probably also be in jeopardy by meeting with him.

For dedicated terrorists, the political cause is everything. There is no personal profit motive for their covert political or criminal acts. Although they surely know that some of their activities are illegal, they feel no guilt because the ultimate political objective provides them with justification. Some terrorists are religious, and therefore have an additional reason for not having guilt—they believe that God approves of their actions. Security is the key to the continuing existence of a dedicated terrorist. The security issue extends well past the individual member to include all group members and the organization itself. A true terrorist will take no action that will jeopardize his movement and fellow group members. Security is so important that a group member who believes that he is under law enforcement surveillance may leave his movement before he will lead surveillance personnel to other group members and to safe houses.

A clandestine member of the Weathermen group was accidentally discovered while removing the ventilation grate in the restroom of a large corporation's headquarters. (It was assumed that he was casing the area for the placement of a bomb.) Although he displayed quality false identification and was released from custody without ever revealing his reason for trespassing, this man chose to surface from his covert position in the movement and apparently never again functioned in a clandestine manner. Clearly this man feared that because law enforcement had become aware of his suspicious behavior, he had become a liability to his cause. He probably assumed the worst—that he was either under surveillance when confronted in the restroom, or would be watched in the future because of the restroom encounter. Regardless, in his mind it was better that he curtail his clandestine activities rather than jeopardize his group.

In 1986, five members of a clandestine cell that possessed explosives and weapons and functioned in California discovered that a concealed microphone had been installed in one of their vehicles by a surveillance team. All fled, and two were subsequently placed on the FBI's Top Ten Fugitive list. Ultimately, after almost a decade spent as fugitives, the two surrendered. It was learned that neither had engaged in any terrorist activity from the time that they had located the microphone, thereby "making" the surveillance, until their surrenders.

Two different members of the United States-based Puerto Rican terrorist group known as the FALN became aware that law enforcement officials had learned of their clandestine membership in the group. One man responded by totally dropping out of the group, while the other man relocated to Puerto Rico.

It is difficult to imagine that there is any terrorist group that does not know that law enforcement uses surveillance to develop information. Virtually every terrorist group stresses security. In this context, they emphasize surveillance, and instruct their members to always be alert for anyone observing their activities. The strategy taught is "if in doubt, abort." Certainly some criminal conspiracies also stress security and caution their members about police surveillance. However, the idea of totally aborting a planned criminal activity, and possibly even relocating to another area, is not usually a part of what they emphasize. Many common criminals fail to even consider surveillance until they accidentally detect it.

Terrorists may practice counter-surveillance techniques even in situations in which they are doing nothing illegal, or have no cause to suspect that anyone is observing them. Obviously, the great emphasis that terrorists place on security makes police work that much more difficult. However, it also slows the terrorist and complicates his activities.

Many terrorist groups study police investigative techniques. Some train to combat the police activities. Others distribute documents that outline how police conduct business, and discuss methods for avoiding coverage. Few common criminals are as educated about police investigative techniques as are terrorists. The idea of the Mafia, a street gang, or a burglary ring issuing pamphlets on counter-surveillance to their members is unlikely. Even if they did, the leaders would have difficulty making their members actually study them. For terrorists such instructional documents are reviewed because members know their importance to the security of the overall political cause.

Despite their dedication to a political agenda that causes many of them to greatly limit the scope of their lives, terrorists are human and therefore have normal human frailties. At times they will become careless, especially if they are in a rush and do not suspect that law enforcement knows about their clandestine activities. Law enforcement must attempt to capitalize on these lapses.

Surveillance personnel are wise to study the security procedures followed by any subject. This is often easier to do with respect to terrorists than it is with normal criminal targets. Terrorists are usually more structured with respect to their counter-surveillance training, and they frequently study written materials on the topic. Criminals are usually much less organized in their approach to counter-surveillance. Surveillance personnel should try to learn everything that the subject has been taught about surveillance, and should review any written manuals that the subject might have studied. Skilled surveillance personnel can frequently devise methods to overcome subjects if they know what knowledge and experience the target possesses. If the law enforcement agency is not able to study materials available to the terrorist, they probably can create their own "manuals" for the group by watching the activities of several group members, and noting similarities of the different people. For example, surveillance personnel might note that various members of the group often feign tying their shoes (possibly even when they are wearing loafers). The investigators could deduce that group members have been taught to use this technique as a way to view people behind them.

In many respects, ordinary criminals are more worldly than terrorists. Criminals are probably much less gullible when told about the actions, tactics, and capabilities of law enforcement officers. Some of the people who give terrorist groups advice about countering police investigative techniques are less than qualified to provide such training. The quality of instructional manuals and verbal directions in this area vary in quality. What this means is that some terrorists are practicing security methods that really do little to protect them from law enforcement agencies, but severely limit their activities.

In 1999, an essay purporting to describe FBI surveillance methods was presented on the Internet for anyone to review. It was indicated that this essay was typical of what appeared in a magazine that was being promoted. The manuscript was very well written and revealed a number of never-before-released "code terms" supposedly used by the FBI. In actuality, the document contained more false information than it contained facts. The document was so misleading that it would actually have made it easier for the FBI to surveil a person using its advice. In addition, a terrorist who attempted to practice the instructions given by the author would find himself so limited as to be virtually non-functional.

Counter-surveillance training can be a double-edged sword for any subject. It does make the subject more alert, and therefore makes it more difficult for law enforcement to learn of his clandestine activities. However, constant practice of counter-surveillance techniques greatly hinders the subject's ability to function. Keeping appointments can present a serious problem for a surveillance-conscious person. As a result, some people will become careless after having practiced counter-surveillance tactics when they realize that they are running behind schedule. Clearly, terrorists who tend to practice rigid security are more prone to these problems than are common criminals. Some terrorists tend to follow security instructions to the extreme, without applying any reason or common sense to them. Obviously, law enforcement can capitalize on these tendencies.

In one instance, a terrorist had been taught to wear a reversible jacket when on a mission. He was to turn the jacket around at a midpoint, thereby enabling him to lose anyone who might be following. Unfortunately for him, the man was so bound by this instruction that he continued to use his reversible jacket in the middle of the winter, when it was clearly inadequate and therefore likely to attract attention. With time, surveillance personnel came to realize that whenever the subject wore the jacket, he was going to do something related to his cause.

Another terrorist mission was compromised when a false mustache worn by a subject fell off during a police interview. This subject had followed his disguise instructions to such an extreme that he wore a false mustache, despite the fact that he had a natural mustache. He should have realized that he could not expect a false mustache to stick to real facial hair.

Types of Surveillance

There are three basic types of surveillance that are conducted by law enforcement agencies—moving surveillance, fixed surveillance, and combination surveillance.

Moving Surveillance

In a moving surveillance, investigators literally follow the subject wherever he or she goes. If the subject stops for a lengthy period, the investigators stop also, and do the best they can to observe his or her activities. When the subject resumes movement, the investigators follow. This is the best-known type of surveillance.

Of course, the idea of an effective surveillance is to observe the subject without him knowing that he is being watched. Successful moving surveillance involves a lot more than merely assigning vehicles to follow the subject as he drives around town. There is a degree of finesse involved in a successful surveillance. The following is an example of how a productive surveillance may occur.

A brown Mercury acting as the "eyeball" (person designated to observe the subject as he departs from a location) notifies the other units that the subject is leaving his residence. A blue Ford falls in behind the subject's car a block down the street. The subject may or may not notice the Ford; however, he does not become suspicious, because it pulls into a parking space within a short distance. When the subject next looks into his rear-view mirror, he sees a red pickup truck that is not involved in the surveillance. The green van driving behind the red pickup truck is now the unit observing the subject. Soon this van turns, and the coverage is picked up by a tan Dodge that is two vehicles behind the subject. Later, the original "eyeball" in the Mercury falls in behind the tan Dodge. The Mercury becomes the primary surveillance unit when the Dodge turns. Several blocks later, the Mercury passes the subject and a black Chevrolet several cars behind assumes the role as primary observer. The green van pulls in behind the Chevrolet. While this is occurring, the Ford and the Dodge are keeping up with the subject by driving on parallel streets.

If, at this point, the subject parks his car, the black Chevrolet will probably pass him and pull to the curb several blocks ahead, preferably out of the subject's view. The green van will slow and attempt to observe the subject's direction and destination as he drives past. Either the Ford or the Dodge will attempt to set up in a secure manner where they can observe the subject's car. One of them will become the "eyeball" who will call out the subject when he returns to his vehicle.

If it is possible to accomplish with security, one of the surveillance officers, preferably one parked nearby, but not the "eyeball," will walk to the location and attempt to watch the subject. If it appears that the subject will be at the location for an extended period, the investigator will summon one or more additional officers to leave their cars and join the foot coverage.

Obviously, the surveillance above is ideal. No one can predict traffic situations, so there are no set rules concerning the length of time that vehicles will be in certain positions during a surveillance. In heavy traffic, a surveillance vehicle could find itself trapped directly behind the subject for many blocks. On other occasions, it may not be possible for any surveillance vehicle to get closer than six or seven cars behind the subject. The goals of the particular surveillance and the information already known about the subject will influence the kind of coverage that is afforded to him. If the surveillance agents know where the subject is going when he parks his car and departs on foot, they may not feel the need to cover him during that period. Similarly, if the goal of the surveillance is to observe the subject meeting with an unknown person, the team is likely to give the subject's movement on foot as much coverage as they can muster. This may mean placing everyone, including the "eyeball," on foot surveillance, making it difficult for the team to resume vehicular coverage when the subject returns to his car.

Fixed Surveillance
(Also Known as Stationary and Picket)

In a fixed surveillance, only the subject moves. The investigators assume stationary positions along what they believe will be the subject's logical route. Each investigator will note the subject's activities as he passes through each assigned station. In theory, each investigator remains at his or her assigned post until the subject has left that area. No effort is made by any investigator to actually follow the subject. Fixed surveillance has been greatly enhanced by the advent of compact radio transmitters and cellular telephones. Each investigator now has the ability to notify an operations center and his or her fellow investigators about the subject's activities within his assigned area. Clearly, such communication makes it easier for each post to pass the subject to the next.

Fixed surveillances are often the best type of coverage to use against meetings and events that will occur within limited areas. Good examples would be the exchange of ransom money in a kidnapping case, or the transfer of classified documents in a counter-intelligence investigation.

In elaborate fixed surveillances, certain investigators, particularly those used in early stages of the coverage, are assigned to cover more than one fixed location. After the subject has left their posts, these investigators are assigned to move to a distant location and establish another fixed post from which to observe the subject. Probably the most efficient method to use in such a surveillance is to provide each investigator with a map on which each post is numbered. After the subject has passed through a position, the investigator assigned there either knows that he is to move to a specific secondary position, or he is instructed by the command post to make the move. If an elaborate fixed surveillance is to succeed, only a few of the investigators will be able to perform double-duty assignments. It would certainly appear suspicious if there was continual movement of people out of an area as the subject proceeded on his route. The elaborate kind of fixed surveillance requires a great deal of planning and a highly skilled organizer in the command center who has the talent to move people from position to position. The key to success is for each investigator to appear as though he belongs wherever he is posted. This could mean using such props as bicycles, school books, baby carriages, and wearing work clothes and carrying tools. Most law enforcement agencies will not be able to successfully perform an elaborate fixed surveillance due to manpower constraints.

Combination Surveillance

Combination surveillance involves a mixture of both moving and fixed surveillance. It is intended to limit some of the risks involved in the former type, while reducing the number of personnel required in the fixed surveillance. It can also be used if the person's destination is totally unknown. The idea is to have some form of fixed coverage at the point of the surveillance's initiation so that no one near that point moves when the subject does. Ideally, fixed posts would also be established at secondary locations so that the subject could travel several blocks without anyone moving after him. The moving coverage would commence at some point along the way, most likely after the subject feels secure in the belief that he is not being followed.

Another variation on this type of surveillance is for an agency to flood a given area with fixed posts that will give the subject coverage while he is in that territory. Moving surveillance personnel can be stationed along the perimeter so that they can follow the subject when he departs the target area.

The combination surveillance method can also be initiated when the subject being followed stops and enters a stationary location such as a business, restaurant, or place of entertainment. At that point, fixed posts can be established to afford coverage in and around the stationary location. Of course, when the subject exits, the nearest fixed post can notify moving outside surveillance personnel so that they can resume moving coverage as he departs the area.

All three surveillance methods have strengths and weaknesses. The fixed method is probably the most secure, and least likely to be detected by either the subject or someone providing counter-surveillance on his behalf. Unfortunately, the fixed method is very complex and manpower-consuming. Fixed surveillances are usually only effective in restricted areas or for relatively short distances. The fixed method also has a tendency to go against the very nature of the personalities of some police officers. The idea of only watching a criminal or terrorist as he walks past, but not being able to follow him, is difficult for some officers to accept. In fact, some officers will follow the subject as he leaves the area covered by their posted position despite instructions not to do so.

Moving surveillance is probably the simplest of the three methods to orchestrate; however, it is also the easiest for the subject to detect—there is always someone moving behind the subject. There is a real danger that counter-surveillance personnel will be able to detect such coverage if the subject himself does not see it.

The combination method requires more manpower than does moving surveillance alone; however, it is simpler to use than the fixed method, and is nowhere near as manpower-intensive. Indeed, most well-established surveillance teams rely heavily on this method. They realize that in order to ensure secure coverage, they must at least be able to get the subject away from the place of initiation before they begin moving surveillance.

Methods of Conducting Surveillance

There are various methods for conducting surveillance that can be followed within the three general types of surveillance.

Around-the-Clock Coverage

As the name suggests, this surveillance method calls for covering the subject 24 hours per day for a set or indeterminate number of days. Unless the subject is known to have only limited movement within a fairly confined area, it would not be practical to attempt to use this surveillance method during a fixed type of surveillance.

Around-the-clock surveillance is extremely time-consuming. It is also the least secure surveillance method. The longer a subject is continually covered, the greater the opportunity for detection. This is especially true during late evening hours when streets are deserted, and anyone sitting in a car or just hanging around the area will appear suspicious. The value of using a combination type of surveillance in connection with this method is clear. During periods of inactivity, the subject would be covered by a fixed post, which would allow the moving personnel to remain some distance away where, if observed as being suspicious, they would at least not alert the subject.

Limited Hour Coverage

In this surveillance method, coverage is restricted to what are believed to be the subject's most active hours. Usually coverage is not done when the subject is at his place of employment, attending school, playing sports, sleeping, or engaged in some other noncriminal activity. The idea is to cover the subject when he is most likely to have an opportunity to engage in criminal activity. The obvious weakness of this method is that it excludes the possibility that the subject may in fact participate in criminal activities during the times that are not being covered. For example, a person could leave work for a short period when he was not being surveilled during which time he would engage in some act that would, if it had been observed, be beneficial to building a prosecutable case against him.

Specific Coverage

The concept behind this surveillance method is to cover the subject only during periods when it is believed that he will engage in acts in furtherance of a criminal conspiracy. Clearly, this surveillance method relies heavily on intelligence developed through other investigative techniques. Possibly an informant or a wiretap has provided information that leads investigators to believe that the subject will do something worthy of coverage on a particular evening. Maybe a review of historical information on the subject and his comrades may reveal that the subject prefers to engage in criminal actions over the weekend or on his day off from work.

Capsule Coverage

This method of surveillance is intended to develop a complete picture of the subject while expending minimal manpower. The subject's life is divided into segments, and coverage is provided to each segment for a given period in an effort to develop a pattern of behavior. Capsule coverage is usually used when the investigator has no other information to suggest when a subject might be engaged in illegal activity.

The capsule method has several variations. One creates capsules based upon the days of the week. Surveillance might be staged for 24 hours during each Monday for a month. If nothing is developed, surveillance may be conducted throughout each Tuesday during the next month. If still nothing is developed, surveillance might be conducted on Saturdays during the third month. Another variation divides each day into segments that are then covered on a regular basis. For example, a capsule of 6:00 A.M. to 12:00 noon may be given coverage for a week. If nothing significant occurs, a capsule of 12:00 noon to 6:00 P.M. might be surveilled during the next week. The concept behind the capsule method is to eventually cover a subject during every part of a 24-hour period on each day of the week. Certainly, if the coverage reveals a particular time or day that the subject is doing something illegal or otherwise worthy of coverage, surveillance will be repeated during that period.

Capsule coverage is an excellent method by which to learn about a subject's daily activities. However, like most of the other surveillance methods, it is possible that the subject could commit a criminal act during a period that is not covered. If a subject does not do anything noteworthy during a capsule of 12:00 midnight to 6:00 A.M. during the first week of the month, it does not mean that he does not normally commit crimes during this period.

Event Coverage

This is a specialized surveillance method designed to cover a person or location in conjunction with a particular event. It is perhaps more commonly used in terrorism investigations than in other kinds of cases. The event that prompts the surveillance could range from a holiday or other significant date to the time of an actual terrorist attack. This surveillance may be planned in advance, or it may be initiated in immediate response to an incident. Some terrorist groups have a history of attacking on dates that have significance to their cause. In response, a law enforcement agency might initiate surveillances of logical targets on those dates in the hope of catching the terrorists in the act of committing a crime. Another use of this method might be in reaction to a terrorist attack. A police agency might assign surveillance teams to initiate coverage of certain individuals immediately following a terrorist attack in the hope of observing these people engaging in suspicious behavior.

Event coverage can be a wasteful surveillance method unless very specific information has been developed that a particular target will in fact be attacked, or that a specific subject will be directly involved in conducting the attack. More often than not, this method is used by agencies that have no other direction to go in their investigation.

Spot Check Coverage

Almost every law enforcement agency uses spot checks on occasion, and many use this method frequently. Some investigators do not regard spot checks as falling within the realm of surveillance, but they should. Essentially, a spot check involves an investigator going past a given address for the purpose of determining what activities are underway, and who is there. Some spot checks are well-planned and conducted with regularity. Most, however, are done sporadically, and with little forethought. Some are conducted during off-duty hours when an officer happens to be in the area, and does a drive- or walk-by of an address.

Spot checks can be very valuable during the course of complex investigations, including terrorism cases. They are easily done and the risk of detection is minimal. The major weakness with respect to spot checks is the failure of investigators to document what they have observed. Because spot checks are concluded within minutes, if not seconds, there is a tendency for investigators to forget to make notes about them. The danger lies in the fact that the investigators conducting such a surveillance could acquire knowledge that they will use, yet when asked in court how they got that information, either will not recall, or will not be able to produce documentation supporting how they learned it.

In one terrorism investigation, several officers stated that they had often observed the subject at a particular location. When the prosecutors attempted to study the documentation of this information so that they could include it in an affidavit, they could find nothing to reflect that the subject frequented the address. It turned out that the officers drove by the address whenever they were in the neighborhood, and looked to see who was present. Although they made mental notes when they observed the subject at the address, they failed to reduce their observations to written form. In essence, the officers' spot checks were useless in connection with the prosecution of the case because they could not remember the specific dates or times when they had seen the subject.

When to Conduct a Terrorist Surveillance

Surveillance should not automatically be instituted in every terrorist investigation. In fact, careful consideration should be given before using this technique, especially in situations in which other investigative techniques are yielding valuable information. A wise investigator should assume that all terrorist group members believe that they are under regular surveillance despite the fact that nothing has occurred that would reinforce such a belief. They should also assume that their terrorist target has had some training concerning law enforcement surveillance techniques. Clearly, a terrorist's fear of being watched by law enforcement increases whenever he actually engages in clandestine activities. A person who believes that he is being continually surveilled becomes extremely cautious in his behavior. This is a double-edged sword. While it restricts the terrorist in what he is able to do, it also makes it extremely difficult for law enforcement officers to observe him.

If a decision is reached to institute surveillance, an effort should be made to limit its scope as much as possible. The longer and more extensive the surveillance, the greater the opportunity for detection. It makes little sense to initiate around-the-clock surveillance on a subject when other techniques, such as a wiretap or informants, are able to provide regular coverage during portions of a 24-hour period.

Surveillance has been used during the course of numerous successful terrorist investigations to develop valuable information. However, the technique should not be attempted unless the law enforcement agency is dedicated to the philosophy of not "getting made" by the subject. This commitment involves more than just verbiage. It means that the agency will devote sufficient and proper personnel to the project and will equip these investigators with adequate vehicles and suitable means of communication. It also requires that the coverage be carefully planned and organized, and that there will be a definite goal to be achieved.

The "Don't Get Made" Philosophy

The most effective terrorist surveillance is one that is based on the premise that the subject will never become aware that he is being watched. Unlike many common criminals who tend to accept law enforcement surveillance as a "cost of doing business," terrorists often regard the detection of a police surveillance as a kind of warning that their operation has been compromised and therefore must be aborted and abandoned. The wise law enforcement officer attempts to avoid "getting made" by the terrorist subject.

The term "getting made" means that the target is convinced that he is being watched by a law enforcement agency. The fact that the subject observes an investigator in his neighborhood, or even makes eye-to-eye contact with him, does not mean that he has "made" the surveillance. The fact that the subject directly approaches the surveillance investigator, and accuses him of watching him, does not necessarily mean that the surveillance has been "made." Similarly, the fact that the subject jots down the license number of a surveillance agent's vehicle, or takes a photograph of him, does not mean that he has "made" the surveillance. However, it does illustrate that the subject is suspicious, and that the wrong response by the officer could blow the surveillance. A number of terrorists have been taught to take such action—they have been told to periodically accuse people around them of following them, and to jot down every license number in their vicinity. Obviously, if the investigator is aware that the subject has taken similar actions in the past with strangers, he can probably assume that the subject is only guessing, and will let the issue go if the officer responds appropriately to dispel suspicion.

Because being "made" means that the subject is virtually certain that the person observing him is connected to a law enforcement agency, it is imperative that investigators do nothing to reinforce a subject's suspicions. An investigator who finds himself confronted by a subject could easily resolve the dilemma by displaying his badge and credentials. However, this would prove to the subject that he had correctly identified the surveillance. Surveillance personnel should make every effort to avoid revealing their official position to the target or anyone else who is in the proximity of the subject. Sometimes a subject will stop a uniformed police officer and report that a person nearby is following him. The subject hopes that if the person he has identified is indeed connected to law enforcement, he will display his credentials when questioned by the uniformed police officer. In such a situation, it is better for the surveillance agent to claim a false identity and deny any wrongdoing rather than identify himself.

Operating under the "don't get made" philosophy forces the surveillance investigators to adopt a much more complex operational plan. It almost always ensures that the surveillance will take considerably longer to accomplish its mission. It requires that all investigators involved in the operation be trained, knowledgeable and, above all, prepared for every eventuality. It also means that officers who are known to the subject on sight should not be involved in surveillance of him. This can present problems for some investigators. They may find it difficult to convince their colleagues or their supervisor to assist them in conducting a surveillance in which they, themselves, are not going to participate. Conversely, it may be difficult for an investigator to follow an order from a superior that he not be involved in a surveillance in his own case. To alleviate such a dilemma, a case investigator might offer to work or be assigned to work in a fixed location such as inside of a van or in a lookout perch.

Clearly, the simplest way to resolve the situation for an investigator who has come under suspicion by the subject is for that investigator to leave the area without comment, or to remain in the area if the subject is departing. The subject will be suspicious, but will not be certain that he is correct. In situations in which the subject has directly confronted the investigator, it may not be possible to retreat without arousing even more suspicion. The investigator should be prepared for such situations. He should be able to provide some plausible explanation for being where he is. The following are actual examples in which confronted investigators extricated themselves without confirming the subjects' initial suspicions that they were surveilling them.

A subject slammed on his brakes and stopped in the street, forcing the surveillance investigator to do a panic stop in order to avoid a collision. The subject immediately jumped from his vehicle and began screaming that the investigator was following him. The investigator also immediately exited his vehicle, and began yelling to passersby that he was not that kind of guy, and that he was not going to accept the advances from a "queer." He stated that everywhere he had gone that day, he had encountered this "queer." He continued by stating that he was a war veteran, and did not have to stand for such behavior. Soon other people had gathered, and a backup in traffic resulted. By the time that the commotion concluded, the subject departed believing that he had encountered some kind of "weirdo."

In the situation above, the investigator responded with such haste that the subject was taken aback. The officer also brought innocent passersby into the situation by addressing his remarks to them, thereby avoiding a face-to-face confrontation with the subject. The "icing on the cake" was the fact that the investigator admitted that he had encountered the subject several times during the day, but made himself out to be the victim. He suggested that the subject had been following him in order to make improper sexual advances. Obviously, the subject wanted no part of such accusations, and left the area without even getting a good look at that investigator. Had the surveillance officer been female, she could have accused the subject of being a "masher" who was trying to pick her up. Another ruse the officer could have used would have been to accuse the subject of being a professional accident-causer, out to defraud insurance companies.

A subject confronted an investigator as he sat in a vehicle in a small park across the street from the subject's residence. This well-prepared veteran investigator responded by providing the subject with the telephone number of the union hall where he could lodge his complaint. Taken off-guard, the subject questioned the reason that he should call the union hall. After some deliberately confused talk, the investigator told the subject to immediately return to his bus, or he would have to file a formal complaint against him. Now thoroughly confused, the subject listened respectfully as the investigator explained that he was the city inspector sent to clock the buses servicing the intersection. He made it clear that the union was fully aware of his assignment. Suddenly the subject "realized" that the investigator had mistaken him for the driver of the bus that was stopped near the intersection. He apologized for bothering the investigator, and returned to his residence.

In the situation above, the investigator realized that someone might question his sitting in a car in the park, so he concocted an explanation to be used if he was approached. He even went so far as to jot down times and comments concerning bus tardiness onto the top page of a clipboard that he had on the seat next too him. There was little question that this clipboard helped convince the subject that the investigator was in fact a bus inspector.

A good surveillance officer will always be able to satisfactorily answer a subject's "Why are you here?" question. This skill comes with experience.

An agency practicing the "don't get made" philosophy must be willing and able to make changes to avoid detection. If a subject has taken particular note of a surveillance vehicle, such as carefully looking into its windows when seeing it parked at the curb, it is best to remove that vehicle from future surveillances of that target. Similarly, investigators who have attracted a subject's attention should probably not participate in future surveillances in which face-to-face contact could occur with that subject. Such an investigator could possibly function in fixed posts rather than in moving coverages. In the example of the investigator who claimed to be the bus inspector, he was not used in future coverage of the target, because the subject had a close and lengthy view of him. Conversely, the investigator involved in the street confrontation returned to the assignment after a cooling-off period. This time he drove a different car and wore a hat and different clothing. This was considered safe because the subject had not gotten a close look at the investigator's face.

An agency planning terrorism surveillance must make a commitment to ensure success. This means that the proper number of investigators and vehicles should be assigned to the project. Adequate radio communications are imperative. Everyone must follow the "don't get made" philosophy. It will be necessary to exclude any "hot dog" officer who insists that he will never lose a subject. Investigators must prepare themselves for their mission. False identification, assorted believable disguises, props to explain various situations (such as the "bus inspector's" clipboard) are all necessary to facilitate the operation. Investigators must purge themselves of all observable "police" items. Included in this category are law enforcement rings, belt buckles, official-issue sunglasses, shoes, pens, and key rings that have handcuff keys and police emblems.

A review of a team's vehicles during a pre-surveillance inspection revealed that one officer had an agency decal on the notebook that he used to keep his log. Another officer had an official police department cap on the rear floor. While it was true that neither item could have been seen during a moving surveillance, had the subject been able to look into one of these vehicles when it was parked, they could have easily seen the incriminating item, thereby "making" the surveillance.

Even though an investigator is working on a surveillance project, he should still have his police identification with him. He should also have an approved firearm (often not the same type that he would carry while in uniform), handcuffs, and other necessary police equipment. These items must be concealed. Any subject who "makes" a surveillance could respond by attacking the surveilling agent. This could certainly occur if the subject was carrying contraband (to include explosives or incendiaries) at the time that he "made" the coverage, and mistakenly believed that his arrest was imminent. Surveillance officers must be able to protect themselves at all times.

Final Preparations for a Terrorism Surveillance

Once the commitment has been made to conduct the surveillance under the "don't get made" philosophy, final planning can begin.

Subject's Background. The investigators who will be conducting the surveillance need to be thoroughly briefed with respect to their target. They should be given photographs of the subject and his known associates and relatives. The team should be made privy to the information that is known to case agents. Equally important is that team members be aware of what is not known about the investigation, so that they can attempt to develop the missing facts. Team members should know the goals and objectives of the surveillance. Unfortunately, surveillance personnel all too often are left in the dark concerning aspects of the investigation. Some case officers even believe that surveillance personnel can be more impartial if they are not given all of the facts. This logic may hold true on some occasions with respect to undercover officers and informants, because these people could encounter serious difficulties if they accidentally let slip information that should not be known. However, with respect to surveillance officers, this logic makes little sense.

These officers would not normally have any personal contact with the subject. As trained investigators, they should not allow previously developed information to taint their conduct. Worse, the surveillance personnel could end up in taking unnecessary risks developing information that they know will be of value, only to discover that the case officer already had that information.

In one surveillance, the point car was set up down the street from the subject's residence. The investigator was assigned to alert his team of the subject's departure from his residence so that the surveillance team could pick him up several blocks away from his home. Unfortunately, a close relative of the subject lived in the house in front of which the investigator was parked. This person noticed the coverage. Fortunately in this case, the target never "made" the surveillance. Because there was so much criminal activity in his neighborhood, it was assumed that the investigator was looking at someone else. This was a situation in which the case officer failed to pass information on to the surveillance team about his subject's relative that he should have given to them.

Intelligence sharing should continue throughout the surveillance. The team should expeditiously submit its surveillance logs and related reports to the case officer. Information of a more immediate nature should be provided even before the logs are prepared. Similarly, the case officer should provide the team with information of value that he develops through other techniques. It is important that if more than one team is following the subject, they share information as quickly as possible. When one team is relieving another, the departing team should provide updates to the arriving team. Scheduling slight work overlaps is useful in accomplishing this objective. Perhaps one team can work 6:00 A.M. to 2:15 P.M. with the relieving team assigned to work 1:45 P.M. to 10:00 P.M. In this way there is a 30-minute overlap during which updates can be given and personnel rotated into position without anyone being forced to work on their own time.

Vehicles and Equipment. Most surveillances will involve vehicles. In fact, in many instances, the entire surveillance will take place using vehicles. Surveillance vehicles should be reliable and well-maintained. Vehicles that fail to start each day or that do not accelerate rapidly can cause failed surveillances. Vehicles that have mechanical problems, including noisy mufflers and squeaky springs, attract attention and are useless for surveillance operations. Any vehicle that will cause the average person to give it a second look should not be used in surveillance. This could include brand-new, sports, custom, and luxury vehicles. Bright-colored cars such as red and electric blue can also present problems for surveillance teams. Any vehicle that has noticeable body damage is a liability on surveillance, because it will probably be remembered by anyone who sees it. Investigators should use vehicles that blend into the community, and generally go unnoticed even if observed several times in a single day.

Unfortunately, some departments have difficulty acquiring appropriate vehicles. They may be forced to use older cruisers, seized and confiscated vehicles, rejects taken from the impound lot, and vehicles claimed from other agency auctions or giveaway programs. Clearly, many of these vehicles are not useful for surveillance purposes. A department that cannot provide proper vehicles to a surveillance team is better off not doing a vehicular surveillance in sensitive cases such as terrorism investigations.

If a surveillance extends long enough, even a drab, plain-looking car will be noticed if the subject sees it frequently. Ideally, a constant exchange of vehicles would solve this situation, but this is extremely costly. Surveillance personnel can alter their vehicles to make them appear different each time the subject sees them:

Remove or change wheel covers

Frequently change items hanging from the rear-view mirror

Place an ever-changing variety of items on the rear window ledge, including stuffed animals, hats, clothing, trash (empty cans, cups, etc.)

Place a changing array of items on the dashboard, including cupholders, compasses, note pads, tissue dispensers, and parking permits

Tape (not glue) and rotate various decals on the windows, depicting everything from advertising to city inspection stickers, school emblems, and parking passes. In cities in which it is common for private firms to place illegal parking notices on the windows of improperly parked cars, tape such notices on the windows on a rotating basis.

Affix and change decals on windows to make them appear cracked and broken (obtain from novelty shops)

Rotate various license plates, license plate holders and, if no front plate is required by the state, rotate vanity and advertising plates

On a rotating basis, place various props inside the car, including baby seats, folding wheelchairs, boxes, and briefcases

Place and remove bike racks (with or without bikes), roof carriers, and ski holders

Place, change, and remove mud, dirt, tree drippings, and other forms of debris from the vehicle's exterior

Place and remove glue/tape-on sport ornamentation to the vehicle's exterior, including racing stripes, pen striping, and decals

With respect to vans and trucks (and, in some instances, cars), rotate magnetic or cardboard signs bearing business names (Joe's Market, Jones' Surveyors, Ace Plumbing, Arrow Delivery Service, etc.).

Even if none of these techniques is utilized, a vehicle can be made to look different by changing the driver, especially if that change is significant. A subject who sees a drab five-year-old Ford in his neighborhood driven by a young, slim, blond white man is not likely to recognize that vehicle on another day if it is driven by an older black woman or an overweight, balding, middle-aged white man. Sometimes having multiple people in a vehicle previously driven by one person can change its nature, especially if a prop (like a baby carrier) is added.

Disguises. No matter how nondescript surveillance investigators are in appearance, it is still wise for them to have some ability to modify their appearance. Clothing can be a simple way to accomplish this. Shirts, blouses, and sweaters that can be properly worn inside or outside of pants or skirts are ideal. An officer can quickly alter his appearance from somewhat formal to casual by merely pulling out or tucking in an article of clothing. Jackets and coats can also be used to alter one's appearance. A person in a coat can look very different when that coat is removed. Unfortunately, coats can present a problem during a foot surveillance, because the investigator will likely have no place to dispose of it when he removes it. A simple solution to this problem could be for the officer to wear reversible outerwear. Some terrorist groups teach their members to do just that in order to elude law enforcement surveillance.

Hats are ideal disguise props and many professional surveillance officers maintain a wide array of them. Particularly valuable hats are the soft fabric types that can be easily folded. Such hats can be kept in coat pockets and worn and removed as needed. Wigs can also be valuable props, but they can cause problems because surveillance personnel often cannot take the time to fit them in front of a mirror. A way to compensate for this is to use a wig in conjunction with a hat so that anyone looking at the person will not realize that the wig does not fit properly. One trick is to wear a long-haired wig under a construction worker's helmet.

Disguising eyes can alter one's appearance. A person wearing glasses looks different from one who does not. Surveillance personnel who normally wear glasses should have several pairs with different frames. Investigators who do not wear glasses should purchase nonprescription window glass-type glasses. Having an array of sunglasses of differing styles is another good way for an officer to alter his or her appearance. Facial hair alterations are also a way to change one's appearance; however, as with wigs, it is sometimes difficult to apply a false mustache, beard, or sideburns without a mirror.

Some professional surveillance investigators maintain elaborate makeup kits, complete with mirrors and lights. These kits contain everything from cosmetics to false facial hair. These investigators also have props that include such items as walking canes, crutches, "superfly hats," eye patches, false arm casts, umbrellas, lunchboxes, or bandannas.

One terrorist group was found to not only have a complete makeup kit, but to have converted the rear of one of their vans into a room that resembled what would be used on location by a movie studio to make up their performers. If a terrorist group can accomplish this, certainly a full-time surveillance team could do something similar.

Another trick that some surveillance personnel employ is a highly visible prop that draws attention away from the person. It is useful in foot surveillances, especially in situations in which the surveillance officer may have a face-to-face encounter with the subject. The highly visible props often used include large belt buckles, big cigars, campaign badges, distinctive earrings and other jewelry, and highly visible bandages. The idea is to make people focus on the prop rather than on the face. After an encounter, the investigator removes the prop and hopefully is no longer recognizable to the subject. Criminals have long used this gimmick. Many law enforcement officers have interviewed witnesses who can provide vivid descriptions of the bright bandanna or unusual sunglasses that the perpetrator wore, but cannot recall anything about the perpetator's appearance.

Surveillance Personnel

Manpower Required. There is no simple answer to questions about the number of investigators required to conduct an effective surveillance. There are many variables—including the type and method of surveillance to be used, and the movements that the subject may make during the span of coverage. The goal of the surveillance will be a decisive factor in assigning manpower.

Some fixed surveillances can be effectively conducted by one or two investigators. For example, the surveillance target may be a clandestine location used by terrorists to stage covert meetings. The goal of the coverage might be to identify people entering and leaving the target address. To accomplish this objective, a fixed "perch" located in the attic of a building across the street could be established. It is reasonable that one person could handle such a location. A second investigator could possibly be assigned to the attic lookout position to assist so the first investigator would not become so fatigued as to miss something. Perhaps the second investigator could also take occasional walks near the target in an effort to record the license plates of vehicles used by people observed entering the target address. Fixed-perch surveillances are fairly common in law enforcement. In this type of coverage it is important not to flood the area with investigators. Someone is likely to become suspicious if six or seven people try to cram themselves into a small attic, or if there is a constant parade of strangers in a lightly traveled neighborhood.

Moving surveillances will usually require many more investigators than would be needed to operate fixed-perch lookouts. Surveillance-conscious subjects will require more personnel than those who are not looking for surveillance. Investigators should assume that terrorists are always on the alert for surveillance. What is already known about the subject will dictate the proper number of personnel to assign to a given surveillance. If it is known that the subject has a tendency to drive for a while, park his car, board public transportation, and ultimately end up traveling on foot for lengthy periods, a fairly large contingent of surveillance investigators will be required. It might be desirable to use vehicles operated by two or more investigators, so that when the subject leaves his vehicle, several surveillance officers will be readily available to follow him when he boards public transportation or travels on foot.

Ideally, a vehicular surveillance team will consist of between five and eight investigators. Using less than five officers is risky, because it is likely that the subject will either lose or make the coverage. Using more than eight investigators, especially if each is driving his own car, can become a logistical nightmare. That many vehicles in a residential area could cause a traffic jam that would result in the subject becoming suspicious. In congested business locations, the problem would in part involve "lost" investigators who could become separated from the team because of traffic signals, stop signs, and people pulling in and out of traffic.

Fixed surveillances, other than from a lookout situation, could involve many investigators, although a dozen is more likely the case. In a crowded downtown area, investigators could saturate several blocks without drawing suspicion, because their assignment is to blend into the scene and not actually follow the subject.

In one major terrorism investigation, moving surveillance personnel consistently lost the subject when the public transportation he used entered into the heart of the city. To determine where the subject was going on his weekly trips, a fixed surveillance team consisting of more than 100 investigators was assigned to posts throughout a six-square-block area. After several unsuccessful efforts, a heavily disguised subject was ultimately observed by several investigators. Once the fixed coverage had determined the subject's route, a moving surveillance team was able to follow him through the downtown area when he made his next trip a week later.

Characteristics of Surveillance Personnel. It is important that surveillance investigators blend into the location where the coverage is being staged. Surveillance is one of the few situations in life where an average or plain-looking person is the most desirable. Unfortunately, finding such people is not as easy as it may sound. Many law enforcement officers have a kind of "cop" look. They fall within certain height and weight limitations, and they keep themselves physically fit. When they enter a room, they command instant attention because of the way they look and conduct themselves. They are the last people that a department would want on surveillance. Even in departments in which there are employees who fit the mold of "plainness," there may be all kinds of problems with using these employees on surveillance. Various federal and state laws forbid discrimination. Similarly, many police labor contracts dictate procedures for transfer and promotion that involve seniority, ratings, and examinations. Consequently, a department may not be able to assign the "best looking" people to a surveillance assignment. Conversely, they may be forced to accept applicants for such an assignment who really should not be performing surveillance.

Ideally, a surveillance team will have a variety of different-looking people who generally fall within the range of "average looking." The demands of physical appearance increase in direct proportion to the amount of time during which foot coverage will be required. Even exceptionally tall, short, or possibly handicapped people look "average" when in vehicles. On foot, however, distinctive looks are likely to be noticed.

If the right personnel are not available, a department will probably be best served by not conducting a surveillance, or by limiting the scope of the coverage. This is especially true in terrorism investigations, in which a "made" surveillance can destroy a case. It may be difficult to employ a team comprised largely of black investigators in an all-white neighborhood, or a team of white officers in an all-black area. Similarly, a team of older officers might stand out surveilling in a young singles scene. A group of clean-cut officers would probably be "made" rather quickly in a neighborhood infested with drug dealers and motorcycle gangs. In any surveillance, investigators who, for whatever reason, do not fit into the area being covered should either be excluded or used in fixed locations or backup roles.

What to Do If Confronted During Surveillance

Investigators may face confrontations from several different directions during the course of a surveillance operation, including:

- the subject
- an associate of the subject
- an uninvolved person, such as a neighbor or security guard
- a law enforcement officer performing his duties
- a criminal
- a mentally ill person

During the course of a terrorist surveillance, gunshots suddenly rang out, and surveillance investigators realized that they were under attack. A call to 911 brought marked police cars to the scene. A lengthy barricade situation resulted. When it was finally resolved, it was discovered that the man involved in the attack on the surveillance team was a local resident who had observed the investigators from his apartment window, and had become convinced that they were after him. In response, he had chosen to "defend himself." The offender was not involved with the target of the surveillance, or with any terrorist group. By wisely calling 911 instead of returning fire or otherwise attempting to handle the situation, the investigators were able to preserve the security of their surveillance. The target of the surveillance coverage never learned the identities of the "citizens" upon whom the barricaded man had fired.

How the investigator responds to such confrontations can make or break a case. Even if the subject or an associate is not involved, the investigator must not lose his sense of responsibility to the security of the surveillance. The subject could be observing the investigator's response to the confrontation, or he could later learn about it from the involved person or a witness.

Surveillance personnel should constantly be asking themselves, "How do I explain why I'm here?" This is especially true in the case of fixed surveillances and situations in which moving coverage has come to a halt. The following are examples of reasons an investigator could give if challenged:

- Insurance investigator verifying a claim
- Husband/wife trying to catch his or her spouse in an extramarital affair
- Freelance writer working on a story involving anything in the community—from architecture to street people
- Accident investigator developing information for a lawsuit
- Conducting a traffic survey
- A land surveyor
- An inspector checking on city, state, county, or private employees who are supposedly working on a project in the area
- Waiting for a rendezvous
- Pretend to be intoxicated or under the influence of drugs
- If able to speak a foreign language, claim not to speak English
- Act as though mentally ill

- Claim car trouble (use a cutoff switch so that the engine will only grind, but never start—can ask the challenger for assistance)

- Claim that vehicle has been vandalized and you are waiting for police to arrive

- Act like a victim and accuse the challenger of harassing or following you. Point out others in neighborhood as also following you.

- Claim that your spouse locked you out of your residence

- Claim to be living in your car because you are homeless (helps to claim that you were just released from prison or a halfway house)

How Terrorists Negate or "Make" Surveillance Coverage

Many terrorists are trained to be alert for law enforcement surveillance. They are also taught how to avoid surveillance. Things that terrorists do to ruin a surveillance or to "make" it include the following:

Constant Observation of Surroundings. The terrorist is always aware of his surroundings. He tries to be aware of people around him and becomes immediately suspicious of anyone that he observes on several occasions. Some terrorists are very open in their observations, clearly looking at people. Others use less obvious methods, including using reflective surfaces such as glass windows and chrome surfaces. Some glance back while tying shoes or retrieving dropped objects. Some retrace their steps to obtain a better view of people in the area. U-turns are a method that some terrorists commonly use while driving.

Erratic Driving. A terrorist who drives in an unusual or erratic manner can often spot surveillance vehicles attempting to maintain close coverage. Such behavior can include rapid acceleration, sharp turns, sudden stops, driving too fast or too slow, parking along the road, driving the wrong way on a street, driving through alleys, parking lots, and private property, driving into dead-end streets, and pulling into private drives.

Confronting People on the Street. Some terrorists will blatantly stop people on the street and accuse these people of following them. They figure that even if they are wrong most of the time, it is worth the embarrassment and inconvenience if they identify even one surveillance officer. A variation of this is for the subject to inform a uniformed police officer that a particular person is following him. If nothing else, they may delay the surveillance long enough to enable them to leave the area undetected.

Using Public Transportation. Public transportation, which can consist of everything from buses to subways to taxis, can be effectively used to both elude and detect surveillance. A subject who suddenly parks his vehicle and boards a bus may be able to observe cars trying to follow. He will certainly become suspicious if he sees someone else exit a vehicle and board a bus. A person on foot can also use public transportation to elude and detect surveillance. The simplest method is to get off the public transportation within a block of entering it. Anyone else who does the same will be identified as following the subject.

Using Associates to Detect Surveillance. Some terrorists use fellow group members or even innocent people to watch them as they leave a certain location in an effort to determine whether anyone is following them.

Using Public Restrooms to Identify Surveillance. Restrooms can be located anywhere—from public buildings to service stations. Remaining in a restroom for a long time can cause surveillance personnel to enter in an effort to determine whether the person exited by another means. If a surveillance agent follows the subject into a restroom, the subject can immediately exit without using the facilities. If the surveillance officer also leaves, he is "made." If he remains in the restroom, he loses the subject.

Aircraft Surveillance

Aircraft can greatly augment most vehicular surveillances. They can also assist in some foot coverages, depending upon where they are conducted. Aircraft enable the surveillance investigators to maintain a safe distance behind the target, thereby making detection of the surveillance much more difficult. Aircraft are excellent in affording coverage to many locations, particularly in rural areas. They are also of value in covering subjects in open areas such as parking lots and fields.

In theory, anything that flies could be used to support surveillance. This includes airplanes, helicopters, blimps, and even satellites. For the most part, single-engine, fixed-wing planes are the aircraft most commonly used to support surveillances. Multi-engine, fixed-wing aircraft can also be used, but they often are too noisy, fly too fast, and are too expensive for many departments to operate. Helicopters have numerous advantages that make them ideal for surveillance support. They can fly low, can take off and land in most open areas, and can almost come to a dead stop in the air. Unfortunately, helicopters are noisy and can leave a distinct shadow on the ground that the subject can identify. Also, most police helicopters have agency markings, which are dead giveaways if seen by the subject. In cities where there are numerous law enforcement, traffic, military, and media helicopters, they can often be used to support surveillance because people have come to accept them. Blimps might be of value to augment surveillances in or around sporting contests or other major events where people might expect that such an aircraft would be employed by the media or for promotional purposes.

Photographic Surveillance

There is an old saying that a picture "is worth a thousand words." Certainly this is true in police work. An investigator's testimony is most convincing in the courtroom, especially if he can support it with a written surveillance log. A photograph or video submitted to support the investigator's testimony and surveillance log is the crown jewel of evidence. It is very difficult for a defense attorney to rebut this kind of testimony.

The camera is a commonly used surveillance tool. Photographs should be taken on a regular basis, but only if they can be taken securely. It would be wise for a department to offer training for all of its surveillance personnel with respect to the proper use of the cameras. Sending officers to a general school of photography certainly has value, especially for the novice. However, it is important that the investigators receive specific training in the use of their department's equipment. Great advances in the field of photography occurred during the 1990s and early twenty-first century. Even as recently as the 1970s many people had difficulty using anything more complicated than the basic point-and-shoot family camera. Modern cameras can quickly be mastered by most investigators. If possible, photos should be taken by the most photographically skilled officers on the surveillance team.

Modern cameras are small and can be easily concealed. Indeed, the placement of most cameras is limited only by the imagination of the photographer. Cameras can be mounted in one location and remotely operated from another, more secure station. Cameras can also be set in such a manner that they will automatically take photographs at certain intervals, or take photographs when a subject does something to trip the shutter. Cameras can be remotely shifted so that they can follow a subject as he leaves a location. Color film that was once never even considered for surveillance photography because of its cost, is now commonly used. By using longer and more efficient lenses, quality photographs can be taken from long distances away from the subject. Photographs can also be taken successfully in very dark conditions, using only a minimal amount of ambient light. Digital cameras have become the norm in the 2000s and their pictures can be sent via computer to command centers and other surveillance personnel. Very recently the camera cell phone has become a "must have" toy. They, too, can be used to a certain extent in surveillance assignments, especially in close-up situations.

Photographs have many uses for the surveillance team. They support surveillance logs. However, on some occasions, the camera may actually record activities that surveillance personnel were not able to observe. Photographs can also be used to augment future surveillance by enabling all personnel to observe the subject's appearance. Furthermore, many people tend to wear the same clothing repeatedly, which might be the apparel depicted in a photograph. In addition, photographs also can be used to connect the subject with an address, vehicle, or associate. Another use for photographs is that they can assist an agency in determining a subject's physical attributes. If a subject is pictured standing next to a store entrance, a subsequent check of that doorway could help ascertain the subject's height. Similarly, if a subject was pictured with another person whose weight was known, it may be possible to accurately estimate the subject's weight.

Video cameras can be used in fixed or combination surveillances. From a remote location, a surveillance agent can observe the subject leaving a point of initiation and alert the surveillance team of this movement. Modern technology is such that a video camera could be placed in the front of surveillance vehicles and record much of the subject's movements. Indeed, many police patrol vehicles are now equipped with such equipment. Television coverage of stock car races often features live video being shot from race cars traveling close to 200 miles per hour. In foot surveillances, video cameras placed in briefcases and other hand-carried items can record the subject's activities. Some cameras are now so small that the surveillance officer can have a camera attached to his body in such a manner as to enable him to film what he sees during a surveillance. If a video camera is to be used in conjunction with a fixed or combination surveillance, it is best placed in a secure location with an investigator. This is not always possible; thus, a remote camera must be considered. The following are possible locations where a remote still or video camera can be concealed:

> On power or telephone poles, parking meters, street signs, traffic signals, or various other fixed structures along a street
>
> In parked empty vehicles
>
> In moveable objects, including baby strollers, shipping boxes, curb trash, or items carried by a live person, including the subject
>
> On building exteriors, including the roof, ledges, rain gutters, signs, shutters, or doorways
>
> In buildings, including inside exit signs, light fixtures, trash cans, molding, smoke alarms, fire extinguishers/hoses, and lobby furnishings
>
> In conjunction with existing security systems, which may or may not be visible
>
> In public buildings, including restaurants, bars, office buildings, modes of transportation, recreational facilities, and stores

Logs should be maintained for pictures taken during a surveillance. If this is not done, the team is likely to end up with numerous photographs that cannot be connected with their surveillance.

Other Closed-Circuit Television Coverage

Closed circuit television (CCTV) has become a part of the very fabric of many large cities, and is also commonly employed in many other parts of the country as well. Even the smallest businesses deploy CCTV to ensure security for their employees and to deter their customers and employees from stealing from them. Costs have dropped so dramatically for CCTV that an increasing number of private homeowners are protecting their property with it. It is very likely that at points during a law enforcement surveillance officers will determine that the subject they are following has come under CCTV coverage. It would be wise for officers to note on their log or on a separate report CCTV coverage in instances where they have not been able to continuously observe the subject, such as when he entered a building. Also in situations where a surveillance team realizes that the subject is being covered by CCTV, especially one that is operated by the city, they may be able to give the subject some slack, thereby reducing the danger of detection. A team member or someone else in the department could subsequently retrieve the film of the CCTV coverage. If nothing else CCTV can be used to support what surveillance personnel report in their logs.

Technical Surveillance Tools

Beepers. The beeper transmits a sound that can be monitored through the radios in surveillance vehicles. Beepers can be wired into the electrical system of the subject's vehicle, or they can be "slapped on" and held in place by a magnet or other means. Wired beepers (also called parasitic) require that the surveillance team actually take possession of the vehicle. This usually requires a court order. Few agency leaders are willing to authorize the "borrowing" of a subject's vehicle for any reason unless authorized by a judge. Installation of a wired beeper requires the skills of a professional technician. The parasitic beeper feeds from the vehicle's electrical system. Improper installation can short out the vehicle's wiring—disabling the vehicle or causing a fire.

During a terrorism investigation, officers "borrowed" the subject's car and had a parasitic beeper installed. Although the beeper functioned as it should have, the subject experienced frequent malfunctions seemingly caused by the installation. This forced the investigators to "borrow" the vehicle several more times, to make repairs. The department learned a valuable lesson—when authorized to install a wired beeper, attempt to locate an identical vehicle, and practice wiring it before actually "borrowing" the subject's car.

Portable "slap on" beepers can easily be installed without any trespass to the vehicle. A surveillance investigator walks up to the parked vehicle, bends down, and clamps the device under the car. Although the "slap on" is simple to use, it does have drawbacks—anyone who looks under the car will be able to see it.

During one terrorism surveillance, the officers observed the subject drive into a garage where the serviceman lifted his car in order to change the oil. Two surveillance officers were forced to immediately enter the garage. One engaged the serviceman and the subject in a subterfuge conversation, while the other sneaked under the car where he removed the "slap on" beeper and concealed it under a newspaper.

Even if no one actually looks under a car, a "slap on" beeper can occasionally be seen. The installation is usually made near the edge of the car, often at the rear. This means that if the vehicle is parked on a hill or on slanted pavement, a person walking up to it might observe the beeper's antenna.

Another weakness of the "slap on" beeper is that it is battery powered. This means that it must be removed and repowered periodically. Clearly, any approach to the subject's vehicle is risky. It may have an alarm that will sound at even the slightest disturbance.

Beepers allow surveillance vehicles to locate a vehicle if it should become lost during a surveillance. It enables surveillance investigators to maintain a safe distance behind the subject, yet always be able to find him or her. It must be remembered that beepers can sometimes be detected by using scanners that are available at electronics stores. Some beepers can also interfere with FM radio reception.

Tracking Systems. During the 1990s, private firms began offering satellite monitoring systems that would enable a vehicle to be traced within certain areas, such as within the borders of a city or county. Soon some trucking and taxi companies employed such systems to keep track of their vehicles. Security firms also began employing the systems to locate stolen vehicles. By the 2000s numerous individuals, government agencies, and businesses had found uses for such systems. Many General Motors car dealers sell tracking devices on their vehicles that enable the driver to receive instant assistance in case of an accident or other emergency. Obviously, if a tracking device can be monitored by a private company, it can also be monitored by a police agency. However, a law enforcement agency should check with their legal counsel and/or prosecutor before attempting such coverage. Of course, the police agency could go to the monitoring company, and request information and assistance—which they would probably provide if given a court order. Some parents have even installed tracking systems on the cars of their teenage children in order to monitor their drving habits. In police work, a tracking system transmitter can be installed in or on a vehicle just as one would install a beeper. It is then possible to track the whereabouts of the vehicle from a control center or other monitoring location.

Surveillance Used with Technical Coverage

The federal government and many state governments allow for court-authorized electronic coverage of conversations conducted within vehicles. Surveillance conducted in connection with such coverage is mainly for the purpose of monitoring conversations held in the vehicle, rather than for aiding in the observation of the subject's activities. Court orders authorizing the coverage also allow for the vehicle to be "borrowed" without the owner's knowledge. The monitoring devices used are almost always wired into the vehicle's electrical system. Although equipment has greatly improved in recent years and twenty-first century microphones are almost impossible to see, it is not always easy to clearly hear and record all conversations being held in monitored moving vehicles. Sometimes this results in surveillance personnel following the target too closely in an effort to hear everything that is being said in the vehicle. Aircraft can also be used to monitor the transmissions.

A court order can be procured that would permit an agency to place a video camera in a vehicle to either film the activities inside (such as the interior of a van) or to film where the vehicle goes. Surveillance teams could well be the law enforcement personnel entrusted with monitoring such operations. If so there should be two officers in the monitoring vehicle, and the coverage should be recorded.

Surveillance Documentation

In many respects, surveillance is only as good as its documentation. From a law enforcement perspective, if the surveillance has not been reduced to written form, it might as well not have happened. There is little question that surveillance logs are time-consuming; however, they must be done even in instances where nothing believed to be of value has been learned. A prosecutor who intends to introduce surveillance evidence, or who plans to introduce evidence that arose from surveillance, knows that he must be able to produce documentation to support that surveillance. He also knows that the court will not tolerate the prosecutor concealing the results of surveillance that do not support his case. The defense will demand all surveillance logs germane to the investigation. If they are not given them, they will argue that the logs not turned over must contain information that is either favorable to their client or that implicates someone else as the guilty party.

Often when surveillance is conducted no one really knows the full extent of what will be developed during the course of the investigation. Some of the seemingly unimportant information learned during a surveillance may turn out to have some significance at a later stage of the case. This, in itself, should be an excellent reason for maintaining good logs for every surveillance conducted during an investigation.

Surveillance logs are usually handwritten. They are better if they are recorded onto an agency form, or in a standard format. Usually the log will reflect the date of the surveillance and the names of the investigators involved in the operation. The first entry of the log should reflect the initiation of the surveillance. It might read something like, "10am, surveillance commenced at the residence of Joe Smith, 897 Green Street, Anytown, United States." Each subsequent entry describes an observation, and the time that the observation was made is noted. Entries might read something like: "10:17am, subject departs front door of residence wearing green coat and brown pants," "10:19 A.M., subject enters blue Ford, Illinois license ABC1234, parked at curb in front of residence," "10:20 A.M., subject drives blue Ford south towards Jones Street." There is usually only one log maintained for a surveillance, even though there are several team members actively engaged in the coverage.

After the surveillance has been completed, each member of the surveillance team should sign the log. Many agencies take the procedure a step further by requiring that each team member also initial the entries that they personally observed. This is more time-consuming, but it is a good procedure to follow.

Although the surveillance log is usually handwritten, many agencies subsequently have the log typed so that it can be read more easily. The original handwritten version must be maintained as evidence. Modern computer technology is such that information entered into a system can be maintained, correlated, and organized. As departments procure state-of-the-art computers, they will want to have the results of all investigative techniques entered into the computer in order to allow officers to assemble and use it. Therefore, the future trend will likely be to have handwritten logs typed.

Some surveillance teams maintain audio logs using handheld tape recorders. It is important that these recordings be reduced to written form, and both the tape and the written log be maintained as evidence. In the future surveillance teams will most likely use laptop computers to type actual logs during a surveillance. If the person maintaining the log is assigned to a fixed-perch location, he or she could certainly do that now. Presently there is commercially available software that can convert spoken language into written form on a computer. Surveillance officers may simply speak aloud what they want in the log as they follow a subject, and print out a final draft in the office later.

In one large-scale criminal investigation, the prosecutor found himself in a predicament when he discovered that the law enforcement agency that had conducted many of the surveillances in the case had not maintained surveillance logs. Amazingly, several of the investigators bragged about the quality of their memories, and offered to testify about observations that they had made several years earlier. Wisely, the prosecutor chose not to use any of the fruits of their surveillances even though several of them had developed information that would have bolstered the case.

The fact that a subject is practicing counter-surveillance techniques in and of itself can be very useful information with respect to the prosecution of a case. This is especially true of terrorism investigations in which efforts to avoid surveillance are common. The fact is that most counter-surveillance actions are abnormal. They are not the kinds of things that average people do during the course of their lives. Jumping on and off buses, driving the wrong way on a one-way street, stopping on the highway, changing clothing, applying and removing disguises, and stopping and accusing people on the street of following them all are unusual behaviors. A surveillance team should make note of such behavior in their logs and make sure that the case officer is aware of it. A wise prosecutor can use such behavior as part of probable cause to obtain search warrants and other court orders. If nothing else, an outline of such behavior can help to convince the jury that the subject was using counter-surveillance techniques.

On occasion, surveillance teams will perform investigative work that is related to, but not directly a part of, the surveillance. For example, a subject may be seen entering a hotel and checking with a desk clerk before entering an elevator. A surveillance officer may immediately contact the desk clerk in order to determine the nature of the conversation. A surveillance team may observe a subject purchasing something at a hardware store. Following the surveillance, an investigator may return to the hardware store in an effort to determine what the subject purchased. A subject enters an apartment building and rings a doorbell. After the subject leaves the building, a surveillance agent notes the name of everyone on the building's directory.

Any investigation conducted in connection with a surveillance must be documented. It is usually better to do so on a separate report than in the surveillance log, which is supposed to reflect the subject's movements and activities. The method of reporting will vary from department to department. For example, if a particular agency has an interview form, it would be wise to use it when documenting an interview conducted in conjunction with a surveillance. If an agency uses a certain kind of envelope to protect evidence, the surveillance officer should use this to store evidence that he recovers in conjunction with a surveillance.

Other Investigative Techniques Used During Surveillance

Trash Cover

Trash cover is a valuable investigative technique. It should be considered by anyone conducting a surveillance. Items discarded by the subject may prove to be of great value and should be retrieved, if possible.

In a major cross-country terrorist task force investigation that covered thousands of miles, two surveillance officers were assigned to handle trash covers. By the end of the coverage, their vehicle was filled with assorted items that the subjects had discarded.

One major objective that a trash cover can achieve is verifying the identity of the subject. Subjects will often discard materials that bear their names, such as bills, receipts, newspapers, and magazines. Much of what is discarded could be sent to an appropriate police laboratory for fingerprinting and even DNA testing. This can be extremely important if there is a question about the subject's identity.

In one very important terrorism case, investigators had followed a subject to a "bomb factory" on a number of occasions. Although the investigators were certain that they had correctly identified the subject, they realized that they might have difficulty proving it in court if the defense argued that the subject being followed was not the person on trial. This was a special problem in this case, because the subject had several brothers (who were similar in appearance) with whom he had close association. One evening, the officers observed the subject discard a food container in a dumpster as he walked from the building. This container was subsequently retrieved and sent to a police laboratory, where a technician lifted the subject's fingerprints from the food container.

Some care must be employed in connection with the recovery of discarded items. A subject could return to the area to see if anyone has taken an article that he dropped. Some foreign spies have been taught to do this in an effort to detect surveillance. It is possible that they might even have an associate watching them to see whether a discarded item is recovered. However, this is usually not an issue in terrorism cases because the item will have been discarded in such a way that it could have innocently moved by the time a subject returned to the scene. However, if the subject makes a point of leaving something where it might not normally become dislodged—such as jamming a wrapper between the slats of a bus bench—the surveillance team should wait several hours before recovering it. In fact, they might even leave an officer to watch the location in case the "discard" is actually a message for an associate. For a broader discussion of trash covers, see Chapter 12.

Mail Cover

Mail covers are not physically employed during the course of a surveillance. However, surveillance officers should make note of any correspondence that the subject mails. These items can be often "marked" by dropping something like a large envelope addressed to the surveillance officer into the mailbox immediately after the subject departs. In that way the subject's communication can be readily located by looking for the letter just below the officer's envelope. Usually the case officer will make the decision regarding the feasibility of obtaining a mail cover to view the subject's mailing. The department's legal counsel and/or the prosecutor should be consulted if there is not an established policy with respect to such a situation. The best that the law enforcement agency can hope for is a view of the outside of the subject's mailing. Obviously, if there is reason to believe that the item dropped into the mailbox is dangerous, such as a letter bomb, a judge should be contacted for an order to open it.

Telephone Record Checks

Subjects commonly use public or business telephones to place calls while under surveillance. If a surveillance officer can safely stand near an open telephone, he may be able to overhear the conversation. Some people "doodle" while talking on the telephone. A surveillance officer may be able to safely retrieve this writing after the subject departs. If it appears that the call is important, the case officer can be notified so that he can make a decision about procuring the call records from that telephone.

Overt Surveillance

Some agencies periodically assign investigators to observe subjects openly. This may involve an officer in a four-door sedan parking in front of the subject's residence, and plainly making notes whenever the subject moves. The idea behind this form of coverage is to intimidate the subject into either voluntarily cooperating with the agency, or scaring him away from committing future crimes. Although this technique involves a law enforcement officer viewing a subject, it is not a true surveillance. Agencies employing this technique are often treading in the gray area of legality and morality. The subject could easily accuse the agency of harassment and file a civil complaint against the agency. The subject is certainly not going to commit a crime when he knows an officer is watching him.

If, for whatever reason, an agency decides to use overt surveillance, it should not use its regular surveillance personnel to conduct it. It should also not use its agency's normal surveillance vehicles. Clearly, in such coverage, the subject is going to become familiar with the investigator and his vehicle. This will render both useless in any normal surveillance of the subject. If the subject is involved with an extremist cause, he will likely confront the surveillance officer, jot down the license number, and take a picture of the vehicle and officer.

Summary

Surveillance is a valuable investigative technique because it places a law enforcement officer in a position in which he or she can observe a subject conspiring to commit, or actually committing, a criminal violation. Unfortunately, the technique has the drawback of being extremely labor-intensive and therefore may not be viable for smaller law enforcement agencies. Surveillance in terrorism cases is particularly difficult and should not be attempted unless the agency has sufficient manpower, vehicles, and resources. Terrorists are very security-conscious and are often aware of how law enforcement agencies conduct surveillance. Many terrorists routinely practice "dry cleaning" tactics designed to identify surveillance or to elude tailing officers.

Surveillances are usually mobile in nature, with the officer following the target. However, there is a valuable form of surveillance in which the subjects will move through a maze of stationary officers who never leave their posts, but who observe the subject's activities while that person is in their area. In terrorism cases, a combination of both of these types of surveillance is recommended. There are various methods of surveillance coverage that can be employed. They range from observing the person on an around-the-clock basis to coverage that will be quite restrictive in duration. Each method has advantages and drawbacks.

Terrorists often differ from common criminals with respect to being aware that they are being surveilled. A terrorist subject who "makes" coverage is likely to inform his group of the breach in security. Frequently the group will respond by aborting the operation and possibly relocating to another area. It is therefore recommended that officers conducting a terrorist surveillance adopt a "don't get made" philosophy, meaning that they discontinue the coverage at the first hint that the subject may be suspicious. Furthermore, it is recommended that an officer always have in his mind a reason for being where he is so that he can explain it to the subject should he be challenged. In that way, the subject will never be certain that he was being surveilled by the person that he has accused of following him. Investigators involved in surveillance should always be alert for items that a subject may discard and recover them if possible.

Documentation must accompany surveillance. Agencies should adopt a philosophy that a surveillance that is not documented never happened. Prosecutors will be very reluctant to allow an investigator to testify from memory about a surveillance that occurred months earlier and was never documented.

⑪ Informants

An informant is an individual who covertly provides accurate information to a law enforcement agency on a continuing basis. Law enforcement agencies use a variety of terms to refer to informants. Among these descriptors are "sources," "contacts," and "assets." The most common term used by street police officers seems to be "CI," which usually stands for "criminal informant," or possibly "confidential informant." Often the media, citizens, criminals, and even some investigators apply uncomplimentary slang terms when referring to informants, including "stoolie," "stool pigeon," "squealer," "snitch," "rat," "fink," and "turncoat." Some agencies have specific titles for informants who provide coverage on particular criminal specialties. These might include "top-echelon organized crime informant," "gang informer," or "narcotics source." Some agencies have separate categories for informants based on the way they develop information. For example, a person who provides coverage to a subject's residence or employment might be called a "neighborhood source" or an "employment source," respectively. A person who develops information of value on a variety of subjects through the course of his employment might be known as an "established source" or "business source."

An informant should provide current information to an agency on a continuing basis. People who are no longer active in a criminal or terrorist conspiracy, but who will provide historical information when asked by law enforcement agencies, are not true informants. Nonetheless, such people are of value to law enforcement agencies, and should be contacted when necessary. Obviously, if one of these people is able to acquire current information, he or she can be used as an informant.

Along this same line, there are members of criminal conspiracies who agree to cooperate in order to engineer a "deal" with respect to charging and punishment, or for some other reason, including self-protection. These people can provide recent and even historical information, much of which may be of value in prosecuting other members of the conspiracy. In fact, these people will often testify against their former cohorts. Because such individuals have left the criminal or terrorist side and have joined the law enforcement camp, they are usually not able to provide current information on a continuing basis. Therefore, they cannot be used as informants in the true sense of the word.

Despite this, some agencies still refer to them as informants. Other agencies have special categories for these people, including "cooperating witness" or "cooperating subject." Clearly, if such a person's cooperation is not known to the criminals/terrorists, and the person is able to report on the current activities of the conspirators, he or she should be used as an informant.

People who provide historical information to a law enforcement agency, and people who cooperate with a law enforcement agency after leaving the criminal/terrorist conspiracy are valuable and should be cultivated. Working with such people often involves money, either to motivate the person or to give him or her protection. Some agencies have no way to provide funds to such people. As a result, investigators are forced to create informant files on them so that funding is available.

Short-Term/Limited Use Informants

The short-term/limited use informant is a person who has such restricted access to the target that he is only able to provide a minimal amount of information on a one-time (or possibly several times) basis. These types of informants are very common in police work. In some agencies, investigators create files on such people, and operate them as "official" informants of their agency. A code name or number would likely be assigned to the person to protect his or her identity. The files would contain some background information on the source, and list a telephone number, e-mail address, or some other means for contacting him or her. In many instances, short-term informants are never officially opened as informants by the officers who deal with them. Virtually all officers who have experience in fugitive investigations have used short-term sources. They are the friend, relative, or other contact of the subject who tells the officer where to locate the wanted person. Frequently such people know nothing of value about the violation that caused the person to become a fugitive. Of course, in the case of someone who has already been indicted or convicted of a crime, any information about the crime would be of little importance to the investigator whose job it is to locate and arrest the subject. Another common use for short-term informants is in the area of street-level narcotics crimes. It is fairly routine practice for arresting officers to offer a deal to a drug user or a low-level dealer who is selling narcotics to support his own habit. If the person will give up the name of his supplier or make a deal with that supplier so the officer can witness the person selling drugs or perhaps even make a buy himself, the investigator will make sure that the prosecutor and judge are aware of the cooperation. Usually in such cases the investigator does not intend to make any further use of the informant because the source's drug use calls into question his reliability and credibility and he probably does not have any further information of value to give to the officer. Investigators also use short-term informants in a variety of other cases including robberies, burglaries, fraud, and street gang violations.

Another form of short-term informant is the person who voluntarily provides a police agency with information concerning a crime, and who is willing to take another step to better enable the authorities to act upon that information. An example might involve a person who reports that he has, on several occasions, observed a particular individual shoplifting at a local store. A police investigator might ask the person to call him when he next observes that individual in that store, so that the officer can facilitate an arrest. As in cases involving fugitives and narcotics, the investigator is probably not going to open this type of person as an official informant and is not likely to ask that person to provide any further information after he has made the arrest.

Still another commonly used short-term informant is the person who has the ability, usually because of his employment or station in life, to develop single items of information on a number of people. These individuals are often opened by law enforcement agencies as official informants, and many are paid on a cash-on-delivery basis. In fact, some police agencies often depend upon such people to provide them with the seeds on which new criminal cases will be opened. A person falling into this category might be the operator of a pawn shop who reports suspicious people who attempt to sell or buy items. Or the person might be a firearms dealer who reports possible criminals who make suspicious inquiries about guns. Bartenders, bellhops, and taxi drivers also fall into this category, depending upon the nature of their clientele. This category of informant is extremely valuable; from a case standpoint, however, they are nonetheless short-term because they usually cannot provide much more than one or two items of information on any single investigation.

Short-term sources are frequently used by law enforcement officers, and they often prove to be quite important. However, because such people do not provide information on a continuing basis, it is highly questionable if they really fit the true definition of an informant. Furthermore, many officers never conduct any background investigations on sources of this kind. These people rarely testify in court, or if they do, they are treated like an ordinary witness and not as an established informant.

Short-term informants should be developed and used whenever they can provide information of value on a case. However, other than perhaps providing initial seed information, such people are, by and large, not of great importance in complex, lengthy investigations—which usually describes most terrorism cases. For that reason the bulk of this chapter on informants is devoted to longer-term sources—people who are willing and able to provide information of value on a continuing basis on a single case, whose backgrounds are checked and who are vetted to ensure reliability.

Informant Targets and Their Development

There are essentially three types of informant targets—inside target, periphery target, and outside target.

Inside Target

The inside informant target is a person who occupies a position within a criminal or terrorist conspiracy in which he knows about the operations of that group. He could be a lead person (but not the top leader), an active member, a trusted contact, or an advisor. He may not know everything about a group, but he does know a good deal of information and is in a position to continue to learn about the group's activities.

From a law enforcement standpoint, the inside target is the ideal informant. He either knows what the group is doing, or has the ability to learn about the group's activities. He possesses at least some historical knowledge about the group and can learn about the group's future activities. He knows where evidence exists that an investigator can use to build a case against the group. He can be used as a direct witness against group members in court.

Unfortunately, of the three informant target areas, the inside target is the most difficult to develop. The very fact that the person is on the "inside" reflects that he is dedicated to the cause, whether it is criminal or terrorist in nature. He is a trusted insider because he has done things that have caused group members to have confidence in him. Approaching such a person is difficult. Convincing him to turn against his own group is likely to be even more problematic. And trying to safely operate him as an informant could prove to be a nightmare.

In the case of terrorism investigations, an inside informant may not be as valuable as would a similar informant in an ordinary criminal conspiracy. Many terrorist groups have developed cellular structures that separate members from each other and isolate operations. Consequently, even a senior member may not know all of the members of the group and may not be aware of who in the group is working on specific projects. As a result, a top-level informant may not learn about an attack until after it has occurred, and may not be able to learn who in his own group perpetrated it.

How To Develop Inside Informants. "Know thy enemy" may sound cliché, but it certainly applies with respect to developing inside informants. An officer who expects that he can blindly knock at the door of a member of a criminal or terrorist group and immediately turn that person into an informant is naïve at best. Indeed, it may be counterproductive, especially with respect to terrorists. Such a contact could reveal that law enforcement has certain knowledge about the group in general, and about the member approached in particular. This could cause a clandestine terrorist group to scatter, negating all of the investigation that led up to the contact with the group member.

Success might be possible if direct contact is made by an officer who is truly knowledgeable about the group and the contacted person. The officer must be an actor of sorts, in that he needs to make an initial impression that will attract the attention of the potential informant. The officer must exhibit a "look" that will be accepted, and his initial words must be sufficient to encourage some degree of conversation. Obviously, a male officer who approaches a feminist subject with a greeting like, "Hey babe, how's it going?" is not going to achieve much success. Similarly, an officer who begins his conversation with a high school dropout group member by delivering a "college professor" lecture will probably fail to develop that person as a source.

Motivation (to be discussed in detail later) is the key to informant development. The person must be made to want to become a source. The officer must be able to hold a "carrot" in front of the person that will cause that person to want to have that carrot more than he wants to remain in his conspiracy. The motivation might be money, or it might be a promise not to arrest the person. It might be an appeal to patriotism, or it might be an over-ture of attention to their needs. Whatever is offered by the officer, it must be something that will appeal to the would-be informant.

Most law enforcement officers are outgoing and gregarious. If they were not that way when they began in police work, they have developed these qualities because of the nature of the job. A shy individual who has diffi-culty relating to people may experience difficulty in carrying out the duties of a police officer. Law enforcement officers soon learn on the job how to deal with all kinds of people. The outgoing nature of police work gives the law enforcement officer an advantage during most interviews. Many police officers become outstanding salespeople—what this means is that if a law enforcement officer can engage a group member in conversation, the officer will usually have the upper hand. If he can begin that conversation, he will have an opportunity to convince that person to cooperate.

Law enforcement officers are often able to engage criminal conspiracy subjects in conversations. With terrorists, however, this can be a serious prob-lem. Certain terrorist groups, such as some right-wing militias and some spe-cial interest organizations, are actively engaged in recruiting law enforcement officers. Consequently, their members may converse with investigators, but for the selfish reasons of their political cause. Many other groups stress that their members avoid any contact with police. They school their members in this and distribute literature to them explaining the reasons for avoiding law enforcement contact. Some even have attorneys on standby who will come to the rescue of any group member who is contacted by a law enforcement officer. In their literature, these groups outline the skills that officers have in interviewing and they urge their members not to say anything to law enforce-ment personnel. Obviously, members of groups that harbor this philosophy are going to be very difficult to interview. No matter how skillful an officer is, and no matter how many motivating factors he has gathered, that officer is going to have difficulty trying to "turn" a person who has slammed the door in the officer's face.

Some investigators have achieved success in developing inside informants by running a "smile campaign," by which they make their existence known to the subject, but do not make an immediate direct approach. If rebuked on his initial contact, the officer courteously exits. He may attempt another contact several weeks later using a different ruse. Again, courtesy is used. Perhaps the next time the subject sees the officer, it is at a protest demonstration, and the officer may smile and walk away. The officer's idea is to show that he is a decent human being who is reasonable and approachable. The "smile" approach can also be used with members of a conspiracy who have been arrested. The officer should be professional. An offer to loosen handcuffs or to provide a chair on which the person can sit can go a long way toward softening a person. An officer can take a few minutes to explain the charges against the person and outline the next steps in the booking process. The subject probably already knows these things, but the fact that someone is willing to explain them to him will be remembered. If, in the future, things occur within the criminal or terrorist conspiracy that upset or frighten the subject, he may reach out to the friendly officer instead of running away or dialing 911. Some very good informants have been developed through the "smile" approach.

Perhaps the most serious barrier to developing informants involves the creation of parameters that would-be informants must fall within in order to be considered for contact. Simply put, the officer decides beforehand exactly what "credentials" his informant must have. A few investigators actually create specific profiles of would-be informants, including their sex, race, creed, age, educational background, work experience, and other factors. The problem is that some profiles are so specific that an investigator has to conduct a kind of "fugitive investigation" in order to find a candidate who can meet the qualifications. Of course, many people who could provide good information are excluded from the list because they fail to meet all of the requirements. Ironically, some leading members of the criminal or terrorist conspiracy will not meet the parameters established by these officers.

With respect to inside target informants, anyone who is within the conspiracy or who has direct contact with the inside people should be considered for informant development. The only possible exception to this rule would be the group leader. Certainly, if a group leader consents to an interview, he should be interviewed. To actually open and operate the leader of a criminal or terrorist conspiracy as an informant against the members of the group under his control and command can create problems. In a court case, each conspiracy member would defend himself by claiming that he was merely obeying the orders of the group's leader who is a police informant. If the group's leader agrees to cooperate and confesses guilt, it is probably best at that point to procure warrants for the other members of the conspiracy and arrest them. Of course, if for some reason the leader of a group offers to provide information of value concerning another group or a person not under his command, it may be possible to operate him as an informant against that other entity.

Periphery Target

The periphery informant target is a person who holds a lesser position within the criminal/terrorist conspiracy, or may be on the fringes of the group. He or she may be someone who associates with some group members, or who has some reason to visit the group's gathering place. He or she may occupy a position outside the group that nonetheless enables him or her to be able to develop information. The periphery target may or may not be in a position to join or move up in status within the conspiracy.

Periphery informants may have an advantage in terrorist conspiracies, especially those that involve cellular structures. It is possible that they can develop relationships with certain group members without others in the group even being aware of these inroads. Of course, if a group is rigidly divided into units, such a source will probably never be able to move himself into a position where he will know everything about the group. However, inside target informants in such an organization will also have difficulty developing such information.

How To Develop Periphery Informants. Periphery informants are usually not as desirable as inside target informants. They are much easier to develop, however. If a case is long-running, investigators should attempt to develop periphery informants even though they have inside sources. No logical candidate should be overlooked. (Mentally ill people, proven liars, and children below whatever minimum age the agency has established should not be recruited to be informants. Drug-addicted people probably should not be used as informants, especially against terrorist groups.) Anyone who is in a position to develop information should be considered even though he or she is not actually a member of the conspiracy. Investigators should avoid establishing "qualifications" for their would-be periphery informants. The determining factor should be whether the person can provide information of value.

Officers should remember that it is not the informant's job to develop the investigation; developing the investigation is the officer's job. It is the officer's task to take the fruits of a number of investigative techniques and blend them together to resolve the case. With this in mind, an officer should not expect that a single informant is going to open his mouth and give the officer the entire case on a silver platter. On occasion an inside person can be developed who will provide a considerable amount of information; however, it is unlikely that a periphery person is going to do this. Instead, the periphery informant will provide some information on part of the case. Sometimes this information will be evidentiary in nature, while in other cases the information will provide a lead on which an investigator can develop information.

Some people who are on the fringes of a criminal or terrorist conspiracy can, with cultivation and direction, become inside informants. Many, however, cannot penetrate the conspiracy. A number of these people could not do so even if they wanted to. Indeed, some periphery informants are not even aware of the true nature of the target conspiracy.

Periphery informants can come from many walks of life. They can be old or young and of either sex; they can be of any race or creed; they can be able-bodied or physically impaired. They could be very similar to the members of a target conspiracy or they could be completely dissimilar. The following are examples of people who could be periphery informants:

Spouses, relatives, and girl- or boyfriends of group members

People who work with group members

Business associates of the group or of its members

Employees of businesses that cater to group members, including restaurants and stores

Neighbors of the group members or of locations frequented by group members

Associates of group members

Legal and illegal suppliers to the criminal conspiracy

Employees of the group or its members

Members of other criminal or terrorist conspiracies who have contact with the group

In the case of terrorist conspiracies, people who participate in overt support activities, including marches, protests, fundraising, legal support, and publications

Anyone within earshot or sight of the conspirators, regardless of their reason for being there, as manifested in the following example:

Thefts are taking place from the loading dock of a trucking company. None of the employees of the dock who would be the most likely suspects will not cooperate, thereby negating the immediate possibility of developing an inside informant. Possible periphery informants might include:

- Truck drivers making deliveries to the dock

- Maintenance and cleaning employees occasionally visiting the dock

- Office clerical employees who never visit the dock, but who associate with dock employees

- The security guard at the trucking company's gate

- Employees of the local restaurant and tavern where dock employees socialize before, during, and after work

- Residents and employees of nearby buildings that face the dock

- Friends, relatives, and associates of dock employees

In the above situation, anyone visiting the dock, even on an occasional basis, such as truck drivers and cleaning employees, could see something that could give an investigator a clue as to the identity of the thieves. The security guard might be able to provide information concerning vehicles driven by employees, which might indicate to an investigator how the stolen merchandise was taken from the facility. The clerical employees might be able to report on dock employees who are big spenders, or they might be able to relay to an investigator innocuous-sounding comments they heard dock employees making. Restaurant and tavern employees might be able to provide similar information based on what they overheard and observed. The residents of nearby buildings might have observed merchandise being placed into vehicles without even being aware that it was stolen. Friends and relatives of dock employees might have observed the stolen merchandise at a subject's residence, seen signs of overspending, or heard comments that could assist investigators.

The Outside Target

The outside informant target has little or no relationship with the criminal or terrorist conspiracy. He is, however, a person who cooperates with a law enforcement agency and is willing to allow that agency to place him in a position from which he can develop valuable information. In some cases, this will involve making efforts to actually join the conspiracy. In other cases, it will involve him being situated in a marginal position from which he can develop information about the conspiracy. In time, the outside informant may be able to work himself into an inside position. Obviously, if the outside informant cannot reach a position from which he can report at least some information of value on the target within a reasonable period, the agency will have to cease using him as an informant. There are two types of outside informants.

Lukewarm. This person has some obvious natural relationship with the conspiracy against which he is directed. If the conspiracy is involved in car thefts, this person might have a car theft conviction. If the group is a right-wing hate organization, this person might have had a previous association with a group like the Ku Klux Klan or the Nazi Party. If the conspiracy involves some form of financial fraud, this person might have an accounting background.

Cold Start. This person does not know the conspirators and has no clear connection to either them or their activities. All he has going for him is his willingness to attempt to develop a relationship with the conspirators in order to provide information to a law enforcement agency.

Many law enforcement officers shy away from cold-start informants because they think that it will require too much time for such a person to work his way into the conspiracy. If the investigation is one that can be solved in a matter of weeks or even a few months, these officers are probably correct. If, however, the case appears to be long-running, as are many terrorism investigations, it may well be worth the effort to develop a cold-start informant.

What law enforcement agencies must remember is that, with respect to cold-start informants, they are starting at essentially the same point as undercover officers. Neither have credentials that would qualify them to be inside members of a group. An agency that uses, or intends to use, an undercover operation against a conspiracy should also consider using a cold-start informant. In fact, it might be an excellent way to test the waters before initiating an expensive and manpower-intensive undercover project. If a cold-start informant can gain some degree of success with respect to developing information, it would certainly suggest that an undercover officer should also be able to succeed. Indeed, the cold-start informant could actually be used to help facilitate the undercover officer's acceptance by the conspirators.

Where to Find an Outside Informant

Potential outside informants are everywhere. Some walk into police agencies asking to become informants. Many either are not familiar with the term *informant*, or do not want to be categorized as an informant. Nonetheless, they visit police agencies anyway. Such people often have innocuous information to provide or have routine questions to ask. What they really want to do is help law enforcement. Some of these people are encountered during investigations. When contacted either as subjects, victims, actual or possible witnesses, or for any other reason, they will ask questions and offer nebulous information about anything that they think will be of interest to the investigator.

Law enforcement officers encounter many people during their daily lives who express interest in assisting them in their job. Of course, many of these people do not directly express a desire to become informants. Such people might include the gas station attendant who expresses interest in the officer's work while servicing his patrol car. An officer's neighbor or fellow church, club, or civic group member may express such an interest. It might be someone who visits locations that law enforcement officers frequent so that he can associate with them. Essentially, these people are "police groupies" or "would-be" police who want to be involved with law enforcement officers and police work.

Another place where potential cold-start informants can be found is in other investigations. There may be a periphery person in one case who would like to make a "deal" to avoid prosecution, but who has little of value to offer. An officer might be able to use such a person as a cold-start informant in another criminal conspiracy investigation.

Still another excellent source of cold-start informants is in the area of closed informants. Many of these people benefited in some manner from their informant experience and would like to do it again.

Law enforcement officers face two major problems with respect to initiating outside informant operations—ethical problems and financial problems.

Ethics. Before using someone as an outside informant, the investigator must ask himself if he is being fair to that person. Just because someone offers to help does not mean that his offer should be accepted. For some, the danger that a particular investigation presents will outweigh the possible gain. Another problem could involve the person's status in the community and with his family. It might be one thing to use a young single man to perform a mission, but to use a married father of several children might be a very different thing. It could destroy his marriage. A more likely problem will involve the person's reputation. If the willing person has a respectable position in the community, it may not be proper for the law enforcement officer to tarnish it. The town barber might be very willing to help the local police because he is really a "police groupie," but what will happen to his business if he joins a terrorist hate group on behalf of the local police department?

Law enforcement officers also encounter an ethical problem with respect to employing some ex-offenders as informants. It is usually not proper to take a person who is now living a "clean" life, and place him into a criminal conspiracy in which he will associate with people who could tempt him to return to his former life. Some of these people are on parole or probation and are, therefore, forbidden to have contact with known felons. It is not proper to ask such a person to violate his parole or probation.

Financial. Cold-start informants are not likely to produce any information of value on the target case during the initial phase of their operation. In fact, it may be many weeks or even months before they are able to get close enough to the conspirators to produce any worthwhile intelligence. For some agencies, this is simply unacceptable. Everything is "cash on delivery." No money can be given to the source for services or expenses unless the source provides information commensurate with what is paid. If an agency adheres rigidly to such rules, it will be very difficult for that department to employ cold-start informants, unless the particular informant is willing and able to shoulder the financial burdens of the operation.

How to Operate an Outside Informant

An investigator should devote some time to preparation before directing an outside informant against any conspiracy. Regardless of how good the person is, he simply does not have the knowledge about the investigation that the law enforcement officer has. It is unreasonable to tell the outside informant to "see what you can find out about this group." A plan and specific direction should be involved.

The investigator should learn everything that he can about the outside informant. It is helpful to list the various attributes on paper. Essentially, the informant's life should be outlined—including his previous residences, employment, relatives, education, life experiences, associates, interests, hobbies, talents, and other pertinent data. The investigator then compares these attributes with the targeted conspiracy and its members. The idea is to develop a "marriage" between the source and the target. If multiple investigators are assigned to the case, all should be encouraged to review the potential source's background in an effort to identify ways in which the source can penetrate the conspiracy. Often no direct ties can be found. Surprisingly, however, there are usually some common areas upon which a link can be constructed. The stronger the connection, the easier the "marriage" will be. Once the area of commonality has been established, the officer must decide how to exploit this area to the benefit of the informant.

In one case it was known that a particular terrorist group had an interest in a specific foreign country. It was learned that the outside informant had previously resided in that country. Through other investigation, the case officer learned that the group was going to conduct a protest demonstration on a particular date and time. It was arranged for the informant to have "business" at the building being picketed. The informant was carefully counseled as to how he was to act so that a protester would speak to him. He was also schooled in how to let the protestor know that he had lived in the foreign country. Everything worked as planned, and within months the informant was actually living in a residence operated by the terrorist group.

In another case, it was known that a terrorist group was seeking a communications system, but did not want to deal with a commercial firm. Through a review of the potential outside informant's background, it was learned that he possessed the technical skills needed by the group. The case officer provided props that enabled the informant to visit various neighborhood business entities, including one run by the target group, selling electronic components. The informant was taught how to start a conversation. When the group realized that the source could handle their communications system, they hired him. Soon he was a group member.

In still another situation, an outside source was found to have once belonged to the same youth club as several current members of a terrorist group. Although years had passed and the informant had never been close friends of the terrorists, he could claim to recognize them. The case officer placed the informant in a position in which he could encounter one of the group members, at which time he said, "aren't you Joe Smith of the Fairchild Boys' Club? Do you remember me? I'm Tom Jones, I used to be the batboy." One thing led to another, and the source eventually gained membership in the group.

A tactic that can be used to facilitate the acceptance of a cold-start informant by a group is the so-called "confession method." Something almost magical occurs when one person feels such an ease and trust with another person that he admits to a weakness or confesses to an indiscretion. This can be used by an informant, but it must be carefully choreographed by the handling officer. The idea is to find something embarrassing in an informant's past that can be confessed to an influential person in the targeted group. The informant begins by telling the person that he feels very guilty, because the group has been so good to him, but he has not been totally honest with them. He then "forces" the person to drag the "secret" out of him. Tears, blushing, shaking, and other appropriate gestures can accompany the confession. Obviously, what is confessed must be something that the group can easily accept. In one case, a source confessed that she had had an abortion when she was a teenager. It was something that the group could care less about, yet it was something that could cause a person to feel guilty. Regardless, the confession resulted in a strong bond being formed between the informant and the group member. Other confessions could include everything from admitting to cheating on college exams, to having had an extramarital affair, to having once been arrested for shoplifting.

Motivation

Motivation refers to factors that cause human beings to respond in certain ways. Being an informant for a law enforcement agency is not something that occurs naturally. It is not an involuntary action like breathing or digesting food. There are reasons people become informants. Conversely, there are reasons that explain why some people will not give information to law enforcement agencies. The reasons vary from person to person. What will cause one person to assist a law enforcement agency may not cause others to do so. The best informant developers are officers who successfully identify the factors that motivate the people they are targeting, and then capitalize on them. Once they have encouraged a person to cooperate, these investigators stimulate the person by continuing to stress the factors that motivate him or her. For example, if a person is providing information because he is truly patriotic and believes that he is helping his government, the handling officer should logically "wave the flag" with the informant whenever he can. Such a handling officer would never criticize the government within earshot of this kind of informant, because it could "demotivate" him.

Most laypeople would respond with the answer "money" when asked what motivates informants. While many law enforcement officers would concur with this, a number of them would suggest that "working off a beef" was the most common motivating factor. Of course, both of these responses would be correct with respect to a large number of informants. Many people provide information in exchange for money, and many others do so to avoid arrest or to get a deal in court. However, these are not the only factors that cause people to cooperate. In fact, some people would actually be turned off if offered either of these inducements by an investigator. Some things that motivate people to become informants are relatively simple and can be easily met, while others are quite complex and may not be viable for an agency to undertake. Some motivating factors can even be bizarre.

There are some investigators who simply cannot employ certain motivating factors because they find them to be personally offensive, or they lack the skills to use them. It helps for an investigator to possess some acting ability in order to use at least some motivating factors. This is particularly true if the investigator is handling multiple sources, all of whom are motivated by different things. How an investigator talks, acts, and even dresses can be used to motivate an informant.

What follows is a list of 20 motivating factors. These are not the only motivators of informants, but they are among the most common.

Financial

Often, money talks. It is said that many criminals will sell or sell out their own mothers for a few dollars. Money is an excellent motivator inasmuch as it causes the informant to return to the law enforcement agency on a regular basis. It also forces the informant to provide information because he will not be paid unless he does so. Of course, there are problems with sources who are primarily motivated by money. For example, some will expect more and more money as they continue with the agency. Eventually, they will reach the limit of what the agency can afford to pay. Some informants become so desperate for money that they will create or exaggerate information in order to get paid. Additionally, some informants will develop information through questionable means, including stealing it. Some informants will even sell the same information to several agencies. Money can also present problems in court. A defense attorney will attempt to make the informant out to be like Judas, "selling out Christ for 30 pieces of silver." Juries can become suspicious about the honesty and character of people who have been given large sums of money in exchange for providing information about their "friends."

Money can often be tied to other motivations. Everyone needs a certain amount of money to live. It may be possible for an investigator to ensnare a person who is motivated by factors other than money into the money trap. This can be done by slipping the informant a few dollars for expenses or for his time. Somewhere along the way the informant becomes accustomed to receiving the regular flow of money and it becomes a secondary motivating factor.

Money will influence some people to report on terrorist groups; however, it does not seem to have the same kind of allure that it has for ordinary criminals. Most people who are members of a terrorist group and who choose to function as informants do so for reasons other than financial reasons, although reimbursement may become a secondary motivating factor. It is possible that a periphery or cold-start informant may be convinced to give coverage of terrorists by the promise of financial gain.

Working Off a Beef

This is a common motivator used by local police agencies. A person avoids prosecution for a crime by agreeing to become an informant. A variation of this involves the police agency or prosecutor offering to put in a good word with the judge if the subject performs well as an informant. Neither of these promises is likely to motivate many true terrorists, because they do not view incarceration as an end of their activities in the same manner as do other criminals. The terrorist wants to do something for his cause regardless of his situation. In prison he can spread his message to his fellow inmates. Of course, there are some exceptions to this rule. Freddie Mendez, who was a member of the terrorist FALN Puerto Rican organization, agreed to cooperate against his fellow group members when he realized that he was destined to spend the rest of his life in prison. He hoped that by providing information he could receive some relief from his prison term. Mendez and people like him are not actually informants, because their most valuable information is historical in nature. In short, they are better witnesses than they are informants.

With respect to terrorism investigations, law enforcement officers may find that periphery and cold-start informants will be more motivated by a promise to avoid punishment for an illegal act that they committed than are actual inside informant targets.

A man who was married to the relative of a terrorist group member was convinced to cooperate after he was arrested for a narcotics violation that would probably have resulted in a 10-year prison term. The man subsequently worked himself into the group and functioned as a source for more than five years before becoming convinced that he had served the equivalent of a prison term. Fortunately, the agency had started paying the informant for information during the early part of his cooperation. By the time he had "worked off his beef," his standard of living had come to depend upon the money; consequently, he remained an informant for another five years.

Law enforcement officers should be guided by ethics when using the "working off a beef" motivation. People should not be promised rewards that the officer cannot give them. If the person does what he has been instructed to do, the promised reward should be given. A person who does not get what he has been promised can spread the word within the criminal/terrorist community, thereby causing other would-be informants to decline future offers made by the agency. The person can also turn against the agency in court.

Blackmail

Although the word "blackmail" sounds ugly, the fact is that it can influence people to cooperate with a law enforcement agency. Many people have secrets about themselves that they do not want other people to know. Some of these secrets involve illegal activities, while others are more of an embarrassing nature. A law enforcement officer who uncovers such a secret could induce a person to cooperate in order to protect the secret.

Obviously, this is a very difficult motivator for many law enforcement officers to use. If not used wisely, it can make the officer appear to be a criminal himself. It could cause a person to take drastic action, including attacking the officer or committing suicide. An investigator may want to have his agency's legal counsel review the scenario before using this tactic.

A newspaper almost destroyed the status of an important Nazi activist in America when it reported that his grandmother was Jewish. Had a law enforcement officer developed this information, he might have been able to use the threat of its revelation to convince the Nazi activist to cooperate.

Not all secrets can be used effectively against a subject. In one international terrorism case, a law enforcement agency's surveillance team observed the subject having intimate contact with a female in a parked car. Had this subject been a bank officer associated with some kind of fraud conspiracy, it might have been possible for a law enforcement officer to let the man know that he was aware of his secret. To save his marriage, the man might have cooperated. In this terrorism case, however, it was known that the man felt no guilt about having a mistress and that his wife probably assumed that he had one. Therefore, the secret could not be used to intimidate the subject. In fact, if the agency had approached the subject about the situation, it would probably have exposed the surveillance.

Ironically, some of the secrets that would cause a terrorist real concern would probably not cause much upset to the average criminal or even the ordinary citizen. An animal rights extremist may not want his fellow activists to know that he enjoys an occasional hamburger. Similarly, Muslim and Jewish extremists would likely have great concern if their associates were informed that they ate pork products. An anti-abortion activist may fear that that her friends might reject her if they discovered that she had undergone an abortion earlier in her life.

Would-Be Cop

The idea of using a "would-be cop" as an informant is a cause of concern for many law enforcement officers. Nonetheless, some of these people can become excellent sources. Certainly people with this motivation should not be ignored. A would-be cop really wants to be a law enforcement officer; however, for some reason he or she cannot become one. The reason should be a key factor in determining the person's potential as an informant. If the person suffers from a mental illness or is extremely cruel and violent, he or she should be avoided. However, many would-be cops do not fall into these categories. Some have physical problems, some have educational deficiencies, some lack residency, some are too old, and some have background situations that include arrests, debts, and poor employment histories that preclude them from being hired as law enforcement officers.

One effective terrorist informant was denied police employment because of poor vision. Another high-level informant could not become a police officer because of a bad conduct discharge from the army. Still another informant had once been employed as a police officer, but had been dismissed due to poor job performance.

When the first person was told that he had failed to eye examination, he asked if there was something else he could do in police work. The second voluntarily appeared at the police department asking if he could do something in law enforcement despite his bad conduct discharge. The third person expressed a continuing love of police work when interviewed during a routine investigation.

Police Groupie

A "police groupie" is different from a "would-be" cop. In the latter situation, the person wants to function as a police officer. They want to conduct investigations. They dream of carrying a badge and weapon. By contrast, the police groupie simply enjoys being in the presence of law enforcement officers. Like the "would-be cop," he may dream of being a police officer, but is fully aware that his dream is not going to come true. In that sense, he is like the groupie who hangs around a rock star. While he may imagine himself as a rock star, he knows that his lack of talent makes that impossible. Nonetheless, he is happy to be around the star.

Many law enforcement officers have difficulty imagining that their profession attracts groupies. Police groupies generally do not act like the people who follow rock stars, professional athletes, and movie stars. They can be the neighbors and friends who insist upon introducing the officer by both his name and profession. "This is my friend Joe Brown of the state police." They can be the people who take active roles in the "associate" wing of the local chapter of the fraternal order of police. Police groupies often hang out at establishments frequented by police, including taverns and restaurants. They may become involved in police-sponsored activities like police athletic league baseball or a bowling league. Many join organizations like the St. Jude League or a police shield group that raises funds for the families of deceased officers. They are the people who let everyone know that they have a police friend who confides in them. Sometimes they hang around the police station offering to help.

A schoolteacher in a large city often told his fellow teachers about "inside" information involving news articles dealing with crimes. He made it clear that he was getting his information from his law enforcement friend. A typical account might be, "My buddy, Joe, the FBI agent, told me that he was involved in this big arrest that's on the front page of the Daily Bugle today. Yeah, he said that it was dangerous, but nobody got hurt. I'll get more details from him tonight."

Police groupies have the potential to be excellent informants. However, an officer must use ethics and common sense before making such a person a source. In the above example, the teacher held a respected position in the community. His FBI agent friend was in fact a neighbor. The teacher was so taken by his friendship with the agent that the agent could easily have induced the teacher to join a terrorist group or even a criminal syndicate if he had asked him to do so. Although police groupies are rarely criminals or terrorists, some can be engaged to work as informants without creating serious ethical concerns. A groupie is willing to cooperate and will usually be trustworthy and reliable as long as the law enforcement officers maintain close contact with him or her, thereby reinforcing the "groupie" motivation.

The Would-Be Spy

The would-be spy is similar to the would-be cop except that the scope of his fantasy is focused somewhat differently. He or she may be better suited for foreign counter-intelligence and terrorism work than he or she is for criminal investigations. Nonetheless, it might be possible to use such a person to gather criminal intelligence, if elements of spy tactics are used in dealing with him or her. Would-be spies probably have read all of the best spy stories and have seen the movies and television programs involving counter-intelligence. Many want to be spies. Others have dreams of being a spy, but in reality do not want to be a "real" spy operating in a foreign country against a hostile target.

The would-be spy can be an excellent informant, providing that he or she is not mentally ill. Most can be easily controlled if they can be convinced that the police officer handler is the leader, and that all orders must be obeyed. Because many of these people are espionage buffs, they have studied spycraft and technique, and they know how to develop good information. Of course, the handling officer must carefully outline the law to such informants, so that they do not engage in illegal activities or sabotage against the "enemy."

A man walked into a law enforcement agency asking to do anything that he could to help his government. In talking with him, it was learned that this foreign-born man had once functioned as a "spy" for his native country. In the 30 years that had passed in between, the man had drifted aimlessly in the United States and had accomplished nothing of significance. He had come to realize that his time as a spy had been the happiest period of his life. He wanted to return to it. The man was subsequently directed against a terrorist group in which he gained membership. He became an outstanding informant in no small part because he knew how to gather information without appearing suspicious.

In order to operate this man as an informant and keep him motivated, the handling officer had to employ "spy" tactics. He used secret codes, hand signals, and dead drops to receive information and give instructions. The more "security" the handler used, the better the informant liked it. The informant was reliving his glorious "spy days." The handing officer knew that his instructions to the informant would be followed. After all, the informant was a "spy," and the handler was his "chief." The spy knew that he must obey his chief's orders.

Patriotism

Many people want to do something to help their country. People sometimes walk into police agencies and volunteer their services. These people are also encountered during routine police investigations. They should not be overlooked. They are not motivated by money or reward. Some are military veterans who, on reflection, believe that the most useful part of their life was when they were in the service. Others are immigrants who want to repay their new country for what it has done for them.

In some cases, patriotically motivated people will turn to a police agency to report criminal or terrorist activity occurring around them. If this is the case, these people can be used as informants reporting on that situation. In other cases, these people do not have information about criminal activities.

The investigator will have to decide if he can ethically and properly direct the person into illegal or terrorist activity upon which he can report.

In some situations, patriotism can be used to turn someone who is actually engaged in criminal or terrorist activity into an informant. This involves convincing the person that his criminal enterprise or terrorist group is involved in activities that endanger the country. This will be difficult to do with respect to people belonging to domestic terrorist groups, because their members want to drastically change the government. With respect to special interest groups, however, the situation can be quite different. Most of these groups have a single agenda that does not require any great change in the government. It might be possible to show a member of such an organization that the group's objective presents a threat to the nation's security. A member of an organized crime syndicate may not like law enforcement, but may hate people who are plotting to overthrow the government, and therefore might provide information against such people.

The Do-Gooder

These are people who have the need to perform good deeds. It is part of their nature. They often join organizations in the belief that they can accomplish worthwhile objectives. Law enforcement officers can capitalize on the do-gooder's desire to help by convincing them that their agency is committed to performing worthwhile deeds.

Do-gooders who join terrorist groups, or who become involved in scams in the belief that they are performing good deeds, can be ideal informant targets when they become disillusioned with these entities. Some will voluntarily visit a police agency to report the crimes they have discovered. Others will agree to cooperate when it can be shown that the best way that they can make amends for having helped the "bad guys" is for them to help the "good guys" (the police).

Soldier of Fortune

The soldier of fortune is a mercenary who sells his services. Informants with this mentality are usually "would-be" mercenaries. They may dream of traveling the world to fight in guerilla wars, but know they will never even vacation out of the country. However, they may be motivated by the excitement of being an informant on a "mission." A law enforcement officer can capitalize on this. By offering money and excitement, the officer can bring the person on board for a "mission." On the surface, it appears that the soldier of fortune is just another source motivated by financial inducements, but this is not really the case. In order to keep this person going, the handling officer will have to stress the "mission" and the source's important role within it. He will also have to emphasize the secrecy surrounding the project. Money is involved because the informant knows that it is what true soldiers of fortune receive in exchange for services rendered. Sometimes the informant can be motivated by the promise of a big payoff to be received at the end of a successful operation, although he may not be paid at all during the course of the operation.

The Need for Excitement

Many people lead relatively mundane lives. Their jobs offer them no challenge and they have no hobbies that interest them. Working with a police agency can alleviate their boredom. Even though they will not be carrying a gun or arresting people, the idea of being a part of the team is important. To some, their informant work is the most important aspect of their lives.

People who are motivated by excitement should receive regular stimulation to keep their interest. This may not be easy, especially if the case under investigation is itself mundane and routine. With respect to terrorism, interest can usually be maintained because something is always going on somewhere in the world. A wise handling officer can often maintain the source's interest by discussing terrorist events worldwide and encouraging the source to read and monitor the Internet and news media for terrorism information.

The Need to Feel Important

This motivation is similar to the need for excitement. Many people lead ordinary lives in which they believe that they are little more than a number. They are in charge of nothing. They do not direct anything. They believe that no one respects them. Yet these are the very needs that dominate their lives. They want prestige and respect. A good investigator can fulfill the needs of such people. By stressing the importance of investigative work, he can make the position of informant appear desirable. By making it clear that the person is the best operative, he can fulfill the person's need for importance. By asking the person for his opinion and advice, the officer can continue to build on the informant's need to feel important. The officer can also do things like bringing in "bosses" within the department to meet the informant to further enhance the informant's sense of worth. (These people do not even have to be superior officers. They can be officers who are older and therefore appear to have authority. It could also be a recognizable person in the department like the agency's press officer or someone who gives speeches for the department.)

Some people become involved in groups and conspiracies in order to gain prestige. A man might be a maintenance worker during the week, but on the weekend, he puts a Klansman's robe and parades in front of public buildings. An investigator who senses that a particular member of a group is involved in order to gain recognition might be able to capitalize on that need in order to turn the person into an informant. The approach might be something like, "I come to you because you appear to be the leader and the most important person in the group, and my boss has instructed me to learn something about this organization. Are you able to help me, or should I contact someone else?"

The Need for Attention

Almost everyone needs some amount of attention from his or her fellow human beings. Informants are no exception. There are many informants who function entirely or in part because of the attention given them by their handling officers. Some people become involved in criminal conspiracies and terrorist groups because they receive attention from the members of these groups. If a law enforcement officer determines that a particular person has joined a conspiracy in order to receive attention, he may be able to turn that person into an informant by paying more attention to him or her.

Law enforcement officers encounter people who need attention on a regular basis. Some come into police agencies asking innocuous questions or making insignificant reports. Others are contacted in relation to any number of law enforcement situations, but prolong the interview unnecessarily. Often they will seek future contacts in order to add irrelevant information to their initial statement.

Many people go through life seeking meaning for their existence. Many join cults or other groups to receive attention. Law enforcement officers can cultivate these people to become effective informants provided that they offer them attention and direction.

Liking the Handling Contact Officer

Almost everyone wants to have one or more close friends. Obviously, the best kind of friend is one whom the person really likes. Sadly, there are many people who do not have enough friends. Con artists are aware of this and have developed expertise at becoming "friends" with their victims. Law enforcement officers encounter many such people during the course of their job. Some of these people will take a liking to the officer and will want to develop a friendship with him or her. If the officer encourages the association, it is possible that the officer could develop that person into an informant. Clearly, the officer will not want to open every friendly person as an informant, but there are some who will fit the mold and be useful. When using the "liking an officer" motivation, the officer will sometimes have to employ a degree of acting, because he may not have the same amount of affection for the person as the person has for him. Although many officers do not identify "liking an officer" as an informant motivator, the fact is that a number of them try to use it with regularity. In interviewing some criminals and members of a conspiracy they try to present themselves in a likeable manner and try to befriend the person. Some subjects accept the friendship and return it by cooperating with and assisting the officer.

One law enforcement officer was nicknamed "the monsignor" by his fellow investigators because he had such a talent for making people like him. His skill made him one of his agency's foremost informant developers. He had such a facility for listening to people that many people confessed their problems and secrets to him.

The weakness of the "liking the contact officer" motivation is that it usually is not transferable; consequently, if the handling officer leaves the assignment, the agency will probably lose the informant. This can sometimes be averted if the agency rotates through a series of assistant handling officers to work with the informant until one or more are able to develop a compatible relationship with the informant.

The Need for Association with Status, Professionalism, and Education

This motivation is often overlooked, but it certainly exists with respect to some criminal informants. Because of their illegal activities, arrests, and prison incarcerations, many criminals have essentially excluded themselves from a position in "respectable" society. They are relegated to living in flophouses, eating in greasy spoons, associating with low-lifes, drinking beer with fellow ex-cons, using foul and vulgar language, and engaging in bull sessions about easy scores and past successes. Yet some of these people are intelligent and are not completely comfortable in such surroundings. To these people, a law enforcement officer, particularly one who wears a suit rather than a uniform, and especially one who is college-educated, can appeal to them in a way that can cause them to become an informant. This type of person wants to be able to escape from the life that he has created for himself, at least temporarily.

A man was arrested for the first time shortly after his high school graduation. What followed was a life of repeated arrests and incarcerations, mostly for burglaries and robberies. The lure of easy money and the desire to avoid the tensions of life were too much for this man. He simply did not want to get a job and assume any responsibility. Nonetheless, he hated his life. He was brilliant. He was very well read, and could discuss a variety of topics with expertise. Unfortunately, no one in his environment cared about his knowledge, and few could hold an intelligent conversation with him. Along the way, he encountered a law enforcement officer who had a master's degree. This officer was willing to engage in discussions with the man about complex subjects. He was willing to meet with the man in decent restaurants and talk about culture. In exchange, the man was willing to function as a top-level informant for the investigator, and penetrated a terrorist organization on behalf of the officer's agency.

Advisor

Sadly, there are many people walking the streets who cannot or will not handle the administrative burdens of their lives. They are behind on their rent, have overdue utility bills, are on the verge of losing their possessions, and have employment problems. The license plates on their cars have expired, and they cannot find their overdue library books. They transform even the simplest problem into a major catastrophe. Although they are basically decent, honest people, they cannot get their lives together. They need someone to keep them organized, and to give them counsel and advice about every aspect of their lives. Many of these people are considered ripe candidates for a cult.

Most law enforcement officers are fairly well-organized people. A "marriage" can be made between the organized officer and the disorganized person. Many good informant relationships involve this very situation. The informant constantly calls the officer about one crisis or another, and the officer either counsels the person or handles the problem. In exchange, the person functions as an informant.

This type of relationship must benefit the law enforcement agency. The handling officer is going to be burdened by the informant, so the information provided must be worth the officer's effort.

Revenge

Revenge can be a powerful motivator. If it is used to motivate an informant, it must be carefully monitored by the handling officer. People who are driven by the desire to get even can be totally dedicated to that objective. If an officer can guide the revenge motivation in a law enforcement direction, he can have an outstanding informant. For example: a man is out to get even with his organized crime boss, because the boss was behind a relative's murder. The investigator convinces the man that the best way to really hurt the boss is to put him in prison for the rest of his life. Now the two can work together to accomplish this objective, which satisfies the needs of both. Another example might involve a terrorist group member who becomes upset because the group's direction has shifted from the way he feels that it should go. The investigator convinces the person to get his revenge by helping him to develop a criminal conspiracy case against the group leaders.

The revenge motivation can even be created by a law enforcement agency. A group member may not even be aware that something alien to his interest has taken place until a law enforcement officer brings it to his attention. This could cause the person to seek revenge.

Revenge is a difficult motivator to use, however, especially in connection with members of a violent criminal conspiracy. The person could become so upset that he may turn to violence to achieve his objective. A police informant killing someone would present a serious problem for a law enforcement agency. Also, unless money or another factor is brought into the operation as a secondary motivating factor, it is likely that the informant will be lost when the specific target of his anger has been eliminated through death, relocation, arrest, or some other factor.

Fear

Fear can also motivate people to become informants. Some people become involved in a criminal conspiracy or terrorist group to such an extent that they fear for their lives or the lives of others. Law enforcement can represent a sense of security. As a result, the person becomes an informant in order to gain the protection of a law enforcement agency. For example, a member of a terrorist group may become frightened for all humankind when he discovers that his group plans to perpetrate an attack with a biological agent.

> One professional criminal boasted to a member of a terrorist group that he had access to explosives. When the terrorist subsequently asked him to obtain explosives for his group, the man found himself in a dilemma. He no longer had the access that he once had, and could not provide the explosives. He feared, however, that the terrorist would kill him if he refused to cooperate. Believing that his life was in danger, he turned to a law enforcement agency, which used him as an informant against the terrorist group.

Often people who cooperate out of fear are not really informants. Instead they become cooperating witnesses or cooperating subjects. They provide historical knowledge of the conspiracy but are no longer in a position to develop current information because the group is aware that they have turned to law enforcement. For example, an organized crime figure turns to law enforcement when he discovers that a "contract" has been put out on his life.

The weakness of using a fear-motivated source is that their desire to provide information ends once the fear dissipates. Unless the handling officer is able to introduce a secondary motivating factor, such as money or personal friendship, the informant will likely be gone when the source of the fear has been eliminated.

"Other People Are Doing It"

Some people become informants because they know that other people are supplying information to a law enforcement agency. Clearly, it is unwise for anyone outside of the law enforcement agency to know that a person is functioning as an informant. Unfortunately, some informants cannot keep the situation confidential. There are also instances in which the source's informant status is placing such a strain on him that it is necessary to reveal his or her status as an informant in order to reduce the pressure.

In one instance, an informant's constant meetings with radical political activists caused a strain on his relationship with his live-in girlfriend. Furthermore, the girlfriend came to suspect that the informant was engaged in drugs or other illegal activities because he always had unexplained money that supported them. Eventually, the informant told his girlfriend that he was a police informant. When she refused to believe him, he introduced her to his handling officer. Shortly thereafter, the girlfriend asked to become an informant, and joined a sister terrorist group on behalf of the handling officer.

In another situation, a source who had a particular fondness for his handling officer was forced to move to a distant state to be near a relative. Before departing, he introduced the handling officer to a "friend" who would be taking his place as an informant handling the area that he had covered. The "friend" effectively took over reporting on the target in the same manner as had the original informant.

Relatives of informants can often piggyback on the credentials of their family members in order to be accepted by criminal and terrorist conspirators. Consequently, using such people as informants should not be overlooked. Often the informant can encourage a relative to cooperate.

Problem Solver

Some people have a need to solve impossible problems. They may be the people who are constantly seeking the most difficult crossword puzzle or the most irrelevant trivia tidbits. They are driven by the compliments they receive after solving a problem that has stumped others. This kind of personality can be tapped by law enforcement officers, although not easily. Essentially, the officer must—on the surface—yield his superior position. He must make it seem that the investigation facing him is impossible to solve. He must draw the person into a position where he wants to help solve the problem.

Using this motivation involves many pitfalls. The person may be uncontrollable. He may go too far or arouse the suspicions of the people he is working against. It may not even be possible to give this kind of person any kind of advice, counsel, or direction. He may be a terrible witness in court because he may come across as arrogant. Nonetheless, these people are usually very intelligent and driven to succeed.

The Town Crier

There are people who, by their nature, like to be the possessors and providers of information. They are like children who proudly proclaim "I know something you don't know!" Sending them out to develop information that they in turn report back to an enthusiastic audience is just the excitement that they need. The key to keeping such a person motivated is for the handling officer to appear excited and interested in the news being provided.

Town criers can make excellent informants. They are driven by the need to develop information that they think others do not know. The high point of their day is when they can stand at center stage and tell someone what they have learned.

Unfortunately, some town criers tell everything to everyone. Therefore, they may not be able to maintain the confidentiality that an informant relationship requires. Some town criers like to be coaxed into providing the information. Consequently, they can be very annoying for officers to deal with.

There are many reasons people become informants. Those listed above are probably the most common reasons people choose to cooperate, but they are not the only reasons.

It is important that investigators understand what motivates the people they intend to hire as informants. These factors must be stressed during the initial contacts. Once a person has been "opened" as an informant, the factors that motivate him must be exploited so the person will continue to provide reliable information. Motivation can change over the course of time. The handling officer must always be on the alert for changes and modify his approach in order to keep the informant interested.

A member of a group became an informant for financial reasons and provided quality information for several years in exchange for money. As time passed, the alternate handling officer came to realize that money was no longer the only factor motivating the source. He noticed that the informant was spending more time with the officers during his personal contacts. He was also placing more telephone calls to his handling officers. The alternate handling officer concluded that the informant had developed a great liking for his handling officers and wanted to associate with them. To fulfill his changing motivation, the handling officers arranged more luncheon meetings with the source, and made concerted efforts to spend more time with him during debriefings. Even when the handling officers plateaued the informant's money payments, he continued to provide quality information.

Documenting Informant Information

Documentation of the informant's information is very likely the single most important aspect of the overall informant investigative technique. From a law enforcement perspective, if an informant's information has not been documented, it does not exist. An officer who has acted on undocumented information is walking on thin ice. A prosecutor who attempts to use undocumented informant information in a trial is courting danger. Some old-timers continue to employ "hip pocket" sources, who are not carried as agency informants, and whose reports are never filed anywhere. As long as their use is strictly limited to giving the officer some general intelligence about neighborhood activities, there is little danger. If, however, the officer allows information from "hip pocket" informants to move him from Step 1 to Step 3 in an investigation, he may face serious problems in court, where he will be expected to explain how he made the leap between steps. This is particularly true with respect to terrorism cases, in which all evidence will be closely scrutinized.

The debriefing of an informant should be very similar to any official business interview that a law enforcement investigator would conduct. Possibly because informants are debriefed on a continuing basis, some investigators tend to forget the basic questions that should be resolved during the course of any interview—"who, what, when, where, why, and how?" If these questions are not covered adequately, the debriefing will be unsatisfactory. The main failing usually involves the "How?" question. All too often investigators fail to ask the informant how he or she knows something is true and correct. Investigators should constantly ask their informants how they developed the information that they are providing. If this is done from the outset of the informant relationship, many informants will become accustomed to this question, and will give the information without being asked.

Labeling is something that is often done in small talk. Informants cannot be permitted to do this. If an informant labels someone, he must explain how he arrived at his conclusion. An investigator cannot place statements like "He's a member of the Mafia" "He's a bomb maker" or "He's a communist" in an informant's report. When asked for further explanation, some sources respond with comments like, "Everyone knows that" or "It's common knowledge." These are unsatisfactory reasons for including such labels in an informant report.

Informant reports should stand on their own. Unfortunately, because informants are contacted on a continuing basis, some investigators think that they can limit what they include in a report. This can present serious problems, especially if the case on which the informant is reporting has multiple parts handled by several investigators. If each investigator only receives reports pertinent to his aspect of the case, they may find that none of them makes any sense. Furthermore, if only some of the reports are used in an affidavit or brought into court, they could be misleading or misunderstood.

On January 1, 1999, an informant code-named Topper told Detective Tom Jones that Louie and his brother Hank met Jerry Jones and Big-mouth Larry at Joe's Place to discuss last week's action. Hank was heard to say that he had personally ordered last week's hit. Bigmouth stated that he was there when it happened.

The information above appears to be of value. Unfortunately, it does not stand alone. Who are Louie and Hank? One may assume that they were identified at least by their last names in a previous informant report. Where is Joe's Place, and who is Bigmouth Larry? Again, they were probably identified in a previous report. What was last week's action? It was probably mentioned in the source's report of the previous week.

Informant documentation should be done by subject, not by date of debriefing. This is not a major problem in most situations, because the source is reporting on only one case. However, it can present a serious security breach if the informant is working on several cases. If the informant is reporting on a gambling operation on Broadway and on a house of prostitution on First Avenue, these cases have no relationship to one another. Even if the informant supplies information on both of these cases during the same debriefing, separate reports should be prepared on each piece of information. If a single report is done, it means that each case file will receive information about the other case. This can present significant difficulties when either case comes to court and the defense attorneys are given pertinent discovery materials. They will be given information dealing with the other case. It would be no different than if an investigator put two different subject surveillances in the same log or documented interviews conducted on different cases on the same report form.

Informant reports should be prepared in a timely manner. This helps case officers by giving them current information. It also enables the handling officer to determine whether there are loose ends that need to be addressed. If the officer realizes that he has not obtained complete information, or if his notes are confusing, he can immediately contact the informant for clarification and additional information. In some instances the information provided by the informant requires immediate attention and must be verbally relayed to a case officer for action. If this is done, written documentation of the informant's information should be prepared rapidly so that there is no danger of the verbal information being markedly different from the written documentation.

The ideal informant report will contain the name of the officer conducting the debriefing, the date of the session, the dates pertinent to the information provided, and the name, code name, or code number of the informant. Each informant should have his own control file into which copies of reports should be placed. Each report should contain a routing number so that copies of that report can be directed to the control file. The exact manner in which reports are written will vary from department to department. Some agencies record informant information in the manner in which it was given to the handling officer. Consequently, a statement like, "The informant advised that yesterday he was with Joe Brown when he murdered Tom Smith" will appear in the written documentation. The weakness of this kind of reporting is that it identifies the informant. Some departments prefer that informant reports be prepared from an observer's viewpoint. As a result, the report might state something like, "The informant reported that Joe Brown and another white man encountered Tom Smith yesterday, whereupon Brown murdered Smith." In this form of report, it does not indicate that the informant was the man with Brown. The source could have been a witness unobserved by either Brown or his associate.

All informant reports should have some indication of the source's reliability so that recipient investigators will be able to better assess the intelligence contained in the report. Following is a sampling of reliability statements that can be used.

"The source known as 'Topper,' who has provided reliable information in the past, reported that ..."

"Topper, reliable informant, reported ..."

"A Criminal Informant known as Topper, who has supplied insufficient information to determine reliability, reported ..."

"An informant, Topper, who has been a reliable source and who is in a position to know, reported that ..."

"An informant, Topper, who has provided reliable information in the past concerning car thefts, but who has not provided previous information in the area of animal rights terrorism, reported the following information concerning the Animal Liberation Front ..."

"The source, Topper, who successfully testified in three narcotics cases during the year 1999, reported the following information ..."

"The informant known as Topper, who has reported accurate information since 1997, and who has never been known to have provided any inaccurate information, advised that ..."

Operating an Informant

The actual operation of an informant will vary according to the kind of informant involved, the target, experience, reliability, level of fear, overall intelligence, and need for attention and guidance. The amount of time that the handling officers have and the overall importance of the target case will heavily influence the extent of attention that the handlers will be able to give to the informant. The following are general rules that will apply to the operation of most informants.

An official handling officer should be responsible for each informant. There should also be a secondary or alternate handling officer who knows the informant sufficiently well to fill in for the handling officer should he be unavailable. There is nothing wrong with both officers meeting the informant on a regular basis. One large federal agency even requires that two officers be present when payments are made to an informant. The two officers must work together, or the informant may play one against the other. There is probably nothing wrong with one or two additional officers knowing the informant well enough to communicate with him on a limited basis. It will be difficult to convince the informant that his identity is truly being protected if more than about four officers have contact with him.

A control file should be established on each informant. A control file should contain personal information, the results of background checks, copies of his reports, and the results of the vetting operations that were done to verify his honesty and reliability. Access to this file should be limited to both the handling agent and alternate handling agent, and to certain agency managers.

A "probationary period" should be established for new informants, during which their backgrounds can be examined and their ability to develop reliable information can be assessed. Information developed by a probationary informant and given to other investigators or placed in investigative files should be flagged so that recipients are aware that this source's credibility has yet to be established. Agencies should develop criteria by which they can designate an informant as reliable. No matter how good a new informant appears to be on the surface, he should not be designated as reliable until the criteria have been met.

Informants should never visit the law enforcement agency's office or any other agency facility overtly. On occasion, an agency may want the informant come to their office to undergo a polygraph examination or to review photographs or evidence. If this is done, the source should be brought to the department's facility covertly, possibly in the back of a van, and secretly taken into the office in such a manner that few, if any, employees observe him. Similarly, security should be practiced whenever a prosecutor wants to interview an informant, and when an informant appears before a grand jury.

Meetings between the informant and handlers should be at locations where no person involved in the investigation can observe them. Additionally, they should be held in such a manner as to avoid arousing suspicion. For example, a handling officer should not spread a group of wanted posters on a restaurant table in view of a waiter or waitress.

Telephone calls between the informant and the handler should be done with security in mind. Due to Caller ID technology, the handler should avoid calling the informant from his law enforcement office. The informant should not use his residence telephone to call the handler. He should definitely not call the handler from a subject's telephone. Cell phone to cell phone calls are a safer way for handlers and informants to communicate. Informants should avoid keeping the handler's number as a favorite on his telephone. The informant should be instructed to dial the handler's number on each call. It is simply too easy for a subject to ask to use an informant's telephone to make a call, and then check to see what numbers the subject calls on a regular basis. Text messaging is now becoming very popular with many younger people. Care should be used in handling an informant through this medium. If used, it should be limited to arranging through pre-arranged code, where and when to meet.

Pagers were once a good way for the informant and handler to make contact, however, they are rapidly losing popularity. If used, the handling officer should avoid paging the informant to his or her office number. Someone with the informant might be able to see the number on the pager screen and recognize it. Further, officers must be careful when instructing an informant to employ pagers for contacts. With the advent of inexpensive cell phones, pagers are rapidly becoming a thing of the past, and an informant may appear suspicious if he carries both a cell phone and a pager.

E-mail is rapidly becoming one of the most common ways for people to communicate, and can be used by a handler and his or her informant. However, this mode of communication is risky. Many people leave their computer on for hours at a time. It is possible for someone else to pull up e-mail when the informant stepped away to use the restroom or simply allowed another person to use his computer. Some political extremists are into hacking, and could retrieve an informant's e-mail messages if they became suspicious of him. As with telephones, the handler's e-mail address should not be saved as a favorite on the informant's computer.

The handler must practice good security techniques with respect to meetings with the informant. If he does, the informant will be encouraged to practice good security habits. Promptness is important with respect to informant meetings. From a security standpoint, it is not prudent for either the handling officer or the informant to hang around waiting for the other to arrive. The handling officer must set the tone by always being on time. If the informant is late, the handler should stress the importance of promptness. There should also be an "abort" signal between the handler and the informant. Each should know that if the other uses the signal that the area is not secure, no contact should be made at that time and place. Similarly, each should know not to wait more than a certain period of time, possibly 10 minutes, for the other to arrive.

The handler must avoid wearing or displaying anything police-related when meeting an informant. He should certainly not wear a uniform when meeting a source in a location where others can see the two of them together.

Secure meeting locations, including safehouse-offsites and hotel rooms are encouraged for source contacts. This is especially true if the informant is of great value, or if documents and photographs are to be reviewed, and/or if the debriefing is expected to be lengthy.

Vehicles can be used for meetings, but proper security precautions must be taken. A handler should not pick up a source at his residence or drive him around in areas where subjects routinely go. If it is necessary for an informant to be driven in an area where the suspects are active in order for him to point out locations or identify people, the informant should be concealed. It is probably best to have the informant hidden in the rear of a van or a car with heavily tinted windows.

The more "shaky" the informant is with respect to fear and inexperience, the more attention the handling officers will have to give him or her.

Debriefing should take place shortly after an event so it is fresh in the informant's mind. Written documentation of a debriefing should be completed shortly after the contact. For newer informants, older informants about whom some questions have arisen, and in the case of significant information, it might be wise to allow the informant to review the written documentation to ensure that it is correct. It might also be prudent to have the informant sign the report.

If an informant is paid money either for services or to reimburse him for expenses, he should be asked to sign a receipt. Money should not be flashed around in a public place. If the meeting is in a restaurant or tavern, the informant should not be using some of the money given to him by the handler to pay for the handler's meal. Similarly, the informant should not use his payment money to buy other things for the handling officer, such as books, cigarettes, or gifts. The department should maintain records concerning all monies paid to an informant. Besides being good budgetary practice and common sense, the payment information may become evidence in court in the event of a trial. How much each informant has been given for his work on behalf of the department may be brought up in a trial. For this reason, handling officers should not give informants more than token gifts, even if these gifts are paid for by the handling officer.

Handling officers should never borrow money from informants. Lending money to an informant should also be avoided. If it is done, however, the handling agents should make an effort to have it returned. Otherwise the loan becomes an informant payment for which there is no record. This could present a problem in court.

Sources can be reimbursed through bank accounts. A handling officer can simply place the payment into the informant's bank account and keep the deposit slip as his agency's receipt. Some informants are motivated by actually seeing and counting the money, so it may be better to pay them in person. Many agencies prefer that informants "believe" that they are being paid "Cash On Delivery-COD," which means that the money given them is commensurate with the quality of the information that the source provides during the debriefing. This concept is reinforced if the handler gives the money to the source immediately following the debriefing.

Whether they are handling officers or not, law enforcement officers should not become involved in business ventures with an informant or their agency. They should also not work for informants in outside jobs and should not hire informants to work for them in business ventures they run outside of their police employment.

Although friendships of sorts do develop between some informants and their handling officers, the handling officer must maintain a barrier that prohibits a true close friendship and association from developing. A handler and his informant should not become "drinking buddies." A handler should not allow the informant to become a part of his life to the extent that the informant visits the handler's home, gets to know his spouse, and plays with his children. Serious problems can result from this kind of relationship. The informant is not a fellow police officer. He also should not be housed in a police officer's personal residence. If the informant needs a place to live, the officer should try to get him into a hotel, apartment, or house.

In situations in which a transfer of handling officers takes place, the previous handling officer must remove himself as soon as is reasonably possible. In some cases, it may take weeks or even several months for a smooth transition to be accomplished. Once it is done, the former handler should vanish from the scene. If this does not occur, the informant may use one officer against the other.

Informant Security and Confidentiality Issues

The confidentiality of the informant-law enforcement agency relationship must be protected. Virtually all law enforcement agencies have policies to ensure that the names of informants are not released to the public. Obviously, if the informant must testify in court, his or her name will be released. Officers must exercise care even within their own agency and within the general law enforcement community with respect to the names of informants. "Need to know" should be the byword. Usually a code name or number is all that many fellow officers need to know about an informant's identity. Experienced investigators get into the habit of never referring to an informant by his true name. It is not unusual for them to make statements like, "Let me check with the Falcon about that" or "I'll see if the Big Guy can cover that meeting" or "I'll show that photograph to CI 8895 to see if he knows his name." Some investigators even go so far as to refrain from using the informant's true name when conversing with the informant himself. Good investigators use care in how they package their informant's information before disseminating it to fellow department members or to other law enforcement agencies. It does no good to conceal the source's true name and then give out information that is documented in such a way that it identifies the informant to the recipients.

Security must begin with the handling officer. The informant will likely be afraid of detection and therefore will want security. However, informants often have little knowledge about what constitutes good security. The handling officer must educate the informant. Often this is best done by example rather than through lecture. A handler who practices proper security techniques will influence an informant to do the same.

Ethical considerations are also related to the issues of confidentiality and security. If an investigator realizes that a person's identity cannot ever be revealed as an informant, he must act accordingly. It may mean that he cannot open the person as a source even though that person may be capable of developing quality intelligence. It may mean operating the source, but not using potentially valuable information that he provides in affidavits that will probably be made public in the future. It may mean not using that person in such a manner as to require his testimony in court. It is a situation that many law enforcement officers face at least once during a career. Do they open as a potentially valuable informant a person whose life will be destroyed when it is later revealed that he is cooperating with a police agency? If the person is an upstanding member of the community who can be induced to function as an informant due to patriotic motivations, the answer is probably "no." If, on the other hand, the person is a career criminal with a long arrest record, the answer might be "yes"—if the information he can produce is of vital importance to a significant investigation. Officers who find themselves in this dilemma should consult with their agency's legal counsel and their prosecutor before opening and directing the person as an informant. It may be possible that the person could be safely used to a certain extent, or it may not be possible to open the person as an informant without placing him or her in jeopardy.

Investigators must remember that if an informant's information is used to procure a search or arrest warrant, his or her name could possibly be compromised. Similarly, if a source's information is used to obtain authorization for technical coverage, his identity may be revealed. It will be very difficult for most agencies to conceal the name of an informant who has worn a wire or otherwise recorded a conversation with a subject. It may, however, be possible for an agency to use an informant's information in internal documents without compromising his identity. For example, an agency may be able to use an informant's information in an in-house proposal to create an undercover operation directed against a particular target. However, if the informant is used to actually facilitate the entrance of the undercover officer into the conspiracy, it is very likely that his identity will not be protected. (Even if the informant's name could be kept out of court in such a situation, it is likely that when the subjects learn of the undercover officer's identity, they will recall the name of the person who introduced him to their group.)

Informants should be told that they are not to reveal their status to anyone else. Security should be strongly stressed. It is useful for a handling officer to cite examples in which the informant should not reveal information. Particular attention should be given to arrest situations. The informant should be told that he cannot try to talk his way out of a traffic ticket by revealing his informant status. Similarly, he will receive no break if he is arrested for a more serious violation. It should be emphasized to the informant that anyone, including a best friend or a traffic cop who knows about his position as an informant, presents a threat to his security. The informant should not trust anyone outside of his handlers with this secret.

Informants should be counseled with respect to names, numbers, notes, and other items that could identify them as sources. Obviously, carrying around the name or telephone number of his handling officer should be discouraged. Telephoning his contact officer from his personal residence or business telephone should also be discouraged.

One valuable terrorist informant was exposed because he used a telephone in his group's safe house to contact his handling officer. The informant was not aware that the group had "bugged" its own telephone with a recording device.

Informants should be warned against making notes while in the presence of subjects. Notes made out of the subject's view should be carefully guarded and destroyed as soon as possible. Informants who are "police groupies," "would-be cops," "would-be spies," and "patriots" often tend to gather police and government documents, decals, shoulder patches, hats, books, and other items that would create suspicion if ever observed. The handler who knows the motivations of his informants should give such people particular cautions about keeping such items.

Vetting the Informant

Vetting is a term used by law enforcement to refer to the process by which the correctness of an informant's information is verified. The word *vet* means to examine and check for accuracy. Vetting should be a continuing project. Some informants lie. Some informants exaggerate. Some informants develop information through questionable means. Some informants simply cannot accurately report what they see and hear. Some informants become impaired due to alcohol, drugs, or mental illness. The fact that an informant was once very reliable and accurate does not mean that he or she will always be reliable and accurate. It is important that an investigator make periodic efforts to verify the accuracy of his informant's information. Vetting can be accomplished through a variety of means, including the following:

> Thorough debriefing and stressing the "who, what, when, where, why, and how?" questions. Any signs of hesitation should be noted and explored further.

> Revisiting previous debriefings to determine whether the informant will give a different account.

> Having another officer debrief the source. Sometimes an outsider can see things that a case officer overlooks because of familiarity.

Bringing in a superior officer to attend a debriefing can often change the whole tenor of the session. The case officer may note changes in the way that the source presents his report, which could suggest that he is exaggerating or has exaggerated in the past.

Using other investigative techniques to verify what the informant has stated. Sometimes this can be done in retrospect. If the source claims that he met with a subject on a certain day, a review of surveillance logs of the subject for that date might verify this fact. Wiretaps and other technical coverage might be able to verify what the informant is reporting. Vetting can also be done proactively. If the informant says that he will be at a particular location, a surveillance can be established to cover him.

Asking other informants about this informant. Obviously, this must be done without identifying the person as an informant. Another informant can be shown surveillance pictures of a group of people, including the informant and case subjects. He can be asked to identify and discuss each person. In theory, the description that he gives of the source should be similar to how the informant describes himself with respect to the criminal conspiracy.

Conducting agency checks. When an informant is initially opened, most law enforcement departments check their agency's files and the files of other agencies for any record of the informant. This should be done periodically to ensure that the informant has not engaged in criminal activity of which his handling officer is unaware.

Polygraph testing an informant can present problems because some informants will regard it as an indication of distrust. It should be considered, however, especially if there is any suggestion of dishonesty. A handling officer can usually explain that his superior officer is ordering it or that it is department policy. It might also be explained that the informant has reached a certain financial plateau that cannot be exceeded unless a polygraph is passed. Sometimes just the suggestion of the polygraph will cause an informant to want to "clarify" some of his or her statements.

Signing reports can also cause some informants to want to "clarify" their statements. The handling officer could hand the informant a copy of the report that he prepared from the source's last debriefing. After the informant has read it, the handler could ask that he sign each page, saying that his superior has requested that it be done because the information is of such high quality. For some sources, the idea of signing something is sufficient to make them want to correct it.

Complete honesty on the part of the informant is something that should be sought at all times, but it is not likely to occur. Honesty with respect to information provided is a goal that is achievable and must be sought. A source who deliberately gives false information must be terminated. An informant who provides incorrect information due to exaggeration, assumptions, and personal opinion must be schooled and corrected. Usually a handler who asks the key interview questions can resolve such problems. A source who provides incorrect information because he simply cannot interpret what he sees or observes will probably have to be closed unless the situation can be rectified.

One terrorist informant had no concept of time. He never wore a watch and rarely even knew the day of the week. He did not work or have family responsibilities. He slept when tired, ate when hungry, and moved around when he felt the urge. His handling officer found that he was repeatedly inaccurate with respect to times, days of the week, and dates. To alleviate the situation, the handling officer debriefed the source at least once, seven days each week. By doing this, the officer was able to be sure that the events upon which the source was reporting had occurred since the last debriefing. Had the handler debriefed the informant on a weekly or monthly basis, the value of his information would be greatly lessened because his indication of the dates and times of events would have been questionable.

Honesty and the Informant Relationship

The law enforcement agency-informant relationship is not a completely honest relationship. The handling officer caters to whatever motivates the informant rather than having a truly honest relationship with him or her. To varying degrees, the handler manipulates the informant in order to make him or her produce as much information as possible. Although many handlers try to convince their informants that they are working together against a terrorist or criminal conspiracy, they rarely actually give any information to the informant. In that sense, the sharing of information is strictly one-way—from the informant to the handler. Often the handling officer uses deceptive statements to foster the relationship, explain unpleasant situations, and encourage the informant to produce.

For example, a handling officer may tell an informant that he has given him the maximum amount of money available for his information, when in fact there is additional money that could be paid. A handling officer may claim that it is department policy that the informant undergo a polygraph examination, when in fact the department has no such rule. During the early stages of an informant's development, the handler will usually encourage the source by telling him that his information is important and previously unknown. More often than not, the handler already knows the information and its value is minimal. A handling officer may tell an informant that he cannot meet him or her at a particular time, possibly over a weekend or late at night, because he will be on surveillance. In actuality, the officer is off-duty and wants to spend his free time with his family. He fears that if he tells his informant the truth, the informant will subsequently decline to cover something because he "is off-duty and with his family."

Even though an informant may be completely honest with respect to his reporting of information, he may be dishonest about personal matters. For example, a source who wants more money will give his handling agent what he believes will be an "acceptable" reason before he will tell him the truth. A source who has spent his money at the racetrack may tell his handler that he lost his wallet or that he had to buy medicine for his sick mother. If a source is instructed to attend a particular function that conflicts with a night of drinking with his friends, he will probably tell his handler that he has a church meeting to attend. If the handler specifically asks the informant why he is helping the department, the informant may give a response like, "I'm a good American" or "I hate what those guys are doing." In reality, he is an informant for the money or in order to get revenge. In some instances, the "little lies" almost become jokes. One "tough guy" informant regularly informed his handler that he needed money because he had been mugged. Eventually, the handler began to respond by stating that he really wanted to give the informant extra money, but he, too, had been mugged.

Both officers and informants separate their professional lives from their personal lives. Both sides will tell the other what they believe will be acceptable. Few handling officers will tell informants much about their personal lives other than in generalities. What they tell them will be facts that the informant will find favorable. If the informant is a family man who stresses family bonds, it is unlikely that the handling officer will talk about his own marital problems. Similarly, if the informant knows that the officer is religious and attends church regularly, the informant is unlikely to criticize religion, especially if he is motivated by money, and he knows that his handling officer has control over what he is paid.

Some young law enforcement officers become extremely upset when they catch their informant in a lie. If the untruth involves information being provided by the informant, it is indeed a serious problem and must be addressed immediately. It could mean that the informant must be closed. If, however, the untruth involves something of a personal nature, it need not jeopardize the informant relationship. Many things that an informant may do are unacceptable to law enforcement officers. Consequently, an informant who wants to remain an informant will probably try to conceal from his handler aspects of his life that the handler might dislike.

Illegal Activities and the Informant

Being an informant is not a "get out of jail free card." Informants must be told at the outset that they cannot violate the law either while "on the job" or while off-duty.

"On The Job"

With respect to "on the job," the informant must be told that the ends do not justify the means. The fact that the informant is performing a good deed with respect to developing information for a law enforcement agency does not justify breaking the law in order to gain that information. The informant cannot break into residences, steal property, conduct wiretaps and similar coverages, or beat people up in order to develop intelligence. The handler must encourage the informant to ask about any questionable techniques that he is considering using to gain information. If the handler cannot give an opinion, he should bring it to his agency's legal counsel. Questions of this nature might include:

> The informant believes that he can seduce the wife of a leading conspirator and develop information during "pillow talk." Should he do it?

> The informant has been left alone in a room where a safe has been left open. Should he look at the papers in the safe?

> The informant has access to the "books" used by the conspirators. Can he borrow them and show them to the handler? If not, can he use the group's photocopier to copy the books to give to the department?

> The informant can get himself appointed as "night security officer" for the group-operated location. If he accepts the post, can he search the location?

> The informant knows that group members use narcotics in their residences. While visiting these residences, he could easily take samples of the drugs without getting caught. Should he do this?

Away From the Job

It is certainly easy for an informant to believe that he can get away with minor violations of the law because he is working for a law enforcement agency. The handling officer must set the informant straight before the issue even arises. Not only will the informant not get any breaks with respect to law violations, but an arrest or other problem could cost him his position as an informant.

Drugs and Informants

In most cases, people who are using drugs should not be used as informants. This is certainly true with respect to terrorism investigations. Most terrorists do not use drugs, particularly hard drugs like cocaine and heroin. Consequently, it would be difficult for a drug user to get close to group members. In fact, some terrorists avoid anyone who might give police a reason to look at them. A narcotics user is an arrest waiting to happen. A drug-using informant would make a poor witness in a terrorism trial because the defense attorney will use the drug usage to discredit the informant's testimony.

Some law enforcement agencies that specialize in drug investigations are often forced to use drug users as informants because no one else can get close to the subjects. It is certainly prudent for such agencies to make as limited use of such people as possible. They are probably best suited for making individual drug purchases that can be documented through surveillance and videotape. Another function for drug-using informants is for them to introduce undercover officers to the target subjects. Although informants in narcotics cases will usually not undergo as rigorous a cross-examination as an informant in a terrorism investigation, such informants, nonetheless, do not make good witnesses during trials. Indeed, by the time the case goes to court, the drug-using informant may not be in condition to testify.

Drug addiction has a command over people that exceeds almost any other form of control. No matter how much of a "hammer" a law enforcement agency believes that it has on a person, drug addiction will likely exceed it. No agency can ever be certain that it will be able to direct an addicted person. Furthermore, drugs can cloud the mind of anyone. As a result, the accuracy and correctness of the reports of many drug-addicted people must be questioned. Expecting such people to be where they should be at any given time is questionable at best. They cannot be characterized as reliable, which in itself is sufficient reason to not use them as informants.

Subsources

A subsource is a person who reports information to an informant who in turn relays it back to the handling officer. Essentially, a subsource is an informant being operated by an informant. It is clear that most informants develop some information by talking to other people, particularly those close to the criminal conspiracy. However, for the purposes of this discussion, a subsource is a person who is actually directed by a source to develop information. Although some intelligence-gathering agencies use subsources, such people should not be used by criminal investigative agencies. This includes agencies conducting terrorism investigations, because these agencies hope to prosecute the subjects. Using subsource information as probable cause for a search or arrest warrant, or to procure electronic coverage, is questionable at best.

The very concept of the subsource should cause law enforcement officers to shudder. It is difficult enough to direct and control an informant and to ensure that his information is accurate, complete, and timely. Attempting to do this with a subsource whose identity is usually not even known to the handling agent is almost impossible. In some instances, the subsource will not reside in the same town, state, or even country as either the informant or the handling officer. What this all means is that the handling officer has to rely on the informant to determine the reliability of the subsource. This is simply not a wise practice for a law enforcement agency.

Of course, there are other problems involved with using subsources. The handling officer has no way to determine how the subsource is gathering his or her information. It could be through illegal means. He also has no way of knowing what the informant has used to motivate the subsource. It might be money or promises, or it might be a threat of some kind. The handling officer does not actually know that there is a subsource. Conceivably, an informant could be conducting illegal wiretaps or thefts to gather information and telling his handling officer that the information is coming from a subsource. The informant could be getting his information from public sources (or even making it up) and crediting his subsource with obtaining it.

The Pretext Informant

A pretext informant is an individual who regularly provides current information about a target to a law enforcement officer without being aware of the officer's true employment. Although the officer is functioning in an undercover capacity, the project is actually an informant operation. The officer himself is not attempting to penetrate the target conspiracy. His mission is to develop a relationship with the pretext informant through which he can develop information. More often than not, the person providing the information is not even aware that the officer has an interest in the target. To many in law enforcement the concept of a pretext informant seems bizarre, but it is a technique that is used by some agencies.

To a certain extent, many undercover officers use people on the periphery to learn about a target or to gain access to a target. These people are unaware of the officer's true identity and profession. The difference between an undercover operation and a pretext informant project is that in the latter situation, the focus is on a particular periphery person, whereas in an undercover operation the focus is on the target. In an undercover operation, the officer wants to place himself in a position in which he can personally develop the information, whereas in the pretext project, the officer wants the information to come from the periphery person.

Pretext informant projects are often conducted under some form of business cover. However, they can also be accomplished through professional associations, hobbies, or just about any way in which one person can form an association with another person.

The following outlines how a pretext informant project might work:

The target of the investigation is the local leader of a violent militia organization. The target is married to a fairly submissive woman. The couple have several children and live a working class existence that allows for few luxuries. A covert female law enforcement officer comes to town from the "big city" after her "divorce," and opens a small handi-craft store. The officer arranges to meet the target's wife at a school function. The officer explains that her new shop is floundering because she does not know the townspeople, and therefore has not attracted crafters to place their wares in her store, and cannot draw customers. "Discovering" that the target's wife "knows everyone" in town, the officer proposes that the wife help her locate local crafters. She offers the wife a "big city" wage for her efforts. The wife accepts, and her husband concurs because it means easy money for his family. With time, the officer becomes a close friend of the target's wife. She tells the wife about various problems that she had, and still has, with her ex-husband.

The idea behind this project is to get the target's wife to talk about her husband. Of course, the project would not necessarily have to be aimed at the target's wife. It could have gone after the target's parents, brother or sister, or best friend. Instead of a female officer, the operative could have been a male officer opening a hardware store. If the project had been a true undercover operation, the officer would have used the wife to get to the husband. Once that had occurred, the undercover operative would have done whatever was necessary to foster a relationship with the husband, even if it meant largely ignoring a relationship with the wife. In the pretext project, the undercover officer has no real plan to actually meet with the target, and if she did, would probably not attempt to cultivate a relationship with him. Her objective is to get information from the wife.

In one pretext informant operation, the investigator befriended the brother of a target who lived in a hostile foreign country. The officer attempted to acquire information by telling stories to the brother about his own "black sheep" brother who supposedly lived abroad. It was reasoned that if a man talks about his own brother, the other man would respond in kind, especially if there were similarities. It was also reasoned that if the brother was honest with respect to general things that he talked about with the officer, he would also honest when talk-ing about the target.

The problem with the pretext informant concept is that it predisposes that unequal or dissimilar people will communicate in an honest and complete manner. It also assumes that an honest relationship developed in one sphere (such as through a hobby) will result in honest exchanges of information in all areas. These assumptions are simply not true. In the handicraft store example, the undercover officer and the target's wife are not, and cannot be, equals. The officer is the "boss" who controls the fate of the target's wife, who is the overpaid "employee." The target's wife is not likely to tell her boss things about herself or her spouse that will jeopardize her job. It is difficult to imagine her telling her boss that her husband advocates the violent overthrow of the government, or that he is stockpiling automatic weapons in his basement, or that he wants to kill all members of a particular minority group. Yet this is exactly the kind of information that the law enforcement agency is seeking. Similarly, if the wife needs to take a Saturday off from work to participate with her husband in a KKK rally, it is unlikely that she is going to tell this to her employer. Instead, she will offer an "acceptable" reason for needing the day off, such as to attend a family reunion.

Summary

Informants are important in all areas of criminal investigation. In the field of terrorism, however, they are often difficult to develop and continue to operate because the cases are frequently of long duration. The informant most likely to provide information of the greatest value is the inside person—an individual who is a part of the conspiracy, and has firsthand knowledge of current activities. Unfortunately, these informants are very difficult to develop within terrorist conspiracies. A second informant target is the person who is on the periphery of the conspiracy. These individuals are close to, but not members of, the conspiracy. They are sometimes overlooked by investigators because they usually cannot provide key inside information that can be immediately used to prosecute the subjects. However, these people can provide tips and leads that will enable an investigator to use other investigative techniques to develop valuable information. With skillful direction, some periphery informants can be guided into inside positions. The third category of informant is the person who is willing to cooperate but is outside of the conspiracy. With careful guidance from the handing officer, some of these "cold start" informants can be directed into periphery or inside positions within the investigation.

Motivation is the key to informant development. The investigator must determine what factors cause a person to do something and then capitalize on them in order to encourage the person to function as an informant. Common motivating factors include money and "working off a beef" for a police agency so the agency will go easy on the person in connection with a criminal violation. There are also a number of other motivators that can be effectively used with informants.

The identity of a source must be protected. Security and confidentiality should be emphasized and the source should be told that he cannot use his relationship with law enforcement to violate the law. He should also be given guidance with respect to what he can and cannot do with respect to developing information.

Documentation of informant-produced information is extremely important. This is especially true in terrorism investigations, in which group members are likely to challenge all evidence presented against them. Informants must be reliable and honest with respect to the information that they provide in connection with the criminal or terrorist conspiracy. They must be vetted (checked for honesty) on a regular basis. Drug-addicted persons should not be used as informants in terrorism investigations.

12 Trash Cover

Trash cover is an investigative technique that involves law enforcement recovery of discarded materials. Often it means going through a person's garbage at his residence or employment. It can also involve recovering materials dropped by a subject during a surveillance. Usually these materials are discarded by the subject, himself. However, on occasion, relevant items pertaining to the subject could be discarded by his or her friends, relatives, or associates. A trash cover can be used effectively in most investigations. Although the phrase "trash cover" seems to imply a structured maneuver, the fact is that many trash covers occur contemporaneously with an investigation and involve little or no planning.

The trash cover is probably the sleeper of all investigative techniques. Many investigators have never conducted a trash cover. Although it often can be accomplished easily, many investigators do not believe that it is worth the effort. Some even regard the technique as "dirty" and beneath their dignity. In many departments, the narcotics officers are the most likely to use trash covers. Any finding of drug residue in a person's trash can provide good probable cause for a search or arrest warrant. Trash covers are also employed during gambling investigations in that losing bet slips, which are often tossed aside, can be used as evidence. At the very least the fruits of a trash cover can validate to the officers that their investigation is heading in the right direction.

Trash covers play a particularly important role in terrorism investigations, because other techniques often fail to produce complete results. In a terrorism investigation, every piece of evidence is important. Indeed, the more varied the techniques, the better the chances are for a successful prosecution. The trash cover can provide intelligence upon which other investigative techniques can be employed. Trash covers can also produce evidence that will confirm the results of other investigative techniques. For example, fingerprints found in a subject's trash could verify his true identity. Trash covers will rarely be the primary investigative technique used—they usually play a supporting role to other techniques.

Perhaps it is human nature. Many people seem to be careless from a security standpoint when it comes to what they discard. Terrorists are as vulnerable to this as anyone else. Terrorist groups preach security to their members, yet they often fail to warn them about careless disposal of their trash.

Trash covers can yield remarkable amounts of valuable information that can be used as direct evidence against the subject. Trash can also provide important investigative leads. Trash can provide background and insight about the subject and his relatives, friends, and business and criminal associates. Some of this information can be used to enhance the quality of interviews with the subject, as well as with others contacted during an investigation.

Trash covers are able to produce quality information because people fail to consider that law enforcement agencies might go through their discards for evidence against them. For many people, trash is dirty, and the idea of some-one going through the garbage is incomprehensible to them. Many people hold the belief that an item no longer of value to them is also of no value to anyone else. Even the most careful people seem to discard incriminating and sensitive materials in their trash. It is amazing that some very security-conscious people, including those who have elaborate alarm systems in their homes, routinely discard in their garbage such items as cancelled checks, outdated credit cards, and bills. A common criminal could have a field day with some of the information contained in residential garbage. In fact, some tabloid reporters regularly develop leads and information through this technique.

Any investigator who questions the value of a trash cover need go no further than his own residence. A quick survey of the discarded items in the various waste receptacles in a typical officer's residence is likely to cause him real security concerns. While the kitchen garbage can may not yield much of real value other than the subject's food preferences, the bathroom waste container may contain prescription medicine bottles, evidence of the use of contraceptives, and packaging from over-the-counter medications. Bedroom waste bins may contain everything from correspondence to clothing tags and receipts, which can reflect buying patterns. Den and office waste cans are likely to contain canceled checks, bills, credit card records, telephone billing reports, letters, computer and fax communications, and a wealth of other personal and employment items. Trash receptacles in a child's room could possibly yield discarded family pictures and mementos, as well school-related items. Garage trash containers will often yield a variety of items that were removed while cleaning cars. Among these materials could be gas and other receipts. Of course, if the survey were carried out during a period of general housecleaning, the yield in the waste containers could be much more incriminating. An investigator could logically assume that the contents of all of the waste containers in his home would ultimately end up in the garbage can that will be placed at the curb for pickup by a waste disposal service. If someone wanted to develop information about the officer, he could certainly get it from the family garbage can.

Obviously, the trash cover investigative technique can only be used effectively against a person if that person is unaware that the technique is being used. This means that investigators should be extremely discreet when recovering trash. If the subject learns that he is being targeted, he will ensure that nothing of value is discarded ever again. Furthermore, he may "booby trap" his trash with everything from feces to tainted needles. A clever terrorist who "makes" a trash cover could plant fabricated information in his trash that could cause investigators to waste considerable time following false leads. It must be recalled that some terrorists are so dedicated to their cause that they will do nothing to jeopardize their fellow group members and their safe houses. A lengthy investigation of a subject can be brought to a halt if the subject catches someone conducting a trash cover on his residence and concludes that law enforcement has learned that he is a covert terrorist.

One Middle Eastern terrorist became aware that investigators had used a trash cover on an associate's residence. He decided to protect himself by purchasing a small barrel in which he burned his trash each day, even though he was aware that open burning violated a local ordinance. He subsequently disposed of the ashes in his curb garbage can. The manner in which the subject burned his trash strongly suggested that he knew that law enforcement personnel were aware of his activities.

The Planned Trash Cover

Legal Aspects of a Trash Cover

Usually when law enforcement officers mention the trash cover technique, they are referring to the recovery of a subject's garbage from his residence or place of employment. The key issue to be considered with respect to this use of the trash cover technique concerns the ownership of the trash. A second issue involves the location of the trash. The mere fact that a subject implies that he no longer wants an item, and therefore discards it into a disposal receptacle, does not automatically mean that he or she actually relinquishes ownership of the item. For example, if a man tosses a cold remedy box into the trash container next to his bathroom sink, it does not mean that he cannot later retrieve it in order to read the directions. The box is still in his home and under his control. If a police officer visits the home to interview the man, and subsequently uses the man's bathroom, he can not take the cold remedy box just because it was in the bathroom trash can.

Even in situations in which it is clear that the person no longer desires an item, it does not necessarily mean that a law enforcement officer can take possession of it. Usually, if an investigator must trespass on private property in order to recover a discarded item, he or she will need a search warrant. As a result, a law enforcement officer for the most part cannot open a person's garbage can and look at or remove trash if the garbage can is physically located on the person's property. Similarly, if a business places trash into a locked container that would be opened by a waste disposal service holding a contract to pick up that trash, a law enforcement officer would almost certainly not be able to legally pick the lock on the container in order to recover the trash. This would be true even if the business owner pushed the locked trash container into a public alley where the waste disposal service would empty it.

Laws vary from locality to locality, and even the smallest difference in circumstances may significantly alter the situation. In some areas of the country, law enforcement officers are all but forbidden to employ the technique. Additionally, various law enforcement agencies have policies and procedures that may govern the recovery of trash. Some of these regulations may even be more restrictive than the statutes. Before an investigator institutes a trash cover, he should explore the circumstances of the project with the agency's legal counsel. Larger departments have attorneys, some of whom are sworn personnel, whose job it is to render such opinions. If a department does not have such a person, the prosecutor's office can give an opinion. In fact, in investigations in which it is anticipated that recovered trash will yield important evidence, the prosecutor should probably be consulted prior to conducting a trash cover, even if the department's legal counsel has given his or her approval. It is the prosecutor who will ultimately have to defend the trash cover in court should it be challenged.

How to Conduct a Planned Trash Cover

Security is at the crux of a successful trash cover. Assuming that all of the legal hurdles have been overcome, and the investigator is certain that the person's trash can be taken legally, the next step is planning. Surveillance of the target location is important to determine when the trash is placed into an area where it can be legally and securely taken. Most residential and business trash collection is done on a schedule. Consequently, it can be determined with some certainty when the subject's trash will be placed in an area for collection by a waste disposal service. Surveillance of the address is often all that is required to determine the trash pickup schedule. Another method for ascertaining the pickup schedule is for an investigator to place a pretext telephone call to the appropriate waste disposal service requesting the information. The investigator can inform the waste disposal service that he is house sitting or visiting the residence in question, and needs to know when and where to place his trash for pickup.

After the pickup schedule has been learned, surveillance should be able to develop a window of safety when the trash can be taken with the least likelihood of attracting attention. When a safe time has been established, the simplest method for retrieval of the subject's trash is for the investigator to walk or drive to the garbage can, remove all or some of the trash, and leave. No effort should be made to go through the trash at the garbage can. It is best to take whatever looks good and leave as quickly as possible.

While the "quick pickup" is the easiest method of conducting a trash cover, it is not the most secure. In fact, if the subject or someone with whom the subject has contact observes the trash being removed, the technique is exposed. The subject could confront the investigator or call the police and report the investigator as a thief, prowler, or would-be burglar. It would be much more secure for the investigator to take the trash container from the residence, and empty it at a secure location for further study. This, however, is not a good idea. The garbage can belongs to the subject. Taking it even for a short period constitutes theft. Furthermore, if the subject notices that the garbage can is missing, and later finds it returned, he will become suspicious.

A safer method for recovering trash is to use a vehicle similar to those that waste disposal companies use, and collect the garbage along the entire block in accordance with the normal pickup schedule. In this way, if the subject is not convinced that the collection is legitimate, he will at least be uncertain that he is the target of investigation because the entire block has been collected.

Another method for conducting a trash cover is to use a dilapidated truck and make slow visits to various garbage cans along the street, taking some items from each. Anyone observing the vehicle might assume that a private refuge collector is taking the "valuables" discarded in the neighborhood. Various props, including an old sink, a broken chair, and assorted small appliances could be piled in the rear of the truck, and roped to the roof and hood, to make the vehicle truly appear to be a junk collector's truck.

A better method is to conduct the trash cover from the actual garbage truck that services the neighborhood. There is very little possibility of being detected by the subject. The weakness in using this method is that people outside of law enforcement (the employees of the waste disposal company), will know that a trash cover is being conducted. There are several ways in which this can be accomplished. If the waste disposal service is operated by the city, the law enforcement agency can make an agency-to-agency contact to arrange for cooperation. If necessary, this can involve the heads of the two agencies making the arrangements. It may be possible for several investigators to simply borrow a city garbage truck and pick up the trash on the subject's block. Another way of conducting this kind of trash cover, however, is for an investigator to ride the truck along with its normal crew, and pick up the trash along the block. When a safe distance from the target location, the investigator leaves the truck carrying the subject's trash. Sometimes insurance regulations or other policies may make this impractical. A modification would be to have one of the regular sanitation workers pick up and segregate the subject's trash as they travel their normal route. When safely out of the neighborhood, the investigator would meet the garbage truck and retrieve the trash. Allowing an employee of the waste disposal service to pick up the trash is not particularly desirable, because that person is the only individual able to certify that the trash came from the subject's container. Sometimes employees of waste disposal services are less than ideal witnesses when testifying in court.

If the trash service is handled by a private company, the company itself can be contacted and arrangements made. Another possibility that is faster is for investigators to contact the employees of the truck that normally services the area, and make a deal with them. Payment may be required to cement this kind of arrangement. If this is a problem, it may be possible that the senior employee on the truck could be opened as an informant of the law enforcement agency and paid. This would depend on the informant operation guidelines of the police agency. If a sanitation worker is opened as an informant, he also could be assigned to give regular reports concerning the subject's residence, including signs of abnormal activity and cars parked at the location. Of course, it may be possible that an investigator could ride on the back of a private waste disposal service truck and pick up the subject's trash, thereby making himself the witness who will testify in court, if required.

Trash covers involving a subject who resides in an apartment building are possible but are often difficult. Many apartment buildings have centralized trash containers in which many, if not all, of the tenants empty their trash. Segregating the subject's trash from that of other tenants can be difficult. Unless the trash can be directly linked to the subject, it cannot be used against him or her in court.

One investigator solved the apartment problem by visiting each apartment in the building on behalf of a nonexistent environmental group. He gave each tenant a box of "free" environmentally safe trash bags. The bags given to the subject were specially marked for identification so that the investigator could locate them in the community dumpster.

Another investigator solved the problem by conducting surveillance from an adjacent apartment. Every time he observed the subject dumping a bag of trash down the common garbage chute, he would drop down a marked bag immediately thereafter. He would then go to the master dumpster in the basement and locate his marked bag, which would be directly on top of the subject's bag.

Even if there is a mechanism for identifying the subject's trash within a community dumpster, various legal questions arise. Usually the dumpster is located on the grounds of the apartment complex. Sometimes it is actually located inside the building. The dumpster may be locked. The waste disposal service comes into the complex often to empty or possibly exchange the dumpster. This system differs from private homes, where residents place their trash cans on the curb or in an alley for pickup.

Investigators are strongly urged to contact their legal counsel before removing trash from an apartment building dumpster. Under normal circumstances, law enforcement personnel can legally take trash from an apartment complex container, if that container is located in such a way that it is available to the public even though it is on complex-owned property. In some instances, the building owner, manager, or engineer can be approached for assistance in locating and removing the subject's trash. Such people can usually make the trash available, provided that they have some form of "custody" over the building's trash, and the trash is truly abandoned. Such employees cannot enter a subject's apartment to retrieve trash for a law enforcement officer unless it is part of their normal job. For example, if the normal routine for an apartment building calls for a maid to enter each room and empty the waste cans along with making beds and other cleaning, she could make that trash available to a law enforcement agency. Clearly, this can be tricky, and the advice of legal counsel should be sought to ensure that nothing that is done will taint the evidence recovered through such a trash cover.

Trash covers conducted at a subject's place of employment can also face limitations. Many of the same problems that exist with respect to apartment complexes will also exist at the business locations. A situation that is unique to businesses is the fact that employee trash is often discarded in waste containers near an employee's workstation. A maid or janitorial employee usually empties the individual waste containers into a large dumpster that in turn is picked up by a waste disposal service. From a legal standpoint, the maid or janitor is the proper conveyor of the trash. Consequently, they can usually turn what they find in the containers over to a law enforcement agency. Of course, they ultimately would have to testify about the source of the trash. It would be questionable if a fellow employee could be asked by a law enforcement agency to rummage through the subject's waste container. Unless the trash container is plainly located in a public place, which is almost never the case, a law enforcement agent would not be able to take trash from an employee's container. Again, advice from legal counsel should be sought with respect to the particularities of a specific business location before a trash cover is conducted.

Handling the Fruits of a Trash Cover. Once the fruits of a trash cover have been obtained, they should be taken to a secure location for examination. Ideally, this location would be something like a parking lot or garage. Unless it can be assured that the trash consists of only paper and other "clean" items, the trash should not be brought into the law enforcement agency's offices until after it has been screened.

In one federal agency, an investigator brought into his office a plastic bag filled with the contents of a subject's garbage can. When he emptied the bag onto a desk, a large rat jumped out and ran through the office before disappearing into an elevator shaft. Fortunately, no one was bitten by the terrified animal.

For safety reasons, gloves should be worn when touching trash. Wearing gloves will also protect fingerprints or residues that might be on the items. Eye protection is also recommended. Items that are to be retained should be placed into clear plastic envelopes. This evidence should be marked and otherwise identified in accordance with departmental evidence procedures. At the very least, the retained items should be initialed and dated by the investigator and assigned an identification number. To examine documents without damaging them, place the plastic bags onto a photocopier, and make copies that can be studied. It is unnecessary to retain the entire fruits of a trash cover. Items that have no intelligence or evidence value should be discarded.

What Can Be Obtained From a Trash Cover. Trash covers can yield a wide variety of items. Some of these items can be evidentiary in nature, and should be retained. What else is kept depends upon the foresight of the investigator. All handwritten items should be studied in order to determine their value. Anything of a financial nature, including bills and receipts, should be carefully reviewed.

The following represents only a partial list of items that are typically found in residential or business trash:

- Canceled checks, deposit slips, bank statements
- Credit card receipts and bills
- Utility bills
- Telephone bills and statements showing numbers called
- Personal correspondence
- Medical bills, receipts, and prescription information
- Mortgage and rent receipts and related correspondence
- Evidence of debt
- Stock, bond, rental property, and other investment correspondence
- Tax information
- Gambling receipts, both legal and illegal
- Magazines, newspapers, periodicals
- Items associated with hobbies and special interests
- Business records
- Information reflecting car, boat, and aircraft ownership
- Correspondence related to clubs and professional groups
- Religious materials
- Remains of specialized foods
- Evidence of weapons ownership
- Indications of alcohol and drug use
- Evidence of illegal activities

Although many of the aforementioned items are of no direct evidentiary value in and of themselves, they could provide leads that might produce evidence of wrongdoing. A receipt paid by a credit card might reveal a heretofore unknown credit card. A subpoena to that credit card company could yield information about purchases of materials that might be germane to the investigation. Old telephone bills could reflect a person's contacts. A subpoena to the telephone company might not be able to recover older billing statements and consequently would not disclose these contacts.

In one terrorism investigation an officer was surprised to find that the subject dumped into his trash a box full of old records for the terrorist group in which he held a leading role. Unfortunately, subsequent regular weekly trash covers conducted during the following months failed to turn up anything of value. The investigator had apparently conducted his initial trash cover immediately after the subject had done some housecleaning.

Discarded food found in most residential trash may not seem pertinent; however, an investigator should still study it. Such waste might reveal an illness. It may also reveal that the subject might not be following the dietary code of his religion or ethnic background. A ham bone found in the trash of a supposedly devout Muslim fundamentalist could suggest that he is not what he presents himself to be to his associates. Such information may be of value if an interview is conducted with this person. Likewise, child pornography found in a person's trash might give an investigator leverage in an attempt to convince that person to become an informant. Information reflecting serious financial problems on the part of a subject could suggest that the person might be motivated to cooperate through promises of payment.

Unplanned Trash Covers

Trash covers need not involve only a subject's home or business garbage. The technique should target anything that the subject discards. During surveillance, investigators should be on the alert for the subject throwing things away. If possible, such items should be examined. Items deemed to be of possible value should be placed in a clear plastic envelope and handled as evidence. Although most items observed being discarded during a surveillance are going to be small and probably paper, such as receipts, notes, and food wrappings, in some instances the discarded items could be large and bulky.

During a surveillance, the subject was observed abandoning a large portable cooler. The surveillance team that recovered it determined that the cooler had been used to transport explosives.

A point frequently overlooked during surveillance is the issue of positive identification. During court proceedings, the most damaging observations introduced from surveillance investigators are going to be worthless if the defense can cloud the issue of the subject's identity. Probably the simplest way to avoid this problem is through fingerprint identification. If a surveillance agent can testify that he recovered a discarded item that was determined to contain the subject's fingerprints, it will be difficult for the defense to successfully argue that the surveillance team was actually following someone who "looked like" the subject, but was not really him.

People are often careless with respect to their residential and business trash. Many people are even worse with respect to what they discard in other locations. People leaving banks can be seen dumping deposit slips and other financial papers in nearby waste cans. Similarly, many people discard receipts before even leaving the store where they made the purchase. People can be seen placing trash from their cars into roadside waste cans.

Of course, there are some people who are security conscious and avoid using their home and business waste receptacles for anything but actual garbage. This creates a dilemma for them. Some might burn such waste, but this would be difficult for people who reside in apartments. Another alternative is for the person to take the materials to a distant location such as a public dump, a dumpster behind a supermarket, or a trash container located on a public street. A surveillance team watching such a trip should make an effort to recover this material. Indeed, a recovery effort should be made anytime a surveillance team observes a person making what appears to be a deliberate effort to dispose of something away from his residence and place of employment. Some people now have shredders in their homes and offices that can be used to destroy paper items. If the investigation is important enough, and it is believed that the shredded item is of significance, a crime laboratory may be able to reassemble the item.

Valuable trash can appear before investigators at any time. A subject may discard something during an interview that may prove to be of value. Sometimes it might be deliberate because the person fears that he will be searched. Many police officers are taught to search the rear seat of their patrol vehicles after transporting a prisoner to determine whether the prisoner had discarded something. In other instances, it might be carelessness, in which the person tosses away something like a matchbook that has a telephone number written on it.

People often leave things behind when they check out of hotel rooms. On occasion, the item might even be a forgotten article of clothing or an alarm clock. More likely it will be food containers, empty packages, and worthless discards. As valueless as these items may appear, they could still contain something of value for an investigator.

People frequently leave items behind when they move from an area that they have occupied for a period of time. Such areas could include: public

conveyances—airplanes, buses, railroad cars, taxis; restaurants; movie the-
aters, and other places of entertainment; park benches; gyms. If surveillance
personnel have the opportunity and can accomplish it securely, they should
check such areas after the person leaves.

People moving from residences frequently leave items behind. These
items can often be found in trash cans. Moving is a time for people to get rid
of things. Some decisions to abandon possessions are made at the very last
minute, when the person realizes that he does not have room in his vehicle
or he becomes just tired of packing. As a result, some of what is left behind
may be of great value to an investigator.

In one instance, a subject left behind various items of trash when he moved.
Included in the discards was a case of clandestine bomb-making manuals.

Final Comments Concerning
the Trash Cover Technique

Common sense should be used with respect to any trash cover. The fact
that a law enforcement officer can legally take a subject's discards does not
mean that he should take them. No law enforcement agency should require
its investigators to conduct trash covers during routine investigations. A trash
cover should be undertaken when conditions are right and legal questions
have been resolved. If taking a subject's trash will reveal the investigator's
interest in the subject, the trash should not be taken. If there is good reason
to believe that nothing of value is in the subject's trash, there is no reason
to risk trying to retrieve it. If taking the trash will cause embarrassment to
the law enforcement agency, it should not be taken. Certainly a trash cover
should not be conducted if it violates the law or an agency policy.

While sitting in a courtroom during a terrorism trial, an investigator
noticed that the subject and his attorneys were putting items into a
small waste paper container under the defense table. During the lunch
recess, the investigator took the contents of the waste container and
examined them. Nothing of value was found. However, a court employee
mentioned the incident to the prosecutor, who became very upset. The
prosecutor subsequently asked the judge to call a meeting with the
defense attorneys in which he explained what had happened. Although
a mistrial was not granted, the law enforcement agency looked bad, and
the judge became more inclined during the rest of the trial to listen to
defense allegations of improper police conduct.

Although it is not truly a trash cover per se, discards should be studied during the service of a search warrant. Investigators will usually do an excellent job searching a residence for whatever is listed in a search warrant. However, they sometimes neglect to look into trash cans within the house, or into the garbage cans outside the residence, even though the language of the search warrant is broad enough to include these containers. If the prosecutor thinks that it can be done, search warrants should specifically mention trash containers so that there will be no question regarding the legality of materials recovered from such locations, and so that investigators will know to look into such containers.

⓭ Pretext Telephone Calls

A pretext telephone call is a covert investigative technique that is used to gather information about a subject. In a pretext call, an investigator or someone representing the investigator places a telephone call to the subject, or someone close to the subject, in which the caller attempts to elicit information without telling the recipient that the caller is associated with a law enforcement agency. The information sought can be very specific, such as determining the subject's whereabouts, or it can be quite broad and include any question for which the investigator believes he can obtain an answer.

The pretext call has a place in law enforcement, but it is not a major investigative tool. Some investigators never use it. In the overall spectrum of investigations, the pretext call is probably used more to augment and enhance other techniques, such as surveillance or technical coverage, than it is to actually develop quality intelligence about the subject. Officers who use this technique often operate in the gray area of legal and ethical behavior.

Information Sought in Pretext Telephone Calls

The following illustrates the kinds of information that investigators often seek through pretext telephone calls.

Verification of a Subject's Location

This form of pretext call is often employed by a surveillance team that has not visually observed their target in some time. They are attempting to determine his or her whereabouts because they realize that, for security purposes, they cannot safely remain in the neighborhood for an indefinite period. Arrest teams and investigators attempting to serve a search warrant will use pretext calls to locate a subject. Law enforcement agencies planning to install microphones and other electronic coverage equipment will also use pretext calls to locate a person and to ensure that no one is inside a targeted location.

Determination of Personal Information

This form of pretext call is intended to learn personal data about the subject, including educational background, work history, family tree, and anything else an investigator needs to know. The investigator, however, must be sure to verify everything that the contacted person tells him through other techniques. It must be remembered that no one is obliged to provide accurate information during the course of a pretext telephone call.

Discovery of Future Plans

This form of pretext call is intended to determine what the subject plans to do in the future. In this context, the call is usually intended to augment and implement another investigative technique. A surveillance team may want to prepare for a fixed surveillance if it can determine where the subject intends to travel. A group of investigators who need to enter the subject's residence to install technical coverage will want to know when the subject will leave, if anyone else will remain at the address, and when the subject plans to return. An undercover investigator may want to have an encounter with the subject, and therefore needs to know the suspect's plans in order to arrange for the "accidental" meeting. It must be remembered that the recipient of a pretext call is under no obligation to provide accurate information during the course of the conversation. In fact, if the content of the call ends up as evidence in court, the investigator may have difficulty convincing the jury that he was even talking to the person he claims to have reached in the call.

Types of Pretext Telephone Calls

There are two basic forms of pretext telephone calls.

Simple Pretext Calls

These calls are usually one-question inquiries. They are commonly used in connection with surveillance coverage. Sometimes they are used in conjunction with the service of a search or arrest warrant. Little preparation is required for simple pretext calls. An investigator telephones the subject's residence and asks for someone. The subject responds that the person is not at that number, and the call is terminated. The investigator has verified that the subject is home. Another form of the simple pretext call is for an investigator to call the subject's place of employment and ask to speak to the subject. When the subject comes to the telephone and says "hello," the caller does not respond, and the subject assumes that the call was disconnected. The investigator has verified that the subject is at work.

A simple pretext telephone call can also be used to locate a fugitive. If the subject answers the telephone, the investigators know that he is at home, and they can plan their arrest accordingly. If the subject is not at home, the caller can attempt to locate him or determine his anticipated arrival by asking for that information from whoever answered the telephone. The investigator could even go so far as to leave a "safe" telephone number with the recipient, or a message in the subject's voice mail, asking for a return call.

Complex Pretext Telephone Calls

Complex pretext calls involve a certain amount of skill and patience. Many investigators are unable to perform them well. The person called is the subject or someone who can provide information about the subject. Usually the caller claims to be a friend or an associate of the subject, or he claims to have something in common with the subject. Sometimes the caller claims to be affiliated with a company, business, or organization that needs information about the subject. Some investigators claim to be conducting a survey. There are no set patterns for pretext calls—successful calls are tailored to the person called and to the specific information sought. If a pretext call is to develop the desired information, it must be convincing and reasonable. It should be fairly short, as most people are not willing to engage in a lengthy conversation with a stranger. The caller should rehearse the scenario in his mind before placing the call. He should try to anticipate the kind of questions that the recipient will ask so that he can respond in a believable manner.

Accuracy with Respect to
Pretext Telephone Call Information

Pretext telephone calls are one of the least credible investigative techniques that can be used. The investigator is, in most cases, using deception. The subject or other recipient of such a call is under no obligation to be truthful. In fact, they have many reasons for providing inaccurate and incomplete information. This is especially true if the pretext involves any kind of sales pitch or survey. Many people respond with rote answers like, "I gave at the office," "I already have the product," or "The survey does not apply to me because …" Some recipients claim that they are not the subject, but instead are a relative, friend, servant, house sitter, etc. As a result, the investigator often cannot even state with accuracy that the person with whom he spoke was the subject of the investigation.

What Should Be Avoided in Pretext Telephone Calls

The pretext call falls within the gray area of what is legal and ethical. To ensure that these lines are not crossed, investigators should avoid the following areas:

Claiming to Be a Professional. Investigators should not present themselves as clergy, physicians, counselors, attorneys, or journalists when placing pretext calls. All kinds of legal problems can arise if the judge learns that an investigator developed information by pretending to be a member of a profession that can claim some form of privilege. Additionally, an investigator should not claim to be a law enforcement officer during a pretext call. The courts might reason that an investigator who felt the need to "pretend" to be a law enforcement officer when in fact he was a law enforcement officer, was engaging in a questionable activity.

Giving Out False Information. Investigators placing pretext calls should avoid giving out false information, especially of a derogatory nature. For example, the caller identifies himself as being with the Board of Health. He states that a person with whom the subject has had sexual intercourse has been diagnosed with a sexually transmitted disease. The investigator wants to ask the subject some personal questions. Another example might involve a call to one of the subject's neighbors, in which the caller identifies himself as being with a collection agency that is trying to locate the subject in connection with a bad debt. Still another example might involve an officer speaking in a tough-sounding voice, asking one of the subject's relatives if the subject will be conducting a card game at his residence that night. If not, where will he be?

Offering Prizes and Rewards. Money talks, and many people will provide information in exchange for a prize. Investigators should avoid offering subjects or anyone else an award unless, of course, the law enforcement agency intends to give an award. A typical way to use this tactic is for the caller to claim to be conducting a survey and offering the person $25 if he cooperates. Of course, as part of the survey, the person will be asked to provide information that the investigator needs, such as place of birth or previous address.

Causing Innocent People to Take Overt Action. A typical ploy used by collection agencies is to call a target's neighbor and explain that they need to contact the target because a close relative has died. The caller explains that he has made repeated calls to the target's residence, but the number is always busy. He asks the neighbor to personally go to the target residence, and try to locate the subject, and have that person call the given number. This method often works because the target and his family do not suspect a neighbor who visits in order to convey a message. An investigator could use this same pretext, but it borders on the unethical. An investigator has no right to covertly ask an innocent person to conduct an investigation of his behalf, especially if it inconveniences or places them at risk.

Avoid Using a Specific Person's Identity. Obviously, an investigator placing a pretext call is not going to use his own name. Many would prefer not to give any identifying information. Under no circumstances should an investigator claim to be another actual person. This would be unethical and may be illegal. Depending on what is involved in the pretext, it could endanger the innocent person.

Avoid Threatening Anyone During a Pretext Call. Law enforcement officers have no right to call a subject or an innocent person under pretext and threaten them in any way. Similarly, investigators should not use pretext calls to harass anyone. Obscene calls should not be placed—they are illegal.

Conducting Interviews that Would Normally Require the Advice of Rights Concerning Self-Incrimination

This is a gray area and should be avoided. If it must be done, the pretext to be used should be cleared through the department's legal counsel or the prosecutor before it is used. Under normal circumstances, an investigator cannot use a pretext to deny a subject his or her constitutional rights. If enough evidence exists against a subject to require an investigator to advise him of his rights with respect to self-incrimination during an interview, that investigator cannot interrogate the subject using a telephone pretext about the criminal aspects of the case without advising him of his rights.

Improving Pretext Telephone Calls

Many people, including terrorists and hardened criminals, are more easily deceived by female callers than by male callers. For some reason, many people still fail to consider females when they think about police officers, and are therefore less suspicious of them. If no female officer is available, a female clerical worker might be employed to make the call.

People who have difficulty speaking English can often fool even the most security-minded people. A caller who begins a conversation in French, Chinese, Russian, or another language will often be able to hold a person on the line if they give the impression that they are struggling to communicate in English. People will try to help the person as best they can.

In one pretext call, an investigator who spoke Chinese held a subject on the telephone for 10 minutes as he "attempted to locate" another Chinese person. Not only did the pretext call determine that the subject was at his residence, it gave the surveillance team enough time to set up in his neighborhood so that he could be followed after he concluded the telephone call.

Investigators who sound like senior citizens are able to carry out successful pretext calls with many people. The pretext could revolve around a proposed senior citizens' center or expanding Medicare.

Surveys that involve a subject's neighborhood or block seem to work better than other ruses in getting people to talk. The issues might involve the creation of a block watch, problems with water pressure, or the need for better trash collection.

Sample Pretext Telephone Calls

Hello, this is Tom at the Glenrock Country Club. Is Mr. Jones there? No? Could you tell me how to reach him? Someone found a set of golf clubs in the parking lot. It looks like one of our members forgot to put them in the trunk of his car. Anyway, one of the caddies thought that they might belong to Mr. Jones. These are expensive clubs, and I'm sure that whoever lost them will soon discover them missing, and report a theft to police. It might be pretty embarrassing, since the clubs are sitting here in the clubhouse. Also, we would rather not have police running around the country club looking for a thief. Are you sure that you can't give me a number where I can contact Mr. Jones?

Hi, this is Terry Smith. I'm from Denver and I went to school with your son, Joe, several years ago at the University of Colorado. I'm getting ready to fly to England to attend a seminar, and I thought that maybe I could get together with Joe for dinner. I had his address in England, but lost it when I moved last year. Do you have it? In case he isn't home, could you also give me his work number?

Mr. Thompson, this is Tom Brown at the XYZ Survey Company. Our firm has been employed to conduct a canvass of the people living in your area concerning television viewing habits. The results of the survey will enable your cable company to better meet the needs of its subscribers. But first let me have some personal information, including your date of birth, employment, number of children, education …

Documenting Pretext Telephone Calls

Pretext telephone calls are an investigative technique and should be documented in the same way that the results of any other investigative technique are documented. The important thing about documenting a pretext call is that it must clearly reflect the fact that the interview was done under pretext.

Under no circumstances should a communication be placed in a case file that simply indicates that on a particular day the subject or another person contacted with respect to the subject, "advised that …" This is wrong because it implies that the person was interviewed and provided information to the investigator willingly. In fact, the person was unaware that he was talking with a law enforcement officer. It is likely that, had the person known this, he might not have provided that information. The overall credibility of the fruits of a pretext call is something lower than that of the results of most other investigative techniques; therefore, it is important for anyone reviewing the report to know the source of the information.

Pretext telephone calls done by surveillance teams and investigators trying to serve arrest and search warrants probably do not have to be documented, but there is no reason why they could not be recorded if an investigator chooses to do so. Some surveillance teams mention pretext calls in connection with their surveillance logs—possibly in a section titled "Notes" or "Other Investigative Activities." There is usually no reason to document attempted pretext calls that go unanswered because an unanswered telephone does not prove anything and does not even mean that there was no one at the residence.

In cases in which there are multiple case agents, such as task force investigations, it is a good idea to document every pretext telephone call that reaches someone. If this is not done, it might be possible that the technique could be overdone, thereby causing the subject to become concerned that someone is watching him. Surveillance teams should share information about the pretexts that they use during the coverage of a subject. A subject would probably become quite suspicious if he suddenly started receiving several calls each day for different unknown people when he had never before received such calls.

Pretext Telephone Calls and Caller ID Technology

In recent years, the use of Caller ID technology has expanded throughout the country, and has become almost a routine part of people's telephone service. Many individuals regularly check their Caller ID before even engaging in a conversation. Law enforcement agencies frequently have protected their telephones from being identified by using "blocks." Recipients are generally leery of "blocked" calls that they receive and will not answer. An investigator planning to conduct a pretext call should avoid using any telephone that will reveal his personal telephone number or the number of a police agency or surveillance lookout. Some agencies have "safe" telephones located in the station or off site that trace to a dummy company or an address that cannot be easily traced, such as a large apartment complex.

To avoid being identified through Caller ID, an investigator might place a pretext call from a pay telephone or from a telephone located in a corporate entity. Calling from a business such as a bar or bowling alley can protect the caller. Regardless of what method is employed, to avoid being identified through Caller ID, the pretext must match the location of the telephone. An investigator calling from a bowling alley can certainly ask for the subject by name or for some unknown person, and not appear to be particularly suspicious. He might have problems, however, claiming to be conducting a senior citizens' survey or verifying a floral delivery while calling from that location.

When cellular phones initially became popular, some investigators were able to safely use them to place pretext calls. Today, Caller ID will inform the recipient that the call is emanating from such a phone and will provide its number. This does not mean that a cell phone cannot be used. However, the pretext being employed should be logical. A person would be suspicious if someone trying to sell magazines or carpet cleaning was using a cell phone.

The Internet

A more recent development has been the Internet as a vehicle for communication. Like the telephone, an investigator could make pretext inquiries with someone over the Internet. However, he should not expect to be warmly received. Unsolicited e-mail (also called "spam") has so invaded cyberspace that many people ignore any messages they receive from unknown parties. Many people have installed blocks to prevent spam from ever reaching them. Fear of computer viruses has also caused many people to delete all e-mail messages they receive that cannot be readily identified. Investigators must be aware that even if they receive a response to an e-mail, they will have no way of knowing who sent the e-mail or if the information sent is accurate. Entering into a chat room in an effort to develop information from or about a subject can present a myriad of problems. It could be considered an undercover operation, and therefore would have to meet the law enforcement agency's policies and procedures for such a project. Most law enforcement agencies have yet to formulate firm policies governing Internet use. Investigators who choose this medium for pretext inquiries should first seek the advice of their legal counsel. In the absence of concrete policies, the general comments relating to pretext telephone calls would seem to apply to Internet pretext contacts as well.

Summary

The pretext telephone call is a lesser investigative technique that can be used to develop valuable leads. It is usually used to augment other investigative techniques—particularly surveillance. The technique should be used with care because it is not always possible to know with whom the officer is speaking. The use of Caller ID has limited the value of pretext calls, because investigators must use telephones that are listed to believable names in order to gain cooperation. Furthermore, the technique operates in the gray area of legal and ethical standards. If the technique is used, any useful information obtained should be documented to reflect how the information was developed. The Internet can be used in a similar manner; however, spam and viruses have caused people to ignore unknown e-mail communications. Furthermore, many law enforcement agencies have yet to develop standards with respect to developing information through the Internet.

⑭ Physical Evidence

Evidence is anything that provides material information on which a conclusion or proof may be based. It consists of information provided by witnesses and by facts developed from real objects. The latter form is called *physical evidence.*

Although physical evidence can play an important part in most criminal cases, it plays an even more significant role in terrorism investigations. A government attorney would have difficulty successfully prosecuting a terrorist case without some physical evidence. In terrorism matters, the defense often challenges every aspect of the case. Eyewitnesses, many of whom are already on edge because they fear the terrorists, will be subjected to rigorous cross-examination. Any deviation in their account or any bias that is exhibited can cause a witness's credibility to be damaged. To counter this, prosecutors want to have physical evidence that can support the eyewitness's account. Physical evidence does not usually change. An expert who testifies about his examination of an article of physical evidence is not likely to modify what was contained in his initial report. Most experts are seasoned courtroom veterans. They are not going to be swayed by intense cross-examination and they are not going to be intimidated by threats. Experts know that whatever they found on an article of evidence will also be found by other experts.

Physical evidence can be found at any time during an investigation. Some cases are actually based on articles of physical evidence. A citizen finds a gun in a park. A jogger finds a purse on a path. A patrol officer finds a car with its ignition pulled. Investigations to discover the circumstances that caused these things to be found are begun. Investigators should always be on the alert for physical evidence, especially in terrorism cases. As the case continues, an investigator may recover items of physical evidence from witnesses, victims, or informants. He may also procure them through search warrants, consent searches, court orders (usually for records), and abandonment. At the time of an arrest, the officer may recover physical evidence from a search of the subject.

When items are taken during the service of a search warrant, a list of such items must be left at the scene or with the person responsible for that scene. Many agencies leave receipts for items that they are given voluntarily. This is especially true if the items are of value, such as jewelry or currency, or if the item belongs to someone other than the subject. Some items of evidence

A Consent to Search Form Used by the FBI.

_____
(Date)

_____
(Location)

    I, _____, having been informed of my constitutional right not to have a search made of the premises herinafter mentioned without a search warrant and of my right to refuse to consent to such a search, hereby authorize _____, and _____, Special Agents of the Federal Bureau of Investigation, United States Department of Justice, to conduct a complete search of my premises located at _____. These agents are authorized by me to take from my premises any letters, papers, materials, or other property which they may desire.

    This written permission is being given me to the above-named Special Agents voluntarily and without threats or promises of any kind.

_____
(SIGNED)

WITNESSES: _____

_____

_____

_____

---

can be purchased. An investigator may buy a book published by a group in which it explains how to elude police. If that officer finds a suspect using the same techniques as outlined in the publication, he might be able to use that as probable cause to indicate that the suspect is a clandestine member of the group.

Some physical evidence can be used to develop a case without an expert examination. A videotape taken by a store security camera, which depicts the subject purchasing the knife that was used in the crime, may stand on its own. It would support the eyewitness report of the cashier who has identified the subject as the purchaser of the knife. A receipt for the purchase of the knife recovered in the subject's garage may also stand on its own. However, an investigator may want to send it to a crime laboratory in an attempt to locate the subject's fingerprints on it.

In fraud cases, canceled checks are physical evidence. They very well may stand on their own. However, an investigator may want to have a crime laboratory attempt to locate the fingerprints or the DNA of the subject on these instruments. Furthermore, the investigator may find it valuable to have a handwriting expert examine them in order to have an expert testify in court that the signatures were made by the subject.

Even in situations in which an examination can be conducted on evidence at the scene, it is often a good idea to send the item to the crime laboratory. For example, many fingerprints can be lifted and "read" at the scene. Investigators specializing in drugs often carry kits of chemicals that can be mixed with suspicious materials to prove that they are illegal drugs. In both instances a professional crime laboratory may be able to go even further than the on-scene analyst. A laboratory may be able to locate more and better fingerprints on the item. The laboratory might be able to state with certainty the exact percentage of the narcotic that was present in the suspicious material. Regardless, the crime laboratory examiner almost certainly has better credentials within his or her field of specialty than does the average street investigator, and therefore has greater credibility in court.

As previously stated, physical evidence can be extremely important in terrorism cases. An investigator should go the extra step with respect to evidence that he or she has recovered. If there is something that a crime laboratory can do to enhance the value of the evidence, the investigator should ask the laboratory to do so.

Steps Involved in Handling Physical Evidence

Assuming that a crime laboratory will be asked to conduct an examination, there are generally five steps involved in handling physical evidence:

1. Collecting the evidence
2. Packaging and shipping the evidence to a crime laboratory

Chicago Terrorist Task Force Investigators with the thousands of articles of physical evidence gathered against the FALN during a terrorist conspiracy case in the mid-1980s.

3. Expert examination of the evidence at the crime laboratory

4. Follow-up investigation based on the laboratory's report

5. Presentation of the evidence in court

Collecting Evidence

Many believe that this is the most important step in the physical evidence process. If the investigator errs here, everything else is for naught. If the evidence is procured illegally, nothing done at a later date will correct it. The prosecutor will never be able to use it in court, no matter how significant it is. Conversely, if an item is not taken when available, it is likely that it will not be recoverable at a later time. Over a career, many officers have said to themselves at one time or another, "I wish I had picked up that item when I had the chance." Not every item observed during the course of an investigation can be collected, but an investigator must use good judgment and not ignore items that may have value.

Physical evidence must be collected properly. Jamming something interesting into a coat pocket or sticking it in the trunk of a patrol car is not the proper way to recover evidence. There are exceptions, however. An investigator watching a subject may pick up an item that the subject threw out of his car window. The surveillance officer continues on with his assignment. No reasonable person would expect the surveillance officer to suspend his mission, put on gloves, initial and date the item, and place it in a bag. However, they would expect the officer to maintain immediate control of the evidence and correctly process it at the conclusion of his assignment.

To a certain extent, circumstances will dictate how evidence is handled. Normally an investigator will wear gloves when picking up an article of physical evidence. At the very least, the investigator will restrict his handling of the evidence so as not to obliterate fingerprints or contaminants on the item. The evidence will be initialed and dated by the recovering officer and will be sealed in a container—usually a plastic bag. A written report describing the item and the details surrounding its recovery will also be prepared.

In terrorism cases, a great deal of physical evidence is gathered at crime scenes, including bombings and arsons. The crime scene is explained in more detail in Chapter 15. Also in terrorism cases, physical evidence is often gathered pursuant to searches made on safe houses, bomb factories, storage lockers, and the residences and vehicles of subjects. While there is certainly nothing wrong with case officers and their assistants performing such searches, it is strongly recommended in terrorist cases that these searches be conducted by crime scene specialists.

In virtually any of the more than 50 metropolitan areas in which there is an established terrorist task force, crime scene specialists will be available or can be brought in from other areas. The FBI can also be asked to bring in crime scene teams to conduct such searches in terrorism investigations.

Chain of custody is one of the most important concepts in the field of law enforcement. It begins at the time that an item of evidence is initially recovered and continues until the evidence is destroyed, returned, or otherwise disposed of in accordance with the law. Essentially, this principle means that someone in a position of authority must have direct control over that article of evidence during the entire time that it is a part of the investigation. The theory is that if law enforcement cannot guarantee protection of the evidence, then no one can state with certainty that the item presented in court is in fact the same item that was initially recovered. No one can state that the item examined in the laboratory

Dynamite and other explosives discovered in a Weatherman bomb factory in Chicago, Illinois in 1970.

is the same item that was brought into the police station by the investigator. Further, if the item was not under constant protection, no one can positively state that it was not damaged, altered, or otherwise contaminated.

Defense attorneys will concentrate on breaking the chain of custody with respect to important items of physical evidence. The best way investigators can combat this maneuver is to handle the evidence correctly. Most agencies establish a property log that accompanies evidence wherever it goes. This log should clearly identify the person responsible for each item of evidence at all times. The first name on the log will be the name of the officer who recovered the evidence. Later names will include the laboratory experts who examined it (and who also usually initial it), and the prosecutor who brings it into court. It will also show who had custody of the item in between these events, which are frequently the longest periods of time. A department will usually have an evidence storage room controlled by an evidence custodian who may or may not be a sworn officer. No one can have access to the evidence without going through this person. Consequently, the evidence is totally protected. Anyone who looks at the evidence for any reason will have his or her name entered in the log.

Packaging and Shipping of the Evidence to a Crime Laboratory

Most law enforcement agencies have a crime laboratory that serves their department. In many cases, it is the state crime laboratory, although in some situations it may be a county or local laboratory. Some areas have several crime laboratories, each of which specializes in a certain criminal offense, such as drugs or weapons. Some law enforcement agencies also use private laboratories to perform certain examinations.

The FBI laboratory also performs examinations for local law enforcement agencies. In connection with terrorism investigations, local law enforcement agencies will probably find that the FBI is the best laboratory to handle their evidence. Not only is the FBI laboratory one of the most respected in the world, it also has the ability to compare evidence on a national basis and, to some extent, an international basis. The FBI laboratory can compare bomb fragments recovered in a California bombing with those recovered in bombings that occurred in Kansas and Florida. State and local crime laboratories cannot do this because they usually do not receive evidence from outside their state. The FBI laboratory is also a full-service facility. Few crime laboratories in the country can perform as many different examinations as the FBI laboratory. Finally, the FBI laboratory maintains relations with law enforcement laboratories around the world, which allows for the sharing of information and for evidence comparisons.

Early crime laboratories were able to perform only a small number of examinations. As a result, veteran investigators could specifically request that the laboratory perform the tests that they required in connection with the case. Today technology is advancing so rapidly that it is difficult for investigators to keep up-to-date. Most police academies provide their new recruits with an overview of what their laboratory can do for them. However, it is likely that even within the period of a year some of this information will become dated.

In view of this, most investigators would be better served if they would explain their needs to the crime laboratory rather than ask for the lab to conduct a specific test. Instead of asking the laboratory to conduct the XYZ test on an article of clothing, an officer might ask the laboratory to conduct an examination to locate blood on the clothing.

Requests for laboratory examination should be accompanied by documentation that explains the case and that requests the kinds of examinations that are required. Sending in an item with a general request to conduct appropriate investigation may not yield the best results. The laboratory needs to know if the investigator wants a check done for fingerprints, a hair and fiber examination, a search conducted for indented writing, handwriting examination, the item studied for internal content, etc. Specific requests are important because an incorrect order of examinations can make certain tests difficult to perform. As an example, a item that has undergone a test that breaks it down or subjects it to alteration may not be able to be subsequently searched for fingerprints.

Some physical evidence must be destroyed because it is too dangerous to be retained. Explosives, volatile materials, chemicals, and poisons can fall into this category. Usually small samples of the material can be safely retained for laboratory examination. Crime laboratories will give instructions on doing so on a case-by-case basis. Some will even send special containers to be used to preserve samples. Although the danger may be so great in some cases that immediate destruction is necessary, it is best to obtain a court order before any material is destroyed. This is very important in the subsequent court case. A defense attorney may be able to make some inroads in the case by arguing that the evidence against his client was destroyed and therefore should not be used against his client. This argument usually goes nowhere if the destruction was ordered by a judge. In fact, the prosecution can influence a jury by reminding them that even a judge thought that the subject's material was so dangerous that it had to be destroyed. If the material to be destroyed is likely to explode or burn, the law enforcement agency might be best served by videotaping the destruction. Only a technician qualified to handle dangerous materials should facilitate their destruction.

In one terrorist airplane hijacking case, the subject used a modified military explosive device to commit the crime. Because the device had been altered, a judge found it to be highly dangerous, and ordered that it be destroyed. The subsequent destruction was videotaped and later presented in court. The film showed an explosion of such a great magnitude that the trial judge greatly increased the subject's sentence.

Under no circumstances should dangerous materials be shipped to any crime laboratory without consulting that laboratory for shipping and handling instructions. In many instances it is a violation of state or federal statute to ship such items, particularly by air. Consequently, it is important that a law enforcement agency act only in accordance with laboratory instructions.

When an investigator sends evidence to the crime laboratory, he or she is hoping that the facility can do a variety of things, including:

Prove that specific actions took place as believed;

Confirm and prove an account given by a witness, victim, defendant, or other party;

Refute and disprove an account given by a witness, victim, defendant, or other party;

Provide information that will identify the perpetrator;

Provide leads that will enable the investigator to develop information to solve the case.

Expert Examination of Evidence in the Crime Laboratory

Crime laboratories can do many things in connection with evidence, including:

Photographing the evidence. This can include blowup shots from every angle. If the item can be taken apart, the photographs can show the item together as well as in various stages of dismantling. The laboratory can also create huge display photographs that can be used as exhibits in court.

Sketching, diagramming, and drawing the evidence as appropriate. A laboratory may be able to create a diagram of an explosive device as it appeared prior to its detonation. They might be able to build an exact copy of the device using the same components.

Taking fingerprints from an item. Modern advancements in this area have made it possible for fingerprints to be identified on materials never before thought to retain them. Investigators should not be reluctant to request a fingerprint examination just because the item does not appear capable of holding a print.

Determining the structure of an item, if appropriate.

Identifying the creator and manufacturer of an item. This can be extremely important because it may enable investigators to ultimately identify the purchaser of the item. An explosive device may have been housed in a gym bag. The laboratory may be able to identify the producer of that gym bag from examining the remnants recovered at the crime scene.

Tracing an item to its origin. Explosives can be identified and traced to their manufacturer. Some are even uniquely coded so that the date and location of the production facility can be identified. Bullets can be similarly traced. Weapons can be traced through serial numbers. Crime laboratories are often able to detect numbers that have been obliterated.

Locating and identifying blood. Until the latter part of the twentieth century, crime laboratories were able to do little more than type blood and identify the species of origin. Presently, crime laboratories can conduct DNA examinations that can identify the person. Obviously, the laboratory must have a known sample of the person's blood in order to make a positive identification. Absent that, the laboratory can only identify the blood by unique characteristics that can later be compared with the suspect's.

Identifying body fluids and, in many instances, also matching them to a specific person through DNA examinations.

Identifying the composition of paper and writing fluids and locating indented writings and images on paper and similar products that were left when someone wrote or stamped something on a sheet that was once above the item. Identifying typewriters and facsimile machines.

Identifying handwriting.

Recovering information from computers, including data that had been deleted.

Locating and identifying hairs, fibers, and other components, including dust.

Determining how events occurred at a crime scene. A crime laboratory will be able to determine a bullet's angle of entry from examining items that it penetrated, including windows, furniture, or even a body.

Identifying chemicals, poisons, or anything else that is desired from an item of evidence.

Offering explanations about how something could or could not have happened.

Creating mockups, diagrams, and other displays depicting evidence for use in court

Follow-up Investigation Based Upon the Crime Laboratory's Report

All crime laboratories will provide the submitting law enforcement agency with a copy of its findings. The report will be written in such a way that it can be turned over to the defense as part of their discovery. Some laboratories will submit supplemental pages in which they will make suggestions about additional investigations that can be conducted. Some will offer suggestions and opinions based upon their examination of the evidence. Some will advise that additional comparisons can be made if the investigator is able to locate certain other items. For example, an examiner might report that there are distinct marks where the metal was cut. If the shears can be located, the laboratory will be able to make a positive identification.

Laboratory reports should be quickly and thoroughly reviewed by investigators. All logical leads that can be gleaned from the report should be identified and set. In many instances, logical leads that are not covered will come back to haunt the investigator when he or she prepares for trial. A knowledgeable prosecutor will try to anticipate any question that a defense attorney might raise in court. Even if the laboratory report is clear and cannot be refuted, the fact that an obvious lead was not addressed might be what the defense attorney can attack in order to dilute the impact of the laboratory's findings.

Some investigations, particularly terrorism matters, can go on for a long time. Many months, or even years, are not unusual for such cases. During this time several things occur. New evidence, both in the form of physical evidence and from witnesses, develops. New scientific technology also develops. In view of these factors, an investigator may wish to revisit his or her evidence. He or she may find that comparisons that were not possible when the evidence was initially examined are now possible. Perhaps new suspects have been developed, or new evidence has been recovered. By checking with the laboratory, the investigator may find that they now have a device that can perform a test that was not available when the evidence was first examined. If these situations exist, the investigator may ask the laboratory to reexamine the evidence in light of the new developments.

Presentation of Evidence in Court

The initial witness to present evidence in court will be the person who recovered it. This could be a law enforcement officer, but it may be someone else. The investigator who received the evidence would be the next logical witness. However, the defense may stipulate to this. If the evidence was sent to a crime laboratory, the expert from that facility who examined it will probably be the next witness. If his testimony is damaging, the defense attorney may not question him at all for fear that he will only magnify the impact of the damage done to his client, or the defense attorney may question the witness's findings. In terrorism cases, the prosecutor should expect a challenge to the evidence and perhaps even to the very integrity of the expert. This is quite risky, because the laboratory scientist is an expert in his or her field, and is usually a courtroom veteran. The defense attorney is more likely to try to attack the person who recovered the evidence in the first place or to challenge the chain of custody. If he is successful in either tactic, it is likely that the evidence will be ruled inadmissible and the expert will never be called to the stand. Laboratory experts can help the case by creating exhibits that can be brought into court to make it easier for the jury to understand. A mock-up of the bomb can help the jury to see how components similar to those found in the subject's home could be utilized in an explosive device.

When to Dispose of Physical Evidence

Following the trial and any subsequent appeals, the evidence should be properly disposed of or returned to its rightful owner. With respect to terrorism cases, investigators may desire to take a much more cautious view with respect to the destruction of evidence. If the terrorist group involved in the case continues to exist, it may be worthwhile to retain the evidence unless it is so specific to the case in question that it would have no other value. The evidence could conceivably be used in subsequent cases conducted against the group. For example, if part of the evidence was a set of diagrams used by the group to construct their explosive devices, it would be wise for an agency to retain these diagrams. It is possible that another part of the group would use the same plans for other devices. The diagrams might be able to prove some kind of conspiracy case against the other bombers. New technology is constantly developing. Articles of evidence that failed to yield fingerprints or significant markings when initially studied by the laboratory may be returned to the laboratory for re-examination using newer technology. Even if the statute of limitations has expired on the specific terrorist attack, it might be possible to use any new findings in some form of conspiracy case against the members of a terrorist group.

Summary

Physical evidence is extremely important in terrorism cases, because it supports the fruits of other investigative techniques. It is also difficult for defense attorneys to challenge physical evidence if the chain of custody has been maintained and a qualified expert examined it.

15 The Crime Scene

There are a variety of ways in which official investigations begin. One of the most common is with the commission of a crime. Reacting to a crime is not what most law enforcement officers would choose. They would prefer to prevent the crime from occurring in the first place, and would like to apprehend the offenders during the planning stages or when they actually commit the crime. This is particularly true with respect to terrorist attacks, because these crimes are often aimed at the government and are intended at least in part to show that the government is powerless to stop the activities of the group. Worse, they are intended to generate fear.

The crime scene is the location where illegal activity has occurred. It could be inside a building or in an open area outside. It could be in a private vehicle or in a public bus. It may be a very small area, or it could happen in a vast expanse. There could be many observers, or there could be no eyewitnesses. The crime scene could be "fresh," in the sense that law enforcement officers came upon it as the crime was occurring or had just taken place, or it could be "stale," in that hours or even days had elapsed before officers came upon the scene. The crime scene could be relatively undisturbed when officers arrived, or it could be badly contaminated. It could be littered with apparent evidence, or it could appear to be devoid of anything of value. Regardless of the circumstances, the crime scene can be extremely important with respect to solving the crime. In terrorism cases some of the most valuable evidence is likely to come from the scene of the attack. If nothing else, photographs of destruction and damaged items can have an impact on a jury hearing a terrorist case.

Problems Facing Law Enforcement Officers at the Crime Scene

Upon arriving at a crime scene, investigators face many difficulties. They must first determine exactly what has happened. An explosion does not necessarily mean that a bomb detonated, and it may not mean that a crime has occurred. A person lying on the street bleeding might have been attacked, or could have accidentally fallen. A report of a gun being fired could have many meanings to a responding officer. A fire does not necessarily have to be an arson.

Helping people who need immediate attention is something that law enforcement officers should prioritize upon arriving at the scene of a crime. This often cannot be accomplished until the investigator has ascertained what has happened. Frequently the responding officer does not even know that someone needs assistance until he has talked with witnesses and victims at the scene.

Attempting to identify and apprehend the perpetrators is likely to be the next priority for many investigators once they have determined that a crime has indeed occurred. Often the same individuals who provided information about the nature of the situation are the people who will provide the most valuable leads about those responsible for the crime.

The crime scene must also be addressed immediately. Its importance in the overall investigation will vary greatly, depending upon the nature of the criminal offense. It is not likely that there will be much in the way of a crime scene investigation in conjunction with a purse-snatching unless the victim has been badly injured or killed, or unless it is clear that the perpetrator left some incriminating evidence behind. By contrast, a terrorist bombing will require a very thorough crime scene investigation in an effort to develop clues about the perpetrators and the victims and about the nature of the explosive device. Crime scenes can yield extraordinary evidence if they are conducted properly. All too often, however, manpower shortages and other problems make it difficult for agencies to conduct good crime scene investigations except in major cases. As many victims of home burglaries, vandalism, and car thefts have found, police agencies do not always conduct thorough crime scene investigations with respect to these incidents.

The owner of a recovered stolen van was told by local police to take his vehicle home from the impound lot, despite the fact that there were several bullets lodged in the fender and blood was spattered on the interior carpet. A widow whose home was burglarized was told by the responding officer that she should keep the broken screwdriver that was found jammed in her door lock as a "souvenir."

In more significant cases, particularly terrorism matters, thorough crime scene investigations should be conducted. If, for some reason, a local law enforcement agency is unable to conduct a good crime scene investigation in conjunction with a terrorist attack, that agency should contact a federal agency, such as the FBI, for assistance.

Often in terrorist bombings, arsons, rocket attacks, and other similarly violent incidents, it is easy for bystanders and even law enforcement officers to conclude that nothing of value could possibly be found in the rubble. There appears to be too much damage for any evidence to have survived. Of course, as the crime scene investigations conducted following the 1993 World Trade Center bombing and the 1995 Murrah Federal Building bombing clearly demonstrated, outstanding evidence can be recovered from what appears to be total destruction. In fact, important evidence was actually discovered within hours in both of these bombings. Many professional bomb technicians operate under the assumption that "everything that was there before the explosion is there after it—although possibly in a different configuration and location."

The crime scene is more than just the exact location where the crime occurred. It can also include the areas adjacent to, above, and below that location. In addition, it may include anything that has passed through the area. The scope of the crime scene will depend on the nature of the crime. In the case of a simple assault, in which one man punched another in the jaw and then ran from the scene, the crime scene is pretty much limited to the specific spot where the punch occurred. The investigation, however, could extend past the crime scene as the officers attempt to locate the perpetrator. For example, they may follow the offender's footprints from the crime scene. In the case of a terrorist bombing, the crime scene will certainly involve the seat of the explosion. However, it will also include adjacent areas where debris was thrown. It will probably include anything above the seat of the explosion, such as trees or nearby buildings. It will involve the earth below the explosion, including subway lines and tunnels. Anything that was traveling through the area at the time of the explosion, such as a vehicle or a passerby on foot, could become a part of the crime scene by virtue of debris penetrating them. Even the bodies of victims are a part of the crime scene.

Protecting the crime scene from contamination can be a key factor to building a case against the perpetrators. Evidence is often left by the offenders. If it can be recovered in a manner that permits it to be brought into court, it can result in a conviction. However, law enforcement often faces a series of immediate problems in guarding such an area following a crime, especially a bombing or an arson perpetrated by terrorists. Some of these problems include:

Rescuing and assisting the injured;

Dealing with immediate dangers—including fires, unsafe structures, toxins, gas leaks, broken water mains, downed power lines, dangerous offenders still in the area, etc.;

Checking on and evacuating neighboring locations as required;

Quickly developing enough information to enable an immediate law enforcement response—including locating and interviewing eyewitnesses;

Dealing with property owners who may be less than cooperative. This could include both the victim location and neighboring properties. These problems may require advice from the department's legal counsel or the prosecutor's office. Depending upon the circumstances, search warrants may have to be obtained;

Searching for secondary devices in the case of a terrorist attack or a bombing;

Addressing and handling rumors or threats of impending disaster and of additional attacks in the case of a terrorist incident;

In the case of a terrorist incident, responding to attacks at other locations

Most of these situations require some penetration of the crime scene, although from a forensic standpoint it is best that only an evidence recovery team should have access to the area. Many crime scene specialists have watched anxiously from the sidelines as firefighters have washed down a crime scene, bomb technicians have moved objects while searching for secondary devices, and utility workers have trampled other objects as they have attempted to cap gas, electric, and water lines.

Despite all the problems confronting them, law enforcement officers must strive to protect and preserve the crime scene as best they can. Entry into the crime scene should be restricted to those with proper authorization.

Filming or videotaping the crime scene is an excellent way to begin the investigation. This should be done as soon as possible. Law enforcement filming should consist of both still photos and video. Logs should be maintained so that the pictures can be identified later. Noting the exact time that the pictures were taken is important because people subsequently entering the crime scene could move or otherwise disturb items. The latest telephone technology should enable officers at the scene to send photos back to their headquarters or a command center to provide superiors with immediate visual information of the crime scene. Charting and mapping the crime scene is also a valuable initial step. Depending upon the nature of the crime, exact measurements can be extremely important.

Someone should be assigned to locate any film that may have been taken before police photographers and crime scene specialists arrived. News photographers and reporters and freelancers often get to the location shortly after the crime and take pictures. With the twenty-first-century popularization of the cell phone camera and the introduction of very inexpensive video cameras, it is now very likely that citizens in the area of any important incident will have also taken pictures. Consequently, any witness who is interviewed should be specifically asked if he took pictures, or if he knows anyone else who filmed the scene.

When to Begin the Crime Scene Investigation

Timely evidence collection is important but should be tempered with common sense and safety concerns. Sending crime scene specialists into a bombed structure that is on the verge of collapse is foolhardy. Similarly, directing them into a crime scene that is contaminated with asbestos is also unsafe. On the other hand, a crime scene investigation cannot be delayed without encountering potential legal problems with respect to the evidence. This is especially true if the crime scene is on private property. If too much time is allowed to pass between the incident and the search, the courts may rule that the law enforcement agency should have obtained a search warrant. There is no specific definition with respect to "too much time." As a general rule, the law enforcement agency should begin its crime scene investigation as soon as is reasonably safe and feasible. If the bombing took place on a Friday evening, an agency might be able to defend delaying its crime scene investigation until the next morning at daybreak. Similarly, they might be able to justify a delay until a storm has ended. However, an agency would have difficulty trying to justify a delay until Monday morning on the basis that it would preclude them having to pay overtime compensation if crime scene specialists were called in over the weekend.

Another problem associated with a delay in conducting the crime scene investigation involves both contamination and decay. Things can change over time. Wind can blow evidence away or bring contaminants into the scene. Heavy rain could wash away footprints. "Wet" items, like those splattered with blood, can dry. If the crime scene is permitted to sit unattended for a period of time, a defense attorney could argue that the evidence is tainted because the scene could have deteriorated or become contaminated in the interim. The defense attorney will probably win his argument if it can be shown that the law enforcement agency failed to adequately protect the crime scene during that period.

At about 10:00 p.m. one evening, a bomb exploded next to the rear alley door of a restaurant. The crime scene area was very dark, and it was raining heavily when investigators arrived at the scene. A crime scene investigation was begun immediately. Investigators used flashlights and car headlights as they spent the night in an unsuccessful effort to locate anything of value as evidence.

The example above is a situation in which a search should not have been conducted immediately following the incident. The restaurant owner was cooperative and gave permission for the search. The alley was on the owner's property, and therefore could have easily been sealed at each end, ensuring that no one gained entry. The search could have been delayed until the next morning when it was light and the rain had stopped. As it was, the investigators packed up their equipment at daybreak and left the scene. Because of the dark, the crime scene photographs were largely useless. Between the rain and investigators walking in the area for eight hours, the crime scene bore little resemblance to what was there immediately following the incident. The alley's configuration was such that the investigators could probably have strung tarps over the crime scene to protect it from the rain.

Beginning the Crime Scene Search

There is no place in modern law enforcement for haphazard crime scene work. Officers wandering around a crime scene picking up an item here and an item there is unsatisfactory. The crime scene should be organized and coordinated even before people conducting the investigation enter the area. When entry is made into the crime scene, the investigators doing it should know exactly what they are supposed to do. 'Wandering around like a tourist" should never be anyone's assignment.

Investigators entering the crime scene should be properly attired and equipped. Clothing, including foot coverings, should be clean and not contaminated with materials from previous crime scenes, practice drills, or from crime laboratories. The same should apply to any tools brought into the crime scene. Gloves should be worn. Depending on the nature of the crime scene, protective equipment for the head, ears, nose, and mouth should be used. Many investigators who arrived at the World Trade Center crime scene in New York following the September 11, 2001 attack, failed to wear adequate respirators, and subsequently experienced a variety of lung-related health problems. Personnel should do nothing to contaminate the crime scene. They should not smoke or eat within the confines of the crime scene.

Evidence at the crime scene should be carefully collected in an organized manner. Ideally, the crime scene should be divided into blocks or squares prior to the investigation. This is often done on a sketch pad, on which someone charts the crime scene and divides it into sections. Each specialist should have a specific assignment and should remain in that area unless reassigned by the crime scene coordinator. Even when a significant piece of evidence is uncovered, it should not disrupt the work of the other investigators. Evidence should be initialed by the investigator who recovered it. It should also be dated and assigned a unique identification number. It should be packaged and the contents of the package should be recorded in a log. Ultimately, the evidence will be forwarded to a crime laboratory where it will undergo whatever study is appropriate, including fingerprint analysis.

Crime Scene Witnesses

Interviews with witnesses and victims of crimes must be immediately conducted by the initial investigators arriving at the scene. These interviews need not be in-depth at this point. The initial responders must determine what happened and learn about the possible perpetrators, victims, and even about other witnesses who may have already left the scene. This information is needed to enable departmental administrators to effectively deploy their officers with respect to the overall investigation. If there are many possible witnesses in the area, priority must be given to those who appear to have the most information of value. A mistake that often occurs on the part of initial responders is that they fail to obtain sufficient background information on the people they interview. Consequently, it becomes difficult to locate these people for a second interview.

Many of the possible witnesses to a crime are unable to provide any information of value to law enforcement investigators. The fact that people were near a crime scene does not necessarily mean that they saw or heard anything. Fortunately, there are often some people in the vicinity who are able to provide information. These witnesses usually fall into two general categories:

1. People who provide direct information concerning the crime or its perpetrators. These people can often provide testimony in court if required.

2. People who provide indirect information about the crime and its perpetrators. These are the people who have not actually seen the perpetrator or the crime itself, but have seen things that can be "clues" upon which the skilled investigator can build a case. Probably most crime scene witnesses who are able to provide information fall into this category.

Efforts should be made to at least identify everyone who may have been a witness to the crime or may have been in the vicinity when the crime occurred. This will enable interviews to be conducted with them later, if it is not possible to interview them at the scene. If a camera is available, pictures of the crowd of onlookers should be taken. Efforts can be made to identify, locate, and interview those who appear in the photographs or video at a later time.

Even if all witnesses can be thoroughly interviewed at the scene, it still might be wise to interview them again at a later date. It is possible that once the initial state of panic and fear has passed, some of these people may be able to recall something that they had not previously mentioned. Also, by this time, the investigators will know more about the facts of the situation and therefore will be able to ask questions from a different perspective than they did during the initial interview. Investigators can facilitate follow-up contacts by ensuring that every person interviewed at the crime scene has been given the officer's name and business telephone number, and has been told to call the officer if they later recall something about the crime. If for some reason the initial interviewing officer knows that he will not be available in the future, he should provide them with the name and telephone number of someone within the agency whom they can call in the future.

The interviews of all crime scene witnesses should be reviewed in order to catalog the reasons these people were in the area. Computers now make it possible for an analyst to conduct such a review almost contemporaneously with the submission of the results of the initial interviews. It is possible that, through this review, additional witnesses can be identified. For example, if several people state that they were passing the location en route to their jobs at the Jones Company, it might be prudent for an investigator to visit the Jones Company in an effort to identify other employees who might also have passed the crime scene while traveling to work. If a witness advised that he had just departed from the Smith Camera shop where he had left film to be developed, it would be a good idea for an officer to identify other people who also left that shop at around the same time. The particular value of these kinds of interviews is that they may locate people who have made observations just prior to the crime without realizing the significance of what they had seen.

Rescue workers and other emergency personnel who were the first to respond to the crime scene are often overlooked as possible witnesses, because they arrived after the incident occurred. However, they should not be forgotten, because they may have arrived soon enough after the incident to have observed something important, such as a perpetrator escaping. If nothing else, they can sometimes identify people who were witnesses, because they observed these people at the scene when they arrived.

Law enforcement agencies should solicit public information concerning a crime, particularly something of the magnitude of a terrorist attack. Using the media, a police agency can publicize a telephone number where possible witnesses and other knowledgeable individuals can provide information. Law enforcement-oriented television programs, including *America's Most Wanted*, can also be used to locate missing witnesses. Despite publicity, there will still be certain possible or actual witnesses who will not voluntarily come forward. Some will not even realize that anyone is looking for them.

Another method that can be used with respect to identifying witnesses involves investigators returning to the crime scene at the same time on other dates to determine who might be in the area. This technique is highly recommended for use in conjunction with terrorism investigations. Many people are creatures of habit. They frequent the same place at the same time each day. Some people are forced to follow a pattern of behavior in order to fulfill requirements of their employment or social life.

Law enforcement agencies usually use the technique on the day following the incident, assuming that the area is again accessible to traffic. They also revisit the scene one week later. It is assumed that by doing this they should be able to locate people who frequent the area at the same time each day, or who visit it on a particular day each week. Agencies having the manpower may desire to return to the scene around the time of the incident on a daily basis for a week or two. It should be noted that some terrorist groups attack on holidays. This presents a problem for law enforcement agencies that try to locate witnesses by returning to the crime scene on the days following the incident. Holiday traffic patterns are usually different from normal activity and are not likely to be duplicated on the following day or the following week.

The victim property owner, lessee, or manager should be interviewed as soon as possible, even if they did not actually witness the crime. It must be determined whether they were threatened and if they know of anyone who would have attacked their facility. They may be able to identify people who should have been present when the attack occurred who can be interviewed as possible witnesses. These owner/managers can also supply valuable information about the target address. This information could be of great value with respect to the subsequent search. For example, they might be able to provide information about dangers such as PCBs, which could now be in the crime scene. While conducting such an interview, it is good practice for the interviewing officer to obtain permission for the law enforcement agency to search the crime scene. If the person refuses, it may be necessary to obtain a search warrant. The owner/manager might be reminded that criminal investigators with the law enforcement agency, as well as his insurance company, could become suspicious about a refusal to cooperate with authorities.

There is no specific time to terminate the process of locating witnesses to a crime. Clearly, any agency must maintain an open door policy with respect to witnesses voluntarily providing information. A person may come forth many months later to provide a firsthand report. This could easily happen if the attack were in an airport or truck stop, where people were traveling through when the crime occurred. Some agency leaders might elect to interview every person who was in the area at the time of the attack. Others may decide to interview only those who can be identified within a given period.

In one terrorist incident that involved multiple bombings, a decision was made to interview everyone who was in one of the victim buildings during the evening when the attack occurred. More than 1,000 people were subsequently contacted. As luck would have it, several witnesses were located who observed the apparent perpetrator bring the explosive device to the building in a box.

None of these people was an actual eyewitness to the explosion, and none was even identified during the immediate response as being a possible witness to the crime. Because law enforcement chose not to publicly release details concerning the box that contained the bomb, these witnesses would not have realized that they had seen something of significance and therefore would not have voluntarily come forward.

The Crime Scene and Security Cameras

In recent years, the video camera and the time-lapse still camera have become a way of life. Not only do communities and businesses employ such systems, many private citizens use them to protect their residences. These cameras can be found inside and outside many locations. Some are live-monitored by security guards, but most probably also record everything they observe. If the crime is serious, such as a terrorist attack, it is imperative that an investigator be assigned to locate every security camera within the crime scene area, and all such cameras that could possibly observe people entering or leaving the crime scene. Some of these cameras can be readily seen because the entity using them publicly warns people that they are being monitored. Others are concealed. Consequently, a law enforcement agency may be forced to conduct a door-to-door canvas for such cameras. The survey should be conducted quickly, because many users of security cameras regularly reuse their film.

Many people carry small still and video cameras on a regular basis. This is especially true with respect to individuals visiting prominent locations, including tourist attractions and historical monuments. Some people carry cameras so that they can film important or unusual things that they might encounter. Such a person in the vicinity of a crime may have snapped valuable pictures just before, during, or after the incident. Efforts should be made to identify people who may have been taking pictures in the crime scene area around the time of the incident. Their film may be just as valuable as that taken from fixed security cameras.

Cameras that yield firsthand information with respect to the perpetrators of the crime can also generate additional leads for a law enforcement agency. They may reflect a possible route of entry or escape. This can lead to an even more extensive survey for cameras that might have picked up the perpetrators at a later or earlier time. For example, a security camera at the crime scene may reflect that a man walked from a van parked on Main Street to the entrance of a government building, where he left a package. Shortly thereafter, the camera reveals that an explosion occurred at the front door of the building. Because the security camera showed that the van arrived from the south and departed to the north, it is logical to believe that some other cameras covering Main Street for several blocks in either direction would also have filmed the van.

Summary

The crime scene is extremely important in a terrorism investigation. Physical evidence obtained from the crime scene is difficult for a subject to dispute in court. Terrorist crime scenes often involve bombings and arsons in which there is serious damage, and therefore investigator safety issues must be addressed. The crime scene must be protected from contamination so that evidence is not tainted or lost. It is important to identify witnesses at such locations. The area should be checked for video security cameras. If possible, the videotapes from these cameras should be recovered.

⓰ Mail Cover

A mail cover is an investigative technique that involves law enforcement review of information that can be observed on the outside of correspondence conveyed in the United States mail. Mail covers are conducted through the authority of the local postmaster. A mail cover does not involve opening mail, nor does it permit the review of materials inside an envelope. (It should be noted that there are certain chemicals that will allow a person to read a letter without opening the envelope in which it is contained. Authority for a mail cover does not permit the use of these chemicals, or any other means that might exist that would permit the reading of a communication contained inside a sealed envelope.) Mail cover authority does not permit an investigator to open a person's mailbox in order to study the envelopes containing his mail. Mail covers are usually conducted by postal employees, with the results given to the requesting law enforcement agency.

The best kind of mail cover is that in which the outside of a target's mail is photocopied. This enables the investigator to see everything on the envelope, including dots and other markings that may be a form of coded communication. It may also enable the investigator to recognize the sender's handwriting. Often in mail covers, postal employees hand-copy the information from the envelopes, rather than photocopying the outside of the envelopes.

Mail cover authority is restricted to incoming communications. It does not cover outgoing correspondence. A law enforcement officer who has the authority to conduct a mail cover would not be able to take outgoing letters that the person might have placed for the postal carrier.

Mail covers usually do not yield much information of primary value. For the most part, it is a secondary technique upon which other forms of investigation can be initiated. Postmarks on envelopes may sometimes be of immediate significance. Return addresses can also be important. On some occasions, a fugitive might be foolish enough to send a letter to a close relative or known associate on which he writes his true return address, but that is not a common occurrence. It would be more likely that the best lead that an investigator could get on a fugitive would be a postmark on a suspicious letter the person received. The basic value of a mail cover is that it reveals some of the parties with whom the subject of the coverage has contact. As such, mail covers help develop an intelligence base on the subject.

For many investigators, the primary use of a mail cover is to identify contacts, associates, and interests of the person that can be explored further. Examples of what a mail cover might develop include:

- Where the person banks
- Where the person works or goes to school
- Who holds the mortgage or other notes involving the person
- Stocks, bonds, and other assets held by the individual
- What telephone company the person uses
- His or her Internet service provider
- Credit card information
- Where the person's vehicle is financed and insured
- The person's medical providers
- What kinds of insurance the person has
- Licenses and permits the person holds
- Whether and where the person is on parole or probation
- Organizations and clubs in which he or she holds membership
- The person's interests and hobbies
- The person's friends, relatives, and associates
- Types of vices that a person may have
- If the person owns other property
- Whether the person uses another identity or title
- If the person is using his or her home for a business or for anything other than a residence

From this information an investigator might be able to conclude that the person has poor credit, is having marital problems, is engaged in off-beat activities, including sexual perversion, has medical difficulties, owns or has an interest in weapons, has a prison record, is active in a church or club, or is active in community affairs.

In most instances, the information developed during a mail cover is so limited that it requires further investigation in order to be of value. Consequently, if the mail cover reveals that the person received a letter from a particular credit card company, a court order would probably have to be procured in order to learn anything about the person's account. If the person received a letter from a probation officer, an inquiry would have to be made with that officer in order to develop information concerning the person.

Many investigators will try to exclude "junk mail" and other advertising correspondence from the results of their mail cover. Unfortunately, some "junk mail" is disguised so that it cannot be recognized for what it is from the outside of the envelope. This is done deliberately by advertisers to encourage the recipient to open the letter rather than destroy it. Such communications could cause an investigator to believe that the mail cover target has an "account" with a firm, when the letter was actually "junk mail." Therefore, the investigator could waste his or her time investigating a lead at this company or obtaining a court order for an account that does not exist.

In reality, so-called "junk mail" may well yield valuable information. People get on mailing lists for a variety of reasons. The fact that a person receives brochures for gun shows and outdoor expositions could indicate that he is a gun owner, or that he is possibly involved with a right-wing extremist group. Similarly, a person who regularly receives advertising from gambling casinos could have a gambling problem. In fact, to an investigator, any unusual advertising received by a subject should raise a red flag. Many mailed advertisements are triggered by something that a person purchased or by some event that he attended. For that reason a brochure for something like pornographic videos is likely to have eminated from some action that the recipient previously took, as opposed to a random mailing.

Many investigators also exclude magazines, newspapers, and other periodicals from their mail coverage. This is a mistake. People pay for magazine subscriptions. As a result, one would assume that the subscriber must have an interest in the subject matter of the publications. Again, off-beat or unusual publications should be of interest to an investigator. For example, the fact that a person receives a Puerto Rican independence publication or a Nazi Party bulletin should be of interest to an officer investigating a person for possible involvement in a terrorist organization.

The fact that a mail cover does not permit the opening of United States mail, and does not allow for coverage of outgoing communications does not mean that law enforcement is totally precluded from conducting such coverages. Courts may issue orders regarding such situations, but good cause will be required. Surveillance personnel occasionally observe subjects mailing letters. If they believe that a particular communication may be important, possibly because it was mailed in a surreptitious manner, they can "mark it" for subsequent recovery. They then obtain a court order and accompany a postal worker to the mailbox. To "mark" a letter, a surveillance investigator may drop a much larger envelope into a mailbox immediately after the subject deposits his letter. Some surveillance personnel drop a newspaper into the mailbox or a sheet of blank paper or cardboard. The assumption is that the subject's letter will be under the item that the surveillance person deposited into the mailbox.

Summary

A mail cover involves reviewing the outside of communications sent to a subject through the United States mail. It does not involve opening any correspondence. The value of a mail cover is limited, and it is unlikely to yield evidence that will solve a case. However, it can identify some personal aspects of a subject's life, such as relatives, friends, bank, creditors, and organizational affiliations.

⑰ The Investigative Task Force

The investigative task force is a relatively new entry into the arsenal of tools that law enforcement agencies use to combat criminals and terrorists. During the 1980s and 1990s the task force became well established as a vehicle to address important law enforcement problems. Although some may argue that the task force is not really an investigative technique per se, most would agree that it is an excellent method for dealing with significant criminal situations.

In an investigative task force, two or more law enforcement agencies formally join together to address a particular criminal problem. The mission of a task force may be broad in scope, including a general area of concentration. Such a task force might address violent street gangs on a city's north side, or deal with car thefts within the entire community. A city experiencing an increase in murders might establish a task force to concentrate on this crime problem. Task forces are often established to address fairly specific criminal activity. Such a task force might look into the illegal activities of a particular group of bunco artists operating in the city. A task force of this kind might also be created to handle a very specific criminal incident. An entity of this type was established to deal with the mass murders that occurred at a Brown's Chicken restaurant in Palatine, Illinois, in 1993.

On occasion, various agencies conducting investigations against the same target will establish a loose confederation in which each agency concentrates on developing evidence of crimes that fall within its specific jurisdiction. A task force is much more than this type of affiliation. In a task force, all of the agencies, regardless of their own jurisdictions, work together to develop violations against the target. Everything that is developed is shared. Investigators from all of the agencies work together on every aspect of the investigation.

A task force is much more than a mutual aid agreement between agencies in which the agencies agree to assist each other in times of need. It is also different from memorandums of understanding, in which agencies generally divide a jurisdiction so that each agency has responsibility for investigating specific portions of a criminal statute. A task force functions in a semi-autonomous state. Each investigator maintains his or her own agency identity, but works under the direction of the task force leadership to accomplish its mission. Each task force member has similar arrest powers and identical security clearances.

In an ideal situation, each member agency will designate personnel to work on a full-time basis. In some instances, a small agency may not have sufficient manpower to do this. In this case, the agency should designate a part-time investigator who can be counted on to provide a certain number of work hours to the task force each week. Investigators assigned to work on a task force should be the only investigators in their department who have access to task force information and operations. There will also be certain ranking officials within each member agency who will receive regular briefings on the task force's targets and progress. Ideally, investigators who are assigned to work on a terrorism task force on a full-time basis should be free from other assignments within their agency. This is not always possible. In such a situation, it would be best that the officer's other assignment be somewhat related to what the task force handles. An example might be a bomb squad detective who works part time on a terrorism task force.

A task force is a vehicle through which the various agencies in a specific region can share their resources, talents, manpower, and legal authority to combat and resolve a specific crime problem. Task forces are created to curtail wasteful competition between agencies. They are also created to ensure that two or more agencies investigating a similar criminal activity in a given region do not accidentally neutralize the others' investigative activities.

Task forces usually arise due to necessity. Something must be done about a crime problem that continues in an area despite efforts by the agencies having jurisdiction to resolve the situation. Often the individual agencies are drawn to the task force concept because they realize that the investigative techniques required to resolve the problem, such as electronic coverage, are not available to their agency. On occasion, a department will attempt to organize a task force because it desires to initiate a long-term project, such as an undercover operation, and it does not want other agencies in the area to accidentally interfere with the project. This will not happen if all of the interested agencies are working together.

Law enforcement agencies have traditionally worked together when the need has arisen. A police department that pursues a fleeing subject across a city boundary usually knows that it can depend on the neighboring town's police to assist. A county knows that it can depend on the sheriff in a neighboring county for help in case of a major disaster. Cities have always shared criminal intelligence with other cities. Many law enforcement agencies cooperate in joint training exercises. For many years police departments have also worked with their counterparts on aspects of criminal investigations. Most of these have been short term, and have usually involved each agency pursuing the areas of the law over which it has jurisdiction, and sharing what it develops with the other agencies in the operation. The task force is a natural extension of this tradition of interdepartmental cooperation. It is perhaps more structured, formal, and autonomous than previous working agreements. The task force is a relatively recent development in law enforcement in the United States. For the most part, task forces did not develop until the early 1970s.

History of the Task Force Concept

It may be impossible to identify the first formal law enforcement task force that was created in the United States. It is likely that the phrase *task force* was not used when the first entity was created. It is also likely that early task forces were not bound by any signed agreements. Instead, they relied on a handshake and promises of cooperation among the members. In fact, one of the country's oldest terrorism task forces functioned for a decade with no formal written agreement. This task force was actually created by individual investigators from various agencies who decided to end bickering and duplicative efforts by agreeing to work together. The agency managers were for the most part unaware of the working relationship that these investigators had formed until the "task force" had achieved a major success. At that point, the task force received overwhelming official blessing from the agency heads. By current definition, a task force should have a written agreement signed by each member agency.

Although the terrorism task force may not have actually been the first task force created, it certainly became the first task force to receive national attention. The New York Joint Terrorism Task Force and the Chicago Joint Terrorism Task Force both produced remarkable results during the early 1980s, and solved a number of terrorist attacks. (It is noted that when first created, these two task forces referred to themselves as "Terrorist" rather than "Terrorism".) Early terrorism task forces blazed the trail for the many task forces that were to subsequently develop throughout the United States. It was the terrorism task forces that resolved the concerns that early critics of the task force concept feared would happen. The worrisome issues included such factors as jurisdiction, legal authority, vehicle use, security clearances, and funding.

The first terrorism task force was developed in the United States in 1981. In the latter part of that year, task forces developed independently in New York and Chicago. Although they were formed for different reasons, the result was essentially the same. The New York Joint Terrorism Task Force was established in response to an armored truck robbery staged in upstate New York on October 20, 1981, in which an armored truck guard and two law enforcement officers were murdered. The perpetrators came from several established terrorist groups. The terrorism task force grew out of a previously established bank robbery task force that was functioning in New York at the time.

The Chicago Joint Terrorism Task Force started when local, state, and federal agencies in the Chicago area joined to work against a common target—the Puerto Rican terrorist group known as the FALN. Its beginning differed from the New York Terrorism Task Force in that it was not founded in response to a particular terrorist attack. Instead, it was designed to prevent the FALN from conducting any further attacks. The New York Terrorism Task Force succeeded in identifying, arresting, and convicting the terrorists responsible for the brutal armored truck robbery and a string of earlier armored truck robberies. The Chicago Joint Terrorism Task Force found the FALN's clandestine safe house bomb factory and ultimately arrested the FALN cell as they made final preparations for a bombing attack that was to take place over the July 4, 1983, holiday.

The successes of both the New York and the Chicago Joint Terrorism Task Forces demonstrated the value of task forces. During the next 25 years, many task forces developed across the United States. These task forces address everything from terrorism to narcotics, gangs, fugitives, bank robberies, major thefts, organized crime, white-collar crime, and many other criminal enterprises. The tragic attacks of September 11, 2001, brought national attention to the joint terrorism task force concept, and within a year terrorism task forces were established in conjunction with every FBI field division. By 2008 there were more than 100 terrorism task forces in operation.

With respect to terrorism, the task force concept revolutionized how the United States law enforcement community addressed this problem. Terrorism became a high-profile crime during the 1960s and 1970s in the United States, although the term "terrorism" was not always used to refer to this form of violence until the mid-1970s. The Vietnam War had galvanized various disenchanted people into action. While most of the anti-war activity consisted of peaceful, yet disruptive, protests, some of it involved violent bombings and arson attacks, particularly during the late 1960s.

Law enforcement found itself unprepared to handle the situation. Numerous violent attacks went unsolved because long-practiced investigative techniques simply did not work when applied to terrorists. The fact that a bomb was detonated in a particular city did not mean that any members of the terrorist group responsible lived anywhere near that city. Although the war issue had brought divergent people together, various other causes were also soon being promoted. These causes included prison reform, civil rights, communism, women's rights, imperialism, and abolition of the capitalist system. During the 1960s and 1970s, and into the early 1980s, several violent clandestine terrorist groups flourished in the United States, attacking government, law enforcement, military, and corporate targets.

For a variety of reasons, the United States law enforcement community had difficulty responding to these terrorist organizations. One high-profile group, the Weather Underground Organization (WUO) perpetrated almost 40 bombings during a seven-year period, including bombings inside the U.S. Capitol and the Pentagon. No one was ever convicted of any of the Weathermen bombings, despite the fact that numerous law enforcement agencies made concerted efforts to solve these attacks. Terrorist fugitives, including Mutulu Shakur, Susan Saxe, Katherine Ann Power, Leo Frederick Burt, Thomas William Manning, Raymond Luc Levasseur, and Cameron David Bishop remained on the FBI's "Ten Most Wanted" list well past the time that criminals normally placed on that list would stay there. Although the Puerto Rican terrorist group known as the FALN perpetrated many bombings during the mid- to late 1970s, the law enforcement community had no success in apprehending these terrorists until the end of the decade. The only exception was one of the leading members, William Guillermo Morales, who was arrested after he was severely injured when the New York bomb factory in which he was working exploded in August of 1978. Morales subsequently escaped from prison and remained free until arrested in Mexico in 1983. Following his release from prison, he was allowed to go to Cuba where he remains in 2008—still a U.S. fugitive.

The initiation of the task force concept in the area of terrorism was to be the death knell to many of the most violent political activists in the United States. Working together, the various law enforcement agencies proved that they could accomplish what they had not been able to accomplish alone. Of course, the success was not only due to the task force concept. Changes in how terrorism investigations were handled were also responsible for the success. However, these changes in investigative approaches were fostered through the terrorism task forces.

What Is Required to Make a Task Force Function ●

The key to a successful task force is cooperation. Each agency must enter with a willingness to share what it has and what it will learn from conducting investigations while on the task force. Task force agencies agree to become involved in organizing and planning investigations. They agree to cooperate, rather than compete, with the other agencies on the task force.

If a task force is to function properly, there are certain factors that should be considered and resolved.

Manpower

The member agencies must contribute their fair share of manpower to the pool of investigators. This does not mean that every agency contributes the same amount of manpower or resources. Usually in task forces, one or two of the agencies has a greater responsibility for the targeted crime problem than do the other agencies. These agencies should contribute more manpower. It would not be reasonable to expect a small agency with a minor involvement in the targeted criminal activity to match the resources being committed by the larger agencies. Every task force member must contribute some manpower to the task force. It would not be fair for an agency to hold token membership on a task force from which they would access the fruits of all investigations yet contribute nothing to the coalition. Ideally, all task force investigators should be assigned on a full-time basis. If a particular agency is so strapped for manpower that it cannot meet this criterion, it should at least dedicate a part-time investigator to the task force on a regular basis. It is not desirable for any agency to rotate personnel through the task force on a short-term basis.

Information Sharing

The member agencies in a task force must share information developed during task force investigations. Furthermore, they must contribute any information about the target that their agency develops outside of the task force to the overall intelligence pool. Examples of this include information an agency learns from an informant, or information discovered in their closed files. The task force will not work if certain agencies are able to conceal the fruits of task force investigations from other member agencies. This does not mean that the member agencies have the right to freely spread the results of task force investigations throughout their own departments. Task force investigations should be treated as "need to know." Terrorism investigations are sensitive in nature and some are classified. Consequently, information regarding terrorism task force investigations should be kept within the task force.

Jurisdiction

Ideally the agencies included in a task force should have some form of jurisdiction with respect to the target of the task force. While it is true that most local police agencies have very broad jurisdiction to handle a variety of criminal violations within their geographic boundaries, the fact is that most other state and federal agencies have restricted jurisdictions. Just because an agency has a physical presence in a particular geographical area where a task force has been established should not mean that agency belongs on that task force. Task force leaders must resist the temptation to accept an agency onto the task force simply to obtain that agency's resources. Serious problems can arise from such a situation. The agency lacking jurisdiction is likely to attempt to redirect the task force into areas where it has authority and interest that may actually be outside the scope of the task force. In addition, task force member departments could easily come to resent an agency with questionable jurisdiction offering opinions on how task force cases should be run. Things changed greatly after the September 11, 2001, attacks. The president and attorney general made it clear that all federal agencies were to work together in the war against terrorism, and that every effort should be made by federal agencies to work with local and state agencies. Departments were encouraged to search their jurisdictions for criminal statutes that could be employed against terrorists and to bring their expertise to terrorist task forces. As a consequence, the number of agencies in joint terrorist task forces greatly expanded.

Participation

If a task force is to be truly effective, it is important that all agencies actually working in the target area join the task force. One of the primary reasons for creating a task force is to eliminate competition among agencies so that cooperative endeavors can be conducted without agencies disrupting one another. Clearly, if one or more agencies continues to function within the target area, but outside the task force, the effectiveness of the task force may be greatly reduced.

Vehicle Agreements

If a task force is to function smoothly, it is imperative that the various member investigators work together as a cohesive unit. This may require investigators to drive each others' vehicles. This is especially true with respect to mixed surveillance teams, in which security may require investigators to change automobiles in mid-surveillance. Similarly, it may be desirable for investigators to be able to switch driving roles when transporting prisoners or even when meeting with informants. It is also likely that one or more of the task force member agencies will be able to contribute a specialized vehicle to the common cause. The vehicle might be a surveillance van or a crime scene truck. It might be a four-wheel drive vehicle or a bus. Regardless, it is important that everyone on the task force who could use such a vehicle have the right to drive it.

Task force vehicle agreements are usually relatively simple. In essence, they place responsibility with the agency of each investigator who drives the vehicle. In a sense, a task force vehicle becomes the "property" of the agency whose investigator is driving it.

Equipment

In a smoothly functioning task force, each agency will contribute whatever equipment it can. This could include basic office items such as pens and paper, or it could involve larger equipment, like photocopiers and facsimile machines. In many task forces the federal agency, especially the FBI, will provide the office space and basic equipment to run the operation. This is true for joint terrorism task forces, in which every such entity functions from FBI-owned or leased space.

In many task forces, the various member agencies will install computer terminals within the task force office space. This equipment allows the agencies to check their own department files and will often allow them to check other records that fall within the purview of their agency.

Training

The best task forces are organized so that investigators can take advantage of training opportunities offered by all agencies within the task force. Consequently, if one agency offers photography in-service training to its members, that agency will make efforts to allow task force members to also attend this in-service training. Similarly, if an agency offers a seminar on surveillance techniques, it will make an effort to permit other agency representatives to attend.

In addition to sharing training opportunities, efforts will be made by larger task forces to stage their own training. Training that task forces have offered to their members have included firearms, bomb recognition, surveillance, crime scene, legal issues, and presentations concerning terrorism and various terrorist groups.

Arrest Powers

It is important that every investigator assigned to the task force have similar arrest powers. When the earliest task forces were created, many viewed the dissimilar arrest powers as an insurmountable problem. It took a little effort and research, but the situation resolved itself. It was found that local, county, and state investigators could be designated deputy United States Marshals, thereby giving them federal law enforcement authority. Similarly, federal investigators from agencies having narrowly defined authority could have their powers expanded by also being designated federal marshals.

Enforcement of state laws creates problems for federal investigators. This is especially true in a state such as Illinois, where federal investigators are not considered "peace officers." This situation could be alleviated by one or more of the local task force agencies designating the federal task force members to be a part of their agency. For example, a sheriff could deputize an FBI special agent, thereby giving him or her police authority in that county. Local police and state police members of the task force could also administer an oath of office to a federal agent.

Prosecution

One of the advantages of the task force concept is that it makes available to member agencies the prosecutors that each agency would normally use in connection with their investigations. Consequently, efforts should be made to employ the most logical prosecutor for the violations developed. In some instances it might be best to prosecute the subject in a local or county court, while in other cases it might be wise to try the person in the federal judicial system. While almost every illegal action constitutes some form of local crime, there is not always a federal violation. However, there are some complex conspiracy statutes that make it possible for federal prosecutors to charge crimes that are not available to local prosecutors. Because of the sentencing guidelines, it might be possible for the defendant to be more severely punished in one court than another. The prison system might also be an issue. People convicted and sentenced to prison in local and state courts usually serve their time in a prison in that state. People sentenced in a federal court can be sent to penitentiaries through the country. In terrorism cases, it is often wise to keep politcal extremists apart. If there are a number of such people in a state prison system, that may not be possible.

Classified Information

The initial joint terrorism task forces concentrated on domestic terrorism. However, it was not long before the task forces encountered domestic groups that had direct contacts with foreign governments and foreign terrorists. As time passed, terrorism task forces became involved in the direct investigation of international terrorist groups that were functioning in the United States. These international terrorism cases resulted in information from foreign intelligence services coming into the intelligence pool of the joint terrorism task forces. Unfortunately, this presented an immediate problem. Much of the information was classified and could only be reviewed by task force employees who held the proper security clearances. Of course, the investigators holding such clearances were usually only the federal agents, especially those from the FBI. The inability to share information presented a serious problem because it violated the very premise upon which the task force was created—sharing and trust. The problem was quickly alleviated, because it was discovered that local, county, and state investigators could undergo the background investigations necessary to grant them security clearances. Similarly, the security clearances of investigators from federal agencies that were insufficient to permit them to review materials could be raised or modified to permit complete sharing. Soon the task forces changed their policies to require that everyone entering joint terrorism task force duty possess a security clearance. In that way, no task force member would be denied an opportunity to review task force intelligence. Many non-terrorism task forces have also adopted a policy of requiring a security clearance in order to avoid situations in which sharing may be precluded.

Task Force Management and Operation

The direction that a task force takes must be mutually approved by all member agencies. In fact, the agencies having the larger presences on a task force usually assume the bulk of the daily management of the unit. Agencies having only fringe involvement in the target of the task force usually have minimal influence on the direction of the task force, although their concerns and opinions are considered. The FBI holds membership in all of the nation's terrorism task forces, and in most instances provides the largest amount of manpower and resources. The top management position (supervisor) in every joint terrorism task force has been an FBI supervisory special agent.

The ability to share unique features, talents, equipment, and powers is one of the strongest features of a task force. In good task forces, the member agencies make available whatever they have that will enable the task force to function. Among the agency resources that may be made available for task force use are: bomb technicians and bomb squad equipment, evidence technicians and laboratory services, SWAT teams, hostage negotiators, electronics technicians, computer specialists, and equipment. In addition, the task force agencies will make available to the task force their established contacts with local, county, state, federal, private, commercial, civic, charitable, religious, and international entities.

Summary

The investigative task force has been an extremely important development in the law enforcement community's efforts against terrorism in the United States. Terrorists are almost always more national than they are local in scope. They travel often and the people who commit violent attacks frequently do not live in the area where the attack occurred. Unless federal, state, and local law enforcement agencies truly work together as a team, each level will experience difficulty in addressing the terrorism challenge. Joint terrorism task forces began in 1981 in New York and Chicago, and by the 1990s had spread to include almost every major metropolitan area in the country and to many rural locations where terrorism presented a problem. The September 11, 2001, attacks led to the creation of joint terrorism task forces in conjunction with every FBI field division. By 2008 there were more than 100 Joint Terrorism Task Forces across the United States. The keys to the success of a joint terrorism task force are trust, sharing, and total cooperation among member agencies.

⓲ Undercover Operations

For law enforcement purposes, undercover is an investigative technique in which a sworn law enforcement officer operates in a covert mode for the purpose of developing intelligence about illegal activities. The undercover officer may occupy a position from which he can provide direct information about criminal activity, or he may occupy a corollary position from which he is able to provide information that, when combined with intelligence gathered through other investigative techniques, can result in the successful resolution of a acase.

The concept of undercover work evokes excitement in many law enforcement officers. For some, it is the rush of adrenaline that the investigator imagines will occur when he, the undercover operative, encounters the "bad guys." For other investigators, it is the idea of a law enforcement officer actually being able to bolster and help resolve an investigation by being present when the "bad guys" conspire to or actually commit illegal activities. Some investigators see the undercover technique as a vehicle through which to avoid the hassles of developing and operating troublesome informants. For other investigators, the intrigue of undercover work revolves around the fact that it enables law enforcement to be somewhat proactive in its approach to crime instead of reacting to crimes that have already occurred. All too often, law enforcement officers view undercover work as being a sure-fire method for solving a complex criminal investigation.

Undercover work is, in fact, highly complex, time- and manpower-consuming, and dangerous. It is fraught with potential problems. However, undercover projects can yield spectacular results that may not be possible through the use of other techniques. Unlike most approaches that are used to solve crimes that have already occurred, undercover operations enable a law enforcement agency to proactively attack a crime problem, and apprehend the subjects as they are committing a criminal act.

Undercover operations can vary greatly in scope and anticipated time span. They can range from a simple covert contact in which some intelligence is gathered, to highly elaborate projects in which the law enforcement agency creates a dummy company. Undercover can involve one covert investigator or several investigators, all functioning at different levels of secrecy. Undercover operations can be augmented by informants, cooperating individuals, and innocent citizens who may have no knowledge of the project.

Undercover, particularly deep cover, operations probably require more overall law enforcement agency involvement than any other investigative technique. An agency must be willing to make a true commitment to ensure that a complicated undercover project succeeds. Undercover projects must be carefully planned, and the project must be outlined very specifically before it is implemented. Every involved part of the police agency must understand its responsibilities. Certainly, the head of the law enforcement agency should personally approve any deep cover operation. In fact, the agency head should probably approve any undercover project that extends more than a few weeks, involves danger to the undercover officer, or deals with sensitive situations that may include national security, public officials, and professionals like doctors, attorneys, clergy, law enforcement officers, and journalists.

Advantages of the Undercover Technique

The goal of an undercover project is to place a law enforcement professional into a position from which he can testify as a direct witness against a subject or criminal conspiracy. Because of his official position and training, he or she is a much more desirable witness than an informant or the average cooperative citizen.

The undercover operative has been trained to conduct investigations and is knowledgeable about the law. He knows what is necessary to develop a prosecutable case within his area of specialty. In these respects the undercover operative is far superior to an informant who rarely, if ever, has any formal law enforcement training. The undercover operative can greatly assist the case officer and prosecutor in developing the case.

The undercover agent is loyal to his department and law enforcement in general. Informants are often selfish and put their own interests above those of the law enforcement agency that is directing them. Both informants and private citizen witnesses can be intimidated by suspects and defense attorneys. Law enforcement officers are rarely intimidated by these people.

The undercover officer is honest. As such, he should not carry any "baggage" with him that would destroy his credibility in court. Informants often are not completely honest. Informants often have criminal records, which can cause juries to be suspicious of their testimony. Informants also must be watched carefully during any operation to ensure that they do not commit criminal acts that could be embarrassing and destroy their credibility.

The undercover operative can be a true partner in developing an investigation. His advice, cautions, and suggestions should be respected and implemented if possible. He is a knowledgeable, loyal, and intelligent person who can be trusted. He is a part of the team. Informants and citizens who provide information can never actually be a part of the investigative team, although in order to keep them motivated, law enforcement agencies sometimes lead these people to believe that they are working in equal partnership with the investigators assigned to the case.

Disadvantages of the Undercover Technique

The undercover technique can be extremely manpower- and resource-intensive. A deep cover operation can overwhelm a police agency and force it to concentrate on the investigation using the technique to the detriment of other cases.

Undercover work has the potential to be dangerous. The undercover agent could be injured or killed because he or she is suspected of being with law enforcement, because of internal strife within the criminal conspiracy, or because of the unsafe nature of the location where he or she must live and function.

The undercover officer can be psychologically harmed by the experience and require rehabilitation in order to return to normal police work. Some long-time undercover agents have serious problems returning to the relatively mundane law enforcement environment.

In certain investigations, particularly those involving terrorists, the undercover officer could become politically indoctrinated with a radical philosophy that conflicts with his or her law enforcement mission. It is difficult for anyone to live in a totally political environment for a long time and not be influenced by it.

The undercover officer's personal life could be damaged due to his or her long absence and the secrecy of the assignment. He or she could be harmed in other ways that would have a lasting effect. These damages could include becoming ill, suffering a disabling injury, or even receiving tattoos, body piercing, or other forms of mutilation.

Types of Undercover Operations

There are three kinds of undercover projects: limited contact, semi-deep undercover, and deep cover operations.

Limited Contact (One Shot) Undercover

This is a very short encounter in which an investigator makes one or more brief contacts with a subject or other knowledgeable person for the purpose of developing intelligence or evidence. It could involve such endeavors as attending a meeting, engaging a person in a conversation, visiting a target location, or even making a "buy" from a subject selling marijuana on the street. Limited contact undercover operations are fairly common. In essence, they involve a law enforcement officer developing information without revealing his identity as an officer. If asked for a name, he will supply a false one. If asked about employment, he will give a response other than "police officer." If asked why he is at a certain location, he will not reveal that he is engaged in an official investigation.

In addition to developing intelligence and evidence, limited undercover projects are sometimes undertaken to determine the viability of instituting a long-term undercover project. For example, if an officer operating as a stranger walking along the street is able to get an invitation to attend a radical group's meeting, then it could be reasoned that a better-documented and better-credentialed undercover agent could also get such an invitation.

Limited undercover projects are also undertaken to ascertain whether a particular person might be open to an official contact by a law enforcement officer. A limited undercover investigator might attend a meeting and talk with several people in order to determine whether any of them might be approachable about becoming an informant.

Sometimes limited contact operations are undertaken to augment a long-term undercover project. Perhaps the investigation has slowed and something is needed to jump-start the project. A one-shot contact might be the thing that will make something happen.

The limited undercover contact can be made in conjunction with a number of activities, including the subject's employment, residence, or hobbies, as well as social, entertainment, criminal, or political activities. Another approach may involve an effort to buy something from the subject, or sell him something. A casual, "accidental" contact could be made on the street, on a bus, at a lunch counter, or while waiting in line at a store.

In the limited contact situation, the investigator usually will not be required to produce false identification, and may not even be asked to provide a name or biographical information. Logically, to avoid any suspicion, the investigator should carry false documentation when making a contact just in case the subject asks for proof of identity. Although the limited contact is often very short-term, it should nonetheless be planned beforehand. Most importantly, the contact should be reasonable. This is particularly true in terrorism investigations. Subjects in such cases are on constant alert for law enforcement coverage. An unusual contact that might cause the average person to do little more than shake his head in bewilderment, could cause a terrorist to become very suspicious and therefore more cautious than usual. For example, it would be normal for an undercover investigator to inquire about a subject's political beliefs if the undercover investigator encountered the subject standing on a street corner distributing literature promulgating a cause. However, for an undercover officer to suddenly start a political discussion with a person he has encountered at a sporting event would be abnormal and therefore suspicious.

How, and even if, limited undercover operations are initiated will depend on an agency's rules and procedures. Some agencies have no objection to an investigator making subterfuge contacts with a subject whenever the occasion arises. Other agencies make it clear that covert contact with a subject cannot take place without management approval. Some agencies limit the number of contacts that can be made before formal management approval must be obtained. Of course, there is always an issue if the subject has been contacted directly and referred an investigator to his attorney. In such a situation a second investigator should consult his department's legal counsel before trying to contact the subject for information via a limited undercover contact.

Documentation is important in all levels of an investigation. While a limited contact undercover operation may be short in duration and develop little evidence, it should, nonetheless, be documented. It is imperative that the nature of the contact be demonstrated so that anyone reviewing the documentation will clearly understand that the person contacted did not voluntarily submit to an interview with a law enforcement officer. Documentation is also important to ensure that other investigators do not conduct any similar limited contacts with the subject that could cause him to be suspicious.

Limited undercover operations should only involve a small number of contacts. If more than three contacts are made with a subject or a target location, strong consideration should be given to designating the project as a semi-deep or deep undercover operation.

Semi-Deep Undercover

In this second level of undercover work, the undercover investigator makes contacts in the target area with some degree of frequency, but he is not functioning on an around-the-clock basis. At this level, the undercover officer should carry quality false documentation. The undercover investigator may have a clandestine residence or employment that the subject can see if necessary. However, it is more likely that the undercover investigator will either claim not to have either, or will decline to provide details about them. Clearly, if the continuation of the project requires the undercover investigator to have verifiable props, including a residence, they should be provided.

In semi-deep undercover operations, the undercover investigator usually has control of his whereabouts. He makes contacts in accordance with what is best for him and his agency. He usually does not make himself available 24 hours a day, seven days a week. The semi-deep undercover officer should have a vehicle that is documented in such a way that anyone running the license plate would be satisfied. Frequently, semi-deep undercover operations are designed to be open-ended, meaning that if all goes well, the agency could expand them into full deep undercover projects.

Semi-deep undercover operations require a certain amount of departmental support. Unlike a limited undercover operation that could occur at almost any time and involve a single contact, the semi-deep undercover technique should be planned. The undercover investigator should have quality false identification that can withstand scrutiny and a reasonable background story about himself, his history, and his daily routine.

It is not unusual for semi-deep undercover officers to work with deep undercover investigators on a project. In some projects, one or more informants are also involved in the operation.

Deep Cover Operations

This is the most complex level of undercover work, and is rarely achieved. Many of the operations that law enforcement agencies describe as being deep cover are actually long-term, sophisticated, semi-deep undercover projects. Essentially, the deep cover operation involves an officer joining the targeted subject or conspiracy on a full-time basis. If the target is a right-wing militia group that maintains a compound in rural Idaho, the deep cover operative would likely live at the compound if other group members did so. If the target is a leftist terrorist who operates a radical bookstore in New York, the undercover officer would work in the bookstore or regularly visit it, and reside in an apartment a few doors away. He would spend his spare time with the subject or the subject's associates. If the project involves the deep undercover officer operating a business that fronts for a fencing operation, the officer would possibly run the store during appropriate hours, live in the area, associate with subjects, and generally hang around in the neighborhood. If the target is a motorcycle gang, the undercover operative would ride with the group and stay in their crash pads.

Deep cover is a full-time assignment. A deep cover investigator should not perform other police functions for his agency. Furthermore, the agency should avoid the temptation to use the deep undercover officer to perform undercover functions in different cases unless they involve the same type of crime and can complement the targeted case. If the undercover officer is operating a fencing operation intended to identify thieves and recover stolen merchandise, he should not be spending his off-duty hours looking for neighborhood fugitives, associating with prostitutes, visiting gambling dens, and inquiring about terrorists. The deep cover officer must function in accordance with the scenario that has been developed for him. Anytime the officer steps outside of the scenario, he risks creating suspicion on the part of the people he is working against. A fence who suddenly begins attending Ku Klux Klan meetings might find his criminal targets distancing themselves from him. Having an undercover operative involved in multiple cases can also present problems in court, particularly in terrorism investigations, in which the defense will often use any challenge possible to defeat the government. It may be very difficult to keep information about other cases on which the undercover operative was or is working out of a trial. If nothing else, the defense attorney will attempt to use such outside activities to cloud the issue and discredit the officer.

Questions to Be Asked Before Beginning a Semi-Deep or Deep Undercover Project

Undercover work involves a great deal more than an investigator telling people that he is someone and something other than what he really is. Even in limited contact undercover work it is wise for the operative to carry quality false identification. Before a law enforcement agency begins an undercover project anticipated to extend beyond several contacts, it should consider the following points.

Have All Other Investigative Techniques Been Exhausted?

Undercover projects are extremely manpower- and resource-intensive. They should not be used if other, less demanding techniques can accomplish the same objectives. One of the major difficulties in using the undercover technique is that it often demands that other investigative techniques be employed to support it. A good undercover project may require the use of wiretaps, microphones, closed-circuit television, and surveillance just to support the undercover officer.

Is It An Emergency Situation?

Where lives are at stake, it may be necessary to employ an undercover operation at an early stage of an investigation if the opportunity presents itself to the law enforcement agency. A common situation where this occurs involves a contract "hit man." A complainant will tell a police agency that he has been contacted about killing someone. The complainant has the capability of introducing an undercover officer pretending to be a killer-for-hire to the individual requesting the murder. Other techniques may be possible, but there is a real chance that they will not be fast enough to save the victim's life. In terrorism cases it could involve an extremist group reaching out to the criminal world for explosives to bomb a target. In order to preclude someone else from responding to the request, a law enforcement undercover operative will assume the role of an explosives provider.

Is There a Suitable Person Available to Function in the Undercover Role?

Most law enforcement officers will not be able to function in semi-deep or deep cover roles even though, for "macho" reasons, they will not feel comfortable admitting this. Some officers find that their morals, standards, and personalities make it impossible for them to convince people that they are someone else. Many investigators are unable to participate in undercover assignments because of the negative impact that such operations will have on their family life. This is especially true with respect to deep cover operations. Some investigators cannot participate in undercover work because they are too well-known as law enforcement officers, or they have future commitments, such as impending trials, in which they may become well-known. Some right-wing groups in the United States target law enforcement agencies seeking new recruits. It is possible that at some time in the future, a law enforcement officer who penetrates one of these groups may find himself face-to-face with a fellow law enforcement officer who is a group member. Law enforcement agencies should be aware of any of their officers or departmental employees who belong to extremist groups that are the subject of investigation.

Some officers will not be able to work in undercover assignments because they also have other specialized responsibilities within their law enforcement agency. Included in this area might be serving on the SWAT team, being a hostage negotiator or explosives technician, or functioning as a training officer or an instructor at the police academy. When engaged in lengthy semi-deep or deep undercover projects, the operative must relinquish such outside responsibilities.

Many departments find it difficult or impossible to find anyone willing and able to work in a proposed undercover project. This may require abandonment or alteration of the operation. Sometimes it may necessitate the agency "borrowing" an officer from another agency or working jointly with one or more other agencies.

The key to the success of an undercover project is clearly the undercover investigator. He must be suitable for the project. Departments sometimes do have volunteers for an operation, but they may not be ideal candidates. Some volunteers come from the fringes of the department. They are the officers who are not the best performers. They have often experienced problems with their written documentation. Some have had difficulties following orders. Some are regarded by their peers as "oddballs." Despite the temptation, caution should be exercised before employing a fringe person in an extended undercover project. Such people often have little difficulty gaining acceptance by the target, because they do not possess the characteristics that the target attributes to law enforcement officers. Unfortunately, such a candidate may prove to be difficult to handle and control. It should be recalled that the advantages of using the undercover technique largely center around the good judgment, experience, professionalism, and skills of a law enforcement officer over those held by an informant or a private citizen. Obviously, a fringe officer is not going to exhibit these traits, thereby negating many of the strong points of the technique.

In some situations, the undercover project may appear on the surface to be exciting and fun. Consequently, the department may find itself with several applicants. This does not guarantee success in the modern world of law enforcement. It is possible that seniority rules, anti-discrimination policies, union agreements, nepotism, and other regulations may force a department to seriously consider a candidate who may not be able to successfully perform the task. Again, it is probably better to abandon the project than to use an inappropriate undercover operative.

No law enforcement officer should be forced to work undercover. The undercover assignment is unlike any other in law enforcement. It is unique and involves certain talents and skills that many people do not possess. The person must be able to act—he must be able to become another person. He must be able to quickly recall every aspect of the background scenario that has been created in connection with his false identity. He must be able to withstand pressure. He must always be alert. He must be able to think quickly and respond rapidly. He must have an excellent memory for both generalities and specifics. People either have or do not have these skills by the time they become adults. Many of these traits cannot really be taught, although they can be refined. A department may be better off not initiating a semi-deep or deep cover operation, rather than beginning one using an investigator who lacks several of these key traits. As an alternative, the department may have to modify the undercover project to fit the natural attributes of the undercover officer.

Is the Department Willing and Able to Make Available a Handler for the Undercover Investigator?

A handling officer must be assigned for any deep cover operative. It is desirable that such a person be designated in semi-deep cover operations, especially if they are long-term and involve a great deal of time on the part of the undercover operative. The handling officer connects the undercover officer to the law enforcement agency. He serves as the conduit through which information is passed from the undercover officer to the police agency, and through which instructions are given to the undercover operative. The handling officer is also the person who assists the undercover officer with personal matters.

In one lengthy, semi-deep undercover operation, the undercover investigator came from an office located a considerable distance from the office in which the operation was being run. This was beneficial because it gave the officer security and allowed him to live a normal life while off duty. Unfortunately, no one was assigned as a handling officer for the undercover investigator. Complicating the situation was the fact that an informant was deeply involved in the case. Because the undercover investigator worked closely with the informant, the agency decided to assign the undercover investigator to also function as the informant's handling officer. This was inappropriate because the undercover officer did not work in the office running the case, had no access to the informant's records, and only had telephonic contact with the overall case officer responsible for the project. It did not take long before a variety of problems developed. The unfortunate undercover officer had only minimal knowledge about the development of the case, because he had no direct link to the office. Additionally, the undercover officer had little knowledge about the informant's background which, as he later learned, was somewhat tainted. Because he had little knowledge of the case, the undercover officer had difficulty giving direction to the informant and even in debriefing him. The undercover investigator and the informant were key figures in the investigation, yet both were left in the dark by the officer running the case.

Can the Department Maintain Complete Security for the Operation?

The undercover operation should be maintained on a need-to-know basis. The fewer people who know about the specifics of the operation, the better it is. The project cannot be common knowledge in the department or the prosecutor's office. The undercover officer's name should probably be dropped from the department's normal rolls. Investigators working on the case should adopt the habit of referring to the operative by a code name, in the same manner as they would refer to an informant. The operative's "departure" from the department should be explained in a reasonable manner. The officer "moved on to a larger agency," "returned to school," "went into private security work," "is working on a federal task force in New York City." People who call the agency looking for the officer should be told that there is no such person on the roster. If the caller persists, he should be told that the agency head maintains all records of past employees, and that a message will be left for him to contact the caller. The handler or case officer should be made aware of the identities of people seeking the officer. Some form of "stop" should be placed in the department's computer system that will flag management and identify anyone who attempts to gather information on the officer's true name or false identification. The computer should be programmed to supply a reasonable response or show "no record" to whoever checks it.

The department must also examine itself to determine whether it has been penetrated by the targets of the investigation or by people who could logically provide information to them. Some right-wing extremist groups are openly recruiting police officers. A police agency that elects to place an undercover officer into one of these groups may wish to reconsider its decision if it determines that some of its employees attend activities sponsored by the group or are members of it.

Some news media personnel offer money for tips about investigations to law enforcement personnel. A department must ensure that an undercover project is not "leaked." Terrorists read newspapers, as do many other criminals. A blurb in a gossip column indicating that the local police have initiated an undercover operation may be enough to send a danger signal to the target of the investigation.

Is the Department Willing and Able to Protect the Undercover Officer?

The immediate response to this question is almost always a resounding "yes." However, it is important that department leaders truly realize what is required to fulfill this commitment. The more dangerous the target, the more protection the undercover investigator may require. An undercover officer working covertly inside a banking institution might not require direct protection during his normal bank working hours, even though he has regular contact with the targets of the case. In contrast, an undercover investigator who has penetrated a terrorist cell could easily require around-the-clock surveillance and electronic protection every time he is with the targets. In the previously outlined example, the officer running the operation often did not know when the undercover investigator was with the subjects of the case, meaning that the operative was virtually left without protection.

Some departments, particularly small ones, simply do not have the manpower or resources to adequately protect undercover investigators. Yet these departments have a responsibility to protect their undercover officers. If protection cannot be given, the agency should consider abandoning the project, limiting the scope of the project, or bringing other agencies into the project to assist.

Security for the undercover agent can involve a variety of precautions. Surveillance is a common form of protection. Another is electronic coverage. Still another might involve closed-circuit television and burglar alarms. Assigning additional officers to function in other undercover roles within the project can also give protection. If the primary undercover officer is frequenting a tavern where he meets with the subjects, a second undercover officer can possibly be placed in the establishment in the role of a bartender so he can keep an eye on the primary officer.

Is the Department Able to Support an Undercover Operation From a Technical Standpoint?

The undercover officer makes an excellent witness in court, but an undercover officer supported by videotape and audiotape transcriptions makes an even better witness. It is always best in a court situation to have evidence that will support an investigator's word against the word of a defendant. This is especially true with respect to undercover operations, because undercover officers often must wait long periods before being able to make notes of what they experienced and observed. Under normal circumstances, an officer makes notes as he conducts his investigation, and then transcribes them into a final report that is submitted to the court. In an undercover project, the undercover officer often must wait hours or even days before he can safely make notes, much less write a formal report. Final documentation could take weeks. A defense attorney may attempt to discredit the undercover officer by challenging his memory. If there is evidence that supports the undercover officer's memory, the prosecutor's case will be much stronger.

Will the Undercover Officer Be Recognized?

In small towns and close-knit neighborhoods, recognition of the officer can present a serious problem. Most people know their law enforcement officers. Some small town newspapers write articles about the town's officers, especially when they are initially hired, promoted, or receive awards. It may be very difficult for an officer to function undercover within his own jurisdiction. It may be necessary for the town to work out an arrangement with another town, or the county, state, or federal government to bring in an undercover operative who can work in the town safely.

A more recent problem involves militias and other right-wing groups who are recruiting active-duty, retired, and part-time law enforcement officers. A police agency seeking to penetrate such groups must be very vigilant for police recruits who might recognize the undercover operative. Environmental, animal rights, and anti-abortion groups may also recruit law enforcement officers, thereby possibly presenting a problem for undercover investigators. Using an undercover officer in an ethnic terrorist group could present a similar problem if the officer used is a member of the ethnic group being targeted. If the town's ethnic community is very small, many members of it will know of other people of the same cultural background, even if they have never met them.

Is the Department Able to Deal With Fallout?

In federal agencies and many state agencies, an undercover officer can be transferred away from the area where the project occurred if it appears that the officer and his family are in danger, or that the operative's ability to resume functioning as a law enforcement officer has been compromised. This situation can create a problem for a city or county law enforcement agency. The nature of the project and the degree of danger that the subjects pose will determine the extent of the problem that may develop from a particular undercover project. Fallout is something that should be considered at the outset of an undercover project. If it appears likely that a problem could develop, and the department has no plan for dealing with this problem, the department probably should alter or abandon the undercover project.

Creating the Undercover Project

Most law enforcement agencies do not create detailed undercover proposals for limited contact undercover operations, although some agencies require management approval for such projects. If a limited contact produces good results and causes an agency to continue it, the department should take the steps to move it into the semi-deep or deep undercover project.

Usually, semi-deep and deep undercover projects are only considered after other investigative techniques have failed to solve the criminal problem. On occasion, however, an undercover operation will "drop" into the lap of an investigative agency as a brand-new case, never before explored by that agency. The situation will be so inviting, or of such an immediate need, that the agency cannot employ other techniques. In a terrorism case it might involve a group seeking someone with criminal connections to get a fugitive member out of the country. Semi-deep and deep undercover operations normally involve a fairly detailed written proposal that must be approved by agency management personnel. Departments that do not do this are taking a serious risk. They may be allowing themselves to become involved in a project that is beyond their ability to support. The FBI not only requires that their agents prepare a written proposal that clearly outlines their undercover project, but also requires that the agents make a verbal presentation and defense of the proposal before a committee of veteran managers and legal advisors. If investigators have done their homework in planning their undercover operation, they should be willing and able to defend it. Conversely, if agency management is willing to support a project, they should be willing to take the time to review the proposal and question it from every angle. Such a process makes it difficult for a manager to rubber-stamp a project that will greatly affect agency resources.

The following is an outline of what should be included in a written proposal for a semi-deep or deep undercover project:

- A description of the crime problem

- An outline of the statutes/laws involved

- A history of the efforts made to resolve the situation to date

- A reason for the proposed project

- The proposed scenario for the creation and operation of the project, including:

  - How the undercover officer will make contact with the target

  - How the undercover operation will develop over time

  - How long the project will take, and how will it end

  - How the undercover operative is going to be selected, and what traits and experience he should have

  - How the undercover officer will be backstopped (false identification and other documentation)

  - How the undercover officer will be protected

  - Who else will be involved in the project (informants, other undercover operatives, private citizens)

- A detailed outline of anticipated expenses
- A list of required personnel, both sworn and support, that the project will require
- A list of personnel required from other law enforcement departments, other agencies, and the private sector to support the project. Also, a statement about the degree of commitment made by these entities to guarantee their support (i.e., signed letters of agreement, memorandums of understanding, etc.)
- A description of buildings, offices, residences, and other structures that will be required for the project
- A list of equipment that will be required for the project
- A detailed description outlining the kinds of support that the department must be willing to provide to ensure the success of the project

- ◆ Statements from the department's legal counsel and from the prosecutor's office giving their approval to the proposal as outlined. These statements should specifically indicate that they do not foresee problems with respect to entrapment if the project is conducted as outlined.

The proposal recommendation will result in a lengthy document that will require investigators to expend a great deal of time and effort in its creation. Similarly, it will force department managers and legal advisors to expend a great deal of their time reviewing the document. However, it must be remembered that, in undercover projects, one or more officers are placing their lives on the line. The careers of department managers can be destroyed by the failure of such a project. The reputation of the department is also often on the line. Extra time and effort at the beginning of the project can do much to avoid pitfalls that can easily occur along the way.

Selecting the Undercover Officer

While it often may not be possible to choose a "perfect" undercover officer, the following points should be considered in order to ensure that a good choice is made.

Compatibility

The undercover officer should be able to blend into the targeted situation with a minimum of effort. He either has to be accepted as "one of the gang" because he appears to be like everyone else, or he has to possess some talent, skill, or quality that causes the group to want to recruit him, or to accept him in some form of working relationship. "Leadership" is a trait that many police officers possess, but it is not a trait that an agency should be trying to sell in an undercover project. The objective should not be to take over the targeted group or to dominate and lead the targeted subject.

It is important not to saddle the undercover officer with a burden that he must continually overcome in order to blend into the targeted group or into the community surrounding it. It is not wise that the undercover officer be the only black, Asian, old, young, female or male, or disabled person involved in the conspiracy, for example. If he is, he will always stand out rather than blend into the group.

Previous success in undercover work does not always guarantee that an officer will be effective in a new project. Similarly, success in a short-term project does not mean that same officer could do well in a long-range, around-the-clock operation. The fact that an officer has had an outstanding record as an investigator does not mean that he will equal that success in an undercover role. In fact, it is possible that such an officer will not be a good undercover candidate. The officer must be compatible with the project and its requirements. If not, the project must be altered to fit that officer's traits, if he is to be used in it.

Experience

One of the main values of undercover work is that it places a skilled investigator in a position where he can use his good judgment and knowledge to develop sufficient evidence to prosecute the suspects. If the candidate for the undercover position does not have these attributes, one of the main reasons for using the undercover technique is compromised. Young rookie officers are often viewed as logical undercover candidates because they often have fewer family ties or other obligations. Unfortunately, many rookies also lack the experience that would enable them to make good judgments and offer wise suggestions during the course of an investigation.

Maturity and Stability

Undercover work can be very demanding. Officers are often on their own when it comes to decision making. There can also be a great deal of loneliness, because undercover operatives do not establish close relationships with the people they are investigating, even though they are with them on a continual basis. Undercover officers will encounter many undesirable temptations, including drugs, sex, and large sums of money. It requires a certain amount of maturity to be able to function in undercover assignments. An immature person placed into such a situation could falter and make poor decisions. Possible mental instability is also something that could manifest itself during the course of a long-term undercover assignment. Many larger departments have professional people who attempt to evaluate the mental condition of candidates for undercover work in an effort to identify and eliminate officers whom they believe may not be able to withstand the pressures of the assignment.

Psychological Issues

Can the undercover candidate function in a manner in which he appears to be loyal to the political cause, yet maintain his true allegiance to the department and his country? This is an issue that must be considered. A department cannot place an officer into a terrorist group only to have that individual switch loyalties and actually join that cause. In a sense, the department must ensure that the undercover officer holds acceptable values and standards, and that he is not searching for something in which to believe. Certainly, it would be unwise to place an undercover officer into a group with which he holds sympathetic political views. Conversely, the operative cannot be a crusader for beliefs that are in opposition to those of the target group. The undercover officer's role is to develop information about criminal violations in order to facilitate the arrest and prosecution of the group members. It is not to convince the targets to change their ways.

Personnel Issues

It is important that the undercover officer be able to testify in court at the conclusion of the case. If the officer's background includes disciplinary actions, these could impair his credibility. This is especially true if he has been disciplined for giving false statements, lying, or failing to follow orders while on duty. Terrorist defendants will make concerted efforts to challenge the integrity of all law enforcement witnesses, particularly undercover operatives, if such people have developed key evidence against them. At the very least, they will attempt to have the judge review such an officer's personnel file. If the judge discovers information in a file suggesting that the officer has been dishonest in the past, he may order the information to be turned over to the defense.

Female Officers as Terrorist Undercover Operatives

The issue of employing female officers in undercover roles in terrorism investigations is worthy of discussion. Many people in society continue to regard police work as a male profession, just as many people continue to assume that nursing is a female profession. In fact, many police agencies did not even employ women as sworn officers until the 1970s. Even a distinguished national law enforcement agency like the FBI did not permit women to be special agents until the early 1970s. Women have made great strides in law enforcement. Today, several women are in charge of major FBI

Field Divisions, and hold executive positions in other federal law enforcement agencies. Nonetheless, the perception that police departments do not hire women to do more than issue parking tickets may well make it easier for a female officer to penetrate a group than it would be for a male. It is possible that the group will not even consider the possibility that the new female potential recruit into their organization could possibly be a cop. Many women in law enforcement possess talents and skills that would make them ideal candidates for all kinds of undercover work.

However, employing women in undercover roles against terrorist groups presents certain difficulties. From about 1960 to 1980, when leftist-oriented groups were quite active in the United States, female members played major roles. The Weather Underground Organization and the FALN are two good examples. Placing a female officer into such a group could present a dilemma. To gain acceptance, the officer would probably have to assume a feminist role and exhibit aggressive behavior and leadership qualities. This is not an ideal situation for any undercover operative. In court proceedings, the defense could portray such an undercover operative as being an agent provocateur who entrapped group members into violating the law.

In some right-wing groups and Middle Eastern terrorist groups, women play secondary roles. In fact, some of these groups do not have female members. This does not mean that a female officer cannot be used in some form of undercover role against these targets. However, if the objective of the operation is to place the operative into the group, it might not be wise to use a female officer in such a situation. (Similarly, some of these groups also do not accept black members, so expecting a black officer to penetrate such a group would not be prudent, either.)

Common sense must be followed with respect to placing people into undercover roles. Although the law of the land may clearly state that all people are equal and must be treated as such, the fact is that many criminal enterprises and terrorist groups do not feel compelled to follow these mandates. No prosecutor in his right mind would take a criminal enterprise to court on charges that it discriminated against women entering their illegal conspiracy.

Safety must also be a concern in any undercover operation. Placing a female into a terrorist group that is primarily composed of men could be inviting trouble. Rape is always a possibility, especially if some of the male members consider themselves to be "macho." In many situations, a woman could develop information by agreeing to engage in intimate relations with group members. However, this is something that no agency should ask, expect, or condone with respect to their undercover operatives. Male undercover officers should also refrain from intimate sexual relationships with targets of investigation. Sexual relations with undercover targets should be avoided. Not only does the officer risk contracting a sexually transmitted disease, he compromises his credibility. The undercover officer will ultimately testify in court. Jurors will look unfavorably at undercover law enforcement officers who engaged in sexual relations with the targets of the investigation.

The Handling Officer

The handling officer functions as the link between the law enforcement agency and the undercover officer. It is absolutely essential that such a person be assigned in deep cover operations. In semi-deep cover, it will depend on the ability of the undercover officer to maintain a normal family life and to visit his police agency. If the assignment restricts what the operative can do with respect to his personal or professional life, the handling agent must step in and function on the undercover officer's behalf. Among the functions that the handling officer could do would be visiting the officers' residence and watering plants, picking up mail, paying bills, and arranging for necessary repairs. He could also care for the officer's personal vehicle and other property. He could assist the officer in filing income taxes and similar obligations. He will also handle administrative matters within the department for the officer.

In addition to these functions, the handling officer acts as a go-between for information dealing with the department and community. He will transmit messages between the department and the undercover officer. He will listen to the officer and offer counsel and advice.

The handling officer will arrange for briefings and debriefings of the undercover officer. In some situations, the handling officer will perform these functions himself. In other instances, he will facilitate meetings between the undercover officer and investigators more involved in the case.

The handling officer also observes the undercover operative for signs that he is weakening or needs relief or assistance. The handler should encourage the operative to express his fears and concerns about security and safety. The handler must convey his observations to the case officer and management personnel. In addition, there should be some form of emergency warning signal established between the handler and the undercover officer so that if the operative needs immediate assistance, he can flag the handler (or surveillance officers or anyone else involved in the project). It could be something as simple as wearing a particular shirt, raising a window shade in his apartment, or uttering a code word that could be overheard on a microphone.

The handling officer should be a mature and stable person. It is beneficial if he has an empathic nature and is a good listener. He must be respected by the undercover officer. It helps if he can present himself as someone who is detached from the investigation and the officers actually running the case. In that way, he can listen to complaints and frustrations from the undercover officer. He should not be the case officer or co-case officer. He should not be a higher-ranking police official. If such a person is employed, it is likely that the undercover officer will not vent his true feelings. Another danger in using a ranking officer is that he has the power to make things happen. As the undercover officer comes under stress, he may make demands on the handling officer out of frustration. If the handler is a line officer, all he can do is report them back to management. However, if the person is a ranking officer, he will be placed in the situation of approving something that perhaps should not be done, or denying something that will unnecessarily antagonize the undercover officer.

The handling officer should be a veteran law enforcement officer who is knowledgeable about the functioning of his own department. It helps if the handling officer has some personal undercover experience. The handling officer is also often functioning in a somewhat covert status. Although he probably should not be also working undercover in the same case as the undercover agent, he will nonetheless carry false identification and drive a falsely registered vehicle. In longer-range and deep cover projects, the handling officer will often maintain a covert apartment or business in which he can make secure contact with the undercover officer.

Securing False Identification

While the written proposal is the foundation upon which the entire undercover project is constructed, false documentation is the foundation upon which the undercover officer is "created." Weak documentation can bring down an undercover officer just as fast as a poorly constructed foundation can bring down a building. Unfortunately, for many operations, false documentation is not treated as seriously as it should be. All too often the undercover officer is told to make up a name and a legend. It is often suggested that the undercover officer retain his true surname and create a false given name. Therefore, Detective Robert Jones becomes Bobby Smith. Sometimes the officer is encouraged to retain his own date of birth or only change the year of birth. It is reasoned that a person using his own first name and proper date of birth will respond quickly if asked, and will not draw suspicion by not answering or giving incorrect information. These suggestions have merit. However, if the proper documentation to support the new identity and date of birth cannot be established, they will end up creating problems for the undercover officer.

Before a department sends an officer into a semi-deep or deep undercover project, it should ensure that he has false identification that will withstand an investigation. The undercover agent's life can depend upon the quality of the false identification. A department would probably be best served by specifically assigning another investigator to help the undercover officer obtain quality false identification, rather than leaving the task entirely to the undercover operative.

It must be realized that procuring false identification may violate local, state, or federal statutes. It is important that a law enforcement agency discuss this issue with its legal counsel, the city's legal counsel, or the prosecutor's office to ensure that the steps taken by the agency to procure false documentation for its undercover officer are legal and defensible in court. In most instances, there are provisions within the law that permit law enforcement agencies to take actions necessary to implement undercover projects.

The cornerstone of quality false identification is a birth certificate. Everyone either has, or knows where to obtain, his or her birth certificate. Consequently, an undercover operative who does not have a birth certificate, who cannot procure one, and/or is unable to explain where such a document is filed, is destined to face problems. This form of identification should be established before any other documentation is obtained.

Some police agencies naively believe that the birth certificate itself is the important document. It is not. Anyone can employ a disreputable printer to create a fake birth certificate or other document, and such a birth certificate will not withstand scrutiny. Furthermore, few people go around waving their birth certificate or have it hanging in a frame on a wall in their home or office. It is fairly easy for someone within a targeted group to conduct a check to verify that a person (the undercover officer) was born as he or she has indicated. They could simply claim to be that person and request a duplicate birth certificate. It can often be done through the mail. A "researcher" could also claim to be conducting a study that requires that he review a person's birth certificate. A good research ploy is a genealogical study of a particular family. Other methods that can be used to confirm a person's birth certificate are for the "researcher" to claim to be an employer verifying an application, an insurance investigator working on a claim, or a private investigator trying to trace a person. In short, a birth certificate is easily checked, so an undercover officer should have one on file in the bureau of vital statistics where he claims to have been born.

During the 1960s and 1970s, many clandestine terrorist groups and some criminals were using the birth certificates of deceased infants for false identities. This method had long been used by foreign spies. A simple way of doing this was to either read the names from graves in the infants' section of a cemetery, or locate the names in the obituary section of old newspapers. During the 1980s, bureaus of vital statistics attempted to curb this practice by noting on birth certificates the fact that the person had died. This became relatively simple to do once an agency had computerized all its records.

Deceased infant birth certificates can still be used, but to a very limited extent. There are still some bureaus of vital statistics in rural areas in which the death of an infant is not indicated on the birth certificate. This can also happen in large cities in situations in which the bureau of vital statistics is unaware of an infant's death. This often occurs in cities near state borders where a child is born in one state but dies in another state. For example, many women residing in northern Indiana or southern Wisconsin use Chicago-area hospitals to give birth to their children. If the child dies more than several days later, the death will likely have occurred in their home states, and Illinois might not be aware of what has happened.

Law enforcement agencies can use the identities of deceased infants to document their undercover officers. In fact, they can probably use just about any deceased infant's identity because the bureau of vital statistics could "remove" the deceased notation from the file at the request of the police department or the prosecutor's office. In that way, if anyone checks to determine if the undercover officer was born as he claims, the records would support the officer's story. As easy as it sounds, some law enforcement agencies, including at least one large federal agency, will not consider using the identities of deceased infants to document their undercover officers. They believe that such a practice would violate the rights of the deceased infant and his or her family. They also believe that the deceased infant's family could be endangered as a result of the use of their child's identity.

Another method for establishing a false identity is to assume the identity of someone who lives far away or who is "unavailable" to the general public. Falling into the latter category would be long-term prison inmates, patients in mental institutions or nursing homes, mentally retarded or brain-injured people, or individuals who have dropped out of society to become hermits or homeless. Criminals and terrorists have procured identifications in this manner. Law enforcement agencies, however, probably should not use this method.

Making up identification is probably the most common method used by law enforcement agencies. The key is backstopping the created name. An official-looking birth certificate can be made by a good printer, or even by many police laboratories. However, few normal people actually display such a certificate, and an operative who carried around a copy of his birth certificate would be suspicious. The important aspect of a created date of birth is that it be backed by a bureau of vital statistics. In some parts of the country, a law enforcement agency can "insert" a record of a nonexistent person into the local vital statistics file. In other areas of the country, policies prohibit this. In still other parts of the country, the records are maintained via computer. In some cases this makes inserting a record simple, but in other cases it makes placement of a false record impossible. Regardless of how it is done, an agency should attempt to support an undercover officer's false identification with a record in a bureau of vital statistics office.

A Social Security number has become a key aspect of a person's identification. These numbers, which were once relatively easy to procure, are becoming more difficult to obtain. During the 1960s, Social Security cards could be procured through the completion of a form. This changed dramatically during the 1990s. People now are expected to apply for Social Security cards as infants. Indeed, a parent cannot claim a child as a dependent on his income tax unless that child has a Social Security number. It is now extremely difficult for an adult to apply for a first-time Social Security number. If the undercover officer speaks a foreign language and "looks foreign," he might be able to claim to be a recent immigrant in order to receive a Social Security card. However, he should have immigration documents to support his claim.

Today, people using false identification will probably either make up a Social Security number or will "borrow" someone else's number. The best "borrowed" numbers will be from people who are not using them for some reason. Included in this category might be prison inmates, disabled people, and homeless people. Made-up numbers have a double risk. They could be nonexistent, which could lead to an inquiry from the Social Security Administration, or they could belong to someone else. In the latter situation, the Social Security Administration could inquire because of improper or impossible payments coming into the actual person's file. Most law enforcement agencies will not permit an undercover officer to knowingly use another person's Social Security number. This means that the officer will probably make up a number and hope that it does not belong to anyone else.

The importance of a Social Security number will depend upon what the undercover officer plans to do with it. If he plans to work using that number, there is an excellent chance that his employer will receive some kind of indication from the Social Security administration that there is a problem. Obviously, no undercover officer wants to have anyone question his false identification. This can be a serious problem if the employment is somehow tied to the project, and the suspect will learn of a Social Security inquiry. Usually it will take a few months for Social Security to inquire about a problem, so if the employment is short-term, the undercover officer may be safe.

Probably the best action that an undercover project can take to skirt the Social Security issue is to either have the undercover officer be unemployed and not even seeking work, or to have the undercover officer "employed" by a dummy corporation set up by the law enforcement agency. Of course, the dummy corporation will never send anything to the Social Security Administration because they are not really paying the officer a salary. The best advice to an undercover officer is to not do anything that will require him to use his Social Security number. That means avoid work unless at a dummy company, and avoid opening a bank account because interest reports may be sent to the Social Security Administration.

When establishing a Social Security number, law enforcement agencies should be aware that the numbers have some significance that the undercover operative should understand. The first three numbers correspond to the state in which the card was issued. For example, numbers 261 through 267 are assigned to the state of Florida. The second two numbers on a Social Security card refer to the approximate year in which the card was issued. These numbers are less important, because they are not as exact. Odd numbers between 5 and 9 were issued to people born before the late 1930s and even numbers 10 and above were issued to people born after that. However, in the 1960s, even numbers between 2 and 8 were issued. The last three numbers have no significance. What this means to the undercover officer is that his background must show some reason that he was issued a Social Security number in the state reflected on his card. An undercover officer who claims never to have traveled west of the Mississippi River may be in trouble if his Social Security number begins with the number "516," which is assigned to the state of Montana. Most undercover officers will probably want to avoid middle Social Security numbers that are odd and less than 10, unless they are claiming to be more than 60 years of age. Possibly the safest and fastest way to create a false Social Security number is for the undercover officer to use the correct first five numbers on his true Social Security card, and then reverse or jumble the last three digits. Of course, he will have to claim to have received his card in the state where he actually did receive it. Obviously, such a "new" number can only be used for a short period for employment purposes, because the Social Security Administration will quickly realize that the number either is already assigned to someone else, or is nonexistent.

False drivers' licenses are usually not a problem for law enforcement agencies. Most states have provisions for issuing drivers' licenses and other forms of state identification to undercover operatives. Care must be exercised in obtaining such a license to ensure that there is nothing unique about it that could compromise the officer. Some states have "flags" on such documents that can alert an officer who encounters someone carrying them. This could be a serious problem if an undercover operative is stopped for speeding while with a subject and is given a "pass" by the trooper because the trooper recognizes him as an undercover operative through a special number on his license, or because he is informed of the officer's status when he runs the license through the state computer.

If a state does not have a special provision for law enforcement licenses, or if for some reason the undercover officer cannot use the provision, the undercover officer can obtain a driver's license in the same manner that the average citizen does—he can take the driver's test. Usually all that is required to do this is for the undercover officer to present proof of identity. In many states, however, an older person will be questioned about his previous license. The operative might be able to admit to having had a license in another state years ago, but having had it suspended for not having insurance. A check of that other state will yield no record suggesting that old records had been destroyed. The undercover officer can also respond safely, by stating that he has lived in New York City for years and could not afford to own a car, and therefore did not have a license. He could also claim to have lived abroad. Another way to avoid questioning is for the undercover officer to enroll in a driving school. Usually applicants from such schools are not questioned seriously when applying for a license, because attending the school seems to be "proof" that the person never had a driver's license before.

Credit cards are excellent forms of false identification. Some law enforcement agencies have arrangements with certain credit card companies through which they can have legitimate credit cards issued to false identities. If, for some reason, an agency does not have such an arrangement, it can usually work through a bank to obtain some kind of a credit card for their undercover operative. If no arrangement is possible, the undercover officer will be forced to do what the average citizen does—apply for a credit card. Another way to obtain credit is for the officer to buy something from an appliance or furniture store, but indicate that he cannot pay for it entirely in cash. Often if the buyer is able to put down a large down payment, the store will agree to finance the rest, rather than lose the sale.

Bank accounts are important forms of identification that many undercover officers need. The best account is probably a non-interest-paying checking account. Many law enforcement agencies have contacts at banks who can open an account. If not, the undercover officer can simply open an account on his own by producing a driver's license, Social Security number, and perhaps a credit card.

The "spice" of a false identification packet will be the numerous miscellaneous forms of identification that the average person picks up, often without asking. Many are best described as "junk ID" because they really do not prove that the person is who he or she claims to be. Hunting and fishing licenses look official and are issued by the state, but often little is required to procure them other than a small fee. The operative probably can avoid questions by applying for an out-of-state license that costs more, but eliminates any need to display in-state identification. A library card is another easy form of identification that looks good. Various museums offer memberships, complete with identification cards, for small donations. Music and DVD clubs provide membership cards for people who buy their products. Athletic clubs, roller rinks, and various specialized sporting operations also offer membership cards, often for doing nothing more than making a one-time use of their facilities. Car washes, grocery chains, restaurants, and other retail outlets give discount cards to customers. Some of these "ID cards" look "official," while others appear to be credit cards. People who see them assume that someone had to have shown proof of identity in order to obtain them. Unfortunately, this is rarely the case. Nonetheless, such documents tend to "prove" that the person is who he claims to be. This is especially true if the person has a number of them in his wallet or scattered around his residence. Undercover officers should assemble a collection of these cards to help make their new identity believable.

It might be prudent for an agency to instruct their undercover operative to spend several days going from location to location pretending to be his new identity, and seeking various forms of identification. It will give him an opportunity to practice being his new self. If the officer finds this mission difficult, the agency may want to reconsider using him on the project. Procuring "junk ID" should be easy compared to the challenge that the officer will face when dealing with the subjects of the investigation.

Assembling the Props

Undercover officers must appear to be what they claim to be. If an undercover officer depicts himself to be a disreputable businessman, he should dress the part, have a car that is registered or leased in his false identity or that of his business, and have an appropriate residence. If the residence will be visited by the targets or anyone who will report to the targets, the residence will have to be furnished so that there will be no question that the undercover officer actually lives there. The department must keep in mind that few people have all new furnishings and clothing. There should be items showing varying degrees of use and wear. It may be necessary to assemble such props from used furniture and clothing stores, or from the "attics" of agency employees. Most larger agencies have some furnishings in storage that came from seizures, forfeitures, abandonments, and previous investigations. Care must be taken when using such items. They should be searched for hidden identification or evidence numbers that might tie them to a law enforcement agency. Also, if the item was used in a previous undercover operation, it should be determined if there is any possibility that the furniture could be recognized by a current suspect or one of his or her associates.

Some "Gray Area" Undercover Projects

By definition, undercover operations involve the use of a sworn law enforcement officer as the undercover operative. The primary advantages of this investigative technique over other techniques involve characteristics of trained law enforcement officers. If a law enforcement officer is not used in an undercover project, most of the advantages are lost.

In some situations, a law enforcement agency will find itself lacking anyone willing or able to perform the role of the undercover officer. However, they might have some contact with a person residing in their community who has a certain skill that would enable that person to assume the role in the project. For example, a right-wing group is engaged in a financial fraud involving the passing of counterfeit securities. A local banker who is friendly with the police department is willing to "allow himself to be recruited" by the group to launder the securities through the banking system. The law enforcement agency could initiate a project using the banker in order to develop evidence against the right-wing group. However, this is not an undercover operation. It is essentially an informant project and should be operated as such.

A second gray area involves the use of nonsworn law enforcement personnel. Most departments employ highly skilled employees who perform support services for the agency. Some of these employees have skills that sworn officers do not possess, but would enable them to infiltrate a variety of criminal organizations. For example, many criminal and terrorist groups would welcome a computer expert into their organizations. A police department computer technician could be directed to join such a group. Police agencies occasionally investigate people who speak foreign languages. They have problems using the undercover technique against these groups because many departments do not have officers who can converse in the foreign language. If the problem is serious enough, larger departments will hire translators to work with the investigators. There could be a temptation to use a translator in an undercover role. However, like the cooperative private citizen, the translator is not a trained investigator. Like the project that used the banker, an operation that uses a nonsworn law enforcement employee should be handled as an informant project.

Final Considerations

A major drawback associated with any kind of undercover operation, especially those in the area of terrorism, is that if the subject becomes suspicious, it could cause him to become more secretive and, therefore, more difficult to investigate. It must be remembered that undercover work is usually initiated because other, less time-consuming investigative techniques have failed. The last thing an investigator wants to do is to make the subject more security conscious. A poorly handled undercover project can be worse than not undertaking the project in the first place.

Entrapment is a word that law enforcement agencies should expect to hear in court when an undercover project results in arrests. Defendants will claim that somehow the undercover officer caused them to violate the law. Terrorists will claim that although they may hate the government, they never actually intended to take any illegal action against it until the undercover officer suggested it. Great care must be taken throughout the course of the undercover project to ensure that the undercover officer does not take any actions that could constitute entrapment. The best method that the undercover operative can take to protect himself is to carefully document his actions. The department can assist by carefully documenting actions taken by other investigators that support what the undercover officer claims he did. Surveillance, electronic coverage, closed-circuit television, and informants can all help to support the undercover agent.

Police officers are often natural leaders and "take charge" people. It is important that undercover officers not exhibit these traits while functioning undercover. It will be very difficult to prosecute a criminal conspiracy in which the undercover law enforcement officer can be shown to be a leader, or essentially "in charge." The defense may accuse the undercover officer of being an *agent provocateur* who basically organized and led "innocent" people into committing illegal acts.

Informants are sometimes associated with, or actually involved in, undercover operations. Because they sometimes work directly with the undercover officer, there is a tendency for some agencies to want the undercover officer to operate the informant. This should not be done. The undercover officer is in no position to operate an informant. He does not have access to the informant's file, and has a major obligation to document his own activities and observations. It would be very difficult for the undercover officer to complete all of his or her own duties and document the informant's activities and reports. In the ideal project, an informant should not even know that there is an undercover officer involved in the case, much less know his or her identity.

19 Technical Investigative Techniques

Technical investigative techniques are also referred to as "sophisticated and sensitive" techniques. They are the most intrusive techniques that are available to law enforcement officers. Virtually all investigative techniques invade a person's privacy to a certain extent. Some, like interviews and the polygraph, are overt and direct. Others, like surveillance and informants, are secretive and unobtrusive. Still others, like trash covers and pretext telephone calls, are deceitful. Technical techniques go a step further, because they invade aspects of a person's life that are intended to be private and personal. For this reason, the government and courts severely restrict the use of these techniques. In most instances, they cannot be employed until other, less intrusive techniques have been attempted and have failed to produce satisfactory results. The primary exception to this rule involves life-and-death emergencies, such as a kidnapping, airplane hijacking, or serious threat to commit an act of mass destruction.

With the possible exception of a camera or video recorder, tracking devices, and consensual monitoring, most investigations will not use sensitive technical coverage. The case either will be solved before such techniques can be used, or the case will not warrant the time and effort required to use this coverage. Some states so severely limit the use of technical coverage that it is not a viable option. Investigations involving terrorists, especially those in which there are specific conspiracies to commit violent attacks, frequently use sophisticated techniques. Indeed, it is often very difficult to take such a case to court without the fruits of sensitive techniques. Terrorism cases are extremely difficult to prove; consequently, sophisticated coverage that directly shows group members saying and doing things that violate the law are outstanding pieces of evidence. Terrorist conspiracy case officers should begin planning for the possible use of technical coverage that they may ultimately use in the case during the early stages of the investigation.

Officers intending to use technical techniques must be able to justify it by preparing written documents that outline their reasons for believing that the person is engaged in criminal or terrorist activity. The reasons must be supported by probable cause. Personal opinions and unsubstantiated statements are insufficient. Informants must be reliable. Many investigators who have attempted to employ technical techniques have been frustrated by the refusal of their superiors to approve their requests. Some have developed so much probable cause in their effort to justify technical coverage that they have actually been able to indict and arrest the subjects before they were able to gain approval for the coverage.

The fact that "everyone knows" that a person is a criminal or a terrorist is insufficient justification for a court to approve the use of a technical investigative technique. In fact, no law enforcement administrator should grant approval to a proposal to use a technical technique unless there is evidence that the targeted person is engaged in criminal activity that justifies the use of the technique. In general, the idea is for the investigator to prepare a written document that so clearly demonstrates that the target is engaged in criminal activity that a reasonable person would accept that conclusion. Obviously, the statements contained in the document should be supported by the results of other investigative techniques. Another issue with respect to technical coverage involves the specific elements to be targeted. The fact that a person can be demonstrated to be a terrorist who is likely to be engaged in illegal activity, is not sufficient to justify technically monitoring his whole life. The investigator must show justification that the targeted person is using his telephone, or computer, or FAX machine, or whatever other device the person has, in connection with the criminal activity. As an example, an investigator might have difficulty getting authorization to listen to calls made from a separate telephone line in the bedroom of the subject's minor child, unless he can show that the targeted subject has in fact made use of that instrument on occasion.

Advantages of Technical Investigative Techniques

The main advantage of most technical investigative techniques is that they get to the heart of the criminal or terrorist violation. While most other investigative techniques can be exploratory in nature, and often initially produce only peripheral information, most of the technical techniques cannot even be used unless it can be shown that they will be productive.

Technical techniques usually produce firsthand evidence that is extremely difficult for a subject to refute in court. This evidence often consists of tapes and films of the subject saying and doing things that are elements of the conspiracy.

Technical techniques can identify a variety of avenues in which other investigative techniques can be used. For example, a wiretap may show when a subject is planning to do something illegal. This information could allow an agency to conduct a very productive surveillance. Similarly, a microphone might show that someone within the group is upset. This could give a department the opportunity to formulate an approach to that person that will ensure that he or she will agree to become an informant. Technically produced information could be used by an agency to better direct an undercover operative into a position from which to gather information.

Disadvantages of Technical Investigative Techniques

Procuring electronic coverage requires a great deal of documentation. Some believe that this time could be better spent doing other investigative practices. Critics also believe that some case officers come to regard the procurement of technical coverage on the suspect to be an end in itself, rather than the means to achieve an end—namely the arrest and conviction of the subject. To be fair, some supporters of sensitive techniques believe that the documentation required to support this coverage has a great deal of value in itself, because it forces someone to assemble every item of evidence gathered to date into a logical, comprehensive document. They believe that because a document of this nature will ultimately have to be prepared for use in the prosecution of the case, assembling it to justify technical coverage will go a long way toward preparing for trial.

Electronic coverage is manpower-intensive. Some agencies simply cannot provide enough investigators to conduct it. Most coverage must be live-monitored. In addition, the preparation of transcripts of telephone and microphone coverage can cripple an agency. In solid criminal cases this task may not be as burdensome as it could be, because the subjects may plead guilty or plea bargain. In terrorist cases, it should be assumed that deals will not be possible, and that the defense will demand access to all monitoring tapes, and review them. As a consequence, the law enforcement agency will have to make transcripts of all monitorings, because they risk the defense springing a surprise from those tapes in court.

A great deal of highly sophisticated equipment is required to conduct technical coverages. Highly trained technicians are needed to install and maintain the equipment. There are also additional costs, including telephone line charges and procuring video and audio tapes. All technical coverage should be conducted on a need-to-know basis. This suggests that the monitoring should be conducted from secure locations. Many departments lack the space to provide isolated monitoring rooms. A court order is required to procure most technical coverage. Consequently, someone has to take the time to prepare periodic and final reports to the court summarizing the results of the investigation. At some point the target will likely be notified that he has been monitored. If this happens before the case has been brought to a resolution, it could jeopardize the entire investigation.

Some technical coverage can be very difficult to perform, and can run the risk of breaching the security of an investigation. The subject is going to become aware that he is under intense investigation if he catches someone trying to install a microphone in his home or vehicle. If a terrorist target finds a monitoring device targeting him, he will likely cease his activities and perhaps relocate from the area.

Types of Electronic Coverage

Wiretaps

The wiretap is an electronic means by which a law enforcement agency can listen to conversations made over a specific telephone. Usually when courts grant authority for a department to conduct a wiretap, they place certain restrictions on who and what can be monitored. If the telephone is located in a known gambling parlor or in a terrorist safe house, the court is likely to permit monitoring of anyone who uses it. If it is located in a legitimate business where numerous employees have access to the line, the court will probably rule that only the subject of the investigation can be monitored. Certain types of calls are also often restricted. For example, the courts will usually forbid a law enforcement agency to listen to a conversation between someone and his or her attorney regarding a legal matter, or between a person and his or her psychologist concerning a mental problem. The process of limiting who and what can be monitored is called "minimization." Everyone involved in monitoring should review the court order authorizing the coverage. Any questionable situations that arise during the monitoring should quickly be brought to the attention of the department's legal counsel or the prosecutor.

Some courts now permit coverage of a number of telephones if it can be shown that a subject moves from instrument to instrument in order to evade coverage. Because this often involves public pay telephones, the court orders will almost always stipulate that only the subject can be monitored. This will frequently require the agency to surveil the subject in order to be certain that he is using a particular telephone.

Most wiretaps occur at a telephone facility. The picture that novelists and filmmakers paint of officers dangling from telephone poles or hiding in basements listening to microphones spliced into telephone lines is simply not accurate. From a technical standpoint, a disreputable private detective might engage in such practices, but law enforcement officers do not. Telephone companies will make the proper installation when given a court order. There should never be "clicks" or other sounds in connection with such coverage, and the subject should not realize that his line is being monitored.

Modern cellular telephones initially challenged law enforcement, but they, too, can be legally monitored. The Communications Assistance for Law Enforcement Act passed in 1994 mandated that U.S. telephone companies enable federal agencies technical access to their equipment. This ensures that these agencies can monitor digital technology and cellular phone if they have the proper authority from a court. Throw-away telephones—the kind where a person buys minutes as he or she wants them—are likely to present a myriad of problems affording coverage or even procuring court orders to enable monitoring, because the numbers will be different for every telephone instrument that is purchased. Nonetheless, a carefully worded affidavit should allow for such coverage, assuming that the investigators can learn the telephone's number before the subject disposes of it.

Telephone wiretap conversations usually must be live-monitored. There are certain foreign counter-intelligence coverages that can be tape-recorded for subsequent monitoring, but local and state law enforcement agencies should not plan to benefit from such a coverage unless they are affiliated with a joint terrorism task force or in some other way with a federal agency. Conversations that are live-monitored also have to be tape-recorded. Usually when a conversation is overheard, an officer prepares a summary of the conversation. If the conversation is important, it should be transcribed. If arrests are made in the case, the results of wiretaps will almost certainly have to be turned over to the defense. It is at this point that an agency must decide whether it is wise to transcribe all of the monitored conversations. If they do, they will know exactly what is on each tape. If they do not, it is possible that the defense may transcribe them and find something that they can use to their benefit. Preparing transcripts can place a very heavy burden on a law enforcement agency, but such transcripts are important because prosecutors do not like surprises in the courtroom.

Text Messaging and Telephonic Photographic Exchange

The twenty-first century has seen text messaging become quite common, especially among younger people. Cellular phones that take pictures that can be forwarded to other people have also become quite prevalent. Court orders can be obtained to monitor both of these new uses of technology, and many law enforcement agencies have the necessary technical skills to monitor these forms of communication.

Pen Register

From a technical standpoint, a pen register uses essentially the same equipment as a wiretap. However, a pen register usually does not require as much probable cause to have it authorized, and it does not produce as much information as a wiretap. The pen register provides a current list of all telephone numbers called from the subject's telephone. The weakness of the technique is that it does not reveal who specifically placed or received each call. In the past, pen registers burdened investigators with piles of unidentified telephone numbers that were of little value unless an investigator recognized them as being pertinent. Modern technology has greatly improved the situation, and now subscribers to most numbers can be quickly identified.

Microphone

The microphone, often called a "bug," is an electronic listening device that is installed in a particular location to enable investigators to hear what is being said by people inside. Some microphones are battery powered and can be placed in a location by any investigator who is able to gain entry to that area. Unfortunately, this equipment has a short life, and often is not very effective. If it is placed carelessly, it can be easily discovered. Most law enforcement officers use parasitic microphones. Such microphones use the subject's electric power. They are physically concealed in the target location by a skilled technician. They can last indefinitely, and should not be discovered unless the subject employs the services of a technician who uses sophisticated detection equipment. Parasitic microphones require physical entry into the target location. Clearly, this should be done without the knowledge of anyone outside the department.

It should be noted that some terrorist groups have learned a few of the tricks of the trade with respect to the installation of listening devices, and have passed this knowledge on to the members of their organization. Law enforcement technicians should always use care when installing listening devices. However, even greater care should be used in terrorism cases because, unlike ordinary criminals, some terrorists now know where in a room to look for evidence of an installation. A bit of dust or a paint chip that would normally go unnoticed could signal to a terrorist that the location had been wired.

The court order that authorizes the use of a microphone also authorizes a "legal entry" into the target in order to install the equipment. Unlike most burglars, who enter, take what they want, and leave, the law enforcement technicians installing the microphone must enter without leaving any sign that an intrusion has been made. They must make their installation without leaving anything behind that would suggest that someone had been there. They should not remove anything from the target area because that would alert the subject that someone had been there.

Because the entry to install a microphone is a "legal entry," anything that is observed by the technicians can be used as evidence. Obviously, this could cause a problem. If the technicians observe illegal and potentially dangerous items such as explosives, volatile chemicals, biological agents, or high-powered automatic weapons, their agency must decide whether to: (1) seize the items and charge the resident with the violation, which would bring the ongoing case to an end. But it might be premature, and other defendants who would probably have ultimately been arrested will be able to escape without being charged; (2) allow the dangerous items to remain in the location. This would be a difficult choice, because possession of such items is a felony. The department might also face serious liability if the subject subsequently used the illegal items to injure someone or do property damage; (3) substitute or otherwise alter the dangerous items so that they could not function. However, seizing or changing these products would require a court order. The Chicago Joint Terrorism Task Force once opted for this choice when they discovered a terrorist bomb factory. They substituted inert products for the explosives, removed the gunpowder from all of the ammunition, and disabled the firearms.

It is strongly recommended that an agency manager not decide to allow a dangerous product to remain inside an address without seeking guidance from the agency's legal counsel or the prosecutor.

Microphones can provide excellent coverage, but they are not without problems. It is often difficult to hear their transmissions. If a group of people is in a room, they may drown one another out. A major problem is that people often do not identify themselves when they talk face-to-face in the same manner that they do on the telephone. Consequently, it may be very difficult for officers to determine who is speaking. This can be frustrating if incriminating statements are made, and the monitoring officer cannot determine who is making them. Recorded conversations can be "cleaned up" to a certain extent by police crime laboratories or private electronics firms so that they can be better understood. However, this can present a problem in court if the defense argues that what the "cleaned up" tapes appear to state are not in fact what was said during the conversation. An officer who repeatedly reviews a tape may be able to pick up otherwise inaudible statements, but in court the jury may not be able to understand the inaudible comments. The defense will argue that the officer is hearing things that were not actually said.

Some subjects try to render microphones useless by constantly playing a radio. In essence, they try to keep their spoken conversations at the same level as or lower than the radio. This makes live-monitoring extremely difficult. However, there is a way in which radio noise can be "removed" so that only the spoken words of the people in the room can be heard. This technology is expensive and may not be available to most agencies.

Monitoring a microphone can also be impeded by ambient sounds, including those made by refrigerators, heaters, fans, and air conditioners. Through a court order, investigators can disable such devices. Common sense must be used in doing this. Fixing a fan so that it will not work will only cause the subject to buy a new one. If the replacement unit is subsequently disabled, the subject will become suspicious. Courts are usually reasonable. If a judge has authorized something, and an extraneous factor impedes that authorization, he will usually honor a reasonable request to alleviate the situation. It is important, however, that investigators refrain from taking matters into their own hands to fix problems, especially if the solution involves a violation of the law like vandalism or breaking and entering.

In one terrorism investigation, a court order was obtained to disable the motor on a refrigerator. To facilitate this, technical specialists installed a remote-controlled "off-on" switch on the motor. The refrigerator functioned normally except when officers wanted to hear something. When a conversation was being monitored, the listening investigators would turn off the refrigerator by flipping a switch. At the end of the conversation, the motor would be restarted. In that way the subject never noticed anything different about the operation of his refrigerator.

Microphones can be installed in any location where it is technically feasible. Residences, offices and other work areas, and locations where conspirators gather are the most common targets for microphone installations. Another common target is vehicles. Usually, the most satisfactory vehicular installations are parasitic and run off of the vehicle's own electrical system. This involves a "theft" (by court order) of the car unless the installation can somehow be made where the vehicle is housed or when being serviced. The latter alternative usually cannot be done securely. Car microphones can be extremely valuable because many people seem to feel more free to talk in a car than they do in a building.

The downside is that monitoring a vehicular microphone can be very difficult at times. A surveillance will usually have to be in place. This means that risk of detection exists if coverage vehicles tail the target too closely. Vehicular microphones can also be monitored from fixed locations if the vehicle is parked or if it stays within a limited area. Possibly the best way to monitor a vehicular microphone is by using an aircraft. This can present a problem if the vehicle is traveling near an airport where surveillance aircraft cannot fly, or if the weather is bad and the aircraft cannot fly. If the installation is not done exactly right, it may cause some disruption to the vehicle's FM radio, which can cause the subject to become suspicious, or result in him or her taking it to a repair shop. It is also possible that a subject or a citizen using a commercially available scanner can pick up transmissions from the microphone. Poor installations can also cause electrical problems for the vehicle that would probably cause the owner to have the vehicle serviced.

Courts are not usually willing to permit a law enforcement agency complete freedom with respect to where microphone installations can be made within the target location. Unless an agency can present a very convincing argument that criminal activity takes place there, or is discussed there, a court will not permit microphones to be installed in a residential bathroom or bedroom. Similarly, if parties not involved in the conspiracy reside in a location, the court will probably forbid coverage of their exclusive space. Thus, a maid's quarters or a mother-in-law's apartment might be off-limits to the law enforcement agency.

Microphones are also subject to court-ordered minimization. If a subject meets with his lawyer in the living room of his residence and discusses pending litigation, the law enforcement agency monitoring that room will have to exclude coverage of that conversation. Similarly, if the subject makes love with his spouse on the living room sofa, coverage would be restricted.

Pagers

Pagers became so commonplace in the 1990s that almost everyone, including children, had one. In the twenty-first century few people still carry pagers, because the proliferation of cellular telephones has made them largely obsolete. Most pagers receive telephone numbers. However, some can also receive short text messages. Criminals and terrorists have used pagers just like everyone else. Law enforcement investigations can greatly benefit by knowing who is contacting suspects who are under surveillance. Usually pager coverage involves the law enforcement agency maintaining a duplicate pager that receives every number or message that the subject receives. Although some pager companies will readily make a clone pager available to a department, a court order is usually required for a law enforcement agency to conduct coverage of a person's pager.

Facsimile (Fax) Machines

Fax machines are much more popular today than they were even a decade ago. Costs have dropped so dramatically during the first several years of the twenty-first century that fax machines are common in residences, small businesses, and social locations. Wireless fax machines and car faxes will soon also be quite widespread. The requirements for procuring a court order to monitor a fax machine are essentially the same as the requirements for monitoring a telephone. In order to implement a fax cover, the department will have to have a fax machine that can be dedicated to receiving duplicates of the subject's incoming and outgoing facsimile communications. If a department employs a fax cover, it should be done covertly. It is not prudent to have duplicates of a subject's faxes arriving on a machine located in the main work area of a law enforcement agency.

Computers

E-mail messages and other computer transmissions can be legally monitored by a police agency under a court order. It is likely that the number of law enforcement coverages within this area is going to increase markedly in the near future. The computer revolution has created a variety of legal issues that affect police agencies. Many of the basic statutes that enable law enforcement agencies to conduct technical investigative techniques were passed prior to the modern computer boom. To complicate matters, developments in this area occur on an almost daily basis, making it difficult for investigators, lawyers, and courts to even keep up with them. Department attorneys and prosecutors are continually struggling to establish guidelines under which computers can be monitored by police agencies. Obviously, if monitoring is to be accomplished, the law enforcement agency will have to have the proper equipment and the skilled technical people to complete the objective.

Short-Wave and Limited-Range Radio

Because many short-wave radio broadcasts can be monitored by anyone who has a short-wave receiver, and limited-range radio can be monitored by people within the transmitter's range, a law enforcement agency may not need a court order to monitor these broadcasts. An agency's legal counsel should be consulted before monitoring such broadcasts and recording information from them into official agency files. There may be a state law or court order that would restrict such intelligence gathering. Short-wave radio has been used in spy operations for many years. Some have used coded messages while others have used "bursts," which require decoding in order to make sense. Various guerrilla and terrorist groups have also used short-wave radio to communicate. Limited, or low-frequency, radio has been used by right-wing extremists in the United States to promote their philosophy and to communicate with one another. It must be remembered that it may be difficult for investigators to identify the people speaking via short-wave transmissions. The quality is often not good enough to employ voice recognition technology. In the case of limited-range radio, what is transmitted may be recorded material, and the person whose voice is heard may not be anywhere near the station or even know what is happening. Consequently, if the accused person denies having made incriminating statements via short-wave or limited-range radio, investigators may have difficulty trying to use those comments against him or her.

Still Camera and Closed-Circuit Television (CCTV)

Although cameras are technical in nature, their most common law enforcement uses are usually not considered sensitive or sophisticated. Cameras are frequently used in conjunction with surveillances. In fact, some surveillances are actually unmanned and conducted entirely by a video camera or by a time-lapse still camera. Some investigators photograph subjects during interviews and some agencies videotape interrogations. Photographs are frequently shown during interviews and informant contacts. Informants and undercover officers sometimes use cameras during their assignments. Crime scenes should be filmed. The service of search warrants is also sometimes photographed.

However, in recent years, the camera has also been used as a sensitive investigative tool. This became possible through advances in photographic technology. When the Omnibus Crime Bill of 1968 was passed, it permitted federal law enforcement officials to install wiretaps and microphones. However, it did not address cameras, primarily because the technology to install totally concealed cameras inside a room was nonexistent. Modern technology has changed all of that. Today, a camera lens can be made so small that it can be concealed in most rooms, offices, businesses, or vehicles without risk of detection. As a result, through court orders, many law enforcement agencies augment their audio technical coverage with video or still photography. Not only can the investigators hear the terrorist talking about bombs, they can actually watch him making the devices. No longer does a prosecutor have to use voice experts to convince a jury that the person speaking on the tape is the defendant. The members of the jury can see and hear the person speaking. Modern camera installations now permit zooming in on specific parts of a room. Cameras can also be moved remotely to change views within the targeted area. As a result, if a meeting is being covered, the camera can be shifted to show each person as he or she speaks.

Installation of a camera within a private location requires a court order. The best kind of installations are those that permit film replacement without requiring another entry into the target location, or a parasitic CCTV that can be live-monitored. The latter situation is usually the most desirable, but it does require a monitoring station and a method for transmitting the signal to that location.

Body Recorders and Transmitters

Great strides have been made in body recorders and transmitters in recent years. The once-bulky equipment that could easily be detected through a body frisk has given way to mini-transmitters and recorders that should not be discovered by anything short of a very thorough search—possibly even a strip search. The negative side of the improvements in technology has been the cost. The prices of many body recorders/transmitters can run into thousands of dollars for a single device. Another drawback is that switches and controls have become miniaturized. This means that some undercover operatives and informants experience difficulties using the controls on their hidden recorders and transmitters.

Body recorders worn by informants and undercover officers often do not require a court order. It depends upon the circumstances and the statutes that apply to the employing agency relating to consensual monitoring.

Parabolic Microphones

In theory, a parabolic microphone permits a person to overhear conversations that occur at a distance. Unfortunately, the technology that will enable these devices to be of much use to the law enforcement field is lacking at present. The current editions pick up all kinds of interference and are difficult to monitor. Almost all are large enough to be noticeable. Furthermore, they require an uninterrupted line of sight between the target and the monitoring officer. This makes it relatively easy for the target to detect the coverage.

Consensual Telephone Monitoring

Regulations governing consensual monitoring vary from jurisdiction to jurisdiction. In some states, a telephone conversation can be monitored by one of the parties involved. In a few states, both parties must consent, and in still other states, a recorded conversation must be accompanied by a beeping sound. Modern equipment has made consensual monitoring much easier than it once was. A recorder can easily be attached to a telephone and a conversation recorded without the other party being aware of it. Consensual monitoring is often used by informants and undercover officers. Sometimes victims can also use the technique, particularly in cases involving threats, fraud, or blackmail. Investigators should check with their department's legal counsel or with the prosecutor before using consensual monitoring.

Tracking Devices

In many urban areas there are satellite systems in place that can allow a vehicle to be tracked. This can be done on a live basis, or the results can be recorded so that an investigator can determine where a vehicle has traveled during a given period. Some private firms use this technology for a variety of purposes. Examples of this technology include trucking firms and school bus companies that track their vehicles, and anti-car theft companies that use it to trace vehicles that have been stolen. Other firms use it to offer assistance to motorists who need help or directions. Many General Motors dealers offer such a service to their new car buyers. More recently, some detective agencies have used it to help parents monitor the whereabouts of their children's vehicles.

Slap-on and parasitic beepers have been used by surveillance investigators for several decades. These devices emit a "beep" that permits officers to follow from a safe distance and to locate targets that become lost from view. The slap-on type is battery-powered and contains a magnet. An officer merely "slaps" it onto the bottom of the target's car. When the battery runs down or a decision is made to remove the device, the officer simply pulls it off. Obviously, the "slap-on" nature of this tracker makes it desirable. However, the fact that it has to be periodically removed for battery exchanges is a drawback. Also, as the battery weakens, the signal weakens, making it less valuable.

Because it is "slapped on" with the intention of easy removal for battery replacement, the device will not be well-concealed. As a result, someone may find it. In addition, because it is only held in place by a magnet, it can also fall off the vehicle and become lost.

The parasitic beeper or satellite tracker requires a legal "theft" of the vehicle, in that the device must be wired to the vehicle's electrical system. Once installed, it usually requires no further attention. Unless someone has a specific reason to inspect the vehicle's electrical system, the target should not be aware that it is on the vehicle. It is possible that the beeper's transmission will disrupt the vehicle's FM radio or that the beep will be picked up on a scanner.

The legal ramifications for using satellite tracking devices and beepers will vary from state to state. A court order will be required if an entry must be made into the vehicle in order to install the equipment. The same is true if a trespass must be made onto private property in order to place a slap-on transmitter onto a vehicle. Individuals have the right to grant permission to have themselves tracked. Consequently, an informant, witness, victim, or undercover officer can voluntarily consent to a law enforcement officer placing a tracker on his vehicle. A business owner can do the same for his equipment. The issue of legal authority with respect to slap-on equipment that does not involve a trespass into the vehicle or private property to attach it falls in a gray area and must be explored with a department's legal counsel or the prosecutor.

The Future

There is little question that rapid technological advances will continue. Microphones and cameras will become smaller, and their quality will improve. Just in the past few years the digital camera has become more affordable and commonplace. It will soon be standard for all police vehicles to be equipped with computers that can be connected to a digital camera to give officers the ability to instantly view surveillance pictures and video that they have taken. It is conceivable that in the not-too-distant future it will be possible that a camera will snap a picture of a subject, and a computer will generate a biographical profile of that person based solely on the picture. Police will undoubtedly deploy camera cell phones in conjunction with surveillances and technical entries.

In the near future it is likely that it will become technologically feasible to covertly "bug" a person's apparel so that his conversations can be heard regardless of where he is located. Indeed, it might also soon be possible to literally "bug" an individual's body with a tracking device, if not a microphone. Similarly, it is likely that cameras will become so small that one could be secreted in a person's clothing to permit investigators to observe that individual's movements. Already the technology exists that would allow for a microphone to be secretly placed into certain items that many people regularly carry with them, including briefcases, cellular telephones, radios, pagers, and laptop computers.

Lawmakers and judges will continue to be challenged to address issues being generated by the new technology. As innovative products develop, police agencies will want to employ them. Criminals and terrorists will attempt to use any new technology available against their victims and law enforcement personnel. Private security firms are often the first to use the latest equipment. The primary issue that often develops in conjunction with technological advances centers around the questions of invasion of privacy and personal liberty. Courts will have no choice but to address this situation, because government attorneys will seek court orders approving the use of some of the new technology. Lawmakers will be similarly challenged to pass legislation governing the proper the use of new equipment. These issues already exist and cannot be ignored.

Telephone technology is another advancing area. Law enforcement agencies are already experiencing a variety of difficulties. Issues involving mobility of cellular telephones, expansion of services available through telephone and Internet companies, the ability of customers to rapidly change service providers, caller identification, and the large numbers of telephone companies, are only a few of the problems that investigators encounter. The throw-away telephone is posing additional issues. Compounding the situation is the fact that whenever new legislation is proposed to address a problem created by technological advances, civil libertarians oppose it because they fear that it will lead to government encroachment on the constitutionally guaranteed rights of citizens.

In the future, law enforcement agencies will be forced to employ increasing numbers of technically trained personnel in order to install and service specialized equipment. They will also have to assign certain personnel to design ways in which the new technology can be employed to meet the specific needs of the police agency. In the past, many agencies neglected the latter aspect of technology. The idea of an agency having a camera installed in a single briefcase that must be used in every investigation that requires a hidden camera will become a thing of the past. Instead, investigators will come to expect that trained specialists will produce unique concealment props to fit the needs of their individual cases.

Storage and maintenance of tapes, films, disks, monitoring logs, and other results of technical coverage will become a major burden for the law enforcement community. The employees who are assigned to oversee such evidence will have to be a level above the average clerical employee. More and more of them will have junior college or college degrees, and they will command higher wages than are presently being paid. Their work must be nearly perfect with respect to detail. Furthermore, they should expect to testify in court if a challenge is made to the security of the evidence or to the chain of custody.

⓴ Investigative Review

Investigative review involves a complete study of an entire case by an investigator who has not worked on the matter. The reviewer should be a veteran investigator with experience directing criminal cases. If a terrorism investigation is involved, the reviewer should have specific experience in administering or investigating terrorism matters.

Investigative review is a unique investigative technique, in that it should only be implemented in cases that have been pending without success for an extended period. It is likely that most other investigative techniques will have been used before investigative review is even considered. The fact that many investigators do not see investigative review as an investigative technique per se does not mean that they do not see its value. During the past several decades, some large police departments have created "cold-case" squads. The investigators assigned to these units carefully review older cases in an attempt to bring them to a conclusion. These cases often have languished in inactive status for years before being re-examined. They usually involve murder, because there is no statute of limitations on this crime. Most law enforcement agencies do not have the luxury of reviewing cases that cannot be prosecuted, therefore older cases involving such crimes as robbery, burglary, and assault are not usually re-evaluated unless it is possible that an innocent person is in jail.

Investigative review in the area of terrorism is used somewhat differently than is the cold-case concept. The terrorism case is more likely to be in a pending status when the review is conducted. The involved terrorist group is probably still functioning and committing violent attacks. This means that it is possible that a conspiracy charge linking present and past violations can be used to prosecute the perpetrators. As a result, the statute of limitations will not necessarily prevent a successful prosecution. Even if the particular offense cannot be prosecuted, it would not negate the value that an investigative review could have in an older case. Solving such a case could lead to the identification and possibly apprehension of people conducting current attacks.

In terrorism cases, it is recommended that investigative review be conducted as soon as a year, but probably two years, after an unresolved case was initiated, especially if the matter has come to a standstill. Most other criminal cold-case reviews begin after several years have elapsed and the case has become inactive or closed. There is also merit in conducting an investigative review in terrorist fugitive cases after a year or two has elapsed and nothing of consequence has been developed to locate the fugitive.

Terrorism investigations and terrorist fugitive hunts are complex investigations. Terrorist bombings, assassinations, and other acts of extreme violence are often difficult to solve, and these cases can drag on for prolonged periods without even one suspect being identified. Terrorist fugitives can be among the most difficult subjects to locate. It is not unusual for investigators to have made little progress in such cases even one year after their initiation.

The primary reason for using the investigative review technique in a criminal case is to ensure that nothing has been overlooked. Terrorism investigations are different from routine criminal matters. The following unique features of a terrorism investigation give rise to the use of an investigative review:

> It is possible that the initial investigators handled the case as they would any routine criminal matter and failed to consider the unique aspects of terrorism. This could easily occur in situations in which the case revolved around robberies, burglaries, frauds, and other "normal" criminal violations as opposed to bombings, arsons, and "traditional" terrorist political attacks. A fresh investigator who looks at such a case from a terrorism viewpoint may be able to develop new inroads that could lead to resolution of the matter. If the case was initially approached from a criminal perspective, it is possible that terrorist suspects were never considered as perpetrators. It is also possible that terrorist informants were not contacted, and that the crime laboratory was never asked to compare the evidence recovered in the case with other evidence known to be associated with a terrorist group.

> Actual terrorist attacks generate large amounts of publicity and bring great pressure to bear on local law enforcement agencies. Many investigators and police management personnel are not accustomed to such oversight. The media and public pressure can force the investigation to take illogical twists and turns. It can make investigators address issues much more quickly than they normally would. As a consequence, leads can be overlooked or not addressed as well as they ordinarily would. A reviewing investigator who is not operating under the direct view of the media a year or two after the incident may be able to clearly see areas that deserve more attention.

> New information developed through the course of subsequent investigations on other attacks and crimes committed by the same terrorist group could help resolve the matter. While it is almost certain that the initial case officer ran the names of suspected perpetrators (both by group and individually) through law enforcement agency indices as they were developed, it is possible that he never rechecked these names. As a result, he may not be aware that the same group and individuals have arisen in connection with

more recent cases. Terrorist groups often commit crimes all over the country on a continuing basis. One of the first steps that the reviewing officer should take is to conduct a thorough review of logical law enforcement indices for all pertinent names developed during the course of the investigation.

Witnesses who were reluctant to cooperate with law enforcement immediately following a terrorist attack because of fear of retaliation from the involved group may be willing to provide information now that a period of time has passed. Victims, especially those from a bombing who have since healed, may now be able to recall details that they could not remember when initially interviewed.

Informants may have been developed based on coverage on the terrorist group since the case was opened. Similarly, defectors may have left the group during the investigation period. A group member may have been arrested for another violation since the initiation of the case. Any of these people may be able to provide information that could resolve the case. It is also possible that they could supply new leads regarding the location of terrorist fugitives.

The Concept Behind the Investigative Review Technique

The person assigned to conduct the investigative review has several major advantages over the initial case officer. He has the ability to view the case from an overall perspective. The case officer has lived the case on a day-to-day basis, but this may have curtailed his or her ability to view the situation in its entirety. In a sense, the reviewing officer is like a person who flies over a forest, viewing it in its totality from above. This person will probably have a very different insight into forest than will a person who walks through it, carefully studying each tree. The person who has viewed each tree will probably have a much greater knowledge of the individual components of the forest than the person who observed it from above. However, the person who flew over the forest may actually have a better understanding of it.

Obviously, the reviewer also has the advantage of hindsight. He knows what worked and what did not work. He knows what suspects have been linked to the case, and which ones have been excluded. He knows where time was wasted following dead-end leads. He knows what errors were made.

The reviewer does not have to endure the pressure that the case officer experienced while directing the case. The reviewer does not have to constantly explain to superiors why the case has not been solved. He does not have to resolve the problems that routinely arise during the course of an investigation with respect to manpower, resources, work hours, and equipment. He does not experience the media pressure to resolve the matter that the case officer must endure. In short, the reviewer can concentrate his full efforts on the "meat and potatoes" of the case without distraction.

The investigative review should not be conducted from the standpoint that criticism of the case officer and his assistants is warranted because the case has not been resolved or the fugitive has not been apprehended. Even the fact that the reviewer discovers leads that were apparently overlooked does not necessarily mean that errors were made. It is possible that at the time there was a good reason that some logical investigation was not conducted. That good reason may or may not continue to exist. It is also possible that the investigation was conducted, but was never documented, or that the documentation was misplaced or never filed. An informant's report may have ended up in the informant's administrative control instead of in the case file. A surveillance log may still be in an officer's desk waiting for him to sign it. A crime laboratory report may have been stored in the department's evidence storeroom instead of in the case file.

The case officer will continue to be involved in a case that is undergoing investigative review. He should handle incoming and outgoing communications during any pending investigation. He can also set out leads based upon what the reviewer has found in his study of the file. The investigative review should not be treated or regarded as an adversarial situation between the case officer and the reviewer.

Who Should Conduct the Investigative Review?

The investigator conducting the review should be a neutral person who has no proprietary interest in the investigation. If the reviewer has some previous involvement in the case, it is possible that he may be prone to take actions designed to justify what was previously done in the investigation. In contrast, if the reviewer is bent on making a name for himself, he may devote the bulk of his time to finding fault with how the case was run rather than trying to solve it. Regardless of who is selected to review the case, it is important that this person have experience in conducting complex investigations. While it may be argued that assigning a rookie officer to conduct such a review may bring in a fresh, enthusiastic approach, it may not work because he or she might not know what can and should be done during the course of a complex investigation. The reviewer should have investigative and clerical assistants to facilitate his assignment.

What Should Be Included in the Investigative Review?

The review should be complete. All aspects of the case should be studied with the intent of asking "who, why, where, when, what, and how?" If the case involves a crime rather than a search for a fugitive, a smart investigator might find it valuable to try to construct a prosecution report that could be used to bring the matter to court, assuming that one or more specific suspects are ever identified. If the report is properly prepared, it will reflect the aspects of the investigation that are missing or have not been adequately addressed. A similar kind of document could be constructed with respect to a fugitive-oriented investigation. The reviewing officer could construct an outline of everything that should be done to locate the particular fugitive in question, and then locate in the case file the items that address each category listed in the outline. Obviously, any category that remains incomplete after the file has been thoroughly reviewed would indicate an incomplete investigation.

The case review should involve all evidence and any materials obtained by subpoena or other court order. Quite often, such materials are not thoroughly reviewed during the early stages of the investigation, probably because they do not offer information that would resolve the matter or apprehend a fugitive. However, as the case progresses, someone should have reviewed the material or at least determined that the material was of no value. If this has not been done, the reviewing investigator must study the material. If it was worth obtaining in the first place, and if it has not been found to be irrelevant to the case, it should be studied.

Crime scene evidence and materials that were obtained as a result of search warrants, voluntary contribution, and other means should be reexamined to determine whether they were directed to the appropriate crime laboratory for review. Occasionally, in major cases, some recovered materials are allowed to remain in police agency evidence rooms, because no one ever gets around to sending them to a laboratory. This is not necessarily a criticism of those involved in the initial part of the case. It is possible that when the material was initially received, there was no real reason for sending it for further examination. However, a review might provide cause for having the evidence studied at a crime laboratory.

Scientific advances occurred rapidly during the latter part of the twentieth century, and will continue to do so in the twenty-first century. Tests and other research that could not be done in one year may well be possible in a subsequent year. The officer assigned to conduct the investigative review should make himself familiar with the latest advances in the crime laboratory that his agency uses. The reviewing investigator should examine evidence with the idea that modern laboratory tests might be able to yield more information than ever before. DNA testing is an excellent example of this. Police agencies are now resubmitting blood evidence in older cases in the hope that modern DNA tests will identify the subject. Lawyers representing prison inmates convicted of rapes are demanding that their clients' DNA be compared with semen samples, saliva, and other bodily fluids recovered from the victim. Until the latter part of the twentieth century, crime laboratories could do little more than identify and match blood types.

Fingerprint technology is another area in which great changes have occurred during recent years. Previously, in many situations, crime laboratories did not examine items constructed of certain materials because the technicians knew that fingerprints could not be retrieved from their surfaces. Modern advances in this area have now made it possible for laboratories to locate identifiable fingerprints on items from which they previously could not. A reviewing officer may want to submit evidence that was not previously submitted to a laboratory to check for fingerprints. He may also want to resubmit certain items on which a crime laboratory previously was unable to find fingerprints.

Surveillance logs and reports from informants, citizens, and investigators from other agencies should also be carefully reviewed to determine whether they were properly and thoroughly addressed. Quite often such sources of information are overlooked and the information becomes "lost in the cracks."

> The reviewer should ensure that everything was done properly. He should ask questions such as:
>
> Was evidence properly inventoried, and were indices and agency searches conducted on names, addresses, and telephone numbers developed from that evidence?
>
> Was the evidence sent to the proper laboratory, and did that laboratory conduct the appropriate tests?
>
> Were tapes from consensual monitoring transcribed and properly acted upon? Were closed-circuit television tapes reviewed? Were the results of a polygraph examination studied properly? Was film from surveillances developed and reviewed?
>
> Were all records checks conducted? Were appropriate documents requested? Were appropriate rechecks of records done?
>
> Were sources of information, including informants, other police agencies, and the Internet, queried?

A thorough case reviewer will study outside accounts of the investigation before reviewing the case. It is likely that there was a fair amount of news media coverage when the crime initially occurred, especially if it was terroristic in nature. Magazines, especially the weekly news periodicals, should also be reviewed. If a year has passed, it is possible that the media has compiled an "anniversary" review of the investigation. If the case was very high-profile, one or more books or films may have been released since the crime occurred. It is also possible that a television news magazine or crime program has done a story on the case. All of these potential sources of information could be avenues of new information not known by the case officer, and not reflected in the case file. While some of this information may be more "fluff" than substance, and may be of little value, it is possible that some significant information may also be included. For example, the media may have located witnesses to the crime that the law enforcement agency never knew existed. They may also have interviewed someone formerly with the terrorist group that the police agency did not know would talk with them. They may have developed historical information that is unknown to the case officer. They may have pictures that the investigators never saw. Photographs can be especially helpful in fugitive investigations.

Many people will talk to the media before they will talk to a police agency. This is especially true of individuals associated with extremist groups who want the media to promote their views. Some media agencies can also offer money to people who provide them with photographs and eyewitness accounts. Law enforcement agencies usually cannot do this. Even the sensational "trash" publications that specialize in shocking stories about people in the entertainment field may offer something of value. Some will write about sensational crimes including terrorist attacks. If nothing else, such publications are heavy on photographs, and may have printed a picture of a fugitive that the law enforcement community never knew existed.

Media personnel are often unwilling to provide information to law enforcement agencies unless they are convinced that they will receive something exclusive in exchange. However, after a year or more has passed and the story is no longer considered newsworthy, some reporters might be willing to share insight into a case. Contacting a reporter who wrote quality articles or an interviewer who was involved in television or radio reports on the terrorist incident might yield some heretofore unknown information.

Perhaps the most important part of the investigative review is the correlative aspect of the process. The reviewer should ensure that all aspects of the investigation have been logically meshed together. If surveillances, consensual monitorings, wiretaps, microphones, CCTV recordings, and informants were all providing information about a suspect during a given period, the reviewer must make certain that the fruits of all of these investigative techniques have been blended together. Often they have not, and some information may have been lost as a consequence. For example, a microphone may yield information from the voice of an unknown male. A CCTV recording might have a picture of that male, and a surveillance team might have a license number for the person. Until the fruits of three sources of information have been correlated, no single item may seem to have value.

Concluding the Investigative Review

The investigative review may not solve the case or locate the fugitive. However, it should result in new leads that can be followed by the investigators who handle the case after the review has been completed. The reviewing investigator may be selected to continue working on the case, or the person who was assigned to the case at the outset of the review may continue to administer it. A new case officer may be assigned, especially if the review has reflected that the previous case officer was less than efficient in handling the case, or if the case officer declines to follow the suggestions made by the reviewer. The results of the investigative review should be documented so that any future case officer or reviewer will know what was done and suggested.

Subsequent Investigative Review

If the case continues for another two years without resolution, or if the fugitive has not been located or apprehended during that period, serious consideration should be given to conducting another investigative review. During this new review, particular emphasis should be given to the period between the two reviews. Efforts should be made to determine whether leads developed since the initial review were adequately covered, and whether all shortcomings noted during the initial review were resolved.

Partial Investigative Review

Because manpower is often a problem for law enforcement agencies, a manager may consider having a partial investigative review conducted in a long-standing case. Instead of a reviewer studying an entire case, he could home in on one or more specific aspects of it. Such a review could stress physical evidence, surveillances, electronic coverage, informants, or any other investigative technique employed in the case. Hopefully, the person assigned to conduct such a review would have a strong background in the area of concentration. If the specific area to be stressed was surveillance coverage, the reviewer would carefully study the fruits of every surveillance conducted to determine whether all of the logs can be located. He would ascertain whether the fruits of each surveillance were integrated into the case. He would identify every logical lead that developed from each surveillance and determine if they had been properly set and resolved. He would attempt to identify targets of possible future surveillance that could help to resolve the case or locate the fugitive.

Summary

Investigative review is a concept that many investigators never experience because they are able to solve their cases within a short period. In terrorism situations, cases of long duration are not unusual. A terrorist conspiracy may be able to operate successfully for several years without law enforcement agencies being able to develop much information about it. It is beneficial in such situations for an experienced investigator outside the case to be brought in to conduct a thorough review of the case file. Such a person will not be under the same pressure that the initial officers were during the early stages of the case. He or she will have the ability to see the case as a whole before beginning to look at the specific aspects of it and will probably be able to see weaknesses in the case and find areas where more investigation could be conducted.

21 Locating Clandestine and Fugitive Terrorists

Over the years, law enforcement agencies have enjoyed a fair amount of success in locating fugitives. Modern communications has certainly helped police in this area. Experienced police officers have developed tried-and-true methods for locating criminals who have become fugitives either because of warrants being issued for them, or because they have escaped from custody. However, terrorist fugitives have proven to be a problem for more than 30 years. The difficulties in tracking such subjects continue to present a challenge into the twenty-first century.

Politically motivated people who are dedicated to the use of fear and violence in an effort to force a change in their government and society usually practice extreme security. They conceal their most sensitive activities from the outside world—especially actions that violate the law. Some of these people will vanish, only to appear somewhere else where they are unknown. They do not act like the average criminal and they do not think like the average criminal. Indeed, many do not consider themselves to be criminals, despite the fact that they have violated laws. The problem is compounded by the fact that terrorist fugitives often associate with highly secretive people who themselves employ security as if they, too, are wanted subjects, despite the fact that they have no outstanding warrants. Terrorist groups provide support for their fugitive members and even for fugitive members of related groups. Surface support groups also provide assistance. In some instances, these overt groups do not even know the name of the person they are shielding.

Types of Clandestine Terrorists

Clandestine terrorists are violent extremists who exist covertly in order to avoid detection by the government and law enforcement agencies. They generally fall within one or more of the following categories:

Federal and state fugitives sought on one or more felony warrants. It is noted that state fugitives wanted for terrorism-related charges are also usually sought on federal Unlawful Flight to Avoid Prosecution (UFAP) warrants issued at the request of the state that holds the local process.

Local fugitives sought on less serious warrants. The charges may have arisen from protests, sit-ins, or other forms of civil disobedience, or they may involve ordinance violations or lesser misdemeanor charges. The local agency may not wish to or be able to extradite such a person. Consequently, the subjects of such warrants are in essence "local" fugitives who need not conceal themselves from authorities while in another area of the country. Federal authorities will not be able to obtain UFAP process on such a warrant, and probably will not be able to initiate an investigation solely on the basis of such process.

Terrorists who believe that they are being sought on a warrant even though none has been issued for their arrest. Such people have usually violated a law and therefore assume that a jurisdiction is seeking them.

Terrorists who have chosen to submerge into an "underground" status in order to better engage in a guerrilla struggle against the government and to conceal their activities, but who are not sought on any warrants. These people have probably not violated any felony statutes. Some of them have never publicly associated with the terrorist group, so law enforcement agencies have no way of knowing that they are in fact functioning with a clandestine group.

"Part-time" clandestine operatives who, on occasion, submerge from overt positions to perform a role in the underground. Such people could function as couriers of communications or supplies, could "case" targets, act as lookouts during attacks, or perform other services for the "underground."

The Nature of the Terrorist "Underground"

Individuals who fall into any of the above categories may be described as "underground." In fact, one of the nation's first true domestic terrorist groups, the Weathermen, later renamed themselves The Weather Underground Organization (WUO). The term "underground" can be extremely misleading. It suggests a situation of people hidden in caves, basements, and behind false walls who venture out in the dark of night to gather food and commit crimes. While this may in fact be a true picture of the life of counterinsurgents living in a war zone, it does not describe the terrorists residing in the United States. "Underground" terrorists in the United States usually live a fairly open existence. Many maintain houses or apartments, hold regular employment, and do pretty much what any other person in their neighborhood would do. They look and dress like anyone else in their community. They often associate and befriend others who are not "underground" and who do not know their status. "Underground" people usually do not reveal their true identities to any surface people, and they do not tell outsiders about their terrorist mission and activities.

Seeking the location of a clandestine terrorist can present law enforcement agencies with a variety of problems. If the person is not a fugitive, some agencies will encounter legal restrictions that will prevent them from investigating someone who is not sought on a warrant. Procuring search warrants or authoritizations to conduct electronic coverage of such an individual may be prove to be quite a challenge. Even if the agency is permitted to conduct intelligence investigations that do not require a criminal violation, they nonetheless may be limited in what they can do because these may be considered low-priority cases. It is obviously easier for a law enforcement agency to legally justify and internally explain time spent seeking a person who is a fugitive or is suspected of committing a specific crime, than someone who is not a fugitive and is only linked to a violent group.

Seeking Fugitive Terrorists

Basic Investigation Steps

The first step in a fugitive investigation is gathering information about the wanted person, including his or her photograph, fingerprints, physical description, and other identifiers. Gathering information about the person's relatives and friends, skills and education, most recent and previous residences, and current and former employment is also important. Much of this information will already be known at the time that the warrant is issued. If it is not known, it should be gathered immediately. The investigator should add to and update this information throughout the investigation.

The next step is the notification process. The proper people must be alerted about the warrant. This should be done immediately after the warrant has been issued. One hundred years ago, this might have involved personal conversations between members of the law enforcement community and telegrams or wanted flyers being mailed to neighboring jurisdictions. Today, this requires placing the subject's name into local, state, or federal "wanted person" computer databases. Probably of equal importance is placing "stops" with any agency that might have contact with the subject. This would involve the subject's bank, credit card providers, driver's license and motor vehicle agencies (in case he or she attempts to become licensed in another state), passport agency, and any other entity that the fugitive might contact, attempt to use, or encounter. A fleeing subject may be forced to write one last check in order to obtain escape funds, charge an airline ticket, or abandon his or her car in a parking lot. Appropriate "stops" with proper agencies might quickly tell an investigator the direction that the subject has taken. The placement of stops and the modification of existing stops should continue throughout the investigation as new information is developed about the subject.

The first two steps are essentially done simultaneously. The former was designated as the initial step only because it would be impossible to enter a fugitive into a database without appropriate identifiers. If appropriate facts like date of birth, description, and identifying designators, including arrest and Social Security numbers, are known when the warrant is issued, the person's name should immediately be entered into appropriate databases.

The next step often involves alerting the general public to the fact that the person is a fugitive. A century ago, this might have been best accomplished by the posting of wanted flyers in appropriate locations. Now, it involves everything from official agency press releases to exposure on television programs like *America's Most Wanted* and similar local and cable television shows, newscasts, the Internet, and books or magazines. (Of course, in some situations, it is not prudent to let a wanted person know that a warrant has been issued for his or her arrest. Consequently, notification of the public is bypassed and any contacts with friends, relatives, and others who might know the subject are conducted under some form of ruse or without mentioning the existence of a warrant.)

The initial "street" investigation usually involves direct contacts by the investigators to the fugitive's friends, relatives, and associates. Related to this would be visits to current and previous residences, and to present and past places of employment. Visits should also be paid to schools, clubs, bars, and other places the person was known to frequent. Quite often these visits and contacts consume many hours and may take weeks, or even months, to complete. These contacts should also be made in other areas of the country where the subject has resided or has friends and contacts. In federal agencies, this is fairly easy to accomplish, because they have branches throughout the country. For local agencies, this usually involves asking fellow law enforcement agencies to assist by conducting investigations in their jurisdictions.

The next step involves contacting more distant friends, relatives, and associates. Hangouts that the subject visited infrequently should be checked.

In connection with efforts to locate the fugitive, the law enforcement officer would employ a variety of investigative techniques. He would use the interview technique. He would also probably contact informants and would employ the services of any undercover officers who might be in a position to locate the subject. He would conduct surveillance at places where he had good reason to believe that the subject might come, and might follow people whom he suspected might contact the fugitive. He might use closed-circuit television to cover certain locations. He might request that suspected contacts of the subject "clear" themselves by undergoing polygraph examinations. In order to locate the subject's fingerprints or DNA, he might send items from places where he believed the subject had visited to a crime laboratory.

Unique Aspects of Fugitive Terrorists

Fugitive terrorists are often much more difficult to apprehend than average criminals. Because they do not regard themselves as criminals per se, even though they have violated a law, they frequently do not act like the average criminal. Their political cause is all-important to them. If they are to be apprehended, it is often the political cause that will lead the investigator to the person. Unfortunately, people involved in, or supportive of, the cause are very unlikely to cooperate with law enforcement officials, especially in locating a person who became fugitive due to cause-related activities. Many people who become fugitives for a cause abandon their family and friends unless their family and friends are also sympathetic to the cause. Therefore, the traditional fugitive investigative step of interviewing friends and relatives will often fail to yield anything of value. Terrorist fugitives usually do not contact former employers and distant friends, because these people have nothing to lend to the cause. Consequently, a law enforcement officer who finds a cooperative relative or associate who may have the ability, for whatever reason, to develop information about the fugitive, should treat that that person with great respect and care.

The average fugitive has no support that he can truly trust outside of his family and friends. If he needs assistance, or even just a friendly conversation, he must turn to these people. Law enforcement agencies have relied upon this for years, and have been highly successful in locating fugitives by concentrating on these known contacts. Terrorists have a network of people who will lend them assistance whether from their own or another terrorist organization. Many of these people are not even known to the authorities. Those who are known will probably not assist law enforcement officials in locating the subject. Politically involved people are often not tempted by promises of financial reward, and they are not usually intimidated by threats. In contrast, friends and relatives of common criminals have been known to provide information in exchange for a reward. Some cave in to pressure when a police officer indicates that they could be arrested if they have assisted a fugitive.

Detection of a Fugitive Terrorist through His or Her Organization

The best way to locate a fugitive terrorist is to combine the usual steps used to locate any fugitive with an emphasis on finding the person through his or her terrorist group. A terrorist investigator who is able to discover the existence of a clandestine cell of a terrorist group will probably discover the location of fugitives through his coverage of that cell. This was clearly demonstrated in Chicago, when members of the Chicago Terrorism Task Force discovered a clandestine cell of the Puerto Rican independence FALN organization. Through covert investigation of this cell, the task force found the hiding place of long-time FALN fugitive member William Guillermo Morales in Mexico. Morales was subsequently arrested through this information.

Informants and undercover officers working in conjunction with a terrorist group will probably develop information about fugitive members of the group even though the fugitive may not be from their jurisdiction and may not be wanted by their department. Similarly, surveillance of a clandestine cell may locate fugitives. Additionally, wiretaps and other electronic coverage of a terrorist group may develop information about fugitive members of that group or other related terrorist organizations.

Locating the Subject through Relatives, "Cause-Relatives," and Associates

While it true that terrorists will not likely have much, if any, contact with family members unless those people are supporters of the cause, investigators should, nonetheless, identify as many relatives as possible, and determine their whereabouts. Modern computing makes this much more feasible today than it was even a decade ago. The names of cause-sympathetic relatives should be highlighted because they are probably the most likely to render assistance to the subject. Of course, they are also going to be the most security-conscious, and therefore the most difficult to cover. It might be wise to use a family-tree program as a basis for charting these people. Next, the subject's "cause family" should be plotted. Because they are not usually relatives, it will be necessary to create a layered chart that will reflect the degree of closeness of each person to the subject. Some of these people will themselves be clandestine, and their whereabouts unknown. However, the information about their relationship to the subject is nonetheless extremely important, because if that person is located, the subject may be in close proximity. Surface support people who have a relationship with the subject will clearly be the first people for an investigator to use to try to locate the fugitive. The third category of people who might lead the investigator to the subject are non-cause-related friends and associates.

The value of identifying and charting relatives and associates was clearly shown in the apprehension of Iraqi dictator Saddam Hussein on December 13, 2003. This apprehension was due in large part to the outstanding work of two U.S. military intelligence analysts who, from a collection of approximately 9,000 names, painstakingly plotted the identities of 300 people that they could determine were directly connected to Hussein through either blood or tribal lines. They gathered as much intelligence as possible on each of the names, and eventually were able to narrow the list to the people closest to the fugitive and most able to assist him.

Locating a Fugitive Terrorist
Using Personal Attributes

A technique that can be used to locate any fugitive, but that is best used against a terrorist, an organized crime subject, or other person involved in a complex group conspiracy, is exploiting both the important and largely insignificant information that has been developed about that subject. The method will most likely bear fruit if the agency employing it has national coverage or is working closely with other local agencies on the same conspiracy. It would seem an ideal tactic for a joint terrorism task force to employ. A computer database of information about the targeted conspiracy and its members is required.

This technique is a modern refinement of the traditional method of gathering facts about the subject and notifying other investigators about this information so that they can recognize him or trace the logical leads gleaned from information to locate him. The difference involves using the computer to store and compile all information about the subject, including the many "little things" that previously were never recorded in police files.

The basic premise of this method of locating fugitives is that virtually every human being is unique, and can be identified if enough information is known about him or her. Traditionally, investigators have developed general facts about fugitives, including physical description, biographic legend, profile, and the identities of relatives, friends, and associates. Other lesser-known facts are also learned, but many end up gathering dust in the fugitive's investigative file or in a detective's notepad. Some are never even documented, because there really is no vehicle through which this can be accomplished. An investigator would be wise to record all information learned about a suspect. If that investigator is reassigned, the volume of facts developed would be available to his replacement as opposed to being carried away in the initial investigator's memory.

Most people are creatures of habit. They do certain things because they work for them. They may engage in these activities because they bring them pleasure, or relieve pain and anxiety. They may do certain things because they have been taught to do them. They may be forced by their physical or mental situation to engage in certain activities. This kind of information can lead an investigator to a fugitive. These factors allow an investigator to isolate the subject from scores of look-alikes.

When a person is trying to hide from law enforcement, he will attempt to change in a variety of ways. His first move will be to divorce himself from his former identity, which he knows is on wanted posters and is in police computers. His new false identity may be made up or stolen, or it may have been purchased from someone on the street. He may or may not have good documentation to support it. Terrorist fugitives are likely to have strong false identification. The fugitive's next logical step will be to modify his appearance, especially if he knows that the police have a good photograph of him, or can identify him on sight. These changes might include shaving or growing hair or changing hairstyles. Men will often grow, remove, or change beards, mustaches, and sideburns. Some people will lose or gain weight. Some will add tattoos or remove or change body adornments. Scars and other identifying marks may be removed or covered. Modern law enforcement agencies usually attempt to counter some of these measures by releasing altered photographs of the subject depicting him as he might appear with different hair or other disguises. The computer has greatly enhanced the ability of law enforcement to create images of fugitives as they might appear in various disguises.

Although the fugitive is likely to make a concerted effort to change the more overt aspects of his appearance, especially anything that is mentioned on wanted notices, he will have difficulty modifying the small, or less apparent, aspects of his personality, speech, and appearance. Indeed, even if he tries to change some of these things, he probably will revert back to many of them within weeks or months, because they are a part of his very nature.

Someone who is always nervous and fidgets constantly is likely to continue that way even in a clandestine status. A person who is always "cold," even in the summer, is not likely to suddenly become warm because he becomes the subject of a law enforcement dragnet. A person who tends to fear the unknown will not lose this tendency when going into an underground status. It is unlikely that a person who loses his temper frequently will become calm and peaceful upon fleeing authorities. A person who is organized and neat will probably continue to be this way. Even if that person is forced to live in a filthy hideout, he will probably arrange his possessions in an orderly fashion. All of these traits, some of which are physical, some of which are mental, and some of which are learned, are a part of the person, and he or she will have great difficulty altering them. The very fact that fugitive status is very tense and uncomfortable may cause a magnification in certain traits that people have, such as a bad temper or moodiness. It could also lead people to seek tranquility by emphasizing activities and traits that are comfortable for them, such as wearing particular clothing or eating a certain food.

In the United States, people have the freedom to purchase a large variety of products. This may not be true in less developed parts of the world, where there are fewer choices available. By the time people reach adulthood in the United States, many are brand-loyal to a variety of products. The fact that they become fugitives does not alter this tendency. A person who smokes Camel cigarettes is likely to continue smoking this brand. Similarly, a man is not likely to change his brand of deodorant, shaving cream, or toothpaste just because he is a fugitive. A woman who prefers to wear jeans as opposed to dresses is probably going to continue to wear jeans even if wanted posters depict her in jeans.

Affinity to brands and styles is not the only aspect of someone's personality that is unlikely to change when that person is hiding. An individual's interests will probably stay somewhat the same. A person who likes to bowl or fish or play tennis will probably continue to have those interests regardless of the circumstances. A person who hates to iron or do housework prior to becoming a fugitive will probably not want to do such things after becoming a fugitive. A person who drives aggressively is probably going to continue to drive in this manner.

Personal habits, including food preferences, will not change a great deal when a person becomes a fugitive. He or she might not be able to eat in the restaurants he or she once did, because he or she may not have the resources to do so, or might fear being recognized. However, if he or she liked a certain food prior to becoming a fugitive, he or she will probably continue to like that food after becoming a fugitive.

Certain physical aspects of a person will almost always remain a constant. The way a person walks or holds his body are significant aspects of his uniqueness. Hand gestures and positioning of legs are unique. Some people naturally touch their chins, cover their mouths, or put their hands in their pockets at certain times. Some people fold their arms when relaxing. Some pick their noses. Some pull on their hair. Some cross their legs or wiggle their feet. Some people bite their nails. Other people take great pains to grow long fingernails. Some people like to show off parts of their body, while others try to conceal certain areas of their body.

Personal habits become part of an individual's nature. Some people wear jewelry while others do not. Some men carry their wallets in a particular pocket, while others prefer to carry a billfold in their coat. Still others do not like to carry a wallet. Some criminals (or even law enforcement officers) prefer shoulder holsters to belt holsters. Others like to carry their weapons in ankle holsters or fanny packs. Some people chew on toothpicks. Others chew on pencils and pens. Still others like to have an unlit cigar in their mouth. Some people belch openly and make other bodily sounds, while others would be embarrassed to do so. Some people always wear a certain piece of jewelry. Others never even wear watches.

People cannot do much to change their patterns of speech once they have reached adulthood. Regional accents are difficult to overcome, especially if a person is caught off-guard. Catchphrases that people use are also difficult to abandon. Similarly, words or comments that a person uses when angry will probably continue as a part of that person's vocabulary and way of expressing himself.

To the investigator, this means that the more information he can develop on the wanted person, the easier it will be to locate him or her. With computers, it is now possible to record and access hundreds of details about people. This can make it possible for a skilled investigator to locate a missing person without even seeing him or her.

For example, an informant in California might report that someone new has been attending meetings staged by certain environmental activists. In a thorough debriefing of this informant, the source might reveal that this unknown person is of a certain race, weight, height, and age; has peculiarities that include chewing a specific brand of tobacco, using a certain type of deodorant, wearing blue pullover sweaters, enjoying stock car races, having a vast knowledge of rock and roll of the 1950s, having a "Type A" personality, wearing necklaces, frequenting Kentucky Fried Chicken restaurants where he always orders a dark meat, three-piece combo meal with an orange soda, swinging his arms when he walks, speaking with a southern accent, and often saying "gol darn." Individually, these facts may have little significance. However, together, they describe a very particular person. It is possible that a computer database will be able to determine that all of these factors are associated with a fugitive sought for an environmental crime in New York state. Even without a picture, this investigator can be pretty sure that he has found the fugitive if enough matches occur.

Of course, the process can also be done in reverse. An investigator in New York can enter into a computer all the details he has about his environmental fugitive, and ask that computer to identify someone with similar traits. If the investigator in California has entered the same or similar characteristics into his computer, both investigators will get a "hit" on this person.

Escaped Prisoners

Although most fugitives are sought on initial warrants, there are some who have already been arrested, convicted, and have subsequently escaped from prison. With respect to common criminals, the apprehension of an escaped prisoner can often be accomplished quickly because the inmate's options are somewhat limited. His primary objective is to get away from the general area of the jail or prison. Many, if not most, escapees are apprehended because they cannot accomplish this feat. Guards find them or local residents turn them in. If the prisoner manages to distance himself from the institution, he usually finds himself in need of help because he lacks the resources to survive. It is then that he must turn to his friends and associates. Knowing this, experienced law enforcement officers immediately give such contacts close coverage, and often apprehend the subject through these friends and associates.

The circumstances of the political extremist escape are often quite different from those of ordinary criminals. Frequently the terrorist escape has been engineered and facilitated by his terrorist group or supporters. As a result, it is likely that he has a means for quickly leaving the immediate area of the penitentiary. He will likely already have support people in place who are either uncooperative to law enforcement or know security procedures to counter police, or are generally unknown to investigators. Indeed, some of the people may not even know the subject, but will lend him assistance anyway, because they support the political cause.

Ordinary criminal escapees usually have little more than the clothes on their backs, and even these are of little use because they are prison-issue.

As a result, most are forced to quickly turn to criminal activity to obtain the most basic needs in life—including food, shelter, and suitable clothing. Every crime they commit jeopardizes their liberty. Because authorities are looking for the escapee, any crime that occurs near the prison will help to direct investigators to the subject. The terrorist has a support network that can get him what he needs.

Most terrorist groups have access to quality false identification—some of which they produce themselves. If the escape has been planned by the group, it is a virtual certainty that the fugitive will be given false identification shortly after leaving the prison. Ordinary criminals usually do not have anyone who can quickly give them quality false identification. They either make up a name or procure false identification of unknown quality off the street. In order to accomplish the latter, they must somehow raise money to pay for it.

Another factor that differentiates fugitive terrorists from ordinary criminals is the availability of foreign shelter. Many terrorist groups have foreign connections that can be used to hide a fugitive. Lacking false identification and funds, most common criminals cannot even consider entering a foreign country, much less finding someone there who will give them shelter. Convicted police killer Joanne Deborah Chesimard (now known as Assata Shakur) and William Guillermo Morales, convicted of illegal possession of explosives and incarcerated for a time in Mexico, are examples of escaped terrorist prison inmates who were able to enter a foreign country (Cuba) that sympathized with their political causes. Few average criminals would even be able to enter Cuba, let alone find help there.

For these reasons, terrorist escapees are usually more difficult to apprehend than are ordinary criminals. Often the best way to locate such individuals is through close study of the people who visited or corresponded with the fugitives prior to their escape. At least some of these individuals probably facilitated the escape. Because this is a crime, it is possible that one of these people could be convinced to cooperate, especially if he can be shown that evidence implicating him in the escape has been developed. Careful investigation of the escapee's terrorist group will also be a viable avenue of investigation. If the case is national in scope, word should be sent to all investigative agencies involved in the case to look for the subject, or to merely be aware of intelligence regarding new members, visitors, or strange communications with their local group.

The best way to handle a terrorist prison escape is to prevent it in the first place. Any terrorist who is in custody should be considered to be a flight risk. Prison officials should be made aware of the person's political group. Any intelligence developed during the course of a terrorist investigation indicating that an incarcerated group member is planning an escape, or that group members are studying ways for a jailed group member to escape, should be treated seriously.

Summary

Terrorists often function in an "underground" status, in which they live what appears to be a "normal" life except that they use false identities and created backgrounds to conceal who they really are. Within this "underground" are people sought for terrorism-related crimes. Fugitive terrorists often present problems for law enforcement officers because they do not act like ordinary criminals. Their crimes are almost never motivated by profit or personal benefit. They frequently abandon relatives and friends who do not support their political cause. Unlike ordinary criminals, fugitive terrorists usually have an organization that will assist them. They also frequently have "surface" supporters who are not directly involved in terrorist activities, but who agree with the general philosophy of the group, and who will render them assistance without any questions being asked. If an incarcerated terrorist is able to escape, he, too, usually has politically involved people who will help him. Indeed, they may well have facilitated his escape. This makes him very different from other criminals who break out of prison. One of the best avenues to explore with reference to locating a terrorist fugitive is his group. Cause-related people are more likely to know the subject's whereabouts, and to be assisting him, than are even close relatives and friends. Nonetheless, there is value in identifying as many relatives as possible and concentrating on those who support the cause. "Cause-relatives" should be similarly plotted, to distinguish those who are the closest to the fugitive.

SECTION III

Factors to Be Considered When Implementing Investigative Techniques Against Terrorists

22 The Terrorist in Court

Trial

Before the trial begins, there will be hearings during which the defense will attempt to obtain rulings from the judge that will be favorable to their side. The defense will have been given access to the evidence that the government plans to present and may well challenge some of it if they believe it to be unfair. They may also attempt to have highly damaging evidence ruled inadmissible, because they know that it will be difficult to counter during trial. Pretrial motions could involve a number of hearings, and ultimately a trial date will be set.

The trial will usually be before a jury in complex cases, although in some situations the defendant may want a judge to render the verdict. A jury must be selected, and both the prosecution and defense can challenge prospective jurors. As the trial commences, the prosecutor will outline his case during opening arguments, the defense will outline how it intends to challenge the case, and will explain weaknesses that they believe exist in the prosecution's case. Following this, the prosecutor will present his case. He will call witnesses, most of whom were initially interviewed by investigators. It is likely that he will also have crime laboratory experts testify concerning physical evidence that was recovered by investigators. In addition, various law enforcement officers will probably testify about information they developed during the case.

The defense will challenge the evidence presented by the government. This will involve cross-examination of witnesses presented by the government and the presentation of their own witnesses.

Following the presentation of evidence, both sides will deliver closing arguments. The government will summarize the evidence that they presented and explain how it proves that the defendant is guilty. The defense also will review the evidence and will attempt to convince the jury that it does not prove the defendant guilty. Ultimately, the jury (or judge in cases without a jury) will render a verdict.

The courtroom process is restrained and proper. Everyone is professional in appearance and actions. There are certain unwritten rules of decorum that all parties follow. Political issues rarely have any part in criminal trials.

What Occurs in the Courtroom during Many Terrorism Trials

In a terrorism case, the first difference that investigators and court personnel may observe will be the presence of supporters of the defendant demonstrating outside the court building. If this occurs, the protesters usually also be will promoting the political cause of the defendant in addition to expressing support for him. Such protest actions are almost unheard-of in connection with non-terrorism criminal cases. Protest supporters may be present during all proceedings involving the case, not just the trial.

The motions that will be made during pretrial hearings will often be typical of those that are made in many criminal cases. However, there are likely to be some variations that can cause court personnel, including judges and prosecutors, concern. The judge may be asked to disqualify himself, which is in itself is not an unusual motion. However, the reason given may be that the judge is biased against the political cause embraced by the defendant, or is prejudiced against people of the defendant's racial or ethnic background. This argument may surprise the judge especially if the judge is a minority or a civil libertarian. Requests for wiretap records will also likely be made. This is fairly typical in many criminal cases. However, in terrorism cases the defense may follow this motion with accusations that the government deployed illegal techniques. This is not a normal motion made in routine criminal proceedings. A number of political extremists truly believe that the government routinely employs illegal tactics against them in order to maintain the status quo. Some are convinced that all of their telephones are tapped and their residences are bugged. Of course, the government will deny that any illegal actions took place. However, this may lead to the defense demanding that every law enforcement agency involved in any way with the investigation be polled with respect to electronic coverage on the subjects.

Plea bargains are usually fairly common in criminal cases, and in fact many cases never make it to a jury trial. Terrorists are not likely to make deals unless the arrangement is so favorable that it cannot be passed up. For many terrorists, the very idea of bargaining with the government is out of the question. This is especially true of some right-wing radicals who do not accept the lawful existence of the government, much less its courts. Some political extremists believe that the exposure that their political cause will receive in connection with a trial, and the information that may be developed about the government's operations during court proceedings is worth the extra time they may spend in prison by not accepting a deal.

Courts are usually on high alert during important terrorism cases. Consequently, additional security personnel will be present. If the court does not increase security, it should do so. If there are picketers outside of the court building, they will very likely be cause-related supporters, rather than friends and relatives. It should be assumed that political supporters will also try to pack the spectators' area of the courtroom.

The terrorist defendant may or may not be represented by counsel. Usually by the time of the trial, the investigators and court personnel will know whether the defendant plans to represent himself or employ an attorney. This will have been determined during the course of the hearings that will likely have been held before the trial.

The investigators and court personnel, including the prosecutor, must realize that the terrorist is politically driven. His political agenda is his whole life. Unless he has cooperated with authorities, which is rare, it must be assumed that he will attempt to use the court as a vehicle through which to promulgate his philosophy. Many extremists, both on the left and the right, view the government as their enemy. They view courts and law enforcement officers as agents of the government and, therefore, feel no reason to respect either. If a terrorist could somehow embarrass an investigator in court, he would consider that a victory of sorts for his cause.

Some of the attorneys who represent terrorist clients have a degree of sympathy for their cause. This is not to say that these lawyers advocate violence. However, if they are sympathetic to the cause, they will devote considerable time to the case, and will make an effort to represent their clients to the utmost degree. Investigators can expect to be cross-examined quite thoroughly about any evidence that they present. Some attorneys will attempt to bring the political philosophy of their clients into court. Even if the attorneys do not, the defendants often will make efforts to do so.

Some terrorists will be represented by the public defender. However, there is no guarantee that these people will cooperate with him or her, or that the public defender will be able to exercise any degree of control over them in court.

Right-wing extremists frequently refuse to hire attorneys or to have anything to do with them. People who fall into this category are often affiliated with the sovereign citizen movement and the Posse Comitatus philosophy. They generally believe that they are citizens unto themselves, and not subject to the control of a central government. Some might allow a "legal advisor" to appear in court with them, but most will represent themselves. Many believe that a mysterious Thirteenth Amendment to the United States Constitution was passed in 1810 that forbids anyone holding a title of nobility from being a United States citizen. Because attorneys may use the term "esquire" after their names upon being admitted to the bar, these extremists believe that lawyers are holders of titles of nobility and, therefore, not eligible to be citizens. They also believe that during the 1800s, lawyers concealed this "real" Thirteenth Amendment from the people in order to protect their own interests.

Some terrorists will claim to be "prisoners of war" (POWs) and will not cooperate with the court because they believe that they are entitled to some form of special treatment. FALN members and some left-wing defendants during the 1970s and 1980s claimed to be POWs. Support groups for left, right, and special interest groups frequently refer to incarcerated members of their cause as POWs, although not all of them use this form of defense in court.

Some defendants will not respect the judge. Left-wing extremists of the 1960s and 1970s often would not stand when the judge entered the courtroom. Right-wing extremists of the 1990s will sometimes refuse to cross an imaginary bar that they believe separates the judge's area from the spectators' section of the court, because they believe the court to be military in nature. In a mid-1990s trial in Missouri, more than a dozen sovereign citizen defendants refused to cross the "bar" in the courtroom.

In some cases, the subject will refuse to remain in court during his trial. In the FALN cases of the early 1980s, the defendants spent much of their time in a room outside of the courtroom because of their disruptive behavior and their unwillingness to remain in the courtroom. As recently as January 2001, a white supremacist on trial in Missouri spent much of his trial outside the courtroom because he refused to participate in his own defense.

Jury selection may well involve questions to prospective jurors from defense attorneys concerning their political views. This can result in objections from the government.

Investigators should be well-prepared when they testify in court. They should not be surprised if they are asked about specific aspects of the Constitution or about their "oath of office." They should also not be taken aback if they are asked if they have committed any illegal activities during the course of the investigation. Some attorneys/defendants will jump on any aspect of testimony that does not seem to have a logical nexus with other facts presented in court. They will allege that the government obviously employed illegal techniques or undisclosed sources to move from point A to point C. Consequently, a clear logical presentation of evidence is important in terrorist cases. Questions about the officer being affiliated with the CIA, FBI, or another agency are also fairly common in extremist cases. If an officer has functioned in an undercover capacity during the case, he will probably be questioned in detail about entrapment issues. Thorough documentation of the investigation can do much to support the investigator's testimony. If the defendant is representing himself, the investigator must be aware during cross-examination that the questioner has both a fear of and possible hatred for him because of his position with the government.

Other Courtroom Tactics Used by Terrorists

Civil Actions

Some right-wing defendants of the 1990s adopted a tax protester tactic of the 1970s by taking civil action against investigators and other court personnel in an apparent effort to prevent them from conducting investigations into their activities. Lawsuits were filed against some personnel. Liens were also filed against the property of court employees and officers. In one Missouri case in the mid-1990s, a multi-million dollar lien was filed against the property of a judge because he found a person guilty of a traffic violation. False Internal Revenue Service (IRS) 1099 forms have been filed reflecting payments to police officers that were never actually made. Such action can lead to an IRS audit of the officer for failure to report the income.

Common Law Courts

During the 1980s and 1990s, people who considered themselves to be sovereign citizens (not subject to any central government's control) began establishing their own "common law courts." These entities had no legal authority whatsoever. Often the participants in such bodies attempt to make their courts look and operate like real courts, but they have difficulty doing so because almost no one involved has any legal training. Nonetheless, they issue orders and even warrants and liens. In the 1990s, one high-ranking police official in Utah received a summons to appear before a common law court that contained a notation that his presence for his trial was not even required! A few weeks later, he was informed by that court that a warrant had been issued for his arrest. In Missouri during the mid-1990s, a woman told a judge that she could not be tried for a traffic offense in his court because she had already been found innocent in a common law court. She cited the principle of double jeopardy in her argument.

Jury Nullification

According to *Black's Law Dictionary* (1999), jury nullification is "a jury's knowing and deliberate rejection of the evidence or refusal to apply the law either because the jury wants to send a message about some social issue that is larger than the case itself or because the result dictated by law is contrary to the jury's sense of justice, morality, or fairness." Many right-wing extremists believe that jurors should make decisions based on the nature of the law rather than from the evidence; and they believe that juries will decide in their favor if they are able to hear their political view with respect to the charges against them. Some extremists believe that trial juries function as a fourth avenue of the checks and balances system in the U.S. government after the executive, judicial, and legislative branches. They believe that trial jurors should regularly review the laws passed by Congress involved in a case to determine if they are valid, fair, and in accordance to the Constitution. If they find that a law is not proper, they cannot convict a person of violating it. The *Black's* definition implies that the entire jury needs to render a verdict. However, for right-wing extremists, a single juror making a decision based on something other than the evidence is often satisfactory to them. It may not win them an acquittal, but it will cause the case to conclude with a hung jury. In some instances, the prosecutor may not wish to retry the case. This will also be a victory for them. If a retrial is ordered, the defendant will be given a new forum for presenting his political views.

Various booklets concerning jury nullification are promoted by political extremists. These publications can be found at gun shows and some political rallies. Militias will also likely have them. Law enforcement officers should be alert for such materials, especially in conjunction with right-wing cases. Supporters of some extremists may attempt to distribute jury nullification documents to everyone entering a courthouse in the hope that a juror will get one. If such a booklet makes it into a jury room, it could mean a mistrial or a hung jury if a juror reads and follows its instructions. There is a good chance that it will not be illegal to distribute such documents unless there is some kind of leafleting restriction around a courthouse, which, of course, would have to apply to any form of leafleting. If, however, someone specifically targets a sitting juror in the vicinity of the courthouse or at his or her residence or other location, the judge should be immediately notified because this could constitute jury tampering at the very least.

Leaderless Resistance Subjects

The concept of leaderless resistance, by which extremist groups encourage sympathizers to perpetrate their own attacks consistent with the philosophy of the group, has generated a defendant that may not be typical of a hard-core political terrorist. Because the terrorist group is not aware of the identities of such people until they are arrested (and sometimes not even then, if the arrests are not publicized), they may not offer them assistance. Furthermore, such individuals are not as likely to be entrenched in their beliefs to the same degree as are long-time group members. And even though they probably have studied the group's security directions, they are not as likely to have the same kind of understanding of these mandates as would an actual member of the group. What this means is that the circumstances involving the arrest and prosecution of leaderless resistance followers is likely to be more similar to what law enforcement officers usually encounter with ordinary criminals.

On January 12, 2004, three young men in Virginia pleaded guilty to multiple counts of vandalism that resulted in hundreds of thousands of dollars in damages during 2002. The attacks were claimed by the Earth Liberation Front (ELF). There was no evidence to suggest that these men—all of whom were high school students at the time—had any direct contact with the ELF, or were specifically directed by that group to commit the attacks. They were engaging in leaderless resistance—doing what they believed that ELF wanted. After being arrested, they responded more like teenagers in trouble for the first time than hardened political terrorists. There were no protests in the streets on their behalf, and no disruptions in court designed to promote the cause. The three men essentially pleaded guilty and placed themselves at the mercy of the court. Sadly for the law enforcement community, no matter how cooperative that these men would be, it is doubtful that they possessed any intimate knowledge of the ELF or about the perpetrators of other ELF-claimed attacks around the country. A similar situation occurred in December 2004 and early 2005, when four young California adults perpetrated several arson attacks on construction projects near Sacramento under the name of the ELF. They subsequently pleaded guilty in late 2005 and early 2006, and were sentenced to prison terms. They, too, were engaged in leaderless resistance, and had no knowledge about the leadership of the ELF.

Summary

For the police officer, the case does not end when the investigation is completed. The subject must be tried and convicted and properly punished. If this does not happen, a large amount of time and effort will have been for naught. Taking a terrorist to court is not easy. He will usually have supporters from his political cause nearby. If he defends himself or hires an attorney, it is likely that he will not agree to a plea bargain, and instead will choose to go to trial. If he can interject his political philosophy into the proceedings, he will. If the subject belongs to an anti-government movement, the investigator should assume that the defendant will view him as a representative of the state that the defendant hates. The best weapon that an investigator can bring into court is a well-prepared case. The investigator should not expect the defense to stipulate to anything. The investigator must be prepared to provide excellent testimony, and must be able to undergo a rigorous cross-examination.

23 Ethical Issues and Investigative Techniques

Law enforcement officers have a demanding, complex, and dangerous job. They are often taken for granted by the public they serve. Compounding the situation is the fact that officers usually encounter people during the worst of times. Some of the people whom officers meet in the line of duty are completely honest and candid with them. Unfortunately, other people are not as honest and law-abiding. It is not unusual for officers to be verbally and physically threatened and abused while attempting to perform their duties. Others may attempt to intimidate the officer by claiming position and influence that can be used against the officer.

Regardless of how hard they work on a case, officers are often criticized for not solving it quickly enough to suit the parties involved. Along this same line, officers are sometimes criticized for not having prevented the crime from happening in the first place. Frequently, officers find themselves pulled in several directions with respect to enforcing the law. City officials, politicians, corporate leaders, and even prosecutors and judges may demand rigid enforcement of certain statutes, while citizens' groups may want other laws stringently enforced.

Work conditions are not always ideal for law enforcement officers. Work hours can be long, and schedules can be erratic. Holiday and weekend work are more the rule than the exception. Many police stations, particularly in large cities, are crammed and unpleasant. The "crime workplace" is often in the poor, more run-down parts of a city. Additionally, although most people do not go into law enforcement to become wealthy, there is a perception among officers and the public that law enforcement officers are underpaid.

Despite all of the hardships that law enforcement officers deal with, they must always behave professionally. Their primary responsibilities must be to uphold and enforce the law, and to provide protection and assistance to the community. In some situations this may require officers to protect the constitutional rights of people who show them no respect. Fortunately, officers also encounter citizens who appreciate the work done by sworn law enforcement officers.

Professional Conduct

The code of professional conduct that governs every law enforcement agency and each individual officer is essentially comprised of five components:

1. Federal, state, and local laws, statutes, and ordinances;

2. Policies, rules of conduct, and procedures set by law enforcement agencies, prosecutors, and governmental bodies;

3. Court edicts, orders, and directives;

4. Memorandums of understanding and other agreements established between agencies;

5. The morals, ethical standards, and values held by the law enforcement officer himself, his superiors, his agency, and the community in which he lives.

Laws, Statutes, and Ordinances

Every law enforcement officer should be familiar with the laws he is charged with enforcing. He should also be familiar with laws that specifically govern how he conducts investigations.

Most law enforcement agencies have legal counsel. Sometimes the department employs such a person, or uses one of their own officers who holds a law degree. If the department has no such person, the city, county, or state should employ an attorney. Every law enforcement agency has access to a prosecutor's office. Law enforcement officers who have questions about the laws they enforce or about the laws that govern their conduct should bring these concerns to their legal counsel.

Policies, Rules, and Procedures

Department rules and regulations govern a variety of facets of the law enforcement officer's life. They deal with everything from work hours to uniform requirements. Some involve how officers relate to their superiors and the public. Others deal with the manner in which reports are to be completed. There are rules concerning sick leave, vacations, and retirement. Some of the policies concerning officer conduct come from prosecutors. Some rules are restatements of laws, and are often more stringent than the statutes upon which they are based. Many new officers discover that there are more rules and policies regarding their behavior as police officers than they experienced in other jobs.

There are many procedures and policies in law enforcement regulating the conduct to be followed during an investigation. While it is true that officers should be mindful of all rules concerning their profession, they must be especially cognizant of those dealing with investigations. Violations in this area can cause the most problems and can result in serious trouble for the offending officer.

Examples of law enforcement agency rules, procedures, and policies include the following:

> An officer must wear a protective vest while on duty;
>
> Two officers must be present during such situations as the interview of a subject, the taking of a signed statement, or the payment of an informant;
>
> High-speed chases of more than a certain distance must be approved by a superior officer;
>
> Handcuffs must be double-locked;
>
> Interviews must be reduced to written form within a certain number of days;
>
> Police vehicles cannot be used for personal business;
>
> Long-distance calls made from department telephones must be logged on a register;
>
> Recovered property must be checked through the stolen property computer terminal within a certain number of days;
>
> Officers must qualify with their approved firearm every month;
>
> Officers must transport prisoners and suspects in the rear seat of a police vehicle.

The rules listed above represent only a small sample of the procedures and policies that a police agency might have for its officers to follow. It is important to note that most rules of this kind are not statutes or laws. As a result, an officer who violates them does not usually risk arrest and prosecution. Nonetheless, officers should always follow them.

Law enforcement officers must realize that violations of agency policies can be used against them in court. In cases in which there is an aggressive defense, as is frequently the situation in terrorist trials, it is likely that any policy violation will be used to show that the investigator cannot be trusted, because he does not even follow his own agency's guidelines. Any rule violation can also result in civil action being taken against the officer and his department. Of course, officers who violate department policy are subject to internal disciplinary action that could include suspension or even termination.

Court Rulings and Guidelines

Officers are usually taught about court decisions and guidelines before they are sworn in to serve in a department. The courts interpret the law. Departments want to ensure that their officers know both the content of the laws that they enforce and what the courts believe these laws to mean. Most agencies have lawyers who monitor court decisions, particularly those that involve their agency. These attorneys quickly pass on information about changes in interpretation. It makes little sense for an investigator to defy a court mandate, especially if it has been rendered in the judicial district in which he works. It could cost him a case and could cause him to be punished by the court or his agency.

Memorandums of Understanding and Other Agreements

Documents signed between agencies often restrict what an officer can do. They are usually prepared in situations in which two or more agencies have concurrent or similar jurisdiction. Some are rigidly enforced while others are informal. Regardless of the nature of an official agreement, investigators should be aware of the existence and contents of such documents so that they do not inadvertently violate them.

Agreements between agencies could involve one entity yielding its jurisdiction to another in a particular criminal violation. It could also involve some form of division of the violation between the agencies. For example, one agency might agree to handle crimes that involve a financial loss below a certain level, leaving crimes with larger losses to the other agency. One agency might agree to handle a specific violation when it occurs within the city limits, whereas the other agency agrees to handle that crime when it occurs in the county.

A large municipal police department has an agreement with the state police, by which the state agency patrols and handles all traffic enforcement and accidents that occur on state expressways that pass through the city. From a legal standpoint, city police officers have the right to enforce traffic violations occurring on these expressways, but this agreement has caused the police chief to instruct his officers not to become involved in traffic enforcement on any of the city's expressways.

A mutual aid agreement is one in which two or more agencies agree to assist each other in certain situations. Often it involves serious emergencies that exceed the response capability of a single agency. Among these situations are riots, multi-alarm fires, and serial murders. Mutual aid agreements usually do not involve agencies relinquishing jurisdiction and authority. In fact, these agreements actually extend the jurisdictions of the involved agencies (although that is not the reason for agencies entering into such an arrangement). More often than not, such agreements permit departments to work in another law enforcement agency's district but under certain rules of conduct. Officers working on cases falling under a mutual aid agreement should understand the restrictions on what they can do.

Ethics

The behavior of all law enforcement officers is tempered by their own sense of morality, the standards of conduct set by their superiors and their department, and by the principles followed by the community in which they serve. Ethical behavior is not necessarily the same as legal behavior.

One department may be highly competitive and have standards that encourage competition with other agencies for quality cases. The department may also have values that encourage internal competition, so that individual investigators feel comfortable engaging in rivalry for cases with their fellow investigators. In contrast, another department may stress the value of cooperation, and may encourage its investigators to work closely with one another, and to share intelligence with other agencies having similar jurisdiction. Clearly, the standards of the two departments with respect to the value of cooperation are markedly different. Top management in the former agency may question the ethics of an officer in their department whom they discovered was sharing information with another agency that had concurrent jurisdiction with their department. In the latter situation, top management would likely commend one of their officers for engaging in intelligence sharing.

Some police managers are sticklers for detail and demand that solid and complete documentation accompany every investigation. Other police administrators may stress the importance of the investigation itself, and may tend to regard written documentation as something of a necessary evil. Again, the standards of behavior are likely to differ with respect to these two schools of administration.

In the case of a minor traffic accident in a service station parking lot, the investigating officer prepared a report that contained an incorrect address and several inaccurate facts. He also failed to include the statement of one of the two drivers involved in the mishap. When questioned about the report by an investigator employed by another agency, the officer explained that because the neighboring towns did not investigate accidents occurring on private property, he did not feel the need to waste his time being particularly accurate in documenting his findings in such a minor incident. He did, however, offer to change his report to indicate whatever the investigator wanted to have included, even though he knew that the investigator was not involved in the accident, and was not even a witness to it.

The situation above demonstrates the values of the particular police officer involved. The example may also reflect the values of his or her superiors and department. In essence, the officer implied that he was only willing to prepare a complete and accurate report in cases that he deemed important. In this case, he was even willing to modify his report to place into it whatever another investigator wanted to include, regardless of its accuracy. It is hoped that most law enforcement officers believe that any official report that they submit should at least be accurate, if not complete. This officer's conduct in the aforementioned traffic case could be used to seriously damage his credibility as a witness if the case were to go to trial.

The Concept of Common Sense

The fact that something is legally proper and falls within moral and ethical standards does not mean that it should be done. Common sense should be used in all investigations. Investigative techniques should be used to resolve a case, not impede its solution.

Interviewing people under adverse circumstances, when it is unlikely that they will cooperate, fails the "common sense" test. Subpoenaing large numbers of records with no intention of ever reviewing them also fails the "common sense" test. Administering a polygraph examination to a person who is under the influence of a narcotic or is mentally ill is improper. Requesting agency records checks in a situation in which it is likely that the subject will learn of the inquiry also fails the "common sense" test if the investigation is supposed to be discreet. Failing to conduct a thorough interview with a cooperative and knowledgeable witness has come back to haunt many investigators and simply does not make good sense.

In one fugitive terrorist investigation, the fugitive's brother was the only member of the family who would provide any information about him. The brother had no love for law enforcement, but he believed that if his sibling remained a fugitive, he would be killed by police or while committing a terrorist attack. During one interview, the brother volunteered that his father had told him that the fugitive had recently paid a surprise visit to the father's residence. The investigator immediately responded by contacting the father's neighbors to determine whether they had seen the subject at the family residence. Previous investigation had already found the neighbors to be friendly with the father and sympathetic to the fugitive son. The neighbors quickly notified the father of the contacts. As it turned out, the only person that the father had informed of his son's visit was the subject's brother. The father quickly deduced that either the brother had informed law enforcement of the visit, or had carelessly told someone else who had in turn told the authorities. Regardless, the father chastised the brother and cut him off from any further information about the fugitive. The brother subsequently ceased his cooperation with the law enforcement agency.

What the investigator did in this case was legal and ethical, but it lacked common sense. It cost the investigator the only informant that his agency had in this case. Of course, after the interviews of the neighbors, the fugitive never again visited the father's residence. This robbed law enforcement of any opportunity to use such techniques as surveillance or CCTV to apprehend him at that location.

After a terrorist bomb had exploded at a corporate headquarters, causing a large amount of damage, a commanding officer felt obliged to make some kind of statement to the media concerning the attack. Unfortunately, the man knew little about the group that had taken credit for the bombing. Checking with other agencies in several cities, he discovered that a cross-country search was underway for several key fugitive members of the group. The agencies had discovered the false identities that these fugitives were using, and had an excellent description of their vehicle. The fugitives, who were using a monitored credit card to buy gas, lodging, and make telephone calls, were unaware of the pursuit or that their false identities were known. The agencies felt that they would soon have them in custody. Wanting to appear knowledgeable during his press conference, the commanding officer revealed the information about the fugitive hunt, and even went so far as to name the fugitives as suspects in the bombing, even though there was good reason to believe that they had nothing to do with it.

As soon as the information appeared in the media, the cross-country trail of the fugitives went cold. It was clear that they had abandoned their vehicle and false identities as soon as they heard that they were being tracked and their identities were known. This was another situation in which common sense was not used.

While monitoring a court-authorized wiretap on a terrorist suspect's residence telephone, a law enforcement officer heard a suspicious telephone call to the subject from a heretofore unknown man. The investigator subsequently asked another investigator to identify the caller through the name and address learned from the content of the telephone call. The second investigator responded by hastily going to the man's residence and asking him about his relationship with the subject.

Within an hour of the contact with the man, the previously productive wiretap went dry and never again produced any useful information. It was learned that immediately following the visit to his residence, the caller had contacted the subject at his employment telephone and told him of the contact. In discussion the men concluded that the law the enforcement agency must have had a wiretap on the subject's home telephone because the men had had no other recent contact with one another. Careless followup on information developed during the course of a productive wiretap cost this law enforcement agency the use of a valuable investigative technique and, even worse, alerted the subject that the agency was investigating him.

Use of Questionable Investigative Techniques

Violating the Law in Order to Enforce the Law

Virtually all law enforcement officers in the United States undergo legal training prior to or immediately upon being employed. Most officers receive periodic legal training throughout their careers. Law enforcement agencies must field investigators who are familiar with the laws they must enforce. Agencies make concerted efforts to train their investigators with respect to the rules and regulations they must follow in their enforcement of the law. Few law enforcement officers deliberately commit illegal acts in order to solve a crime. Rarely does an investigator encounter a situation in which his or her department will instruct him or her to violate a law.

Nonetheless, law enforcement officers are human beings subject to fear, anger, and other human frailties. It can be difficult for an officer not to at least consider responding excessively in situations in which he or she is being threatened or actually attacked by a subject. Similarly, officers sometimes consider entering the gray area between legal and illegal action when they believe that a dangerous person will go free to commit other crimes due to "technicalities," or because the person has somehow intimidated the witnesses against him. Human nature itself may cause an officer to consider an irresponsible reaction to a person who is abusing him, cursing at him, or lying to him. The temptation to take extraordinary action will certainly manifest itself in situations in which the officer realizes that a subject's refusal to cooperate could result in harm and danger to innocent people. This could include situations in which a kidnapper refuses to reveal where his hostage is being held or a bomber will not reveal where he put a bomb. On occasion, an officer may encounter a situation in which he believes that a subject may avoid a criminal charge because of an oversight or error made by that officer or another investigator. In such situations there is a temptation for the officer to correct the problem by back-dating or modifying a report, or doing something that was not done before.

The entertainment industry's portrayal of law enforcement personnel often inaccurately depicts investigators operating in gray areas of legality. Some television dramas and films show police officers committing illegal acts for supposedly "good" reasons. A person who frequently watches such programs could easily come to believe that occasional illegal and unethical actions are acceptable behavior.

Despite the many temptations to violate the law, officers cannot compromise their principles and those of their agency. An investigator who violates laws in order to enforce other laws is no better than the criminal he or she is investigating.

A more recent problem that must be considered by all law enforcement officers is that defense attorneys do not allow law enforcement personnel "free passes" with respect to their courtroom testimony. Instead, they will challenge an investigator's integrity whenever possible. Prosecutors are not always able to protect the personnel files of officers who will be testifying. Anything contained in such files that involves questions of honesty can be used to damage the officer's credibility as a witness. Some prosecutors maintain a list of investigators who have credibility problems, so that they will know not to use these people in any court situation. They will not even allow these officers to swear to the accuracy of arrest and search warrants. The advent of computer technology has made it very easy for both prosecutors and defense attorneys to maintain the names of investigators with credibility problems. In fact, some lists may contain complete details of the transgressions committed by these officers. Anything in a law enforcement officer's history that shows dishonesty can greatly impair his or her ability to function in the profession.

Quite possibly, terrorism investigation is the area in which the temptation is the greatest for law enforcement officers to violate the law for the greater good. Terrorists threaten the government itself. Some want to overthrow the government, while others hope that, through the use of force and violence, they can make the government alter its stance on certain issues. Most terrorists place their political cause above anything else. Completely innocent people are often the victims of terrorist attacks. Some terrorists directly attack law enforcement personnel. Some terrorists operating in the United States are based in foreign countries or are sponsored by hostile foreign governments. Compounding the situation is that, in many instances, the public openly opposes terrorist groups, and looks to the government and law enforcement to counter the threat through any means possible. This can lead to an environment in which the law enforcement officer believes that he has public support to do what is necessary to solve the case.

The Vietnam war in the 1960s and early 1970s was a very unpopular conflict, and generated massive anti-war protests, riots, and college building takeovers. Various clandestine terrorist cells developed in the United States during this period. There were numerous bombings and arsons associated with the anti-war fervor. In 1969, power transmission lines were bombed in Colorado, and a clandestine group in Michigan bombed military targets. In 1970, four individuals destroyed a huge building on a college campus in Wisconsin, and in Massachusetts a terrorist cell killed a police officer during a bank robbery. Between 1969 and 1977, the Weather Underground Organization bombed almost 40 buildings, including the United States Capitol and the Pentagon. In the 1970s, the New World Liberation Front attacked scores of West Coast targets. Also during this period, black activists spoke of "offing the pig," and engaged in direct confrontation with police. The law enforcement community in the United States had never before experienced such a situation. Much of the population was demanding action.

Law enforcement reacted to the anti-war activities in a number of ways, including penetrating groups with informants and undercover agents, conducting open photographic coverage of protesters, and conducting investigations on many citizens. Unfortunately, some departments and investigators went too far. For some of these officers, the objective of solving and preventing terrorist attacks justified their investigating and disrupting all anti-war groups, including religious, cultural, and student organizations. Some engaged in "dirty tricks" to solve the problem. A few investigators violated laws in their efforts to locate terrorist fugitives. Many of the investigators and departments that went too far found themselves facing criminal charges or lawsuits. Fortunately, the use of questionable tactics did not yield much information of value. Had there been success, it could have resulted in serious problems in court, and at least some defendants would not have been convicted or would have been freed after being jailed. Additionally, success could have encouraged other investigators to roam into gray areas of legality.

"Dirty Tricks"

"Dirty tricks" are small actions that can be taken to disrupt a person's life or the operation of a business, organization, criminal conspiracy, or other enterprise, including a terrorist group. "Dirty tricks" designed to disrupt criminal activities or to "get even" have no place in proper law enforcement. In some instances, such tactics may be illegal, while in other circumstances they may only skirt the limits of the law. The overt support network for terrorist groups certainly poses a tempting target for such tactics because clandestine operatives depend upon their assistance, and dirty tricks could hamper the activities of these surface supporters. Despite this fact, these tactics should not be employed against either overt or underground people.

"Dirty tricks" can range from almost childish pranks that can irritate people and enterprises, to intricate plots that can destroy the reputation and operations of the target. In some cases, such tricks can cause a major disruption in the illegal activities being conducted by a person or enterprise. They can cause people to leave a group, and cause supporters to pull away from a cause. Sometimes innocent people may be harmed. If the officer is caught doing something like this, the consequences can be very serious. The major problem with using such tactics is that no one can know precisely what the outcome will be when such a trick is perpetrated. Even a simple prank could result in someone being killed.

The following are examples of "dirty tricks":

> Starting rumors that could turn group members against one another. A rumor could be started that the leader of a right-wing extremist group is actually Jewish, has a black relative, or is of Hispanic ancestry.

> Using false information to start internal strife. A few well-placed telephone calls from a female to a Mafia member's home might create marital discord. Notes left near a gang hangout suggesting that a gang member is a police informant could result in retaliation against that person.

Suspending or initiating services. Electricity or telephone service could be suspended to a boiler room operation, thereby curtailing their fraudulent activities.

Ordering deliveries of anything from pizzas to pornographic magazines to loads of fertilizer to the target address could disrupt their activities.

Disrupting the activities of a "front group" for a terrorist organization by disabling their printing press or distributing leaflets bearing their name but advocating a philosophy alien to their cause.

Using the Internet to depict a person or entity in an unflattering light.

These tactics are not necessarily limited to covert, secretive activities. An investigator can damage a person or entity through the use of direct "investigative techniques." Examples of this include the following:

Contacting a person's employer claiming to be conducting an investigation on terrorism, organized crime, or other criminal activity. Asking the employer if he has ever seen the subject carrying a gun or heard him talking about explosives. Following such a contact, many employers would seriously consider terminating the employee.

Conducting a neighborhood investigation by asking if anyone had ever seen the person building bombs in his backyard, or heard him talking about using biological agents of mass destruction.

Visiting a business location while driving a vehicle bearing markings like "Bomb Squad," "Vice Team," or "Police Crime Scene Investigation."

Disruptive tactics such as these, whether overt or covert, have no place in law enforcement, even if they might succeed in neutralizing a criminal subject or enterprise. All too often such tactics eventually come to light, and the reputation of the agency is tainted, and prosecutions are possibly negated. In addition, such activities might be afforded priority over legitimate investigative techniques that could properly resolve the case.

Foreign Investigative Techniques

There are investigative techniques used in some foreign countries that are not legal in the United States, even in situations in which the subject is a foreign national. Many of these techniques are specifically prohibited in the United States Constitution and the Bill of Rights. Among these practices are the following:

Lengthy detention without charge. Although the specific number of hours that an officer may hold a person will vary from location to location, the general rule in the United States is that a person cannot be held without being charged for more than a few hours. Ultimately, when a person is charged, he or she must be brought before a magistrate where bond is considered. Many foreign countries allow for this type of detention for days or even weeks. Some have no formal provisions for bond even when a person is charged. In many countries, people believed to have information (witnesses) can be held for long periods even though they are innocent and will never be charged.

Explanation of rights. In the United States, people have the right to remain silent and are not required to talk with law enforcement personnel. No one is required to incriminate himself. People who are arrested must be advised of their rights by law enforcement officers. These rights include the right to consult an attorney. Many foreign countries have no rules that require officers to inform subjects that they have any rights. In fact, in some countries, suspects have very few rights.

Torture. Although the days of medieval torture devices have largely passed into history, many countries still use some forms of torture to encourage people to cooperate. Modern torture is more likely to include beatings, electroshock, sleep deprivation, threats to harm the person and family members, and isolation. All can be effective, but do not ensure honesty of the part of the person. In order to end the torture, a person might confess to anything.

Warrantless Search. In the United States, a person's property is protected from intrusion by the government. Law enforcement officers cannot enter a person's home without permission, a court order, or an emergency—such as chasing a fleeing felon, a fire, or an explosion. Many countries do not have such protections, or have more liberal provisions for making such an entry.

Electronic Coverage. Federal and some state statutes permit limited electronic surveillance by law enforcement. The electronic surveillance can include wiretaps on telephones, fax machines, computers, tracking devices on vehicles, closed-circuit television, body recorders on informants and undercover investigators, and microphones. The laws in other countries vary. Many allow more liberal use of electronic surveillance than the United States.

Mail Entries. In some countries, investigators can open mail in order to develop information. In the United States, a federal court order is required, and the opening of mail is highly restricted. Most law enforcement officers will never be able to justify opening mail.

Membership in unpopular and even anti-government organizations. Some countries have lists of groups that are "banned"—and in which membership constitutes a crime. No such prohibition exists in the United States. However, claiming membership in a known terrorist group could justify a law enforcement agency investigating the person as a possible suspect in the group's criminal activities and violent attacks.

Summary

The result, no matter how praiseworthy, cannot be used in law enforcement to justify the use of unlawful or questionable means for obtaining that objective. Illegal, improper, and unethical behavior on the part of law enforcement personnel should not be tolerated. With the modern trend in court for defense attorneys to challenge law enforcement witnesses and their techniques, improper investigative activities are bound to eventually come to light. Not only will this result in acquittal of the defendant, it can lead to the offending officer being labeled incompetent and can result in civil actions against the officer and his or her department.

It must be remembered that illegal and improper law enforcement conduct is not subject to a statute of limitations with respect to the victim's ability to appeal a conviction or to seek civil recourse. A convicted person who learns that an investigator used an illegal technique to help send him to prison can seek a reversal of conviction on the basis of the officer's improper action, despite the fact that many years have passed since the officer's transgression occurred.

A law enforcement officer's integrity is one of his most important assets. An officer who compromises his integrity in either a work-related situation or in a personal matter, has severely damaged himself, possibly to the point that he may not be able to continue to function in his profession. To be effective, a law enforcement officer must be able to testify in court. A person who has been shown to be a liar, especially in the records of his own department, or who has committed a criminal violation, such as stealing money or assaulting his spouse, will be forever tainted to some extent. Compromised law enforcement officers should not be assigned to work on terrorism investigations because defense attorneys in such cases often attack the integrity of the investigators. If they discover a "tainted" investigator, they will capitalize upon it to the detriment of the case and the reputation of the department. An otherwise good case could be lost in court because of such an officer's involvement in it.

24 The Law Enforcement "Offsite" Location

For purposes of this text, an offsite location is defined as a covert location maintained by a law enforcement agency to provide support for its investigative mission. An offsite is not an investigative technique per se. Instead, it is a tool that assists investigators in their use of such investigative techniques as surveillance, informants, undercover operations, and trash covers. Offsites are intended to be covert in the sense that the subjects of the investigation are unaware that these places are in any way connected to a law enforcement agency. Ideally, no one outside law enforcement should be aware of the true identity and employment of the renter/user of the location. In some instances, a private citizen or landlord who is totally unrelated to any investigation will be aware that a law enforcement agency is using his or her property. In such situations, it is best that the citizen or landlord not be informed of the target or nature of the investigation.

Virtually any kind of structure can constitute an offsite. Included in this category are houses, apartments, condominiums, townhouses, mobile homes, offices, businesses, trailers, and warehouses. Some offsites serve a single operation within an individual investigation, whereas other offsites support several operations in a variety of cases. Offsites are proper and legal. At one time or another, most law enforcement agencies will use them.

Offsites are often used in long-running and complex investigations. Terrorism cases fall into this category. Security is the key to successful terrorism investigations. Terrorist groups are often able to conduct investigations on people and locations that they suspect are being targeted against them. Offsites can be used to ensure the integrity of many of the investigative techniques used by law enforcement agencies against terrorist subjects. Over the years, many successful terrorism investigations have used one or more offsites.

With respect to undercover operations, offsites should not be confused with a covert residence or business that an undercover officer uses as a cover. These locations are tools and props of the actual undercover operation, and do not really fall within the definition of an offsite.

Similarly, offsites are not safe houses. From a law enforcement perspective, a safe house would be a place where a protected witness might be hidden while waiting to testify. It might also be a place where an undercover officer could escape from his clandestine existence. With respect to terrorism investigations, the term "safe house" is more often applied to a location where terrorists feel safe. It might be an apartment where a terrorist group can conduct secure meetings. It might be the rear of a store where terrorists can make their contacts. It might be a location where people could hide following the commission of a terrorist or criminal attack. It might also be a location where a terrorist group hides a fugitive member.

How an Offsite Can Be Used

Surveillance

Offsites used in direct support of surveillance are often referred to as "lookouts," "eyeballs," or "perches." Frequently they are established in houses, apartments, or businesses within line of sight of a subject's residence, place of employment, or other known haunt. When the subject departs the area, the person manning the offsite calls out his direction, mode of transportation, and clothing description to surveillance officers who are staged several blocks from the location. Cameras and closed-circuit television are often operated from such an offsite. Investigators involved in terrorism investigations must be aware of counter-surveillance and other methods being used by the subject to detect law enforcement coverage of him. For this reason, terrorism surveillance often uses lookout offsites.

An offsite can be used to house the covert vehicles employed by an agency's surveillance investigators. Such vehicles should not be housed in a law enforcement agency's parking garage. Many agencies that maintain professional surveillance teams operate offsites where these investigators can stage, meet, store appropriate disguises and props, and prepare their written documentation. Investigators who regularly work on surveillance should not report to any known law enforcement location such as the police station.

Undercover Operations

Offsites are used as safe havens where an undercover officer can be briefed and debriefed by his handling investigators. An offsite can also serve as a place of "recreation and relaxation" for the undercover officer so that he can "recharge his batteries" and regain composure required for his duties. Offsites may also be used to protect the undercover agent. A surveillance team may observe the undercover officer from such a location. Agencies may also operate electronic coverage intended to support and protect the undercover officer from an offsite. The more intricate and dangerous the undercover operation, the greater the need for offsites to protect the undercover officer. Terrorism cases in which the officer is in direct contact with the subjects of the investigation are extremely dangerous and officers need maximum support.

Informant Operations

Although many sources can be successfully operated without the need for offsites, the quality and security of most informant contacts can be enhanced if an offsite is used. Security is the name of the game with respect to informants. These people are literally placing their lives on the line in order to assist law enforcement. If anyone within an informant's target area becomes aware of his cooperation with law enforcement, it could present serious and perhaps deadly consequences for him, his family, and his associates. Every time an investigator meets a source, there is a risk. The jeopardy increases if the meeting is in public such as in a restaurant, tavern, vehicle, city park, museum, or on public transportation. Meeting in a hotel room is usually safer, but still presents some risks, especially if an employee, guest, or other person notices an officer renting a room and then observes the informant using the elevator to go to the guest area of the facility. Also, because of cost considerations, agencies often use "contact hotels" that give them special rates. Unfortunately, this means that certain hotel employees will come to know when covert police operations are taking place. They may also come to know informants coming to the hotel.

Informants are extremely important in terrorism investigations. They are difficult to develop and maintain. Many terrorist groups make continual efforts to identity informants within their ranks. Every effort must be made to protect their identities and to give them a sense of security in order to ensure their continued cooperation. Offsites can do much to enhance terrorist informant operations.

Offsites should be considered for informant meetings in any situation in which the informant is particularly valuable, and the risk of someone observing a meeting is great. An offsite should definitely be considered in instances in which the officer wants to be present when the informant contacts a subject. These situations could include telephone calls (possibly consensually monitored or recorded), contacts via the Internet, and fax transmissions.

Trash Covers

When trash is obtained from a subject, it should not be brought directly to a law enforcement agency. An offsite, particularly a commercial site, like a warehouse or garage, can be an ideal location for an initial survey of recovered trash.

Covert Communications

Offsites can be used to receive mailings from target individuals and groups. Efforts should be made by law enforcement agencies to read documents distributed by subjects of their investigation. This is particularly true with respect to terrorist groups that are driven by their political beliefs. Although these groups try to promote their views and hope to win converts, many will not knowingly send direct mailings to police agencies. Even if they did, it could be an embarrassment to the agency if the public became aware that the agency was on the mailing list of a terrorist group. Consequently, such documents can be received at an offsite. An agency would not want to have literature from a group sent to the same offsite that is used to debrief an informant who reports on that group, or to an offsite that is used to surveil someone in that organization.

Offsites can also be used to place pretext telephone calls. Caller ID technology is making it very risky for police agencies to make pretext calls. It is too easy for the recipient to determine that a call came from a police facility. Additionally, if an officer places such a call from his personal residence, the recipient may learn the officer's home telephone number. As with receiving mail, an offsite used directly in connection with other investigative techniques used in a case, should not be used to place a pretext call to people involved in the investigation. Traditionally, officers assigned to a fixed surveillance offsite would place pretext telephone calls to the subject in an effort to ascertain whether he was in fact at home, at work, or at another location. This now must be avoided. A subject who receives a telephone call from a building across the street from his residence or employment is going to be very suspicious, especially if he has received previous calls from that number.

The Internet is a terrific information resource. Many terrorist groups have their own Web sites, which can be accessed by anyone. There is always a fear, however, that a highly skilled computer expert can identify individuals who visit a Web site. For a variety of reasons, a law enforcement agency may not want a group to know of their interest in them. An offsite is an ideal location to use for Internet research. An offsite can also protect a police officer who enters a chat room to have a discussion with members of a terrorist group. Law enforcement officers should use great care in engaging subjects of an investigation in conversations via the Internet. An agency intending to do this should consult their legal counsel before becoming involved in such conversations.

Issues to Consider When Developing an Offsite

Legal Issues. Any law enforcement agency planning to establish an offsite should present its proposal to its legal counsel, city attorney, or other competent authority to ensure that all statutes, policies, and procedures are followed. It must be remembered that written or verbal contracts are commonly involved in such transactions. It is usually illegal for anyone to sign a contract under a false name backed with fictitious documentation for a falsely stated purpose.

It may be easy for Detective John Jones, a high school graduate with no business expertise, to claim to be Charles Brown, a certified public accountant, when he rents an office for the stated purpose of operating as a tax consultant. However, it is probably a violation of the law for Detective Jones to sign a lease as "Charles Brown, CPA." Similarly, it may constitute a violation of the lease for Detective Jones to use the location to meet informants, rather than operating a consulting business.

Virtually all government agencies have provisions under which law enforcement agencies can conduct undercover operations. These must be understood and followed. Not only can problems occur for the agency and its officers if the procedures are not followed, but difficulties can also arise during subsequent court proceedings in the case. It would not be very advantageous during a trial for the defense to be able to show that the arresting officers themselves had committed criminal violations in connection with their investigation. Additionally, the department and its officers could find themselves civilly liable for damages.

Costs. Offsites will usually involve some expenses. On many occasions, they can be quite costly. Offsites are often obtained completely covertly, and are rented just like any other property would be rented—a lease, security deposit, first month's rent, last month's rent, and monthly rent. Occasionally, an offsite can be obtained from a cooperative citizen who does not want to know the nature of the law enforcement agency's intended use of his property. Examples of such situations include:

> A law enforcement officer encounters a citizen who states that he is a retired military officer, postal worker, or firefighter who loves his country. If asked, such a citizen might volunteer the use of his barn for police use and never want to know the specifics.

> A law enforcement agency may find a citizen who will allow the agency to use his garage, but wants rent of $100 per month, with no questions asked.

> A law enforcement agency uses a friendly "contact" within a real estate management company to locate and rent an offsite. No lease or deposit is required. In this case, the contact knows the true identity of the tenant, but other employees of his firm are not aware of the law enforcement agency's involvement in the property.

Regardless of how an offsite is obtained and established, it is important that the financial obligations associated with it be handled in a timely manner. The rent and utility bills should be paid when due in order to avoid bringing attention to the property. The payments should be made covertly, using suitable documentation. Although it may seem that paying in cash would prevent problems, it is often not a good idea. The idea is to make the property blend into the community. Very few people pay rent and utilities in cash except in very transient, poor neighborhoods. Virtually no business entity pays its bills in cash. In many situations, money orders will also appear suspicious because most individuals and businesses pay expenses with checks or credit cards.

Security. The key to an effective offsite is security. Nothing about the offsite should connect it with law enforcement. This means no people who are readily identifiable as police officers can be seen entering or leaving the location. It also means that no identifiable police vehicles should be associated with the address, and no marked police equipment can be maintained at the location.

Security concerns also mandate that the address not draw any attention to itself. The idea is for the offsite to blend into the community so well that it generally goes unnoticed. There should be nothing strange or unusual about it. If the façades of the houses in the neighborhood are generally shabby and dilapidated, then the front of the offsite must also have similar chipping paint and a dingy appearance. On the surface, making an offsite blend into the community may seem to be a relatively simple project. However, it must be remembered that an offsite is not what the other buildings in the neighborhood are. For this reason, a number of factors must be addressed in order to make it truly unobtrusive. For example, if it is to be used late at night, blackout curtains must be installed so that it will not stand out as the only illuminated house in the neighborhood. It may be necessary to allow for covert entry so that an unusually high number of people are not seen entering and leaving the location. However, if the site is in a high-traffic area, it will be necessary to have several people come to the location every day so that it will not stand out from the neighboring buildings.

An offsite must be secure from criminal activity. Losing police agency property to burglars is undesirable. Similarly, attacks on covert officers working in the offsite will cause problems. Homeless people, gangs, and drug users cannot be permitted to use the offsite for any reason.

Types of Offsites

Offsites fall into two broad categories: unoccupied and occupied locations.

Unoccupied Offsites. If the offsite is in a building that would not normally be occupied, such as a garage, shed, barn, abandoned structure, or warehouse, it will be necessary to devise methods by which investigators can enter and exit covertly without being seen or heard. Because any indication of activity in such a structure would call attention to it, efforts must be made to keep every movement inside the location from being observed from the outside. This might involve constructing barriers and walls inside the building so that lights, sounds, and movements cannot be seen by passersby. Law enforcement vehicles, both unmarked and marked, should be parked a safe distance from any address that would normally be unoccupied.

Occupied Offsites. If the offsite is in a structure that would normally be occupied, it is important that the type of activity that can be observed or heard from the outside be appropriate to that location. Neighbors would soon become curious if a constant parade of different people could be seen entering and leaving a small studio apartment. Similarly, a constant stream of older men entering an apartment supposedly occupied by a young woman might draw suspicion. A house in which no one mowed the lawn or put out the trash cans on pickup day would soon stand out as strange.

Within the occupied offsite category, there are a variety of uses.

Business Offsites. Offsites that are presented as businesses are difficult to establish and operate. Such offsites usually have to be manned by a front person on a fairly regular basis. They have to be structured in such a manner that neighboring businesses and passersby do not become suspicious. A butcher shop that has no meat in its counter, or a shoe repair shop that will not repair shoes for local residents will attract unwanted attention. Similarly, an insurance agent who is rarely open for business will stand out in the community. By contrast, local residents might not be suspicious about a business specializing in uniforms for a particular profession, school, or fraternal organization only having "strangers" not living in the area as customers. Additionally, regardless of the nature of the supposed business, the offsite must be prepared to deal with a local person who enters as either a customer, salesperson, job seeker, or other passersby. If such a person is handled improperly, the word can soon get around the neighborhood that something is amiss.

Office Offsites. Offsites that are established as offices are much easier to operate than are storefront businesses. The office scenario that is used should limit contact with area residents and neighboring offices, yet not be suspicious. A good ruse might involve a limited client specialty. Examples of this include accountant, business consultant, telephone solicitor, translator, or writer. Although the office would not be open to the public per se, the office must be able to withstand scrutiny by anyone who is able to view it. The office must look like it is conducting whatever business it is supposed to be conducting. The law enforcement agency establishing the office may not want anyone to enter, but the office must nonetheless be set up in such a manner that it will not draw suspicion from the landlord, a building maintenance employee, a city inspector, or a neighboring businessperson who drops by for a visit.

House Offsites. Private residences, including houses, apartments, mobile homes, and townhouses, are often used as offsites. Of these, the house, and to a slightly lesser degree, the townhouse, are probably the most difficult to operate successfully. Houses require outside maintenance, which can present a problem. Houses are also clearly visible to neighborhood residents. Anything out of place will attract attention. Local residents usually expect owners or tenants to actually reside in their homes. People expect to at least get to know their neighbors on a "Hi, how are you?" basis. People expect to see their neighbors do normal things, including washing their car, playing with their kids, sitting on the front porch, bringing groceries into the house, jogging or walking around the neighborhood, dragging trash cans to the curb on the appropriate pickup day, gardening, attending local parades and sports, social and church events, mowing the lawn, and shoveling the walk. Obviously, if a law enforcement agency truly hopes to make a home offsite blend into the neighborhood, it will almost certainly be to their advantage to have one or more investigators actually living in the house and doing the "normal" homeowner activities.

Apartment Offsites. Apartments are easier to operate as offsites than are houses. They require virtually no outside maintenance, and frequently there is not the same kind of "neighborliness" that exists with houses. Apartment dwellers often do not even know their close neighbors. This is especially true in large complexes. Because windows almost never face hallways, residents rarely see their neighbors and therefore do not know much about their comings and goings. In areas where large apartment complexes are common, law enforcement agencies would probably be best served by procuring offsites in such buildings.

Entry into the apartment building should be considered before an apartment is rented. The best kind of situation is one in which there are multiple entries and exits. If a building has only a main entry that is guarded by an attendant, security may quickly be compromised. The attendant will come to know everyone visiting the offsite. Furthermore, visitors could be required to stand at the front door while the attendant calls the apartment in order to receive permission, or they could be required to sign a register.

"Illegal" Offsites. In some instances, law enforcement agencies create offsites that are intended to appear to be illegal operations. These are risky situations, but they may be the best that can be established in some high-crime areas. A warehouse may be made to appear like a chop shop. An apartment may be made to look like a brothel. A business may be made to appear to be a front for a gambling or fencing operation. Such offsites are fraught with danger. Local criminals may want to get involved in the operation or a gang or local mob boss may demand protection money. Neighbors could demand that authorities investigate the location. The site could be raided by local police.

An illegal offsite is very different from a sting-type undercover project, in which a law enforcement agency creates an "illegal" activity, like a fencing operation, to snare thieves. It is also dissimilar from an "illegal" employment established as a prop to give an undercover officer credibility.

Operating an Offsite

Having decided on the kind of offsite that is to be established, the law enforcement agency must then decide how it is to be operated. This is not much of an issue if the offsite is to appear to be unoccupied. In that situation, there is no need to display a front-man tenant for neighbors to see. However, it is best that someone be assigned to handle security, supplies, and repairs for the unoccupied offsite.

Occupied offsites must have a "front man," or several front men. If the offsite is a business or office, someone must appear as the proprietor. In the case of a residence, at least one person must appear to be the owner or tenant, and appear to live there at least part of the time. Whoever is assigned to be the owner or resident must have appropriate false documentation to assume the role. He or she must be able to play the role in a convincing manner, and must be familiar with the scenario that has been developed for the offsite. It must be understood that the front man is functioning in semi-deep to very deep cover, even though he probably has no direct contact with the target of any investigation. No law enforcement agency should force one of its officers to work in a lengthy semi-deep or deep undercover role unless the officer is willing to assume such an assignment. Many people have great difficulty trying to live a lie—which is in essence what undercover work involves. It is almost impossible for some officers to pull off an undercover assignment. They blush, tremble, and exhibit other nervous habits whenever they try to pretend to be something they are not. The front person should not be someone who will likely be recognized as being a cop.

Selecting an undercover officer to be the "front man" in an offsite may present serious problems for an agency. Insofar as an offsite operation does not involve direct contact with suspects, it is usually fairly safe, and often does not ultimately involve court testimony. It can be rather attractive to some officers. This is especially true if fringe benefits are involved, such as free rent, a luxurious building, pool, gym, and car. A department may find itself with several applicants. A department may find itself being pressured to accept a less-than-ideal candidate by nepotism, union policies, seniority procedures, or even equal opportunity regulations. Of course, if the offsite has negative aspects, such as being in a bad neighborhood or requiring poor work hours, a department may not have any applicants for the assignment.

Just as the offsite must blend into the neighborhood and go unnoticed, the officers assigned to the project must also blend into the community. It makes little sense to assign a black officer to live in a house in an all-white neighborhood. Conversely, a white officer would stand out living in an apartment building otherwise totally occupied by blacks. A 55-year-old police sergeant will certainly be out of place living in a townhouse complex mainly occupied by young singles. A department that finds itself forced to accept an offsite front man who simply cannot do the job because he does not blend into the community is probably best served by abandoning the offsite project.

While it is not required, it is probably best that a full-time front man be employed in connection with an occupied offsite. If the offsite is a business, it would be ideal for the front man to report each day at a certain time, and to remain until a certain time each afternoon or evening. Hours of an office offsite can be more varied, but should still have some regularity. Ideally, the front man would actually live in an offsite residence, which would mean that he would sleep, eat, and relax there. He should also leave the residence for eight-hour blocks during the day or night in order to "work," unless the scenario for the offsite calls for him to work at home, be on disability, or be unemployed. Actual, live-in/work-in front men make business, office, and residential offsites more believable. They also make such locations more secure. Live-in personnel enable the mission of the offsite to be handled in a much more efficient manner.

In one instance, a major fire erupted in an apartment building where an offsite was maintained. The "front man" officer actually lived there, and was able to conceal camera and recording equipment before being forced by firefighters to abandon the apartment. Although the offsite was one of the few apartments that was not destroyed, it was entered by firefighters who would have uncovered the true nature of the off-site had it not been an actual residence. Furthermore, because he was known to live in the building, the front man was able to return after the fire was extinguished to "recover belongings." It was at this time that he was able to sneak to the roof with a "friend" (an agency technical expert), and remove the antenna that the agency had installed on the roof before fire investigators could discover it.

The offsite should have furnishings that match its function. One would certainly expect to see a bed or furniture that could be used for sleeping in a residential apartment. An office should have a desk, chair, and perhaps some filing cabinets. Depending on the nature of the scenario, a computer would probably also be expected in an office. A store should contain merchandise of the kind that the business purports to sell. Occupied offsites should be created with the idea that some outsiders, including landlords, neighbors, and repair personnel, will come in on occasion. It should be remembered that the offsite must blend into the community. The offsite should appear to be what it claims to be.

With respect to offsites, investigators cannot do much to prove that the location is what it claims to be without calling unwanted attention to the site. An investigator cannot stop his neighbors in the lobby of an apartment building and try to convince them that he actually lives in the apartment. If he does, the neighbors will suspect that something is not right with the apartment and its tenant. Similarly, the proprietor of an offsite that purports to be a store cannot place large posters in his window urging passersby to believe that his business is really a store. The offsite must stand on its own appearance and scenario. The props must fit the premise of the business. People must accept the location for what it claims to be without hesitation.

The big props, like furniture or display cases, are very important in making the offsite look authentic. Equally important are clothes in the closets and in dresser drawers of residences, and papers, ledgers, forms, pens, computers, desks, tables, and filing cabinets in offices. Food in kitchen cabinets of residences and a coffee pot in an office are important touches.

All occupied offsites should receive mail on a regular basis. In the beginning, investigators can send themselves mail to fill up the box. Later, magazine subscriptions will do the job. Shortly after the periodicals begin to arrive, so will the unsolicited advertisements that make everything look normal. Bills for rent, utilities, and the telephone will round out the mail situation.

Making an Offsite Believable

Often it is the small touches that remove all doubts that may exist about the legitimacy of an offsite. The following are small touches that should be considered in order to make an offsite appear legitimate:

Residence—House/Apartment

- A slightly worn throw rug inside the entrance—possibly a muddy/salty/dirty pair of boots near the door

- Coats, hats, umbrellas hanging in the entrance closet

- A dirty dish in the kitchen sink and several washed dishes in a drain board alongside the sink

- Opened and resealed containers in the refrigerator, and some empty containers stacked on top of the refrigerator

- Empty food containers in a kitchen trash can, and crumpled tissues and a soap wrapper in the bathroom trash can

- A grocery cart hanging inside the kitchen closet, pans or a kettle on the stove, a broom, mop, and dust pan in the corner

- A filled spice rack hanging on the kitchen wall

- Kitchen magnets on the refrigerator door possibly securing the shopping list or the photograph of a child

- A toaster, mixer, blender, and other small appliances on the kitchen counter plugged into wall sockets

- A kitchen clock with the correct time hanging on the kitchen wall

- Salt/pepper mills, napkins, placemats on the kitchen or dining room table

- A crumpled newspaper on the living room coffee table along with several folded back magazines

- A half-empty glass or can of soda on a coffee table

- A TV Guide folded open to the current week, lying on the television

- A CD in the stereo and several others near the stereo

- Opened mail lying on a desk or coffee table and crumpled remnants of mail in a waste container in the living room

- Loose change lying on the bedroom dresser and maybe a half-full can of pennies on the nightstand

- A laundry tag on the floor near the closet

- A ticking windup clock with the correct time anywhere in the bedroom

- A book with a bookmark lying near the bed

- An eyeglass holder or maybe a pair of reading glasses lying on the nightstand

- Linens and pillows on the bed

- Shoes under the bed and in the bedroom closet

- A partially filled laundry basket in the bedroom or bathroom

- A radio, electric toothbrush, hair dryer, and maybe a small electric heater in the bathroom

- A half-used tube of toothpaste lying near the sink and a medicine cabinet filled with miscellaneous partially used bottles and other containers

- A shower curtain, towels, soap, shampoo, and washcloth in the tub/shower area

- Suitcases in a closet

- Wall decorations throughout the residence and what appear to be family pictures in frames placed around the unit. An unframed snapshot of a person, maybe an older woman or a child, stuck in the frame of a mirror or taped somewhere

- A small aquarium containing a few fish anywhere in the residence

- Plants anywhere in the residence

The clock, aquarium, and plants all "prove" to people that someone at least frequents, if not actually "lives," in the residence. In fact, a good windup clock does not have to be wound every day, fish can go for several days without attention, and plants like aloe vera and cactus need water only about once a week.

Certainly the best way to create the "lived in" look is to actually have one or several people live there on at least a part-time basis. If they do, the aforementioned items that "prove" residency will naturally occur.

Business and Office

- A bell that rings when the door opens
- Local advertisements in the store window promoting club meetings, youth baseball, a charity run, etc.
- An electric fan
- Mail on the store counter or office desk
- In an office, a sweater, umbrella, coat hanging behind the door
- A calendar marked with various notations like telephone numbers, messages, and scheduled meetings
- In an office, a bottle of aspirin, a box of stomach pills, and maybe a container of cough drops on a window sill or in a bathroom
- Scraps of paper, general discards, and some fast-food containers in a trash container
- In an office, a paper shredder with shredded paper in a container next to it
- In an office, several well-used telephone books complete with handwritten numbers on the covers and a Rolodex®
- In an office, CDs or DVDs in a container or lying on or near a desk or computer
- In a business, calendars from appropriate vendors, either hung on a wall or lying somewhere
- In an office, a bookshelf containing books related to the nature of the operation
- Magazines appropriate to the office or business
- In a business, a dog or cat that could in theory provide protection from intruders and vermin. In an office, a small aquarium to give a homey appearance
- Framed pictures of family members, especially in an office
- In a business setting, a bulletin board filled with notes

Procuring Offsite Furnishings

Some offsite furnishings will be purchased new. Other furnishings can be purchased from used furniture and clothing outlets. Still other items can be bought at flea markets and from yard/garage sales. Members of the department can be asked to donate or lend furnishings. Just about everyone has at least one household item that they no longer need or use. New and used furnishings can be rented. In some instances, rented furnishings can be purchased at the end of a contract. Most police departments have some furnishings that they have seized or have recovered as abandoned property. Some of these items can be used if care is taken to remove identification numbers that can be traced to law enforcement. Some actual police department furnishings can also be used in office or business settings if their identification numbers are removed.

In most instances, regardless of the size of the budget involved in the project, some used furnishings should be used in offsites because few normal persons or companies have all new items. People would become suspicious of a residence in which everything from major furnishings to knick-knacks was brand-new.

Summary

Offsite locations are valuable to investigators in a variety of ways. They can support surveillance and undercover operations. The can be used as informant debriefing locations. They can also be employed by law enforcement agencies to receive covert communications, monitor the Internet, or make pretext telephone calls. If an offsite is to be of value, it must be operated covertly and maintained in such a way that it does not create suspicion.

SECTION IV

Applying Investigative
Techniques to
Terrorism Investigations

25 When a Clandestine Terrorist Is Identified

The ideal situation is for the police agency to prevent the terrorist attack from happening and to successfully prosecute those responsible for the conspiracy to commit the act. Unfortunately, many terrorist investigations begin in response to a violent terrorist attack.

Occasionally, a law enforcement agency will learn about a terrorist conspiracy before the violent attack occurs. This presents an opportunity for that agency to not only prevent the act, but to also seriously impair the ability of that terrorist group to function. Such intelligence should be handled with care.

Intelligence about a terrorist group is difficult to develop, but it does periodically come to light, especially if a law enforcement agency has investigators who specialize in the field. The following are some of the sources that might provide a law enforcement agency with information with respect to terrorist groups:

- Informants

- Disgruntled or fearful group members

- Suspicious people, including a landlord, educator, employer, friend, business associate, or relative

- Investigators working on other cases within the agency or in other agencies

- Anonymous individuals who provide unsolicited tips

- Foreign intelligence services

- News media

- A past or potential victim

The information that is provided by the sources listed above is often not specific in nature. Sometimes the reporting person will not even know the true significance of his information. For example, a news reporter may call an investigator asking questions about a hate crime. The investigator may decide

377

to explore the situation to determine whether it could have been committed by a terrorist organization. A game warden may tell a local sheriff that he encountered some people "playing soldier" in a remote part of his county. The sheriff may assign a deputy to look into the matter. Unfortunately, the people who discover such activities do not always take appropriate action.

In one situation, a citizen reported to a law enforcement agency that a man of a particular nationality was attempting to purchase a heavy military missile for some unknown reason. The agency representative discounted the information because he did not believe that people of that nationality would be involved in criminal activity within the geographic area of his agency's responsibility. The representative suggested that the citizen take the information to another agency, which he did. That agency began a successful investigation that resulted in several arrests. Unbeknownst to the representative, his own department did have a pending case related to the situation at the time the citizen visited the office.

In some instances, the information received from sources will be direct and specific. Its quality will be such that it compels that action be taken.

One terrorist case was initiated when a narcotics wiretap picked up information that certain members of a drug conspiracy were being recruited by a hostile foreign power to perpetrate terrorist attacks in the United States.

Another terrorist investigation began based on information from an informant that a man was seeking mercenaries to participate in some kind of military action in a foreign country.

An informant caused another case to be opened when he reported hearing a conversation between two known terrorists in which they indicated that another person in the community, who appeared to be apolitical, was in fact "underground."

Still another terrorism investigation began when a foreign intelligence service reported that it had traced weapons to an address in the United States.

In many situations, it is the line-level manager within an agency who makes the ultimate decision that causes a proactive terrorism case to be initiated. The line manager usually holds a rank or title like squad supervisor, group leader, or sergeant. He or she is a leader responsible for a team of street investigators. The line manager reviews incoming information. If he or she misses something, that information is likely to end up in a closed miscellaneous file. If the manager opens a case but gives improper directions to the investigator, the information may become useless. For example, in the scenario above in which the person was "underground," it would be unwise for a manager to direct an investigator to interview that individual in order to determine whether he was really a terrorist. The line manager is also the person who can authorize a street officer to conduct an investigation based on information that the officer has developed.

A Possible Terrorist Scenario

For simplicity's sake, it will be assumed that a local law enforcement agency has received information from an employer that strongly indicates that a employee, whom we will call Joe Bomber, is a member of a clandestine terrorist group that has claimed credit for a series of bombings. The employer is a person of good standing in the community and has no reason to lie. The employer reported that he observed his employee, Joe Bomber, experiencing difficulty operating the company photocopier. A technician who was called to repair the equipment discovered that a sheet of paper had become jammed inside the photocopier. The employer gave the crumpled paper to the police agency. It appears to be a rough draft copy of an official "communiqué" from the terrorist group, in which the group is making demands of the government. The letter is printed on paper with the official logo of the terrorist group. This is of significance, because neither police agencies nor media sources have ever displayed this logo, nor even mentioned its existence. The fact that Joe Bomber has such a document strongly suggests that he is a member of, or has a close intimate affiliation with, the terrorist group.

The information about Joe Bomber should be treated as vitally important, because no member of this covert terrorist group has ever before been identified. There is nothing about Joe Bomber that would suggest that he is a terrorist. He is married and has children. He is steadily employed and rents a modest residence in a nice neighborhood. He is not overtly politically active, and he seems to be an average person.

Possible Investigative Approaches

Based on this information, it would certainly appear that Joe Bomber is connected to the terrorist group in some way. He may be their primary bomb maker, or he could be a lesser rank-and-file member. He may be a member of a small "cell," or he may function in some kind of advisory role, perhaps as the group's philosopher or writer. Regardless of his position, Joe Bomber appears to have direct contact with other group members, none of whom are known to law enforcement.

Direct Approach. The law enforcement agency could directly confront Joe Bomber and even show him the communiqué. It is possible that Joe

Bomber might admit his guilt and offer information about his group in order to gain favor with the authorities. If Joe Bomber were a street thug or a burglar, the direct approach might produce both an admission and an agreement to function as an informant. A good interrogator could probably turn the crumpled communiqué into something much broader in scope, and convince Joe Bomber that the police were aware of his activities.

Unfortunately, law enforcement agencies should not anticipate this response from a member of a terrorist group. He may refuse to participate in an interview. He may demand to contact his attorney. Because he has probably been instructed about police interview tactics, Joe Bomber is unlikely to allow himself to be bluffed. The interrogator will have to produce more than one communiqué in order to induce Joe Bomber to cooperate. The interview is likely to end with Joe Bomber demanding that he either be charged or permitted to leave the interview. If directly approached, Joe Bomber's life as a terrorist in the city has probably drawn to a close for a long time, if not forever. In that sense, the law enforcement agency has been successful, because it has neutralized him. However, if Joe Bomber declines to cooperate, the law enforcement agency has burned its only inroad into the terrorist group. Essentially, they have returned to square one with respect to the other members of the terrorist group.

Take No Action. A police agency that cannot commit the time and manpower to conduct a meaningful investigation but recognizes the value of the information about Joe Bomber can store that information for future use. Of course, taking no action only refers to the use of labor-intensive investigative activities. The agency certainly could conduct background checks on Joe Bomber and procure records from such areas as utilities, credit cards, banks, and Joe's home and work telephones, without jeopardizing the confidentiality of the investigation.

Give the Information to Another Agency. If a local agency believes that it cannot conduct an appropriate investigation based on the information about Joe Bomber, it can turn over the information to the FBI, which has the primary federal responsibility for handling terrorism matters. In a situation of this nature, the FBI usually would attempt to work with the local agency rather than handle the matter independently. Oftentimes, a state or county law enforcement agency might be available to take over a case from a local department. They, too, would probably include the local agency in the overall investigation. Given the fact that joint terrorism task forces are now in operation throughout the United States, every local agency has a place where a terrorist case can be referred. Given the emphasis now being given to cooperation among law enforcement agencies, it is likely that the local department will not find itself cut out of such a case.

Initiate a Full-Scale, Discreet Investigation. If a thorough investigation was conducted on Joe Bomber on an around-the-clock basis, it would probably identify other members of the terrorist group. It is also possible that such surveillance could lead to the discovery of safe houses, covert vehicles, secret mailing addresses, false identities, and weapons caches. Through the use of more sensitive investigative techniques, it might be possible to learn about the group's current activities and their future plans.

Unfortunately, around-the-clock coverage is very labor-intensive. Many agencies cannot do it for extended periods. Furthermore, such coverage will probably be detected by the subject if it continues for long periods. The main issues that the agency must address are Joe Bomber's degree of dedication to his cause and the extent to which he will protect his group.

If Joe Bomber is a truly dedicated terrorist, his political cause is the most important aspect of his life. He regards himself as being an important cog in his movement. However, he regards his cause as being even more important than he is. He will not do things that will compromise the group. Joe Bomber is clandestine, as are his cohorts in the group. As long as he is able to function at that level, he is an asset to the cause. If, however, Joe Bomber comes to believe that the police have learned of his role within the terrorist group, he will realize that he could compromise his beloved movement. He will quit his own group before he will endanger it. He will abandon his role within the organization before he will lead law enforcement officers to his group's members and safe locations. In short, if the law enforcement agency is careless and Joe Bomber learns that he is being investigated, he will ensure that they will never develop anything of value by monitoring his activities. Joe Bomber may even quit his job and move to another city. The law enforcement agency will not only lose its initial intelligence on Joe Bomber, but it will lose whatever else it learned throughout the course of the investigation.

If a decision is reached to begin an active investigation of Joe Bomber with the intention of not allowing him to discover that he is under investigation, there are certain steps that should be taken:

Establishing Case Objectives. Building a case against Joe Bomber is certainly an objective, but it should not be the primary goal of the investigation. The main objectives should be aimed against the terrorist group as a whole, the bombings that it has already done, and the bombings that it is currently planning. These objectives should include identifying all clandestine members of the group and the locations of the group's weapons, explosives, safe houses, and assets. Another objective should involve developing a conspiracy indictment against various group members.

Procuring Cooperation From Other Agencies Conducting Terrorist Investigations in the Area. As difficult as it is to give up a case to another department, it sometimes has to be done. If there is the possibility that another agency working on terrorism cases in the area will stumble upon Joe Bomber, a contact will probably have to be made. Clearly, if any law enforcement agency makes a direct approach to Joe Bomber for any reason related to terrorism, Joe Bomber is going to assume that he has been compromised. Therefore, it is imperative that everyone keep away from Joe Bomber.

Since the attacks of September 11, 2001, joint terrorism task forces have been established in conjunction with every FBI field division. Consequently, there are agencies working on terrorism in almost every area that already know what the other agencies are doing. As a result, there will be no need to worry about an agency compromising the Joe Bomber case. In rural areas that might be quite a distance from a terrorist task force, the information developed on Joe Bomber could easily be used as a foundation for the creation of a sub-unit of the closest task force. The Chicago Joint Terrorism Task Force, which is one of the original such entities in the United States, was established based on information similar to the Joe Bomber example. One of the three agencies conducting terrorism investigations in the Chicago area developed information concerning a clandestine member of the terrorist FALN organization. Realizing that it had a manpower deficiency, and knowing that if either of the other two agencies accidentally made contact with the clandestine individual, he would cease his activity in the FALN, the initiating agency chose to bring the other two agencies into the case as equal partners. The result was a highly successful investigation that resulted in arrests of the entire FALN cell, and the prevention of a major terrorist bombing that was being planned by the group.

Gathering Sufficient Manpower. Manpower is a key element in building a case against a terrorist organization. One person is not going to be able to accomplish much, although he or she can perform some valuable activities while the other personnel are being assembled. Building a case against a target like Joe Bomber will require a division of responsibilities. Although one investigator should be designated as the "case officer," it is unreasonable (and unworkable) in a sensitive and potentially massive investigation to expect one person to coordinate surveillances, run an undercover operation, work with the prosecutor on court orders, prepare written reports, handle agency checks, perform trash covers, and operate informants. The work should be divided, and the coordinators of each aspect of the case should work closely with each other and the case officer in order to accomplish the objectives that have been established for the case.

Staffing should include all of the agencies involved in the investigation. Any agency that participates in the case should provide some manpower and equipment. While it is prudent to allow agencies to practice their specialties, it is also a good idea to integrate investigators from the various agencies into general investigative projects. For example, there is no reason investigators from several agencies cannot work together on Joe Bomber's trash cover.

Bringing a Prosecutor on Board. If the investigation is to succeed, it will be necessary to bring a prosecutor (or prosecutors representing several levels of government) on board at an early stage of the investigation. Many investigators refrain from doing this during the course of routine investigations. They prefer not to notify the prosecutor's office of the existence of a case until they have developed sufficient information. Many prosecutors do not want to be briefed on a case until the investigator has conducted enough investigation to indicate that it is viable.

With respect to investigating a clandestine terrorist like Joe Bomber, it will be necessary to use investigative techniques that require court orders during the early stages of the investigation. Consequently, a prosecutor must be brought on board. It might be desirable for the management representatives of the law enforcement agencies to meet with their counterparts in the prosecutor's office at the outset of the investigation so that everyone agrees with the importance and significance of the investigation. In that way it can be assured that a prosecutor will be available when needed, and that he or she will become a part of the team working on the case.

The prosecutor may want to bring the Joe Bomber investigation to the attention of a standing grand jury, preferably one that will sit for a number of months. In this way he can procure grand jury subpoenas for records as required.

Conducting the Least Intrusive Investigative Techniques. Due to the sensitivity of a clandestine terrorism case like that on Joe Bomber, it is imperative that every effort be made to keep the subject from learning about the law enforcement interest in him. An excellent way to do this is to initially use noninvasive investigative techniques in an effort to build a wealth of intelligence on the target. These techniques should include:

Law Enforcement and Public Agency Records Checks. Everything about the subject that can be checked should be done at the beginning of the case. Law enforcement agency records should be reviewed to determine whether the subject has ever been arrested. They should also be checked to determine whether he has ever been a crime victim, witness, complainant, traffic offender, or employed by a business that conducts police checks on their workers. Birth and marriage records should be reviewed, because they can provide information on relatives. Vehicle and driver's license checks should also be performed. Hunting, fishing, firearms, voting, property ownership, and tax records should be reviewed. All of these records can disclose some valuable information, yet there is virtually no chance of the subject ever learning about these checks.

Credit Records. The value of a credit check on the subject is that it can identify previous employment, former addresses, banks, loans, and credit cards. A number of leads can subsequently be set from this kind of information. Unfortunately, many credit bureaus insist upon documenting every record review of the person's credit history. If this is the case and the credit bureau refuses to waive the rule, a credit check should not be conducted. Many terrorists are instructed to periodically check their credit record in an effort to learn whether any law enforcement agency has been looking into their affairs. If Joe Bomber finds an indication of a police review of his credit record, he will assume that his clandestine status has been compromised.

Financial, Utility, Telephone, and Credit Card Agency Checks. These kinds of records checks can yield outstanding intelligence on a subject. This is especially true with respect to banking and telephone records. Reviewing information provided by these entities will often require a great deal of time and patience, but the results are usually worth the effort. It is a good idea to use a computer to correlate and store the results of this research. Court orders are often required to procure these kinds of records.

Internet Checks. The Internet is a newly arrived investigative technique that has yet to be fully exploited by the law enforcement community. It can be of great value in terrorist investigations. It would be wise for an investigator to run the name of a terrorist subject and his group through a search engine like Google or Yahoo just to see if there is any information about him or the organization. Clearly, information on the Internet cannot be taken as positive proof of anything, and it should not be used in search warrants or even as evidence in court. Before placing it into an official file, an investigator should check with his department's legal counsel to determine whether material of that kind can be maintained. Nonetheless, Internet information can provide excellent lead material. This is especially true if the Web site can be traced to its source where interviews can be conducted to verify the authenticity of the information. Many an investigator has been surprised when, on asking an informant how he knows that information that he is providing is true, the source has responded "everyone knows that" or "it's common knowledge on the street." On checking further, the investigator does indeed find that a large number of people are aware of something that he, the investigator, never knew. Of course, it may turn out that what "everyone knows" is not entirely correct. The investigator may want to view Internet search results in that same manner. An inquiry may reveal various Web sites providing certain information about his subject that is totally new to the investigator, yet appears to be known by numerous other people. If for no other reason than developing fuel for an interview with the subject, the Internet should be searched. When contacting the subject, the investigator could suggest that he became aware of the subject's activities because a citizen had reported that certain Web sites had described him as a member of a particular terrorist group or as being involved in a break-in at a mink farm or some other crime.

Mail Covers. A mail cover is not likely to locate a "smoking gun," especially in a situation like the Joe Bomber case, but it can yield information about banking, credit cards, and other agencies with whom the subject may have a relationship. Subsequent checks with these business contacts can yield valuable information. If, during the course of the investigation, it is discovered that Joe Bomber has a covert mailbox or secret address, a mail cover on that location may yield much better intelligence, even though the technique does not permit entry into personal or business correspondence. Care must be taken with respect to checking on people who communicate with the suspect. A careless contact can make the subject suspicious. For example, making inquiries at the local Jones Plumbing Company about the suspect could get back to him. Just because that firm sent a letter to the suspect does not mean that it requires investigation.

Contacting Informants. At this stage in the investigation of Joe Bomber, talking to informants can be risky and must be done with care. There is always the danger that an informant might make inquiries about the subject that may get back to him or her. For this reason, it is best during the early stages of a case to restrict informant contacts to only reliable sources who afford coverage to the terrorist group in question, or who are logically in a position to know something about the subject. Even with these limitations, contacts with these sources should be of a general nature. Questions like these could be asked: "We got a tip that there is a communiqué from the XYZ terrorist group floating around town. Have you seen it?" "The New York Police Department has information that there is a clandestine member of the XYZ group living in our town. What do you think about this?" or "You work at the Smith Company, we have some information that some employee down there has a false identification. Do you have any idea who that may be?" Hopefully, through vague questions like these, an informant who has information about the XYZ group, or about suspicious people at the Smith Company, will volunteer it. Obviously, if the source mentions Joe Bomber by name, the handling officer can pursue that information without revealing previous knowledge about Joe Bomber.

Once the non-intrusive techniques have been used and their results studied and correlated, the various coordinators and agency representatives should meet to discuss the steps that should be taken next. Prior to such a gathering, it would be a good idea for someone to prepare a report in which everything of value developed about the subject is assembled. In that way, everyone present will be aware of what has been learned. During this meeting, decisions about the deployment of more intrusive investigative techniques must be reached.

Deploying More Intrusive Investigative Techniques. Surveillance is likely to be the next step. In order to be successful, it must be conducted with a philosophy of not getting "made." If the subject learns that he is under surveillance, the case is compromised. Probably the best tactic to employ at the beginning is a fixed-picket or combination surveillance. An investigator in a stationary location can monitor the subject at his residence and employment in order to establish his patterns of arrival and departure. If an offsite surveillance location can be procured, this should be used to provide the coverage. If it cannot be done securely, a vehicle parked in a stationary location can be used. A closed-circuit television camera could also be used. Once a pattern has been established, it should be possible to begin additional surveillance coverage from several blocks from the where the subject makes his departure. It would probably be wise to employ a fixed-picket coverage for several blocks during the early surveillance in an effort to learn whether the subject is practicing dry cleaning tactics—including making U-turns, stopping in the street, making unsignaled turns, increasing and reducing speed, and driving in alleys—and whether he has any contacts nearby. Later surveillances could be of the moving variety, initiated from points several blocks from the subject's point of departure. To avoid detection, sufficient manpower and proper vehicles should be used during any surveillance of the subject.

Documentation of surveillance results will be extremely important. The subject is clandestine. He should know how to function in a secure manner. He may be so skilled that he will be able to do clandestine things directly in front of average people without being noticed. Attention must be paid to everything that he does. Anytime the subject does anything that suggests "dry cleaning" or the use of security procedures, these should be carefully documented. They can be extremely valuable in justifying future court orders. Surveilling the subject on an around-the-clock basis will determine his routine, but it will be difficult to accomplish without being detected. A capsule surveillance should be used over a period of weeks or even months, in which each part of the subject's day is given coverage, but not all on the same day. Hopefully, this will reveal certain times where it can be established that the subject is doing something clandestine or at least has the ability to do covert activities during that period. Once these windows have been developed, intensive surveillance coverage can be given to the subject during these periods. Fixed-picket surveillances, which are labor-intensive, may now be practical because they will only be employed for limited periods each day.

Trash covers are another more intrusive technique that may yield excellent results because even terrorists can be careless with their discards. Extreme security should be practiced when using this technique. It is probably best to pick up the trash from the actual waste disposal service truck rather than risk using a car. During surveillance, discarded items should be recovered—but carefully in case the subject is using such items to determine whether he is being followed.

Developing informants may be considered at this point, but great care should be used to avoid allowing any potential informant to know the exact target. A neighbor of the subject who has been carefully selected from a background check may be contacted under the guise of a narcotics investigation involving an area street gang. Over time, the neighbor could be asked to report any suspicious activity in the area. If the neighbor should mention something about the subject, the handling officer should express interest and suggest that the source try to develop additional information. This should be done in such a manner that the neighbor does not become aware of the investigator's previous interest in the subject.

Intrusive Investigative Techniques

As more information is developed about the subject, consideration can be given to using much more intrusive investigative techniques, which actually involve some degree of risk. One of these is the undercover technique. It is probably unrealistic to believe that an undercover officer will actually be able to penetrate a clandestine terrorist group. If such a feat is feasible, it will probably require a lengthy period. However, such a person might be able to get close enough to Joe Bomber or another covert member of the group to develop some valuable information. Intelligence developed during the course of the investigation will have to be used in developing a scenario for such an endeavor. Surveillance may have revealed that Joe Bomber regularly works out at the Sunset Gym. Perhaps the undercover agent could join this facility and develop a relationship with him. The investigation may have revealed that the subject and his cell members conduct clandestine meetings at Tom's Bar. Maybe the undercover officer could get a job there as a bartender and work himself into a position where he could overhear conversations or possibly even develop a friendship with members of the cell. If it has been determined through an informant that Joe Bomber is seeking an explosives supplier, maybe the undercover officer could enter the picture as a member of the military who supplements his income by selling stolen explosives.

Informants can be directed against the target in much the same way as an undercover officer would be directed. Obviously, great care must be used with informants because they do not have the reliability or trustworthiness that an undercover operative has.

Using Invasive and Sensitive Investigative Techniques

As the amount of intelligence builds, it may be possible to use very invasive and sophisticated investigative techniques. Even though these techniques are intrusive, most are actually quite secure. They include wiretaps, fax and e-mail coverage, cameras, video recorders, and microphones. All of these techniques require court orders based on well-documented information. The evidence presented in court need not be absolute in the sense that someone must have actually seen or heard the subject do things, but it must be compelling enough to strongly indicate that the subject is involved in violent illegal activities.

A great deal of intelligence showing clandestine and illegal activity will have to have been gathered before sensitive technical coverage will be authorized. However, in order to prove a terrorist conspiracy, it will probably be necessary to employ technical coverage. Similarly, in order to effectively prevent the group from committing a terrorist attack, technical coverage will most likely be required.

Procuring technical coverage will vary among agencies. Some local, county, and state agencies may not be able to procure authority to effectively use technical coverage. A federal agency like the FBI, which is involved in every joint terrorism task force, has the power to employ all forms of technical coverage, provided that there is sufficient cause to justify its use. A usual prerequisite for the FBI to procure technical coverage is a showing that less intrusive investigative techniques have been attempted or used without success. However, in case of an immediate violent threat—like a group gathering explosives to perpetrate an attack in the near future—it will be possible for the FBI to secure technical coverage without having to show that lesser techniques have failed.

There is a logical progression with respect to the various levels of investigation. The more intrusive and invasive steps should not be employed until the less intrusive techniques have been used. In fact, in some cases, the more intrusive and sensitive techniques require the results of less technical methods in order to be authorized. The fact that very intrusive techniques are being used does not mean that simpler and more basic techniques cannot also be used. For example, agency checks should be conducted throughout the investigation. Surveillance certainly should continue if an undercover project is initiated. Trash covers should be used, if productive, during the entire duration of the case.

Ideal Results. If all goes well, the various investigative techniques will yield results. They should show that although Joe Bomber lives what appears to be a relatively normal existence, he also engages in clandestine activities during certain periods of his life.

The case of the FALN member who caused the Chicago Terrorism Task Force to be established was very similar to the theoretical life of Joe Bomber. For most of every week, this man lived a very normal life. However, the investigation disclosed that on one night each week after work, he would do things that were unlike anything that he did on the other six days of the week. His actions were furtive, and it was obvious that he was "dry cleaning" himself. Obviously, great emphasis was given to this one evening each week. Eventually, surveillance observed the man changing into a disguise.

Coverage continued for many months, until the man was ultimately followed to an apartment building on the opposite side of the city. Coverage of the building identified other clandestine members of the FALN, who, like this man, were living otherwise normal lives. Finally, a court order was procured that permitted entry into the apartment that the group was using, and microphones, cameras, and wiretaps were installed. Weapons, explosives, and other terrorist paraphernalia were located in the apartment.

At this point, a choice had to be made. The dangerous materials could not be left with the terrorists. Arrest warrants could have been procured and the cell members arrested, or the dangerous materials could have been taken and made to appear as though a burglary had occurred. The terrorists would probably not assume that they had been compromised. The third choice, which is the one that was used, was to substitute every dangerous item in the apartment with inert and disabled facsimiles. Within a very short time after the apartment was "wired," investigators were able to watch and hear the man constructing explosive devices. Conversations were also overheard involving cell members as they planned both criminal and terrorist actions.

When to Stop. Although the objectives in a case like that of Joe Bomber involve a lot more than just developing probable cause to arrest Joe Bomber, they do not clearly indicate when the case should be brought to a conclusion. Certain things are very clear. The group cannot be permitted to commit a terrorist attack if the investigators can prevent it from happening. The group cannot be allowed to perpetrate a violent criminal action to raise funds or to gather weapons and supplies. Group members who can be indicted for terrorist or felony criminal violations cannot be permitted to escape unless there is no other choice. Of course, Joe Bomber cannot be permitted to flee or perpetrate a felony or terrorist attack. The case should be permitted to continue if it appears likely that additional conspirators can be identified and intelligence developed that will lead to the solution of attacks and criminal violations. Remember that just because an investigator has developed sufficient information that Joe Bomber committed a violation of the law does not mean he has to be arrested.

It is very difficult for the law enforcement investigators and their managers, as well as the prosecutors involved in a highly successful terrorist investigation, to consider closing it. A case of this kind can generate an excitement unequaled in law enforcement. Many investigators and prosecutors know deep-down that this is a "career" case. They may never again experience anything like it. Something new is developed each day. No matter how many clandestine terrorists are identified, there is always the belief that others can be uncovered. No matter how many safe houses and weapons caches are found, there is the feeling that there are more. Even if no ties have been developed between the targeted group and other terrorist groups, there is always the belief that there must be some that will be identified if given enough time. Investigators forgo sleep, vacations, family gatherings, and everything else that would normally occupy their time in order to remain in the action. In one terrorism case, a truly dedicated officer not only worked seven days each week, but actually slept with the surveillance team's radio under his pillow at night so that he could monitor the subject's surveillance.

There may come a day when a case will have to be concluded because it has become too large and complex to manage securely. The investigators and managers will no longer be able to function at maximum efficiency. The number of investigators will have risen to the point that no single manager or investigator can even identify all of them by sight, much less by name. The geographic scope of the case will have come to include many cities across the United States and possibly some areas outside the United States. Criminal violations are being developed in other jurisdictions, which has necessitated the inclusion of a number of additional prosecutors representing those areas. While the managers actively involved in the case hope that it will last until every conceivable charge can be developed and all group members are identified, upper-echelon managers in the involved agencies want to bring the matter to a conclusion because the manpower and resource drain are crippling other operations within their agencies.

It must always be remembered and emphasized that any act of carelessness on the part of law enforcement can bring the case crashing down around them. Clearly, the bigger and broader the case, the greater the potential for disaster. For example, if any of the subjects under surveillance makes the coverage, word would quickly spread through prearranged signals, and the entire terrorist cell could vanish. This actually occurred in California in 1986. An extensive investigation of a six-person terrorist cell came to a abrupt end when one group member discovered a concealed microphone in his vehicle. Within hours, all six members disappeared. Officials searched for thousands of hours, but it was not until almost a decade later that the two leading members of the cell voluntarily surrendered to authorities.

The Aftermath. The indictments, arrests, and seizures of clandestine paraphernalia, including weapons and explosives, do not end the terrorism investigation. It is here that open interviews are now conducted with the group members and anyone associated with them. Searches are likely to be conducted at such locations as safe houses, residences, and vehicles. Trial preparation and the actual trial must now take place. In theory, preparation should not be as difficult as it might appear. Even though the case was large, every investigative step should have been carefully documented as it occurred. If they were not, serious trial preparation problems will arise.

Investigators will face two main problems as they prepare for trial. One is the preparation of a comprehensive prosecution report, in which all of the evidence that will be used against the defendants is assembled into a single, smooth-flowing comprehensive document. The better the quality of this document, the easier the prosecution of the subjects will be. The second problem involves the results of technical coverages. It is likely that during the course of the case, summaries were prepared in connection with pertinent wiretap and microphone intercepts. For trial, word-by-word transcripts will have to be prepared for the conversations the government will use against the defendants. In addition, detailed logs will have to accompany video and still camera evidence. Preparation of the audio transcripts can cause a significant manpower drain on the involved law enforcement agencies.

Court proceedings involving terrorism are unlike court proceedings that most law enforcement officers and prosecutors usually encounter. The subjects and their attorneys may attempt to interject their political philosophy into the courtroom. Disruptions, threats, actual attacks, and other forms of intimidation are typical. The defense will often not stipulate to what is otherwise normally accepted without question. Witnesses undergo arduous questioning that may include attacks on their reputations and character. Every facet of the evidence will be questioned and highly scrutinized.

Guilty verdicts and long prison sentences do not conclude the matter. The subjects will appeal and make various demands that will require written responses from the prosecutors. Once in prison, the subjects will disrupt the institution and will be major escape risks. They will spread their political philosophy to fellow inmates and prison employees and attempt to recruit new members wherever they can. They may make themselves martyrs. They may go on hunger strikes or claim that they are being abused or being denied proper medical care. Their outside supporters may make demands and possibly contact the media and influential people on their behalf.

Summary

Many terrorism cases begin with a violent attack. This requires a response that hopefully will lead to the identification of the perpetrators and their apprehension and prosecution. This is certainly not the ideal situation. Most law enforcement officers would prefer to prevent the attack and apprehend the perpetrators during the planning stages. Periodically, information will develop that will identify a member of a terrorist group. The law enforcement agency must then decide how to handle this information. For some agencies, it is best to turn the intelligence over to a larger agency or to an agency that has a broader jurisdiction. Some agencies may choose the direct approach of confronting the person in the hope that he will cooperate. Unfortunately, terrorists often will not agree to help police agencies, and a direct approach may force the entire group to flee the area or to engage in such tight security that a successful investigation will be unlikely.

There is great value to initiating a long-range, discreet investigation based upon the receipt of information that identifies a member of a terrorist group. It will have to be carefully planned and followed so that the group does not become aware of it, but the results will be very rewarding.

26 Handling a Terrorist Attack

A terrorist attack has occurred—and it is in your jurisdiction!

No law enforcement agency wants to hear those words. Prior to three decades ago it was likely that only the police agencies in large cities like New York, Chicago, and Washington, D.C. would have received such a notification. During the 1960s and early 1970s Vietnam war era, law enforcement agencies located near universities that were experiencing large anti-war protests may have also encountered terrorist attacks. Similarly, there were southern towns and cities where there might have been violent attacks staged by Ku Klux Klan-type extremists in connection with the integration issue. Otherwise, most law enforcement agencies probably would not have been worried about terrorist attacks taking place within their jurisdiction. Much has changed during the past two decades. The scope of terrorism has expanded with the growth of single-issue extremism and the threat of international terrorism. Law enforcement agencies must now place terrorism somewhere on their radar screens, if not in the middle of the viewing area. In today's world any law enforcement agency, regardless of its size or location, could receive the call to respond to a terrorist attack. The target may be something like the World Trade Center, located in the center of a huge city, or it could be a minority church in a medium-sized town, or it could be a mink farm located in an unincorporated area many miles from the nearest sheriff's office. Similarly, law enforcement agencies anywhere in the county could find terrorist safe houses, bomb factories, and weapons and explosives training sites within their jurisdiction.

Regardless of where the terrorist incident occurs, the law enforcement agencies responsible for conducting such investigations can expect to face a serious challenge. It is probable that the case will be unlike any other they have handled. The media will respond with haste and force, and will demand information. The incident will receive nationwide, and possibly worldwide, attention. Local citizens and business leaders in the area are likely to become more concerned about this kind of incident than they ever would about most other criminal violations. City, county, state, and federal law enforcement agencies will arrive at the scene and expect to be included in the investigation. Political leaders will also respond to the incident. Some will make demands, others will make inquiries, some will offer assistance, and still others will attempt to capitalize on the situation in order to bolster their own careers.

A terrorist attack can take many forms. Almost anything that causes extreme fear can be used by a terrorist group. In the United States, bombings and arson have traditionally been employed in no small part because they are force multipliers. Film of the damage can be shown repeatedly for months or years. Still pictures can be used repeatedly in newspapers, magazines, and on the Internet. The damage from such attacks is difficult to conceal and requires time to repair, so people passing by will be constantly reminded about what happened. In South America, kidnappings occur frequently. In Northern Ireland, physical attacks, including beatings, "kneecappings," and murders, have been used over several decades. These too, are force multipliers. Vandalism is a tool often used by single-issue terrorist organizations in the United States and Europe. It can take many forms—ranging from spray painting and gluing the target's door locks, to destroying a laboratory's expensive equipment or using acid or smoke bombs to make a location unusable. Anti-abortion militants have assassinated doctors and shot into abortion clinics.

The Immediate Response

For simplicity's sake, it will be assumed that a terrorist group has bombed a building in the downtown area of a medium-sized city in the United States. The law enforcement community must respond to this incident.

As the local police arrive at the scene, they observe destruction and chaos. The time and date of the incident will have a measurable impact on the number of casualties, as well as on the number of bystanders who may be in the area. Fire and other rescue workers will converge on the location at the same time that the local police arrive. The first responsibility for all responders is the protection of citizens and the rendering of assistance to the injured. The fire department will attempt to extinguish any fire that may have resulted, and rescue whomever they can from the area. Ambulance crews will provide immediate assistance to the injured. Police will attempt to clear the immediate crime scene and establish a safety perimeter. If they suspect or know that the explosion was caused by a bomb, they will attempt to procure the services of explosives technicians from their own department or from another agency, so these experts can search for secondary devices that may have been left at the scene.

The first investigative task for the local law enforcement agency is to ascertain exactly what happened. Sometimes this is known almost immediately, because a terrorist group may have already claimed credit for the attack. Other times, eyewitnesses will be able to pinpoint the cause. Often the firefighters will make this determination. Sometimes bomb technicians or crime scene specialists will be able to determine the cause of the explosion.

Assuming that it can be quickly determined that a terrorist bomb has caused the incident, the local law enforcement agency must organize itself in order to handle the investigation that must begin immediately. That agency should have a contingency plan that clearly outlines the proper response. If it does not have such a plan, the agency will have to quickly establish some kind of investigative strategy. If it fails to do this, the crime scene will probably become contaminated. It is possible that various components of the police department may compete for control over the operation. The lack of a plan could also result in some members of the department unwisely releasing information to the media. If the local police agency cannot get its act together quickly, it may find that other police agencies will converge on the crime scene. If the situation cannot be coordinated, major problems can and will develop. If the area has a formal joint terrorism task force, that entity will assume control of the investigation because it should represent all of the law enforcement agencies in the area that logically would have jurisdiction in such a case. In addition, task forces should have in place an emergency response plan that has received the approval of all of its member agencies.

The Crime Scene

The crime scene is an extremely important aspect of the investigation. It must be addressed immediately. If cleared or contaminated, the crime scene cannot be reconstructed exactly. Firefighters and other rescue workers will do a certain amount of damage to any crime scene as they perform their missions, but this can be kept to a minimum with good management and security procedures. The police must cordon off the crime scene so that entry is either completely prohibited, or at least restricted. The crime scene should be filmed with still cameras and video recorders before it is entered by investigators.

Crime scene investigation must be carefully planned. A police agency cannot allow open entry into the area. This prohibition should also cover members of their own agency. A plan must be made to recover evidence. Some larger law enforcement agencies have crime scene investigation teams whose job it is to recover evidence. Some teams have crime laboratory personnel attached to them. If a department has such a unit, it should use it in connection with a terrorist attack.

All law enforcement personnel should have received at least minimal evidence recovery training during the course of their police career. If there is no specialized crime scene unit available, the management of the department will have to organize evidence recovery teams. These teams should plan carefully for their assignment. They should not enter the crime scene until each member of the group knows what to do. People who have no crime scene experience should not enter the area until they have at least received some instruction about preserving evidence.

The federal government has an interest in all terrorist attacks. The FBI has been designated as the primary federal agency responsible for terrorism matters. When it comes to terrorism crime scene investigations, local police agencies should strongly consider using the FBI to conduct searches. The FBI has highly trained personnel with a great deal of experience in these investigations. It maintains one of the finest crime laboratories in the world. Unlike some crime laboratories, which concentrate on specific violations such as narcotics, the FBI laboratory conducts investigations on virtually all forms of evidence. Because they are national in scope, and even conduct many international investigations, the FBI laboratory has the ability to compare evidence from one crime scene with evidence from other crime scenes. They can also compare crime scene evidence with materials recovered during searches conducted all over the country of such locations as residences, businesses, vehicles, and people. This national comparison ability is something that local and state crime laboratories usually lack. Terrorist groups often function wherever they choose, and do not limit themselves to particular towns, counties, or states. For a group to attack in several different states is not unusual. Unfortunately, if each state sends its evidence to its own state or local laboratory, or to a private laboratory for analysis, it becomes difficult, if not impossible, for any one laboratory to compare that evidence. As a result, a great deal of intelligence is lost, and the ability to charge group members in a conspiracy is compromised. The FBI laboratory also has relationships with prominent foreign police laboratories, which can prove to be quite valuable in international terrorism investigations.

Local authorities could certainly conduct the crime scene investigation and send the results to the FBI laboratory. However, if the FBI is willing to conduct the crime scene search, it is probably better to allow their personnel to at least participate, if not orchestrate the search, because they have a greater familiarity with the strengths and capabilities of their laboratory. In major terrorist attacks, the FBI laboratory will often send laboratory technicians to the scene to assist FBI crime scene specialists in the recovery of evidence. As of 2008, all areas of the United States have joint terrorism task forces available to them. These entities are attached to every FBI field division. As such, FBI crime scene experts are readily available to conduct investigations.

Regardless of who conducts the crime scene investigation, it must be thorough. Even in a bombing or arson, where it appears that nothing could have survived, the fact is that the potential exists for the recovery of a great deal of valuable evidence. Every effort must be made to avoid contaminating the crime scene. Each article of evidence must be clearly marked with the identity of the recovering officer, along with the date. It should also be assigned some form of unique identification number. A log should be maintained describing each article recovered, and indicating where and when each item of evidence was found. Many crime scene specialists use computers to enhance the quality and speed of their work. The computers generate bar codes that can be affixed to each article of evidence. The computers also record information about the recovery, including a description of the item, where it was discovered, who found it, and when it was recovered.

Recovered items must be packaged separately. An investigator cannot simply dump a desk drawer into a trash bag and identify it as, "Item Number 1, contents of the desk located in Mr. Jones' office at the Smith Company, recovered on 1/1/04 by Detective Joe Dokes, Star Number 1234." Similarly, some items must be packaged differently based on their condition. An article of clothing covered with wet blood should be packaged differently from an article of clothing covered with dried blood. Suspected explosives cannot be packaged in the same manner as a written document. Certain burned materials, especially paper items, require special treatment. Chemicals require appropriate handling depending upon their nature and condition.

Crime scene investigators must avoid the "I found it" syndrome, in which everyone runs over to look at an item that appears to be of significance. Not only does the overall crime scene become damaged by such behavior, there is also a tendency for the other investigators to become less thorough after learning that the "key" piece of evidence has been found. The fact that an important article of evidence has been recovered should not mean that the crime scene investigation should be discontinued. Investigators and law enforcement managers should use care in jumping to conclusions about recovered evidence prior to a laboratory being able to analyze the material. There is certainly nothing wrong with setting leads to trace the origin of such articles, but refocusing the direction of the investigation can be problematic. For example, a watch found at the crime scene could have been the timing device for the bomb, or it could have been blown off the arm of a victim, come from a jewelry store destroyed in the blast, or been a broken timepiece discarded in a trash can.

A crime scene should not be released to its owner until it has been thoroughly processed. Not only will any item of evidence found subsequent to the release prove embarrassing to the law enforcement agency, it is likely that it will not be admissible in court because it will have a questionable chain of custody.

Witnesses

Locating witnesses is another important task that must be undertaken almost immediately after police arrive at the scene. Witnesses are one of the first resources that will enable authorities to determine what happened. However, most officers will not have the opportunity to interview every available witness in order to determine what occurred. They will probably be forced to rely on the people whom they find closest to the scene, and those who are the most willing to provide information. It is nonetheless incumbent upon authorities to quickly identify, at least by name and address, as many witnesses as possible. The more time that elapses, the more difficult this mission will become. If earlier arriving officers have a video camera, they should film the crowd so that at least some concrete record will exist to help investigators later identify additional witnesses.

It should be remembered that there is no guarantee that all of the perpetrators of the attack were able to flee the scene prior to the arrival of emergency response personnel. It is possible that one or more of the "witnesses," "victims," or "innocent bystanders" could actually be a terrorist. For this reason, it is important to ask people who are contacted to produce identification to prove that they are who they claim to be. Suspicious people, particularly those who cannot show identification and cannot explain why they are at the scene, probably should be interviewed in more detail.

The rejects of society should not be overlooked as being witnesses. Homeless people, drunks, narcotics users, prostitutes, runaways, and even common street criminals who are in the area can provide valuable information. Obviously, the reliability of such people is suspect. One often-overlooked aspect of these people is that they are a part of the overall fabric of the neighborhood, consequently they know who should be in their area. In that sense they may be able to supply the names of more credible people who frequent the area and who could logically have seen things of interest.

Claim of Credit for the Attack

A claim of credit can be an important avenue upon which to direct an investigation. Although not all terrorist groups claim credit for what they have done, many groups in the United States do so. These groups want to ensure that everyone knows why they have committed the attack. For these terrorists, it makes no sense to commit a violent act unless it promulgates their cause. Therefore, they want to publicly explain the reason for their action.

Terrorist claims have often been made by telephone or by written communiqué. Traditionally, communiqués have been sent to victims, the news media, or law enforcement agencies via the U.S. Mail. Some groups have left their communiqués at the scene or in other locations where they will be found. More recently, a number of groups have used the Internet to disseminate their claims of credit. It is likely that in the future the Internet and e-mail will be the method of choice for most groups to get their messages out. Some extremists, particularly those in the animal and environmental areas, use a third party, such as a surface support organization, to distribute their claims of credit.

The claim of credit is important because it identifies the perpetrator. This can give an investigation some direction. It is particularly important if a law enforcement agency has already developed intelligence about the group in question, or has a pending investigation involving the group. The claim of credit almost always outlines the reason for the attack. Often it makes comments about future group plans, including threats. All of this information can be of value in developing an investigation. The communiqué can also be used against the terrorist group and its members in subsequent prosecutions.

If the claim is made by telephone, it is important to determine exactly what was said. Consequently, an investigator should immediately conduct a personal interview with the recipient of the telephone call. If it will be some time before the investigator can visit that person, he should instruct that person to make a written record of the exact words the caller used. The investigator should then tell the person not to talk to anyone else about the call. These points are important, because the recipients of terrorist telephone calls are usually caught off-guard and therefore do not always understand everything the caller has said. Many will know little or nothing about the extremist group or cause involved. Frequently the caller is nervous, and attempts to disguise his or her voice. He or she assumes that the recipient has some method for immediately tracing the call, and wants to make his or her statement and quickly terminate the conversation. As a result, many callers begin talking before the recipient can begin to comprehend what is being said. They are often reading scripts and do not repeat what they have stated, even if the recipient claims not to have heard or understood what was said. Efforts should be made to determine if the call was recorded, and to obtain a copy of the recording even if a court order is required. In some cases the person receiving the call may not even be aware that his or her employer records calls, therefore it might be necessary to talk to management personnel to find out this information.

It is important that the investigator document everything that the recipient recalls hearing before he or she forgets, or before someone else taints his memory. A well-meaning co-worker or a member of the media could easily make "suggestions" about what the caller might have stated. The recipient could come to accept a suggestion as being correct. For example, a switchboard operator may recall that as she was responding, "Hello, Daily Star Newspaper," the caller was saying something like, "this is the garbled L garbled just bombed your downtown warehouse." The operator's supervisor could suggest that the caller must have said that he was with the JDL because that group has committed violent attacks in the past. By the time the investigator arrives, the switchboard operator has come to believe that the caller did in fact say JDL. In actuality, the caller might have said ALF or ELF, or possibly the name of a previously unknown group.

Terrorist telephone calls can take several forms. Some will warn that there is a bomb in a target location. Others will claim credit for an attack that has already occurred, possibly simultaneously with the call. In either of these calls, an explanation for the attack can be given. Another type of call that some terrorist groups use is one in which the group provides directions to the location of a communiqué that has been left.

Records Checks

From the beginning of the incident, investigators should check records for intelligence about the perpetrators of the attack. The name of the group claiming responsibility should be checked through all logical law enforcement agencies. Records checks should be done on suspicious people and vehicles. The names of people who were on the scene as "witnesses" when the initial officers responded should also be checked. Anything that immediately stands out at the crime scene should undergo a records check.

> At a multiple-device terrorist bomb scene, explosives technicians found a name and address label on the box that contained an unexploded device.

Terrorism experts should be quickly consulted for advice and counsel, especially if no immediate claim has been made, or the group making a claim is unknown. These specialists can review their own intelligence files and study terrorist literature for information. They may be able to identify the perpetrator based on what initial investigators learn from the crime scene and from witnesses.

> Several hours after a devastating terrorist attack, an investigator who had considerable knowledge about several terrorist groups viewed a photograph of the remains of one of the arson devices recovered at the crime scene. He immediately recognized the device as being identical to one used by a group that had attacked in several other cities in the past. Several days later, a communiqué from that group, in which the group claimed credit (postmarked the day of the attack), arrived. The investigator's information allowed his agency to focus in the proper direction almost from the outset, even though that particular group had previously never been active in that city.

Informants

Investigators who have informants capable of providing terrorism information should be instructed to contact these sources as soon as possible to determine whether they have any valuable information. Most will not have direct information about the bombing, because if they did, they would have provided it to their handler prior to the attack or immediately thereafter. Some might be able to provide information regarding recent visitors to the city, strange conversations they overheard, or unusual activities they saw, but deemed unimportant at the time. Now that an attack has occurred, these innocuous incidents might take on a new meaning.

Even if the sources cannot provide any information about the bombing, they can often capitalize on it. They can use the publicity generated from the attack to "make conversation" and openly ask questions. Informants can often use a terrorist attack to make inroads that would otherwise not be possible.

Creating and Organizing a Command Center

Getting organized must be a major priority in the response to any terrorist attack. The violent incident itself is enough to cause confusion. The media, politicians, and the arrival of personnel from other agencies all add to the turmoil. The need to take immediate action to protect the crime scene and locate witnesses will add to the pressure. A command structure must quickly be established or the investigation will fail. If the crime scene is removed by a waste disposal service, it cannot be replaced at a later date when a law enforcement agency is finally ready.

The deployment of a well-written contingency plan will address the key issues. Unfortunately, some agencies have no such plan. Other agencies find their plans to be outdated. In still other situations, agency leaders refuse to implement their plans, possibly because they were never aware that they existed.

Creating a command center is an important aspect of administering a terrorism investigation. The command center should be established close to, but not actually at, the crime scene. Managers responsible for coordinating the various aspects of the investigation should be assigned to work in the command center. The head of the law enforcement agency or his or her designee should be in the center or be housed adjacent to it, because he or she must be available to render key decisions.

It is not the purpose of the command center personnel to actually conduct the investigation. Instead, it is their responsibility to ensure that a proper investigation is performed. Command center personnel are there to both lead and serve the street investigators. They should use their power and authority to give orders and instructions, and to procure for the investigators what they need to complete their assignments.

Command center managers should not actually be covering leads in the case. If they do, they leave a leadership void in the command center that may cause serious problems for the street officers who need their support and direction. Furthermore, command center personnel who elect to become directly involved in lead coverage can cause morale problems. A street investigator who identifies an eyewitness will become quite upset if a command center manager insists upon interviewing that person. Communication difficulties can also result from such actions. A crime scene specialist is not likely to immediately inform the command center of the discovery of an important article of evidence if he or she believes that he will be told that someone in the command center will come to the scene to personally "recover" that article.

While it is true that the command center personnel should manage the investigation, it is not reasonable to believe that they can or should handle every minor aspect of the case. The command center officials must know that the crime scene investigation is being conducted, and they must be informed of significant findings. They also must know if the crime scene personnel require certain equipment, and they must assist in procuring it. However, the command center should not be involved in assigning shovels to individual investigators, or in dividing and assigning crime scene quadrants to specialists. There is no reason for command center personnel to arrange the work or lunch break schedules for crime scene personnel. These "local" responsibilities should be handled by an on-scene manager. If the crime scene is large, it may be better to establish a crime scene command center that will be subordinate to the main command center. The crime scene center should be located adjacent to the crime scene. In addition to the on-scene manager, this center might house coordinators for equipment, scheduling, evidence storage, and any other activity that requires supervision. Similar localized on-scene managers or command centers could be established for a variety of activities, including the location of witnesses, SWAT, hostage negotiation, media contacts, and lead coverage.

In theory, the main command center will issue the orders and provide the direction for the investigation. The on-scene managers or local command centers will follow the directives that apply to their specialty. They will report their results to the main command center, where the appropriate managers will gather significant information, issue appropriate instructions, and disseminate information where necessary. Consequently, if the crime scene command center reports that a name and address have been found on the container that housed the bomb, the main command center manager will ensure that the manager responsible for lead coverage will be given that information. This manager will in turn provide the information to the lead command center, where an investigator will be assigned.

The main command center should have a broad view of every aspect of the investigation, whereas the on-scene localized command centers will have only a specific knowledge of their area of concentration. This situation carries many responsibilities. The main command center must ensure that proper investigation is being addressed on all fronts, and that every area of concentration is adequately manned and equipped. It must establish goals and objectives for the investigation, and make sure that they are addressed. It must handle immediate needs quickly. It must ensure that the investigation is being properly documented. The main command center is really the only entity that has the ability to make sure that nothing "falls though the cracks."

> In a terrorist attack in which multiple explosive devices were used, the command center informed investigators at the scene of one of the incidents that a particular crime scene specialist would arrive and take control of the remains of the explosive device. Unfortunately, the command center neglected to inform the specialist of the assignment. Many hours later, investigators who were packing evidence for shipment to the laboratory discovered that the remains of the device were missing. They subsequently returned to the crime

scene where they discovered that the remains had been thrown into a locked trash dumpster by a building janitor. Fortunately, the dumpster had not been emptied by the waste disposal service, and the evidence was recovered.

The weaknesses illustrated by the above example are obvious. The command center should have created a local command center to handle the crime scene aspect of the investigation, or it should have created individual crime scene command centers at each crime scene. The main command center should not have been making street-level manpower assignments. In this case, the command center did not even appoint an on-scene street-level manager to direct the crime scene investigations. Consequently, there was no one to realize that one of the crime scenes had been left unassigned.

Rumors, personal opinions, and hunches are bound to arise in any major investigation. It is the responsibility of the command center to keep these in check. The command center must ensure that the investigation is based on a solid foundation. Managers in the command center must constantly deal with the "who, what, where, when, why, and how" questions in connection with the direction of the investigation. The command center must also ensure that personnel understand their assignments and fulfill them. They also must make certain that completed work is rapidly and correctly documented. The immediate responsibility for the latter two points rests with the on-scene command center or the on-scene manager. Ultimately, however, the responsibility is with the main command center.

In one terrorism case, the direction of the investigation swung to a belief that the fugitive subject had fled to a particular foreign country because he was fluent in that country's language. After several days, an investigator trying to locate the documentation for this information discovered that the fugitive actually had a "mental block" that made it virtually impossible for him to learn a foreign language. This factor made the idea of him fleeing to any non-English-speaking country quite improbable. Further tracing of the intelligence led to a specific investigator who admitted that he had introduced the foreign language information into the intelligence pool of the case. He explained that he had once had a friend who was employed in the same profession as the fugitive. Because he knew that his friend was required as part of his job to speak the language in question, he "knew" that the fugitive would also be required to do so. As a matter of fact, subsequent investigation revealed that the profession had waived the language requirement for the subject when they learned of his "mental block." In this case, command center personnel directed that various items of intelligence and leads be sent to police agencies in the foreign country to look for the fugitive, without ever asking about the origin of the information.

In another terrorism case, an investigator assigned to interview the residents of a small apartment building located above the office that had been bombed reported that he had completed his assignment within an hour, but had been unable to locate any witnesses. A week later, when a resident of the building voluntarily came forth with some information, a recheck of the initial investigator's documentation was conducted. It was found that he had contacted less than half of the building's actual residents. When questioned about the situation, the investigator stated that he had interviewed all of the residents that he had found home at the time of his visit, which was immediately after being assigned the lead. The Leads Coordinator had meant for the investigator to interview all of the residents of the building, not just the residents who happened to be home when the investigator visited the location. In fact, most of the residents of the building who were present when the bomb exploded were at their jobs by the time the investigator came to the building. This was a situation in which the investigator did not understand his instructions, and the coordinator giving the assignments never reviewed the results to ensure that they were followed.

In another terrorism case, two teams of investigators were assigned to conduct a neighborhood investigation on the street where the bombing occurred. The teams divided the work, and one team immediately commenced its interviews. The other team delayed an hour before they began work. Neither team developed anything of value. Several days later, the Lead Coordinator reviewing the documentation presented by the two teams discovered that the names and addresses of the people interviewed were similar. Apparently, when the team leaders divided the work, they did so by one agreeing to take the left side and the other the right side of the street. The problem was the two men were facing each other when they made their decision. In this situation, the error was caught because there was a Lead Coordinator who was performing his duties.

Speed, accuracy, and thoroughness are important in the initial response to a terrorist attack. It is imperative that an appropriate number of personnel be assigned to cover leads. It is important that the initial response not be treated as a 9-to-5 job. The command center must make arrangements to work around the clock, if necessary, or as long each day as is practicable. This means that shifts must be established so that employees do not become overtired, and therefore inefficient and careless. Shifts must also be created for the main command center, and for any on-scene local command centers that are established. Managers, including the agency head, should not attempt to function as "iron men" because fatigue will cause them to make mistakes.

Including Other Law Enforcement Agencies

In terrorism investigations, it is probably best that the various agencies having jurisdiction work together. Working in opposition will be counterproductive. The best situation occurs when each agency concentrates on its strengths with respect to the overall investigation. The various agencies working on a terrorism case should be represented in the overall command center. However, there should be nothing to prohibit each agency from maintaining its own command center to coordinate its manpower and equipment, and to administer leads that fall within its unique purview.

There are virtually no citywide terrorist groups in the United States whose goal is to overthrow a city or to force a single city to change its philosophy. Terrorists travel freely and perpetrate violent attacks and criminal acts nationwide. They maintain safe houses and weapons caches everywhere. It is extremely difficult for a local jurisdiction to successfully investigate a terrorist group separately from other law enforcement agencies.

The joint terrorism task force concept, which started in the early 1980s, became a national reality as a result of the September 11, 2001 attacks. Virtually every part of the country is covered to some extent by a task force. The larger and more vulnerable cities have task forces that are quite active, and are composed of investigators from almost every law enforcement agency in the area. Terrorism task forces are attached to every FBI field division. Some task forces have subdivisions in cities away from the main FBI office covering their area.

Involving Prosecutors

At an early stage of the investigation, the appropriate prosecutors must be brought on board. This could mean the local district attorney's office, the county prosecutor and, at the federal level, the United States Attorney's Office. It is very possible that investigators will require court orders and search warrants in the early stages of a terrorism investigation. If a suspect is identified, arrest and search warrants may be required. Terrorism cases can offer special legal problems that are not usually encountered and that may require the immediate assistance of a government attorney. For example, a building owner may not cooperate with respect to a crime scene, and demand that he be permitted to clean the debris in order to reopen his business. The recipient of a communiqué may refuse to allow investigators to have, or even view, the original document. Picketers, demonstrators, and other supporters of the involved political cause may disrupt the investigators. Suspects may refuse to cooperate with authorities, and attorneys representing them may cause problems by demanding information, or by filing complaints about the investigators. The news media may interfere with the investigation or refuse to allow investigators to review their film of the crime scene.

As an immediate outcome of the September 11, 2001 attacks, the U.S. Attorney General instructed every U.S. Attorney's office in the country to establish a task force to respond to terrorism issues. These entities were not intended to compete with joint terrorism task forces or to conduct street investigations. The intent was for the management personnel of law enforcement and prosecutive agencies to come together to study the problem, and ensure that their area was being properly protected. In most areas the relationship between the United States Attorney's task force, now known as the Anti-Terrorism Advisory Council (ATAC), and the joint terrorism task force complement each other.

Lead Coverage

Witness interviews often develop leads. Witnesses usually will report on suspicious people and vehicles they observed. These leads must be investigated. The crime scene will probably develop some leads, although the best leads may not come until later, when the laboratory examines the evidence in detail. The publicity generated by the case will probably yield tips that should be investigated. The communiqué or other claim of credit will also yield some leads. Law enforcement informants will probably supply some leads. There may already be a current investigation on the group who claimed responsibility for the attack. It is possible that leads in that case will take on a new urgency.

In short, almost any terrorist attack will generate leads that require immediate attention. The command center should have a manager who is responsible for leads. This person, in turn, should designate someone to coordinate and assign specific leads to investigators. Often this assignment will be given to an on-scene command center or an on-scene manager.

On the surface, assigning leads appears to be a relatively simple task. Unfortunately, many managers treat it as such. As a result, leads are assigned in a haphazard manner. In other situations, no record is maintained as to who has been assigned what lead. The results of such leads are handled in a similar manner. In one major case, the command center set up a large cardboard box where investigators were instructed to place the results of their leads. The problem with the system was that no one maintained a list of the assignments, so there was no way to match the results with the leads. Some leads were covered more than once, while other leads were apparently never assigned. People who had insufficient background were assigned to conduct highly specific leads, while terrorism specialists were assigned to conduct routine inquiries.

Coordinating leads is a tedious and demanding responsibility. It must be given to a competent person with a talent for organization. Preferably, the coordinator should be an experienced investigator who has a good deal of time on the street, so that he knows how to cover leads. The pool of investigators should contain many experienced investigators. Agencies often employ rookie officers and other inexperienced personnel to cover leads. This is acceptable if these officers can partner with veteran investigators on covering more complex leads.

Computers have solved many of the problems relating to lead assignment. There is no reason an agency cannot use a computer to assign leads and record their results. Using a computer, a command center should be able to track every lead that has been assigned to determine its status and, if completed, determine its results. The FBI has established an excellent computer program that does just this. This program has been used in several major terrorism investigations. Other law enforcement agencies also use effective lead-tracing computer programs. The names and backgrounds of investigators can also be computerized so that expertise can be factored into lead assignments. For example, if there is a lead for an investigator to observe the autopsy of a victim in an attempt to locate bomb fragments, it would make sense to assign it to an officer who had a medical background, such as a former nurse or military medic. Similarly, it would make little sense to send a computer illiterate investigator to trace the origin of an e-mail communiqué.

It is important that the results of leads be properly documented in some kind of standardized format. This is particularly true if the investigation is being conducted by a group of agencies. It is certainly true if the case is being computerized as it progresses. Obviously, information developed during the investigation that is of immediate importance must be reported before it can be reduced to written form. There must be a way to do this. Every investigator who thinks that he or she has found something of significance cannot bring it into the main command center. This is one reason on-scene local command centers are important, because the coordinators of these entities will review the results of investigations under their control, and report significant information to the main command center on a regular basis.

The Transition from Crisis Response

As time passes, the need to immediately deal with leads will dissipate. The crime scene will be conducted and cleared. The laboratory will return the results of its examination, and the appropriate leads will be set, with the most pressing being given priority. Witnesses that can be located will have been interviewed and possibly reinterviewed several times. The most pertinent and pressing leads will have been handled. If good fortune prevails, the perpetrators will be identified and arrested. In terrorism cases, however, the offenders often will not be identified or, if they have been, at least some will be missing. Regardless, there will come a time when the sense of urgency dissipates. The departments involved in the investigation can return to a sense of normalcy. The main command center will begin to reduce personnel and hours of operation, and will eventually cease operations. The local on-scene command centers will similarly reduce in size, and will also come to an end. A core of investigators will assume control of the case with one of them being designated as the case officer. If the case officer is fortunate, his main task will be in the area of trial preparation, but it is more probable that he will have a great deal of work to do with respect to identifying the perpetrators and then arresting them.

There is no set time frame for "immediate response" periods to come to an end. Some will end shortly after the crime scene is cleared. Others may extend for many months. It will depend on the size of the attack, the group involved, the extent of media coverage, and the amount of public concern. An Oklahoma City or World Trade Center-type of attack will require a command center to maintain operation for a year or more, because the crime scene is so massive and the leads so numerous. The bombing of an unoccupied one-room military recruiting office by an established terrorist group may see its "special" designation being dropped with the closing of the command center after a few days.

Summary

When a terrorist attack occurs, an immediate response to the scene will be required, and quick action will be demanded by the community. Helping victims will be the first concern. Following this will be the tasks of securing the crime scene and locating witnesses. Establishing some form of command center to control the investigative operations is imperative in attacks of any size or consequence. Ideally, law enforcement agencies will have contingency plans in place that will outline how such an investigation is to be structured. In terrorism cases, it is important to coordinate the efforts of the various investigative agencies that might have jurisdiction in the case. In almost every part of the country a joint terrorist task force is in place, and the agencies will already have a working relationship. With time, the number of investigators will decrease, and the command center will be closed. A single investigator or small squad will continue the investigation.

㉗ Crisis Preparation

All agencies should prepare for crisis situations. This is particularly true for agencies that will respond to terrorist attacks. Such an incident will require an immediate response. Terrorist attacks cause great fear and concern in the community. They also create a media frenzy. The more the media learns, the more the public becomes aware of the very worst aspects of the situation. When a terrorist incident occurs, a department must react immediately to protect the public, save lives, prevent additional attacks, preserve the crime scene, and identify the perpetrators. Such incidents require an expeditious, comprehensive, departmental response. The department head or other high-ranking officer must assume responsibility for the operation. A command center should be established to run the investigation. It is foolhardy for a law enforcement agency to attempt to handle a terrorist attack in the same way that it would address a more routine criminal violation.

The case should be separated into investigative components, and management personnel within the agency should be placed in charge of each component. Investigative components might include leads, crime scene, surveillance operations, SWAT, hostage negotiators, electronics specialists, media, bomb technicians, and intelligence gathering. Investigators throughout the department should provide the manpower required by each component to complete its mission. There must be regular and continuous contact between the various investigative components and with management so that each entity complements and supports the others. Briefings should also be given to all investigators so they can have a broad understanding of the investigation.

It is a natural tendency for a department to pride itself on its ability to respond to criminal violations that occur within its jurisdiction. Agencies will find that, with respect to terrorist attacks, they will be forced to work in harmony with other agencies if they hope to solve the case. Terrorist attacks are high-profile crimes that will draw the response of every local, county, and federal agency that can find a reason to become involved. Even if an agency does not immediately enter an investigation, the publicity generated by a terrorist incident will soon force its top leadership to take some form of action to become involved. Furthermore, the complex nature of terrorist incidents often requires a joint endeavor because a single agency will have difficulty resolving a terrorist attack.

Since September 11, 2001, joint terrorism task forces have been established throughout the United States. Consequently, it is likely that a plan of sorts is already in place that will call for various law enforcement agencies to work together in response to terrorist attacks. Also as a result of September 11, 2001, U.S. Attorney's offices throughout the country were ordered to establish task forces now called Anti-Terrorism Advisory Councils (ATAC) with local and federal agencies within their jurisdiction. These entities are not investigative in nature, but instead bring the management of various law enforcement agencies and local, county, state, and federal prosecutors together to formulate a response to terrorism in their area. They usually work in conjunction with the joint terrorism task forces that conduct the actual investigations of terrorist groups and their attacks. The United States Attorney's offices throughout the country have sponsored numerous training programs in the area of terrorism to local, state, and federal investigators and to the management personnel of law enforcement agencies.

Usually some, if not all, of the perpetrators of an attack are from outside the area where the incident occurred. This presents a major problem for a local law enforcement agency. The federal government is better able to trace the terrorists around the country, but they must rely on the local authorities to handle everything from crowd control to crime scene security. They also need the local law enforcement agencies' manpower, informants, and intelligence base. Contingency plans must take these factors into consideration. A local police department that does not include state and federal agencies in its terrorist attack contingency plans is likely to face a rude awakening when an incident occurs. Similarly, a federal agency that creates a contingency plan that fails to include local and state law enforcement agencies is bound to encounter trouble when it attempts to implement their plan at the crime scene.

Preparation for major crisis situations, including terrorist attacks, can take several forms. Personnel ranging from the highest-ranking agency official to the lowest-ranking rookie officer should be aware of what will be expected of him or her in the event of a crisis incident.

Contingency Plans

The contingency plan is the most basic form of crisis preparation. Essentially, a contingency plan is a written document that outlines how a department intends to respond to a crisis situation. The plan should explain the roles that agency employees will assume during a crisis. It should also make it clear where, and to whom, all employees will report. The plan should outline what each employee is to do. Some departments have several crisis contingency plans, each designed to address a specific type of problem. If a department elects to have multiple plans, they should probably be similar in structure, and, if possible, investigators should be assigned to perform the same tasks in each situation, regardless of the nature of the crisis. Employees who possess special skills and training should be assigned accordingly in contingency plans. It makes little sense to assign a detective who has extensive crime scene experience to handle media calls or coordinate hostage negotiations. The departmental leader should ensure that all employees review the agency's crisis contingency plans prior to an actual emergency situation. In fact, it makes sense for the plan to be discussed either during an all-employee conference or during squad meetings. Employees should be encouraged to give their input about the plan, especially if they think that something has been neglected or they have been improperly assigned.

One of the main problems with contingency plans is that they can become dated rather quickly. Employees retire, resign, or are reassigned. The availability of equipment and command centers and other work sites can change. An outdated contingency plan can cause confusion when a crisis occurs. Key people may be missing. Investigators may report to locations that are no longer usable. Communications can be nonexistent because the employees assigned to handle them cannot operate newly acquired equipment. To avoid such problems, several things can be done.

Someone in a ranking position within the department should be designated, at least on a part-time basis, as the crisis coordinator. Most large law enforcement agencies should have such a position. This person's job would be to review all agency contingency plans on a regular basis, at least every six months, to ensure that each plan can be instituted as written. This employee should be aware of all personnel movement within the department so that he or she can make plan modifications as necessary. He or she should visit all locations mentioned in the plans in order to determine if these areas remain viable for use. He or she should be aware of purchases, changes, and repairs that the department has made involving major equipment in order to ensure that people designated in the contingency plan to operate this equipment can indeed perform their assignments. Many departments regularly update their computer systems. It is imperative that the coordinator make employees assigned to use computers in the plan aware of significant changes. It would be helpful if this coordinator is given sufficient time that he could monitor crisis situations around the country, and attempt to learn how well the appropriate law enforcement agencies responded to them. In that way he could update his department's plans with new ideas, and attempt to avoid shortfalls that other agencies experienced.

A second way that an agency can maintain its contingency plan in a current status is to make assignments by position rather than by individual. Instead of writing that investigators John Smith and Mary Jones will handle the crime scene during a crisis, the department's plan can indicate that members of the agency's evidence recovery team will have this responsibility. Thus, if Jones has been promoted to patrol sergeant, he will know that he will have no crime scene responsibility because he is no longer a member of the evidence recovery team. Instead of indicating that Lt. Brown will be in charge of the command center's lead desk, the plan would designate this responsibility to the chief of detectives. If Lt. Brown holds that position when a crisis occurs, he will assume command of the lead desk. If he has retired, his successor as chief of detectives will handle this function. The weakness in doing this is that the person occupying a particular position at the time of a crisis may not have the kind of expertise that his predecessor had, and may not be able to perform the assignment very well.

A third method of ensuring that an agency's contingency plan is current, is to place it into the agency's computer network where it can be accessed by all employees, and can be updated instantaneously with any personnel or equipment change. If a crisis occurs, all employees can refer to their agency's server to know where to report. A danger with this concept is that the agency may find itself with no plan at all if the crisis involves the agency's computer system. There seems little question that terrorist groups will at some time in the future attack computers because of the large amount of damage that can be done to such a target with little risk to themselves. The most obvious way that an agency can protect itself from this situation is to make hard copies of the agency's contingency plan available on a monthly or quarterly basis to the leaders of each of the agency's subdivisions. Another way to ensure that plans are available would be to encourage employees to save each revision onto either their computer's hard drive or a CD or DVD. In that way employees would still be able to bring up their agency's plan even if the terrorist attack wiped out the department's overall computer system.

Responsibility Agreements

Few law enforcement agencies have the ability to handle all aspects of a major crisis situation, especially if it involves a terrorist attack. Even if an agency has the capability, it is bound to encounter other law enforcement agencies that also have jurisdiction for aspects of the crisis. When preparing a response to a crisis situation, a department should identify the other federal, state, and local agencies that have jurisdiction. In addition, efforts should be made to determine what emergency services, including fire and rescue, will respond. These agencies should be contacted, and efforts should be made to develop a working agreement with them, so that when a crisis does occur, the various investigative and emergency entities are not impeding and competing with one another. It may be prudent to establish a joint command center to direct the law enforcement and overall emergency response entities in a major crisis. A written agreement is desirable, and will be similar in structure to an agency contingency plan.

Mutual Aid Agreements

Because a crisis is likely to tax the resources of a town and its agencies, it is important that some form of backup for critical responsibilities be arranged in advance with neighboring communities. Many cities already have agreements with fire departments to assist them in case of major fire and/or to man their empty fire stations when their firefighters are battling a significant blaze. Police agencies should also have such plans, especially with respect to important specialties. For example, multiple bombings could tie up a city's bomb squad, so there should be arrangements for other nearby bomb squads to assist as needed. Similar situations could involve SWAT teams, crime scene specialists, and hostage negotiators.

Of course, a mutual aid agreement is a two-way street. An agency should be cognizant of the commitments that it has made to neighboring communities with respect to terrorist attacks that might occur. Investigators as well as managers should be made aware of what their responsibilities will be with respect to an attack outside of their normal jurisdiction. It is quite possible that what investigators will be expected to do in connection with a terrorist attack in another jurisdiction may be different from what their agency's contingency plans call for them do in their own area.

The Tabletop Exercise

The Tabletop Exercise is an excellent form of crisis training that can be conducted with a minimal amount of disruption to a department. A Tabletop Exercise can be organized and run by a department employee, or it can be staged by a professional. The latter is usually preferable, but can be costly. Professionals can come from universities, government agencies such as the Federal Emergency Management Agency (FEMA), or private companies. A Tabletop Exercise is essentially a "role-play" type of practice session that puts a department's contingency plan into operation. (A department that does not have a contingency plan, or that has an outdated or poorly written plan, will quickly come to regret it when they attempt to conduct a Tabletop Exercise.)

Tabletop Exercises are used to familiarize employees with how they are to respond to a crisis situation. A "paper" crisis is created over a period of several hours. The session usually begins when the departmental leaders have gathered in a command center. However, a Tabletop Exercise could start from scratch with a facilitator suddenly announcing over an agency's public address system that a building has been bombed in what appears to be a terrorist attack. Everyone in the department must respond appropriately, which for leadership means to open and operate a command center.

Once the Tabletop Exercise has begun, the facilitator keeps it going through a regular infusion of developments. The command center personnel are expected to express how they would address each new infusion of information. In most instances, the command center personnel will only state verbally how they would respond. In more elaborate exercises, the command center personnel would actually go through the motions of ordering subordinates to take appropriate actions. Usually it goes no further than this stage, because a Tabletop Exercise rarely includes investigators conducting crime scene investigations, surveilling subjects, or arresting people. The facilitator wants people to learn and wants the employees to understand why they are doing what they have been assigned to do. When the facilitator interjects something new into the crisis situation, he wants the employees to understand who within the command structure will handle the new development, and the reason this person has been given this responsibility.

A typical Tabletop Exercise might proceed as follows:

Department managers have gathered in a command center at assigned stations. The facilitator announces that an unknown group has kidnapped the city's chief judge and is holding him at an unknown location. A communiqué from the group has just been brought to the department by a reporter who stated that it was left at his newspaper office. The facilitator holds up the communiqué and asks who in the command center should handle it? He also asks whether the reporter should be interviewed and, if so, who should do it?

After these questions have been resolved, the facilitator advises that the communiqué states that a group calling itself the "Environmental Saviors" is holding the judge until the city stops its project to dam the local river. The facilitator asks, "Who does what with this information?" The facilitator next advises that an informant has just told a detective that the Environmental Saviors have a hideout in the old mill. The facilitator asks, "Who does what with this informant information?"

Eventually, the command center will take actions that will result in the old mill being reached, and the facilitator interjects that the judge is being held in the old mill. The facilitator mentions SWAT and the department negotiators, asking, "Who in the room is responsible for these entities, and what orders should be given about their use?"

At this point, the facilitator brings in a factor from left field. He explains that a prominent athlete has arrived at the old mill, and has offered to negotiate with the kidnappers because he was formerly married to one of them. The facilitator asks, "How does the command center want to respond to this man's offer?" Now the facilitator advises that a department sniper team member is on the telephone, reporting that he has a clear shot at the leader of the kidnappers. The facilitator wants to know what instructions the command center has for this sniper. If the center managers fail to mention legal issues that could be involved, the facilitator will ask if perhaps the department's legal counsel or city attorney or prosecutor should be contacted for advice on this issue.

Next, the facilitator reports that the mayor has arrived at the old mill and has pushed his way to the front line. The facilitator asks the center personnel how they will deal with this situation. He also reports that the SWAT leader is expressing fear that the kidnappers might shoot the mayor.

Following this, the facilitator advises that someone inside the old mill has shot into the police line and has hit an officer. The facilitator wants to know how this development changes things and what action the center plans to take.

By this time, the facilitator has brought everyone in the command center into the scenario. He has forced various department managers to render opinions. In some instances, the wrong official has rendered a decision. In other situations, the proper official remained mute or incorrect decisions were made. In other cases, logical options were not explored. For example, the officer who was shot may still be lying on the ground, because the command center became so concerned about deploying SWAT that they forgot to direct someone to help him. Members of the command center may have sent directions to the sniper about what he should do, without realizing that the sniper should have contacted his tactical superior and not command center personnel directly. The idea of the Tabletop Exercise is to illustrate the importance of every command center manager having knowledge of his or her responsibilities.

An effective facilitator can create a situation that is so real that the command center managers almost believe that what is being discussed in the center is actually happening. Some facilitators can build the tension even more by introducing visual aids. Instead of telling the group about the communiqué, the facilitator can actually have someone enter the command center carrying the document. Center personnel could then read and interpret it for themselves. The detective's report from the informant could arrive at the center via police radio or through a fax machine, supposedly from a police substation. A picture of the old mill can suddenly appear on a large-screen television in the center. The information about the shooting could be relayed via telephone to one of the command center assignment posts.

Tabletop Exercises can be very beneficial and are encouraged. They require few resources and can be conducted in a matter of hours, or can be extended for several days. They force everyone in authority to delineate how they envision their roles and responsibilities in a crisis situation. If run properly, they can resolve problems that could manifest themselves during an actual crisis. They often reveal confusion that exists at the management level concerning areas of responsibility. Tabletop Exercises are also valuable for identifying shortcomings in verbal and written communications.

Tabletop facilitators are usually familiar with the law. They will often ask under what authority an employee is acting. They also know command structure and authority. They will usually see incorrect assignments before problems develop. They can maneuver the exercise so that the participants will discover these shortcomings. They will want to know whether the person making a decision has the authority to do so and, if not, who should be making the decision. Because there are usually no actual incidents being staged during the program, the facilitator can set the pace for the operation. If it appears that there is confusion about a particular issue, the facilitator can stop everything by declaring a "time out." He or she can then attempt to resolve the problem even if it means seeking a legal decision or studying agency procedure manuals. Working together with the facilitator, it may be possible that management can actually create a policy to deal with questionable issues during the "time out" period.

It is important that a department treat the Tabletop Exercise as a serious training session. The head of the agency and his or her immediate subordinates should participate, unless their positions would not normally hold leadership positions in the command center. If, for some reason, the head of the agency would not be in charge of a crisis involving his agency, it should be made clear in the agency's contingency plan exactly who will have the ultimate authority. Although it is desirable that all management personnel participate in a Tabletop Exercise, it is not necessary that vacations, sick leave, court appearances, public presentations, or major investigations be interrupted or canceled to accommodate the exercise. The fact that few agencies can expect to have perfect attendance during an actual crisis is one of the reasons that contingency plans should provide for replacing missing personnel.

Many Tabletop Exercises encourage onlookers to observe the proceedings. Ideally, this group will include managerial assistants and individuals who would replace missing personnel. Representatives of the tactical team, which normally would be performing the aspects of the investigation that are being simulated for the exercise, should also attend as observers.

The major weakness of the Tabletop Exercise is that it is largely based on an imaginary scenario in which there is no real jeopardy to the participants. In this sense, during a Tabletop Exercise, many systems are not actually used, much less tested. Telephone traffic into the command center is largely fabricated by the facilitator, who advises that the center "just got a call" in which something was said that requires someone in the center to respond. Similarly, radio, fax, and computer transmissions usually do not actually take place. If they do occur, they happen in a very limited manner. For example, a radio operator may transmit a message to the command center from the department's main radio control console rather than that message coming from a car radio, as it would in an actual crisis. The emphasis during a Tabletop Exercise is on the person and his position within the command center, not on the equipment. Consequently, a Tabletop Exercise can lead an agency to have false confidence in their communications and technical equipment because the Tabletop Exercise does not actually test these systems. Also, because the facilitator is controlling the exercise, the tension that can build in a command center during an actual crisis never really develops during the practice session. Employees whose only crisis experience is the Tabletop Exercise may be shocked when they are called in to work in a real command center.

Full Field-Training Exercise

The Full Field-Training Exercise is essentially a real-life response to a mock crisis situation. Unlike the Tabletop Exercise, which usually involves very little planning by the department itself because much is simulated and the facilitator prepares the entire scenario before he even arrives, the Full Field Exercise requires a large-scale agency manpower commitment. Many weeks, if not months, of preparation are required. Unlike the Tabletop training, in which the facilitator feeds command center personnel a steady stream of developments to which they are to respond, in a Full Field Exercise, the events are in fact taking place in a mock fashion. They are being reported to the command center as they would in a real-life situation.

The command center is aware of the results of a surveillance because they have monitored the radio traffic of an actual surveillance team following an "actor" portraying a suspect. The center is aware of the fruits of an interview because investigators who conducted that interview with an "actor" portraying a witness have faxed their written documentation of that interview to the center. The fruits of a hostage negotiation between an investigator and an "actor" playing a kidnapper are being provided directly to the command center. In turn, command center personnel respond by giving instructions to the investigators available to them in an effort to resolve the crisis. Investigators are expected to follow the instructions and orders of their superiors.

In a Full Field Exercise, the command center is forced to endure problems that can develop during a real crisis. In some instances, it is the shortage of space, or the computer system that shuts down and has to be rebooted. It might be the radio system that cuts out, or the constant distraction of ringing telephones. It might be the lack of restrooms or the scarcity of food and drink. It might be too hot or too cold.

Although the facilitator has a general plan during a full training exercise, command center personnel who are not usually aware of the intended direction of the exercise can make decisions that will alter the plan. Similarly, the investigators can take actions during the course of their assignments that can alter the planned course of action.

The concept behind a Full Field-Training Exercise is to truly test an agency's response to a crisis. Ideally, such an exercise will simulate exactly how an agency will respond in such a situation. Even better than a Tabletop Exercise, a Full Field Exercise should expose weaknesses in an agency's contingency plan. It should highlight areas where confusion of authority exists. It should demonstrate communication difficulties. It should indicate problems with respect to proper documentation of investigative activities.

Full Field-Training Exercises can be exciting for a department. They can offer an opportunity for all personnel, both investigative and clerical, to demonstrate and use their specialties. Above all, they allow a department to come together in a common cause. All too often, the various components of a department do not work together, and therefore they do not appreciate or even understand one another. In some instances, specialties and expertise are largely unknown to most of the employees until a Full Field Exercise or real-life crisis occurs. Suddenly, members of the department realize that they have a capable SWAT operation or highly skilled electronics experts. They come to realize the talents of the department's surveillance and evidence recovery teams. They develop confidence in their leaders.

Despite their many strengths, Full Field-Training Exercises have several weaknesses that are worthy of comment. The most obvious shortcoming revolves around the time, energy, and expense involved in staging such an event. Many departments simply lack the resources to conduct a true Full Field Exercise. Therefore, they are either forced to forgo the exercise entirely, or stage a watered-down version that may not offer much training value. A department has to realize that a full training exercise that lasts for several days will have a negative effect on the law enforcement functions of the agency during that period. Many agencies, especially local police departments with direct responsibility for protecting the public, cannot suspend operations for an extended period.

A second weakness is much less obvious, but is nonetheless noteworthy. It is one that the facilitator should prevent. It is essentially a sense of false security that a department derives from an improperly staged training exercise. A crisis exercise that shows that there are no problems can lead an agency to believe that it can handle an actual crisis without experiencing significant difficulties.

The problem starts with preparation. The head of the agency wants to ensure that everything goes perfectly during the exercise. He appoints a committee of managers to prepare all aspects of the project. He provides them with a budget to enable them to achieve their objective. He invites city officials and other important people to attend the exercise as observers. He also invites the media to cover the event. Given such a situation, it is likely that the Full Field-Training Exercise will be a success. Everyone, ranging from top city officials to the newest agency employee, will leave the exercise with a sense of confidence that the department can properly respond to a major crisis. Agency managers spend the weeks following the exercise patting themselves on the back rather than addressing problems that the trainer should have identified. When an actual crisis does occur, the agency finds itself in chaos.

If a Full Field-Training Exercise is to be truly meaningful, it should be conducted in the same manner as a response to an actual crisis. It makes little sense for a department to borrow a corporate conference facility for a training command center when such a location would not be available for use during a real crisis. Likewise, it makes no sense to rent all kinds of radio and communications equipment from an electronics company if this equipment could not actually be procured when an actual crisis had to be addressed. Similarly, cancelling all leave and rearranging work schedules to ensure that everyone in the department can be involved in the exercise may sound like good training logic, but it does not prepare the agency for what will probably occur during an actual crisis.

One agency staged an elaborate crisis training exercise that involved several hundred employees. The agency head appointed a team of managers, who spent months preparing for the event. The agency procured an ideal command center location. Vacations were canceled, and employee schedules were altered to ensure that everyone could be involved. The exercise was a great success, as was mirrored by the glowing comments made by managers and employees during a post-exercise meeting. Many agency employees left with a feeling of confidence that their agency could rapidly and effectively respond to any crisis.

Unfortunately, the exercise was totally unrealistic. In fact, the agency did not have a command center, and had no plans to procure one. Instead, they planned on using a small conference room in their office to run operations. The command center used during the exercise was located 40 miles from the agency's office, and would almost certainly not be used during an actual crisis. The furnishings in the training command center all belonged to the firm that owned the building. The agency itself was short of furniture, and could not properly equip a command center even if it was able to procure one. Some of the communication equipment used in the training was borrowed. In addition, the technicians spent several days installing the equipment prior to the exercise. Ironically, despite the many preparations, various communication problems occurred during the exercise. However, when these shortcomings were mentioned by participants, management discounted them, saying that they were "unique" to the area where the command center was located. They were confident that the problems would not occur during an actual crisis, because the command center would be located in their own office.

Practice exercises should use the facilities and equipment that an agency plans to use in an actual crisis situation. These should be outlined in an agency's contingency plan. Facilitators should demand this. Managers and employees should be forced to practice with what they have available. If nothing else comes from the training session, perhaps the attendees can devise ways to overcome their limited resources. In fact, in situations in which it is obvious that there are resource problems, the facilitator should use frequent "time out" periods during which he addresses the inadequacies and attempts to seek solutions to them. These problems may involve major impediments, including insufficient space to hold assigned employees, computer inadequacies, or communications shortcomings. Other problems could be irritants, including poor ventilation, noise, inadequate parking, or the lack of food, water, or restrooms.

Leadership and Crisis Preparation

An agency that prepares itself to deal with a crisis situation will almost certainly have more success in meeting an actual emergency than an agency that makes no preparations. However, contingency plans, mutual aid agreements, Tabletop training, and full-fledged crisis exercises are only as valuable as the ranking members of a law enforcement agency allow them to be. It is an agency's leadership that creates the atmosphere through which a department approaches a crisis. All too often, egos and lack of competence within the leadership negate what has been gained from practice sessions, and what has been outlined in well-written contingency plans. The top leader in an agency must make decisions. If, for some reason, he fails to do so, or makes himself unavailable to make decisions, the entire response to the crisis can be negatively affected. Secondary leaders often view a crisis as an opportunity for them to demonstrate their ability and to impress their superiors. While there is nothing wrong with this, it is important that these people also fulfill their assignments. Unfortunately, some try to make a good impression by trying to perform what they view as high-profile tasks, even though these tasks are not within their area of assignment. Others try to remain in close proximity to their superior, which causes them to neglect their own area of responsibility.

In one crisis situation, the overall leader came upon an investigator who had just developed an important piece of information. Responding to the leader's inquiry, the investigator told him about the information. The secondary leader, under whom this investigator worked, became quite upset when he learned about the investigator's conversation with the top leader. The secondary leader was heard muttering in anger, "What's left for me to tell him?"

In this situation, the secondary leader wanted to make a name for himself, and thought that he could best do this by personally informing the top leader of big developments in the case. In fact, this secondary leader spent so much time trying to position himself close to the top leader and to function as something of a "town crier" with respect to information that he failed to perform many aspects of his own assignment.

If a department is to perform well during a crisis, the leader must do his job, and must ensure that his subordinates do their jobs. A few weak management personnel can greatly hamper, if not destroy, a department's investigation of a major crisis situation. Top managers must ensure that competent employees are where they belong. In a crisis, members of an agency must function as a team. Each element of the department must support the other. The failure of one unit within a crisis command center can have a negative impact on all other units represented in that center. For example, a weak legal counsel component can stall everything from the investigators on the street to SWAT operations. Ineptitude from a manager responsible for technical support can slow the investigators, hostage negotiators, SWAT, and even the mechanical operations of the command center itself. A neglectful manager in charge of intelligence gathering can cause those assigned to cover leads to perform unnecessary work, and place investigators in danger.

An agency head must make certain that his management personnel are assigned where they are best suited and needed. It makes no sense to place the manager who heads the police motor pool in charge of tactics or lead coverage, when a crisis response clearly dictates that vehicles will serve a vital role. Similarly, it would be illogical to assign the lieutenant who heads the department's intelligence division to manage the media desk in the command center. Yet these things happen. If a department has a squad that handles terrorism investigations, the manager of that unit must play an important role in a terrorism-related crisis. That person cannot be tied to a managerial assignment in the command center that is unrelated to his or her area of expertise. If he or she must be assigned to a position in the command center, he or she should be assigned to head the intelligence desk or to be in charge of basic investigation. An agency head would be wise to give the terrorism manager a great deal of leeway with respect to specific assignments in a crisis situation. The agency head may find that he is best served by having his terrorism manager function as an advisor reporting directly to him. In that way, the terrorism manager could provide expert counsel to the agency head while at the same time being able to give direction to his squad, which should consist of the most knowledgeable terrorism personnel in the department.

The joint terrorism task force already has a management structure, and that should be taken into consideration with respect to formulating a management staff during a terrorist crisis. These people should be assigned so that their unique expertise is exploited. If the task force is large and already has a manager in charge of intelligence gathering, it does not make sense to assign another department manager to handle this responsibility during a terrorist attack crisis. Similarly, the investigators on the task force have both the training and experience in conducting investigations involving terrorism. They should be assigned to handle significant leads.

Summary

All agencies should prepare for crisis situations. This is especially true for agencies that are likely to face a terrorist attack. Large cities fall into this category. Law enforcement agencies should have contingency plans that outline responsibilities in the occurrence of a major crisis. It is important that these contingency plans be tested through Tabletop and Full Field-Training exercises. Leadership is a key element to any crisis response. It is important that everyone involved be aware of the leadership structure that will operate during a crisis. If a joint terrorism task force is active in the area, it should be factored into an agency's terrorist attack response plan.

SECTION V
The Future

28 The Future of Terrorism Investigation

The very phenomenon and nature of terrorism has changed dramatically during the past 100 years. Modern technology has made it possible for virtually anyone, living almost anywhere, to perpetrate a meaningful terrorist attack. The objective of the terrorist is to use fear to make the government or population change its direction with respect to whatever the extremist desires. For some political extremists, the change being sought is drastic, and involves major alterations in how the population will live. For many other extremists, the desired changes are fairly specific in nature, and do not require the overthrow of the government, and will not greatly alter the way in which most people live their lives. The terrorist is impatient. He want the change to occur immediately. He is also not usually interested in compromise. He wants everything that he demands, not just part of it.

Almost everyone is upset about something. The concerns may range from broad topics, including a lack of meaningful employment, the rising cost of living, high taxes, the inability to receive a good education, or maybe even fears for retirement security, to more specific complaints about such concerns as the local river being polluted, the presence of an abortion clinic in town, unfair zoning laws, or a store selling furs. In the distant past—100 years ago or more—there was little the average person could do about issues that upset him. And what action he could take garnered little more than localized publicity, and maybe not much of that. If the person became so upset that he decided that he wanted to perpetrate a violent action to express his anger and force a change, he usually lacked the knowledge and weaponry to do much more than token damage, or attack a government official in such a manner as to ensure being arrested. Furthermore, the would-be militant or revolutionary of past centuries was often isolated from others in the state or country who harbored similar concerns, and who might have been willing to join him in a conspiracy if they had been aware of it.

During the latter part of the twentieth century and the early part of the twenty-first century, the primary factors that previously limited people from turning to terrorism fell by the wayside. Today an average person who becomes extremely upset about an issue can perpetrate horrific violence in order to express his anger and exert pressure for a change. A great deal of knowledge with respect to the use of potent weapons, including explosives and incendiaries, is but a few clicks of a computer mouse away from almost anyone in the country. This is assuming that the angry person cannot glean the right information from the television, radio, movies, and the print media. Of course, some people already possess knowledge that can be used for terrorist purposes. They may have learned it in college or technical schools or in the military. Publicity for what the person has done can be almost instantaneous, and can quickly spread across the country. The angry farmer upset over a factory that is polluting the river near his home can be assured that if he bombs the target of his anger and issues a communication outlining his reasons for the attack, he will receive widespread, possibly even worldwide, publicity for his action. If before or after his violent expression, he chooses to join together with like-minded people, or join a group dedicated to addressing similar pollution problems, the Internet allows him to do so with relative ease. If the farmer does not know how to attack, current communications technology certainly permits him to rapidly learn without anyone else even being aware of what he is doing. In fact, he might be able to actually get like-minded people to come to his area and conduct the attack for him.

The objective of the terrorist is to use fear to force a change. Modern technology has made it relatively easy to carry out actions that will accomplish this end. In many ways, if the person can conjure up in his imagination an action that will frighten people in general or his target in particular, he can probably find a way to perpetrate an attack that will capitalize on that fear. The September 11, 2001, attackers used commercial airliners, filled with innocent people and loaded with enough fuel to make cross-country journeys, as airborne missiles to attack the World Trade Center and the Pentagon. Undoubtedly, in the case of the World Trade Center, the terrorists hoped that the structures would topple over onto other large New York buildings, causing even more mayhem than actually did occur. The modern terrorist needs do little more than watch a few hours of television or take a walk or drive around his town in order to compile a list of targets worthy of attack—a taxi running into a group of people on a sidewalk, a train derailing into a church or school located near the track, poison spread onto fresh produce in a grocery store, random shootings into crowded market places, acid thrown into the face of a city official, a bridge leading into the town being knocked out of commission, the town's electricity, water, or gas being suddenly terminated, a crowded restaurant being bombed, or a movie theatre being torched during an evening showing. These are the types of things that one could envision that could paralyze a town with fear. Sadly, in the modern world it would not take a great deal of time or skill to accomplish most of the aforementioned forms of attack, if the angry person were so inclined.

Even as recently as four decades ago, most law enforcement agencies in the United States did not even have to consider the threat of terrorist attack as an issue of concern. This is no longer the case. While it is true that certain areas of the country are more likely to be struck by criminal political extremists, the fact is that just about anyplace can be the target of an attack. Instead of assuring themselves that no self-respecting terrorist would attack their jurisdiction, law enforcement officials everywhere must now be constantly vigilant for targets within their jurisdiction, and for issues that might cause a person to stage an attack in their area. This requires that law enforcement officers be knowledgeable about the kinds of targets that terrorist groups are presently attacking, or threatening to attack, in order to protect such locations and people in their community. It requires these officials to know how to recognize a terrorist attack when it does occur, because it could sometimes be mistaken for vandalism, hooliganism, or straight criminal activity. It necessitates that the law enforcement authorities know how to respond to a terrorist attack, and from whom to receive assistance in conducting their investigation. Every law enforcement agency in the country should know where their nearest joint terrorism task force is located, and be aware of how to contact it.

The Nature of the Current Threat

Between January 1, 2000 and the beginning of 2008 there have been about 500 political extremist terrorist attacks inside the United States, Most of these were perpetrated by animal rights extremists with environmental (or eco) radicals causing the next highest number. Early in the twenty-first century there were more than 35 attacks generated by opponents of agricultural genetic engineering. The last of these attacks occurred in December 2005. There have been about 20 attacks each perpetrated by apparent anarchists and anti-abortion extremists during the twenty-first century. The attacks of September 11, 2001, were conducted by international terrorists. Rounding out the attacks during the twenty-first century have been several right-wing activist incidents.

Single-Issue/Special Interest. In many respects, single-issue or special-interest terrorism is a modern phenomenon. Pure activists falling into this area are not attempting to overthrow a government or make drastic widespread changes in society. There is a specific issue that has so agitated them that they have elected to use violence in order to foster the change that they desire. Often these people support the government and, indeed, rely on a strong government to pass laws that will accomplish their objective. While the issues promulgated by true single-issue extremists are clear and easily definable, they are not always the exclusive domain of the special-interest activist. Anti-abortion is a single-issue terrorist concern. However, some white supremacist right-wing extremists also oppose abortion. Of course, their interest in this issue is a little different from that of the single-issue activist, because right-wing extremists often only want to see the abortion of white fetuses outlawed. They have little concern for non-white babies.

More recently, it has become difficult to discern the true nature of some of the activists engaged in animal rights and environmental causes. While many of these extremists truly fall into the single-issue category, others are really left-wing anarchists who see the evils of capitalism causing the destruction of the environment and the abuse of animals. There seems to be little question that anarchists are targeting animal and ecological activists for recruitment into their much broader political agenda. Clearly, some anarchists have heavily committed themselves to ecological and animal rights issues. Anarchists usually argue that the changes that animal rights and ecological extremists seek are only going to happen if the morally corrupt capitalist government is overthrown.

There has been a violent aspect to the anti-abortion movement for two decades, and abortion providers have been murdered. By contrast, animal rights, ecological, and anti-genetic engineering activists have traditionally made it clear that they are opposed to causing injury or death to human beings. However, some people involved in these movements in the early twenty-first century have expressed a belief that it is permissible to perpetrate violent attacks against the perpetrators of abuses against the environment or animals, and those who protect them. It remains to be seen if violent actions against people will become commonplace in the animal rights, ecological, and anti-genetic engineering areas. In late 2003, animal rights activists claimed responsibility for two bombings targeting companies in California that had relationships with animal testing firm, Huntingdon Life Sciences. Even though the devices did little damage, and seemingly were not meant to harm anyone, they nonetheless represented a great stride in the direction of increased violence in the animal movement. The fact that there was not a hue and cry among animal rights extremists in opposition to these bombings suggests that many people had no objection to this shift in direction of the clandestine movement.

The vast majority of the approximately 500 terrorist attacks that have occurred in the United States during the twenty-first century were committed by single-issue extremists. Within that category, animal rights activists have committed the largest number of attacks with environmental, or ecological, militants falling into second place in the number of attacks, but being very possibly in first place with respect to the damage caused by their violent actions. Most of the animal and environmental attacks involved vandalism although both factions also employed arson as a tactic, These militants have made it clear that their intent is to cause economic damage as opposed to harming people. Some of the attacks carried out by these factions have resulted in little damage and have been more of a nuisance than anything else. However, other attacks have caused millions of dollars in damage and/or resulted in the losses of years of research that could not be replaced. Indeed, the August 1, 2003, Earth Liberation Front (ELF)-claimed arson of a nearly completed condominium complex in San Diego, California, resulted in a loss of some $50 million, and would have to be considered in economic terms as one of the worse terrorist attacks in United States history. By liberating animals, activists have put some fur farmers out of business. Extremist attacks on some laboratories have resulted in the loss of years of research on which no value can be placed.

From 2005 to 2008 the law enforcement community made great strides with respect to solving animal and environmental attacks, and in stopping conspiracies to perpetrate new violent actions. A number of arrests were made that resulted in convictions and lengthy prison terms. Significant attacks, particularly from the late 1990s and early 2000s, were solved. Undoubtedly, these law enforcement successes have shaken these extremist movements. During the 1980s, 1990s, and early 2000s, most animal and environment attacks were not solved. There were few arrests, and those that did happen often resulted in lesser punishments. As people began to be arrested in 2005 the numbers of attacks dropped dramatically. The number of attacks in 2006 was only a third of those that happened in 2005 and less than half of 2004. The total number of attacks in 2007 was higher than 2006, but still less than half of 2005. Furthermore, most of the 2006 and 2007 attacks were nuisance in nature.

It remains to be seen if either the radical extremist animal or environmental movements will be able to regenerate themselves to perpetrate the number of attacks that they did during the 1990s and early 2000s. Both of these movements have come to rely heavily on the concept of "leaderless resistance" wherein they present their platform and recommended methods, and encourage sympathetic people to commit acts of their own. The fact that in the past few perpetrators of attacks were ever identified or prosecuted, certainly encouraged people to commit acts on behalf of the movement. The recent arrests not only demonstrated that security from arrest is no longer guaranteed, but it also showed that these movements do not really have the ability to do much to help those who have been arrested other than to lend them moral support.

Most anti-abortion activism consists of protest demonstrations. However, there has been an average of at least two abortion clinic attacks each year during the twenty-first century. Most have involved actual or attempted arsons. There have also been four actual or attempted bombings and five incidents in which unknown people have fired into closed clinics. Although several abortion providers were shot and killed or wounded during the 1990s, the last such incident in the United States was the sniper murder of Dr. Barnett Slepian at his Amherst, New York, home on October 23, 1998.

Left-Wing. Left-wing extremists seek to overthrow the present form of government and replace it with a socialist state in which all people would be equal and the means of production would be commonly owned. During the 1960s, 1970s, and the early 1980s, this form of political violence was common in the United States. Groups like the Weather Underground Organization, the New World Liberation Front, the United Freedom Front, and the Armed Resistance Unit all perpetrated violent attacks, usually bombings, in an effort to promulgate their agenda, which included the overthrow of the capitalist government. The end of the war in Vietnam, the decline and eventual downfall of the Soviet Union, and the successes of the American law enforcement community all combined to bring this threat to an end.

During the 1990s and into the twenty-first century a more modern form of left-wing threat arose in the form of anarchy. In the extreme, these people do not want any form of government, and believe that all people should be self-governing and essentially islands unto themselves, associating with others only as they choose. Because these people oppose formalized organization and government, they are not likely to join together in large structured groups. However, they will battle their enemy in less formal, short-term entities, such as black blocs formed to confront authorities and commit violence during protest demonstrations. Many modern anarchists are less than thrilled at being labeled as "leftist," and a larger number do not like to be referred to as "communists." In fact some believe that, historically, communists have overthrown dictatorial governments only to assume totalitarian positions themselves under the guise of having to rule until the people have been educated to function in the new society. In that sense, they see communists as hypocrites who do not practice what they preach. Given the size of the population presently on earth, it is difficult for modern anarchists to truly believe that humankind can live with absolutely no government. Consequently, many seem to be promulgating a socialist view of very limited government on a local basis with direct democratic procedures being followed. In short, no representatives speak for the people. They tend to speak of such bodies as town meetings and tribal councils functioning as forums where people can resolve issues that affect them. At the very least, it is fair to say that most anarchists in the United States today believe that the capitalist form of government is wrong and exploitative. During the early twenty-first century, some anarchists, or people claiming to follow this philosophy, have attacked government structures in protest of the war in Iraq, and have become involved in violent ecology-related attacks concerning road and house construction, and off-road vehicles. While twenty-first-century anarchists are often concerned with environmental and animal rights issues, it would be unfair to conclude that all ecological and animal rights activists are anarchists.

Right-Wing. The right wing in the United States encompasses a variety of philosophies that are generally opposite from left-wing views, but are not necessarily similar to one another. Some people characterized as right-wing extremists are neo-Nazi in direction, and seek a strong central government that will cater to a special class of people to the disdain of others. This would be similar to the Aryans of World War II Germany, and their efforts to dominate the Jewish and Gypsy populations of that country and countries that Germany conquered. However, other people generally characterized as being right wing in nature are opposed to any strong centralized government. Indeed, some are against any government at all, and are more anarchist than they are neo-Nazi. Some right-wing activists believe that there is an imminent takeover threat from the peoples of the world in the form of the United Nations. More recently a few right-wing activists have expressed fears that there is a secret conspiracy afoot to merge the United States, Canada, and Mexico into a single nation. Some right-wing extremists are strong constitutionalists who believe that the true nature of that document has been subverted over time, and that what the government practices today is very different from what our founding fathers intended when they formulated that Constitution. Other anti-government activists do not even believe that the Constitution was properly ratified in the first place, because they claim that the Articles of Confederation were never properly repealed. The English common law is very important to many right-wing activists who believe that this tradition and the Magna Carta and the English Bill of Rights essentially assure that each person is a self-governing or a sovereign citizen, not subject to any centralized government. By the mid-twenty-first century, many right-wing militants became concerned with illegal immigrants coming into the country from Mexico. Because these people believe that such immigrants have Indian blood in their veins, they do not accept them as being of the white race, and therefore, they do not want them coming into the country.

Regardless of the foundation of their beliefs, many right-wing extremists have similar objectives, fears, and hatreds. Anti-the-present-government is common. Fear that foreigners, minorities, or Jewish people have, or are going to, take over the government is typical. The belief in white supremacy is a factor that unites many right-wing people, as is the feeling that the country's borders should be closed to non-whites. Another fear that brings these people together is the belief that the government will take away citizens' guns, thereby leaving the average citizen at the mercy of the government, stated and unstated oppressors, minorities, and criminals.

Those who believe that the government is illegal or has been subverted often want nothing to do with it. To accomplish this objective, they refuse to allow themselves to be subject to anything that they regard as being a contract with the government. Common manifestations of this include refusal to obtain a driver's license or license plates for their vehicle. Failing to file income tax returns or pay property taxes is also a part of the protest against the "illegal" government. Some do not even want their births to be recorded with the government, and will add punctuation marks into their names to differentiate themselves from the "blind" followers of the government.

The right-wing movement in the United States had seen a great change during the twenty-first century. Old-time revered national leaders like Dr. William Pierce and Richard Butler have died and no one has risen to their stature to replace them. The large extremist groups like the National Alliance and the Aryan Nations weakened when their leaders, Pierce and Butler, respectively, died. The latter group barely exists in 2008 and the former group has undergone at least two splits and is a shell of what it once was. The white supremacist World Church of the Creator (WCOTC), which was to subsequently change its name to the Creativity Movement, all but vanished when its leader Matt Hale was sentenced to 40 years in prison in 2005 for conspiring to kill a federal judge.

During the twenty-first century there have only been a handful of relatively minor terrorist attacks perpetrated by right-wing extremists. However, this fact is misleading in that the law enforcement community across the country has been highly successful in stopping right-wing conspiracies and arresting and prosecuting the people involved in them. There is little doubt that had law enforcement not been so successful there would have been a number of attacks perpetrated by these people

International. The international terrorist threat become a major concern for the law enforcement community in the United States following the attacks of September 11, 2001. This is not to say that the potential for attack was not already known to police agencies before that attack. The world has been ever "shrinking" with the rapid advances in transportation and communication. Virtually every ethnic and religious group in the world has some form of representation in the United States. Many of the more recent immigrants came to the United States because of political problems that existed in their homelands. Although they may have immigrated to America to establish a new life, they still have relatives and friends in their native land, and they harbor allegiances and sympathies with respect to the political problems of that area of the world. Any of the people from volatile parts of the world can become involved in situations in United States related to their homeland. They could be targeted for funds, or asked to assist a fleeing militant, or enlisted to help procure weapons. They could become involved in actual conflicts in the country with respect to such tasks as attacking enemies from their homeland who have also come to the United States. Or they could attack their former nation's diplomats or their establishments in America. They could continue the battles of their former country from the shores of the United States—traveling to the former home to perpetrate an attack and then returning to the safety of their adopted country. In the 1970s and 1980s, United States law enforcement officers investigated Serbs, Croats, Armenians, and Sikhs living in the United States for their involvement in terrorist incidents, including attacks on foreign diplomats, directly arising from problems in their native countries.

Of course, United States government and corporate interests abroad have been attacked over the decades, especially by Islamic extremists during the past 15 to 20 years. The September 11, 2001, attacks made it clear that at least some of the world's terrorists were no longer satisfied with striking America at a distance. It served as a wake-up call that the mainland of the country could be attacked. It was not long before law enforcement agencies began discovering cells of people in the United States who were preparing to commit attacks. On October 21, 2002, six men of Yemeni origin who were United States citizens living in the area of Lackawanna, New York, were charged in a federal grand jury indictment with providing material support to a foreign terrorist organization. They admitted to having received training at an al Qaeda terrorist camp in Afghanistan for the purpose of someday staging attacks in the United States. The six men subsequently pleaded guilty, and during December 2003 all were sentenced to prison terms ranging from seven years to ten years in custody.

As with right-wing extremists, the law enforcement community has been successful during recent years with respect to identifying and arresting international terrorists who have been conspiring to perpetrate attacks in the United States. In May 2007, government agents arrested five men of foreign birth on charges of allegedly plotting to kill soldiers at the Fort Dix Army base in New Jersey. Only weeks later, in a totally unrelated case, authorities arrested members of an Islamic militant cell on charges that they were allegedly plotting to blow up a major jet fuel line under the John F. Kennedy International Airport in New York. Clearly, if these conspiracies and the various similar conspiracies that law enforcement officers have disrupted during the past eight years had not been interrupted, vast amounts of destruction and many deaths would have resulted from the violent attacks that these people had planned.

There is every reason to believe that international terrorism will continue to present a threat, both internally and externally. There are and will continue to be groups of foreign people in the United States who could perpetrate an attack on the country. Similarly, there will be people who will try to enter the country from abroad in order to stage an attack, after which they will leave. In the latter situation, there is no question that an attack of that nature would be classified as international terrorism. In the former case, the issue is not as clear. It could be argued that if the attack takes place in the United States by people who actually live in the United States, it is a domestic terrorist attack even though the cause involved a largely foreign issue. For the law enforcement community, the concern is more the crime than it is an issue of foreign versus domestic. The investigators must address the attack with immediacy and professionalism, because the fear generated in the community will demand such a response.

Also of concern with respect to international terrorism is the United States-born citizen who comes to accept a foreign militant philosophy and elects to perpetrate attacks in the United States on his own, on behalf of the philosophy. In December 2006, law enforcement authorities arrested a U.S.-born man who had converted to Islam and allegedly became convinced that he should stage terrorist attacks in the United States. He was taken into custody because he had conspired to procure hand grenades that he intended to use in an attack in a shopping mall in Illinois during the Christmas shopping period.

The Law Enforcement Response to the Terrorist Threat

The law enforcement community enjoyed a good deal of success in dealing with left-wing and right-wing terrorists during the 1980s and early 1990s. However, single-issue violence—particularly in the areas of animal rights and environmental issues, was a different story. Very few of the many hundreds of attacks, ranging from minor vandalism to major arsons, were solved, and most have seen their statute of limitations pass without a clue being developed. The leaderless resistance nature of these movements appears to be one of the major reasons for their success. By spreading their philosophy on the Internet, and telling sympathizers to use the group's name in attacking a logical target, these causes have presented the law enforcement community with a significant challenge. Compounding the problem is the fact that various Internet sites set up by activists direct would-be attackers to logical targets, and tell them how to perpetrate an attack. They even go so far as to explain how to avoid arrest and prosecution when they actually perpetrate an attack. Things changed in 2005 when the law enforcement community charged a number of people in several different states with serious felonies. The number of attacks dropped dramatically in the years 2006 and 2007 seemingly because of the many arrests.

The law enforcement community can successfully address the terrorism problem in the United States. The willingness to share information and work as a team—something that arose in the aftermath of the September 11, 2001 attacks—will go far to address the challenge. It is important that the joint terrorism task forces established in all parts of the country since 2001 be kept in operation, and that logical investigative agencies continue to provide manpower to them. Responding to terrorist attacks in a proper, organized manner, and conducting exhaustive crime scene investigations will pay off in success in the long run. Using modern technology, including computers and the Internet, is also certain to prove valuable. Prosecuting the crime in a manner that truly reflects the serious nature of the crime and its impact on the community will have a chilling effect on potential recruits who today believe that they either will not be apprehended or will escape with a slap on the wrist.

Appendix ⬤I

What to Do in Response to a Terrorist Attack

Most terrorist attacks in the United States, outside of the liberation of animals, will involve the use of explosives, incendiaries, or chemicals (such as stink bombs and acid), or extreme forms of vandalism. Kidnappings, physical assaults, airplane hijackings, and assassinations are more common outside of the United States than they are in the country, although personal attacks have occurred in the United States in the area of anti-abortion extremism. The September 11, 2001 attacks involved suicide bombers—a factor that led some in law enforcement to believe that people blowing themselves up in an effort to kill people and damage property would become a problem for the United States. As a matter of fact, during the period between 2004 and 2007, suicide attacks around the world have averaged well over one instance each day. However, this form of terrorism has not become popular within the United States itself although such attackers have targeted U.S. troops in both Iraq and Afghanistan. As the year 2008 commenced, the September 11, 2001, attacks remained the only terrorist suicide attacks that occurred in the Unites States during the twenty-first century.

Law enforcement agencies, especially those in parts of the country where political extremists are known to be active, should have contingency plans in place that articulate the kind of response that the agency will take in the event of a terrorist attack. All of the suggestions below should be addressed in these plans either in generalities or in specific detail. The contingency plan should clearly outline the command structure that will be utilized to direct a terrorist attack investigation.

The contingency plan should call for the establishment of a command center, and describe, at least by position, if not by name, the personnel who will operate the command center. If, at the time of a terrorist attack, an agency has no contingency plan, its leadership should nonetheless immediately establish a command center to direct the investigation. If some form of command center is not created, it is unlikely that many of the suggestions

435

below will be properly executed. In fact, it is probable that various investigators/agencies will compete to cover the most logical leads and responsibilities as outlined below, while neglecting lesser duties, to the overall detriment of the investigation.

In areas where several law enforcement agencies will logically respond to a terrorist incident, it is imperative that these agencies establish guidelines under which to function in harmony in response to an attack. Preferably these agencies will create contingency plans that address a multi-agency response. If a joint terrorism task force is operational in an area (and most metropolitan areas now have such entities as a consequence of the September 11, 2001, attacks), any contingency plan that is formulated must factor in the responsibilities, expertise, and authority of the task force. It makes no sense for an agency to participate in a joint terrorism task force, yet ignore it in their contingency plan and actual response to a terrorist attack.

Below are suggestions for what the responding agency and its investigators should do when a terrorist attack occurs within its jurisdiction:

Render assistance as required to the victims of the attack. As much as investigators might be tempted to begin their crime scene investigation, the victims must be given first consideration. In many instances the assistance will consist of helping paramedics and other first responders as they attempt to aid and move the injured people from the scene.

Remember that the victims are also a part of the crime scene. Their bodies and clothing may contain evidence. Furthermore, they may have seen the perpetrators, or possibly have been the specific target of the attack. For these reasons it is important that investigators be assigned to monitor where the victims have been taken so that appropriate follow-up investigation can be undertaken. If it is not practical for an investigator to accompany a victim as he is taken from the scene, investigators should at least request that medical specialists preserve the victims' clothing and other foreign materials located on their persons. If little information with respect to what has happened is available, it may be desirable for investigators to attempt to briefly interview victims at the scene or in an ambulance en route to the hospital, provided that such action will not cause further harm to them.

Secure the crime scene. Obviously, emergency personnel, including firefighters, bomb technicians, and medical specialists must have access to the crime scene area until they have completed their missions. However, it is important that other people be kept out of the crime scene. In some situations, unauthorized people may have to be restrained or arrested if they attempt to enter the secure area.

Film the crime scene with both still and video cameras. Once the crime scene has been disturbed, it has been forever altered. Consequently, it is important to have a record of the way it originally was found.

Film the crowd. Although in a terrorist case it is unlikely that the perpetrators will remain in the area to see the damage, it is possible that the device initiated prematurely, and the responsible parties were unable to flee. More importantly, such a film will make a record of possible witnesses to the incident who may leave the scene before investigators can interview them.

Begin interviews with actual and possible witnesses at the earliest opportunity. If nothing else, attempt to obtain the names, home and employment addresses, telephone (including cell phone) numbers, and e-mail addresses of potential witnesses so that they can be contacted when sufficient resources are available.

Immediately set out leads to conduct appropriate investigation. This must be done if the initial interviews of possible witnesses yield intelligence of value, or if the initial survey of the crime scene gives reason for rapid follow-up investigation. Setting leads with appropriate dispatch should continue throughout the crime scene investigation and could result in the capture of the terrorist before he can make a clean get-away—as an example, Oklahoma City bomber Timothy McVeigh.

Before entering a bomb crime scene, ensure that a trained explosives technician surveys the area for secondary devices. This is a real danger in terrorism cases. Many terrorists view law enforcement as the enemy, and therefore could have placed delayed bombs deliberately intended to injure law enforcement officers and first responders. It is alleged that former FBI Ten Most Wanted Fugitive, Eric Rudolph, did this in two of his bombing attacks. Also, in any bombing there may be more than one device placed by the terrorist. The first bomb may have somehow jarred the other devices so that they did not explode as planned. A subsequent disturbance of such a damaged device by an investigator could cause it to detonate.

Through experts, including the fire department, bomb technicians, and building owners/managers, determine if there is anything of a dangerous nature at the crime scene that should be addressed prior to crime scene investigators entering the location. It makes little sense to inadvertently broaden the scope of harm caused by the terrorist attack by having investigators injured or killed while conducting the crime scene investigation. Dangers could involve structural problems, toxic chemicals, or contaminants such as asbestos and PCBs. By aware that in the months and years following the September 11, 2001, attack on the World Trade Center, many of the crime scene workers and emergency responders reported various respiratory problems allegedly due to inadequate protective equipment.

Formulate a plan of action with respect to the crime scene. Once a crime scene has been entered, it will never be the same. Consequently, the crime scene investigation must be organized and coordinated. Responsibilities should be assigned, and investigators should be properly equipped and trained to do their jobs. If the right investigators are not available, wait until they are before entering the crime scene. All activities should be carefully documented, and all evidence clearly labeled as to its origin and the person who recovered it. Continuous filming should be considered during the crime scene investigation, especially with respect to the recovery of important pieces of evidence.

It is important that unauthorized people be kept out of the secure crime scene. These people can include everyone from law enforcement officers and managers who are not involved in the crime scene investigation, to the news media, building owners, and curious citizens. It is equally important, though sometimes overlooked, that no one take "souvenirs" from the crime scene.

Crime scene personnel must make a concerted effort not to contaminate the crime scene. Clothing worn into the scene must be clean and not contain foreign materials that came from another crime scene. This is particularly important if there are several crime scenes and investigators are moving between them. Prepackaged and unused coveralls are highly recommended.

A good neighborhood investigation must be initiated to locate witnesses as soon as possible. Anyone in the area of an attack could be a witness—including the homeless, prostitutes, and other street people. Remember that people in the area who did not actually see the crime or anything directly related to it still could be of value, because they might be able to identify others who were in the vicinity, and who might have been eyewitnesses to the crime.

Security video cameras located on the target building and on surrounding buildings should be checked to determine if they recorded the incident and perpetrators. Efforts should immediately be made to retrieve these videotapes to ensure that they are entered into evidence, and to keep them out of the hands of the media. If a logical route of entry and escape can be determined, efforts should be made to identify security cameras on that route, and to secure their film. Remember that closed-circuit television cameras have become so common in the twenty-first century that it is highly likely that there are some cameras in the proximity of almost every terrorist attack—especially those in metropolitan areas. Due to the present relatively low cost of such cameras, some private citizens have them "patroling" their residences; consequently, if the attack has occurred in a residential area, efforts should be made to locate home and apartment owners who are using such cameras for security.

Any claims of credit, especially in written form, should receive immediate attention. This may involve efforts to recover the original written communiqué or to trace a telephonic or e-mail claim. Web sites that may function as spokespersons for known terrorist groups should be monitored for claims of credit.

Intelligence bases within the agency and other law enforcement agencies should be queried about the names of any groups or individuals developed as possible perpetrators of the attack.

Review extremist materials and the Internet. Web sites, magazines, "e-zines," and extremist newspapers should be studied for any information about the incident. Some may contain claims of credit, others may have stories in support of, or opposed to, the attack. Depending upon the situation, the very fact that certain publications do not have stories concerning the incident may be of some significance.

Monitor legitimate news services, including television, radio, and newspapers for information on the attack. Because the Internet is widely used by the media of the twenty-first century, go to Web sites of the various forms of media where there may be stories and film footage of the incident.

Ensure that the victim of the crime has been notified of the attack. Determining who is the victim may not be as simple as it appears. The victim may be the owner/operator of the structure that was attacked. However, in the case of a large commercial building, or even a sizable government facility, the actual victim could be a single tenant. When the specific victim has been identified (usually through a claim of credit from the perpetrator, or through police intelligence), he should quickly be interviewed. He may have been threatened in the past, and/or he may have some knowledge about the identities of the perpetrators. Also, he may own/manage other locations that could possibly require immediate protection. Remember that conducting investigation through neighbors, closed-circuit television cameras, and other techniques at these other victim-associated locations might yield information about the terrorist group. It is possible that the group may have cased several locations related to the victim before settling on the one that they did strike.

Make certain that all evidence has been removed from the crime scene before the location is returned to its owner. Evidence found later by the owner or someone else may not be admissible in court because the chain of custody may be considered to have been broken when investigators left the crime scene.

Appendix ⓘ

What *Not* to Do in Response to a Terrorist Attack

Do not deny that an attack has occurred. This is especially true in cases in which the evidence of the attack is visible, and a known terrorist group has claimed credit for it. Denying it is not going to make the attack disappear. However, downplaying it can reduce the priority that agency investigators give to the incident, and it can restrict the amount of assistance the community will voluntarily offer to help solve the crime. It will also hinder other law enforcement agencies from entering the investigation when they might be able to provide valuable help. Denying a terrorist attack and the resultant failure to notify the appropriate joint terrorism task force of it, could cost the jurisdiction the services of an entity that could be of great value in addressing the crime.

Do not assume that evidence of value will not be found at the crime scene just because there is a huge amount of destruction. Physical evidence is vital to solving terrorist crimes. Experience has repeatedly shown that valuable items of evidence can even be recovered from crime scenes as massive as the World Trade Center attacks of 1993 and 2001, and the Murrah Federal Building bombing in 1995.

Do not yield to the temptation to clean up the crime scene as quickly as possible in order to give the citizens the impression that the terrorists have not hurt the city. Doing this can lead to the loss of valuable evidence. It can also cause investigators to believe that the incident does not warrant the kind of attention that it should receive.

Do not rule out terrorism as the motivation behind an attack just because the target does not appear to make "common sense," especially if a viable terrorist group has claimed credit for the incident. What makes sense to an extremist may not make sense to the average citizen. What will make a terrorist feel the need to commit a violent attack may not be something that would cause a similar response in the average citizen. In addition, terrorists have been known to hit locations by mistake or through improper intelligence concerning the target. Some animal activists have struck at otherwise innocent and uninvolved targets whose only mistake is that they provide a service to the entity that the terrorists actually oppose.

Do not discount a claim by a group that it perpetrated a terrorist attack just because the victim has not reported it. And do not assume that a victim will always report a terrorist attack. Some victims will not inform authorities of a terrorist attack for a variety of reasons, including fear of more attacks, concern for loss of insurance, and unwanted publicity for what it is that their business really does—such as using animals for tests. Some victims, particularly those in remote areas, may not even realize that they have been attacked.

Do not assume that a terrorist attack must cause a large amount of damage or result in deaths and injuries. Some terrorist attacks are designed to result in vast damage and scare everyone in a country. Other attacks are aimed a very specific victim, and may be designed only to generate only enough fear to cause that person to modify his behavior. In such a case the fear could be generated by the terrorists breaking windows in the victim's home or vandalizing his car. Terrorist attacks do not have to kill or even injure people. A good number of the true terrorist groups that have functioned in the United States over the past 40 years, and many that function today, have deliberately gone out of their way to avoid causing injuries.

Do not criticize a terrorist group for hitting the "wrong" target. Terrorists usually choose their targets for a reason and plan their attacks carefully. However, they are human and mistakes can occur, resulting in an incorrect target being attacked. Openly criticizing the group for their mistake does not do much to further the investigation. Indeed, doing so may lead citizens to question why the authorities are unable to catch the culprits, if they are as stupid as they are depicted. Furthermore, there is the danger that the group may be goaded into making a return visit to hit the "right" target.

Do not downplay the amount of damage that the group or the media claims resulted from a terrorist attack unless there is a valid reason for doing so. The fact that the group's bomb only caused $500,000 in damage instead of the million dollars that they or the media claimed, really does not make enough difference to validate a criticism. Such statements could cause the group to return for a repeat performance. In addition, when the perpetrators are apprehended, the prosecutor will want to express to the judge and jury the horrible damage that was done. Statements made by officials that downplay the extent of damage could be introduced by the defense and result in a reduced sentence.

Do not deny the validity of a verbal or written claim of credit by a known or even unknown terrorist group, issued in conjunction with an incident, unless it is certain that it is a bogus claim. Such denials can cause investigators to go in the wrong direction. They may also cause the group to release additional communiqués in which they give specific details to prove that they were the perpetrators. Such communiqués will receive heavy media coverage, and probably give the group even more publicity than it would have received if authorities had never made the denial.

Do not tell the media that the group could have done far more damage if they had attacked in a different manner or in a different location within the victim target. Nothing is gained when authorities tell terrorists where they should attack in order to do the greatest amount of damage. Some groups may return to do the job right, or will modify their modus operandi during their next attack at a different location.

Do not emphasize investigation of overt surface supporters of the terrorists following an attack. There is certainly nothing wrong with contacting local activists who support the overall political cause of the group that perpetrated the attack to determine if they have information of value about the crime. However, harassing and threatening them, and generally making their lives miserable, will likely not help the investigation. If they knew that there was to be an attack, it can logically be assumed that they would have arranged good alibis to ensure that they could not be connected to the incident. Targeting surface people too frequently can result in investigators being unable to find the time to follow more logical leads. Furthermore, some of the surface people could possibly lead to the perpetrators if subjected to discreet investigation. Finally, it is possible that a specific attack—in the present or future—may turn off a particular support person, either because of the nature of the victim or its violence. Such a person might be inclined to lend a law enforcement agency assistance if he or she has been treated with respect by them in the past.

Do not think that immediately following a terrorist attack the law enforcement agency must give a statement to the media in which it tries to prove to the media that they have logical suspects and leads, when in fact they do not. This gains nothing if it is not true. In fact, if a law enforcement agency makes such statements, yet does not quickly solve the case, it could cause the media and community to demand explanations. If the agency has good leads, nothing is gained by telling the media about their success because the information will likely drive the perpetrators further underground. Also, at some point during such talks with the media, the agency may inadvertently release information that will damage the investigation.

Do not tell the media that the law enforcement agency has no direction to go in solving the attack. Often this is in fact true; however, there is nothing to be gained by expressing this belief. It certainly does not bolster the morale of investigators. Even worse, it may cause the group to feel sufficiently safe to perpetrate even more local attacks than it had planned. It is better to offer nebulous statements about following logical leads or awaiting laboratory results than it is to claim to have no direction.

Do not "pass the buck." Blaming the "feds," or the state, or local law enforcement agencies for making mistakes that allowed the terrorist attack to take place does nothing to further the investigation. In some instances, a particular agency may have done something that was improper; however, such failings should be handled behind the scenes, and not in a public forum. If the media uncovers such shortcoming, there is nothing to be gained by other law enforcement agencies ganging up on the offending agency.

Do not make threats or promises that cannot be carried out. A large reward may sound impressive, but it should not be offered unless the money is available to pay it, and there is an intention to pay it in accordance with the stated provisions. Threats to put the offenders in jail for a hundred years or to pursue the death penalty should not be issued unless these are viable options.

Do not give expert opinions concerning the nature of the "weapon" used in the terrorist attack unless it is clearly known, and even then there should be some reason for providing such specific information. An investigator who ventures a guess that a case of dynamite was used to blow up the target could jeopardize the prosecution, if in fact an L.A.W. rocket was the weapon employed by the terrorists. The investigator could end up in court as a defense witness countering the testimony of a law enforcement laboratory expert or his own agency's bomb technician. Furthermore, such a statement could send other investigators in the wrong direction.

Do not release information about the terrorist group's unique methods and intimate traits unless there is a need to do so. Doing this can result in "copycat" crimes that investigators will be unable to distinguish from those done by the terrorist group. Furthermore, such information can be used to determine if an informant or group turncoat actually has the intimate access that he claims to have in the group. For example, there is really little reason for the media to know that the group's incendiary devices are always concealed in empty "Jell-O" boxes, or that the communiqués the group sends to the police following an attack are always duplicate copies rather than the originals.

Do not assume that because the attack was political in nature, the perpetrators are less than capable, or are a bunch of "crazies." As a rule, most terrorists are usually intelligent and well-organized. They are often much more difficult to identify and apprehend than the average criminal.

Do not go it alone when an attack occurs. If an agency is part of an established joint terrorism task force, it should work with the member agencies of that entity when responding to a terrorist attack. Attempting to exclude fellow task force investigators at the time of an actual terrorist incident is not going to stop these agencies/officers from responding, and will result in confusion, conflict, and inefficient duplication of work.

Appendix ⓘ𝐈𝐈𝐈

In a Nutshell:
Bringing Terrorists to Justice

Go after the terrorist group. If the group has perpetrated a number of attacks, it is likely that many of these attacks can be solved if the group structure can be identified and monitored.

Identify anyone who is in the covert, clandestine group. Homing in on that one person should eventually lead to the other members of the organization.

If an actual clandestine member of the group cannot be identified, find someone from the surface support group who has direct contact with the covert group members. Monitoring this person should eventually enable investigators to find at least one covert member of the group. (It is important that investigative guidelines be followed when monitoring the activities of an overt person so as not to violate his or her rights.)

A covert member of a terrorist group or a surface person having direct contact with a clandestine organization can be identified through any of the following means:

- **Informants:** The source may only be on the periphery of the group's surface support network. Nonetheless, he may learn something that will enable an investigator to determine that someone is functioning in a covert manner. It should be remembered that informants are not trained law enforcement officers. They may not realize what is pertinent. Consequently, it is important to employ the appropriate "who, what, when, where, why, and how" questions when debriefing a source. Do not assume that an informant will tell everything he knows—ask specific questions. The source may assume that the investigator already knows the information or that something is not important.

- **Citizens:** The average person will not be a member of a covert group but, like a periphery informant, might be able to offer some information that could lead an investigator to identify a covert group member.

- **Physical evidence and crime scenes:** Usually obtained from a terrorist attack crime scene, however, evidence could come from something like an abandoned address or recovered trash. Possibly a note, a fingerprint, or DNA could identify a covert group member. Crime scenes must be carefully processed and every effort must be made to locate as many witnesses to the terrorist attack as possible. If it means interviewing hundreds of people who may have seen something, it should be done. Efforts should also be made to determine how the attack was orchestrated. It might be beneficial to create a computer reenactment of the crime. This could help investigators locate additional possible witnesses.

- **Technical or other coverage on related extremist groups:** Wiretaps and microphones can yield a great deal of information. Although it might not identify a group member, it might give an investigator sufficient direction so that he can identify a member of the targeted group. Similarly, informants and undercover investigators working in other groups might come up with information of value. It is not unusual for clandestine groups to have some contact with, or knowledge of, other covert groups of similar political persuasions.

- **Surveillance:** Following a suspected clandestine contact person could lead to the identification of a covert extremist. Conducing surveillance of a potential target of attack might identify a clandestine group member casing that location.

- **Intelligence about the group:** The more that investigators know about the group, the better the chance that they will develop a vehicle through which to identify a member. An investigator who learns how a clandestine group communicates with its members may be able to identify covert members through coverage of this system. Similarly, an investigator who learns how a covert group procures its supplies and weapons might be able to capitalize on this intelligence to identify members of the covert cell.

- **Gossip:** Many people just naturally talk about current activities. Investigators and informants who can keep their ears open to conversations among overt support people immediately following a terrorist incident might learn something that could identify a clandestine operative.

- **Other law enforcement agencies:** It is possible that some agency has information of value regarding terrorism without realizing it. This is especially true with respect to agencies whose missions do not normally involve terrorism (game wardens, food inspectors, forestry agents, building inspectors). Following the

September 11, 2001, attacks, the president and attorney general of the United States made an all-out effort to encourage the broad spectrum of law enforcement agencies to work together in the "war against terrorism" in order to avert this failing.

- **Private intelligence-gathering entities:** There are a number of non-law enforcement companies and not-for-profit groups that monitor political extremists for a variety of reasons. Some of these organizations have excellent information and may be able to identify a clandestine operative.

- **Do not forget law enforcement retirees who continued to work in the area of terrorism after leaving their agency.** Some of these people are now teaching, writing, and doing research, and can prove to be a wealth of information to current investigators. A few might be able to engage in proactive endeavors that could glean valuable intelligence.

- **Thorough organizing of information:** Law enforcement agencies usually do an excellent job of assembling their information for prosecution purposes. However, when a terrorist is unknown and no prosecution is imminent, investigators may find it difficult to take the time to review and organize all of their information into a single coherent document. If they did, many would likely discover that they knew more than they thought. One of the great values of organizing information is that this process clearly shows what is and is not known.

- **Being alert for the use of false identification:** Any information that someone associated with the political movement is using false identification should be regarded as an indication that the individual is operating clandestinely.

- **Being alert for "missing" people among cause-related overt activists.** Some clandestine groups recruit from overt support groups. A person who suddenly vanishes from an overt group may have gone underground. Also be alert for overt people who seemingly "disappear" for short periods on a periodic basis.

- **Be alert for a new person who associates with overt cause-related people.** Insofar as political extremists are usually suspicious of people they have not known for a long period, particular attention should be afforded to a stranger who appears to be trusted by local activists. That person could be a clandestine activist, and possibly a fugitive, from another part of the country.

Once a covert person is identified, give that person coverage through a variety of investigative techniques. However, take no action that will reveal to that individual that law enforcement is on to him. Trying to interview this person in the hope that he will confess or reveal the names of his cohorts, is not likely to yield satisfactory results. However, it will probably cause him and his associates to abandon the project and perhaps even flee the area.

Avoid the temptation to "take down" the single covert terrorist on a lesser crime in the belief that he will "talk." Most terrorists will not provide information of value about their group during an interview, so little will be gained by such action. Also, such an arrest is likely to cause the group to flee the area or lay low for a lengthy period. If an agency is pressured into making such an arrest, an effort should be made to stress the criminal offense, and not discuss the terrorist angle. A terrorist group may not scatter or discontinue their activities if they believe that their incarcerated member was arrested on a straight criminal charge that the law enforcement agency had not linked to terrorism. The law enforcement agency may know full well that the subject intended to use the stolen car that he was driving to do a bombing. However, by only mentioning the car theft charge without citing the terrorist link, the terrorist group may feel free to continue their activities. If the subject proves cooperative during the interview, the reason for the theft could possibly be asked about at that point. If the subject responds truthfully, at that time a pitch can be made to "turn" the person against his group.

Carefully document any and all illegal actions in which covert people are engaged. Always be alert for information that may arise out of previous illegal actions that group members may have undertaken, and conduct investigation to verify these violations and develop prosecutable cases around them. Such criminal violations can be used to ensure that an arrested terrorist cannot easily bond himself out of custody and flee the jurisdiction.

Attempt to identify other cells of the group or of associated terrorist groups before taking the group down. When the decision is ultimately made to arrest the cell members, ensure that coverage is afforded to these other cells. Have sealed warrants for their members. Unless there is an indication that they are trying to flee as a result of the arrests of the targeted groups, consider not arresting them immediately. If they remain in place, give them complete coverage and determine their activities and contacts.

Do not allow the covert cell to actually perpetrate a terrorist attack. In addition to the loss of life and property damage, this could cause a law enforcement agency irreparable harm if it later became public that the agency had been in a position to prevent such an incident.

If something can be done to prevent the group from committing a terrorist attack without the group being aware of it, this should be considered, especially if there is more information to be developed through additional covert investigation. There is also added value in extending the investigation in this manner, because a conspiracy to perpetrate an attack is, in itself, a serious charge. One way to prevent such an attack might be to have a number of marked police cars near the target when the group "cases" that target. This will likely cause them to reconsider attacking such a location. Another method might be to have a security guard clearly posted inside the group's target when they had assumed that the location would be unguarded.

Carefully plan the arrests of the terrorists so that no one can escape and so that all possible intelligence is developed.

Have sufficient teams of law enforcement arrest/processing and interview personnel available so that the terrorists can be offered an immediate opportunity to talk to investigators, should they desire to cooperate.

Have sufficiently strong charges against the terrorists to ensure that they cannot easily bond themselves out of custody and flee. Ensure that the prosecutor has sufficient information to enable him to make a strong argument for no bond or a high bond.

Have search warrants and other appropriate documentation prepared before the arrests of the terrorist group members. Have appropriate search personnel ready so that all locations and vehicles associated with the terrorists can be processed without delay.

Know what the terrorist knows. Because many terrorist groups provide instructions to their members with respect to what they should expect and do if arrested, law enforcement agencies should attempt to become knowledgeable about this training and act appropriately (and legally) to counteract what the subject expects.

Appendix **IV**

Domestic Terrorist Attacks during 2005 through 2007

Below are listings of political extremist/terrorist attacks that occurred in United States during the years 2005 through 2007. They are proceeded by summations of the attacks during each year. It should be noted that the information contained below is from public sources, including newspaper accounts, communiqués of credit released by terrorist groups, and accounts displayed on activist Web sites. Because most of these attacks have yet to be solved, there is no way to be absolutely certain that the extremists who either claimed them, or who are strongly suspected of doing them, did in fact perpetrate them. However, based on the targets and victims, all of the incidents appear to be have been staged by political extremists in order to engender fear and force changes in the government or society.

It is quite apparent that following 2005 there was a great drop in the number of attacks that occurred in the subsequent years. In the six years between January 1, 2000, and December 31, 2005, there were almost 450 terrorist extremist attacks in the United States. However, over the next two years there were only about 70 incidents. These low numbers continued into 2008. Although no one can state with certainty why there was such a drop, it is highly likely that several significant arrests, prosecutions, and convictions of animal and environmental activists beginning in 2004 explains this phenomena. The most significant of these situations involved more than a dozen animal and environmental extremists who comprised the clandestine activist cell known as the "Family." Most were charged with serious felonies in December 2005 or during 2006, and subsequently pleaded guilty. All of those who were taken into custody received lengthy prison sentences during 2007. Several defendants were able to avoid arrest by fleeing, and are being actively sought by federal authorities. They will also likely receive heavy prison terms when apprehended. One subject committed suicide in his jail cell rather than face trial. In May 2004, six animal activists were charged with inciting violence and terror in connection with a campaign to close down the animal testing firm, Huntingdon Life Sciences (HLS). They were subsequently convicted and sentenced to several years each in prison in 2006. In February 2008, four alleged environmental activists were indicted by a federal grand jury in Michigan for allegedly perpetrating a number of attacks in Michigan and Indiana dating back to 1999. All were subsequently arrested. If convicted, these defendants will face lengthy prison sentences and could be ordered to pay millions of dollars in restitution. It is difficult to imagine that arrests of these kinds have not had an adverse reaction on both animal and environmental activists. Previously, these people had come to believe that they were not in jeopardy from the law enforcement community. There had been few arrests of people who had committed animal and environmental attacks during the 1990s and first five years of the twenty-first century. Insofar as the largest number of terrorist attacks perpetrated during the twenty-first century in the United States has been done by animal and environmental extremists, anything that would cause these extremists to back away from perpetrating attacks would cause a huge drop in the overall terrorist statistics.

The Year 2007 in Review

The total number of attacks during the year 2007 was down considerably from those perpetrated during each of the years between 2000 and 2005; however, it was around 75 percent higher than the number committed during 2006. Most of the attacks were relatively minor in terms of damage, and none resulted in injuries. The most noteworthy attack occurred in April 2007, when an attempt was made to bomb an abortion clinic in Austin, Texas. Had the nail-filled explosive device not failed to explode due to wiring problems, the explosion would have likely have been quite devastating and deadly. Another abortion clinic attack in December 2007, in Albuquerque, New Mexico, may have also been devastating had not the Molotov cocktail fire-bomb thrown onto the building's roof set off a motion detector that brought firefighters to the scene to extinguish the flames. The vast majority of the attacks during 2007 fell within the animal rights category. Almost 20 involved people engaged in research using animals, and/or those connected to the animal testing firm, Huntingdon Life Sciences (HLS). The actions against HLS associates were intended to force the victims to terminate their connection with HLS in an effort isolate HLS, and put that firm out of business. Four incidents involved attacks against people allegedly engaged in animal cruelty. Three of the 2007 attacks involved the liberation of animals from farms. In one incident hens were taken from an egg farm, in another case rabbits were stolen from a farm that raised them for food, and in a third situation minks were liberated from a fur farm. There were also six actions were against stores selling furs. A meat market was vandalized, as were restaurants serving foie gras.

During 2007 there were two attacks on SUVs by apparent environmental activists; however, these were the only actions by ecological extremists during the year. Also during 2007 there were three vandalism attacks in opposition to the war in Iraq including an attack on the office of a U.S. Congressman. Anarchists are suspected in each of these incidents. A lone individual attempted to bomb an abortion clinic in Texas, but the device failed to function. The perpetrator was subsequently arrested, pleaded guilty, and was sentenced to 40 years in prison. Another abortion clinic in Kansas was vandalized by apparent anti-abortion extremists in July 2007 while one clinic was fire-bombed and a second suffered window breakage in New Mexico during late December 2007.

Terrorist Attacks—2007

January 5, 2007—South Jordan, Utah: In a communiqué the Animal Liberation Front (ALF) claimed responsibility for vandalizing a home at 11739 South Lampton View Drive, South Jordan owned by University of Utah scientist Audie Gene Leventhal. The communiqué claimed that Leventhal's residence was targeted because of his alleged experimentation with cats and other primates. The residence was vacant at the time and it was for sale. The activists claim to have destroyed six windows and a sliding glass door by applying glass-eating acid to them. They also claim to have covered the house with paint including with the graffiti, "CAT KILLER." In addition the communiqué, gave the addresses of other properties owned and/or used by Leventhal, and threatened to attack them if he continued to engage in animal abuse.

February 3–4, 2007—Philadelphia: In a communiqué released by the animal activist Web site, Bite Back (www.directaction.info), animal activists claimed responsibility for spray-painting the residence of David Stout, President of GlaxoSmithKline over the weekend of February 3–4, 2007. The communiqué stated that the home was targeted to protest Glaxo's relationship with animal tester Huntingdon Life Science (HLS). They also indicated that the attack was intended to protest against the Glaxo drug, Seroxat, that they alleged has caused teenagers to kill themselves. In their communiqué, the activists allege that this is the third time that Stout's residence has been vandalized.

February 17, 2007—Inglewood, California: In a communiqué the Animal Liberation Front (ALF) claimed to have attacked the Hubnet Express company office at 1014 Hillcrest Blvd. in Inglewood on the night of February 17, 2007, because that firm does shipping for Huntingdon Life Sciences (HLS), a firm that ALF claims tortures animals. Specifically the ALF claimed to have spray-painted on the outside of the building, demands that Hubnet sever ties with HLS. They also claimed to have glued shut the locks on the company's doors. Inside the building, they claimed to have sprayed red die tainted with concentrated liquid smoke onto the carpets. In their communiqué the ALF warned that if Hubnet did not sever its ties to HLS, "… the smell of smoke will not be from a liquid concentrate."

February 19, 2007—Fountain Inn, South Carolina: By communiqué the Animal Liberation Front (ALF) claimed to have liberated 20 rabbits from Blue Chip Farm, Inc. in Fountain Inn because that firm raises rabbits for meat. With respect to the rabbits the ALF stated that 4 were "… to be placed in homes." The ALF also warned that "Last night's action will be repeated if (sic) farm is not shut down."

March 6, 2007—Portland, Oregon: In a communiqué the Animal Liberation Front (ALF) claimed that on early Tuesday they vandalized the residence of Jason Bratt, 1425 Southeast Viquil Street, Portland. Specifically the ALF stated that they painted "Drop SSK" on Bratt's garage door, and sprayed the letters "ALF" in black paint across the side of his car. The communiqué identified Bratt as the first vice-president of Wachovia Securities in Portland; and stated that Wachovia owns more than a half-billion shares in GlaxoSmithKline (GSK), which the ALF claims is the largest customer of animal testing company, Huntingdon Life Sciences (HLS). The communiqué warned Wachovia to sell its shares in GSK, or they would continue to target the homes and property of Wachovia employees.

March 19, 2007—Lansing, Michigan: Apparent anti-war vandals attacked the office of Congressman Mike Rogers in Lansing. They splattered bright red paint all over the congressional signs on the outside of the building. They also painted anti-war graffiti on the sidewalk in front of the office. Further, the vandals destroyed surveillance cameras protecting the location, and glued the front door locks shut. A sign stating, "Rogers there is blood on your hands" was hung on the front of the office. No group claimed responsibility for the attack. The office has been subjected to peaceful anti-war protests in the past, but had never before been physically attacked.

April 1, 2007—Woodland, California: At around 1:30 A.M., two white males and one female, all described as being in their late teens, vandalized SUVs along Casa Linda Drive and Elm Street in Woodland. A total of nine SUVs were spray-painted in black with the letters, "ELF" and other markings. The perpetrators fled as police arrived at the scene.

April 3–4, 2007—Pittsburgh, Pennsylvania: Overnight, apparent anti-war activists vandalized the Marine Officers Recruitment Station at 5837 Ellsworth Avenue in the Shadyside neighborhood of Pittsburgh. The attackers smashed windows, spilled paint all over the station, and caused other damage. Earlier that evening the center had been the target of an anti-war protest.

April 10, 2007—Portland, Oregon: The Animal Liberation Front (ALF) claimed responsibility for vandalizing the "shiny new" SUV of Kevin Singer, vice president of Wealth Management of Wachovia Securities at Singer's home in Portland, by spray-painting it with slogans and paint stripes. The

ALF stated that the attack was to protest the financial relationship between Wachovia and GlaxoSmithKline (GSK), which is a customer of the animal testing firm, Huntingdon Life Sciences. In their communiqué the ALF promised more attacks against Wachovia executives if the firm did not sell their shares in GSK.

April 21–22, 2007—Naples, Florida: Over this weekend the Collier County Republican Headquarters at 194 U.S. 41 North, Naples was vandalized by apparent anti-war, anarchist activists. "Democracy failed" was spray-painted on the sidewalk outside of the main entrance; an anarchy sign—a letter A in a circle—was painted on the door; "Repaint with Iraqi blood" and "If legality equaled morality, Bush would be in jail"; was painted on either side of the door; and peace signs were painted on three sides of the building. On the rear of the building was painted, "All war is deception" and "Who would Jesus bomb?" Also on one side of the building the attackers painted such slogans as, "I won't kill for capitalists," "Prodigies of Peace," "Fascists," and "Hicks don't mix with politics." On a side door "Stop Bush" was painted. In addition, the red, white, and blue decorations that adorned the entrance to the headquarters were removed, and burned in a small parking lot at the rear of the building.

April 25 and 27, 2007—Austin, Texas: On Wednesday the 25th, a bomb consisting of explosive powder and nails was found in a cooler in the parking lot of the Austin Women's Health Center, a facility where abortions are performed. A police bomb squad subsequently rendered the device safe. The discovery of the device came a week after the U.S. Supreme Court released a decision that banned a controversial form of abortion. On Friday the 27th, Paul Ross Evans, 27, was arrested in connection with the bomb. He was charged federally with use of weapons of mass destruction, and the manufacture of explosive material. Evans was paroled in 2005 after serving three years of a 15-year sentence for a crime spree that included breaking into cars, and using a pellet gun to rob a convenience store and a fast-food restaurant.

April 26, 2007—Riverton, Utah: The Animal Liberation Front (ALF) claimed responsibility for vandalizing a vacant home owned by Audie Leventhal in Riverton. The ALF claimed that Leventhal abuses animals. The ALF stated that they glued shut every lock on the house, smashed the front window, spray-painted slogans all over the deluxe Jacuzzi, and poured a salt-saturated solution all over the front lawn that would kill the grass, and force replacement of the soil. The group claimed their attack caused thousands of dollars in damage. In their communiqué the ALF threatened Leventhal by stating, "Audie can rest assured that we will be back."

May 21, 2007—Studio City, California: The Animal Liberation Press Office in Canoga Park, California, disclosed a communiqué from individuals identifying themselves as Los Angeles (LA) Animal Services volunteers who claimed responsibility for paint-stripping inside and out, the SUV and pickup truck of Heidi Hubner, 1515 Simpson Avenue, Studio City, California, on May 21, 2007. The perpetrators said that they carried out the attack on behalf of the Animal Liberation Front (ALF). They blamed Hubner, who they identified as being the LA Animal Services Volunteer Coordinator, for the deaths of animals at the Los Angeles Department of Animal Services.

June 14, 2007—Johnstown, Pennsylvania: At 4:30 A.M. animal activists vandalized Linda's Fashions and Fur Salons, 903 Old Scalp Avenue in Johnston. The attackers threw a cinderblock through the front door, and spray-painted the letters "ALF" onto the building. In a communiqué the activists claimed to have done the attack to express solidarity with Jeffrey Luers, who they identified as being an Earth Liberation prisoner beginning the seventh year of an almost 23-year sentence.

June 24, 2007—Los Angeles, California: By communiqué, the group Animal Liberation Brigade claimed responsibility for setting fire to the BMW of Dr. Arthur Rosenbaum at 1:30 A.M. The BMW was parked in front of Dr. Rosenbaum's residence at 465 Loring Avenue, Los Angeles. In their communiqué the attackers alleged that Rosenbaum conducted abusive experiments on monkeys. The communiqué threatened Rosenbaum by telling him to watch his back because he might be "... facing injections into your eyes like the primates ..." Rosenbaum is a physician and a professor at the Jules Stein Eye Institute at the University of California Los Angeles (UCLA). Police investigators found that although the incendiary device was lit by the perpetrators, it failed to ignite the vehicle.

June 29, 2007—Washington, DC: The animal activist Web site, Bite Back, www.directaction.info, reported that they had received a communiqué from anonymous animal activists who claimed to have vandalized the residence of John Frederick Richardson. The communiqué identified Richardson as being a director of Abbott Labs, which is a customer of Huntingdon Life Sciences, a company that activists claim tortures animals. Specifically, the activists stated that they painted Richardson's door and stoop with red paint, and broke a window at the home.

July 2–3, 2007—Austin, Texas: Animal rights activists claimed that over the evening of Monday-Tuesday, they vandalized seven eateries in downtown Austin that they say serve veal and foie gras, The establishments were damaged with spray-painted graffiti and obscenities. The victim restaurants were Aquarelle, Eddie V's Edgewater Grille, Fleming's, Restaurant Jezebel, Ruth's Chris Steak House, Spaghetti Warehouse, and Truluck's.

July 3, 2007—Wichita, Kansas: On Tuesday anti-abortion activists climbed onto the roof of the Women's Health Care Services clinic, 5017 East Kellogg, Wichita, operated by Dr. George Tiller. They then drilled holes into the roof, after which they ran a hose from a faucet onto the roof, and directed water into the holes. Following that the perpetrators glued the faucet open, glued the lock to the clinic door shut, and glued shut the lock of the gate on the fence surrounding the facility. Because the running water set off an alarm, police immediately responded, and were able to gain entry through the fence gate before the epoxy had hardened. The water from the hose caused several thousands dollars in damage, and forced staff members to work throughout the July 4th holiday in order to enable the clinic to reopen on Thursday. The clinic performs late-term abortion procedures, and has been the target of anti-abortion activist protests for many years. Dr. Tiller was shot in both arms by anti-abortion extremist Rachelle Shannon on August 19, 1993.

July 4, 2007—Burleson, Texas: A deacon of the under-construction Victory Family Church in Burleson caught Dayton Lee Calaway, 19, Michael Philip Plaisted, Jr., 18, Jered Michael Ragon, 18, and a male minor, attempting to detonate a bomb at the entrance to the church building. After allegedly twice failing to detonate the device, the men attempted to escape when they saw the deacon. However, the deacon caught Calaway and Plaisted when their vehicle became stuck in mud. Ragon and the boy escaped, but Ragon became involved in a bizarre incident shortly thereafter. In a field two to three miles from the church, Ragon attempted to douse evidence from the attempted Victory attack with gasoline and set it ablaze. However, when he lit the fire, Ragon did not realize that he was standing in gasoline, and suffered burns to his feet. A nearby resident heard screaming, saw smoke, and observed Ragon fleeing in a vehicle. During interview Calaway and Plaisted implicated Ragon, who subsequently voluntarily came in for questioning on Thursday. The three men identified themselves as part of a group of around 10 to 15 people who are radical Christians who oppose government and organized religion. They claimed that their act at the Victory church was to test the device, and to get the attention of the community. They stated that their group is attempting to wake up society by committing destructive acts. The group also believes that there are too many denominations and churches, and that there should be only one church. They believe that society has become too focused on self-improvement and self-gratification, and has lost focus on the glorification of God. Two of the men also confessed to involvement in a fire at a recycling bin near the CenterPointe Church in Burleson during the spring of 2007. They claimed that this arson was done because the older generation is making the younger generation clean up their mess. That fire only burned materials in the bin, and did not damage the church. The three men were charged with arson at a place of worship, a first degree felony that could result in a sentence of life in prison. Ragon was also charged with tampering with physical evidence. The juvenile was not charged because the three men claimed that he was not involved. Burleson police spokesperson Commander Chris Havens reported that his department characterizes the entity to which the men claim to belong as being in the category of a domestic terrorist group.

July 5, 2007—New York, New York: The Animal Liberation Press Office in Woodland Hills, California released a communiqué dated July 5, 2007, that they received in which people identifying themselves as ALF members claimed to have spray-painted the home of Ellyn Brown, who sits on the board of the New York Stock Exchange. They claim to have left slogans, "NYSE Puppy Killers" and "Drop HLS" on Brown's house. They also claim that several days later they dropped across Brown's front gate a banner that stated, "Drop HLS from NYSE for Good."

July 13, 2007—New York, New York: In a communiqué dated July 13, 2007, members of the Animal Liberation Front (ALF) claim to have deleted the access of more than 300 associates of Lagrange Capital Management of New York from the Lagrange Web site. In the communiqué the ALF members ordered Lagrange to sell its shares in the animal testing firm Huntingdon Life Sciences.

July 16, 2007—Washington, DC: At around 3:30 A.M., a recently purchased $38,000 Hummer was severely vandalized by two men with their faces covered. The Hummer was parked in front of a residence on Brandywine Street NW in Washington, DC. The men used a bat to break every window in the vehicle, and used a knife to stab each 38-inch tire. They also scratched into the vehicle's body, "FOR THE ENVIRON."

July 29, 2007—Los Angeles, California: Via a communiqué dated July 29, 2007, the Animal Liberation Front (ALF) claimed responsibility for mailing an "interesting package" to the home of Arthur Rosenbaum. They warned Rosenbaum to be careful, because "We are only just getting started. This action is a mere token when compared to the other things that we can and will do." The communiqué called Rosenbaum a sick and twisted animal torturer and murderer involved in the primate vivisection program at UCLA.

July 31, 2007—Lake Oswego, Oregon: The Animal Liberation Front (ALF) claimed Via a communiqué dated August 2, 2007, that they had "recently" vandalized the residence and vehicle of Eliot Spindel. The attackers identified Spindel as an employee of the Oregon National Primate Research Center who was involved in research using animals. The communiqué stated that the attackers used chemicals and spray paints to damage Spindel's home and vehicle. They warned Eliot to "Quit the torture industry and issue an apology or we swear we will make an example out of you." They continued their warning, "… what's going to be next, Eliot, spray paint, broken windows, or fire bombs?" More specifically, the communiqué warned, "Whatever they pay you in one year, we promise we can match in damage in one night." On July 31, 2007, a contractor discovered "ALF eyes on you" spray-painted on the garage door of Spindel's residence, and found Spindel's daughter's car covered with a white foam.

August 5, 2007—Ocean City, Maryland: Via a communiqué released by the animal activist Web site, Bite Back (www.directaction.info), the Animal Liberation Front (ALF) claimed responsibility for vandalizing boats in connection with the 34th annual White Marlin Open being staged in Ocean City between August 6–10, 2007. The White Marlin Open describes itself as being the world's largest bill fishing tournament. The ALF claimed to have used scuba gear and tactical equipment on the evening of August 5, 2007 to attack and disable eight of the approximately 400 boats scheduled to participate in the tournament. Specifically, the ALF stated that they welded the props on the boats, and cut into the hulls, allowing water to enter the crafts. Also, in their communiqué the ALF listed the names, home ports, and owners of some of the boats that participated in the tournament, and stated "We urge activists to take appropriate measures" against these vessels.

August 13, 2007—Hinsdale, Maine: More than 300 mink were "liberated" from their cages at Berkshire Furs in Hinsdale on early Monday by unknown people assumed to be animal rights extremists. Although the farm keeps between 10,000 and 30,000 mink at the location, the liberated animals came from a group of between 400 and 500 minks maintained for breeding purposes. To gain entry, the attackers cut a barbed wire fence at numerous places. Earl and Jeanne Carmel, the owners of the mink farm, sustained a loss of between $75,000 and $100,000 from the attack. In 1996 animal activists "liberated" 1,000 mink from the same location when it was known as Chatham Ranch.

September 2, 2007—San Clemente, California: A building owned by Farajollah Mahjoor, the owner of Phenomenex in San Clemente, was vandalized. The Animal Liberation Front (ALF) claimed that they stained the front walk of the building with blood red paint, destroyed 20 windows in the building with etching fluid, and painted, "We found you" on the building. In a communiqué sent to the Animal Liberation Press in Woodland Hills, California, the ALF stated that the attack was done because Phenomenex is a key supplier to the animal testing firm Huntingdon Life Sciences (HLS). The ALF warned that unless Mahjoor and Phenomenex severed their association with HLS, the group would attack again.

September 3, 2007—Auburn, California: The Longhorn Meat Market was vandalized by apparent animal rights activists. Unknown people spray-painted slogans, including, "Meat is murder" and a drawing of a decapitated cow onto the building. In addition, "PETA" was written with the last letter encircled in the manner of an anarchist symbol. The graffiti extended the entire length of the building.

September 23, 2007—Fullerton, California: The residence of Paul Moravek was vandalized by the Animal Liberation Front (ALF), who claimed to have destroyed the paint on a BMW automobile and on an SUV at the home. They also claimed to have stained the white cement driveway with red paint. In their communiqué, the ALF warned that Moravek's gated neighborhood had not protected his residence, and that the attack had occurred while Moravek's television was playing inside the home. They threatened to return to the residence unless Moravek Biochemicals ceased doing business with animal testing firm Huntingdon Life Sciences (HLS). Moravek is the vice president of Moravek Biochemicals.

October 8, 2007—Washington, DC: Animal activists claimed to have vandalized Miller's Furs and Rizik Brothers in Washington, D.C. by gluing the locks to the stores. They also claimed to have vandalized Furs by Gartenhaus in Washington, D.C. by gluing the lock to the metal safety gate and smashing two windows with rocks. These attacks were claimed in a communiqué sent to the animal activist Web site, Bite Back.

October 18, 2007—Santa Clara, California: Anonymous animal activists claimed to have vandalized Tarlows Furs in Santa Clara by gluing shut three door locks and using two cans of spray paint to damage the outside of the building. These actions were claimed in a communiqué sent to the animal activist Web site, Bite Back.

October 20, 2007—Beverly Hills, California: By communiqué the Animal Liberation Front (ALF) claimed to have vandalized the residence of Edythe London by smashing a window and inserting a running garden hose into the house in the hope of flooding the inside of the residence. They indicated that although their first choice was fire, they chose to flood the house instead of burning it, because they feared starting a brush fire that might harm animals. The attackers also claimed to have clogged the intake drain on the pool pump in the hope that it would run dry and burn itself out. The group warned that they would not stop until UCLA discontinued its primate vivisection program. University officials subsequently reported that the flooding to the London residence caused between $20,000. and $40,000 in damage.

October 22, 2007—Portland, Oregon: Animal activists claimed to have vandalized Nicholas Ungar Furs by gluing two locks shut, smashing windows, and destroying glass blocks. They also claimed to have vandalized the fur dealer, Asia America, by smashing "many" windows with rocks. These attacks were claimed in a communiqué sent to the animal activist Web site, Bite Back.

November 5, 2007—Spanish Fort, Utah: Activists from the Animal Liberation Front (ALF) claimed responsibility for entering a shed at Shepherd's Egg Farm located near Spanish Fort, Utah, and taking 102 hens from the farm, and giving them "good homes." In a communiqué sent to the Animal Liberation Press Office, Woodland Hills, California the activists stated that they had liberated the hens to commemorate the sixth anniversary of the death of British animal liberation activist Barry Horne, who died at age 49 while on a hunger strike. At the time, Horne was serving an 18-year prison term for placing incendiary devices in stores selling animal products in England.

November 9, 2007—Los Angeles, California: Activists from the Animal Liberation Front (ALF) claimed responsibility for pouring super glue into the card access slot to the entry gate to the walk-up teller of a Wachovia bank satellite office in downtown Los Angeles, thereby knocking the teller machine out of service. The activists made their claim via a communiqué to the Animal Liberation Press Office, Woodland Hills, California, in which they indicated that the action was done to demand that Wachovia sever its ties to the animal testing firm, Huntingdon Life Sciences (HLS).

November 10, 2007—Laguna Woods, California: The Animal Liberation Front (ALF) claimed that they had dropped a small incendiary device into the after hours deposit box at the Wachovia Bank branch at El Toro Road and Paseo de Valencia in Laguna Woods. In a communiqué that they sent to the Animal Liberation Press Office, 6320 Canoga Avenue, California, 91367, Woodland Hills, California, the activists stated that Wachovia had been targeted because it held investments in the animal testing firm Huntingdon Life Sciences (HLS). They warned Wachovia that they would attack again if Wachovia did not sell its HLS shares; and they encouraged other activists to take similar actions against Wachovia.

November 12, 2007—Rowland Heights, California: Animal activists claiming to be from the Cat and Dog Liberation Army stated that on Monday night they vandalized the residence of Deborah Villar, who is the sister of Los Angeles Mayor Antonio Villaraigosa. Specifically, the activists claimed to have poured red paint over the steps, walkway, and ornamental light fixtures outside of Villar's home, and to have covered Villar's black SUV with stripper. They claimed to have conducted the attack to pressure Mayor Villaraigosa to stop the abuse and killing of animals at Los Angeles animal shelters. The claim of responsibility was sent to the Animal Liberation Press Office, who released it on their Web site. The activists ended their communiqué with the warning, "Villaraigosa deserves to be bumped off like the dogs and cats we witnessed with their eyes wide, terrified before they were bumped off. He got off way to (sic) easy."

November 13, 2007—Brea, California: Activists from the Animal Liberation Front claimed responsibility for painting the front of the Wachovia bank branch in Brea with red paint. The activists made their claim in a communiqué to the Animal Liberation Press Office, Woodland Hills, California, in which they said they vandalized the bank to demand that Wachovia sever its ties to the animal testing firm, Huntingdon Life Sciences (HLS).

November 23, 2007—Los Angeles, California: In a communiqué sent to the Animal Liberation Press Office in Woodland Hills, California, the Animal Liberation Front (ALF) claimed that on Friday evening they poured paint stripper on a white Ford Explorer parked in front of the house of Los Angeles Deputy Mayor Jimmy Blackman. In their communiqué, the ALF demanded, "Stop the murder of innocent shelter animals at LA Animal Services, Mr. Deputy Mayor."

December 6, 2007—Portland, Oregon: In a communiqué sent to the Animal Liberation Press Office in Woodland Hills, California, the Animal Liberation Front (ALF) claimed that they had vandalized the vehicles of Miles Joseph Novy, at his home. Specifically, the group stated that they had painted graffiti and poured paint stripper on the vehicles. Novy is a medical researcher at the Oregon Health & Science University. The communiqué claimed that "Novy's reproductive research on primates has resulted in this senseless torture of one of natures (sic) most magnificent (sic) creatures.

December 13, 2007, Bremerton, Washington: Unknown individuals vandalized the Kentucky Fried Chicken restaurant on Naval Avenue in Bremerton. They painted the following slogans onto the building: "Meat is Murder," Mess with Animals get Served," and "ALF." They also squirted caulking onto the windows and doors.

December 18, 2007—West Hempstead, New York: At around 11:50 P.M. unknown individuals threw a brick through the glass door of Strathmore Furs, 433 Hempstead Avenue, West Hempstead. Authorities found attached to the rock a note that warned the owner, Thomas Szenes, to stop profiting from the suffering of animals. The note also told him to close down his store. Szenes was inside of his business when the brick was thrown.

December 24, 2007—Brooklyn, New York: Individuals stating that they were from the Animal Liberation Front (ALF) claimed that on Christmas Eve they sprayed a noxious fluid called, "Liquid Ass" inside of a boutique selling fur in Brooklyn. They indicated that by spraying carpets and fur clothing items, they made the store smell so badly that customers would not shop there. In their communiqué of claim the activists warned that anyone in Brooklyn selling fur should stop selling it or face their locks being glued, their windows being broken, or "worse."

December 25, 2007—Albuquerque, New Mexico: On Christmas unknown individuals vandalized two abortion clinics in Albuquerque operated by Planned Parenthood. At around 4:30 A.M. a Molotov cocktail fire-bomb was thrown onto the flat roof of Planned Parenthood's Surgical Center on San Mateo Boulevard. The cocktail started a small fire, and it also set off a motion detector alarm that resulted in firefighters responding to the scene and rapidly striking the fire. A small hole in the roof and a broken front door was the only damage. At around the same time an alarm sounded at the Planned Parenthood's Central Clinic four miles away at Central Avenue and Carlisle Boulevard. Responding authorities found three large front windows broken. Neither attack resulted in any injuries. Both clinics were able to open on December 26, 2007. No one immediately claimed responsibility for the incidents.

The Year 2006 in Review

The total number of attacks in the year 2006 was only around one-third of the number that occurred during 2005. As was the case during the previous years during the twenty-first century, the largest number of the attacks was in the area of animal rights. However, in terms of damage, environmental attacks led the field. No one was injured by any of the attacks during 2006, and only one—involving a Molotov cocktail incendiary device—appeared to have the potential to cause harm to anyone. Most of the attacks fell into the area of vandalism, with animal liberation coming in a distant second. In the animal rights arena there were five animal-raising facilities raided with animals being released or taken. Several of these attacks resulted in considerable losses to the operators. At least four businesses engaged in the sale of fur were attacked during 2007, and two individuals and entities using animals in research were the subject of vandalism. Individuals and businesses engaged in business with animal testing firm Huntingdon Life Sciences (HLS) were attacked by vandals on four instances. Two fast-food establishments serving meat products were also victims of vandalism. In December 2006, a group calling itself the Animal Rights Militia claimed to have tampered with bottles of pomegranate juice because the company producing the product allegedly used animals to test their products.

Environmental extremists began the year with a major attack when, on January 17, 2006, they claimed credit for burning a home under construction in Washington State because they disagreed with where it was being built. The fire caused approximately $2 million in damage. Near the end of the year in October 2006, the Earth Liberation Front (ELF) claimed responsibility for vandalizing logging equipment near Hilt, California. The damage in this incident ran upwards of $500,000. There were also two other vandalism attacks against housing being built in areas that the activists thought were inappropriate. In addition, there was an action in April 2006 in California where 15 SUVs were vandalized by apparent environmental extremists.

Finally, on September 16, 2006, a lone individual drove a vehicle into a closed women's health facility, and set it ablaze, causing around $170,000 in damage. This attack was done in an apparent effort to stop abortions, although the facility does not provide such services.

Terrorist Attacks—2006

January 17, 2006—Camano Island, Washington: On early Tuesday an arson fire almost totally destroyed an almost completed 9,600-square-foot, three-story home overlooking Skagit Bay. On arriving at the scene, firefighters found a pink bed sheet containing a spray-painted threatening message draped across a masonry gate in front of the house. The bed sheet contained the name Earth Liberation Front (ELF). The damage to the $3 million home was estimated at around $2 million. The home is owned by Mark and Karla Verbarendse, who had planned to move into it in February 2006.

February 1, 2006—North Carolina: The animal rights activist Web site, Bite Back, www.directaction.info, reported that anonymous animal rights extremists broke into the home of Mike Pucci, an executive at GlaxoSmithKline, and stole his credit card. The burglars claimed to have subsequently used the card to make a $1,000.00 dollar donation to an unknown charity selected by the extremists.

The activists stated that they entered the home in response to GlaxoSmithKline's investment relationship with Huntingdon Life Sciences (HLS).

February 14, 2006—New Jersey: The animal rights activist Web site Bite Back, www.directaction.info, reported that animal rights extremists claimed to have held a "smashing" nighttime demonstration at the home of Kevin O'Leary, a senior Vice-President of HLS customer, Roche Pharmaceuticals. The activists said that they smashed out windows, and threw items around O'Leary's front porch.

March 11, 2006—Salem, Oregon: Environmental activists vandalized three Salem properties under construction with spray-painted slogans used by the Earth Liberation Front. The slogans read: "Quit building ant farms," "E.L.F.," "Rent is theft," "Viva E.L.F." and "Don't kill my air." Vandals also broke a window at one of the properties.

March 25, 2006—Litchfield, Connecticut: The animal activist Web site Bite Back reported on April 13, 2006 that it had received an anonymous communiqué from animal activists who claimed to have entered an egg-laying chicken farm in Litchfield, Connecticut on March 25, 2006. The activists stated that they rescued 120 chickens that they claimed were now living in peace and comfort in a sanctuary where they will never again have to endure the terrible conditions on factory farms.

April 15, 2006—Santa Cruz, California: Unknown vandals slashed tires and spray-painted more than 15 SUVs on the West side of Santa Cruz. The vandalism included smashed mirrors, broken windows, and "keyed" doors. The spray-painting consisted of slogans, including "Oil equals blood" and "Guzzle." One victim observed about 30 to 40 young men wearing black trench coats and riding bicycles, slashing the tires on her new GMC Yukon SUV.

April 29, 2006—Howard Lake, Minnesota: In the early morning animal activists claiming to be from the ALF (Animal Liberation Front) broke into the Latzig Mink Ranch in Howard Lake, Minnesota. They opened cages and released hundreds of breeding mink, and they removed and destroyed all breeding records that they found. The attackers claimed that the raid on the farm was to express solidarity to Peter Young, who is serving a federal prison term for liberating mink in Wisconsin.

May 21, 2006—Old Town, Maine: According to the July-August, 2006 edition of *Earth First Journal*, a group calling itself the Acadian Green Brigade (AGB) issued a communiqué claiming responsibility for a May 21, 2006, vandalism of equipment owned by the Owen Folsom Company in Old Town, Maine. The AGB claimed to have used fire to destroy three pieces of the company's heavy equipment. They stated that the attack was done because Owen Folsom was supplying sand and fill to the Juniper Ridge Landfill, which the AGB described as being one of the top polluters in New England.

June 3, 2006—Mokena, Illinois: On Saturday apparent environmental activists vandalized equipment at the McNaughton Development home construction site located on 110 acres in Mokena. The damage included broken windows on three bulldozers, three scrapers, and a pickup truck. Grease was also poured into several of the vehicles. The attackers wrote in the dirt with pink spray paint, "No more new houses" and "F—K Mokena." Several racist slogans were also sprayed at the scene. Some local residents have expressed dissatisfaction with the chopping of numerous mature trees on the plot.

June 3–4, 2006—Delaware: Through the Web site Bite Back, www.directaction.info, animal activists claimed responsibility for freeing 35 hens from a large cage egg facility in Delaware over the weekend of June 3–6, 2006.

June 30, 2006—Los Angeles, California: Members of the Animal Liberation Front (ALF) claimed to have left a Molotov cocktail at the doorstep of the residence of UCLA psychiatry professor Lynn Fairbanks in the Bel-Air neighborhood of Los Angeles. The activists stated that they had placed the incendiary to protest Fairbanks' experiments with monkeys at the university. Authorities reported that the device failed to ignite as intended. They also noted that the device was incorrectly left at the residence of a 70-year old woman who was a neighbor of Fairbanks.

July 15, 2006 (?)—Los Angeles, California: On August 2, 2006, the Animal Liberation (ALF) Front Press Office released a communiqué they claimed to have received from unidentified animal activists in which the activists, "(Two) weeks ago the Animal Liberation Front paid a visit to our old pal Dave Dilberto. A half-gallon paint bomb was left to blast red paint all over his home. We hope the mess was good enough to remind you the blood is on your hands, Dave. Stop the killing now." Dilbero is the man who oversees the operations at five city animal shelters in Los Angeles where animal activists claim that thousands of animals are killed every year.

August 25, 2006—Portland, Oregon: In a communiqué sent to the Web site Bite Back (www.directaction.info), animal activists claim to have glued locks and spray-painted the Schumacher fur store on Friday. In their claim of credit the activists warned the owners to close their store, or they would close it down themselves.

September 11, 2006—Edgerton, Iowa: At 4:30 A.M. on Monday David McMenemy, 45, of Sterling Heights, Michigan, drove his car into the Edgerton Women's Health Center in Edgerton, Iowa, ending at the counter in the clinic's central lobby. He then allegedly spread gasoline over the interior of his car and lit it on fire. The resulting blaze caused $170,000 in smoke, fire, and water damage; and forced the clinic to close for two weeks. McMenemy allegedly attacked the clinic because he believed that abortions were performed at the facility. In fact, the health center does not perform abortions or provide abortion referrals.

September 13, 2006—Philadelphia, Pennsylvania: By communiqué dated September 13, 2006, animal activists claimed to have broken the windows of a Kentucky Fried Chicken restaurant that was presently closed for the season. They claimed sales had been hurt by a previous protest at the eatery.

September 18, 2006—California: By communiqué dated September 18, 2006, the ALF (Animal Liberation Front) claimed that over a 20-minute period they spray-painted "F—k MC'D, Meat is murder, ALF was here, and Mcmurder killers" at four McDonald's restaurants located two miles from each other at an unstated location in California. They also claim to have covered every bathroom with red spray paint.

September 19, 2006—Hardwick, Massachusetts: By communiqué dated September 19, 2006, animal rights activists claim to have liberated 23 rabbits from the Capralogics laboratory in Hardwick, Massachusetts. They claimed that the action was taken in honor of the SHAC-7 defendants who were convicted on March 2, 2006, in Trenton, New Jersey, of animal rights activism actions in violation of the Animal Enterprise Protection Act.

October 2, 2006—Hilt, California: Workers discovered that unknown individuals had heavily vandalized logging equipment owned by Hilltop Logging, Inc. at a parcel of the land that they were logging around 10 miles west of Hilt. The damage included dirt and debris in fuel tanks, cut hoses, lines and belts, and computer components ripped out of log loaders and tree-shearing and de-limbing machines. The initials of the Earth Liberation Front (ELF) were found scrawled on some of the machines. The damage was estimated to be as high as $500,000.

November 4, 2006—Winter Springs, Florida: The animal activist Web site, Bite Back, www.directaction.info, released a claim that it had received from anonymous activists who stated that they had broken a window and spray-painted "Dump HLS" at Lancer USA.

November 10, 2006—Lloyd Harbor, Long Island, New York: Unknown animal activists used red paint to write "Leland Hairr Is a Murderer" on Hairr's EEA, Inc. office building and on Leland Hairr's parking spot. In their claim of responsibility the activists accused Hairr, as mayor of the town of Lloyd Harbor, of playing a role in the killing of 20 deer by authorizing a deer hunt that they stated had already devastated the deer population. The attackers warned that if Hairr did not stop the killing, they would be back.

November 27, 2006—Minnetonka, Minnesota: The animal activist Web site, Bite Back, www.directaction.info, reported on November 30, 2006, that they had received a communication from animal activists who claimed to have attacked the offices of Antares Pharmaceuticals in Minnetonka on, or immediately before, Monday, November 27, 2006. The activists claim to have used a glass etching solution to damage more than 30 windows at the facility. The activists stated that Antares had been chosen because of its ties to Huntingdon Life Sciences (HLS), a major animal testing company. The attackers warned that every company working with HLS had to realize that if they do not stop their affiliation with HLS, they will be forced to spend thousands of dollars on repairs to their offices.

December 2, 2006—Hanover, Pennsylvania: The Animal Liberation Front (ALF) claimed responsibility for using a pellet gun to destroy a large etched glass display window at Furs by Susan in Hanover. In their communiqué the ALF dedicated the attack to incarcerated animal activist Peter Young. The communiqué was released by the Animal Liberation Press Office via their Web site, www.animalliberationpressoffice.org.

December 14, 2006—East Coast, United States: Via a communiqué dated December 14, 2006, a group calling itself the Animal Rights Militia claimed that it tampered with 487 bottles of Pom Wonderful Juices, pomegranate juice, along the eastern seaboard in stores like Wild Oats, D'Agostino's, and Food Emporium. They claimed that while the contamination would not cause death, it would cause diarrhea, vomiting, and headaches. They claimed that the action was taken to protest the cruel use of animals in testing the juice. The communiqué was released by the Animal Liberation Press Office via their Web site, www.animalliberationpressoffice.org.

December 18, 2006—Manhattan, New York: On Monday animal activists claimed that they had glued and tampered with the locks on every fur, leather, and wool store on Orchard Street between Delancey Street and Houston Street in Manhattan. The communiqué from the activists was released by the Animal Liberation Press Office via their Web site, www.animalliberationpressoffice.org.

December 18–19, 2006—Princeton, New Jersey: Via a communiqué dated December 19, 2006, the Animal Liberation Front (ALF) claimed responsibility for liberating around 250 birds from the Griggstown Quail Farm owned by George Rude in Princeton overnight Monday-Tuesday. The ALF claimed to have clipped the fencing, cut through large sections of the canopy covering three pens, and then flushing some 250 quail, pheasants, and partridges to freedom. Upon investigating the incident, the FBI determined that the actual loss was closer to 2,500 birds valued at around $80,000. Furthermore, the FBI reported that the birds represented the farm's entire breeding stock for 2007. The FBI also found that the birds were not wild as the ALF members seemingly believed, but instead were domesticated fowl. The FBI stated that some of the liberated birds had been hit by passing vehicles and that the remaining fowl would also likely be killed or die from lack of food, water, and shelter.

December 22, 2006—Towson, Maryland: In a communiqué the Animal Liberation Front (ALF) claimed responsibility for using a pellet gun to destroy a large etched glass display window at Kent Fisher Furs in Towson. The activists dedicated the attack to incarcerated animal activist Peter Young.

The Year 2005 in Review

There were more than 75 extremist attacks in the United States during 2005. Most were perpetrated by animal rights activists. Around 35 directly involved attacks on individuals or entities associated with the animal testing firm, Huntingdon Life Sciences (HLS). These attacks were intended to force the people and companies to discontinue their relationships with HLS, thereby isolating HLS and forcing it out of business. There were at least four attacks against alleged animal abusers, and four break-ins intended to liberate animals—three at farms and one involving a laboratory. During 2005 there were around seven vandalism attacks at McDonald's and Kentucky Fried Chicken restaurants to protest their sale of meat. There was also one rather unique attack claimed by both the Animal Liberation Front (ALF) and the Earth Liberation Front (ELF). On September 9, 2005, activists vandalized an American Legion post by spray painting the outside of the building, defacing memorials, and destroying Legion property. The attack did not involve the Legion per se, but was aimed at the Minuteman anti-illegal immigration group who was slated to hold a recruitment meeting on the following day at the Legion hall. The ALF and ELF claimed that the Minutemen were racist and had a homicidal agenda. Neither group had ever before staged an attack for such a cause.

Around 20 percent of the terrorist attacks during 2005 were perpetrated by environmental extremists. Most involved attacks on construction projects that the activists claimed were being built in areas that should not be developed. Four of the actions happened at construction sites in California during the first two months of the year, and were not hugely successful. An apparent environmental attack occurred in February 2005 in Albuquerque, New Mexico, where a home being built was destroyed by an arson fire resulting in a loss of $350,000. Another house under construction in Sammamish, Washington, was burned in April 2005 by ELF activists and resulted in approximately $300,000-$350,000 in damage. Still another home was burned in Maryland in November 2005 for a loss of around $300,000. There were also three attacks on SUVs during 2005.

In addition, during 2005 there were two vandalism attacks on army recruiting stations seemingly by anarchists opposed to the war in Iraq. In still another form of attack, at the beginning of December 2005 vandals broke into a science laboratory at the University of California at Davis, and vandalized the location by spraying slogans in opposition to genetic engineering and damaging equipment. Although there had been a number of attacks during the late 1990s and the early twenty-first century expressing opposition to genetic engineering, there had not been one since mid-2003. The December incident was to prove to be something of an aberration because no agricultural genetic engineering attacks occurred during either 2006 or 2007.

During 2005 there were four attacks involving the anti-abortion issue. In early January 2005, an arson fire at an abortion facility in Olympia, Washington, caused about $500,000 in damage. Another abortion clinic in Florida was heavily damaged by an arson fire in July 2005. A Molotov cocktail failed to ignite a fire at a Louisiana abortion clinic in December 2005, and a small fire set in an abortion clinic in Bloomington, Indiana, in March 2005 did not spread enough to cause significant damage.

Finally, on December 21, 2005, two bombs exploded outside an Islamic mosque in Cincinnati, Ohio. No one was injured by the explosions and no one claimed responsibility for the attack. On the surface it would appear that the perpetrators were upset with Muslims possibly in connection with the September 11, 2001, attacks or the war in Iraq.

Terrorist Attacks—2005

January 2, 2005—Miami, Florida: Through animal rights Web site Bite Back (www.directaction.info), anonymous animal activists claimed to have conducted a harassment program against the Florida-based staff of Primate Products, a supplier of Huntingdon Life Sciences (HLS). During 2004 they claim to have filled out stacks of magazine subscription cards, and requested hundreds of mail-order catalogs for Primate employees Donald Bradford, President; Eileen Sylvester, Office Manager; Donna Steiner, Head Veterinarian; and John Resuta, Operations Manager. They also claim to have subscribed their targets' names to every book club and dating service that they could find, and to have placed free ads in local papers for products that their targets were purportedly selling. Furthermore, they claim to have accessed Sylvester's airline frequent flier accounts, and donated miles to a charity, and used miles to subscribe her to magazines. The Web site communiqué also published the addresses, telephone numbers, and e-mail addresses of the four people the activists targeted.

January 9, 2005—Olympia, Washington: An arson fire heavily damaged the roof of the Eastside Women's Health Clinic, an abortion provider, at 2:00 A.M. Sunday, causing heat, water, and smoke damage to the offices in the building. No one was injured. Damage was estimated at around $500,000. The clinic was opened in 1981, and serves 30 to 40 patients each day. Although the clinic has had anti-abortion picketers come to their building every Thursday, the day that abortions are performed, for the past 20 years, they have had no recent threats of violence. No one immediately claimed responsibility for the fire. The Bureau of Alcohol, Tobacco, Firearms, and Explosives (BATF) assumed federal jurisdiction in the case, saying that it appeared that the arson was a "... random act at this time." For this reason the Federal Bureau of Investigation (FBI), the agency that normally investigates domestic terrorist incidents, withdrew from the investigation. The co-owner of the clinic expressed disbelief that the attacker chose the clinic at random, saying, "The first thing that comes to mind is they're anti-abortion."

January 12, 2005—Auburn, Placer County, California: On Wednesday authorities successfully disabled five fire-bombs found at the under-construction three-story Parkhill Professional center. The devices employed gasoline and red dye diesel fuel commonly used in farm equipment. Although there was no graffiti to indicate who might have placed the fire-bombs at the location, the devices were like three fire-bombs that were found at a home construction site in Lincoln, California on December 27, 2004. In that case graffiti including "Quit destroying their homes" and "U will pay" was found spray-painted at the scene. The timing devices employed in all eight fire-bombs were similar. The Auburn complex has been the subject of controversy involving the destruction of old trees. Eco-terrorists are suspected in both attacks.

January 14, 2005—Pensacola, Florida: The Animal Liberation Front (ALF) claimed credit for using acid to damage all five windows and the back window of the red Lexus sports car of the owner of the Madame de Elegance fur store.

January 14, 2005—Port Jefferson, New York: Animal activists vandalized the residence of John DiBella, the Research and Development manager of Forest Laboratories. The street in front of his home was spray-painted with "DiBella Kills Kids," the front porch was spray-painted with "puppy killer" and "murderer," a light bulb filled with red paint was thrown at the front door, and the front door locks were filled with super glue.

January 18, 2005—San Miguel, California: The Animal Liberation Front (ALF) claimed responsibility for cutting away one-fourth of the fence around a pen, thereby releasing the entire deer heard from the GNK Deer Farm in Monterey County during the early morning hours. The ALF identified the owner of the farm as former Los Angeles Police Sergeant Gerd Konieczny, and said that the farm is one of the three largest deer farms in California.

January 19, 2005—Pennsylvania: Animal activists claimed to have covered four cars with paint stripper at the residence of George Barrett, the CEO of Teva Pharmaceuticals-USA.

January 19, 2005—Pennsylvania: By communiqué, animal activists claim to have sent dozens of magazine subscriptions to three executives of Teva Pharmaceuticals because of the firm's relationship with Huntingdon Life Sciences (HLS). They also claim to have sent a letter from the president of the board of the Middle States Tennis Patrons Foundation informing them that Teva CEO George Barrett had been removed from the board for his horrible cruelty to animals. In addition, they claim to have sent letters from Barrett to the President and Vice President announcing his resignation because he did not want to work with "the complete idiots on the board." Finally, they claim to have sent the names, addresses, phone numbers, and e-mails of all of the board members to above-ground animal activists.

January 29, 2005—Pennsylvania: Animal rights activists claim to have glued the locks to the residence and vehicle of Ayne M. Klein, Associate Director of Sales for Teva Pharmaceuticals, a customer of Hundingdon Life Sciences (HLS). The activists also claim to have strewn bags of garbage across of the lawn of Dr. Nydia Ramos, Technical Services Director of Plantex USA, a Teva subsidiary, and to have left her a warning note not to contract with HLS.

January 2005—Edmund, Oklahoma: On February 8, 2005, through the animal activist Web site Bite Back, http://directaction.info, animal activists claim to have vandalized the offices of Legacy Trading "several weeks ago." The activists claim to have broken a shatter-proof window and detonated smoke flares inside the Legacy office seemingly causing the sprinkler system to damage laptops and paperwork therein. The activists threatened the business owner, Skip (Boruchin), with a return visit if he did not stop doing with business with Huntingdon Life Sciences (HLS).

February 1, 2005—Manhattan, New York: An army recruiting center in the Flatiron section of Manhattan was the target of a thrown rock that cracked the front door. An unidentified attacker also used red paint to scrawl an anarchist symbol and an expletive that mentioned the war in Iraq at the location.

February 1, 2005—Bronx, New York: David Seigel, 19, of Litchfield, Connecticut, was arrested for allegedly throwing a burning rag at an army recruiting center in Parkchester in the Bronx. The rag caused some charring and minor damage to the building.

February 2, 2005—Brookland, Arkansas: Apparent animal activists vandalized Shopher's Taxidermy shop by covering the walls of the building with obscenities, and disassembling the propane tank. The attack was publicized on the Bite Back animal activist Web site (http://directaction.info)

February 6, 2005—Torrance, California: Apparent animal activists vandalized the McDonald's restaurant at Crenshaw Boulevard and Skypark Drive by shattering the glass doors and spray-painting slogans, including "McMurders Killers" on the windows and the initials "ALF" on the building.

February 7, 2005—Sutter Creek, Amador County, California: At around 3:00 A.M. fire erupted at the recently opened 128-unit Pinewoods Apartment Homes complex southeast of Sacramento. On arriving, firefighters found seven individual fires started by incendiary devices. One apartment was destroyed and three others received some damage. A fire suppression system confined the fires and limited the destruction damage. There were only two occupied apartments in the complex, and they were not in the targeted building. Authorities found graffiti indicating, "We will win – ELF" sprayed on a storage box at the perimeter of the complex site. A spokesman for the complex owner, the Jackson Rancheria Band of Miwuk Indians, estimated the damage at more than $100,000.

February 8, 2005—Franklin Lakes, New Jersey: Animal activists claimed to have gained access to the credit card of George Svokos, President of

Plantex, a subsidiary of Teva Pharmaceuticals, and used it to buy Svokos an inflatable sex doll. They also claim to have given his address and credit card information to others to use. The claim was made through the animal activist Web site Bite Back (http://directaction.info).

February 13, 2005—Carson, California: The Animal Liberation Front (ALF) claimed responsibility for vandalizing the Kentucky Fried Chicken (KFC) restaurant at Carson and Figueroa Streets in Carson on Sunday. The attackers broke windows and spray-painted animal rights graffiti on the building. Damage was estimated at around $20,000.

February 13, 2005—Torrance, California: The McDonald's restaurant at 24650 Crenshaw Boulevard was vandalized sometime prior to 5:00 A.M. on Sunday morning by individuals who smashed windows, and spray-painted the graffiti, "McKillers" and "ALF," on the building, The same McDonald's had been similarly attacked on February 6, 2005.

February 13, 2005—Auburn, Placer County, California: Authorities found a fire bomb at the foot of an entrance to the Placer County Courthouse. A walker noticed a purple duffle bag outside of the east entrance of the courthouse and, upon smelling a suspicious odor coming from it, contacted Auburn police. The device was subsequently handled by the Placer County Explosives Ordinance Disposal team. Early indications were that the device ignited, but failed to explode fertilizer. Although no one immediately claimed responsibility for the device, the fact that the Earth Liberation Front (ELF) has been linked to five fire bombs left at the Parkhill Professional Center in Auburn on January 12, 2005, was noted by the local media. None of those devices ignited. However, on February 7, 2005, an arson fire attributed to the ELF caused more than $100,000 in damage to an apartment complex in nearby Sutter Creek in Amador County. On February 9, 2005, Ryan D. Lewis of Newcastle was arrested for the Auburn arson attempt.

February 15, 2005—Auburn, Placer County, California: At around 7:00 A.M. a pipe-bomb was found, and safely dismantled at the back of a Department of Motor Vehicles office in Auburn. Although this bomb was different from the fire bomb found at the entrance to the Placer County Courthouse in Auburn on February 13, 2005, authorities cannot rule out that the two incidents are not related. Nor can authorities rule out that these attacks are not connected to an Earth Liberation Front (ELF)-claimed unsuccessful fire bomb attack at the Parkhill Professional Center in Auburn on January 12, 2005. On February 9, 2005, Ryan D. Lewis of Newcastle was arrested for the Parkhill arson.

February 18, 2005—Albuquerque, New Mexico: An arson fire destroyed 3,000-square-foot home (valued at $350,000) that was under construction in the Volcano Cliffs neighborhood. The home was the first to be built on land at Unser and Universe NW near the Petroglyph National Monument. The house was on Shiprock Court in an undeveloped area west of Taylor

Ranch. The arson was not the first attack on the home. On February 3, 2005, the builder's generator was stolen; on February 12, 2005, all of the newly installed windows were broken, and around the time of the fire, someone vandalized the electric power pole near the home. A number of billboards put up by developers in the area have also been vandalized. On February 28, 2005, a spokesperson for the FBI called the arson an act of "eco-terrorism." The building project to extend Paseo del Norte through the petroglyphs to development in the area has been the subject of vehement protests by groups dedicated to protecting the ancient rock art.

February 19, 2005—Chino Hills, California: Apparent animal rights activists vandalized the home of Casandria Smith, the chief veterinarian for the city of Los Angeles. Several windows at the residence were broken by attackers who left leaflets behind bearing Smith's picture, and accusations that she was involved in animal cruelty.

February 27, 2005—Tranquillity, California: The ALF (Animal Liberation Front) claimed responsibility for breaking into a farm owned by Woodland Farms, a subsidiary of Maple Leaf Farms, and taking 12 ducklings. The ALF accused Maple Leaf Farms, which they describe as being the largest producer of duck meat in North America, of abusing ducks by allowing them to immerse themselves in water.

March 3, 2005—Redmond, Washington: Two incendiary devices were found at a housing-construction site in Redmond. The devices failed to set fires. Although no one claimed responsibility for the attempted arson, the devices were similar to those previously used by the Earth Liberation Front (ELF).

March 5, 2005—New Orleans, Louisiana: Animal activists claim to have spray-painted "Stop Dogfighting" and "ALF" on the house of Cleveland J. Harris, because Harris was charged for the second time with dog-fighting and cruelty to animals. In their claim, the activists described Harris as being a prominent dog-fighter, and indicated that: "If the courts won't stop dog-fighting, we will."

March 7, 2005—Fair Oaks, California: Two residents found their full-sized pickup trucks, and another resident found his Ford Expedition SUV, spray-painted with the letters, "ELF" and the license plates painted over. Fortunately, the victims found the damage before the paint had dried, and were able to remove the paint before it did permanent damage. Police note that similar damage was done to at least four other similar vehicles in the area since February 2005.

March 9, 2005—Polk, Craig, and Clarks, Nebraska: Animal activists claimed to have attacked the homes of relatives of Skip Boruchin in the cities of Polk, Craig, and Clarks in Nebraska. They claim to have covered Boruchin's brother-in-law's house and RV with spray-paint, and to have also done the same thing to a neighbor's home. They claim to have then covered with spray-paint the residence of Boruchin's uncle-in-law. Finally, they claim to have gone to the residence of Boruchin's sister-in-law, where they spray-painted the house, several vehicles, and a boat. Boruchin operates Legacy Trading in Edmund, Oklahoma, and his business has been previously attacked because of its involvement with Huntingdon Life Sciences (HLS).

March 13, 2005—Pennsylvania: Via the Web site http://directaction.info, animal activists claim to have vandalized the residence of Richard S. Egosi, General Council, Teva Pharmaceuticals, USA by spray painting his three-car garage with the slogan, "Drop HLS." They also claim to have covered his SUV with paint stripper. Animal activists indicated that Teva is a customer of Huntingdon Life Sciences (HLS), a firm they have targeted for alleged mistreatment of animals.

March 13, 2005—Pennsylvania: Via the Web site http://directaction.info, animal activists claim to have vandalized the row house of David M. Stout, President of Pharmaceutical Operations, GlaxoSmithKline, by spray-painting the large white garage door with "PUPPY KILLER DAVE." They also claim to have spray-painted the door and porch of the residence, and they threatened that this was only the beginning until his company dropped its relationship with Huntingdon Life Sciences (HLS), a firm that the activists claim abuses animals.

March 14, 2005—Franklin Lakes, New Jersey: Via the Web site http://directaction.info, animal activists claim that more than a month prior they contacted the pastor, secretary, and several parishioners at St. Nicholas Greek Orthodox Church where George Svokos, the president of Plantex-USA, and his wife are members, and told them that they were parishioners who along with other parishioners, had observed Mr. Svokos inappropriately touching young children. They asked the pastor to intervene before they would call the police. They made it clear that they intended further action at the church in an effort to ruin Svokos' reputation as long as Teva ruins animals' lives. Plantex is a subsidiary of Teva Pharmaceuticals of Franklin Lakes, New Jersey, which in turn is a customer of Huntingdon Life Sciences, a firm targeted by animal activists for alleged mistreatment of animals. Previously, on February 8, 2005, activists claim to have gained access to Svokos' credit card, and said that they had used it to buy an inflatable sex doll. At that time they claimed to have given the credit card information to others to use.

March 25, 2005—New Jersey: Animal activists claimed via the animal activist Web site, http://directaction.info, that they had vandalized the residences of four employees of Roche pharmaceuticals because of Roche's association with Huntingdon Life Sciences (HLS). They claim that the damage consisted of throwing paint bombs, gluing door locks, and dousing front porches with brake fluid. They also claim to have spray-painted slogans, including "pervert," "puppy killer," and "your $ your fault" at the victims' homes.

March 27, 2005—Pennsylvania: The animal activist Web site, http://directaction.info, presented a claim by animal activists that they had vandalized the home of Dimitri Gunasekera, an executive with Teva Pharmaceuticals, and covered the entire front of the house, the columns, and the mailbox with spray-paint and slogans. They also claimed to have glued the front door locks. The activists threatened to return to the house if Teva did not drop its association with Huntingdon Life Sciences (HLS).

March 27, 2005—Pennsylvania: The animal activist Web site, http://directaction.info, presented a claim by animal activists that on Sunday they had glued the locks shut to Eisenhower Fellowships because Glaxo CEO J. P. Garnier is on the board of directors. They also claim to have vandalized the residence of John G. Sommer, vice-president of programs at the Eisenhower Fellowships. They claim to have spray-painted in large letters, "John Sommer kills puppies" on the white wall by Sommer's house, and to have painted Sommer's door and porch. They also claim to have glued his locks. They stated that Sommer will continue to suffer until Garnier was removed from the Fellowship's board.

March 28, 2005—Hattiesburg, Mississippi: The animal activist Web site, http://directaction.info reported that by anonymous communiqué dated March 29, 2005 animal activists claimed responsibility for vandalizing on the previous night a Kentucky Fried Chicken restaurant in Hattiesburg by spray-painting slogans, and putting Fix-A-Flat into the order box speaker.

March 30, 2005—Pennsylvania: The animal activist Web site, http://directaction.info, presented a claim by animal activists that they had vandalized the residences of Program Analyst March Bondurant and Sales Channel Director Cheryl Posavac of GlaxoSmithKline warning Glaxo to drop its affiliation with Huntingdon Life Sciences (HLS). They claim to have covered the employees' homes in Center City with spray-paint, and to have glued the door locks.

March 30, 2005—Pennsylvania: The animal activist Web site, http://directaction.info, presented a claim by animal activists that they vandalized the home of Peter McCausland, Chairman and CEO of Airgas, Inc., because GlaxoSmithKline President David M. Stout is on the board of directors of Airgas. They claim to have covered two vehicles, including a new Porsche, with paint stripper, and to have spray-painted McCausland's house and property. They warned that Airgas would continue to be targeted until Stout is removed from the Airgas board.

March 30, 2005—Bloomington, Indiana: An employee arriving for work on Wednesday at the Planned Parenthood office found the remains of a small fire in the foyer of the office. The glass entry door had been broken. There was a small amount of smoke, and the windows were covered with a thin layer of soot. On March 19, 2005, burned papers were found near the same office. The FBI joined the Bloomington police department in the investigation of the incident. No one immediately claimed responsibility for the attack.

April 1, 2005—Bluffs, Illinois: The Animal Liberation Front (ALF) claimed responsibility for an early morning raid on the fox farm of Kerry Littig, who they describe as being the top breeder of silver foxes in the United States. They claim to have removed the majority of the surrounding fence, removed all of the breeding information, and finally opened every single cage, releasing dozens of foxes to the surrounding countryside.

April 13, 2005—Sammamish, Washington: At around 5:00 A.M. firefighters responded to a report of a house under construction burning. The home was three weeks from completion, and it was determined that it had cost the owner between $300,000 and $350,000. Although the firefighters were able to save the basic structure, there was heavy damage to the home. While the firefighters were battling the fire, someone noticed a paper in front of another under-construction home on the same street. This paper bore the initials, "ELF" and several slogans, including "Where are all of the trees?" and "Burn Rapist Burn." Firefighters entered this house and discovered that the gas had been turned on, and that an incendiary device had been placed to seemingly detonate the gas. Authorities were able to defuse the incendiary device before it caused an explosion or fire.

April 15, 2005—Philadelphia, Pennsylvania: The animal activist Web site, http://directaction.info, presented a claim by animal activists that they had paint-stripped the car of Steven A. Smith, a scientist at GlaxoSmithKline in the Philadelphia suburbs.

April 17, 2005—Laurel Hollow, New York: The Animal Liberation Front (ALF) claimed to have followed Maria Ryan, the wife of Chuck Ryan, the director and chief patient counsel to Forest Labs, a customer of Huntingdon Life Sciences (HLS). After observing her park her Mercedes CLK at Stony Brook University, ALF members claim to have entered the unlocked car and to have taken information and possibly items from the vehicle. One of the items identified was the Ryans' Capital One credit card. With that information, the ALF members claim to have procured Capital One Travelers Checks from the account which they wrote and distributed as follows: $5,000 to Boston Area Rape Crisis Center; $5,000 to Help Iraqi/Global Exchange; $4,000 to Save the Manatee Club; $6,000 to Global Greens Grant Fund—Tsunami Relief Fund. The ALF members warned the Ryans that they had their vehicle insurance information, and could have cancelled their car insurance, and then burned the Mercedes leaving then with an uninsured loss. Finally, in their communiqué, the ALF released a volume of personal information about the Ryans including their home address and telephone number, assorted financial records—bank account and credit card numbers—and the names of personal friends.

April 19, 2005—Torrance, California: The Animal Liberation Front (ALF) claimed responsibility for vandalizing the home and cars of Flora

Sadeghi, the CFO of Phenomenex, a supplier to Huntingdon Life Sciences (HLS). The group claims to have painted the garage doors and three cars, including a brand-new Jaguar. They gave Sadeghi an ultimatum to drop HLS within seven days or face further attacks.

April 20, 2005—Pennsylvania: Through the Web site www.directaction. info, animal activists claim to have vandalized the home of James W. Hovey, who sits on the same board as GlaxoSmithKline President David Stout. They claim to have defaced the front doors and windows and two sides of the house with tire blackener, which they claim leaves stains. They also claim to have taken personal photographs and written documents from the Hovey trash can. They closed their claim by warning that Hovey can expect a return visit. The activists then claim to have visited the home of Erin Hillman, who is Programs Manager with the Eisenhower Fellowships where GlaxoSmith-Kline CEO J.P. Garnier is a member of the Board of Directors. They claim to have poured paint stripper on two cars at the residence. The activists warned that they will continue to target the Eisenhower Fellowships until they drop Garnier from their Board.

April 21, 2005—Pennsylvania: Animal activists used the Web site www. directaction.info to claim responsibility for throwing a brick through the front window of the residence of GlaxoSmithKline President David Stout. (Activists previously claimed to have vandalized the residence on March 13, 2005).

April 21, 2005—Baton Rouge, Louisiana: The Animal Liberation Front (ALF) claimed responsibility for liberating 21 mice from the Biology Department at Louisiana State University during the early hours of April 21, 2005. They claim to have broken through a vent in a side door on the building's seventh floor. They claim to have given the mice to loving homes, and not to have released them into the wild. They also claim that while in the college they smashed aquariums, broke windows, spray-painted slogans, glued locks to any doors to rooms that did not house animals, and poured paint stripper on outer walls.

April 22, 2005—New Jersey: Animal activists used the Web site www. directaction.info to claim to have vandalized with spray-painted slogans and paint-bombs, the residences of the following three employees of Roche Pharmaceuticals, a customer of Huntingdon Life Sciences (HLS): Janet Lee, a scientist; Barbara Sennich, Vice President of Sales and Marketing; and Dr. Vishna Singh, a Roche executive.

April 26, 2005—Hollywood Hills, California: Animal activists attacked the residence of Andrew Baker, an executive of animal testing company, Huntingdon Life Sciences (HLS). Police caught five activists allegedly breaking windows and defacing the property of Baker. Arrested on felony vandalism charges were Colin Birock, 35; Lorena Perez, 20; Linda Greene, 57; Sandra Sepulveda, 34; and Jessica Chervat, 20.

May 13, 2005—Rockville, Maryland: Via the Web site Bite Back, www. directaction.info, animal activists claim to have attacked the residences of Medifacts employees because of Medifact's ties with CentraLabs and Huntingdon Life Sciences (HLS). The door, porch area, and driveway of President and CEO Sandra Garrett were spray-painted and their locks were glued. The residence of Executive Director and COO Doug Cowart was spray-painted and the locks glued. Two of his cars were also covered with paint stripper. The home of Consultant Bert Spilker was also covered with spray-paint and his locks were glued. The residence of CFO James Krejci was spray-painted on its front, back, and side, its locks were glued, and the fence and sidewalk were covered with slogans, including "puppy killer" and "drop Central Labs." At the residence of Senior Vice President and Executive Director Vincent Lagrotteria, the house, porch, furniture, and walkway were covered in spray-paint and the locks were glued.

May 22, 2005—Aspen, Colorado: Three vehicles: a Mercedes SUV, a Volkswagen Vanagon, and an Audi were attacked by apparent environmental activists on Garmisch Street and Durant and Copper Avenues in Aspen. The initials "ELF" was spray-painted on one of the vehicles, "Sucks" was spray-painted onto the Mercedes. In addition, the words "Zulu nations," was spray-painted onto the wall of the Aspen Ice Garden ice rink. A police officer estimated that repairs from the damage will run into the thousands of dollars.

May 26, 2005—Richard Township, Pennsylvania: Animal rights activists vandalized a nursery that is a proposed housing site for monkeys waiting to be shipped to medical research laboratories. The vandals overturned and destroyed around 1,000 peonies at Peonyland in Richard Township on Thursday night. They also poured paint stripper on two vehicles and spray-painted graffiti mentioning the primate plans, and stating "ALF is watching" on buildings and greenhouses. The proposed transformation of the nursery into a commercial kennel to house up to 500 monkeys on the 47-acre site has been met with community opposition. Damage was in the thousands of dollars.

June 12, 2005—Irving, Texas: Animal activists claim to have used acid to etch 18 windows at an Abbott Laboratory complex in Irving in an effort to force Abbott to drop any involvement with Huntingdon Life Sciences (HLS), a firm engaged in animal testing.

June 23, 2005—Portland, Oregon: Anonymous animal activists claim to have thrown three paint stripper-filled light bulbs at a United Parcel Service (UPS) truck at the UPS main facility on North Basin Avenue in Portland. They claim the attack was done in an effort to force UPS to stop delivering for Huntingdon Life Sciences (HLS). They warned that if UPS continued dealing with HLS, "We intend to make the contract less profitable for them."

June 24, 2005—Melville and Woodbury, New York (2 attacks): The Animal Liberation Front (ALF) claimed responsibility for using a paint-filled and recharged fire extinguisher to throw gallons of paint across the building of the Wachovia Securities Financial Network at 510 Broadhollow Road, Suite 308, Melville, New York, 11747-3606. ALF also claimed credit for splattering paint and thinner across the entire front of the Wachovia Securities office at 88 Froehlich Farm Boulevard, Suite 110, Woodbury, New York, 11797. Windows were also broken at the Woodbury location. The attacks were done to protest Wachovia Corporation's holdings of stock in GlaxoSmithKline, which does business with animal testing company, Huntingdon Life Sciences.

July 4, 2005—San Carlos, California: Via the animal activist Web site Bite Back, www.directaction.info, the Animal Liberation Front (ALF) claimed responsibility for recently spray-painting and breaking windows at the offices of Bachem/Peninsula Laboratories to protest this firm's association with animal tester, Huntingdon Life Sciences.

July 4, 2005—West Palm Beach, Florida: A fire broke out in the Presidential Women's Clinic in West Palm Beach. The abortion clinic had been the target of weekly anti-abortion protests for more than a decade. The fire caused extensive damage to the building. The fire was immediately deemed as "suspicious in nature," and evidence of some form of fire accelerant was found at the scene. The fire occurred a year and two days after another fire destroyed the inside of the Women's Care Center abortion clinic in nearby Lake Worth, Florida on July 2, 2004. Still another abortion clinic, that of Dr. Michael Benjamin, was damaged by an arson fire in Tamarac in adjacent Broward County, Florida on May 25, 2003. The West Palm Beach facility was the only remaining abortion clinic in the county.

July 6, 2005—Port Jefferson, New York: The Animal Liberation Front (ALF) claimed responsibility for vandalizing the office of Wachovia Securities, 414 Main Street, Port Jefferson, New York, 11777, Suite 101. They claimed that on Wednesday night they spray-painted the first floor storefront with animal rights messages and the acronym, ALF, and to have splashed black paint on the second floor. The attack was to protest Wachovia's relationship with GlaxoSmithKline, a firm the activists claim is associated with Huntingdon Life Sciences, a company engaged in animal testing.

July 21, 2005—Brant Beach, Long Beach Township, New Jersey: Animal activists vandalized a home on 65th Street in Brant Beach by spray-painting "puppy killers" and other slogans on the house and gluing the locks, and by painting orange stripes on the BMW parked in the driveway and gluing its locks shut. Police believe that the attack was a case of mistaken identity in that the residents of the address are not affiliated with Hoffman-LaRoche or Huntingdon Life Sciences, firms currently being targeted by animal activists in the state.

August 16, 2005—Seattle, Washington: According to the Web site Bite Back, www.directaction.info, animal activists vandalized a Kentucky Fried Chicken restaurant in Seattle, Washington, by etching ten of their windows with acid.

August 23, 2005—Manhasset, New York: On Tuesday the Animal Liberation Front (ALF) claimed responsibility for a vandalism attack on the Manhasset Bay Yacht Club to protest the fact that Walter Carucci and Stephanie L. Bass of Carr Securities frequent the club. The ALF claimed to have completely covered the club area with red paint and slogans. They also claim to have made the attack because Carr Securities began to market stock in LSRI (Life Sciences Research, Inc.). Animal testing company, Huntingdon Life Sciences (HLS), is a wholly owned subsidiary of LSRI.

August 25, 2005—Oyster Bay, New York: The Web site Bite Back (www.directaction.info), reported that individuals calling themselves the ALF Pirates for Animal Liberation claim to have used a boat to get to Center Island in Oyster Bay, New York, where they vandalized the Seawanhaka Corinthian Yacht Club by spray-painting fences and outside structures with anti-HLS (Huntingdon Life Sciences) slogans and with the huge letters, "F- - K YOU CARR". The attack was aimed at Walter "Wally" Carucci, President of Carr Securities for marketing HLS, an animal testing firm. The attackers demanded that the yacht club oust Carucci as a member.

September 9, 2005—Seattle, Washington: The Bite Back animal activist Web site, www.directaction.info reported that on September 9, 2005, animal activists had attacked a Kentucky Fried Chicken restaurant in Seattle by etching nine of its windows and spray-painting slogans.

September 9, 2005—Babylon, New York: On early Friday the Animal Liberation Front (ALF) and the Earth Liberation Front (ELF) claimed responsibility for vandalizing American Legion Post # 94 by destroying property, defacing memorials, and spray-painting the entire building with anti-hate slogans. The attack targeted the Minutemen group, who were scheduled to stage a recruitment meeting at the facility on September 10, 2005. The ALF and ELF claimed that the Minutemen, who seek to secure the United States borders against illegal immigration, have a racist and homicidal agenda. The information about the attack was released by the Animal Defense League of Long Island, New York, who claimed that the North American Animal Liberation Front Press Office censored the ALF attack, and refused to publish information about it.

September 11, 2005—West Old Town, Maine: On Sunday evening vandals attacked the West Old Town landfill, causing at least $30,000 in damage. The assailants left graffiti initials, ELF," on numerous locations and also left the initials, "G" with an overlapped A" which some believe refers to "Green Anarchy." Most of the damage was to equipment owned by Sargent & Sargent, a general contracting company working at the landfill. Damage included flattened tires, a smashed console on a new tractor, keys broken off in nearly every piece of large equipment, windows broken in the main building and the scale house, and hoses inserted, and the water turned on into these structures.

September 16, 2005—Los Angeles, California: The Animal Liberation Front (ALF) claimed responsibility for igniting military-strength smoke grenades on the floor of the residence of Gordon Stuckey, general manager of the Los Angeles Animal Shelter. In attacking Stuckey the group stated, "Stuckey you are a disgusting human being who takes pleasure in the murder of over 50,000 animals a year. You are a target. Sleep light."

October 2, 2005—Seattle, Washington: The animal activist Web site, Bite Back, www.directaction.info, reported that that on October 2, 2005, animal activists had anonymously claimed to have vandalized two Kentucky Fried Chicken restaurants in Seattle by using acid to etch four windows at each site and by spray-painting slogans on the buildings.

October 3, 2005—Bozeman, Montana: On Monday workers constructing the Kenyon Noble Lumber & Hardware store on West Oak Street in Bozeman discovered that equipment had been vandalized by unknown individuals who spray-painted the letters "ELF" at the scene. An electrical box, two forklifts, a man lift, and several bags of cement were damaged for a total loss of around $3,000. No one reason for the attack was immediately known.

October 25–26, 2005—Chicago, Illinois: Overnight, apparent animal activists vandalized Cyrano's Bistro and Wine Bar on Chicago's near-north side. A window was broken and splattered with a red liquid resembling blood, and flower boxes and a fence surrounding the outside eating area were smashed. On Tuesday, Didier Durand, the chef at the restaurant, had spoken before the Chicago City Council against a proposed ordinance to ban the sale of foie gras in city restaurants.

October 29, 2005—Chino Hills, California: At 9:25 A.M. San Bernardino County sheriff's deputies were called to the 2700 block of Calle Luna, Chino Hills to handle a possible bomb. On arriving they found a device consisting of two red cylinders inside of a box with antennae protruding outside of one end. While the officers were at the scene, the *Daily Bulletin* newspaper received a telephone call from a female claiming to be from the Animal Liberation Front (ALF). She stated that a device had been placed at the exact location where the officers were then located. The caller said that the resident of the address was a veterinarian with Los Angeles County. The sheriff's bomb squad was called to the scene, and used a robot to determine that the device was inert and could not have exploded. While this operation was ongoing, neighborhood residents were ordered to evacuate their homes for several hours. The Animal Liberation Front (ALF) subsequently released a communiqué claiming responsibility for the attack, and stating that the target was Cassandra Smith, the head veterinarian at the Los Angeles Animal Services at her home. In their statement, the ALF reported that they had told Smith that they would deactivate the bomb if she released a public statement resigning from her position (That demand was seemingly made during the ALF telephone call to the *Daily Bulletin* on October 29, 2005).

October 31, 2005—Commack, New York: Through the Web site Bite Back, www.directaction.info, the Animal Liberation Front (ALF) claimed on November 4, 2005, responsibility for vandalizing the Citibank branch in Commack with paint and graffiti slogans and other damage during the last week of October 2005.

October 31–November 1, 2005—Oakland, Greenville, Fairfield, Hallowell, and Augusta, Maine: Suspected environmental activists vandalized properties of the Seattle, Washington-based Plum Creek Timber Company and its employees and people associated with the company over Monday and Tuesday night. The residence of Plum Creek General Manager Jim Lehner in Oakland was attacked with rocks and small containers filled with orange paint. Four windows were broken. The damage was estimated at around $8,000. The residence of project manager Luke Muzzy in Greenville was defaced with animal feces and a chemical poured onto the porch that penetrated the home with the odor of vomit. Plum Creek's offices in Fairfield, and a real estate office formerly owned by Muzzy in Greenville were vandalized with paint, and animal parts were left on the doorknobs. The lock to the door of the real estate office was also glued shut. Other locations vandalized were the Augusta law office of Preti Flaherty Beliveau Pachios and Haley, whose partner, Severin Beliveau, serves as Plum Creek's attorney, and the residence of the next-door neighbor of Beliveau in Hallowell. The attackers apparently mistook the neighbor's historic home for that of Beliveau. Plum Creek Timber has been under fire for proposing the rezoning of around 10,000 acres of timberlands around Moosehead Lake so that two resorts, 975 house lots, campgrounds, and other uses can be made of the property.

November 15, 2005—Huntington, New York: On Tuesday night activists from the Animal Liberation Front (ALF) vandalized the residence of Leland M. Hairr, Mayor of Lloyd Harbor, New York. The ALF activists claimed to have completely covered the Hairr residence in red paint with slogans demanding that Hairr put a stop to the deer kill scheduled to take place in Caumsett State Park, the Seminary of Immaculate Conception, and Lloyd Harbor town park.

November 16, 2005—Westhampton, New York: Activists from the Animal Liberation Front (ALF) claimed to have followed Kenneth J. Greiner from his home at 105 5th Avenue in New York City to his weekend getaway in Westhampton, New York. During the night the activists claim to have covered Greiner's Honda sport utility vehicle and Lexus with paint and broke a back window. They also claim to have covered the house with paint and the words, "drop HLS" and "sell Isri.ob."

November 20, 2005—Hagerstown, Maryland: Shortly before 4:00 A.M. on early Sunday a fire at the Hagers Crossing housing development on U.S. 40 in Hagerstown, Maryland, destroyed one townhouse and damaged three others. All of the units were unoccupied at the time, and there were no injuries. Finding four separate points of ignition, firefighters quickly determined that the blaze was an arson. An anonymous e-mail sent to news organizations including the *Herald Mail* newspaper following the fire, claimed responsibility for the attack in the name of Earth Liberation Front (ELF) stating that they "… put the torch to a development of Ryan Homes … to strike at the bottom line of this country's most notorious serial land rapists." When the 160-acre Hager's crossing development is complete, it will contain more than 700 units. Damage from the arson was estimated at $300,000.

December 1–2, 2005—Davis, California: Overnight, unidentified individuals entered the Life Sciences addition building at the University of California at Davis, and defaced walls, doors, and refrigerators in 20 locations throughout the building by spray-painting, "No GM," "No to Frankenfoods," and peace symbols. They also broke six glass beakers and overturned several plants.

December 12, 2005—Shreveport, Louisiana: At around 10:45 P.M. a female threw a Molotov cocktail at the Hope Medical Group for Women. The incendiary device landed short, and the fire did not spread to the abortion clinic.

December 21, 2005—Cincinnati, Ohio: At around 10:10 P.M. two bombs detonated outside of the Islamic Association of Cincinnati Mosque complex on Clifton Avenue in Cincinnati. The mosque had closed after evening prayers had ended at about 8:00 P.M. The complex consists of a house used for daily prayers, and an attached worship center that opened two years ago that is used for large gatherings. The explosions occurred in front of each building and damaged the doorways. There were no injuries. The reason for the bombings were not immediately known as there had not been any recent threats, and no one claimed responsibility for the attack. The complex is located near several churches and the Hebrew Union College, and a mile from the University of Cincinnati campus. The FBI offered a $15,000 reward for information leading to the arrest of the perpetrators of the attack. The Council of American-Islamic Relations offered a $5,000 reward in the case.

December 23, 2005—Woodbury, New York: The Animal Liberation Front (ALF) claimed that they vandalized the residence of Stuart Rabinowitz, 2 Victor Lane, Woodbury, New York, by covering the whole house with spray-painted slogans. They claimed to have done this because Rabinowitz, the President of Hofstra University, had selected Collin Goddard, the CEO of OSI Pharmaceuticals, to be the keynote speaker at the mid-year commencement ceremony of the college. The ALF claimed that Goddard's financial partner is GlaxoSmithKline vice president Robert Ingram, and that Glaxo is one of the largest customers of the animal testing firm, Huntingdon Life Sciences (HLS).

Appendix Ⓥ

Key Terms and Concepts

The definitions used in this section emanate from law enforcement usage with respect to terrorist investigations. As such, some of the definitions may be quite different from what would be found in a conventional dictionary or used in the secular world.

agent provocateur—According to Webster's Dictionary, an agent provocateur "is a paid agent who, by pretended sympathy, seeks to induce suspect persons to expose themselves, esp. one who provokes seditious movements in order to justify official reprisals." In a more practical sense, the government will likely hear the agent provocateur accusation used as a kind of entrapment defense in which the defendant claims that he was not predisposed to commit the crime for which he was arrested. In the entrapment argument, the defendant claims that the undercover operative (who is usually an undercover officer, but who could be an informant) directly caused or facilitated his commission of a specific crime that he otherwise would not have committed. The agent provocateur defense is usually not as specific. The defendant does not accuse the officer of direct involvement in a particular crime. Instead, he accuses the officer of creating the general environment that inspired the commission of the crime. For example, a terrorist might state that his group was only engaged in legal protest activity until the time that the undercover officer joined and convinced them that violent actions were the only vehicle through which they could achieve their objectives. Inasmuch as there is no claim that the undercover officer facilitated the specific crime for which the terrorist was arrested, the agent provocateur defense will probably not be accepted in court. However, if not challenged by the prosecution, it could have an adverse impact on the judge and jury.

bomb factory—Usually refers to a covert location used by a terrorist group for building explosive devices. The term has also been broadened to include a clandestine location used by terrorists to make incendiary devices or to store weapons.

bug—A concealed listening device placed by a law enforcement agency to overhear the target of an investigation. A court order or consent is usually required for such an installation.

bumper lock—The law enforcement practice of following a vehicle so closely that the officer cannot possibly lose sight of it. Inevitably, the subject becomes aware that he or she is being followed. This method is not recommended during terrorism surveillances because terrorism coverages should be designed to avoid detection.

burned—A term used to describe the fact that a target of investigation has identified a person following him as a law enforcement officer. It could also include the fact that a terrorist group identified an undercover officer or informant as being connected to a law enforcement agency. An informant might be "burned" if he is seen meeting with a known police officer or making a call to a law enforcement telephone number.

casing—refers to subjects observing a target that they plan to attack

C-4—A powerful military plastic explosive that can be molded into a variety of configurations.

chain of custody—An important concept with respect to evidence. It involves a tracking record of a piece of evidence from the time of its recovery through the time of the trial. Defense attorneys will attempt to show a break in the chain of custody by demonstrating that there was a period during which the exact location of the evidence was unknown. If this is successful, the evidence will probably be ruled inadmissible regardless of its importance to the case.

CCTV (Closed-Circuit Television)—CCTV is often used by police agencies to monitor people and locations. It consists of a television camera and a television screen receiver that monitors what the camera films. CCTV is used quite extensively by businesses to bolster security, and in the twenty-first century has become so commonplace and inexpensive that many private citizens use it at their residences.

contingency plan—An outline that explains how a law enforcement agency intends to respond to an emergency situation. An agency should have a such a plan to handle crisis situations, including terrorist attacks.

countersurveillance—The practice by which the subject of surveillance takes actions that allow his associates to detect coverage by a law enforcement agency. The associates may actually follow the subject in an effort to detect officers who are also following him, or the subject may take actions that force surveillance officers to react in such a manner that an associate will be able to observe them. Often an associate of a subject will covertly observe the subject as he leaves a particular location in an effort to determine whether anyone is tailing him. The term may also be used to refer to surveillance efforts by the subject and his associates against selected law enforcement officers. For example, a terrorist group may surveil a police parking lot to observe personnel and identify vehicles being used by that agency.

dangle—A term often used with respect to informants in which a source is placed into a situation that enables the targets to observe, meet, and possibly recruit him. An undercover officer could also be "dangled" by his agency so that the targets of the investigation will find him suitable for recruitment.

deflagration—A term used to describe burning with great heat, as with an arson. (For prosecution purposes, deflagration can be contrasted with detonation, which means "to explode.")

detonation—A term used to describe an explosion, such as with a bomb. (For prosecution purposes detonation can be contrasted with deflagration, which means burning with great heat, as in an arson)

DNA—Deoxyribonucleic acid. The principal component of cellular chromosomes, DNA is a unique identifier within every human being. Unlike fingerprints that can only be left when a person touches something with his or her hands, DNA can be left through blood, saliva, and other body fluids and skin shavings. As careful as terrorists have become to avoid leaving fingerprints, it will be difficult for them not to leave behind DNA, especially in safe houses and bomb factories where they have spent time. In its early uses during the 1990s DNA testing was costly and time-consuming. Modern technology has greatly shortened the time required to conduct these examinations.

dry cleaning—A process by which a subject takes actions that enable him to "lose" anyone who is attempting to follow him. A person may "dry clean" himself by entering a crowded movie theatre and leaving soon after through a rear door. Undercover officers and informants should also undertake "dry cleaning" maneuvers before meeting each other.

dumpster diving—A slang term for a trash cover.

entrapment—A situation in which a law enforcement officer causes a subject to commit a criminal act that he was not predisposed to commit. This defense is often made by people who have been arrested as a result of an undercover operation. The defendant will claim that the undercover officer encouraged or facilitated his commission of a crime that he had not previously considered, or could not have committed without the officer's assistance. Investigators should expect this defense to be claimed in any terrorism case in which an undercover officer was involved. The argument can also be used against an informant.

exemplars—Items of physical evidence of known origin that can be compared with other items. An investigator might obtain exemplars of a person's handwriting to compare with unidentified handwriting.

eyeball—This is the law enforcement officer who has the direct view of the subject during the course of a surveillance. Often during a surveillance, when the subject is not moving, one investigator will be designated as the "eyeball," meaning that it is his or her responsibility to watch the subject. Other surveillance officers will then move to more distant locations.

handler (handling officer)—The law enforcement officer whose job it is to bridge the gap between an undercover officer and his department. He transmits information and provides physical and emotional support for the undercover operative. The handler himself may be undercover in the sense that he carries false identification and maintains a safe location where meetings can be held.

Joint Terrorism Task Force (JTTF) (originally called Joint Terrorist Task Force)—An investigative entity comprised of various federal and local law enforcement agencies operating in a given area to investigate terrorist violations. JTTFs operate under a signed memorandum of understanding that outlines each agency's responsibilities. JTTFs are characterized by sharing information and investigative responsibility. The concept was started in 1981 under the name Joint Terrorist Task Force in New York City and Chicago, Illinois, and initially concentrated on domestic terrorism. Over the years JTTFs were developed in other parts of the country, and JTTFs expanded their responsibilities to address all forms of terrorism in the United States including that perpetrated by foreign extremists. The attacks of September 11, 2001, resulted in the JTTF concept becoming the norm with respect to law enforcement response to the terrorist threat in the United States. By 2008 there were more than 100 JTTFs covering virtually the entire country.

Light Anti-Tank Weapon (L.A.W.)—A disposable, handheld, military anti-tank rocket that is popular among terrorists. Puerto Rican terrorists have used these devices against federal buildings in Puerto Rico.

log—A written record of events. In law enforcement, logs are commonly used to record the subject's activities during a surveillance (surveillance logs). Logs can also be used to record incoming and outgoing telephone calls during electronic coverage, and to document the recovery of evidence. Some agencies maintain logs in conjunction with a subject's interview to reflect the exact time the interview began, when the person was advised of his rights, when he agreed to waive his rights, and when the interview ended. Logs are also frequently used to track photographs taken in connection with investigations. Police agencies often have pre-printed log forms that are used for specific purposes, such as surveillance. Many modern logs are maintained on computers.

lookout—A term used in surveillances to refer to a fixed location from which an investigator is able to view a person or an address.

made—A slang term that refers to a subject identifying someone who is following him as a law enforcement officer. It is said that the subject has "made" the surveilling officer. The term can also be used to refer to a subject identifying a person as being a police informant or undercover agent.

material witness—A person who is not the subject of an investigation, but who nonetheless possesses pertinent information about a criminal activity. Because of the fear generated by terrorists, reluctant witnesses may have to be convinced to cooperate by being held in custody as material witnesses in order to ensure their testimony before a grand jury or in trial.

minimization—The process that an investigator uses to avoid listening to and documenting certain "privileged" conversations during the operation of a wiretap or microphone. When a court order is issued authorizing a wiretap or microphone, the court will usually specify that certain types of conversations cannot be monitored, thereby requiring listening officers to minimize listening to privileged conversations. For example, monitoring a call between a lawyer and the subject would almost always be minimized, as would coverage of a microphone that could hear a subject and his spouse engaged in sexual activity.

Molotov cocktail—An incendiary device that usually consists of a bottle filled with gasoline and possibly other slower-burning flammables like fuel oil or soap flakes, and ignited with a rag or fuse. The device is intended to burst into flames when it is thrown and strikes something, thereby breaking the container.

Memorandum of Understanding (MOU)—An agreement signed by two or more law enforcement agencies that outlines the duties and responsibilities of each agency with respect to a certain crime problem. Local and county police agencies in a particular state might sign an MOU in which the local agency agrees to handle bombings that occur inside the city, and the county agrees to respond to incidents that occur in any other area of the county.

Off-site—A covert location maintained by a law enforcement agency to provide support for an investigation.

parasitic device—This refers to an electronic monitoring device (a beeper or microphone) that uses the target's power source, usually from his vehicle's battery. In most instances, a court order will be required to use such a device, because a "trespass" of the subject's property will be required to place it.

pen register—A device that records numbers dialed from or to a targeted telephone.

perch—A slang term for a lookout.

picket—A manpower-intensive form of surveillance in which only the subject moves. The law enforcement officers remain stationary and observe the subject as he passes through their line of sight. Each surveillance officer is called a "picket." This form of coverage is sometimes referred to as "stationary" or "fixed." It is often used in connection with ransom drops and espionage cases.

plant—In terrorism terms, this refers to a person from an extremist group who has been able to covertly penetrate a law enforcement or government agency to benefit his political cause. In spy terms, the word would be "mole." The term plant is sometimes used in surveillances to refer to an officer who remains in a fixed location, or to a lookout post itself.

pretext call—a telephone call to a target or someone who can provide information on the target during which the investigator does not reveal his police position or the true reason for the contact.

pretext interview—An interview conducted by a law enforcement agency with someone able to provide information about the subject, in which the officer does not reveal the true nature of the interview. The officer may or may not reveal his official position.

proactive investigation—In terrorism cases, this term refers to an investigation conducted to prevent a violent attack from occurring.

Prosecutive (or prosecution) report—A document prepared by a law enforcement officer outlining the evidence against a subject that will be used by the prosecutor at trial. Federal officers are usually required to prepare such a document. A prosecutive report can be extremely important in terrorism cases because it should clearly answer the "Who?" "What?" "Where?" "When?" "Why?" and "How?" questions that defense attorneys will attack in court if not resolved. It also lets investigators know if any aspect of the investigation has been overlooked.

reactive investigation—In terrorism cases, this term refers to the response that occurs after a terrorist attack has taken place, designed to determine the responsible parties.

ruse—An action taken by an investigator to mislead a target and conceal from the target the real reason for his interest in that person. A ruse is like a subterfuge and can be verbal or physical in nature.

Safe house—A clandestine location established by a terrorist group to give them protection and security for their operations. The safe house is often used for meetings, and to place and receive telephone calls. It could also be used as a hiding place for fugitives, and as a staging area for terrorist attacks. Some law enforcement agencies also use the term to refer to a location where an undercover officer can get away from the subjects for relaxation and debriefing. It can also be a place where a police agency can hide a terrorist group member who has agreed to cooperate with the department, and is being sought by the extremists.

scanner—A device that can pick up radio broadcasts. It is of concern to investigators because a scanner might be able to monitor police radios and identify the presence of court-ordered microphones.

Semtex—A Czechoslovakian plastic high explosive that has been used by several major international terrorist groups.

slap-on—This refers to a magnetized electronic monitoring device that a surveillance team can "slap on" to the undercarriage of a subject's vehicle in order to follow him or her.

Stake-out—Often used as another term for surveillance—the visual observation of a person or location. However, the term is more likely to be applied when the purpose of the surveillance is to arrest the targeted person.

stop—The practice of placing a lookout notice with an agency that may encounter a subject. This notice usually asks the agency to notify the requesting department of any contact that the subject has with it.

subsource—An "informant" who is operated by a police informant. This is not a desirable situation because the law enforcement agency has no control over the informant's informant, and often does not know his or her identity. The reliability of information provided by a subsource cannot be determined, thereby severely restricting the use that a law enforcement agency can make of the information that he or she provides.

subterfuge—A deceptive practice designed to develop information without allowing the target to know that a law enforcement agency is involved. A surveillance team may use the subterfuge of a picnic to permit them to observe a suspect in a city park.

Tabletop—A training session for crisis/emergency response conducted in a theoretical rather than an actual manner. Usually those in a law enforcement agency who would be involved in a particular emergency situation, such as a terrorist bombing, will gather in a room where a "facilitator" will introduce a situation that requires action. He will then ask the appropriate personnel to explain how each would respond. Following this, the facilitator will bring in additional facts. No investigator actually conducts an investigation. Instead, it is a matter of each person learning what role he would be expected to play if the emergency were real. Tabletops are usually aimed more at managers than street investigators.

taint—Anything that can cause the credibility of a witness, a written document, or an article of evidence to be successfully challenged. An informant may be described as being "tainted" if it can be shown that he lied in testimony given in a previous unrelated court case. An article of evidence may be described as "tainted" if it can be shown that it was altered in some way or that its chain of custody had been broken.

terrorist task force—See joint terrorism task force

toxin—A poisonous substance.

tracking systems—Electronic devices that can be placed on a vehicle or inside a container so that a law enforcement agency can monitor the movement of that object.

trash cover—An investigative technique through which an investigator recovers a subject's discarded items. Trash covers are usually conducted at a subject's residence or place of employment, but they can also be conducted in connection with items that a subject discards at any other time, including during a surveillance.

vetting—The process by which a law enforcement agency verifies the reliability and honesty of an informant.

wire—A slang term that refers to a covert monitoring device (either a recorder or a transmitter) that an informant, undercover officer, or citizen wears while meeting with suspects.

witness—An individual who has observed something of interest to a law enforcement agency. In some right-wing cases, a "witness" is someone who an extremist will insist be present during an interview. This kind of "witness" is usually not an attorney or a relative. He may, however, be a person who is also involved in the criminal activity at issue, and may even have mentored the subject with respect to his or her political development.

Appendix Ⅵ

Selected Extremist Terms

The definitions and descriptions herein apply to law enforcement usage with respect to terrorist investigations. As such, definitions are likely to differ from those that would appear in a traditional secular dictionary.

ALF/Animal Liberation Front—A clandestine terrorist group that has claimed credit for hundreds of attacks in the names of animal rights. The group was originally founded in England in 1976. ALF moved into Canada in 1981 and into the United States in 1982

American Dissident Voices—A weekly radio program intended for white people and sponsored by National Alliance, a group founded by the late William Pierce, who died July 23, 2002.

Anarchist Cookbook—A publication originally circulated in the 1960s but is still available today. This book describes the construction of explosive devices and has been popular with a variety of political extremists.

anthrax—A highly infectious, usually fatal disease. It is possibly the single most feared biological weapon of mass destruction. Threats to use anthrax closed scores of abortion clinics in the late 1990s and the early twenty-first century.

Army of God—A name taken by various anti-abortion activists who have committed violent attacks. The name was first used by three men who kidnapped an abortion doctor in Southern Illinois in 1982. There is also an *Army of God Manual* that instructs people how to construct bombs, sabotage clinics, and use weapons.

Aryans—White people from Northern Europe. Many right-wing extremists in the United States describe themselves as being Aryan, and believe that the white race is superior to all others.

Aryan Nations—A group based for many years in Hayden Lake, Idaho, that seeks to establish a white-only nation in the northwestern part of United States. It is heavily influenced by the Christian Identity religion. Its founder and long-time leader, Richard Butler, was a Christian Identity minister. Many people associated with the Aryan Nations have committed acts of violence over the past several decades. The Aryan Nations compound was sold in a bankruptcy proceeding in 2001 after Richard Butler lost a civil suit filed by two people who were accosted by compound security guards. In the early twenty-first century, a competing group also using the name Aryan Nations, and claiming to be the successor to the original organization, established a presence in Pennsylvania. They, too, were heavily influenced by the Christian Identity religion. When Butler died on September 8, 2004, he did not leave a designated heir to his position, and the group's membership dissipated. The Pennsylvania group relocated to Florida, and ultimately to South Carolina, where it continued to maintain an active Web site into 2008. Others claiming to be successors to Butler moved to Alabama and eventually ceased used the Aryan Nations name in 2007.

Atomic Dog—A nickname of former FBI Top Ten Fugitive James Charles Kopp, who was sought for the murder of Dr. Barnett Slepian, a New York abortion doctor. Kopp was arrested in France on March 29, 2001, and subsequently extradited back to the United States in 2002. On March 18, 2003, Kopp was found guilty in a New York state court in Buffalo of the second-degree murder of Dr. Slepian in his home in Amherst, New York, on October 23, 1998, and was sentenced to a 25-year prison term. On January 25, 2007 Kopp was convicted in federal court of violation of the Freedom of Access to Clinic Entrances Act (FACE) and illegal use of a firearm in connection with the Slepian murder. On June 19, 2007, he was sentenced to life in prison plus ten years.

booting—A term employed by Skinheads to refer to kicking people whom they oppose, often minorities and gays. Skinheads are known for wearing heavy steel-tipped boots.

Brady bill—A federal law passed in 1994 that restricts handgun ownership by requiring that a background check be done before a weapon can be sold. Right-wing extremists fear that this is the first of many laws that will eventually make all handgun ownership illegal.

butyric acid—A poisonous and noxious chemical that has been used by anti-abortion activists to attack abortion clinics. Its odor penetrates the clinics, causing them to shut down temporarily.

cell—A small clandestine unit within the group that performs violent attacks or illegal acts for the group. Cells usually contain four to five people.

chosen people—A term used by the Christian Identity Church to refer to European, particularly English, white people whom they believe are direct descendants of the "lost tribes of Israel" who were chased from the promised land about 722 B.C. Many other religious-based groups also believe themselves to be "chosen" by their god.

clandestine—A term used to refer to the secretive operations of a terrorist group. Group members who are clandestine do not inform non-group members about the true nature of their activities. Clandestine people usually carry false identification and live apart from people who would know them.

Christian Identity (CI)—A religion developed in the United States during the mid-1950s from the Anglo or British Israelism philosophy that emanated in England during the nineteenth century. CI believes that the white people of Europe, particularly those in England, are the true chosen people of the Christian Bible who were carried from the promised land in about 722 B.C. They believe that the people who now call themselves Jews are actually directly descended from Cain, who was the child of Eve and Satan. They refer to non-white people as "mud people," and believe that these individuals are no more than higher forms of animals, which have no soul.

common law court—An entity through which residents of the United States who consider themselves "sovereign citizens" settle their own disputes. Common law courts are not sanctioned by any government entity in the United States. They have no legal basis for existing although supporters try to trace the court's roots to English common law traditions and the Magna Carta. They are usually composed of local residents, frequently living in rural areas, who have no legal training or experience. They attempt to emulate the proceedings of an actual court. These courts render decisions that "release" people from governmental restrictions and mandates. For example, they may revoke a person's citizenship, relieve a person from paying taxes, or excuse an individual from a traffic citation. Often they operate under the concept that a crime only occurs when a person is harmed. In some instances they have worked with militias and indicate that the militias will carry out their mandates.

commune—A term often used by left-wing extremists of the 1960s and 1970s to refer to locations where people of similar political beliefs resided and engaged in political activities. Communes often were in urban areas—houses or apartments.

communiqué—A document issued by a terrorist group claiming credit for a violent attack. Communiqués can also be released to state a group's political philosophy, or to make a threat. Communiqués of the 1960s and 1970s were often sent by U.S. Mail or were left in a place like a telephone booth where they could be found by authorities. During the 1990s, many terrorists turned to the Internet as a vehicle for their communiqués, and that trend has continued into the twenty-first century. During the twenty-first century the trend has also been to send communiqués to overt entities that represent the group's views, and have them release the communiqué, as opposed to sending them directly to the media.

compound—A location where people of similar political beliefs reside and engage in political activity. Compounds are often somewhat self-sufficient. Many political compounds are also rooted in religion and have a belief that the country or world is coming to an end.

Cosmotheist Church—An anti-Semitic "church" concept formulated by the late National Alliance leader William Pierce, who died July 23, 2002.

Covenant, Sword, and Arm of the Lord—A 224-acre Christian Identity-oriented right-wing compound led by James Ellison. The compound, which straddled the Arkansas-Missouri border, functioned from the early 1970s until 1985, when it was raided by federal agents who recovered weapons, explosives, and cyanide.

creativity—A basic concept of the entity formerly known as the World Church of the Creator (WCOTC), and subsequently calling itself the Creativity Movement, involving the advancement of the white race. The WCOTC calls what it believes and does "creativity." The church professes five fundamental beliefs of "creativity," including that race is their religion, the white race is the finest, racial loyalty is the highest honor, what is good for the white race is the highest honor, and that their religion is "the one and only, true and revolutionary White Racial Religion—Creativity—is the only salvation for the White Race." (see Creativity Movement)

Creativity Movement—A name taken by the World Church of the Creator (WCOTC) in 2003 after a federal judge ruled that the group's former name infringed on the copyright of another church. Founded by the late Ben Klassen in the 1970s, the group was resurrected under the leadership of Matt Hale of East Peoria, Illinois, in the 1990s. The church does not worship a deity, and believes that if a god did create the world, he has since left it on its own. A white supremacist group, the movement believes in its version of the Golden Rule: "What is good for the white race is the highest virtue. What is bad for the white race is the ultimate sin." The religion is also extremely anti-Jewish. The Movement was severely jolted in January, 2003, when Hale was arrested on charges of conspiring to murder the federal judge involved in the copyright case that resulted in the church being forced to change its name. Hale was convicted of the charges on April 26, 2004, and sentenced to 40 years in the federal penitentiary on April 6, 2005. The WCOTC/Creativity Movement was left in disarray without Hale to lead them, and by 2008 had no central presence, and was essentially defunct. (see creativity)

de facto government—A term used by right-wing "sovereign" citizens to refer to the current government of the United States, which they believe is illegitimate and was formed without the knowledge or blessing of the people.

de jure government—A term used by right-wing "sovereign" citizens to refer to the "original" form of the government in the United States that they believe was replaced by the current "de facto" government. In the de jure government, people were self-governing, not ruled by a central government.

dirty bomb—An explosive device usually intended to spread radiation. Unlike a nuclear bomb which in itself causes massive destruction and the dispersal of radiation, the dirty bomb uses a conventional explosive device to spread radiation—most likely from radioactive waste products such as would be produced by a nuclear power plant. In theory, a dirty bomb could also involve a conventional explosive device dispersing biological or chemical agents into the atmosphere. The fear is that a terrorist group would blow up a railroad train or truck carrying radioactive waste.

"Dirty Dozen"—A group of abortion providers depicted on wanted posters distributed in the mid-1990s by anti-abortion extremists.

distributionism—The basic economic concept of the Third Position. It calls for the wholesale spreading of a nation's wealth as broadly as possible. It encourages the establishment of small family businesses, producer co-ops, profit sharing, and the creation of a modernized guild system.

eco-crime or eco-terrorism—Violent or illegal acts undertaken to promote the environmental extremist philosophy. These can be any crime committed in the name of saving the environment. The perpetrators sometimes call themselves "eco-vandals."

Ecodefense: A Field Guide to Monkeywrenching—A book written in the mid-1980s by Earth First founder Dave Foreman. This publication lists a variety of methods by which environmental extremists can attack their targets in the interest of protecting the environment.

economic sabotage—A term used primarily by environmental extremists to refer to attacks intended to disable companies that they believe are committing acts that are harmful to the environment. These attacks often include damage to equipment and corporate structures.

Eco-Raiders—One of the first of the environmental terrorist groups established in the United States. This group caused millions of dollars in damage by staging numerous raids between 1971 and 1973 on housing projects being built in areas around Tucson, Arizona, which they believed should be left in a natural state. They were arrested in September 1973.

Ecotage—An early 1970s book that outlines methods of sabotaging the equipment of companies that present a threat to the environment.

Earth First—An environmental action group founded by a group of people (including Dave Foreman) in 1980. The founders believed that the earth was in danger of destruction due to technological advances. Many environmental activists continue to be called "Earth Firsters."

ELF—The Earth Liberation Front. Self-described as an international underground organization consisting of autonomous groups of people who carry out direct action according to ELF guidelines. Economic sabotage and property destruction are considered proper ELF actions.

Elohim City—A right-wing Christian Identity compound in eastern Oklahoma, founded by Richard Millar, who died in 1999.

Elves—A name that clandestine members of the Earth Liberation Front (ELF) call themselves.

Evan Mecham Eco-Terrorist International Conspiracy (EMETIC)—This high-profile terrorist group was named after a former Arizona governor who was impeached. This group perpetrated several environmental attacks in the southwestern United States in the late 1980s, and its members were ultimately arrested in mid-1989. Most were convicted in 1991 and sent to prison.

fag bashing—An attack on a homosexual person. Usually done by Skinheads and other right-wing extremists (also called "gay bashing").

Fourteen Words—A sentence authored by former Order member (see The Order) David Lane who died in prison on May 28, 2007. This sentence has become something of a rallying slogan for right-wing extremists. "We must secure the existence of our people and a future for white children." In 1995 Lane's wife, Katja Lane, began operating a publishing company and Web site called the 14 Word Press in St. Maries, Idaho, that served as a vehicle for her incarcerated husband to promulgate his philosophy of white supremacy. The operation moved from Idaho in 2001, and has since become defunct.

free agents—A term usually used to refer to international terrorists who are not directed by, or tied to, a national government or a revolutionary movement centered in a particular nation.

Freeman—A concept that residents of the United States are sovereign citizens who are not bound by any government, particularly a federal or national government.

"Franken"—A term derived from the Frankenstein monster story. Anti-genetic engineering and environmental activists apply this term as a prefix to the names of genetically altered plants and animals. Examples: "Frankenplant." "Frankentree," "Frankenfood."

gay bashing—See fag bashing.

"GE"—Refers to genetic engineering (see genetically altered crops).

genetically altered crops—A target of violent attacks by environmental terrorists during the late 1990s and early 2000s. Anti-genetic engineering extremists believe that man should not alter the genetic makeup of crops or animals. They have destroyed crops and seeds and have vandalized laboratories engaged in genetic engineering research.

globalization—The concept of viewing economic, financial, and social issues from a worldwide perspective rather than from the viewpoint of a single nation.

guerrilla theater—A form of play in which the participants act out a political issue. Often used to promote protests against the government. Sometimes the performance depicts acts of violence. Very popular among leftist-oriented extremists in the late 1960s.

Hunter—The second significant novel of the late National Alliance leader William Pierce (using the pen name Andrew Macdonald). Written in 1989, this novel outlines the struggle of Oscar Yeager against the federal government, Jews, and blacks. It promotes the idea that a single activist can perpetrate significant attacks on his own. This novel never gained the prominence of Pierce's earlier *Turner Diaries*, and many right-wing extremists do not accept parts of its philosophy.

Jihad—When used by extremists it refers to a "holy war." It is often applied to a philosophy of violence espoused by Islamic militants to justify the use of force intended to spread or defend their religion.

JOG—"Jewish Occupied Government." A variation of the more popular right-wing extremist term, "ZOG." Refers to the right-wing belief that Jewish people control the United States government.

JTTF—Joint Terrorism Task Force (originally Joint Terrorist Task Force). Federal and local investigative agencies working together as a single entity against the terrorist threat. The first JTTFs were founded in 1981 in New York City and Chicago, Illinois and gradually spread to larger metropolitan areas of the country. As a direct result of the attacks of September 11, 2001, JTTFs were established throughout the United States in association with every FBI field Division. In 2008 there were more than 100 JTTFs serving the entire United States.

jury nullification—Refers to the idea that a trial juror will render a decision based on factors other than the guilt or innocence of the accused as presented during the trial. For example, a juror may find a person not guilty in a tax evasion case because the juror decides on his own that the tax laws are invalid. Right-wing extremists have made efforts in some trials to convince members of the jury to render decisions based on the political cause advocated by the defendant, rather than on the evidence presented in court by the government against the defendant. Right-wing radicals also preach that under the concept of jury nullification a trial jury is a fourth party in the country's checks and balances system. They argue that a jury has an obligation to review the laws involved in the case and determine if they are legal. If they do not find the law to be proper, they should find the defendant innocent for that reason despite the evidence.

leaderless resistance—A concept that has gained great popularity during the past decade, although it dates back to Brazilian revolutionary Carlos Marighella's *Mini-Manual of Urban Guerrilla Warfare*, released during the 1960s. Several extremist groups believe that the best method for avoiding arrest is for small, self-directed units to perpetrate attacks on behalf of the political cause, but without the knowledge of anyone in the group. Both animal rights and environmental extremists support this concept.

liberation—A term used by animal rights activists to describe actions in which they release animals being held for food, products they produce, including fur, milk, and eggs, and for laboratory experimentation. Fur farms and college and private laboratories are common targets of animal activists liberations.

lien—A right-wing tactic to attack the government and stop government officers from investigating them. A lien is a legal document that attaches the title of property until the owner pays the person filing the lien the amount of money supposedly owed. As a principle of law, a lien is intended to force a person to pay a debt before he disposes of property upon which that obligation was incurred. In right-wing circles, the tactic is designed to harass government officials or law enforcement officers, and to impede the operations of the court, because there is no actual debt owned to the person who filed the lien.

Lone Wolf—A form of leaderless resistance in which one person acting on his or her own commits violent or illegal acts on behalf of his or her political movement without the direction or knowledge of others involved in the political cause.

militia—A concept of a citizen army that was championed by Posse Comitatus founder William Potter Gale in the 1980s. Militias started forming during that decade, and received publicity with the 1995 bombing of the Murrah Federal Building. The media suggested that the bombers were affiliated with the militia movement. The bombing caused authorities to look into militias, resulting in some arrests and unwanted publicity. (see also unorganized militia.)

monkey wrenching—Sabotage employed by environmental activists against equipment and tools used by people and businesses.

Monkey Wrench Gang—An influential environmental activism book written in 1975 by Edward Abbey.

Montana Freemen—A right-wing group that refused to pay federal income taxes and that issued large numbers of fraudulent financial certificates. They became famous when they staged an 81-day standoff with FBI agents who were attempting to arrest them. Ultimately, the Freemen surrendered, and most were convicted of various crimes.

National Alliance—A Hillsboro, West Virginia-based right-wing neo-Nazi extremist organization founded by the late William Pierce, who died July 23, 2002. The group espouses a belief in natural law and states that people are responsible for everything over which they have a choice. It heavily stresses that white people have a responsibility for making themselves the best they can be. The National Alliance opposes race-mixing and preaches that Jews control the media in the United States. Following Pierce's death the National Alliance suffered defections and splits, and lost many of its members as well as the influence among right-wing extremists that it once had.

National Vanguard Books—A distributor of right-wing books, comic books, audiotapes, and videotapes. Operated by the National Alliance.

The New Order—A group of right-wing extremists who conspired to perpetrate violent attacks in southwestern Illinois near St. Louis, Missouri, in the late 1990s.

New World Order—A concept that there will be a single entity that will rule the entire world. Right-wing extremists fear this concept, and many believe that it is part of a Jewish conspiracy. Some claim the concept dates back to Plato and has continued throughout history. Most people look to the philosophy of Andrew Carnegie, Cecil Rhodes, and H.G. Wells (who wrote a 1939 book titled *The New World Order*) as initiating the movement. Right-wing extremists believe that a single world government will be run by non-whites to the exclusion of American whites.

New Year's Gang—A name given to the four individuals who perpetrated the 1970 fatal bombing at the University of Wisconsin-Madison Army Math Research Center. At the time, it was the worst terrorist act to have occurred in the United States. One of the four, Leo Frederick Burt, remains a fugitive. The other three were convicted, sentenced to federal prison, and have been released.

Nuremburg Files—An Oregon-based Web site that listed the names of more than 200 abortion doctors who were called "baby butchers." In early 1999, a federal jury ordered the operators of the Web site to pay more than $100 million in damages to those mentioned on the list. Although the site has been closed, other sites continue to display its contents.

Odinism—A long-defunct Norse religion that has seen some resurgence among right-wing extremists. The new followers believe that Christianity, with its "love thy neighbor" and "turn the other cheek" philosophies destroyed Odinism when it spread into Europe. They view Odinism as a religion of the white man, and believe that it encourages white people to fight for their people and for their gods. Many right-wing extremists have adopted Odinist symbols that they display through tattoos and jewelry. They have particular love for the Odinist God of Thunder, Thor. (Not all people who claim to be Odinists are right-wing extremists or terrorists.)

one world government—The idea that the entire world will soon be ruled by a single government. Right-wing extremists fear that when this happens, white people will be dominated by non-whites, primarily Asian or African people.

Operation Rescue—An anti-abortion group founded by Randall Terry that staged many disruptive protests against abortion providers.

(The) Order—The violent fictional clandestine terrorist cell that was a central player in the late William Pierce's 1978 novel, *The Turner Diaries*. Also the name of a real clandestine terrorist group that eventually contained more than 20 members, established and led by Robert Mathews in the northwest United States in the early 1980s. The group disbanded when Mathews was killed on December 8, 1984. Most of the group's members were subsequently sentenced to lengthy prison terms for crimes ranging from bank robberies and counterfeiting to murder.

Phineas Priesthood—A concept based upon the Old Testament book of Numbers, Chapter 25. Phineas Priests believe that this section of the Bible instructs them to be men of action, and to use force as necessary to do what God wants. There have been several examples during the past 20 years of violent people or groups that claim to be following this message. In 1996, a group of Phineas Priests robbed banks, bombed a newspaper office and an abortion clinic, and stole vehicles in the Spokane, Washington, area. The late Paul Hill, who murdered abortion provider Dr. John Bayard Britton in 1994, had written in support of this concept.

Pontifex Maximus (supreme leader)—The title originally used by Ben Klassen and more recently used by Matt Hale as the leader of the Creativity Movement, formerly known as the World Church of the Creator (WCOTC). Hale was arrested in January 2003 on a charge of conspiracy to murder a federal judge in January 2003, and was sentenced to 40-years in prison on April 16, 2005. No person of prominence presently uses the term Pontifex Maximus.

Poor Man's James Bond—A book by Kurt Saxon that gives directions for building bombs and weapons. It was very popular among left-wing extremists of the 1970s and is still available today.

Posse Comitatus—A Latin term meaning "power of the county." The people adhering to this concept disdain the idea of a federal or even a state government. They regard the sheriff as being the highest authority because he is an elected police official. Some supporters of the concept wear jewelry depicting a hangman's noose, which is a warning to the sheriff that he must cooperate with the people and follow the Bible, or he will be hung. The concept was created by William Potter Gale and Henry "Mike" Beach around 1970.

prisoner of war (POW)—A term employed by incarcerated, left-wing, right-wing, and international terrorists to suggest that rather than being criminals, they are in fact freedom fighters engaged in a war with the United States. They will often demand that they be treated in the same manner as an enemy who was arrested during wartime.

RAHOWA—The slogan of the Creativity Movement, formerly known as the World Church of the Creator. It is based on the first two letters of the phrase, "Racial Holy War." Group members often sprayed the phrase "RAHOWA" in graffiti in areas where they were recruiting members. Although the Creativity Movement is largely dead following the 2004 conviction of its leader, Matt Hale, some white supremacists might still use the RAHOWA term.

redemption—A right-wing financial scheme that suggests that the United States government went bankrupt during the Great Depression, but saved itself through raising money by placing a value on the work that its citizens could do. The argument is that people can now reclaim their "value" by issuing checks against the government.

Resistance Records—The largest distributor of neo-Nazi music in the United States, this firm is presently operated by the National Alliance in Hillsboro,

West Virginia. It was originally founded by George Burdi in 1993 and changed hands several times after Burdi was imprisoned.

ricin—A highly toxic protein that is extracted from the castor bean. Many experts fear that it will be used by terrorists as a weapon of mass destruction. In 1995, four Minnesota right-wing extremists were convicted of attempting to kill law enforcement officers with ricin.

Ruby Ridge—This location in Northern Idaho has become a rallying point for many right-wing extremists who oppose the federal government. When local resident Randy Weaver failed to appear in court on a federal firearms charge, U.S. Marshals attempted to arrest him in August 1992. A gun battle erupted and a Deputy U.S. Marshal and Weaver's son were killed. A standoff developed. On August 22, 1992, an FBI agent shot and killed Weaver's wife, Vicki. The standoff continued for 11 days and attracted national publicity. Weaver became something of a hero to right-wing extremists.

sarin gas—An extremely toxic chemical warfare agent and a potential weapon of mass destruction. The Aum Shinri Kyo (Supreme Truth) group dispersed this deadly gas into the subway system in Tokyo, Japan, in 1995, killing 12 people and causing thousands of others to become ill.

Seedline (Seedliners)—A basic premise of the Christian Identity Church. It holds that white people are directly descended from God through Adam and Eve and that Jews are descended from a liaison between Eve and Satan. Hence, there is a continuing battle between the forces of good (white people) and evil (Jews-the devil).

SHARP—Skinheads against Racial Prejudice. Unlike most Skinheads, the members of this group stand against racism.

Skinheads—The Skinhead movement began in England in the 1960s and subsequently spread to various other parts of the English-speaking world, including the United States. Skinhead members are usually young and white. They are right-wing in political direction and have attacked non-whites, Jews, and homosexuals. They have often been targeted for recruitment by right-wing terrorist groups because of their violent tendencies. Skinheads are known for shaved heads, steel-tipped boots, and tattoos—many of which express violent or political themes. They favor punk rock music, especially songs that promote violence and right-wing political themes.

sight draft—A legitimate financial document that some right-wing extremists have used fraudulently. In a variety of schemes, extremists have issued thousands of "sight drafts" that are not backed by currency or the government, and therefore are worthless.

Simulacrum Candidus (the white emblem)—A symbol consisting of the letter "W" with a crown above it, and a halo above the crown, used by the now largely defunct Creativity Movement (formerly known as the World Church of the Creator).

sovereign citizens—The right-wing belief that each person in the United States is a citizen unto himself and not a citizen of the United States. Some extremists believe that certain conspirators in the country's early history manipulated the government over time to trick people into giving up their individual rights in order to become citizens of the United States. Sovereign citizens often try to repudiate their U.S. citizenship, even to the extent of refusing to pay taxes, use license plates, or be involved with Social Security.

spider web tattoo—Some right-wing extremists tattoo a spider web design on their elbow to show that they have committed a crime of violence, possibly even murder, on a member of a minority race.

Straight-Edgers—A youth group, sometimes associated with Skinheads, that holds both right-wing and animal rights-environmentalist views. Not all young people who call themselves Straight-Edgers are Skinheads or hold extremist views. However, virtually all Straight-Edgers reject drugs, alcohol, and casual sex. The group's name is derived from a line in Ian Mackaye's 1981 song Minor Threat performed by a band of the same name. Straight-Edgers have been convicted of animal rights attacks in the 1990s. Many Straight-edgers are vegetarians. Although founded on the East Coast, the group has a strong presence in Utah.

Third Position—A European movement that developed in the United States during the later 1990s with a claim that it had a philosophy that was neither right-wing nor left-wing, and that it was neither capitalist or communist. The group calls for a total distribution of wealth, opposition to Zionism, support of national states, and protection of animals and the environment. Its influence seems to have ebbed in the United States in recent years.

Thirteenth Amendment—Some right-wing extremists and sovereign citizens believe that a missing "Thirteenth Amendment" proposed by Senator Philip Reed in 1810 was passed and essentially denied citizenship to people holding titles of nobility, including attorneys. They also feel that this amendment took away "honors" enjoyed by judges over other citizens. They believe that lawyers, bankers, and others in Congress at the time hid this amendment from the people. They also believe that the Fourteenth Amendment (which they think should be the Fifteenth Amendment) not only gave citizenship to the former slaves who were freed by the Thirteenth Amendment (which they believe should be the Fourteenth Amendment), but also forced the concept of citizenship onto all other people living in the United States who were previously sovereign citizens not subject to the federal government.

Thor—The Odinist god of thunder.

"tree huggers"—A derogatory term used to refer to people involved in environmental activism.

tree spiking—A tactic used by environmental extremists to prevent the harvesting of trees by lumber companies. Specifically, metal or porcelain spikes are driven into the trunks of trees in such a manner that they cannot be seen. When the trees are cut into lumber in a mill, the metal spike will cause the expensive saw blade to shatter, resulting in damage to the mill and endangering mill employees. If loggers believe that spikes have been placed in some of the trees they intend to harvest, they will often be forced to endure the expense of running the logs through an x-ray before bringing them to a sawmill.

The Turner Diaries—Using the name Andrew Macdonald, the late National Alliance leader William Pierce wrote this racist novel in 1978. It tells the story of Earl Turner, who became disenchanted with the government and ultimately joined a clandestine group that waged war against it. *The Turner Diaries* has been one of the most influential books ever written in the area of right-wing extremism. Order leader Robert Mathews and Oklahoma City bomber Timothy McVeigh read it repeatedly.

underground—A state of clandestine existence in which terrorists overtly and covertly function under false identities.

Uniform Commercial Code—The UCC is a detailed code of law that applies to contracts regarding the sale of goods and commercial matters between the states. Right-wing sovereign citizen advocates have latched onto the UCC as an alternative to the U.S. Constitution and laws passed by the U.S. Congress. They often will place "UCC" or "UCC 1-207" on documents as a vehicle for expressing their common law rights.

Unorganized militia—(See also militia) The unorganized militia is a concept that dates back to the 1800s, when the standing militia for all men between certain ages outlined in the United States Constitution, had become very unpopular. In the 1830s, to maintain the Constitution, yet pacify the people, Congress established an active militia for those who wanted to serve (it subsequently became the National Guard), and the unorganized militia for everyone else. In the 1980s, William Potter Gale developed the idea that people could in fact establish active unorganized militias on their own. These bodies could be used to protect the people from the government, and to guard from threats like the New World Order. There is no legal basis upon which the various unorganized militias that have been established over the past three decades operate.

Vieques—An island near Puerto Rico that has been used as a rallying point for Puerto Rican independence activists for years. The island was used by the United States military for live-fire exercises for about 60 years before protests forced the U.S. Navy to cease its activities in May 2003. Protests continue with respect to the polluted condition of the island that resulted from the military activities.

Waco—The name of this Texas city has become a rallying point for right-wing extremists and anyone opposed to the federal government. On February 28, 1993, Bureau of Alcohol, Tobacco, and Firearms agents raided the Branch Davidian religious compound near Waco in an effort to arrest its leader, David Koresh for firearms violations. A shootout occurred, with four BATF agents being killed, along with several compound members. A standoff continued for the next 51 days, until April 19, 1993, when the FBI attempted to bring it to an end. Millions of people watched on television as the compound burned to the ground, killing 74 Branch Davidians, including Koresh.

White Aryan Resistance (WAR)—A California-based right-wing extremist organization led by Thomas Metzger. WAR has heavily recruited among Skinheads. The group also publishes a newspaper titled W.A.R.

White Man's Bible—Written by Ben Klassen, the founder of a group then called the World Church of the Creator, subsequently called the Creativity Movement. White supremacy as outlined in the publication is the foundation upon which the Creativity Movement was built.

World Church of the Creator (WCOTC)—(See Creativity Movement)

Yahweh—The name that the Christian Identity Church, Phineas Priesthood followers, and certain other right-wing extremists use to refer to God.

Zionism—The desire of Jewish people to have a Jewish state in Palestine. Right-wing groups, the Third Position, and Islamic extremists all oppose the concept of Zionism, and believe that the U.S. government should not support the state of Israel.

ZOG—Zionist Occupied Government. Also called Jewish Occupied Government. A belief held by many right-wing extremists that Jewish people control the United States government.

Index

al Qaeda
 as international terrorist group, 22
 Training Manual of, 62–63, 65
American Dissident Voices, 495
American Revolution, 5
America's Most Wanted, 260, 328
Anarchist Cookbook, 495
Anarchists, 20
 future of investigations into, 428
 as left-wing extremists, 26
 "leftist" label for modern, 430
 and single-issue terrorism, 29
Animal Liberation Front (ALF), 23, 64–65,
  495
Animal rights
 future of terrorist investigations
  into activists for, 428
 as single-issue terrorist group, 28
 terrorist acts of activists, 451–483
Anthrax, 495
Anti-abortion
 activism, religious-based terrorism and, 43
 extremists and The Army of God Manual, 65
 as single-issue terrorist group, 28, 427–429
Anti-genetic engineering terrorist group, 28
Armed Resistance Unit, 16
Army of God Manual, The, 65, 495
Arson-Around with Auntie ALF, 65
Aryan Nations, 496
"Activist Tips" security documents, 63–64
 Richard Butler and, 34–35
 right-wing extremism and, 27, 431
Assassination, 5
Atomic Dog, 496

Bioengineering Action Network, 65
Birth certificate, false, for undercover
  operations, 296–297
Black Liberation Army, 16
Blackmail, as motive for informing, 188
Black's Law Dictionary, 343
Bolsheviks, 20

Boston Tea Party, 5
Brady bill, 496
Branch Davidians, 34
Bugs. *See* Microphones
Butler, Richard
 and Aryan Nations, 34–35, 431
 and Christian Identity religion, 39
Byrdsong, Ricky, 41

Caller ID technology, 237–238
Cameras
 as electronic coverage in investigation,
  312–313
 filming the crime scene, 256
 response to terrorist attack and, 436–437
 security and the crime scene, 261–262
 video, still, and CCTV in surveillance,
  162–164
Chain of custody, physical evidence and,
  245–246
Chicago Joint Terrorism Task Force, 16–17
 and FALN investigation, 387
 and terrorism, 269–271
Christian Identity, 497
 domestic religious-based terrorism and,
  39–40
 as right-wing extremists, 27
Civil action, use by extremists and
  terrorists, 342–343
Civil war and revolution, 33
Classified information, task forces and
  sharing, 275
Closed-circuit television (CCTV)
 as electronic coverage type, 312–313
 in surveillance, 164
 use in intrusive investigation, 385–386
Cold-start informants.
 See Informants, inside
Columbo, interview methods of, 81
Command center, creating and organizing,
  401–404
Common law court, 343, 497

511